MANAGEMENT AND OFFICE INFORMATION SYSTEMS

EDITED BY
SHI-KUO CHANG

Illinois Institute of Technology
Chicago, Illinois

PLENUM PRESS • NEW YORK AND LONDON

Library of Congress Cataloging in Publication Data

Main entry under title:

Management and office information systems.

(Management and information systems)
Includes bibliographical references and index.
1. Management information systems—Addresses, essays, lectures. I. Chang, S. K.
(Shi Kuo), 1944–   II. Series.
T58.6.M328   1984   658.4′038   83-26875
ISBN 0-306-41447-3

© 1984 Plenum Press, New York
A Division of Plenum Publishing Corporation
233 Spring Street, New York, N.Y. 10013

Printed in the United States of America

MANAGEMENT AND OFFICE INFORMATION SYSTEMS

MANAGEMENT AND OFFICE INFORMATION SYSTEMS
Edited by Shi-Kuo Chang

CONTRIBUTORS

PETER S. ALBIN ● *John Jay College, City University of New York, New York, New York*

ADARSH K. ARORA ● *Department of Computer Science, Illinois Institute of Technology, Chicago, Illinois*

BALA V. BALACHANDRAN ● *Department of Decision Sciences, Accounting, and Information Systems, J. L. Kellogg Graduate School of Management, Northwestern University, Evanston, Illinois*

HELMY H. BALIGH ● *Fuqua School of Business, Duke University, Durham, North Carolina*

ROBERT W. BLANNING ● *Owen Graduate School of Management, Vanderbilt University, Nashville, Tennessee*

RICHARD M. BURTON ● *Fuqua School of Business, Duke University, Durham, North Carolina*

C. R. CARLSON ● *Standard Oil (Indiana), Chicago, Illinois*

SAMIR CHAKRABORTY ● *Consultant—Strategic Planning, Telecom Canada, Ottawa, Ontario, Canada*

SHI-KUO CHANG ● *Department of Electrical Engineering, Illinois Institute of Technology, Chicago, Illinois*

BALBIR S. DHILLON ● *Engineering Management Program, Department of Mechanical Engineering, University of Ottawa, Ottawa, Ontario, Canada*

MITSUHIRO HATTORI ● *Computer System Research Laboratory, C & C Systems Research Laboratories, NEC Corporation, Kawasaki-city, Kanagawa, Japan*

MASAHITO HIRAKAWA ● *Faculty of Engineering, Hiroshima University, Higashi-Hiroshima, Japan*

CHEN-HSHIN HO ● *Institute of Information Science, Academia Sinica, Taipei, Taiwan, Republic of China*

YUI-WEI HO ● *Institute of Information Science, Academia Sinica, Taipei, Taiwan, Republic of China*

YANG-CHANG HONG ● *Institute of Information Science, Academia Sinica, Taipei, Taiwan, Republic of China*

FARROKH Z. HORMOZI ● *Pace University, Pleasantville, New York*

YUH-LING HWANG ● *Institute of Information Science, Academia Sinica, Taipei, Taiwan, Republic of China*

TADAO ICHIKAWA ● *Faculty of Engineering, Hiroshima University, Higashi-Hiroshima, Japan*

JYH-SHENG KE ● *Institute for Information Industry, Taipei, Taiwan, Republic of China*

BENN R. KONSYNSKI ● *Department of Management Information Systems, University of Arizona, Tucson, Arizona*

KIICHI KUMANO ● *Computer System Research Laboratory, C & C Systems Research Laboratories, NEC Corporation, Kawasaki-city, Kanagawa, Japan*

TE-SON KUO ● *Institute of Information Science, Academia Sinica, Taipei, Taiwan, Republic of China*

DANIEL T. LEE ● *School of Business Adminsistration, University of Wisconsin-Milwaukee, Milwaukee, Wisconsin*

EDWARD T. LEE ● *Department of Computer Science, Louisiana State University, Baton Rouge, Louisiana*

AUGUSTO A. LEGASTO, JR. ● *Department of Management, Baruch College, City University of New York, New York, New York*

PANOS A. LIGOMENIDES ● *Intelligent Machines Program and Electrical Engineering Department, University of Maryland, College Park, Maryland*

CHING-LIANG LIN ● *Institute of Information Science, Academia Sinica, Taipei, Taiwan, Republic of China*

A. C. LIU ● *Department of Electrical Engineering, Illinois Institute of Technology, Chicago, Illinois*

KENNETH D. MACKENZIE ● *Organizational Systems, Inc., Lawrence, Kansas; and University of Kansas, Lawrence, Kansas*

LEONG SIEW MENG ● *Department of Business Administration, National University of Singapore, Singapore*

JUZAR MOTIWALLA ● *Institute of Systems Science, National University of Singapore, Singapore*

STERGIOS L. MOURGOS ● *John Jay College, City University of New York, New York, New York*

TADAO MURATA ● *Department of Electrical Engineering and Computer Science, University of Illinois at Chicago, Chicago, Illinois*

AMADOR MURIEL ● *Department of Statistics and Computer Information Systems, Baruch College, City University of New York, New York, New York*

YOSHIHIRO NAGAI ● *Computer System Research Laboratory, C & C Systems Research Laboratories, NEC Corporation, Kawasaki-city, Kanagawa, Japan*

J. NATESAN ● *Engineering Management Program, Department of Mechanical Engineering, University of Ottawa, Ottawa, Ontario, Canada*

JAY F. NUNAMAKER ● *Department of Management Information Systems, University of Arizona, Tucson, Arizona*

D. A. OLSON ● *Ford Aerospace and Communications Corporation, Newport Beach, California*

SHUHSHEN PAN ● *Computer Science Department, Purdue University, West Lafayette, Indiana*

ROGER A. PICK ● *Krannert Graduate School of Management, Purdue University, West Lafayette, Indiana*

JAE K. SHIM ● *Department of Accountancy, California State University, Long Beach, California*

TATSUO SHIMIZU ● *Faculty of Engineering, Hiroshima University, Higashi-Hiroshima, Japan*

RICHARD W. SRCH ● *G & W Electric Company, Blue Island, Illinois*

EDWARD A. STOHR ● *CAIS Department, Graduate School of Business Administration, New York University, New York, New York*

HOUSTON H. STOKES ● *Department of Economics, University of Illinois at Chicago Circle, Chicago, Illinois*

CHIOU-FENG WANG ● *Institute of Information Science, Academia Sinica, Taipei, Taiwan, Republic of China*

ARTHUR WEINBERG ● *John Jay College, City University of New York, New York, New York*

ANDREW B. WHINSTON ● *Krannert Graduate School of Management, Purdue University, West Lafayette, Indiana*

NORMAN H. WHITE ● *CAIS Department, Graduate School of Business Administration, New York University, New York, New York*

BAYARD E. WYNNE ● *Arthur Andersen & Company, Chicago, Illinois*

PREFACE

Decision making is a very complex phenomenon. Modern decision makers must deal with very complex problems which are constantly changing and often ill-structured, making modeling and analysis difficult. In order to provide support for the decision makers, computer-based information systems are designed to collect, store, process, and transport information. Recent advances in computer technology, data communications, database systems, office automation, and knowledge engineering have made possible the design of very sophisticated information systems. However, rapid technological advances also create many problems, not the least of which is the lack of integration among the various disciplines in information system design. Without such integration, a costly computer-based information system is at best partially useful and at worst totally useless. The aim of this book, therefore, is to examine the various issues involved in designing management information systems, decision support systems, and office information systems for increasing productivity and providing decision support.

This book is the outcome of the Workshop on Management and Office Information Systems, which was organized by the Knowledge Systems Institute and held at Chicago, Illinois, from June 28 to 30, 1982. Twenty-seven papers from the working papers presented at that workshop were selected for inclusion in the present volume, which is organized into five parts: (I) organization structures and management, (II) decision support systems, (III) database systems, (IV) office information systems, and (V) systems and applications.

The use of information by an organization is a central issue in the analysis and design of an organizational structure. The information substructure of an organization refers to the formal and informal information exchange mechanisms in an organization. The chapters in Part I address various issues related to organization structures, management, and information substructures. Baligh and Burton advance the viewpoint that efficient processes of designing organization structures can be derived from the logical and economic properties of these structures. The information substructures can then be designed in the context of decision rule structure and reward substructure, etc., within the organization structure. They also point out that both the informational aspects and the organizational aspects of information substructures need to be considered, and that the latter involve the proper integration of the information substructure into the total organization structure.

Mackenzie maintains that the the design of an information system should satisfy both the formal and the informal information needs of an organization. He

vii

presents the idea that the organization itself can be considered as an information system called the organizational process information system (OPIS), which is similar to the information substructure of Baligh and Burton. The computer-based information system, or in Mackenzie's term, the technologically augmenting information system (TAIS), relies on a combination of technology and its users to augment human communication. Mackenzie concludes that unless the technologically augmenting information systems are designed to fit the organizational process information system, their development and usefulness will always be limited. Motiwalla, in his chapter, illustrates organizational characteristics typical of major governmental institutions in Singapore and Indonesia. He also emphasizes the importance of understanding these organizational characteristics before attempting to design the management information system.

In their provocative study, Legasto and Muriel discuss the information needs of organizations under crisis. They maintain that database systems and management information systems provide trivial aid to the managers of organizations undergoing severe crisis. The historical data contained in databases of management information systems are useful in satisfying the information needs of stable organizations. The information needs of organizations under crisis are totally different. Legasto and Muriel use the term "proactive" information to describe "forward-looking" information created by the decision support system. They then propose a procedure to generate a set of potential organizational crises, so that each can be treated as a decision option and evaluated by means of a decision criterion. In their procedure, the generation of crisis scenarios requires the involvement of human experts. It is conceivable that expert systems can be employed to augment and/or replace some of these human experts, so that crisis-triggered simulations can be done automatically or semiautomatically.

The chapters in Part I amply illustrate the pitfalls and limitations of technologically augmenting information systems. The so-called "Peter Principle" states that every employee will be promoted to his level of incompetency. A modified form of the Peter Principle seems to be also applicable to information systems—every information system will continue to grow until it reaches its level of incompetency. Instead of designing super information systems, which soon become incompetent, are there other alternatives? The six chapters in Part II attempt to provide new insight in designing decision support systems.

Stohr and White emphasize the need for software tools, which can then be combined to generate customized information systems. Citing Boulden, they observe that approximately one-third of the larger planning systems fail in the first two years after implementation, and another one-third perform indifferently. This observation not only corroborates Mackenzie's point made earlier, but also illustrates that we must examine carefully how recent hardware and software advances can facilitate the development of decision support systems that are more easily used by planning staff and other managers and have increased functionality combined with an ability to adopt to changing assumptions and needs. Stohr and White then present an excellent survey of the software requirements for a planning system generator. They also prescribe some strategies that might be employed in its construction.

In their chapter, Pan, Pick, and Whinston emphasize that database systems and knowledge-based systems should be integrated, and that artificial intelligence techniques are useful in decision support systems. They then proceed to define a class of formalisms for describing decision support systems (DSS). One particular formalism will define a DSS at a conceptual level. Associated with each formalism is a number of possible structures. One particular structure defines the implementation of the DSS in terms of data and programs. This unified formalism illustrates what could be accomplished in formal system specifications, which at least can serve as the reference or the blueprint in actual system design.

Konsynski and Nunamaker address the application of principles of decision support in the facilitation of enterprise analysis. The ill-structured nature of information strategic planning and requirements determination processes has led to the development of a decision support environment that serves as a front-end process in determining information system requirements. Balachandran and Srch have developed a framework for an integrated MIS model that is uniquely directed toward satisfying R&D organizational objectives. Both Wynne's chapter and Motiwalla's and Leong's chapter address information needs analysis of decision support systems. These four chapters not only point out the many facets of DSS design, but also illustrate the need for integration and interface in information system design.

The heart of any management information system or decision support system is the database system, which is the subject matter of the next five chapters in Part III. The five chapters, not accidentally, are all based upon, or can be applied to, the relational database approach, which seems to be the most promising approach of data management for decision support systems.

In his introductory chapter, Daniel Lee examines the existing technologies in decision support system development, and advocates a new approach in DSS design with special emphasis on database design. He employs the entity–relationship model for conceptual system design, which can then be translated into relational, hierarchical, or network database models. Carlson and Arora present a methodology for designing enterprise information system databases. This methodology permits the system designer to specify user requirements in any enterprise model suitable to the needs of the individual application. A formal language, called the update protocol model (UPM), is used to describe data semantics. This methodology is based upon the relational database model, and its view integration strategy results in a database design free of many potential conflicts.

Blanning points out that the function of a decision support system is to integrate data management, model management, and knowledge management. He also suggests that this might be done in the relational database framework. Since the knowledge base consists of objects and relations, the relational database framework is also useful for knowledge management. Blanning presents a model query language (MQL) which is a relationally complete language for model management.

As pointed out by several authors, decision makers are often faced with ill-structured problems. The information system to support decision making, therefore, should also tolerate ambiguity and imprecision. Hirakawa, Shimizu, and Ichikawa describe an augmented relational model, which contains two types of relations, namely, the conventional relations and the semantic relations. The semantic relations represent the relatedness between elements in a domain. With this augmented relational model, the user can specify queries with a certain amount of ambiguity. Stored information can be retrieved through relevancy estimation and similarity estimation. This similarity retrieval technique, as reported by Hirakawa *et al.*, is also applicable to a pictorial database, i.e., a database containing pictures.

The ability to deal with pictures such as sketches, line drawings, signatures, and images, is very important for modern decision support systems as well as office information systems. Edward Lee discusses similarity retrieval techniques for pictorial databases, based upon fuzzy languages and similarity measures. Such techniques will soon find their way to many interesting applications involving pictorial information.

As low-cost personal computers and intelligent terminals proliferate, decision support systems will soon be integrated into office information systems. The six chapters in Part IV deal with the methodology of office information system design. Chang discusses the essential characteristics of office information systems. First of all, office information systems are evolutionary information systems. Second, office information systems combine data management, message management, and activities management (which includes knowledge management and model management). Chang then describes how to enhance a passive database system by introducing database alerters, so that the database system can actively respond to outside messages and events. He then describes a methodology for specifying user requirements in terms of message exchanges, database retrieval–updates, and office activities. This integrated model, called the office procedure model (OPM), can be translated into implementable routines for a relational database system. The OPM model is based upon the Petri-net model, which is also the model used by two other systems reported in this part.

Liu and Olson describe the interaction between database alerters and triggers, and provide an example of applying this technique to design an automated library information system. The design and implementation of another library information system is described by Ke *et al.*, who also use Petri-net modeling technique to specify library procedures for verifying correctness of data flow. The system is essentially the integration of a general purpose data entry system, a relational database system, and an information retrieval subsystem. Hong *et al.* describe a prototype system for office procedure automation, which is mainly based upon an extension of Petri nets for modeling office work as a set of man-machine interaction procedures.

It is clear that Petri-net model is very useful in office procedure modeling. The Petri-net model is essentially a general purpose tool for representing and analyzing concurrent systems where several activities progress in parallel. Murata's chapter is a well-written tutorial on Petri nets, with emphasis on the analysis methods.

As office information systems evolve, more and more software needs to be written. Software tools are needed, according to Kumano, Nagai, and Hattori, to automatically generate new office application programs. It is interesting to note that Stohr has made the same observation regarding DSS software. Kumano *et al.* have developed an office application program generator, which can be used with ease by office workers to specify new application programs for office management and document retrieval.

The last part, Part V, consists of six chapters on systems and applications. Albin, Hormozi, and Mourgos present an information systems approach to the analysis of job design. Baligh and Burton have stated that the composition of decision rules, information exchanges, information processing functions, etc., for an individual define his job. Albin *et al.* address the problem of describing and measuring the content of a job design by using a system of structural representation. In Ligomenides' chapter, the decision-making problem in large open systems is related to a command hierarchy, and the command decomposition problem is formulated and analyzed. Stokes describes the LINPACK linear algebra routines in the SPEAKEASY program, which is a useful tool for many decision-making applications. Chakraborty describes a systems approach to produce the corporate provisioning plan, which has been successfully implemented in a Canadian telecommunications company. Shim describes the primary functions and key features of a grants management system for cost accounting currently in use in New York City. Finally, the various aspects of reliability and maintainability management are discussed by Dhillon and Natesan.

The chapters in this volume demonstrate that a lot of progress has already been made in information system design methodologies. It is hoped that awareness of the impact of organization structures, management practices, and user requirements upon information system design will lead to the formulation of a new methodology which will attempt to integrate many of the methodologies and techniques reported in this volume.

SHI-KUO CHANG

CONTENTS

xiii

PART IV

OFFICE INFORMATION SYSTEMS

PART V

SYSTEMS AND APPLICATIONS

ORGANIZATION STRUCTURES AND MANAGEMENT

THE PROCESS OF DESIGNING ORGANIZATION STRUCTURES AND THEIR INFORMATION SUBSTRUCTURES

HELMY H. BALIGH AND RICHARD M. BURTON

1. The Logic of Design Processes

The processes of organization design are logically identical to algorithms and search procedures, and have varying degrees of efficiency. Unless a logical order is imposed on the choice space in which the algorithm is to operate or the search to occur, there is no way to specify the algorithm or analyze its efficiency. This logical order, or algebra, forms the basis on which one may identify the conceptual steps in the algorithm or search procedure. For example, the process of differentiation for the calculus is directly based on the algebra of real numbers. It is an efficient way to proceed to find a continuous function's maximum. It is more efficient than a totally random search. The same logic applies to processes of designing organization structures. The specification or identification of efficient processes depends on one's capacity to impose a logical structure on the set of organization structures. Furthermore, unless this algebra allows us to map the operational components of organization structures onto it, it will be little or no use as a basis for determining process efficiency or the choice of efficient processes.

Algorithms, or search processes, contain specifications and definitions such as turn left after y miles, go west for x miles, differentiate, add, equate, set to zero,

HELMY H. BALIGH and RICHARD M. BURTON ● Fuqua School of Business, Duke University, Durham, North Carolina 27706.

etc. Analogous concepts and an algebra are now available for the process of designing organization structures.[1] In a paper by Baligh and Burton[2] these concepts and algebra are used to design a specific organization structure which is to solve a specific economic problem repeatedly under varying environmental conditions, i.e., for different parameter values. This structure maps onto one point in the algebraic space developed in Baligh and Damon.[1] The structure is a good example to use in the identification of a number of organization structure design processes, and to specify some of the operational concepts for use in identifying more or less efficient processes.

This paper derives conclusions on the efficiency of organization structure design processes, and uses the described structure to illustrate its concepts, conclusion, etc. The analysis contained in this paper deals with the following specific issues of design:

a. Cost and revenue relations to operationally defined structure components and hence to marginal additions (subtractions);
b. The concept of sequential design and the logical relations, e.g., structure addition, that define the steps;
c. Structure neighborhoods and marginal additions, and the information collected from each small step and used to identify the next step;
d. Efficient and inefficient marginal additions (subtractions);
e. Process decomposition and its allocation to designers;
f. Information substructure design in the context of decision rule substructure, reward substructure, etc.;

We use the specific and detailed structure in Baligh and Burton[2] and others sketched in this paper to illustrate our arguments and our conclusions on a relatively efficient process of design. First we describe the structures then we describe the process of designing them and structures in general.

2. An Economic Problem

A basic economic problem was presented in an earlier paper by Baligh and Burton.[2] It involves a monopolist who sells a single product in two markets, each with a distinct response function. The product is produced in two factories each with a specific production function that employs two inputs. Input prices are independent of amounts bought and are fixed each period, but vary from period to period. The monopolist wishes to make those decisions which maximize his profits. The organization structure, including its information substructure, produces decisions. The problem is intentionally simple, for our objective is to consider designing structures and is not the more limited issue of solving the economic problem.

The basic relations of the monopolist to his economic environment are given by a number of functions. Each function describes a production or exchange transformation available to the firm. Factories one and two are described by the functions $g_1 = f_1(x_{11}, x_{21})$ and $g_2 = f_2(x_{12}, x_{22})$, where g_i is the output amount of the good produced in factory i, $i = 1, 2$ and x_{ij} is the amount of the ith input used in the jth factory, $i = 1, 2$, and $j = 1, 2$.

The exchange transformations in the selling markets are the two market response functions. The two markets are described by the functions

$$p_1 = h_1(r_1, y_{11}, y_{21}) \quad \text{and} \quad p_2 = h_2(r_2, y_{12}, y_{22})$$

where p_i is the price commanded for the sale of the output product in the ith market, $i = 1, 2$; r_i is the total amount of the output product sold in the ith market, $i = 1, 2$; y_{ij} is the amount of the ith marketing effort exerted on behalf of sales in the jth market, $i = 1, 2$, $j = 1, 2$. y_{1j} may represent for example advertising efforts (spots on TV) and y_{2j} may be personal selling efforts, etc.

The remaining exchange transformations are those involving the manner in which the monopolist exchanges money for the inputs of production and marketing. Suppose these transformations are such that we can say that s_i is the price for the ith input of production, and t_i is the price for ith input of marketing, with both s_i and t_i independent of the amount of inputs bought by the firm.

The firm is to operate over a number of periods in the future. We assume that f_1, f_2, h_1, and h_2 remain unchanged through time. However, s_1, s_2, t_1, and t_2 change from period to period. During each period, the correct values of these prices can be obtained for use in each period's decisions. But the values of these parameters must be obtained anew each period if the decision makers are to make decisions based on the correct values of these parameters. We will consider here only the first period situation without inventory carryover and with no financial restrictions. While the intertemporal aspects of the problem are of significant economic interest, they are not necessary to illustrate the design issues we address. The transportation problem of allocating factory output to specific markets is not considered.

3. Description and Design of Organization Structures

The description of the unified single-decision-maker structure includes a monopolist whose goal is to maximize profits. This decision maker d_1 has the decision rule to optimize:

$$
\begin{aligned}
V = {}& h_1(r_1, y_{11}, y_{21})r_1 + h_2(r_2, y_{12}, y_{22})\, r_2 \\
& - [s_1(x_{11} + x_{12}) + s_2(x_{21} + x_{22}) + t_1(y_{11} + y_{12}) + t_2(y_{21} + y_{22})] \\
& + \lambda_1((r_1 + r_2) - (g_1 + g_2)) + \lambda_2(g_1 - f_1(x_{11}, x_{22})) \\
& + \lambda_3(g_2 - f_2(x_{11}, x_{22}))
\end{aligned}
$$

TABLE 1
The Unified Organization

Organizational members	Number and decisions to make	Number and parameters to read	Number of messages to receive	Number of messages to send
d_1	9	4	0	0
	x_{11}, x_{21}	s_1, s_2		
	x_{12}, x_{22}	t_1, t_2		
	y_{11}, y_{21}			
	y_{12}, y_{22}			
	g			
Total	10	4	0	0

Other tasks for the monopolist d_1 in each period is to (1) read the values of s_1, s_2, t_1, and t_2, and (2) solve for the profit-maximizing values x_{ij}, y_{ij}, for all $i = 1, 2$, and $j = 1, 2$, and for g and r. Another description of this structure is presented in Table 1. Note there are no messages to send or to receive. These are internal to the formulation.

An organization structure is a mechanism for obtaining the solution *each period*. With only one person to solve the problem we have an organization structure. However, there are interesting cases where we have more than one. The process of breaking down this total economic problem into subproblems for many people to solve, and putting together all the subproblem solutions to obtain the solution to the whole problem, is the process of designing an organization structure.

We now describe in detail another organization structure for this firm. This structure will also produce decisions that maximize profits† (except as noted later) as defined above for the firm, and yet no one person in the organization ever solves the *whole problem* or decides values to be given all decision variables. The structure with more than one person in it presumes that one person cannot gather the information and solve the whole problem in time (within the time period). This is the Simon[3] condition of bounded rationality. The structure has eight components each of which is a set of elements. The structure is as follows:

1. The decision makers in the structure are d_1, d_2, d_3, d_4, d_5, d_6, d_7.
2. The decisions to be made each period are x_{11}, x_{21}, x_{12}, x_{22}, y_{11}, y_{21}, y_{22}, g_1, g_2, r_1, and r_2.

---

†It can be shown that the decisions made by this organization structure are the same as the optimal decisions for the single-person organization. The approach is to show the equivalence of the Kuhn–Tucker conditions for the two organizations.

3. The parameter values to be read (found out) each period are s_1, s_2, t_1, and t_2.
4. The decision variables are allocated to the decision makers as follows:

d_4 chooses values	x_{11} and x_{21}
d_5 chooses values	x_{12} and x_{22}
d_6 chooses values	y_{11} and y_{21}
d_7 chooses values	y_{12} and y_{22}
d_2 chooses values	g_1 and g_2
d_3 chooses values	r_1 and r_2
d_1 chooses values	$g = (g_1 + g_2)$ and $r = (r_1 + r_2)$

5. The parameters are allocated to the decision makers to read as follows:

d_4 reads values	s_1 and s_2
d_5 reads values	s_1 and s_2
d_6 reads values	t_1 and t_2
d_7 reads values	t_1 and t_2

6. The decision rules used in the organization, and their orginators and users are as follows:
   a. From d_1 to d_2:
      i. Minimize by choice of values g_1 and g_2 the expression $W = C_1(g_1) + C_2(g_2)$ subject to the condition that $g_1 + g_2 = g^0$ (any given value). $C_i(g_i)$ is the function which gives the lowest cost of producing g_i in factory i, $i = 1, 2$.
      ii. From solution of i derived $C(g)$, the function which gives the lowest cost of producing any total amount g.
      iii. Produce g^0 and derive the optimal values g_1^0 and g_2^0 that are associated with it in solution of i. The value g^0 is received by d_2 the decision maker in a decision rule each period.
   b. From d_1 to d_3:
      i. Maximize by choice of r_1 and r_2 the expression $V = R_1(r_1) + R(r_2)$ subject to the condition that $r_1 + r_2 = r^0$ (any given value). $R_i(r_i)$ is the function which gives the highest revenues from selling r_i in market i net of the costs of efforts y_{1i} and y_{2i} expended in market i, for $i = 1, 2$.
      ii. From solution of i derive $R(r)$, the function which gives the highest revenue of selling any amount r net costs of effort y_{1i} and y_{1i} for $i = 1, 2$.
      iii. Sell r^0 and derive the optimal values r_1^0 and r_2^0 that are associated with it in solution of i. The value r^0 is received in a decision rule each period.

   c. From d_2 and d_4:
      i. Minimize by choice of x_{11} and x_{21} the expression $k - (s_1 x_{11} + s_2 x_{21})$
         subject to the condition that $g_1 = f_1(x_{11}, x_{21})$ (any given value).
      ii. Derive $C_1(g_1)$ from solution to i where $C_1(g_1)$ is the function which
         gives the lowest cost of producing any level of output in factory 1.
      iii. Produce g_1^0 and derive the optimal values x_{11}^0 and x_{21}^0 that are associated
         with it by i. The value g_1^0 is received in a decision rule each period.
   d. From d_2 to d_5: These rules are analogous to those for d_2 to d_4.
   e. From d_3 to d_6:
      i. Maximize by choice of y_{11} and y_{21} the expression $Q = h_1(r_1, y_{11}, y_{21})r_1$
         $- t_1 y_{11} - t_2 y_{21}$ subject to the condition that $r_1 = r_1^0$ (any given value).
      ii. Derive $R_1(r_1)$ from solution to i where $R_1(r_1)$ is the function that gives
         the highest revenue net of costs of y_{11} and y_{21} for any value of r.
      iii. Sell r_1^0 and derive the optimal values y_{11}^0 and y_{21}^0 that are associated with
         it by i. The value r_1^0 is received in a decision rule each period by d_6 from
         d_3.
   f. From d_3 to d_7: These rules are analogous to those from d_3 to d_6.
   g. From d_1 to d_1: Maximize by choice of g and r where $g = r$ the expression
      $Z = R(r) - C(g)$.
7. The messages that are to be sent each period and their originators and receivers
   are the following:
   a. From d_4 to d_2: The list that is the function $C_1(g_1)$.
   b. From d_5 to d_2: The list that is the function $C_1(g_2)$.
   c. From d_6 to d_3: The list that is the function $R_1(r_1)$.
   d. From d_7 to d_3: The list that is the function $R_2(r_2)$.
   e. From d_2 to d_1: The list that is the function $C(g)$.
   f. From d_3 to d_1: The list that is the function $R(r)$.
   g. From d_4 to d_2: Values x_{11}^0 and x_{21}^0 and s_1 and s_2.
   h. From d_5 to d_2: Values y_{11}^0 and y_{21}^0 and t_1 and t_2.
   i. From d_6 to d_3: Values y_{11}^0 and y_{22}^0 and t_1 and t_2.
   j. From d_7 to d_3: Values g_1^0 and g_2^0 and s_1 and s_2.
   k. From d_2 to d_1: Values g_1^0 and g_2^0 and s_1 and s_2.
   l. From d_3 to d_1: Values r_1^0 and r_2^0 and t_1 and t_2.
8. The reward system is as follows: (d_i, w_i) where w_i is d_i's money reward each
   period, $i = 2, \ldots, 7$. For d_1 rewards, w_i, are profits. Organization continues
   as long as

$$W_1 = R(r) - C(g) - \sum_{i=2}^{7} w_i - A \geq 0$$

where $r = g$ and where A are structure operating costs other than rewards.

Another, less detailed, description of this structure is given in Table 2.
The above two organization structures of one member and seven members

TABLE 2
The Maximally Partitioned Organization with Seven Decision Makers: Partial Descriptions

Organizational members	Number and decisions to make	Number and parameters to read	Number of messages to receive	Number of messages to send
d_1	2 g, r		2	2
d_2	2 g_1, g_2		3	3
d_3	2 r_1, r_2		3	3
d_4	2 x_{11}, x_{21}	2 s_1, s_2	1	1
d_5	2 x_{12}, x_{22}	2 s_1, s_2	1	1
d_6	2 y_{11}, y_{21}	2 t_1, t_2	1	1
d_7	2 y_{12}, y_{22}	2 t_1, t_2	1	1
Total	14	8	12	12

are extremes. There is a large number of intermediate structures of which we shall describe three in less detail than we have the first two.

A functional organization would associate production decisions for factories 1 and 2 as a subunit, marketing decisions for markets 1 and 2 as a subunit, and have a single coordinating unit. In Table 3, these decision makers are called d_2, d_3, and d_1, respectively. The structure results directly from the seven-member structure. Four decision makers are removed from the latter. All the decision rules given them to use and messages to and from them are also removed from the structure with seven decision makers.

Two divisional organizations are depicted in Tables 4 and 5. The first is an optimally coordinated divisional organization where the structure can obtain optimal overall decisions. Market 1 and factory 1 are associated in a single unit, or division. The decision maker is called d_2. Similarly, d_3 is the decision maker for market 2 and factory 2. This structure permits cross shipments from each factory to each market. This coordination is accomplished by d_1, who sets the level of effort for factory and market, and assures overall optimality.[4] Note that production and sales need not be equal within a division.

A second divisional structure is summarized in Table 5. Each division considers its own factory and market independently. Thus, it can obtain an overall optimal set of decisions by accident, not by plan. Within each division, the market and the factory are suboptimized. However, without the possibility to balance both factories and markets together, it is not possible to assume a global optimal.

TABLE 3
A Functional Organization with Three Decision Makers: Partial Description

Organizational members[a]	Number and decisions to make	Number and parameters to read	Number of messages to receive	Number of messages to send
d_1	2		2	2
	g, r			
d_2	6	2	1	1
	x_{11}, x_{21}	s_1, s_2		
	x_{12}, x_{22}			
	g_{11}, g_{22}			
d_3	6	2	1	1
	y_{11}, y_{21}	t_1, t_2		
	r_1			
	y_{12}, y_{22}			
	r_2			
Total	14	4	4	4

[a] d_1, headquarters; d_2, factories 1 and 2; d_3, markets 1 and 2.

TABLE 4
An Optimally Coordinated Divisional Organization with Three Decision Makers

Organizational members[a]	Number and decisions to make	Number and parameters to read	Number of messages to receive	Number of messages to send
d_1	4		4	4
	g_1, g_2			
	r_1, r_2			
d_2	6	4	2	2
	x_{11}, x_{21}	$s_., s_2$		
	y_{11}, y_{21}	t_1, t_2		
	g_1, r_1			
d_3	6	4	2	2
	x_{12}, x_{22}	s_1, s_2		
	y_{12}, y_{22}	t_1, t_2		
	g_2, r_2			
Total	16	8	8	8

[a] d_1, coordinating units; d_2, for division 1—market and factory; d_3, for division 2—market and factory.

TABLE 5
A Nonoptimizing Divisional Organization with Two Decision Makers

Organizational members[a]	Number and decisions to make	Number and parameters to read	Number of messages to receive	Number of messages to send
d_1	5	4		
	$x_{.1}, x_{21}$	s_1, s_2		
	y_{11}, y_{21}	t_1, t_2		
	r_1			
d_2	5	4		
	x_{12}, x_{22}	s_1, s_2		
	y_{12}, y_{22}	t_1, t_2		
	r_2			
Total	10	8	0	0

[a] d_1 for division 1—marketing and factory; d_2 for division 2—marketing and factory.

In Table 6, there is a summary of the decisions, parameters, and messages for each alternative organization structure and information subsystem.

4. Sequential Design Processes

There are two kinds of organization structure costs. The first is the cost of designing the structure. The second is the cost of operating the resulting organization. The former cost will depend on the process used, and on structure properties such as its complexity, detail, etc. This cost will also depend on the nature of the economic problem the structure is to solve, and on the extent to which the structure is intended to approach the optimal solution to that problem. The operating costs are the cost of operating the structure, of using rules, collecting information, processing information, of implementing the reward substructure, etc.

4.1. Structure Design Costs

The rule for the maximally partitioned organization that d_4 is to minimize $(s_1 x_{11} + s_2 x_{21})$, such that $f_1(x_{11}, x_{21}) = g_1^0$ is obtained at a cost which depends on how the rule is obtained. To obtain the rule, the designer must use some logical process, which in this case involves a problem formulation, and the identification of separable parts of the objective function. If he uses an algorithm to obtain that rule as a partial solution, his cost will depend on the algorithm and the system it involves. For example, paired comparisons of rules on any basis is less efficient than a method by which a given rule is used to guide the creation of the next one. Thus given the rules in Section 7c of the description of the structure above, it is

TABLE 6
Summary of Totals for Organizational Choices

	Number and decisions to make	Number and parameters to read	Number of messages to receive	Number of messages to send
Unified organization	10	4	0	0
Maximally partitioned organization	14	8	12	12
Functional organization	14	4	4	4
Optimizing divisional organization	16	8	8	8
Nonoptimizing divisional organizational	10	8	0	0

logical to create the rules in 6.d. The cost will also depend upon the rule itself. Given a process of obtaining a rule, this rule would be expected to cost more to obtain than one requiring the minimization of the costs of obtaining output amount in a given finite subset of output levels.

For the information substructure, we have the costs of specifying messages to be sent, parameters to be read, etc. The cost of specifying these components of the structure depends on the process we use to determine what message on what decision variable or parameter value, and what list on relations between such sets are to be sent. How did we arrive at the conclusion that a message on $C_1(g_1)$ is to be sent in the maximally partitioned organization? Did we specify it before creating the decision rule or after? If we use logic based on the notion that the rule producing $C_1(g_1)$ is of value only if $C_1(g_1)$ is sent to d_2, the cost of specifying this element of the information substructure would be smaller than it would have been had we randomly chosen messages from d_4 to d_2 and settled on these messages after checking each one in the sequence to see whether it is useful. Furthermore, the cost of specifying this message as an element of the structure depends on the message itself. A message on a subset of $C_1(g_1)$ is usually less expensive to determine and specify than one for all values of $C_1(g_1)$. The cost of sending and receiving a message depends on a number of aspects of the message.

The cost of determining the allocation of decision variables to decision makers also depends on the process. If it is based on the identification of the separable components of the objective function it will likely be more costly to specify than if it were random, or if it ignored a number of interconnections, i.e., created artificially separable components. The point is clear in a comparison of the optimally coordinated divisional organization with the nonoptimally coordinated divisional organization in Tables 4 and 5.

The reward system costs will depend on the choice of decision makers. The nonoptimal divisional structure assigned one factory to each market, with no logical connections allowed between the two divisions. It is, in fact, two separate substructures. Each has one factory and one market. There is no need for a coordinating unit as in the optimally coordinated divisional organization. The cost of obtaining the nonoptimizing decomposition and the cost of identifying the reward system is lower than for the optimizing structure.

If the information substructure design is obtained by a process of searching a space of substructures the costs would be expected to be lower for a smaller space than for a larger one. One would expect that to be the case in all but some of the most cost efficient processes of search, e.g., those analogous to the ones used in maximizing (minimizing) constrained continuous functions. These are not available for the designer of organization structures, nor for the designer of the information substructure only. The cost of design depends on the components: the degree to which they are complete, their number, the detail of their specification, etc.

4.2. The Cost of Operating the Organization

Operating structure costs are made up of the costs of executing the structure. The more complex the decision rules in the structure, the fewer the number of rules may be given to any decision maker to use in any given period, and the larger the number of decision makers needed. The more complex the rules—e.g., minimize $(s_1 x_{11} + s_2 x_{21})$, such that $f_1(x_{11}, x_{21}) = g_1^0$, instead of find the historical cost for some subset of some output levels—the more time needed for their use, and the higher the cost of their use.

Operating costs of the information substructure result from the reading of parameters, the sending and receiving of messages, the process of transforming variable and parameter values into others, and information storage. The costs of information collection in a structure depend on the nature of parameters to be read, and of course, on the nature of the reading process. Thus, finding the price of an input bought in a perfect market is much less costly than estimating the parameters of $h_1(r_1, y_{11}, y_{21})$ which may involve market research and complex information transformations. Messages on $C_1(g_1)$ are more costly to send than those on a subset of $C_1(g_1)$. Reading the exact values of a parameter is more costly than reading the set of values that contain the exact value with a probability π. On the other hand, the message sent in the latter case contains three numbers, viz., upper and lower values of the parameter, and the probability, and it will cost more to send than the other message which has only two numbers, viz., the value of the parameter and the number 1, the probability that it is that value.

Because we have an operational description of a structure, the process of finding its costs can be systematized. The information on a structure cost can be collected or estimated in a systematic component-by-component manner. Small structure changes, i.e., marginal ones, may be made and their costs estimated. The marginal changes chosen at each step in the sequential process described below can be based on the information obtained in the comparisons of costs (and revenues) of the specific components they have. In fact, marginal costs of structure changes may be systematically estimated, and the results used to identify what may be at least the better set of marginal changes to be made next.

The organization's revenues also depend on the structure. Since the structure produces decisions which in turn affect the outputs, different structures may produce different revenues. The arguments made for cost are applicable here, and together, marginal revenue and marginal costs of small structure changes (additions or subtractions at the "margin") may be used to guide the process of sequential structure design. The goal of design is to design a structure that maximizes the difference between its revenues and its costs. In the simple terms of our economic problem and our design, this involves maximizing the discounted present value of the operating profits produced by the structure over its expected life, minus the discounted value of its operating costs, minus its design costs.

5. Limitations of Search Processes: Marginal Comparisons without a Gradient

The efficiency of the process of designing organization structures, and their information substructures, depends on our capacity to make marginal changes and to relate the components of these marginal structures to their operating costs and revenues. As we shall explain in a following section, process rules are derived from some fundamental relations between structure components. On the basis of these relations, we derive useful principles which help us to choose from among the possible marginal changes the ones to use and evaluate on return and cost bases, in order thereby to improve the efficiency of our process. Before we discuss these relations, we need to discuss the process of design in general, now that we have at least one rationale for the process of sequential marginal additions.

One process of design is that of comparing pairs of structures that are given, e.g., U-form and M-form,[4,5] or any two in the list described in this paper or any subsets of any one or two of those in the list. The comparison between the efficiencies of any two leads to a conclusion that eliminates one of them as inferior to, or no better than, the second. The remaining structure is then compared to a third structure, and the process continues. When the process stops, the surviving structure is the best of the subset designed. This subset is created in a totally unguided manner. Each element is designed or copied from a description of a structure. Only if the searched subset of structures contains the optimal one will the remaining structure be the best. However, the designer has no idea how the chosen structure compares to any structures not in the subset involved in the paired comparisons. This process is an unguided search procedure. Nothing is learned from the past to guide the search. In addition, the process of how any given structure is designed cannot be specified by this process. The structure compared must somehow be there, be copied from existing ones, or put together in some manner. This random process is clearly inefficient, and incomplete, and we need to identify a better one.

The algebraic properties of the space of organization structures, particularly the necessary incompleteness of its logical order, make it impossible to obtain design processes analogous to those of the stepwise gradient search algorithm, or one to solve a system of linear equations. This is a major conclusion that is obvious from the presence in the algebra of organization structures of elements that are functions or nonnumber variables, etc.[1] Another major conclusion drawn from this algebra is that one can use the algebra to identify means of making the process more systematic and more efficient. The levels of efficiency allowed by these processes are not those of gradient search.

6. The Rule of Mimic

A sequential process may be identified for the design of organization structures, a process that is more efficient than random search, or paired comparisons. The superiority of the efficiency of the sequential process results from the use of information obtained from completed steps to determine the choice of the next step, so that the step is at least more efficient than many others we might take. The description of the logical process of design is derived from the logical order that exists in the space of organization structures, the identification of the kind of information we need, and the analysis of logical and economic relations between and among components of structures. The process is specified in terms of the concepts of structure addition, i.e., the definition of the steps in the sequence.[1] It is specified in terms of marginal changes (based on the logical order of structure and substructure) and the evaluation of the costs and revenues of structure components based on the clear distinction between components and the specification of the logical structure of the elements of each.[1] It is also specified in terms of general rules to guide marginal structure choices developed below.

The process starts with the specification of a small structure. Marginal costs of its separate components are evaluated and added to obtain the marginal cost of the structure. The same is done for revenues. For example, we can start with the noncoordinated divisional structure, and add to it the components that turn it into a coordinated divisional structure. Based on this information, and the principles given below, another marginal structure is designed and added to the first. The process continues with marginal additions and subtractions, each in part determined on the basis of information gleaned from past additions and subtractions, at least from the previous marginal addition or subtraction. For example, in the maximally partitioned organization, if we were at a stage where neither rule given to d_4 or d_5 was yet in the structure, we might add the structure made up of the first rule. If we did that, and the addition had a net marginal return, then the obvious next step is to add a structure with the analogous rule for d_5 to our present one. This is the rule of mimic because we can expect that its net marginal return will also be positive. The first step identifies one "good" next step. Of course, the process does *not* guarantee an optimal structure after n steps. But it is very likely to produce a better structure than the first process given a level of design effort (cost).

Suppose that we had designed only the substructure related to factory 1 of our structure. The costs of this structure are then calculated, though its revenues cannot yet be specified. Whatever the organization structure chosen, the minimization of the costs of producing any given output in one factory is necessary to the maximization of profits (before we subtract structure costs). Though not necessarily optimum, the next step is clearly the addition to this structure of another structure identical to it, except that it involves factory 2.

As we will show below, there are some rules that may be used in choosing the specific structure to add or subtract at the margin. The rules also guide the design of these marginal structures. Suppose we subtract the rule to minimize $(s_1x_{11} + s_2x_{21})$, such that $f_1(x_{11}, x_{21}) = g_1^0$, and messages from d_4 to d_2 on $C_1(g_1)$. We then add the structure made up of variable x_{n1} (money spent by factory 1), the rule maximize $f_1(x_{11}, x_{21})$ such that $x_{n1}^0 = (s_1x_{11} + s_2x_{21})$, a message from d_4 to d_2 on $Q_1(x_{n1})$ (the highest output obtained from any given amount of money), and the rule for information processing that asks d_2 to transform $Q_1(x_{n1})$ into $C_1(g_1)$. The results of these marginal changes are a total operating revenue and cost that are identical to the first. However, this structure has one information transformation and one decision variable not in the first. It costs more and produces the same result; it is less efficient. However, a couple of more changes, one marginal subtraction and one marginal addition, gives us a structure that has the same number of rules, messages, transformations, etc. as the first, but one in which production is directed by decisions on budgets and the use of money. Whatever implications this specific change has to reward systems and control can now be explored in this process of guided sequential design. The moves from the structure given in detail above and in Table 2 to the structure represented in any of Tables 3, 4, and 5 can be similarly made. There is a series of steps of component additions and substructures that takes us from any one of those structures to any other.

In summary this process involves:

1. A simple systematic and operational procedure of marginal changes;
2. A systematic and operational procedure for evaluating marginal changes, often derived from evaluation of earlier marginal changes;
3. A mechanism for the use of rules that helps us identify the specific nature

of the marginal changes including their size (because of the nature of the algebraic space there is no single marginal structure to any structure, but rather sets of these).

7. Technological Efficiency: Relation between Components of Organization Structures

An analysis of the relations between components of structure may allow us to derive certain rules to help our process of design. The relations allow us to identify technologically efficient structures, and to design such structures. This in turn permits us to derive some principles that will guide the sequential process. The principles give us rules which will, among other things, allow us to exclude certain marginal structures from consideration, even before we evaluate their marginal costs and revenues. Technological efficiency of structures is analogous to the concept of the technological efficiency of production transformations. The place of the former in the problem of organization structure design is analogous to that of the latter in production theory, at the elementary level.

The concept of technological efficiency of structures is exemplified by the concept of the value of information in structures as developed in Team Theory by Marschak and Radner.[6] However, this concept includes more than information value. By definition, a technologically inefficient structure is one which contains a nonempty substructure which when subtracted from it produces a structure that has the same operating profits as the first.[1] It is analogous to the notion of Pareto optimality in classical microeconomics. Operating profits are defined as revenues minus operating costs, with structure design and structure operating costs not yet subtracted. One clear example of a set of technologically inefficient structures is that given in MacCrimmon.[7] There we find structures designed for the Sweetsa Plantation that involve messages on parameter values that are not used in any decision rule, and decision rules without messages or readings on the parameters in their domains. Because technological inefficiency can be related directly to components, it may be used to eliminate marginal changes from consideration, or to specify marginal changes for consideration. As is shown below, technological inefficiency may be easily established by reference to small substructures of the structure. Before any step in the process is taken, such checks for technological inefficiencies will help us to determine what marginal structures not to add, and hence make it unnecessary to evaluate marginal costs and revenues of these structures. The concept of technological inefficiency would be of even greater value if we could use it to derive a set of operational and general rules to guide the sequential process of structure design.

Thus even the process of marginal design may be made partly systematic, in other words "appropriate" marginal structures may be operationally defined.

Evaluation of marginal net returns of marginal structures, etc. need not be made until the result of the addition of a marginal structure results in one that is technologically efficient. The last design in a sequence should be technologically efficient. The last design is the one we choose to implement. But the efficiency of the process will likely be higher if all its steps were made to produce a technologically efficient structure. If we start with a structure s_1 and add to it structure s_2, a marginal one, then $s_1 + s_2 = s_3$ may or may not be technologically efficient. If we check for technological efficiency after the whole addition we may have to reject it. But if we check s_2 (a small structure) with the "appropriate" substructures of s_1 in a sequential manner, we may be able to reject or accept s_2 as a marginal change, before cost and profit evaluation, without checking the whole finished structure s_3. If s_2 passes against the appropriate substructure, then s_3 will be technologically efficient. Furthermore, the element or component of s_2 that causes a technology inefficiency of some s_3 can itself be replaced by one that does not; we now make marginal changes on marginal changes. The logical counterpart to this process is that the design of the marginal structure itself be limited to components and elements which do not produce a marginal structure s_3 for which $s_1 + s_2$ is technologically inefficient.

The kinds of relations between components (and between elements of different components) involved in the concept of technological inefficiency are ones which are identified by a logical analysis of the economics of organization structures in general. Without any attempt to be comprehensive, a few of these relations may be used to produce rules that determine technological efficiency. These rules, if followed, produce an organization structure that is not technologically inefficient. Some of the rules are adapted and expanded from Team Theory;[6] others are new. Any set of rules may be specified, providing the economics of the structure and its goals, etc., are specified. Some rules may be briefly identified as follows:

    a. Parameter and decision variable values are to be read only if the values lie in the domain of a decision rule or reward function.

    b. Messages are to be received on parameter or decision variable values by any d_i only if (1) its object (parameter or decision variable value) is in the domain of decision rule d_i uses, or (2) it or its transform by d_i is the object of a message sent by d_i.

    c. All decision rules for use by any d_i must be accompanied by knowledge by d_i of the values of all elements in their domain, either through reading parameter values, receiving parameter and decision variable values, obtaining functions in the rule from some d_j, or from other rules d_i uses, or obtaining decision variable values from another decision rule that d_i has that produced these values. (Parts of this rule result from requirements on intracomponent relations discussed below).

    d. No parameter is to be read by any d_i unless he has a decision rule with this parameter value in its domain, or there is a message from d_i with this parameter value or some transform of its value as its object to some d_j.

    e. There is to be no decision rule used by any d_i unless d_i is allocated the decision variable in the decomposition the value of which results from the use of the rule (the reverse does not hold).

    f. No d_i is to be in the structure unless there is also in the structure a decision rule for d_i to use, or a parameter for d_1 to read, or d_i is to be the recipient *and* sender of messages on the same subject or its transform.

All these rules are strictly observed in the structures described in detail above. Both those structures are technologically efficient. On the other hand, the structure that remains after we remove any messages from component 7, or any allocation from components 4, is technologically inefficient because it violates rules (b) and (e), respectively. Any addition to the structure of a message from d_4 to d_2 given the optimal values of x_{11} as a function of output g_1 would violate rule (b).

More rules can be identified, some rather trivial like the last one, others more complex than, say, (c). In all cases, technological efficiency can be said to be most likely the outcome of the relations between the information substructure and the decision rule substructure. The above rules are not inconsistent with structures that are more complex and more nearly complete than those described. Such structure spaces as in Baligh and Burton[8] allow for rules in parameter and decision variable value transformations. They allow for feedback information, multiple parameter readings for accuracy required, messages for accuracy and reliability, etc. The set of rules above can be expanded for such more complex concepts of structures. But in all these cases most of the rules apply or need to be modified slightly. For example, the concept of decision rules needs to be expanded to include decision rules that correct decision makers, on the basis of feedback on their use of other decision rules.

Two important statements on the use of the concept of technological efficiency to guide design steps can be made. If s_1 and s_2 are both technologically efficient, then $s_1 + s_2 = s_3$ is technologically efficient. If s_1 is technologically efficient and s_2 is not technologically efficient then $s_1 + s_2 = s_3$ is not necessarily technologically inefficient. We may guarantee that at the end of any step in a sequential process, the structure we have designed is technologically efficient by guaranteeing that every structure in the process is technologically efficient. A number of checks for each marginal structure is substituted for one check and corrections on a much larger structure. This suggests another source of improved efficiency in the process of design.

Regardless of the concept of technological efficiency, we still have to evaluate marginal structures in the sequential process of design. This concept permits us to reduce the number of marginal structures eligible for addition, but we will have to choose one from the remaining set. Marginal structure costs depend mostly, though not totally, on the components of the marginal structure. Marginal revenues of marginal structures, however, depend very strongly on the structure that results from the addition. For example, the value of information depends on its use. But the use of information is not restricted to the decision rule in the domain of which that information is located. Any rule which uses the decision variable values that result from the first rule relies on that information also. The nestedness of decision rules, where the decision variable values that emerge from one belong to the domain of another, make it very difficult to identify the value of a piece of information. If parameter value t_1 is not read, and all messages on it are canceled in the structure, then some small cost saving would result. However if we substitute for this value the value $\bar{t}_1$, the mean of the probability distribution of t_1, we obtain a marginal change in structure revenues. These cannot be obtained from only the rule which uses $\bar{t}_1$ or t_1 directly. The value of t_1 or $\bar{t}_1$ is traceable through a number of decision rules to d_1. Even so, the clearer, more operational, more detailed, and more explicit our concept of the structure is, the easier will this tracing process be. Tracing effects through nested decision rules is likely to be easier if the rules are clearly specified and explicitly laid out. If no rules exist or if the nestedness is not total, i.e., partial, then it would be very difficult to trace the effects of information and hence its value. This implies that the relationship between the decision rules in the structure, those between messages, and those between the elements of any component of structure, may be another source of obtaining rules the use of which would make the sequential process of design more efficient than it would be in their absence. The few rules we have derived are only a subset of the total, and it should be clear that the specific purposes of the structures designed may be used to obtain others.

8. Logical Consistency: Relations between Elements of Any Component of Organization Structures

Any given component of an organization structure is termed logically consistent if there are no logical contradictions or inconsistencies between the elements within it, or within any such element. Logical contradiction and consistency have to be specifically defined for each component's elements, and for some they may not be meaningful. The relation of logical consistency to structure cost and revenues is not as clear as that of technological efficiency to costs and revenues. Nonetheless, if some such relationships can be identified they may allow us to specify rules for choosing marginal additions which may help us improve the process efficiency, at times if not always. Each contradiction or inconsistency directly produces a rule to guide the sequential process of design.

Two decision rules are contradictory if there is any variable for which both produce values, and if the values they produce for the variable are never equal to one another. They are inconsistent if the above holds for some points in their domains but not for others. For example, in our structure, the rule on net revenue maximization given d_5 would be at least inconsistent with the rule that requires the minimizing of the costs of marketing any given output. This latter rule produces zero values for y_{ij}, all i, j. If the first rule never produces these values, they are contradictory. Two transformations of the same set of decision variables and parameter values are inconsistent if they sometimes produce different sets of decision variable or parameter values, and contradictory when they always do so. The transformation of $C_1(g_1)$ into $Q_1(x_{n1}) = C_1^{-1}(g_1)$ may itself be internally inconsistent if $C_1^{-1}(g_1)$ does not exist. The transformation should then specify the transformation of $C_1(g_1)$ into $Q_1^*(x_{n1})$, where $Q_1^*(x_n^0) = C_1^{-1}(g_1^0)$ if and only if $Q_1^*(x_{n1}^0) \geq 0$. The same applies to tranformations on parameter readings, e.g., the statistical methods employed to estimate a parameter, or the mechanical or electronic, etc., process used to read a parameter such as the number of units of inventory.

Such inconsistencies and contradictions may not always be undesirable aspects of a structure. However, their desirability must be established, and until it is, these logical relations supply us with rules to follow in the process of sequential design. These rules can be used to check marginal structures against the relevant substructures of the one to which they are added. No addition is made unless the result of the sum of the marginal structure and the relevant substructure is a substructure that has no inconsistency or contradiction. Every decision rule to be added can be checked for internal consistency and against the substructure made up of the relevant subset of decision rules in the marginal structure. When these decision rules are explicitly stated, and when the order imposed on the structure groups them together, it is relatively easy to identify the substructure against which the marginal structure is to be tested for logical consistency. In fact, only a substructure of the substructure of decision rules is likely to be involved at any step of marginal addition.

The concepts of technological efficiency and logical consistency of a structure allow us to eliminate whole classes of structures from eligibility as marginal additions at each step of our process without evaluating their marginal returns. Suppose we had structure s_1 and s_2 a marginal structure which contained a substructure s_2' of s_2, such that $s_1 + s_2' = s_3$ had a logically inconsistent component. We can now conclude that not only is s_2 not to be added to s_1 in our process but any structure s_n such that s_2' is a substructure of s_n is also not to be added as a marginal structure *in this step*, i.e., the one to be specifically determined. The step of checking s_2 identified for us a whole set of ineligible structures and thus narrowed down our choice set. For help in future steps we can specify the substructure which must have been added to s_1 (or subtracted from it) before any structure in the group identified as ineligible may be added at any future step, i.e., may become eligible. It is, in effect, the basis for making the process systematic.

9. Information Substructure of Organization Structure

The tasks of designing a structure may well be allocated to a number of designers. We may have job designers, one for each d_i as represented by the rows in Tables 1–5. One may also have an information substructure designer, the decision rule substructure designer, the reward substructure designer, etc. These are the columns in Tables 1–5. One can also have both at once, i.e., specialize by specific cells in the tables. This would make the process of designing organization structures one that is itself like a maxtrix organization. Because of our definition of a structure and the algebraic concepts of substructure and addition, we can create a structure s_3 by creating separately each element in a set of substructures $\{s_1, s_2, \ldots, s_n\}$, such that $s_1 + s_2 + \cdots + s_n = s_3$.[1] The nature of s_i is entirely up to us. We may choose to have s_i and s_j be such that the only substructure they have in common is the empty one. We may choose overlapping substructures. The choice may be based on available designing expertise which we may use to advantage, or by a decision to redesign some substructures of a given structure. The sequential process described earlier may be coupled with such a partitioning process. In general, the substructure tasks are not separable. Unless the two processes are connected, there is no guarantee that the resulting structure will be technologically efficient or logically consistent. If the partitioning is based on component groupings and no elements of any component are in more than one group, then each such structure design may produce a logically consistent substructure. The structure s_3 may be logically consistent. Technologically efficiency of s_3 will be obtained, however, only by pure chance, unless the substructure designers work under specific conditions. Other partitionings are also possible.

Individual expertise in the design of information substructures may be enough to produce a logically consistent substructure. It is never enough to produce the *best* information substructure. The best such structure is that which is designed within all the technological efficiency criteria (as well as others not analyzed in this paper), and these criteria by definition cannot be determined by the information substructure designer by himself. The total structure can only coordinate the activities of decision makers if it is designed by coordinated designers. With this as a background we may discuss information substructures and their designs.

The information substructure of a structure is that substructure in which the only components that may be nonempty are the information components. We are not referring here to any information on the structure, e.g., that decision rules given to d_6 be made known to him, or that rules given d_4 be made known to d_6.

These are issues that are ignored at this point, since they really involve metadesign. We assume for the moment that every decision maker will know that substructure that involves him, i.e., his job. The information substructure to which we refer is that which involves parameter and decision variable value readings, logical transformations on these values (functional transformation on numbers or functions relating nonnumber values to others etc.), the messages sent by any decision maker to others, questions asked, and subjects of these messages and questions.

In the detailed seven-member structure above, the information substructure is made up of the elements of components 3, 5, 7. It is valuable to identify what structural changes the information substructure designer may produce on his own, without creating any technological efficiency problems, and which he may not. We seek to identify, in effect, those elements, components, etc., of this substructure that the designer may under certain conditions design without producing any technological inefficiency and those he may not. Perhaps the analysis will produce some generalizations about the kinds of marginal changes in the substructure that may be treated as independent of other substructures, about others that are not, and about the conditions under which these changes may move from one set to the other.

One set may be termed purely informational, i.e., they involve the mechanics of information, and the others organizational aspects of information, i.e., they involve the proper integration of the information substructure into the total organization structure. The first kind of design decisions could be left to the information substructure designer, with results restricted to the substructures. The second, if left to the information substructure designers, will have effects on all of those substructures. Thus the realm over which substructure designers need to be coordinated is narrowed to the second set of changes. The first set can be excluded *ex ante* from any process of coordinating the sequential and partitioned design process.

We may illustrate these points with reference to the structure designed earlier. If that structure had been rich enough to include the decision rules by which s_i or t_i, all i, were to be read, then any variations in those rules that would not affect the accuracy of the reading or its availability would have been mechanical ones. The decision on such changes in the information structure have effects, under these conditions, only on the cost and logical consistency of the information substructure. A change from having d_4 and d_5 read s_i all i, would be purely mechanical, providing d_4 and d_5 both have the values in time. Thus, as in Marschak and Radner,[6] d_4 may read s_1 and s_2 and send two message on the values to d_5 or the reverse, etc. The decision to transmit the equation for $C_1(g_1)$ in a general form, i.e., in a form in which s_i remains s_i, and then the value of s_i each period to d_2, instead of sending a message on the equation of $C_1(g_1)$ in each period with the value of s_i plugged in, is a mechanical design decision. This change produces no technological inficiencies, but the cost of transforming the general equation for $C_1(g_1)$ into the number equation for $C_1(g_1)$ by d_2 and d_4 may not be the same. In that case, though the new structure design preserves technological efficiency, it may involve the added costs of this transformation, along with any savings obtained from sending messages with the value of s_i as subjects instead of messages with the whole equation. Technological efficiency is but one factor in the decision to allow the information substructure to be designed independently of the rest of the structure.

A decision on substituting $\bar{s}_i$ for the real value of s_i, when s_i is the average of the probability distribution on s_i, any i, is not a mechanical design decision. As has been shown, the relative values of knowing and using s_i and $\bar{s}_i$ depend upon the decision rule substructure, and on the functional relation described in the organization's economic problem. In our case, the profits derived from the use of $\bar{s}_i$ by the optimum decision rules are less than those derived from the use of s_i by the optimum decision rules, which in this case are the same as those used in $\bar{s}_i$. For the total structure the former may indeed be better because of the costs of obtaining s_i, but the decision should not be made purely in the information substructure. The same may be said for an information substructure in which s_i is not read exactly each period, and in which $\bar{s}_i$ is not used, but each period s_i is determined with probability 1 to lie between s_i^0 and s_i^{00}. Further refinements, such as identifying the probability distribution of $s_i^0 \leq s_i \leq s_i^{00}$, where s_i will lie in the range with certainty, and then using $\bar{\bar{s}}_i$ the mean of that distribution are of course possible. All these information substructure design decisions have an impact on the technological efficiency of our structure, but not necessarily on other structures we may design to replace it.

If s_i were estimated from other parameters, then the estimation procedure, i.e., the set of decision rules needed to obtain s_i, is a mechanical information substructure decision, providing the value of s_i estimated by each transformation is always the same. If it is not the same, the decision may have technological efficiency and general efficiency consideration. Simon's[3] dictum may be restated in our terms to say that the cost of information transmittal should lead parameter value users to be also parameter value readers. The statement says, in effect, that decision rule substructures, and information and the decision variable and parameter reading substructures, should be of specific kinds, not only should they not be designed separately. Though the case for independent information substructure design is strong (witness the seemingly unchanging, rigid, and organizationally independent information substructures today), the opposite case is equally strong. The concept of technological efficiency and the clear and operationally defined concepts of the space of organization structures should help identify the cost and revenues associated with each case. The determination of the parts of the information substructure that should be designed independently of the other substructures of the organization, and those that should not, should be based on an understanding of the logical nature of an organization structure.

10. Job Design

A frequently adopted approach to organizational design is based on the concept of the job. That is, the composition of the rules, information exchanges, etc. for an individual to define his job. The design of these for a specified number of individuals yields an organizational design. In contrast to the substructure approach, which focuses on the columns in Tables 1–5, the job design approach partitions the organizational design issue by the rows in Tables 1–5.

For example, the organizational designer might approach our illustrative situation by identifying three jobs for a $\{d_1, d_2, d_3\}$ three-person organization of Table 3. He then designs the three jobs by specifying decision variables for each, then the messages each is to send, and so on. The goal would be to create an organization by sequential addition of substructure functions to operating jobs in order to obtain technologically efficient and logically consistent total structures.

A systematic process of job design involves the creation of new jobs from old ones by job combinations, or job splitting. The first takes two jobs and makes them into one, the second does the reverse. The advantage of this process is that search cost is lower than that of other processes, e.g., paired comparisons. Another source of efficiency is the fact that the property of technological efficiency transfers with job addition. Combining two jobs that are technologically efficient gives a job that also has this property. Job splitting is more complex; however, it is possible to take a technologically efficient job and create two technologically inefficient jobs.

Whatever the process of design, one should seek to choose one that is efficient relative to others. The manner of identifying this efficiency, or of creating relatively more efficient processes, should be derived from an understanding of the logical and economic nature of organization structures.

References

1. H. H. BALIGH, and W. W. DAMON, Foundations for a systematic process of organizational structure design, *J. Inf. Optim. Sci.* **1**(2), 133–165 (1980).
2. H. H. BALIGH, and R. M. BURTON, Describing and designing organization structures and processes, *Int. J. Policy Analysis Inf. Sys.* **5**(4), 251–266 (1981).
3. H. A. SIMON *The Science of the Artificial*, MIT Press, Cambridge, Massachusetts, 1981.
4. R. M. BURTON and B. OBEL A computer simulation test of the M-form hypothesis, *Administrative Sci. Q.* **25**(3), 457–466 (1980).
5. O. E. WILLIAMSON *Markets and Hierarchies: Analysis and Antitrust Applications,* The Free Press, New York, 1975.
6. J. MARSCHAK and R. RADNER, *Economic Theory of Teams,* Yale University Press, New Haven, 1972.
7. K. R. MACCRIMMON, Descriptive aspects of team theory, *Manage. Sci.* **20**(10) 1323–1334 (1974).
8. H. H. BALIGH and R. M. BURTON, *Designing Organization Structures* 1983, incomplete monograph.

2

ORGANIZATIONAL STRUCTURES AS THE PRIMAL INFORMATION SYSTEM

AN INTERPRETATION

KENNETH D. MACKENZIE

1. Introduction

An information system consists of a collection of entities and their relationships. Information systems act to collect, store, process, and transport information. This chapter argues that there are two polar types of information systems. The first, the organizational process information system (OPIS), relies upon the organizational structures as its information system. The second, the technologically augmenting information system (TAIS), supplements the OPIS. A TAIS relies on a combination of technology and its users to augment human communication. Every OPIS has had its supporting TAISs ever since the invention of writing. In the past century the capacity improvements in TAISs created by improved communications, improved information processing capabilities, and developments in understanding of decision theory and management science models have created miracles and headaches for those operating organizations.

The expansion of TAISs creates major system incompatibilities with the primary OPIS. It is argued that such system incompatibilities are inevitable until designers of TAISs augment their thinking and methods to incorporate and to understand how the primary OPIS works. It is also argued that the best way to identify, solve, and implement corrections to such incompatibilities is to first learn to model the OPIS and then to design and co-opt TAIS technologies to support it. The current technique of enlarging TAISs without understanding the OPIS has diminishing returns, creates inevitable incompatibilities, and tends to become ineffective. It is argued that while TAIS technologies should always be improved,

KENNETH D. MACKENZIE • Organizational Systems, Inc., P.O. Box 1118, Lawrence, Kansas 66044; and University of Kansas, Lawrence, Kansas 66045.

to the extent that they remain incompatible with the OPIS, they will not be decisive in the running of the adaptive and efficient organization. Because it is more difficult to change humans than it is to change technical processes and because humans control organizations, it is argued that designers of TAISs should expend an increasing amount of resources on understanding the real world OPIS.

For years it was argued that improvements in TAISs would eventually supplant existing OPISs. In part they have. However, they have paradoxically allowed the expansion of the OPIS which in turn has led to improved TAIS, etc.

The purposes of this paper are to explain the ideas behind organizational process information systems, to develop the idea of a TAIS, and then discuss the interdependencies between an OPIS, its supplementary TAISs, and the resulting system incompatibilities.

2. Organizational Process Information Systems

One of the old stories emphasizing the lack of completeness in theory is the "inability" of the bumblebee to fly. Somehow it was not possible for a physicist to explain how bumblebees could fly. A quick scan of business publications might lead to the conclusion that organizations need computers, fast and accurate communication systems, automated office information systems, and workers with more than a classical education to run them. It would seem impossible for a large multinational corporation facing fierce competition and external pressure to change to run well without all of the technologically augmenting information systems. But, just as the bumblebee could fly in spite of conventional wisdom about physics, so can large, complex organizations function without modern TAISs.

History provides numerous examples. Westerners would cite the Roman Empire (whose expanse and longevity was impressive and likely to be greater than any existing corporation), the Catholic Church, and the British Empire. Others might cite the Ming Dynasty in China, the Ottoman Empire at the time of Suleiman, and the Moguls in India. The Romans ran a corporate state which was quite extensive for approximately 500 years without the use of computers, xerography, telephones, satellites, management science, systems theory, or printing presses. They did fairly well with a small educated elite, messengers, parchment, rocks, and quills. The Romans, of course, did not have the technology we have today and had to rely solely on the OPIS with primitive TAIS support.

Another example is a competitive market economy such as that which is approximated in North America which somehow coordinates, controls, and directs the interlocking commercial interests of millions of companies and more millions of customers without the need for a czar or a formal TAIS.

It is neither necessary nor sufficient that a complex organization have a technologically augmenting information system requiring more than the most elemental devices. History provides many examples questioning the necessity. The short survival of numerous organizations with fairly extensive technologically aug- menting information systems (e.g., Braniff, Wickes Lumber, and perhaps Inter- national Harvester) raises questions about the sufficiency. Just as we can see bum- blebees flitting from blossom to blossom, so do we also see technologically primitive organizations survive and prosper for long periods of time. Today we even see very high technology producing firms with rather primitive information systems.

These observations need to be made at a conference on Management and Office Information Systems because they are overlooked in the pell-mell rush to perfect technologically advanced information systems. They are definitely not made in order to criticize the many technological marvels spewing forth from our research and development centers. They should help create curiosity about how the Romans or even Andrew Carnegie and J. D. Rockefeller managed to run sizable organizations without all of the modern technology we now take for granted.

Actually, the answer is very simple. *The organization is itself an information system.* The division of labor, the lines of authority, rules and regulations, inter- personal relationship guide the generation, flow, storage, processing, and trans- portation of data and information. The organization of work, the direction, con- trol, and coordination of work, and the planning are defined by the organizational processes themselves. The role of technological augmentations to this primary information system (the OPIS) is to supplement it. For numerous reasons to be discussed later, the TAIS cannot ever eliminate the OPIS.

The idea that the organization is itself an information system has far-reach- ing implications. The first is the necessity of reformulating the issues of TAIS design to support the OPIS. We need to question our basic thinking and challenge our implicit assumptions in the design of TAISs. The second is the systemic incompatibilities that can emerge as a result of ignoring the OPIS. The third is the need to formulate TAIS in a form that is more compatible with the OPIS. The fourth is the need to be able to understand the conditions under which a TAIS is preferred as a supplement. Fifth is the consideration of where to locate the persons who design, improve, and manage TAISs. Sixth, the very nature of man- agement requires more rigorous formulation. In order to address these implica- tions and to understand an OPIS, we first need to review what is meant by orga- nizational structures and concepts of task processes.

2.1. Organizational Structures

A structure is defined by its entities and the relationships between them. A structure can be represented by

$$S = (X_n; R) \tag{1}$$

Where $X_n = (x_1, x_2, \ldots, x_i, \ldots, x_n)$ represents the n entities of interest and R is a matrix whose rows and columns are defined by X_n and whose entries are a measure of the directed relationship between any corresponding pair. The entry $r_{ij} \in R$ need not have the same value as the symmetric position $r_{ji} \in R$.

A structure represents an interaction pattern among the entities. The entities can be individuals, milestones in a process, elements of a computer program, organizations, machines, etc. Human structures change and the laws by which they change are consistent with the assumption that a structure represents a need-satisfying interaction pattern. Thus as needs change or as the perceived instrumentability of maintaining the current interactions changes, so will the structures tend to change. Laboratory experiments in structural change result in highly predictable processes whose timing and results can be modeled with precision.[1−4]

An organization of people engages in multiple task processes and each task process has its own structure. Thus an organization has multiple structures. For example, the authority structure is just one of many and is usually a convenient fiction bearing only a transient relationship with the actual interaction patterns. The structures of any human organization are fluid rather than rigid, as is generally supposed.

Each structure represents the interaction pattern to complete a particular task process. There is a different structure for strategic decision making and planning than for finance, personnel, marketing, products, quality control, etc. Different persons are usually involved and the interaction pattern tends to follow the lines dictated by the different task processes.

The task processes are related to one another and consequently so are the structures. The task processes change and the structures change to accommodate one another. The organization is a part of a larger system called its environment. Changes in the environment set into motion changes in both the task processes and the structures. Attempts are made to control the environment to suit the task processes and structures preferred by the organization. Structures represent how entities interact to carry out task processes. The organizational structures represent the primal information system. They describe who sends what to whom. The entities collect, filter, process, and change the information as each performs its parts in the various task processes. Thus, the entities, the environment, and the task processes adapt and adjust to one another. They alter the information system as they adapt. Consequently, the OPIS is dynamic, flexible, and opportunistic.

2.2. Task Processes

A *process* is a time-dependent sequence of elements governed by a rule called a process law. All processes have five common ingredients:

    a. The entities participating in the sequence of elements;
    b. The elements which are descriptions of the steps in a process;
    c. The relationships between these elements;

d. The links to other processes; and
e. The resource characteristics of the elements.

A *process law* specifies the structure of the elements, the relationship and the links to other processes. The *state of a process* is an ordered pair of the attribute representing the outcome and the value representing the degree to which the process has been completed. A process law can be represented by

$$y = F(X) \tag{2}$$

where X is the set of elements, F is the graph of the relationships among the elements, and y is the state of the process. Different processes have different X's, F's and y's.

A process is always linked to another process. A process law is activated by an event. There can be multiple events, chains of events, hierarchies of events, and chains of process laws in organizations. There are sequences of events and process laws. The situation is not unlike having a box of Chinese puzzles and opening them to find that parts of each puzzle at one level lead to puzzles at the next, etc. and where there are instructions to go to another puzzle as each is solved.

A useful typology of process laws by variability can be drawn from the second equation, $y = F(X)$. In some cases X is fixed. In other X is variable. In some cases F is fixed and in others F is variable. The classification of process laws is shown in Table 1.

Conservative task process laws are quite common and represent habitual process routines such as standard operating procedures. Variable process laws are relatively rare because usually when the function changes so do its elements. Dynamic process laws have the same function but the values of the elements change. Dynamic process laws are common in the physical sciences. Progress in defining technologically augmenting information systems is roughly parallel with the evolution from conservative to dynamic process laws. Decision support systems extend TAISs into the realm of variable process laws. Open process laws are very significant in organizations and describe the planning, strategic management, and analysis by senior management. Open process laws are currently beyond the reach of most existing TAIS research except for the possible application of artificial intelligence.

TABLE 1
Classification of Process Laws by Variability

Elements, X	Functions, F	
	Fixed	Variable
Fixed	Conservative	Variable
Variable	Dynamic	Open

Another useful typology of process laws can be made that stresses the *level of each process law* and the transitions to others. At the lowest level is the execution process law which is conservative. One can move from one execution process law to another by a sequence of execution events. An *execution process law* is a conservative process law

$$e = E(X) \tag{3}$$

where the elements X are activities or sets of activities, the interrelationships are the sequential interdependencies between the elements, E is the execution process graph, and e is the state of the execution process, and the entities are those who perform the activities and sets of activities. The state, e, of an execution process law is $e = (A, v)$, where

$$A = \begin{cases} 1 & \text{if directing, coordinating, and controlling} \\ & \text{process laws are required} \\ 0 & \text{if not} \end{cases}$$

and

$$v = \begin{cases} 1 & \text{if process is in progress} \\ 0 & \text{if process is not in progress.} \end{cases}$$

The attribute of the state of an execution process law describes whether or not the execution process requires any integrating help from another source.

A directing, controlling, or coordinating (DCC) process law is a variable, dynamic or open process law,

$$d = D(E(X)) \tag{4}$$

where D is a mapping function process for selecting execution process laws to effect choice and to achieve "in common" or compatibility in resource characteristics across two or more execution process laws, and d is the state of a DCC process. The state, d, of a DCC process law is an ordered pair of its attribute and its value or $d = (A_d, v_d)$, where

$$A_d = \begin{cases} 1 & \text{if change in process processes are required} \\ 0 & \text{if not} \end{cases}$$

and

$$V_d = \begin{cases} 1 & \text{if process is in progress} \\ 0 & \text{if process is not in progress.} \end{cases}$$

A *mapping function* is a dynamic process law in which, for a specific situation, the elements are variable, D describes all possible paths from the first variable in the vector of network variables to the resulting states, d. Normally, the person involved is called a decision maker, who may represent an individual, a committee, or a decision procedure applied by a central processor. Note that every variable in a mapping function can be seen as the result of its own mapping function (as in the Chinese puzzle boxes metaphor). In many cases, the determination of the state of each variable in the mapping function rests on different circumstances for each variable.

A third level is the change in process process. A *change in process process law* is an open process whose inputs are states of a DCC law and whose outputs are new DCCs of execution process laws. A change in process process law is represented by

$$\delta = C(D\{E(X)\}) \tag{5}$$

where C is a mapping function on a DCC process and δ is the state. δ is an ordered pair of an attribute and a value, denoted $\delta = (A_\delta, v_\delta)$, where

$$A_\delta = \begin{cases} 1 & \text{if more change in processes are required} \\ 0 & \text{if a transition to a DCC law is required} \end{cases}$$

$$v_\delta = \begin{cases} 1 & \text{if process is in progress} \\ 0 & \text{if process is not in progress} \end{cases}$$

Thus the three levels correspond to how to execute, how to direct, coordinate, nd control, and how to change a process. Table 2 illustrates the hierarchy of process laws and their relationships.

Process laws can also be combined as a sequence of process laws and events. A *compound process* is a time-dependent sequence of activated process laws and

TABLE 2
Hierarchy of Processes and Process Laws

Process law level	Process law level		
	Execution	DCC	Change in process
$e = E(x)$	$\checkmark^a$	$\checkmark$	$\checkmark$
$d = D(e)$	—	$\checkmark$	$\checkmark$
$\delta = D(d)$	—	—	$\checkmark$

[a]Denotes that the process law level indicated by the row can be a part of the process law level indicated by the column.

events. A *conservative compound* process consists of a time-dependent sequence of processes whose events are the preceding processes.

Example of a Conservative Compound Process. Let PL_1, PL_2, PL_3, and PL_4 be the process laws in a compound process; then,

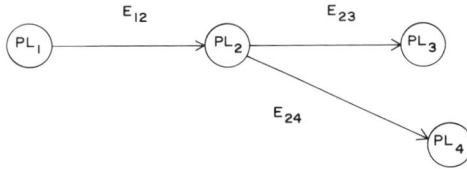

represents the conservative compound process. The events are signaled by the preceding process. Note that the events in a conservative compound process are trivial and may be defined by the links connecting a pair of process laws. In the above example, let

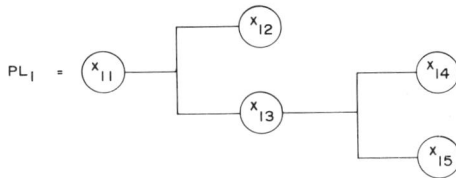

and

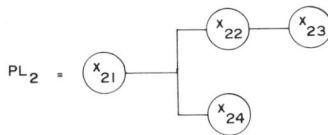

then

An *open compound process* consists of a time-dependent sequence of process laws and events in which at least one of the events comes from processes not in the defined set.

Example of an Open Compound Process. Let PL_1, Pl_2, and PL_3 be members of the compound process and let PL_4 and PL_5 be members of other compound processes.

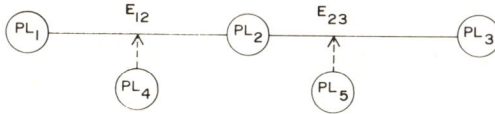

One can place compound processes horizontally within each level and vertically across level as is shown in Fig. 1. The dotted circled portions of the figure represent a composite compound process called a play. Planning plays connect compound change in process processes and DCC processes. DCC plays connect compound DCC and execution processes. Plays become an essential feature of the theory and procedure for studying task processes in real organizations. Plays are discussed in more detail in the next section.

2.3. Task Process Resource Characteristics: In Commonness and Plays

Thus far, the description of process laws has not been concerned with the entities or the resource characteristics, which are two ingredients in the definition of the elements of a process. The consideration of entities ties the task processes to

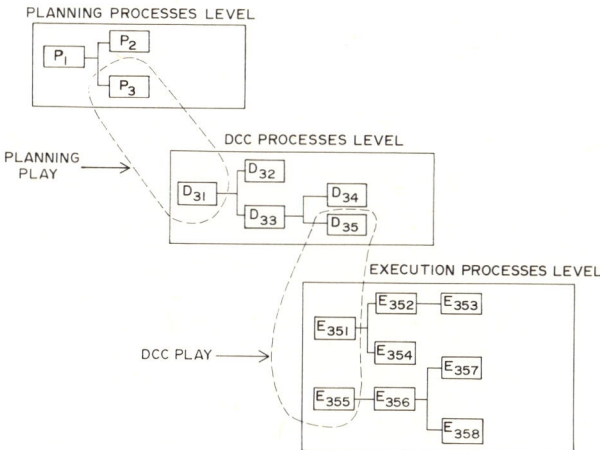

FIGURE 1. Horizontal and vertical compound processes.

the structures of an organization. The *task process resource characteristics* include the following:

    a. Location where performed;
    b. Personnel involved;
    c. Technology involved;
    d. Timing of performance;
    e. Knowledge base employed;
    f. Information used;
    g. Sets of others with whom the task process is contingent; and
    h. Continuity of directing, controlling, and coordinating.

Given any pair of task processes, Table 3 describes the test for whether or not they share the same task process resource characteristics.

For each of the eight resource characteristics, the test for sharing on each for any pair of task processes is described. However, as a whole, two task processes share the same resource characteristics only if they share all eight task process resource characteristics. This is a stringent test that is incorporated in a more sensitive question that is critical to both the concept of management and the relationship between OPIS and its TAISs.

The key question is whether or not two task processes are "in common." Two task processes are said to be "*in common*" if they obey three rules:

    a. They share the same task resource characteristics;
    b. They are on the same task process level;

TABLE 3
Tests for Determining if Two Task Processes Share a Resource Characteristic

Resource characteristics	Test for sharing
(a) Location	Processes are performed in the same location
(b) Personnel	Personnel performing the task processes are in the same organizational unit
(c) Technology	Task processes require the same capital equipment
(d) Timing	Task processes have same general pace and cycle duration in completion
(e) Knowledge	Task processes require the same technical background
(f) Information	Task processes use the same sets of information
(g) Contingent others	Those providing inputs or requiring output from the task processes are in the same classification
(h) Continuity of DCC	There is provision for directing, controlling, and coordinating the task processes throughout the entire length of time of the operation of the organizational units involved

c. They have been brought into common by a predecessor; integrating process.

Two task processes are either "in common" or not "in common." The determination of whether or not they are "in common" can be made using the three rules. For example, rule (b) refers to the task process level. There are two aspects: The first is the level as described earlier. And within one of these three levels, the task process level (or the organizational logic) is further defined by the hierarchy of the task process graph which is normally aggregated into *areas* which subdivide into *groups*, these into *bundles*, the bundles into *modules*, and the modules into basic *activities*. So, if task process T_1 is a DCC level and task process T_2 is an execution level they are not on the same process level. And if both T_1 and T_2 are, say, at the execution level but T_1 is a bundle and T_2 is a module, then T_1 and T_2 are not on the same process level.

The third rule refers to a *predecessor task process* which is one preceding a successor task process in a graph of a task process set. An integrating task process and its special form referred to as a predecessor integrating process in rule (c) needs a few more definitions for clarification.

Two task processes on any process level are *compatible* whenever

a. One is the immediate predecessor of the other;
b. They are in parallel and have a common predecessor not more than two levels higher.

Furthermore, two task processes are said to be *maladaptive* whenever they are incompatible. Maladaptive task processes are commonly created by inserting some TAIS technology into an OPIS where the TAIS is inconsistent organizationally with the existing OPIS. Two task processes are *separable* if

a. They are not "in common";
b. One is not the immediate predecessor to the other;
c. They are in parallel.

Most organizational processes are in parallel to the others. Two task processes are said to be *integrable* if they have a common immediate predecessor and are compatible. Many task processes are integrable but not "in common." To bring integrable task processes into the state of being "in common" it is necessary to create an integrating task process. An *integrating task process* is one that creates an "in common" set of task processes where one did not exist previously.

A *play* is a set of task processes which includes the directly integrable task processes and their directly integrating task process. A *directly supervisory task process* is a DCC process having the same play timing as its integrable execution processes. A directly supervisory task process and its constituent execution processes, taken together as a unit, constitute a *DCC play*. A *planning play* consists of a planning task process directly integrating one or more DCC task processes. DCC plays and planning plays are illustrated in Fig. 1. Every bundle is a play of modules. Every group is a play of bundles and every area is a play of groups.

The play is emerging as the building block out of which organizational designs are created. It is a unit of task processes which combines managing processes (DCC and planning) with execution processes. It usually corresponds to a unit within an organization such as a head teller who performs the DCC or integrating task processes with the tellers who perform execution processes such as paying and receiving financial instruments for deposit services. The key to the play is the integrating task process which brings integrable task processes into "in commonness."

The play leader is an entity that creates "in commonness" among the players. For the eight task process resource characteristics, the play leader provides a superset for each that includes those of the players. Management is defined in terms of play leadership. The different levels and types of plays illustrate the variety of management task processes. An examination of the requirements to create "in commonness" in order to construct a play can be used to define the qualifications for selecting managers. The concept that a manager creates a superset of task processes and task process resource characteristics has many applications. For example, a head teller of paying/receiving tellers provides a location superset (each occupies a location within her sphere of operations). All tellers in her unit report to her. They all use the same technology, they share the same timing, they require the same basic knowledge, information, and serve the same public. A head teller should have the training and experience to provide this superset of resources in order to train, direct, coordinate, and control the tellers of her unit. There are also notes tellers who have a different set of execution processes and involve different technology, timing, knowledge, information, and customers. An assistant cashier over both the paying/receiving tellers and the notes tellers would provide a superset if both supervisors reported to her and she had the necessary experience and knowledge to provide the superset for the sets of both task processes. An assistant cashier who did not understand the notes teller processes could not provide "in commonness" until she learned how to do them. A cashier may involve sets of assistant cashiers, regardless of location, who report to her. Thus, her location encompasses each of the separate locations. In some cases, the cashier integrates the "back room" operations that support the teller line. To provide "in commonness," she should understand both the processes in the "back room" and on the teller lines. The cashier may have a supervisor called the Vice President of Operations who supervises the cashiers, handles personnel issues, etc. for these operations. Again the scope of the activities increases and her job is to provide the integration. Once the activities are understood, the logic of the processes described, one can begin constructing the DCC and planning processes that create "in commonness" up and down the organizational pyramid.

Process maladaptations break up plays by destroying "in commonness." They are seriously disruptive and create organizational maladaptations. Note that many of the lines describing who works with whom on what do not follow the organizational chart. Typically less than 50% of the task processes are compatible with the Organizational Architecture. Lippitt and Mackenzie[5] provide a theory for why such organizational maladaptations occur, and Mackenzie[1,4] provides computational procedures for estimating the magnitude and the impact on efficiency.

The organizational process information system, referred to earlier as the OPIS, is the *organization of plays* within the organization. It depicts how the players and their task processes are integrated into a whole. At each level there are integrating task processes whose properties depend upon the players and the task processes integrated by the integrating task processes. The OPIS is fluid and reacts to change quickly. The integrating task processes collect, filter, process, and transport information throughout the organization.

Every organization, whether the Catholic Church, the Roman Empire, Sears Roebuck, the University of Kansas, etc. has an OPIS. It is the key feature of any organization and remains remarkably untouched by technologically augmenting information systems, especially at the senior management level. An OPIS is, by its very nature, a comprehensive and flexible information system. The OPIS is the primal information system for any organization. All others are supplementary.

3. Technologically Augmenting Information Systems

The variety of technologically augmenting information systems ranges from written words to the newest technology in decision support systems,[6] electronic mail,[7] and office automation.[8] This variety makes it difficult to impose a stable typology for TAISs. Instead of describing this variety, the emphasis is placed on the task processes involved. There are six major points.

The first is that TAISs deal with process fragments. A process fragment is a subset of a task process. For example, there are numerous information services available ranging from newsletters about arson investigations to Dun and Bradstreet financial information. These are helpful, they inform, and they assist in making decisions. But they only deal with a part of the problem of investigating an actual case of suspected arson or deciding to sell a product to a firm whose financial information has been provided by Dun and Bradstreet. A computer information system on daily retail sales in every store in a chain can be very helpful but it is only a part of the ongoing processes of implementing a retail sales strategy. NASA's Mission Control can monitor a space flight, but it is the astronauts aboard who have to take necessary action to correct a malfunction. Research journals, computer search, and electronic mail call help some research and development projects but they are only augmentations of the actual research and development. The list of examples is endless that can be used to illustrate the point that TAISs deal with process fragments within an OPIS.

The second point is that most technologically advanced TAIS have their own internal logic which is driven by needs for internal consistency. A TAIS would not be very good if it were not consistent because that is its strength. For example, Langefors[9] suggests a procedure for all systems analysis, design, or management. He starts by partitioning the systems work into four "separate" tasks (p. 50):

    a. List all parts from which the system is regarded as built-up;
    b. Define all interconnections which make up the system by joining its parts together;
    c. For each single part (or group of similar parts), separately define its properties as required by the system work at hand and do this in a format as specified by the way the systems structure is defined (in task b);
    d. Use the definitions produced by the tasks a, b, and all separate tasks, c, all taken together. Compare with specifications wanted for the system and repeat a, b, c, and d until satisfied.

He continues this line of thought to give concern for the problem of defining the boundary of the system, which is not a trivial task. Later on page 79, he proposes that:

> A system can only be designed to specified properties through a hierarchical system of design processes, in each of which every subsystem specified in a previous process is designed by organizing a workable subsystem structure for it, and the system so designed will itself have a hierarchical structure.

From the viewpoint of the designer of a TAIS, Langefors's writing, as a whole, makes an effective case for the need for one plan of attack in designing a TAIS. However, given the logical necessity for internal consistency, there is pressure to push the boundary of such a system outwards until it comes into contact with more than one unit of an organization. It is at this point that serious conflicts between an OPIS and a TAIS can arise.

The third point is that each TAIS should be seen as an organization having a mixture of human and inhuman entities and human and nonhuman relationships. Seen as an organization within an organization, it has its own task processes, structures, and relationships to its external environment which is often the organization in which it is embedded. The flow of information, for example, will involve a substructure whose entities are involved in input, processing, storage, and transfer. A "supervisor" could be a cpu in a computer as well as its human.

The humans in such a system supervise the subordinated TAIS and are a part of a more extensive OPIS. It is usually safe to assume that the humans will tend to act in accordance with what they believe are their own interests. Thus, the organization of each TAIS is a part of a larger organization and cannot be assumed to be politically neutral. The needs for the internal consistency of a TAIS combine with the personal needs of its directing humans to create conflicts between the TAIS organization and the OPIS.

The fourth point is that there are usually multiple TAIS organizations because there are multiple organizational processes and multiple technologies available for a TAIS. For example, the telephone, telex, electronic mail system may be existing side by side with a dozen computer system TAISs. Because each TAIS strives for internal consistency and because each TAIS should be considered as an organization, there can be and usually are problems in obtaining internal consistency for the organization of TAIS organizations embedded in the human organization. These multiple TAIS organizations constitute a "stack" of suborganizations requiring direction, control, coordination, and planning. Hence, they become a part of the OPIS. These needs are recognized by position titles such as Director of Information Services, Director of Administration, etc.

The fifth point is that there are usually system incompatibilities within the set of TAIS organizations even though each by itself may be internally consistent. For example, the Director of Finance and Accounting may use his own computer for report preparation and the main computer under the control of the Director of Data Processing for input numbers. As both TAISs overlap on use of the main computer and as both require updating the programs, changes in one TAIS affect the operation of the other. This lack of "in commonness" can lead to problems of the logical consistency of both TAISs and this in turn to a power struggle between the two directors which later sets off further changes in the respective TAISs.

The sixth point is that there are usually system incompatibilities between the TAISs and the OPIS. Such incompatibilities are virtually guaranteed if the TAIS organization is not precisely in parallel to the OPIS. These problems are exacerbated if the process fragments integrated by the TAIS cut across organizational units within the OPIS having organizational maladaptations. The organizational maladaptations can generate conflicts between the humans in the organization. The existence of maladaptations between the TAIS and these humans will often lead to attempts to use the TAISs politically to resolve the existing OPIS maladaptations. Thus the organizational incompatibilities, the inter TAIS incompatibilities, and the OPIS–TAIS incompatibilities interact and severely limit the effectiveness of TAISs.

They also create major incongruities within the organizational technology.[10–13] In Fig. 2, a conceptual framework for the means–ends linkages for any organization is illustrated. This diagram, called the ABC model, is a useful device for thinking about the relationships among the organization's environment, its goals and strategies (A), its organizational technology (B), and its results (C). The

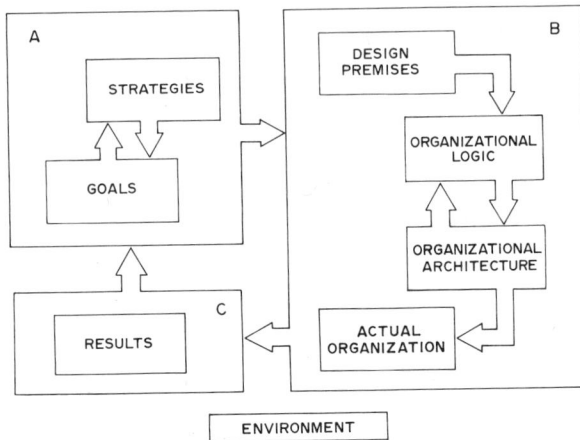

FIGURE 2. The ABC model of means–end linkages.

OPIS is an information system for adapting A,B,C, and E for any organization. The OPIS can adapt informally very quickly to changes in any of the relationships. The reliance on plays in the OPIS provides great flexibility and stability. It is doubtful that any TAIS has such proven capability. It takes time (T_A) to identify, formulate, solve, and implement a change to any system. It also takes time (T_C) for the problem to change. The one great advantage of an OPIS is that it can cope with changes to the organization rapidly and without major upheaval in most cases. The solution may not be optimal and it may not be elegant but the OPIS operates organizationally in a manner which is analogous to the "invisible hand" in competitive markets to adapt itself. Ideally, T_A should be less than T_C for any information system. Currently the OPIS beats the existing TAIS in the ability for $T_A < T_C$ for adapting to change.

However, the OPIS can also fail to react to major change adequately because it tends to "muddle through" by incremental changes. A method for organizational design called the organizational audit and analysis[4,10–13] has been employed to solve the OPIS issues. These methods, based on a theory of group structures, have been employed in a variety of industries and seem to work well. The extension to the design of TAISs and more importantly to the integration of the OPIS and its burgeoning TAISs is feasible.

4. An Example of the TAIS–OPIS Interfaces

This sixth point is illustrated by an actual case involving a supermarket chain. This organization has seven major categories of activities called areas. One of the areas, sales and merchandising, has seven groups of activities broken into 130 bundles of activities. Of these 130 bundles, three involve a person called the Senior Meat Buyer. His three bundles are subdivided into 16 modules of activities having a total of 63 activities. Of these 63 activities, 46 take place within the meat department, nine involve linkages to data processing, two involve interaction with finance and accounting, four involve working with the perishables warehouse, and two involve the meat market managers in the retail stores. The nine activities regarding data processing are broken into seven activities for the input of information into the computer, and two involve direct liaison with members of the department of data processing.

The Senior Meat Buyer has nine process fragments involving data processing alone. As one examines the other 4000 employees in all of the seven areas the same way, it becomes very clear that the operation of the various TAISs by the Department of Data Processing penetrate the entire organization. These relationships between the OPIS and the TAISs under the control of the Department of Data Processing have created the need for a Data Processing Committee to adjudicate and allocate the services and capacities of the Department of Data Processing and to recommend investment in either software or hardware. The criss crossing of the OPIS by the various TAISs under the control of the Department of Data Processing is immense and is the source of much friction within the OPIS.

In some important ways, the Department of Data Processing is a "sovereign state" within the total organization. It is physically sealed off from the rest of the corporation, it determines most of its own priorities, and it controls an important resource for which other units are very dependent. It is a high-technology unit operating in a low-technology industry. It is sufficiently independent that it commissioned its own organizational study during the period that the rest of the organization was being studied by another consulting firm. (This independent study cost approximately 200% more than it would have had it been included in the wider study. The department received a clean bill of health for its internal organization of the Department of Data Processing but the report ignored how its many TAISs impact on the rest of the organization.) Thus the commissioning of an independent study could be viewed[14] as a power play, despite sincere avowals to the contrary.

And although the Director of Data Processing is self-effacing, honest, competent, and canny, he is undoubtedly sincere in his energetic efforts to provide the best possible user services. The problem is that as each program is developed, it creates more process maladaptations for the OPIS even though each separately is incrementally helpful to some in the organization (including the Department of Data Processing). The drive for internal consistency for each TAIS leads to a derivative need for internal consistency across the set of TAISs and, step by step, the process maladaption for the OPIS accumulate.

To give an example, consider the common problems of a retail store chain in balancing the needs of its Corporate Product departments and the separate product departments within each of the stores. Corporate Product Departments perform the functions of procurement and giving merchandising advice. They often buy nationally, they buy for all the stores, they are generally more expert in product knowledge and have talents which are needed in the stores. The corresponding department in each store needs these services but each operates within the authority chain of a store manager, territory supervisor, and a Director of Retail Operations. There is a tug of war over the authority of the Corporate Product Department personnel and the authority of line management in the Retail Store organization. The territory supervisors are also expert and they travel from store to store helping the store managers and their department heads. The competitive needs of the individual store must be matched to the competitors within the primary trading area of each store. Often, the competitive requirements at the store level are in direct conflict with the programs developed by the Corporate Product Departments and control by the Retail Store operations.

Now consider the impact of a TAIS for reporting daily store sales daily back to corporate headquarters. The Corporate Product Departments who reside in the corporate headquarters receive the information as soon as it is available. The territory supervisors who are traveling from store to store are out of touch with this information. Thus the Corporate Product Departments are not only better informed about the technical aspects of the products, they have better information about actual sales than do the leaders of the sales organization. Consequently, the TAIS developed to serve the OPIS exacerbate the conflicts already existing within the OPIS. Control of information and use of information are sources of influence and power. Thus, inevitably by the pull of the need for internal consistency, the controllers of a TAIS are drawn into power struggles created by maladaptions in the OPIS. This conflict can be used by the controller of a TAIS to advance his special interests. It would require an organizational saint to remain neutral in these conflicts.

5. Conclusions

A recent book edited by Landau, Bair, and Siegman[15] entitled *Emerging Office Systems* contained 19 chapters devoted to the study of human and organizational factors in the use of information technology. Lodahl[16] stresses the issues of functional interdependence and the need to understand them in order to develop custom designs interactively. He stresses the need for new design ideas. Conrath[17] discusses the failure of integrated computer-based communication-information systems due to their inappropriateness to the existing organizational structures. He stresses the need for the technology to satisfy "the fundamental work related needs of its users" (p. 157). Turoff[18] concludes that "The key issue in this technology is the design of the social system making up the organization and whether or not that will be a planned process" (p. 256). Driscoll[19] is the most outspoken, entitling this paper "Office Automation: The Dynamics of a Technological Boondoggle." He argues that both from a cost effectiveness point of view and in terms of what can be regarded as known about managerial effectiveness, there are clear and diminishing marginal returns to TAIS technologies. He argues that designers of TAISs will necessarily become more involved in issues of human requirements for worth, dignity, and purpose. Englebart[20] is more positive about the capacity to help humans evolve by augmenting their intelligence and capabilities. The paper by Landau[21] most closely resembles the view of the organizational audit and analysis technology by proposing careful analysis of the processes of both the humans and the new TAIS technologies.[10-13]

A technology for accomplishing such work is well on its way at Organizational Systems, Inc. This technology for organizational design is currently directed at the OPIS. It is just now bumping into the issues of TAISs and the logic for integrating them. When one recalls that structures are need-satisfying interaction patterns and that in the long run the OPIS will always dominate its TAISs, there is little reason to be as pessimistic as James Driscoll or as optimistic as many of the vendors. We have a problem to solve: How to fully integrate the human needs with the technological imperatives of the new TAIS technologies. The approach discussed in this paper will hopefully illustrate that the problem is ancient, that with new approaches it can be solved, and that progress is being made.

In order to provide some specific reassurance let us return to the ideas of "in commonness" introduced early in the paper. In discussing processes, it was shown that organizational behavior, organizational structures, and TAISs are represented as flows of interconnected processes. The most interesting aspect of the levels of process laws lay in the definition of DCC (directing, controlling, and coordinating) processes and planning processes because they define the organizational plays. A play requires that the processes must be integrable and they must share the common task process resource characteristics listed in Table 3. There were seven resource characteristics: location, personnel, technology, timing, knowledge, information, and contingent others. It is difficult to see how a TAIS or a system of TAISs, dealing as they do in process fragments, can allow the integration of task processes across the organization. It is also difficult to see how such systems, by themselves, can provide the necessary integrating mechanisms to bring the task process resource characteristics into the state called "in common."

Thus, it is plausible that continual expansion of TAISs based on technological imperatives contain their own natural limits. What has to be done is to change our thinking from technological expansion of TAISs toward understanding the OPIS and then designing flexible TAISs to serve it. It is doubtful that members of a pluralistic society will allow any other solution to occur.

References

1. K. D. MACKENZIE, *A Theory of Group Structures. Vol. I: Basic Theory,* Gordon and Breach Science Publishers, New York, 1976.
2. K. D. MACKENZIE, *A Theory of Group Structures. Vol. II: Empirical Tests,* Gordon and Breach Science Publishers, New York, 1976.
3. K. D. MACKENZIE, *Organizational Structures,* AHM Publishing Co., Arlington Heights, Illinois, 1978.
4. K. D. MACKENZIE, A process based measure for the degree of hierarchy in a group. Three parts: I. The measure; II. Some empirical experiences with small group data; III. Applications to organizational design, *J. Enterprise Manage.*1, 153–184 (1978).
5. M. E. LIPPITT and K. D. MACKENZIE, Authority-task problems, *Administrative Sci. Q.* **21**(4), 643–660 (1976).
6. P. KEEN and M. SCOTT MORTON, *Decision Support Systems,* Addison-Wesley, Cambridge, Massachusetts, 1980.
7. S. K. HILTZ and M. TUROFF, *The Network Nation. Human Communication via Computer,* Addison-Wesley, Reading, Massachusetts, 1978.
8. M. D. ZISMAN, Office automation: Evolution or revolution? *Sloan Manage. Rev.* **19**, 1–16 (1978).
9. B. LANGEFORS, *Theoretical Analysis of Information Systems* (4th Ed.), Averback Publishers, Philadelphia, 1973.
10. K. D. MACKENZIE, A. MARTEL, and W. L. PRICE, Human resource planning and organizational design, *Work, Organizations, and Technological Change* (G. Mensch and R. J. Neihaus, Eds.), Plenum Press, New York, 1982.
11. K. D. MACKENZIE, Organizational congruency tests, *J. Enterprise Manage.* **3**(3), 265–276 (1981).
12. K. D. MACKENZIE, Concepts and measurement in organizational development, *Dimensions of Productivity Research* (J. D. Hogan and A. Craig, Eds.), American Productivity Center, Houston, Texas, pp. 233–304, 1981.
13. K. D. MACKENZIE, Manpower waste, *Human Syst. Manage.* **3**, 136–142 (1982).
14. J. PFEFFER, *Organizational Design.* AHM Publishing Co., Arlington Heights, Illinois, 1978.
15. R. M. LANDAU, R. BAIR, and J. H. SIEGMAN, Eds., *Emerging Office Systems,* Ablex Publishing Co., Norwood, New Jersey, 1982.
16. T. J. LODAHL, Designing the automated office: Organizational functions of data and text, in *Emerging Office Systems,* Ablex Publishing Co., Norwood, New Jersey, pp. 59–72 1982.
17. D. W. CONRATH, Evaluating office automation technology: Needs, methods, and consequences, in: *Emerging Office Systems* (R. M. Landau, R. Bair, and J. H. Siegman, Eds.), Ablex Publishing Co., Norwood, New Jersey, pp. 139–158, 1982.
18. M. TUROFF, Management issues in human communication via computer, in: *Emerging Office Systems* (R. M. Landau, R. Bair, and J. H. Siegman, Eds.), Ablex Publishing Co., Norwood, New Jersey, pp. 233–258, 1982.
19. J. W. DRISCOLL, Office automation: The dynamics of a technological boondoggle, in: *Emerging Office Systems* (R. M. Landau, R. Bair, and J. H. Siegman, Eds.), Ablex Publishing Co., Norwood, New Jersey, pp. 259–278, 1982.
20. D. C. ENGLEBART, Evolving the organization of the future: A point of view and integrated, evolutionary office automation systems, in: *Emerging Office Systems* (R. M. Landau, R. Bair, and J. H. Siegman, Eds.), Ablex Publishing Co., Norwood, New Jersey, pp. 287–308, 1982.
21. R. M. LANDAU, Some new approaches to the emerging office information systems, in: *Emerging Office Systems* (R. M. Landau, R. Bair, and J. H. Siegman, Eds.), Ablex Publishing Co., Norwood, New Jersey, pp. 309–338, 1982.

3

ANALYSIS OF FORMAL AND INFORMAL INFORMATION NEEDS IN DECISION SUPPORT SYSTEMS DESIGN

Juzar Motiwalla and Leong Siew Meng

1. Introduction

This chapter argues for information needs analysis to be an integral part of the design of a decision support system (DSS). A proper needs analysis ensures effective direction and priorities for the systems design. The data analysis and decision analysis approaches to information needs analysis are reviewed; an experimentation approach to needs analysis is proposed. An empirical study using this approach was carried out in a stockbroking office. A crucial finding was that informal information ought to be included in the design of a decision support system for stockbrokers.

A primary problem facing many information users is that of information overload. This problem has been further compounded, not alleviated, by the availability of cheap small computers and the proliferation of the attendant applications software packages. The information user is able to have greater amounts of information available in a shorter time. It is proposed that an appropriate information needs analysis will considerably aid the design of an effective DSS. The information needs analysis must precede the design of information storage, retrieval, manipulation, and control mechanisms. Nutt and Ricci[1] specify that systematic changes toward office automation require the specification of the information requirements and an analysis of the information flow.

JUZAR MOTIWALLA • Institute of Systems Science, National University of Singapore, Singapore.   LEONG SIEW MENG • Department of Business Administration, National University of Singapore, Singapore.

An important consideration in the process of information needs analysis is to uncover the types of informal information which impact user decisions. The informal communications network in an organization has a strong influence over organizational decisions.[2,3] Before attempting to design methods of capturing and storing informal information, its importance to users and the types of such information required must be well understood.

2. Information Needs Analysis

Davis[4] dichotomizes two methodologies for determining information needs for a given application—data analysis and decision analysis.

2.1. Data Analysis

Data analysis is used to determine information requirements by analysis of the data currently or potentially used. Alternative methods of data analysis are collecting existing reports, interrogating the information user, and building a comprehensive database. The first method of data analysis requires an understanding of what reports are presently being provided as output, and duplicating the information in these with appropriate modification.[5] Kennedy and Mahapatra[6] state that such an approach does not handle the purposes which the reports are to serve. By merely studying what is currently being produced, the analyst may miss the information flowing in informal information systems.[4]

Clifton[7] proposes that information needed can be identified through interviews and questionnaires addressed to users. Craney[8] observes that in practice, the first step in analyzing the information requirements is normally to ask the managers themselves what they need. Kennedy and Mahapatra[6] followed this approach to determine the information requirements of departmental chairmen at a university. Ackoff[9] and Kneitel[10] argue that the assumption behind this approach, which states that "the manager needs the information that he wants," is erroneous.

Krauss[11] pictures the database approach as one which consists of "gathering whatever data may be floating around the company and storing it in machinable form . . . . Usually the data are organized so that they can be extracted and put to almost any inconceivable use." Much of the support for the database approach stems from the impossibility of anticipating in advance all the decisions to be made and the information needs for those decisions.[11] However, Suter[12] comments that the database approach does not indicate how data should be integrated or processed to provide information for a decision maker. This argument leads to the decision analysis approach.

2.2. Decision Analysis

Cooper and Swanson[13] characterize decision analysis as focusing on the identification and modeling of decisions within the problem areas of the organization. Lundeberg[14] proposes an excellent method for utilizing the decision analysis approach. The approach requires the identification of control structures and modes, and the design of control methods and processes. King and Cleland[15] propose a formalized, yet participatory, process of decision analysis which provides greater understanding of the organizational change which this process engenders.

2.3. Experimentation

The crucial element in the identification of information needs is the information user. It is not simply a question of asking the user, as he is often not aware of his own information processing.[9] Decision analysis is appropriate only if one is searching for a normative definition of the decision model and the consequent information requirements.[15]

The approach used in this study is experimentation. Such an approach is classified under model fitting in the framework for managerial information processing provided by Ungson et al.[16] Information needs for a specific decision are explicated by observing the information user's responses to sets of information elements. In order to relate the response to specific information elements, controlled experimentation is carried out.

3. Experimental Setting—The Stockbroker's Office

The stockbroker's office was chosen as the research setting as it receives a significant amount of formal information and it was felt that stockbroking decisions are often influenced by informal information. The research department in a stockbroker's office is the recipient of a considerable amount of information, including published accounting data on company performance, research material provided by investment companies, official announcements of the stock exchange, and economic news and reports on market conditions of foreign stock exchanges. The stockbroker, however, also receives informal information from the grapevine. This type of information can range from market rumors or gossip, "hot tips" about the activities of big traders, or secret and surprising news about company mergers and acquisitions.

The stockbroker setting was used as it is concerned with repetitive though complex decisions.[17] A separation was made between two decision tasks—when to buy (or sell) and which particular stock to buy (or sell). The former decision is determined by such factors as the general economic climate and the market trend.

The latter decision is the focus of this study, and obviously information relating to the particular stock is required.

4. Experimental Design and Methodology

A stockbroking firm in Singapore which was interested in implementing a DSS was chosen for this study. The investment research department in this firm served purely as a conduit for formal information received, with the researchers supplying summary reports to the stockbrokers.

The subjects were 17 stockbrokers. They had an average of eight years of stockbroking experience. Nine subjects were utilized for Experiment 1, while eight were utilized for Experiment 2.

Before the experiments were designed, the respondents were asked to force rank seven selected financial factors to determine their order of importance and the degree of agreement among the stockbrokers in their rankings. The seven factors were total earnings (TE), net tangible asset backing (NTA), average daily volume traded (VOL), support and resistance levels (SRL), earnings per share (EPS), price earning ratio (PER), and dividend per share (DPS). These factors were chosen from a list of factors generally taken into account by analysts in their appraisal of stocks.

To ascertain the order of importance of the seven factors, a modified version of the method proposed by Roselius[18] was used. A neutral point was first established. With seven factors, a rank of fourth was deemed neutral. The number of unfavorable responses (that is, ranks of fifth, sixth, and seventh given by each stockbroker for each factor) was subtracted from the number of favorable responses (that is, ranks of first, second, and third). The difference was then divided by the total number of responses. The quotient, when multiplied by 100,

TABLE 1
Ranking of Seven Financial Factors by Net Favorable
Percentage (NFP)

Factor	NFP
NTA	63.0
EPS	35.0
PER	25.0
TE	−15.0
VOL	−30.0
SRL	−35.0
DPS	−40.0

yields the Net Favorable Percentage (NFP), which has a continuous range from +100 to −100, reflecting a completely unfavorable response.

Table 1 shows the results. Of the seven factors, only three—NTA, EPS and PER—were considered favorable. It is noted that these are fundamental factors. Both the technical factors—VOL and SRL—received poor ratings.

The subjects were also asked to rate the importance of the grapevine. The results indicate that informal information appears to be valuable. Thirteen respondents rated the grapevine as either "very important" or "important," while the other four gave a "neutral" rating. The effects of informal, unpublished, and qualitative information should therefore be considered as carefully as that of formal and published accounting information.

4.1. Experiment 1

This experiment attempted to analyze how stockbrokers evaluate financial information. In particular, the experiment was designed to test whether stockbrokers perform fundamental or technical analysis, and whether they process information differently for investors and for speculators. In so doing, it will be able to establish whether or not they process information configurally.

Fundamental analysis attempts to identify the intrinsic value of a company by evaluating economic and financial statistics. Technical analysis is the study of the action of the market itself. It involves the recording, usually in graphic form, of the actual history of trading in a certain stock or the stock market index. From the pictured history, the probable future trend is then determined. The techniques of technical analysis include bar charting of price ranges, point and figure charts, and oversold–overbought indicators.

The subjects were given 16 hypothetical companies to evaluate, where each company was described by some financial information. This information related to two factors which are used for fundamental analysis—price/earnings ratio (PER) and net tangible asset backing (NTA)—and two factors used for technical analysis—price movement (PRM) and daily volume traded (VOL).

To systematically analyze the impact of the four factors on stockbrokers' decision processes, a 2^4 full factorial design was run. Hence, each subject had to evaluate 16 companies. Each factor was manipulated at two levels, as follows:

Factor	Levels	
PER (Price earnings ratio)	High	Low
NTA (Net tangible asset backing)	High	Low
PRM (Price movement)	Increasing	Stable
VOL (Daily volume traded)	Active	Quiet

For each company, the subject had to rate the desirability of purchase on two seven-point scales, one rating for an investor client, and one rating for a speculator client.

To establish realistic figures for the factor levels, data from eight large diversified companies on the stock exchange were taken. The average for these companies on PER, NTA, and VOL over the past year was provided to respondents.

4.2. Experiment 2

In this experiment, subjects were given information from the grapevine as well as the financial information of Experiment 1. There was thus a better approximation of the information available to stockbrokers under real stock market conditions.

It is well known that there are a considerable number of rumors that pervade the stock market in Singapore. In order to analyze the impact of the grapevine on stockbroker decision processes, it was decided to categorize information by source, pervasiveness, and specificity. Information comes from various sources, some sources being highly reliable while others tend to be of uncertain reliability. Information that is pervasive is information that is widely known and circulated in the market. Information may also be quite specific in content, but at other times, it may be vague (for instance, information that indicates "a major announcement will be made soon"). Each factor was then controlled at two levels.

Factor	Levels	
SRC (Source reliability)	High	Uncertain
PVS (Pervasiveness)	High	Low
SPF (Specificity)	High	Low

Table 2 illustrates one of the companies evaluated. This company has high PER, low NTA, increasing PRM, quiet VOL, uncertain SRC, high PVS, and low SPF.

The design for this experiment then contains seven factors, each controlled at two levels. Hence, the maximum possible number of combinations would result in 2^7 or 128 companies, clearly an unmanageable number to judge. However, Goldberg[19] has shown that is is possible to reduce the number of companies to be evaluated without significantly distorting the results. A set of only 16 companies was presented to the stockbrokers to evaluate. The levels for the factors were chosen based on a set given by Box et al.[20] for a one-eighth fractional replication of the full 2^7 factorial design. Again, two seven-point scales were used—one for the investor rating and one for the speculator rating.

TABLE 2
Sample Company Report

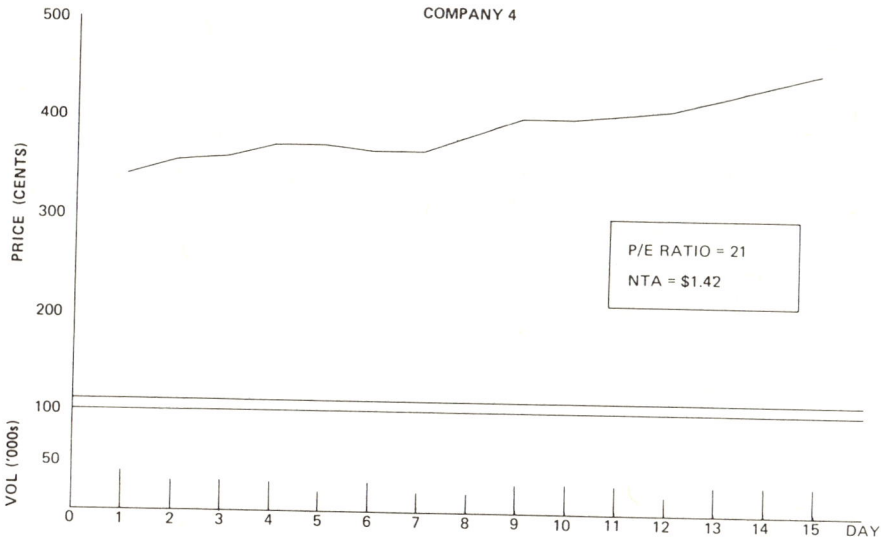

COMPANY 4

P/E RATIO = 21
NTA = $1.42

OTHER DATA

A market rumour circulated by sources unknown to you indicates that the company may be revaluating its assets and expanding its operations this year. Their effects on the company's profitability were not specified.

Speculator Rating:

Poor Buy   1   2   ③   4   5   6   7   Excellent Buy

Investor Rating:

Poor Buy   1   2   3   4   5   6   ⑦   Excellent Buy

5. Results and Discussion

5.1. Experiment 1

The significant effects found in this experiment are shown in Table 3. The results indicated that for clients who are investors, the stockbrokers (a) rated a stock with low PER higher than one with high PER, (b) rated a stock with high VOL higher than one with low VOL, (c) rated a stock with high NTA higher than one with low NTA.

On the other hand, for clients who are speculators, the stockbrokers (a) rated a stock with increasing PRM higher than one with stable PRM, (b) rated a stock with high VOL higher than one with low VOL.

TABLE 3

Tabulated Summary of Significant Effects and Their Confidence Intervals

Experiment 1		Experiment 2	
Rating for investor	Rating for speculator	Rating for investor	Rating for speculator
PER	PRM	PER	PER
$(-1.43 \pm 0.50)^a$	$(1.29 \pm 0.61)^a$	$(0.81 \pm 0.54)^a$	$(-0.61 \pm 0.49)^b$
NTA	VOL	SPF	SPF
$(0.51 \pm 0.50)^b$	$(1.24 \pm 0.61)^a$	$(0.91 \pm 0.54)^a$	$(0.95 \pm 0.49)^a$
VOL			PRM
$(0.71 \pm 0.50)^a$			$(0.55 \pm 0.49)^b$
NTA $\times$ PRM			
$(0.65 \pm 0.50)^a$			

[a]Statistically significant at $p < 1\%$.
[b]Statistically significant at $p < 5\%$.

Evidence of configural information processing takes the form of the NTA $\times$ PRM interaction effect for investors. The interaction arises because a stock with high NTA and an increasing PRM was rated highest for investors since it promises capital gains with the assurance of sound backing in terms of assets.

The type of information used by the stockbrokers reflected the type of financial analysis performed for the various clients. The significant interaction effect (NTA $\times$ PRM), as well as the significant main effects (PER, NTA, and VOL) all serve to indicate that the stockbrokers use both fundamental and technical analysis for investors.

As for clients who are speculators, the stockbrokers appeared to favor technical analysis since the resutls showed significant effects for PRM and VOL. The importance of VOL for both speculators and investors may be that most of the blue-chips on the stock exchange favorable for long-term investment are also actively traded. However, this bias towards technical analysis contrasts with the results presented in Table 1.

5.2. Experiment 2

The significant effects found in this experiment are shown in Table 2. The results showed that for clients who are investors, the stockbroker (a) rated a stock with low PER higher than one with high PER, (b) rated a stock that he had received specific informal information on higher than one that he had received nonspecific information on. For clients who are speculators, the above also applies. In addition, the stockbrokers rated a stock with increasing PRM higher than one with stable PRM.

As can be seen from the above results, the stockbrokers considered SPF and PER for both types of clients in this experiment. Also, it can be observed that there are no significant interaction effects.

These findings have obvious implications for information processing and utilization under heavy information load. Unlike Experiment 1, where only four variables were manipulated, this experiment introduced seven variables to the stockbrokers. The information input affected both the amount and type of information used by the respondents for the various clients.

The use of PER and SPF for both investors and speculators indicates that under high information load, the decision maker may focus on only one or two key attributes in making his decision. This research finding thus supports the propositions of March and Simon[21] and Soelberg.[22]

6. Conclusion

The empirical study described in this chapter illustrates the importance of information needs analysis in aiding the design of a DSS. The directions and priorities for effective design can be identified through proper needs analysis.

For the stockbroker's office, the information needs analysis indicated that informal information is an important factor to be considered in the design of a DSS. Informal information was not collected in any orderly fashion in the office. Implementing a DSS which would simply have automated current formal documentation would not have effectively supported information users. Incorporating informal information in the DSS may require the use of text handling capabilities.

It was found in this study that the specificity of the informal information was significantly related to stock ratings; however, the reliability of the source was not related to ratings. This finding is useful for the DSS designer, as the collection of informal information from the stockbrokers in the firm may not be easily done if they have to identify the source of their information. However, information content is generally not considered sensitive, and may be compiled by the DSS.

The importance of price movement (PRM) to stockbrokers suggests the incorporation of graphics capability in the DSS. This would allow the tracing of price movements over different periods. It is interesting to note that the experiment showed that technical analysis was carried out by stockbrokers. This finding is contrary to what their rankings showed in Table 1. Hence, the traditional approach to information needs analysis of simply asking the user his requirements is not effective. Experimentation as a means to needs analysis is better able to explicate the requirements of information users.

Finally, the conduct of information needs analysis enhances the implementation success of a DSS. Since implementation is a process of change, it is important that managers perceive a need for change.[23] By allowing information users to participate in the process of DSS design, the information needs analysis ensures that users are aware of the rationale for the proposed DSS structure.

References

1. G. J. NUTT and P. A. RICCI, Quinault: An office modeling system, *Computer* **14**(5), 41–57 (1981).
2. C. L. ADAMS How management users view information systems, *Decision Sci.* **6**(2), 337–345 (1975).
3. T. J. ALLEN and S. I. COHEN Information flow in research and development laboratories, *Administrative Sci. Q.* **14**(1), 12–19 (1971).
4. G. B. DAVIS, *Management Information Systems: Conceptual Foundations, Structure and Development,* McGraw-Hill, New York (1974).
5. E. PAYNE et al., *The Scope of Management Information Systems,* American Institute of Industrial Engineers, Atlanta, (1975).
6. M. H. KENNEDY and S. MAHAPATRA, Dynamics for establishing the flows of information for effective planning, administration and control, Paper No 742–74, Sloan School of Management, MIT (1974).
7. H. D. CLIFTON, *Systems Analysis for Business Data Processing,* Auerbach, Princeton, New Jersey (1969).
8. D. L. CRANEY, Management information—a simple and systematic approach, *Proceedings of 5th Australian Computer Conference* (1972).
9. R. L. ACKOFF, Management misinformation systems, *Manage. Sci.* **14**(4), B-147–B-156 (1967).
10. A. M. KNEITEL, Current myths about information processing, *J. Systems Manage.* **26**(5), 36–41 (1975).
11. L. I. KRAUSS, *Computer-Based Management Information Systems,* American Management Association (1970).
12. A. E. SUTER, The management decision making process, *Society for Management Information Systems Proceeding* (1973).
13. R. B. COOPER and E. B. SWANSON, Management information requirements assessment: The state of the art, *Data Base* **11**(2), 5–16 (1979).
14. M. LUNDEBERG, Interaction between information analysis and the design of control process. *MIS Copenhagen* 70, Auerbach, Princeton, New Jersey (1971).
15. W. R. KING and D. I. CLELAND, The design of management information systems: An information analysis approach, *Manage. Sci.* **22**(3), 286–297 (1975).
16. G. R. UNGSON, D. N. BRAUNSTEIN, and P. D. HALL, Managerial information processing: A research review, *Administrative Sci. Q.* **26**, 116–134 (1981).
17. P. SLOVIC, Analyzing the expert judge: A descriptive study of a stockbroker's decision process, *J. Appl. Psychol.* **53**(4) (1969).
18. T. ROSELIUS, Consumer rankings of risk reduction methods, *J. Marketing* **35** (1971).
19. L. R. GOLDBERG, Simple models or simple process?: Some research on clinical judgement, *Am. Psychol.* **23**, 483–496 (1968).
20. G. E. P. BOX, J. S. HUNTER, and W. G. HUNTER *Statistics for Experimenters,* Wiley, New York (1978).
21. J. G. MARCH and H. A. SIMON, *Organizations,* Wiley, New York, (1958).
22. P. SOELBERG, Unprogrammed decision making, Papers and Proceedings, 26th Annual Meeting, The Academy of Management (1966).
23. J. MOTIWALLA, A problem-directed approach for identifying implementable MIS projects, *Proceedings of Western AIDS Annual Meeting, Hawaii,* American Institute of Decision Sciences, Georgia (1981).

4

INFORMATIONAL NEEDS OF ORGANIZATIONS UNDER CRISIS

Augusto A. Legasto, Jr. and Amador Muriel

1. Introduction

The value of data base and management information systems (DBS and MIS) has been dramatically shown in the last few decades. It has been implied in a previous study[10] that these systems provide trivial aid to the managers of organizations undergoing severe crisis. Simply put, it is argued that the current models, techniques, and principles of management are best suited for dealing with the "normal" problems of an organization, that is, with problems typically experienced during periods of organizational stability. During these periods the historical data and the information derived from them become the bases for formulating decisions, strategies, and even policies. Goals and objectives are well defined and broadly accepted. They become convenient points of reference for the organizational system in determining its need for corrective action. The DBS and MIS systems have served well in satisfying the informational needs of the stable organization.

The informational needs, however, of destabilized systems are totally different. In light of the unfamiliar conditions that prevail, a destabilized system no longer enjoys the benefits of well definedness and broad acceptability of its goals. The historical data contained in the DBS and MIS virtually become obsolete. This paper reveals the new type of information that will be needed by managers when steering systems through crises.

The type of information system needed could be described as "proactive."

AUGUSTO A. LEGASTO, JR. • Department of Management, Baruch College, City University of New York, 17 Lexington Avenue, New York, New York 10010.   AMADOR MURIEL • Department of Statistics and Computer Information Systems, Baruch College, City University of New York, 17 Lexington Avenue, New York, New York 10010.

The initial entries would include a listing of the potential major crises that the system may be susceptible to. Unlike the traditional information systems a "proactive" one is forward looking rather than backward looking. Rather than merely derive information it seeks to create information. This paper presents a means by which managers are able to create new information through the generation of new "regimes."

2. Management of Crises

In a previous study we demonstrated the inevitability of crises in social systems.[9] When an organization is defended against a specific crisis, e.g., a labor strike, it is, *ceteris paribus*, made vulnerable to other crises, e.g., insolvency. It was proposed that a radical change in the treatment of crises needs to be made. Rather than being treated as events to be avoided or "designed away," crises must be treated both as opportunities for change and, more importantly, as strategic decision alternatives. In other words, a set of potential organizational crises is generated; each is then treated as a decision option and evaluated by means of a decision criterion.

The modeling procedure consists of the following steps: (1) preliminary listing of potential crises, (2) formation of a panel of experts or key representatives of interest groups, (3) construction of a crisis-triggered simulation model of the organizational system by a modeling expert with the aid of the panel, (4) setting by the panel of the threshold levels or critical values of vital organizational variables, e.g., market share, pollution level, and population density, (5) experimental simulation runs to study the behavior of the system under alternative crisis situations to provide pertinent information for the panel, (6) live-simulation and cost–benefit analysis of each crisis alternative by the panel, (7) generation of alternative "regimes" or new evolutionary patterns of the system with the panel's aid, (8) cost–benefit analysis of each "regime" by the modeling expert, (9) evaluation of each crisis–regime combination using a "net benefit" model by the modeling expert, and (10) selection by an executive in charge of preferred (or "optimal") crisis. The individuals involved in this procedure are an executive in charge of the project, a modeling expert, and a panel of key representatives of interest groups or at least of individuals playing their roles.

Legasto has already developed steps 1, 2, and 6–10 in Refs. 9 and 10. This study focuses on steps 3, 4, and 5. In particular, it will develop a crisis simulation model, demonstrate the way the critical values or "threshold levels" of vital system variables are set, and then produce test simulation runs via a computer to uncover more pertinent information about the system by artificially creating different crisis situations.

Throughout this continuing study a new approach to crisis management is taking shape. Three existing approaches to crisis management have been shown to be largely ineffectual in the handling of crises.[9] These three were (1) the incrementalist approach of Lindblom,[12] (2) the systems design approach of van Gigch[16] and (3) the conflict management approach developed by organizational behavior scientists such as Blake and Mouton.[1] The major arguments against these three are briefly presented here. The incrementalist approach does not address the problem of crisis at all; it is simply displaced by ad hoc emergency measures if and when a crisis occurs. The systems design approach attempts to view the system in its totality, i.e., holistically, so that all potential crises can be modeled and anticipated. The system is then redesigned so as to design away the more likely major crises. The first criticism points to the difficulty of "immunizing" a system against several major crises simultaneously. The second criticism points to its neglect of the problem of crisis management; its full attention is devoted to crisis avoidance. The final criticism laid against it concerns the unrealistic assumptions it makes, particularly the one about the decision maker's rationality and comprehensive knowledge. Several studies cited in Legasto[9] show, for one, that there is considerable confusion about both objectives and the responsibility for making executive-level decisions. In the real world of management where there is, at least at the outset, rarely any agreement on goals the presumption of the existence of a common goal is shown to be unrealistic.

Conflict management, the third approach to crisis management, is too highly reactive in nature providing for drastic interventive measures only after the crisis has occurred. The major problem lies in the fact that there do exist situations where it would have been far less costly, both in economic and social terms, to anticipate and avoid the crisis. It was then shown that the ten-step crisis decision modeling approach outlined earlier is superior to any of these three in terms of realism, cost, usefulness or applicability, and effectiveness.[9] We now begin with the model development.

3. Modeling Such Discontinuous Events as Crises: The State of Current Models

There is no doubt that the methodologies of the physical sciences have almost exclusively dominated the study of systems in the social sciences. Insofar as systems in the physical sciences are said to be largely "subject to gradual transitions and constant regularities"[4] it is not surprising that representations of social systems have been monopolized by models of continuities. In physical science systems discontinuities surface whenever there are unresolved issues requiring further explanation. For example, for many decades electromagnetic theory could not explain the photoelectric behavior of light; this was considered "discontinuous" behavior.[16] In social science systems, discontinuities are also prevalent and natural.

Unfortunately, discontinuities in social systems tend to create a more dramatic effect on the system than do continuities: assassinations, civil wars, and the like.

How useful then are such continuity models of socioeconomic systems as are found in system dynamics,[11] econometrics,[15] and KSIM?[5]

These models of continuity or trends are extremely useful in representing systems under "normal" conditions and, consequently, in aiding our understanding of their behavior. For behavior beyond the normal these models have extremely limited, if any, predictive value. Insofar as these systems spend most of their lifespans in "normality" continuity models will continue to provide significant assistance to system planners and policy makers. (In dealing though with the ongoing operations of the system other methodologies such as decision theory, linear programming, program budgeting, or cost–benefit analysis may offer a more cost-effective alternative to dynamic structural modeling or simulation.)

When dealing with system discontinuities or crises it becomes evident that existing methodologies are simply inadequate. Even the most likely candidate tool of analysis, the dynamic structural simulation model, by and of itself fails to provide us with an adequate crisis modeling tool. (Nevertheless, it will be used as an important building block of our crisis modeling procedure.)

The basic mathematical relationship used by dynamic structural models is the differential equation. It is well known that one of the first assumptions of differential calculus by which the rates of changes are expressed is that surfaces and graphs be continuous. This calculus is therefore not suited to represent processes that undergo discontinuous or sudden changes. When the model system experiences a "disruption" the only way the modeler can represent this is by abruptly switching to a different set of input parameters or, worse, a different set of variables and relationships.

The fact is that most of these continuous models do run themselves down into a collapse mode. To demonstrate this conceptually we first introduce the following terminology:

Let us assume that a system is described by its state variables, denoted by $f(i,t)$, where f is some variable, say population of an urban system, and i denotes the type of variable we are considering. i ranges from 1 to some number N. t is the time, which in the case of numerical simulations from year to year, is an integer ranging from 1 to some value, e.g., 10 or 100 years, depending on the time scale of the problem being considered.

As this theory assumes the availability of computers we will use difference equations.

In general, therefore, we write

$$f(i, t) = f(i, t-1) + \sum_{j,k\,=\,1}^{M,N} g(j, f(k, t-1)) \tag{1}$$

where $g(j, f(k, t-1))$ are expressions describing the changes applied to $f(i, t-1)$ to find this new value at time t. M is the number of contributions to changes in i.

Obviously, the functional forms of $g(j)$ determine the time evolution of the system. The evolution of the system depends on the initial variables $f(i, 0)$ as well as the form of $g(j)$ used. In a sense, once the difference equation is formulated, $g(j)$ determines the type of system that evolves. Nearly all numerical simulations published are of this type. Most systems are Markovian and linear, but we do not discount the possibility that $g(j)$'s could involve nonlinear functions of the $f(i)$'s. Then, instead of $g(j, f(k))$, we could have $g(j, f(k), f(l), f(m))$. In the future, we hope to show systems of such a nature.

Whenever systems in general, and socioeconomic systems in particular, are modeled in this mode, it is quite unlikely that steady state is immediately (if ever) found. To use physical analogies, steady-state solutions are reached only when there is an interplay of a constant external stimulus and a randomizing influence, conditions which are rarely present, if at all, in social systems. In fact, even those systems which are allowed to evolve by themselves using a set of equations do not necessarily reach a stationary state. In nature, collapse situations in the biological world are certainly commonplace.

Therefore, it is our contention here that collapse modes are not surprising at all and may not be all that disastrous given the possibility of intelligent control, or superior mutants of the collapsed system. In fact, it would be more surprising to discover, accidental as it may be, steady-state solutions.

Many dynamic numerical simulations of which system dynamics is the best known lead to catastrophic results.[2,3,13] When such situations are reached in modeling, simulations are generally stopped, the crystal-ball nature of numerical simulations take root, and modelers assume the role of Cassandras. It is doubtful that modelers could ever avoid the image of Cassandras, or for that matter, even optimistic futurologists, depending on their philosophical orientation. For such is the nature of the equations used that the modeler would have to be incredibly lucky to find steady-state solutions. It would mean improbably lucky choices of the initial conditions or an improbably fortunate set of g's.

We now present an approach which can be readily utilized in modeling discontinuities and, more importantly, in aiding managers to better exploit the dynamics of crises more effectively.

4. Modeling and Analysis of Crises

Even if one accepts the virtual inevitability of crisis one is still faced with the problem of not knowing, not to mention preventing, which crisis will occur. (This is where we begin to set up our "proactive" information system.) Simulation models like those of system dynamics can be used to generate the set of probable crises that a particular socioeconomic system may encounter. These crises can be induced and, consequently, studied as follows:

We first assume that the model is equipped with an objective function consisting of a specific set of social indicators. We now introduce three new concepts. The first one is: the critical index $I(i)$, which when reached by a system (or the appropriate social indicator), triggers a crisis leading to a radical change of $g(j)$'s.

The second concept is the set of potential regimes or "recovery modes" of the system; various sets of $g(j, c)$ are generated where c refers to different regimes with $c = 1$ to some small integral value m. For example, $c = 2$ may be used to represent a moderately predictable future-oriented system and $c = 3$a less predictable highly future-oriented system. This is discussed in greater detail in Ref. 10.

Third, is the tacit admission of the existence of regimes, not as natural cycles as determined by one set of $g(j)$, but of different cycles, whose g's are invented by experts. The regimes are certainly not periodicities, such as the sunspot cycles, or even economic cycles, but regimes arising out of the inability of systems to take themselves out of catastrophic evolution.

To formulate these concepts in mathematical terms, we define

$$I(i, L) = \frac{f(i)}{f(i, \min)} \tag{2}$$

$$I(i, H) = \frac{f(i)}{f(i, \max)} \tag{3}$$

Where $f(i, \min)$ and $f(i, \max)$ are preset values, interpreted as constraints. It is tacitly assumed that the variables could easily assume these values if they are allowed to evolve according to the set of g's used. When the system is allowed to evolve, numerically of course, the equations used will be

$$f(i, t) = f(i, t-1) + \sum_{j,k=1}^{M,N} g(j, f(k, t-1)) \tag{4}$$

$$I(i, L, t) = \frac{f(i, t-1)}{f(\min)} \tag{5}$$

$$I(i, H, t) = \frac{f(i, t-1)}{f(\max)} \tag{6}$$

where $I(i, L, t) > 1$ and $I(i, H, t) < 1$. When either of these two inequalities is violated, the system, encountering a discontinuity, is terminated and a new set of g's is activated. Thus, the new equations of evolution become

$$f(i, t) = f(i, t-1) + \sum_{j,k=1}^{M,N} g(j, 2, f(k, t-1)) \tag{7}$$

$$I(i, L, t) = \frac{f(i, t-1)}{f(\min)} < 1 \tag{8}$$

$$I(i, H, t) = \frac{f(i, t-1)}{f(\max)} < 1 \tag{9}$$

Again the model is allowed to evolve using this new set of equations, until one of the state variables hits a critical value and a new set of g's takes over.

In reality, governments are helpless in radically changing the equations of motion abruptly. The functional relationships described by g are not that easily changed. But our modeling approach does not stress such a drastic, discontinuous measure. Instead, we emphasize that long before the attainment of critical indices is reached, the modeler will have come up with altered equations of motion representing a new "life" or evolutionary pattern for the system. It is in this sense that we call our model a crisis-triggered simulation—the crisis may or may not in fact take place in the real world, but the possibility of the crisis is established by the model. In addition we are given insight into the possible choices we have concerning the system's future.

The following information is known either *a priori* or as an output of a series of crisis-triggered simulation experiments: the set of probable crises (as *a priori* information), the severity of the damage done by them (as simulation output), and the set of probable evolutionary patterns, $g(i, c)$'s (as "created" information possibly extracted through a "Delphi"[14] panel of experts and based on the crisis-triggered simulation experiments).

Examples of crises from developing countries abound. The set of potential crises is a large one. This includes economic collapse, intolerable population densities in urban areas, complete loss of traditional values, revolution, etc. Some of the regimes that might be examined are: an agriculture-oriented economic growth strategy as opposed to an industry-oriented one and massive redistribution of land and property. Preliminary development of a model of social unrest in a developing country has been undertaken by Legasto.[6-8]

5. Applications: Societal Development and Education Funding

The first application addresses the problem of societal development. A model of the societal system of a developing country, the Philippines, is developed in Ref. 6. The four most important system variables employed are the growth rate of gross national product (GNP), the degree of fairness of income distribution (DIST), the quality of interpersonal environment (PER), and the population level of a system sector i [POP(i) where i refers to lower-income or upper-income rural or urban community]. The simulation model consists of three modules: economic, demographic, and sociological. The economic module models the size (through GNP) and fairness (through DIST) of the economy. GNP growth rate in sector i in year t is computed as follows:

$$\text{GNPR}(t; i) = \frac{\text{GNP}(t; i)}{\text{GNP}(t-1; i)} \tag{10}$$

The fairness of income distribution (in year t) is measured by the index:

$$\text{DIST} = \sum_{i=1}^{s} \%\text{GNP}(i) * \text{LOGN} \left(\frac{\%\text{GNP}(i)}{\%\text{POP}(i)} \right) \tag{11}$$

where $\%\text{GNP}(i)$ represents the percentage of total GNP shared by sector i, LOGN is the natural logarithm, and $\%\text{POP}(i)$, the percentage of total population in sector i. The demographic module contains the population and migration variables. The population size in sector i in year t is

$$\text{POP}(t; i) = \text{POP}(t-1; i) + \text{DT} * (\text{INC}(t-1, t; i) + \text{MG}(t-1, t; j, i) \tag{12}$$
$$- \text{MC}(t-1, t; i, j))$$

where $\text{INC}(t-1, t; i)$ is the natural addition to population in sector i between years $t-1$ and t. $\text{MG}(t-1, t; j, i)$ is in-migration to sector i from all other sectors j and $\text{MG}(t-1, t; i, j)$, out-migration from i to all other sectors j. MG is determined by the following factors:

$$\text{MG}(t-1, t; i, j) = \text{function}(N(i), \text{MGECM}(i, j), \text{MGEDM}, \text{MGCTM}, \tag{13}$$
$$\text{MGSSM}(i, j), \text{EMOP}(i, j) \text{ parameters})$$

where $N(i)$ is the sector i population, MGECM reflects the economic pull exerted by the perception of higher earnings in sector j relative to i's, MGEDM accounts for the upward pressure applied on MG by increased government expenditure on educational programs that ultimately raise aspiration levels and sharpen the perception of individuals. MGCTM accounts for the upward pressure on MG generated by increased government expenditure on communication and transportation which also raises aspiration levels through various media and, in addition, tends to ease the physical transfer problems of individuals. MGSSM accounts for the upward pressure exerted by the perception of improvements in social services resulting from a move from sector i to j. EMOP operates as a braking factor on

MG. The realities of limited employment opportunities have contributed to the return of potential migrators to their original sector.[6,7]

The sociological module models the quality of the interpersonal environment (in year t); this is measured indirectly as follows:

$$PER = \frac{1}{RMG} \tag{14}$$

where RMG represents rural-to-urban migration rate.

The major potential crises are (1) POP/(area in sector) or the population density in i may exceed some psychologically and sociologically tolerable limit on density; (2) since the quality of the interpersonal environment declines as "RMG" increases, when (1/RMG) exceeds some expert-recognized limit the society may experience an irreversible breakdown in family and other interpersonal ties; (3) GNP growth rate may hold at such persistently negative levels as to precipitate depressionary conditions; and (4) DIST may deteriorate to the point of causing widespread discontent and, conceivably, crime and civil disorder.

Possible recovery regimes include (1) a new society where the distribution of assets is significantly improved, (2) a new traditional society that rediscovers or maintains the value and usefulness of the "good old ways" while integrating certain useful features of the "unsettling new ways," and (3) a ruralization strategy to reverse mass migrations from rural to urban sectors. New simulation equations would have to be formulated at this point since the old simulation equations would be outmoded once crisis sets in and throws the system off its "expected" pattern of behavior.

The second application addresses the problem of funding education. The results of this application are published in Ref. 14. The variables that are critical to the survival of the system in its present structural form are: the amount of surplus funds in the school budget, changes in the enrollment level, changes in tuition charges, changes in the levels of state and county funding, changes in FTE ("full-time equivalence" standards), size of the uncontrollable part of the budget, and the ratio of adjuncts to the total teaching population. A major finding of this study is its demonstration of the impending bankruptcy of a particular community college if it pursues its current practice of funding, i.e., "FTE-based state funding." Bankruptcy becomes imminent if any one of the following takes place: increases in state funding fall below 24%, increases in county funding fall below 25%, or tuition increases fall below 25%. Any realistic increase in tuition, for example, is shown to effect only a temporary respite from deficit spending. The only realistic ways to avoid deficit spending require a crisis mentality and new directions or patterns of evolution for the system: drastic cuts in the budget, drastic reduction in the inflation rate (which we have recently been experiencing), or a total rejection of enrollment-driven funding formulas. The modeling of these new patterns will of course require the creation of alternate models.

6. Crisis-Triggered Simulations: Its Significance

As another approach to numerical simulations, crisis-triggered simulations represent a philosophic departure from most computer simulations. The natural boundary of most simulations is determined by the arrival of absurdly low or high values of the variables. In an activist approach to simulations, the same equations are used but with different assigned numerical parameters, or even radically different initial conditions. Our approach goes farther than these simple numerical fixes. We hypothesize that most intelligence-run systems impose values of an altogether different form of thinking that changes the equations of evolution, instead of simply changing the parameters. The method of crisis-triggered simulations we propose accepts the presence of crisis as a fact of life; it accepts the existence of crisis as unavoidable, and therefore creates provisions for the confrontation of the crisis before and after it occurs. The degree of self-correction applied depends on the assigned values of $f(\min)$ or $f(\max)$. The choice of $f(\min)$ or $f(\max)$ may be such that no crisis is felt or seen at all.

What crisis-triggered simulations demand are the following:

1. A realistic acceptance of the inevitability of collapse in a deterministic system. This is in keeping with the difficulty of arriving at equilibrium states especially in systems that involve competing species.
2. A value-laden approach that allows the recognition of unacceptable values of the parameters.
3. An *a priori*, or ad hoc assumption of alternate equations of motion as soon as the critical indices are reached.

The approach suggested here takes modeling one step beyond present-day modeling. It compels modelers to immediately think of alternate equations of evolution instead of merely correcting numerical parameters.

Who will determine the g's? Here is where planners, or experts may be called upon—to question existing policies corresponding to the g's used for modeling, to come up with several alternate g's, and examine what "regimes" are acceptable, and for how long. These planners must open their thinking to other possible regimes, or g's, and must avoid unquestioned loyalties to conventional thinking or planning formulas. Nevertheless, these planners must subscribe to some acceptable goals, or even principles. Such principles could spring from a humanist or an egalitarian orientation. These planners become truly subjective in one sense, but on the other hand it removes them from the categorical label of "technocrats." With this approach, planning becomes a truly human undertaking, not a simple technical act.

References

1. R. R. BLAKE and J. S. MOUTON, The fifth achievement, *J. Appl. Behav. Sci.* **6**, 413–426 (1970).
2. J. FORRESTER, *Urban Dynamics,* MIT Press, Cambridge, Massachusetts, 1969.
3. J. FORRESTER, *World Dynamics,* MIT Press, Cambridge, Massachusetts, 1971.
4. O. HELMER and N. RESCHER, On the epistemology of the inexact sciences, *Manage. Sci.* **6**(1) (October 1959).
5. J. KANE, W. THOMPSON, and I. VERTINSKY, KSIM: A methodology for interactive resource policy simulation, *Water Resources Res.* **9**, 65–79 (1973).
6. A. A. LEGASTO, JR., The development and application of a quality-of-life index to developing countries, unpublished dissertation, Columbia University Graduate School of Business, New York, 1974.
7. A. A. LEGASTO, JR., A multiple-objective policy model, *Manage. Sci.* **24**(5), 498–509, (January 1978).
8. A. A. LEGASTO, JR., Toward a calculus of development analysis, *Technol. Forecasting Social Change* **14**, 217–230 (1979).
9. A. A. LEGASTO, JR., Crisis decision modeling, unpublished Working Paper No. BML8201, Baruch College, Department of Management, New York.
10. A. A. LEGASTO, JR., The positive-feedback approach to crisis management, unpublished Working Paper No. BMAL8203, Baruch College, Department of Management, New York.
11. A. A. LEGASTO, JR., J. FORRESTER, and J. LYNEIS, *System Dynamics,* North-Holland Elsevier, Amsterdam, 1980.
12. C. E. LINDBLOM, The science of muddling through, *Public Adminis. Rev.,* 1959.
13. D. MEADOWS *et al.,* *Limits to Growth,* Universe Books, New York, 1972.
14. A. MURIEL, A management support model for community colleges, *J. Res. Higher Ed.* (1982).
15. J. PILL, The Delphi method: Substance, context, a critique and an annotated bibliography, *Socioeconomic Planning Sci.* **5**(1), 57–71, (February 1971).
16. A. PINDYCK and J. RUBINFELD, *Econometric Models and Economic Forecasting,* McGraw-Hill, New York, 1976.
17. J. VAN GIGCH, *Applied General Systems Theory,* Harper & Row, New York, 1978, pp. 493–557.
18. L. A. ZADEH, Outline of a new approach to the analysis of complex systems and decision processes, *IEEE Trans. Syst. Man, Cybern.* **SMC-3**, 28–44, (January 1973).
19. E. C. ZEEMAN, Catastrophe theory, *Sci. Am.* 65–83, April 1976.

DECISION SUPPORT SYSTEMS

LANGUAGES FOR DECISION SUPPORT SYSTEMS

AN OVERVIEW

EDWARD A. STOHR AND
NORMAN H. WHITE

1. Introduction

The accelerating complexity and size of modern private and public institutions and their increasing dependence on environmental factors such as multinational trade, world politics, and government regulations point to a need for computer-based decision support systems (DSSs). Several surveys[12,16] have indicated an increase in the use of such models especially in applications such as pro forma financial statement projection and budgeting. These systems can vary widely in both scope and objectives (see Table 1, which is based on Ref. 15). On the one hand a number of comprehensive corporate planning systems have been developed that attempt to model the firm's complete production process in time and across geographic locations. Examples are the Potlatch Corporation[4] and Xerox[21] models. Such systems may contain 50 or 60 submodels and thousands of lines of code. At the other extreme are the currently popular microcomputer-based "accounting spread sheet" packages that are used in small financial and budgeting applications.

Although a number of successful DSSs have been reported in the literature there have been a number of failures as well. According to Boulden,[4] approximately one-third of the (larger) systems fail in the first two years after implementation and another one-third perform indifferently. Surveys by the Financial Executive Search Foundation[27] and by Hayes and Nolan[12] indicate both human

EDWARD A. STOHR and NORMAN H. WHITE • CAIS Department, Graduate School of Business Administration, New York University, 90 Trinity Place, New York, New York, 10006

TABLE 1
Types of Planning Models

Organization level	Strategic objectives setting	Specific multiyear plans	Budgeting
Corporate	Econometric models; judgemental models	Pro forma financial statements Capital investment models	Financial budgeting (top-down, bottom-up)
Divisional	Industry/local econometric models	Pro forma financial statements Capital investment models	Budgeting (financial, physical)
Project or department	—	Marketing models, R&D models, plant/ location, capital investment models	Operations management models (scheduling, distribution)

and technical causes for these failures. On the human side there was inadequate communication between managers and developers, leading to (1) a lack of fit between the model and the organization's planning and control procedures, and/ or (2) models that were too complicated for managers to understand and use. The technical difficulties included inadequacy of the hardware and software tools leading to (1) long development times, (2) expensive use characteristics, and (3) the inability of the model to evolve in response to rapidly changing needs.

Our objective is to examine how recent software advances can facilitate the development of DSS systems that are more easily used by staff personnel and managers and have increased functionality combined with an ability to adapt to changing assumptions and needs. We will do this by examining the language interfaces provided by generalized DSS software. A DSS generator is a set of tools which can be used to build a wide variety of DSS. Some commercial examples include EMPIRE,[8] EXPRESS,[9] IFPS,[13] PLATO,[18] SIMPLAN,[22] and XSIM.[31] Although there are particular environments that need a specialized DSS possessing feature not normally included in a DSS generator, we argue that the similarity of organizational structure and operations makes these the exception rather than the rule.

The discussion is limited to a consideration of the user interfaces provided by DSS generators. In particular, we will be primarily concerned with the language facilities provided. Other aspects of the user interface such as hardware devices, communication speed, graphics, and dialogue style are covered more fully in Ref. 25.

We attempt to define the language functions that must be provided by a DSS. The range of these functions is broader than in most other types of software. In addition the nature of the operations that must be performed by users is qualitatively different. A major thesis of the paper is that these two facts will necessitate the development of new languages that can manipulate quite complex data objects, processes, and abstractions. At present we do not even have a coherent and broad-based terminology for the concepts and operations involved in interacting with a DSS. However, a number of actual DSSs have developed a limited set of special functions at the requisite level of abstraction and aggregation.

In the next section we describe the DSS environment and derive some general software requirements. In Section 3 we describe a software architecture that serves as a framework for much of the discussion. Section 4 lists the types of language that should be made available in a DSS generator. Section 5 discusses some of the trade-offs involved in designing DSS languages. Finally, in Section 6 we outline the major functions that have to be performed by DSS languages for data manipulation and query, model definition, model execution, sensitivity analysis, and specification of output requirements.

2. The DSS Environment

A DSS is used to support decision making in ill-structured or poorly structured decision situations. A decision situation is unstructured to the extent that cause–effect relationships are unknown; there is uncertainty with regard to the possible actions that might be taken and their consequences; important variables are qualitative or immeasurable; there are multiple conflicting objectives and decision makers cannot express their trade-offs in terms of a higher-level goal. The "support" in the above definition implies that human judgement is a necessary ingredient in the resolution of the decision-making process. Thus we see a division of labor between the "structurable" part of the process (which is relegated to the computer in the form of data base retrievals and/or more complex simulation or optimization models) and the "nonstructurable" part of the problem (which relies on human judgment). The important point here is that the DSS generator should provide an environment that will facilitate both facets of the decision process.

We will distinguish the following classes of user of a DSS system: (1) managers—the "ultimate" decision makers, (2) intermediaries—staff personnel who interact with the DSS in a hands-on mode and form a channel of communication between the manager and the "builder" of the DSS, and (3) builders—technically oriented personnel who program DSS applications (build models), perform the

DSS data administration function, and so on. It is of course possible that all three roles might be filled by the same person. In terms of Schneiderman's[19] semantic–syntactic model of computer users the managers can be expected to have a high "semantic" knowledge of the application domain and a relatively low "syntactic" knowledge of the DSS system itself. Conversely, the builders might have low semantic and high syntactic knowledge. Finally, the intermediaries might lie somewhere in between the managers and builders in terms of both syntactic and semantic knowledge.

The DSS generator should provide a variety of interfaces and language types to suit the functions performed by all three classes of user. Moreover, since DSS use is often voluntary, the interface should not only be effective in terms of the direct benefits to the decision-making process, it should be easy to learn and remember and pleasant to use. Moreover, empirical evidence,[31] supports the idea that individuals differ significantly with respect to their perceptual processes and patterns of problem solving. To support these different "cognitive styles" we should provide a variety of interface styles and language types. Moreover we should provide "extensible" languages where new terms and synonyms can easily be introduced.

A DSS is characterized by an evolutionary development process involving a three-way dialogue between the end-user (manager or intermediary), the builder, and the system itself. To facilitate this process the DSS generator should provide languages that are powerful enough to allow the rapid development of models and efficient exploration of the consequences of these models via sensitivity analyses. At the same time the software code produced should be readable and well structured to facilitate maintenance and allow successful models (or at least certain subcomponents of them) to be used in other applications or incorporated in the operational systems of the organization.

Finally, the language interfaces provided by the DSS generator (and/or built using the tools provided by the generator) should have the properties of any good man–machine interface, namely; (1) easy to learn, use and remember, (2) forgiving when mistakes are made, (3) suitable for both novice and expert use, (4) providing immediate response for most user actions and informing the user of likely time delays on complex tasks, (5) providing a means for "undoing" all actions that affect the system integrity. In particular it is always helpful for users of computer languages if the previously entered command is retained and presented back to the user for on-line editing to eliminate mistakes or to allow modification of the command in an incremental fashion. This saves typing and provides a useful short-term memory aid.

The array of DDS language requirements that has so far been enumerated is certainly quite imposing. However, we feel that there are other aspects that get closer to the heart of the DSS design problem. Returning to the definition of DSS at the beginning of this section we see a need for the development of higher-level languages more suitable to the problem-solving environment. These languages would differ from conventional languages in that they would operate at a higher level of abstraction manipulating global data objects and computational processes in a manner more closely resembling human problem-solving processes. Modern data retrieval languages are already approaching this level of sophistication. To give another concrete example, we cite the DSS generators that support the sensitivity analysis process by providing a "what if" language—"what if x is increased by 10%," "what does x impact?" etc. Other areas where there is a potential for such high-level languages will be mentioned below.

Borrowing from the ROMC methodology for DSS development[23] we obtain useful insights for DSS language development efforts. According to this paradigm we need to provide the user with (1) alternative representations (e.g., graphic, textual, tabular) for a single concept; (2) a useful set of operations to allow exploration of alternatives and the construction of yet more complex concepts; (3) a set of memory aids to help users overcome their own cognitive limitations; and (4) a set of control mechanisms that allow users to utilize the three preceding sets of tools. We will use this framework in our subsequent discussion.

3. An Architecture for a DSS Generator

We commence with a brief description of the major software components shown in the idealized system architecture shown in Fig. 1. This is based on Stohr and White[25] (see also Ref. 24).

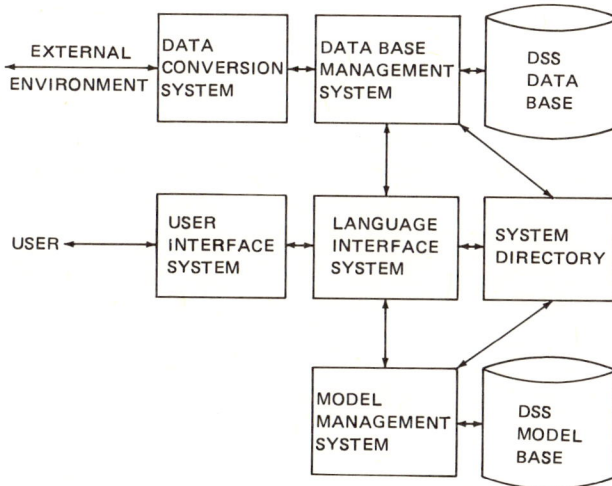

FIGURE 1. Major components of DSS generators.

Data Conversion System (DCS). This subsystem is used to transfer data between the DSS and the external environment including the corporate transaction processing systems.

Data Base Management System (DBMS). This provides the traditional data management and retrieval functions. In a DSS environment some additional capabilities should be provided as discussed later.

Data Base (DB). The repository of DSS data—time-series, productivity coefficients, geographic locations, etc.

System Directory (SD). A repository of "metadata" concerning the structure and contents of the data base and "model base" as well as intelligence about how the various software and data components relate to each other.

Model Management System (MMS). This system allows procedures and models to be defined, documented, stored, retrieved, loaded, and executed. It provides an environment in which more complex models can be constructed from primitive procedures and other models stored in the "model base."

Model Base (MB). A procedure or model library containing useful building blocks from which more complex models can be built.

User Interface System (UIS). A layer of software placed between the user and the other components of the DSS. This provides (1) "device independence" by relieving programmers and users of the necessity to know anything about physical device addresses and characteristics, line speeds, and communication protocols, (2) a uniform set of interface conventions for users, and (3) menu and screen management facilities.

Language Interface System (LIS). A layer of software providing translation (interpretation and compilation) services and message-switching facilities that allow the various components of the system to communicate with one another.

In practice the actual division of functions between the various components of DSS generators will vary from case to case. One possible design would involve a loosely coupled system in which, for example, the DBMS and MMS have well-developed, powerful, and user-friendly languages. In this case the LIS would need minimal translation abilities. Alternatively, the DBMS and MMS might support only terse mathematically oriented "target" languages suitable for system programmers. In this case the LIS would need to contain language translators to provide more natural languages for the end-user.

Our separation of the UIS and LIS serves to emphasize the many nonlanguage aspects of the man–machine interface. These range from physical characteristics such as line speed and quality of CRT displays to "help" features, graphics, and menu and screen management facilities. Even the most powerful and user-friendly of languages will fail to satisfy users if these aspects of the interface are unsatisfactory.[28]

A DBMS relieves programmers of many tedious and difficult data management and manipulation chores. In a similar fashion the UIS will provide higher-level languages for designing screens, menus, reports, and graphic displays. At present these functions can only be provided by separate report writer, screen manager, and graphic packages purchased from separate vendors. Access from available DSS generators is difficult if not impossible. This results in inferior (e.g., prompt-response as opposed to full-screen) modes of interaction in many DSS systems. Obviously there are many advantages to the UIS concept. These include economies in number of lines of code required, reduced application development times, enhanced prototyping capabilities, and the opportunity to present a coherent set of interface conventions to users.

The UIS and LIS jointly perform many complex transformations. A command issued by a user may be in the form of an English-like language, a terse formal command language, or merely the touch of a light-pen on a CRT screen. Alternatively, graphics or even voice media may be used. All of these inputs must eventually be translated to activate a sequence of machine-level instructions. Conversely, the raw output of, for example, the DBMS or MMS may be formatted into screens, transformed into graphs, or formatted and paged by a report-writer. The LIS role in these transformations is to perform the language translations required.

As a more advanced feature the LIS might allow DSS builders to construct their own languages specially tailored to fit particular applications or particular user styles. To do this the LIS would contain a parser–generator.[1] Note that some current natural language interfaces contain this feature to allow application specific vocabulary and grammar rules to be defined.[14]

Finally it is very important in terms of the flexibility and extensibility of the DSS that access to general-purpose languages (FORTRAN, PASCAL, APL, etc.) be provided from the MMS.

4. Types of DSS Language

Table 2 lists some applications of languages in a DSS together with the user roles with which they are most likely to be associated. Although many different languages are listed it should be clear that we are only interested in the range of functions performed and that a common syntax and style across these functions would be advantageous. We must also emphasize that the languages in Table 2 are those made available by the DSS generator. This list ignores both the language(s) used by the designers of the software to build the DSS Generator and the "languages" (or "interfaces") that can be constructed using the tools provided by the generator. In particular the major role of the DSS builder is to use the languages of Table 2 to derive new languages for use by intermediaries and managers. The ease with which useful *"derived"* languages can be built provides a measure of the success of the DSS generator.

TABLE 2
DSS Language Functions

Language	Purpose	Primary users
CL (DSS command language)	High-level control of DSS processes	All
Data base management system		
DDL (data definition language)	Define data and logical relationships	Builder
DML (data manipulation language)	Retrieval and update from application programs	Builder
QL (query language)	Interactive data retrieval; limited update	Intermediary, manager
Model management system		
MDL (model definition language)	Program statements defining operations on data (the "model")	Builder, intermediary
MCL (model command language)	Link, load-execute modules; sensitivity analysis; store and analyze results	Intermediary, manager
Report manager		
RDL (report definition language)	Define report formats and data	Builder, intermediary
RCL (report command language)	Display reports; interactively modify formats	Intermediary, manager
Screen manager		
SDL (screen definition language)	Define screen formats and data; store in library	Builder
Menu manager		
MnDL (menu definition language)	Define menus and hierarchical relationships; store in library	Builder
Graphics manager		
GDL (graph definition language)	Define graph type, scale, axes, labels, etc.	Builder, intermediary
GCL (graph command language)	Display graphs; interactively modify formats	Intermediary, manager
GPL (general purpose language)	High-level language accessible from MDL; extend model base	Builder

Note that most language categories in Table 2 have both "definition" and "command" languages. The definition languages generally describe data objects—the schema for the DBMS, specific types of graphs, reports, screen formats, and so on. However, in the case of models, the model definition language (MDL) describes procedures as well as data objects. In fact MDLs may be general-purpose programming languages with conditional branching, looping constructs, and so on. Usually they include specialized language features that help in building models—for example financial functions such as present value and return on investment. They tend to be formal keyword-oriented languages because of the need for precision and expressive power. They are generally more suited for use by DSS builders or intermediaries. If a definition language is interpreted (as is the case with QLs and some MDLs), it becomes more like a command language. However, the latter operate at a more aggregate, "meta" level.

The command languages are usually interpretive and, as their name implies, they cause processing to take place identifying both the data objects and procedures to be used. As an example, the DSS command language provides interactive high-level access to other DSS components. The simplest form of such a language would be a query–response interface or a menu with options allowing the user to enter various components (cause them to execute). Alternatively the DSS command language may be a key-word language. Often these have the format: COMMAND parameter 1, parameter 2, ... A useful extension of a simple command language involves giving users the ability to store much-used sequences of commands in "command files" for execution on an as-needed basis. Depending on the sophistication of the system it may be possible to pass symbolic parameters to the command files to allow for variations in data names and other specifications. Finally, the DSS command language may support looping and branching constructs, in which case it resembles a full programming language. A second example of a command language is provided by the model command language (MCL) which allows users to execute models and perform sensitivity analyses. When an MMS is present the MCL can be quite sophisticated as discussed more fully below.

Often the statements of a definition language must be typed in a file for later use by the DSS. When these processes cannot be initiated interactively from the main DSS command interface we will call the languages *"separate."* Compiled MDLs are often separate languages in this sense. The DDL, MNDL, and SDL are also usually separate languages. Since the latter three are used only by the builder, little is lost in terms of the interactivity of the interface. However, separate MDL, RDL, and GDL languages can cause time delays that decrease the effectiveness of the DSS.

Any DSS generator must have the ability to perform at least some of the functions of the CL, DDL, (DML or QL), MDL, MCL, RDL, and RCL. However, these may exist only in rudimentary forms. In many ways the language functions in Table 2 together with the type(s) of interface supported provide a good way of describing both the capabilities of a DSS generator and its ease of use. For example one popular system provides a CL imbedded in a query–response type of interface which accesses a powerful MCL and somewhat less powerful DDL, QL, RCL, GDL and GCL languages. The MDL is a separate (compiled) language and the RDL and command file facilities are separate also. The current version of this system supports the standard (text, dumb terminal, typing) interface only. No access is provided to a GPL to allow extension of the model base.

5. Language Trade-Offs

In this section we discuss some major implementation issues concerning the *form* of DSS languages without regard to the domain over which the languages are defined. The latter (semantic) issues are addressed in Section 6 below. Our discussion is in terms of some of the major design choices faced by DSS language designers: compilation versus interpretation; language power versus ease of learning and use; "host-language" versus "self-contained" systems; menu-driven versus command languages; formal command languages versus "natural" languages.

A major consideration in DSS languages concerns the choice between *interpretation* and *compilation*. In compiled languages the definition and execution phases are separate processes and unless the transition is well handled the interface loses the immediacy property mentioned in Section 2. Compiled software executes more rapidly but is more time consuming to develop. Statements in an interpretive language on the other hand are executed as soon as they are typed, thereby providing prompt feedback to the user and aiding the evolutionary DSS development process. Furthermore, it is often possible in interpretive systems to allow users to dynamically define new commands and to create and store new data objects. This provides some measure of language extensibility and allows users to develop more personalized systems. Finally, some systems allow users to develop and test procedures in an interpretive mode and then to translate the developed code using a compiler to obtain an efficient execution. This provides some of the advantages of both schemes.

A DSS is used to accomplish decision-making tasks efficiently and effectively. The ability to do this is closely connected to the *"power"* of the languages used. A language is powerful, with respect to an application domain, if (1) it has high expressive power (operations in the domain can be expressed clearly and succinctly), and (2) it has reasonable computing efficiency in terms of both response times and computing resources used. Figure 2 is a Kiviat Star diagram that illustrates some major language trade-offs and relationships. Two languages, APL and FORTRAN, are plotted on the diagram as examples. If the application involves a mathematical application such as linear programming then the shapes of the two plots might be as shown. Notice that the relative positions of the two languages

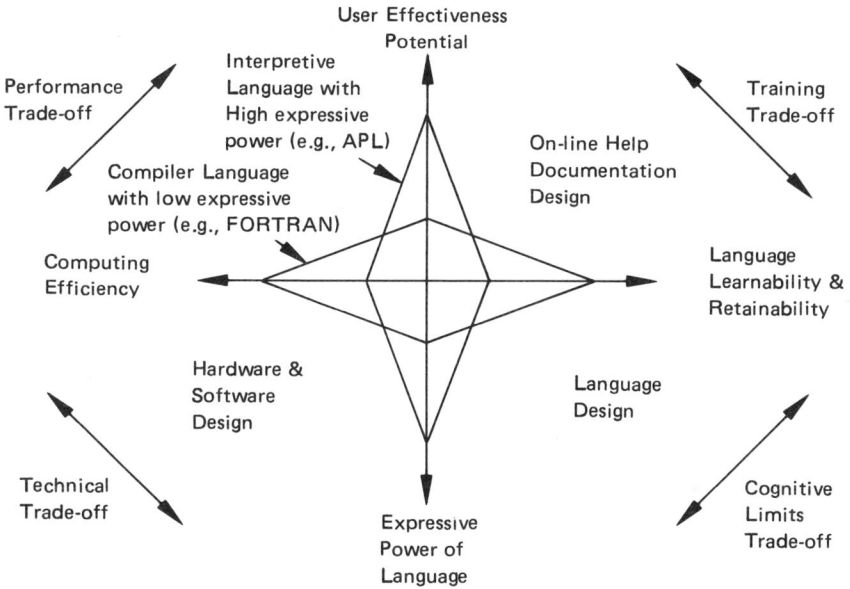

FIGURE 2. DSS language relationships.

on one or more axes might be reversed if another application domain were considered.

We now discuss the trade-offs associated with the quadrants in Fig. 2.

Technical Trade-Off. There is a tendency for languages with high expressive power to be less efficient in execution time and memory usage. Thus a well-written assembler program may be more efficient than the same program written in a high-level language. Similarly CODASYL DML[6] is likely to be more efficient than a high-level relational language for most retrieval tasks. Interpretive languages are, *ceteris paribus,* less efficient than compiled languages.

Performance Trade-Off. Often higher user effectiveness is associated with lower computer efficiency. Usually the effectiveness of users in problem solving will be the most important factor in a cost–benefit analysis. Potential effectiveness will be increased with a language of high expressive power since the necessity for detailed programming is eliminated and prototype modifications will be faster. Again interpretive languages give higher user effectiveness, *ceteris paribus,* because they provide immediate feedback.

Training Trade-Off. In general the languages with the highest performance potential will be the hardest to learn. Human factors studies show that on-line help and documentation aids can effectively reduce the cost and time to train users.

Cognitive Limits Trade-Off. Languages with higher expressive power have both larger vocabularies and more complex grammars; they will therefore be more difficult to learn and retain. Reisner[19] has suggested that languages should be "layered" in difficulty. This means that the most common functions should be expressible in simple forms that can be easily learned by casual users while less common functions can have more complex syntax.

The choice of the "best" language for a given application depends on a cost–benefit analysis taking into account computer and training costs for different levels of user effectiveness.

The designers of a DSS generator must decide whether it is to be constructed as an extension of an existing general-purpose *"host language"* or be *"self-contained"* in the sense that all language interfaces and other functions are coded into the software of the DSS itself. The simplest form of a host-language DSS generator would consist of a package of subroutines or procedures callable from a language such as FORTRAN, PL/1, or APL. A more sophisticated approach is to extend the syntax of one of these languages to provide DSS functions embedded in a unified syntactic scheme. Often this is done by precompiling the augmented language to produce intermediate code in the original host language. Self-contained languages are specially built for the purpose at hand and can be designed to perform efficiently and to present a uniform interface to the user. Their major disadvantage in comparison with host-language systems is that communication with other, more general purpose programming tools may be severely restricted. This can limit the ability of DSS builders to develop new kinds of applications not envisaged by the designers of the system.

As pointed out by Vassiliou and Jarke[30] (and as is evident from our previous discussion), the concept of a computer language has expanded in two directions: (1) methods of communicating with computers are beginning to embrace more of our physical senses (touch, hearing, etc.) and (2) formal key-word languages are becoming more English-like and even "natural." Both of these trends appear to have potential in DSS applications.

Interfaces employing devices such as light-pens, touch-screens, and joy-sticks fall into the first of the above categories. Often these are used to provide an alternative to typing as a means of menu selection. For this purpose they are useful interfaces for managers and other casual users. However, the expressive power of such interfaces is limited to a discrete set of predetermined choices. Empirical evidence[10] indicates that users tend to prefer command languages to menu-driven interfaces after they have gained some initial experience with a system. Furthermore, the complex data retrieval and procedure coding tasks faced by DSS builders require a full language capability. Thus we see a need for both levels of "language" in a DSS. Menu or simple prompt-response interfaces can be used at the higher levels of the DSS to allow all classes of users to select the major subsystems or modes of operation they wish to enter. These simple interfaces can then be extended downwards two or three levels to allow casual users to perform useful tasks such as running predefined models and reports. Full language capabilities must be provided for the builders and intermediaries to build the models, format output reports, and so on.

The second important trend in computer languages is the attempt to make them more like English. To the extent that this can be achieved it is generally believed that managers will be encouraged to interact personally with the computer. In addition, learning and retention properties should be improved. More importantly, perhaps, progress in the field of "natural" computer languages will, of necessity, pave the way for more intelligent (forgiving) interfaces since human speech involves many shortcuts and abbreviations that require a built-in intelligence to understand. Eventually our progress in understanding natural language will be coupled with voice entry of commands and queries to give a truly different dimension to the man–machine interface. At the present time there is at least one successful "natural" database query language on the market,[11] and progress in voice recognition has reached a point where voice commands could be used for simple menu-selection tasks and restricted forms of data entry.

To summarize our discussion so far, we believe that DSS generator MDLs and QLs should be interpretive, have high expressive power, be "layered," and be augmented by a range of help and documentation aids. In addition all language functions shown in Table 2 should be accessible from the main DSS interface (no separate languages).

6. DSS Language Functions

We turn now to a brief discussion of the semantics of DSS data retrieval and modeling languages. We are interested in what these languages can do for DSS users or, more precisely, in the range of functions that must be performed by DSS languages. Lists of the most important functions are given (Tables 3–5), together with some summary comments. However, it is our intention that these functions should be incorporated into the vocabulary of the various DSS languages. In some cases this can be done by simply storing callable procedures in the model base. In other cases, particularly for command languages such as the MCL, the functions and the objects on which they operate might form the verbs and nouns (respectively) of a DSS language. The discussion will be limited to database and modeling functions only since these are closer to the end user and are also most likely to differ from conventional MIS applications.

We will not discuss *DBMS languages* in great detail here since they have been the subject of many articles and books. However, DSS databases have their own unique data management problems that should be reflected in language facilities. First the unanticipated nature of many requests to the DSS and the generation of new data by DSS models implies that the DBMS should allow new data

TABLE 3
Data Management Functions

Concept	Representations	Special data base operations[a]
Time-series	Variable length array Line graph Scatter plot	Extraction from MIS or external data bases Periodicity conversion Missing values Period ranging Concatenation of series Grouping of series Aggregation over series
Multi-dimensional information	Multi-dimensional array	Aggregation Multi-key sorts
Hierarchical groups	Trees, confluent hierarchies	Aggregation Tree search
Meta data	Dictionary format; definitions, cross-reference maps	Multi-key, partial-key and context search; Dictionary maintenance

[a]In addition to the usual retrieve, display, store, add, delete, and modify operations.

TABLE 4
Analytic and Modeling Capabilities

Data transformation operations
  Simple calculations
  Vector and matrix operations
  Recoding of data values
  Concatenation
  Missing value transformations
  Conversion of periodicities
  Grouping of time-series
  Aggregation

Statistical functions
  Descriptive statistics
  Exploratory data analysis
  Time-series forecasting
    Exponential smoothing
    Box–Jenkins
  Regression forecasting
    Multiple regression
    Simultaneous equation techniques
  Multivariate analysis

Financial functions
  Net present value, return on investment, etc.
  Accounting conventions
  Consolidation
  Depreciation routines
  Tax routines

Management science techniques
  Mathematical programming
  Simulation support facilities
  Simultaneous equations

Sensitivity analysis
  Impact analysis
  What-if analysis
  Goal seeking
  Monte Carlo analysis

TABLE 5
Model Management Functions

Concept	Representations	Operations
1. Housekeeping (builder):		
Functions, subroutines, and procedures as building blocks	Source code, object code, data abstractions	Store, retrieve, add, delete, modify
Model dictionary	Input–process–output description, cross-reference maps	Multi-key, partial-key, and context search; dictionary maintenance
2. Construction (builder, intermediary):		
Model built from building blocks	Source code referencing, library functions, and procedures	Store, retrieve, add, delete, modify, execute (compile, link, load, go)
3. Sensitivity analysis (intermediary, manager):		
Assumptions	Model code	Modify
Model parameters	Data items	Modify, range values
Base case	File of data item values	Store, retrieve
Case	Operations on base case data items	Execute, store, retrieve, undo
Sensitivity	How does x vary with y?	Marginal analysis
Goals	What value of y is required to obtain $x = $?	Target analysis
Causality	What impacts x? What is impacted by x?	Impact analysis

relationships to be added dynamically at execution time. This facility is provided most easily by relational systems.[5] Secondly a number of conceptual objects and relationships occur in DSS that cannot easily be represented in a conventional DBMS. Table 3 lists some of these together with possible representations and operations (following the ROMC method—see above).

There are a number of aspects of DSS data manipulation that need special attention:

(1) Many, perhaps most, DSS applications involve planning and forecasting, giving rise to a need for the DSS to handle time-series. There are a number of problems here: (a) conventional MIS usually maintain only recent transactions and store data on a cross-section rather than time-series basis, making data acquisition by the DSS difficult; (b) conventional DBMS often do not handle variable time length data well; (c) there is often a need to store many versions of the same time series with different periodicities and ranges of time.

(2) Accounting data are often conceptualized by managers as having many different *dimensions*—for example sales—by product, by region, by customer

class. Hence there is a need to be able to store, create and manipulate multidimensional arrays.

(3) *Hierarchical classification* schemes (accounting systems, organization structures, project task breakdowns, product explosions, etc.) are a common means for dealing with complexity. The DSS generator languages must therefore allow the user to create and manipulate alternative hierarchically organized data objects.

(4) The DSS System Directory (Fig. 1) contains metadata concerning the meanings and relationships of both data and model objects. Language concepts that can be used to create and retrieve such metadata should also be provided.

Many of the representations and operations shown in Table 5 have been provided by different systems. For example statistical packages provide facilities for handling time series, and some report writers handle the concept of multidimensional objects well. However, research on the semantic and syntactic structure of DSS languages for manipulating these concepts is much needed.

The concept of "model management" has been an innovative feature of DSS research. We have previously mentioned that the MDL (model definition language) should be (1) interpretive, (2) have capabilities (in terms of control structures and input–output) of a full programming language, (3) allow procedural access to a general-purpose programming language to allow additions to the model base to be constructed, and (4) provide a number of commonly used operations useful in planning. Table 4 indicates the major classes of functions that should be provided in the MDL. Many of these can be implemented via procedure calls. Others would be better implemented by incorporating them into the syntax of the MDL. Ormancioglu[17] describes a mathematically based high-level language that provides a number of operations that are useful in data retrieval and model building and would allow DSS models to be stated in a concise form. Another interesting possibility is to build specialized languages containing key words corresponding to commonly used operations such as "Regress," "Forecast," and "Consolidate." Current DSS generators generally provide these functions only through standard procedure or subroutine calling conventions.

Turning now to the MCL (model command language) there are a number of concepts and operations that can be defined over models and their inputs and outputs. Table 5 lists these operations in three groups: housekeeping, construction–execution, and sensitivity analysis.

The model base (Fig. 1) contains a large number of procedures that can be used in models (see for example Table 4). The *housekeeping* functions are concerned with the maintenance both of these procedures and their descriptions. The *construction* functions combine these building blocks into executable modules. While the housekeeping and construction facilities are a necessary part of any application development system much DSS research has been aimed at providing more powerful systems for building models. Database techniques have been used to coordinate the inputs and outputs of cooperating models at different organization levels.[24] Knowledge representation techniques from artificial intelligence might be used to give the system greater self-knowledge in order (1) to assist users in learning the capabilities of the model base and (2) to help builders in the construction of models.[7] Continuing this direction of research, Bonczek *et al.*[3] have shown how predicate calculus and the resolution principle can, in principle, be used to automatically construct models from more basic building blocks. This would allow users to state information results in a nonprocedural manner by specifying *what* is to be accomplished rather than the procedural details of *how* the computation is to be performed.

The ability to explore the implications of models under various assumptions concerning their structural form and parameter values and different management policies lies at the heart of the DSS idea. The MCL interface should support the decision-making process by providing short- and long-term memory aids. These might help the user keep track of sets of parameter values and assumptions cases and their corresponding results.[26] In this context we need to develop language constructs that would allow users to create and modify "base cases" (trial settings of parameters and other model elements), to retrieve the results of previous runs, to compare different solutions, and to modify the underlying assumptions.

In the area of sensitivity analyses we have already mentioned the emergence of languages for "what if?" analyses. At a more advanced level Blanning[2], defines a formal grammar for decision making based on six functions commonly provided by a DSS: selection and aggregation of data, estimation of parameters, solution of simultaneous equations, and optimization. The grammar contains four variables: a decision to be made, a sensitivity analysis, a performance measure, and an environment. Sentences in the language correspond to common sequences used in problem-solving tasks.

7. Conclusion

In this paper we developed a set of general requirements for DSS languages. We then listed an array of languages that should be included in a DSS generator. These were differentiated both according to the function performed (example model definition or data base retrieval) and according to their type (derived, command, definition, separate, etc.). Some of the major implementation issues faced by DSS software designers were also discussed. Next we provided a detailed analysis of some of the special functions that a DSS should perform in the areas of database and model management. For each area we described the desired capabilities from the point of view of the end user or model builder. The next step will be to design specialized, high-level languages that will assist the user in performing these functions. This is seen as an important area for research and development by behavioral scientists, operations researchers, and computer scientists.

References

1. A. V. AHO and J. D. ULLMAN, *Principles of Compiler Design,* Addison-Wesley, Reading, Massachusetts, 1978.
2. R. W. BLANNING, A decision support language for corporate planning, *Int. J. Policy Anal. Inf. Sys.,* 313–324, December (1982).
3. R. H. BONCZEK, C. W. HOLSAPPLE, and A. B. WHINSTON, A generalized decision support system using predicate calculus and network data base management *Operations Res.* **29** (2), 263–281, March-April (1982).
4. J. B. BOULDEN, *Computer-Assisted Planning Systems: Management Concept, Application, and Implementation,* McGraw-Hill, New York, 1975.
5. E. F. CODD, A relational model for large shared data banks, *Commun. ACM,* **13** (6), 377–387, June (1970).
6. DBTG: *Data Base Task Group April 1971 Report,* CODASYL Programming Language Committee, ACM, New York, 1971.
7. J. J. ELAM, J. C. HENDERSON, and L. W. MILLER, Model management systems: An approach to decision support in complex organizations, *Proc. 1st International Conference on Information Systems,* Philadelphia, December, 1980.
8. EMPIRE: Applied Data Research Inc., Princeton, New Jersey, 1983.
9. EXPRESS: Management Decision Systems, Waltham, Massachusetts, 1983.
10. D. GILFOIL, Warming-up to computers: A study of cognitive and affective interaction over time, *Proc. Conference on Human Factors in Computer Systems,* Gaithersburg, Maryland, March 1982.
11. L. R. HARRIS, User oriented data base query with the ROBOT natural language query system, *Int. J. Man-Mach. Stud.* **9,** 679–713 (1977).
12. R. H. HAYES and R. L. NOLAN, What kind of corporate modeling functions best?, *Harvard Business Rev.,* 102–112, May-June (1974).
13. IFPS: EXECUCOM Systems Corporation, Austin, Texas, 1983.
14. H. LEHMANN, Interpretation of natural language in an information system, *IBM J. Res. Dev.* **22,** September (1978).
15. P. LORANGE and J. F. ROCKART, A framework for the use of computer-based models in the planning process, Alfred P. Sloan School of Management, Working Paper WP 860-76, 1976.
16. T. H. NAYLOR and H. SCHAULAND, A survey of users of corporate planning models, *Manage. Sci.* **22** (9), 927–936, May (1976).
17. L. ORMANCIOGLU, An array theoretic specification environment for the design of decision support systems, *Int. J. Policy Anal. Inf. Sys.,* 373–392, December (1982).
18. PLATO DSS Reference Manual, OR/MS Dialogue, New York, 1982.
19. P. REISNER, Human factors studies of data base query languages: A survey and assessment, *ACM Compu. Surv.* 13 (1981).
20. B. SCHNEIDERMAN, *Software Psychology: Human Factors in Computer and Information Systems,* Winthrop Publishers Inc., Cambridge, Massachusetts 1980.
21. R. A. SEABERG and C. SEABERG, Computer based decision systems in Xerox corporate planning, *Manage. Sci.* **20,** 575–584 (1973).
22. SIMPLAN: SIMPLAN Systems Inc., Chapel Hill, North Carolina, 1983.
23. R. H. SPRAGUE and E. D. CARLSON, *Building Effective Decision Support Systems,* Prentice Hall Inc., Englewood Cliffs, New Jersey, 1982.
24. R. H. SPRAGUE and H. J. WATSON, A decision support system for banks, *OMEGA* **4,** 657–671 (1976).
25. E. A. STOHR and N. H. WHITE, User interfaces for decision support: An overview, *Int. J. Policy Anal. Inf. Syst.* **6,** December (1982).
26. E. A. STOHR and M. TANNIRU, A data base for operations research models, *Int. J. Policy Anal. Inf. Syst.* **4** (4), 105–121, December (1980).
27. J. W. TRAENKLE, E. B. CASE, and J. A. BULLARD, Jr., *The Use of Financial Models in Business,* Financial Executives Research Foundation, New York, 1975.
28. J. TURNER, E. A. JARKE, Y. STOHR, Y. VASSILIOU, and N. H. WHITE, Using restricted natural

languages for data retrieval: A laboratory and field evaluation, *Proc. NYU Symposium on User Interfaces,* New York, May, 1982.
29. User Interfaces: *Proc. NYU Symposium on User Interfaces,* Graduate School of Business Administration, New York University, May, 1982.
30. Y. VASSILIOU and M. JARKE, Query languages: A taxonomy, in *Proc. NYU Symposium on User Interfaces,* Graduate School of Business Administration, New York, 1982.
31. XSIM: Interactive DATA corporation, Waltham, Massachusetts, 1983.
32. R. W. ZMUD, Individual differences and MIS success: A review of the literature, *Manage. Sci.* **25,** 966–979 (1979).

6

A FORMAL APPROACH TO DECISION SUPPORT

SHUHSHEN PAN, ROGER A. PICK, AND ANDREW B. WHINSTON

1. Introduction

It is often the case that the existence of a theoretical structure for an object provides for an easier design and implementation of that object. This typically occurs because the theory gives the builder a starting point, an unambiguous definition of the object, and a clear enumeration of the object's properties. Some areas of computer science which have benefited from a theoretical structure include compiler construction, benefiting from formal language theory, and the relational data model, benefiting from mathematical logic. It is the purpose of this paper to describe a formalism which will provide the theoretical foundation for decision support systems.

The formalism we describe, *the higher-level formalism,* is a mathematical logic designed to express knowledge about data and programs. With that formalism there is a structure which precisely defines the semantics of the formalism. That structure may be realized in a decision support system implemented on a computing system. The capabilities of the system are expressed by a set of parameters for the formalism. The nature of the implementation of those capabilities is defined by the form of the structure.

Since the term decision support system (DSS) means something different to everyone who uses it, we will informally define what it means to us. We see a DSS as having three components: a language system (LS), a knowledge system (KS), and a problem processing system (PPS). More details on this may be found in Ref. 2. We will give a formal definition that conforms with this informal definition in Section 2.

SHUHSHEN PAN ● Computer Science Department, Purdue University, West Lafayette, Indiana 47907. ROGER A. PICK and ANDREW B. WHINSTON ● Krannert Graduate School of Management, Purdue University, West Lafayette, Indiana 47907. Research was supported in part by the National Science Foundation, Grant Nos. IST-8108519 and ECS-8116135, and by a gift from the IBM Corporation to the Management Information Research Center.

In this chapter, we will assume the nature of each of these components to be roughly as follows with details to be given in later sections. The knowledge system (KS) contains a database and programs. The database is viewed in terms of a higher-level data model. The problem processing system (PPS) is a mechanical theorem prover. The language system (LS) is a language of the higher-level formalism. The higher-level formalism is a class of mathematical logics whose semantics are defined by higher-level databases. A LS based upon a mathematical language cannot be considered user friendly. We assume that a query language has been defined and the queries are translated into well-formed formulas (wffs) in the higher-level language. These wffs implicitly specify the logical pathway through the KS for answering a query. The nature of the user interface and the translation are irrelevant to the purposes of this paper. What is relevant is that the PPS is presented with a query in the form of a theorem to be proved. The LS will not be considered further in this paper.

The focus of this chapter is upon the PPS and the KS. The KS consists of knowledge about the problem domain contained within the DSS. This knowledge is in the form of data and programs.† The KS is organized according to the higher-level data model. The next section will discuss this briefly, but details are found in another work.[7]

The PPS serves as the interface between expressions of knowledge from the KS and expressions of problems from the LS. This is accomplished by regarding the KS as providing a set of axioms. The LS supplies theorems to be proved. The PPS is a mechanical theorem prover which executes programs and retrieves data as necessary.

The unifying framework for the DSS is the higher-level formalism. This formalism is a mathematical logic defined in such a way that many features of the DSS context are easily expressed. The formalism provides a theoretical language which serves as a basis of the DSS. The PPS is the deductive component of the formalism. The KS provides a semantic structure of the formalism. The LS is the interface between the DSS and its environment.

The rest of this chapter will describe what has been informally introduced in this section. The next section gives a formal definition of a DSS and defines the higher-level formalism. Section 3 describes the KS component of the DSS. The PPS is described in Section 4. The LS is outside the thrust of the paper and is not described further. Throughout this paper, there are three simple DSSs which illustrate how this formal approach works.

---

†We are using the term program in a somewhat narrower sense than the usual usage. By program, we mean a set of executable codes which calculate a set of output values from a set of input values. This definition is often used in the DSS literature to define the term "model." That term has different meanings in logic and in database management, two other areas from which this paper draws heavily.

2. A Formalism of Decision Support

We now define a DSS formally. A *decision support system* is a quadruple (F, K, P, L), where

F is a particular language of the higher-level formalism,
K is a structure for F,
P is a theorem-proving mechanism, and
L is a parser, converting from an external (user) language to the formalism.

This definition is in accordance with the informal definition which appeared earlier in the paper. The definition results in F corresponding to our formalism as an abstract description of the DSS. K, as a structure, defines a particular realization of the KS of the DSS. L corresponds to the LS component (user interface) of a DSS. P corresponds to the PPS.

The definition of a DSS guides the system designer in refining a particular DSS in steps proceeding from abstract considerations to implementation considerations. Initially, the designer must select the parameters for the formalism. These parameters define a particular language among the class of all higher-level formalisms. The designer must provide a set of parameters which are sufficient for abstract descriptions of all situations that may arise in the problem domain. The formalism provides a foundation for defining a particular DSS. The other three portions of a DSS are based upon the formalism.

A mathematical logic such as the higher-level formalism is useful for precisely representing factual information. To achieve the full power which mathematical logic can provide, we must associate with the formalism a semantic notion of truth and a syntactic notion of proof. For any particular formalism, we define a structure by associating meanings (in a way defined below) with each parameter. The system designer may define truth in any way he wishes by defining the structure appropriately. Naturally, he should only select from among those structures which provide a useful meaning for the formalism. These meanings may be provided by implementation of each parameter on a computer. Various parameters may be implemented by means of tables of values stored in files, programmed computational routines, or pointers. The decision as to how each parameter should be implemented is made after the selection of the appropriate parameters. The formalism is concerned with a set of objects and not with how they are achieved. The structure is an implementation of the formalism. The structure embodies the semantic knowledge that accompanies the formalism. The implementation provides a structure, which is the knowledge system for the DSS.

The PPS accepts user inquiries and attempts to answer them from the information contained in the KS. The query can be regarded as a collection of axioms. The PPS attempts to find a deduction of the query from the KS. Thus, the PPS is a mechanical theorem prover. Many existing decision support systems may be regarded as implementations of various ad hoc theorem provers. We advocate the use of a mathematical theorem prover in order to obtain full advantage from the use of a logical formalism. We also advocate the use of a mathematically sound and complete theorem prover such as can be based upon the resolution principle.[14] It is also possible to use other proof mechanisms featuring nonmonotonic reasoning[9] or inexact reasoning.[10]

We will now define precisely the higher-level formalism and the structure which goes with it.

2.1. Higher-Level Formalism

The higher-level formalism is syntactically defined by a set of symbols and a set of rules for combining them. Two kinds of symbols are used. There is a set of logical symbols. The logical symbols are the same for any of the higher-level formalisms. There is a set of parameter symbols, which vary. The parameter symbols distinguish which particular language is being used among the class of all higher-level formalisms.

This explanation of the formalism follows the format of Enderton's[6] explanation of first-order predicate calculus (fopc). The reader who finds the explanation in this paper too terse may find Enderton helpful.

The higher-level parameters are as follows:

1. A finite set of sort symbols $\{S_1, \ldots, S_m\}$. These will correspond to various sorts, which are domains of discourse.

2. For each n-tuple of sort symbols, $(S_{i_1}, \ldots, S_{i_n})$, there is a (possibly empty) finite set of type $(S_{i_1}, \ldots, S_{i_n})$ predicate symbols. We say that these are defined over the sorts $S_{i_1}, \ldots, S_{i_n}$. There are at most a finite number of predicate symbols.

3. For each $(n + 1)$tuple of sort symbols, $(S_{i_1}, \ldots, S_{i_n}, S_{i_0})$, there is a (possibly empty) finite set of type $(S_{i_1}, \ldots, S_{i_n}, S_{i_0})$ function symbols. We say that these functions are defined over the sorts $S_{i_1}, \ldots, S_{i_n}, S_{i_0}$. There are at most a finite number of function symbols.

4. For each sort symbol, there is a nonempty set of constant symbols. These constant symbols may coincide with some of the predicate symbols and function symbols. Constant symbols which are neither predicate symbols nor function symbols are called *atomic symbols*.

There is a restriction upon the predicate and function symbols which may be in any particular sort. We define a hierarchy of levels among predicates, functions, and sorts. No predicate may be defined over a sort of a higher level than itself. No function may be defined over a sort of a higher level than itself. Each sort must be of a higher level than any symbols (atomic or nonatomic) which it contains.

A formal definition of levels consistent with the above restriction is

Level $(i) = 0$, if i is an atomic symbol.

Level $(S) = 1$, if S is a sort which consists only of atomic symbols. Such a sort is referred to as a *first-level sort*.

Level $(P) = 1$, if P is a predicate defined only over first-level sorts.

Level $(f) = 1$, if f is a function defined only over first-level sorts.

Level $(P) = \max_{j=1,\ldots,n}$ level (S_{i_j}), if P is a predicate over sorts $S_{i_1}, \ldots, S_{i_n}$.

Level $(f) = \max_{j=0,1,\ldots,n}$ level (S_{i_j}), if f is a function over sorts $S_{i_1}, \ldots, S_{i_n}, S_{i_0}$.

Level $(S) = \max_{x \in S}$ level $(x) + 1$, if S is a higher-level sort.

We must restrict the language of the higher-level formalism in such a way that the above definition of levels is well defined. This restriction amounts to a restriction on the nature of atomic formulas and terms. We define, using levels, a hierarchy of predicates and sorts. This hierarchy is necessary to prevent self-reference and the paradoxes that it causes. The hierarchy permits the construction of a mapping from the higher-level formalism to fopc.

There is also a collection of logical symbols. The set of logical symbols includes (,), $\sim$, and $\rightarrow$, which are parentheses and the two logical connectives for not and implies. There is also a set of variable symbols: a countably infinite set of variables for each sort; i.e., for sort S_k $(k = 1, \ldots, m)$, there are $v_1^k, v_2^k, \ldots$. In the rest of the chapter, the sort of a variable will be obvious from context and will be omitted. There is, for each sort, a quantifier symbol $\forall_k$. As with the variables, the sort associated with a particular use of the equality or quantifier is almost always obvious and will generally be omitted.

Some of these symbols are used to define terms. A S_k *term* of the higher-level formalism may be one of the following: A constant symbol which is among the set of constant symbols associated with the sort S_k is an S_k term. A variable symbol for the sort S_k is an S_k term. A symbol of form $f(t_1, \ldots, t_n)$, where f is a function symbol of sort $(S_{i_1}, \ldots, S_{i_n}, S_k)$ and each t_j is of sort S_{i_j}, is an S_k term.

An *atomic formula* is of the form $P(t_1, \ldots, t_n)$, where P is a predicate symbol of type $(S_{i_1}, \ldots, S_{i_n})$ and t_k is an S_{i_k} term for $k = 1, 2, \ldots, n$. All atomic formulas must be such that the predicate symbol is of the same level or higher than any of the terms occurring in the formula. That is, level $(P) \geq$ level (t_k) for $k = 1, 2, \ldots, n$.

The *well-formed formulas (wffs)* of the higher-level formalism are defined as follows:

If S is a sort symbol and t is a term, then $S(t)$ is a wff.

An atomic formula is a wff.

If ψ is a wff, then so is $(\rightarrow\psi)$.

If θ and ψ are wffs, then so is $(\theta \longrightarrow \psi)$.
If x is a variable symbol and θ is a wff, then $(\forall x \theta)$ is a wff.

The above recursive definition of a wff encompasses what is usually referred to as atomic formulas, not, implies, and quantification. There are further types of wffs corresponding to and, or, existential quantification, and so forth. These further types of wffs are abbreviations for the minimal set defined above. For example, $\alpha \wedge \sim\beta$ is an abbreviation for $\sim (\alpha \rightarrow \sim\beta)$ and α or β is an abbreviation for $(\sim\alpha) \rightarrow \beta$. Also, $\exists\, x\phi$ is an abbreviation for $\sim\forall x \sim\phi$. Another abbreviation is that we will leave out parentheses whenever they are not necessary for the reader's understanding of a wff. Finally, we will often leave out quantifiers. An unbound variable symbol will be considered as implicitly universally quantified.

2.2. Higher-Level Structure

The structure is the basis for defining the truth of a particular wff in the formalism.

The semantics or meaning (truth value) that goes with the syntax of the formalism is defined by a *structure* M. A structure gives the basis for determining the truth of any wff. This structure defines the meaning of any wffs expressed in the language. The structure is a mapping from parameters of the language to their meaning as follows:

1. For each sort symbol, there is a set called a sort. The cardinality of this set corresponds to the number of constant symbols of the sort, which is required to be finite. For each constant symbol which is a predicate symbol, there is a corresponding relation (as given below). For each constant symbol which is a function symbol, there is a corresponding function (as given below). We will denote the set which goes with sort S_k by S_k^M.

2. For each predicate symbol of type $(S_{i_1}, \ldots, S_{i_n})$, there is either a subset of $S_{i_1}^M \times \cdots \times S_{i_n}^M$ or a program mapping from $S_{i_1}^M \times \cdots \times S_{i_j}^M$ to $S_{i_{j+1}}^M \times \cdots \times S_{i_n}^M$ for $1 < j < n$. This subset is often called a relation. We will call the program a dynamic relation. We will denote the relation or dynamic relation which goes with predicate symbol P by P^M.

3. For each function symbol of type $(S_{i_1}, \ldots, S_{i_n}, S_{i_0})$, there is a partial function mapping from $S_{i_1}^M \times \cdots \times S_{i_n}^M$ to $S_{i_0}^M$. We will denote the partial function which goes with function symbol f by f^M.

4. There is a one-to-one correspondence between constant symbols and elements of the sorts. A logician would say that each element C^M of a sort has a name C.

We have the following recursive definition of truth for a closed wff (no unbound variables—see Enderton;[6] Enderton calls such a wff a sentence) ψ:

If $\psi = S(t)$, then ψ is true iff $t \in S^M$.
If $\psi = P(t_1, \ldots, t_n)$, then ψ is true iff the tuple $(t_1^M, \ldots, t_n^M)$ is in the relation corresponding to P, P^M.
If $\psi = {\sim}\alpha$, then ψ is true iff α is false.
If $\psi = \alpha \longrightarrow \beta$, then ψ is true iff α is false or β is true.
If $\psi = \forall \, x\phi$, then ψ is true iff $\phi\,[x/c]$ is true for all constants c in the sort for which the variable x is associated. The notation $\phi[x/c]$ indicates that the term c is to be substituted for all unbound occurrences of the variable x in the wff ϕ. For example, $GT(x, 0)[x/1]$ is the same as $GT(1, 0)$.

If Γ is a set of closed wffs in a higher-level language L and M is a structure for that language, we write $M \,|\, = \Gamma$ (read M *satisfies* Γ or M is a *model* for Γ) iff all wffs in γ are true in M. If ψ is a wff and Γ is a set of wffs, we write $\Gamma \,|\, = \psi$ (read Γ *semantically implies* ψ) iff all models of Γ are also models of ψ.

To generalize the notion of truth of a given wff to include the case of open wffs, we must define a specification function. An open wff is a wff with unbound variables. Let $s_i\colon V_i \to S_i^M$ be the local specification function from the set V_i consisting of those variables corresponding to sort S_i, and define the global specification function as follows:

$$s(x) = s_i(x), \qquad \text{if } x \in V_i$$

The extension of s, $\bar{s}$, from the set T of all arguments into the union $\cup S_i^M$ can be defined as follows:

1. For each variable v_i, $\bar{s}(v_i) = s(v_i)$.
2. For each constant symbol C, $\bar{s}(C) = C^M$.
3. If $t_1, \ldots, t_n$ are arguments and F is an n-place function symbol, then $\bar{s}(F(t_1, \ldots, t_n)) = F^M(\bar{s}(t_1), \ldots, \bar{s}(t_n))$.

Truth of an open wff with respect to a structure M is ambiguous since the values of the variables are unknown. The specification function eliminates this ambiguity. We define *satisfaction* of a (possibly open) wff α with respect to a structure M and specification function s (written $M \,|\, = \alpha[s]$) as follows:

If $\alpha = S(t)$, then $M \,|\, = S(t)\,[s]$ iff $\bar{s}(t) \in S^M$.
If $\alpha = P(t_1, \ldots, t_n)$, then $M \,|\, = P(t_1, \ldots, t_n)[s]$ iff $(\bar{s}(t_1), \ldots, \bar{s}(t_n)) \in P^M$.
If $\alpha = {\sim}\beta$, then $M \,|\, = {\sim}\beta[s]$ iff it is not the case that $M \,|\, = \beta[s]$.

If $\alpha = \beta \to \gamma$, then $M \mid = \beta \to \gamma[s]$ iff $M \mid = \sim\beta[s]$ or $M \mid = \gamma[s]$.
If $\alpha = \forall x\beta$, where x is a variable symbol for sort S, then $M \mid = \forall x\beta[s]$
iff $M \mid = \beta[x/d][s]$ for all $d \in S$.

3. Higher-Level KS

The KS contains all the stored knowledge of the DSS about its problem domain. Theoretically speaking, it is a structure for the formalism since it can be used to determine the truth of any wff in the formalism. In another work,[7] we have discussed how the structure may be implemented as a database. This implementation approach was called a higher-level data model. The KS component of the DSS may include information coded as either files or programs. This necessitates an extension of the data model to include the case of programs as implementations of predicates.

This section briefly discusses the higher-level data model. We go on to compare and contrast programs and relations. Then, we explain the extended data model which supports the KS. The last topic in this section is a discussion of a diagrammatic representation of the KS. The section concludes with examples.

3.1. The Higher-Level Data Model

Proposed as an implementation of the formalism, the higher-level data model serves as an extension of the relational data model.[5] The extension is useful in its own right, since it alleviates some of the difficulties that exist with the relational model in capturing certain kinds of meaning. The extension was constructed in parallel with the construction of the higher-level formalism so that the new data model would have a relationship with a theoretically strong mathematical logic analogous to the relationship between the relational data model and fopc.

It should be noted that we do not necessarily advocate a relational-based model as the basis for implementing our higher-level data model. Other database models can be accommodated by the formalism. We give an example later in the chapter which is based on a CODASYL network data model. We generally stay with extended relational databases in this chapter. This is because the conversion of mathematical logic predicates to relations is convenient.

The extension of the relational model with the higher-level model comes in two parts. The first part consists of a discipline which permits relations to be defined over relations. This discipline is done in such a way (through the use of levels) that problems of self-reference are avoided and the resulting higher-level database is equivalent to a relational database in first normal form. The second part of the extension consists of permitting the database to include closed wffs over variables and wffs involving logical connectives. This allows much more freedom in expressing knowledge than can be achieved under the relational model (which only permits atomic formulas over constants). This freedom is particularly helpful if one wants to have inference rules and integrity constraints stored as part of the database. A forthcoming paper[8] describes the use of data retrieval and data modification operators upon higher-level databases.

3.2. Higher-Level Programs

We see data and programs as being two different implementations of the same abstract concept. In either case, the question is whether or not a certain collection of values are related to one another in some way. In one case, the list of values for which the relationship holds are stored explicitly. In the second case, the list of values for which the relationship holds are computed according to some algorithm. Blanning[1] has proposed that programs† be regarded as relations and executions of programs be regarded as tuples. His argument is that there are major similarities between models and data, provided each is viewed properly. He points out that one executes a program by supplying its inputs and calling it. After execution, one knows the resulting set of outputs along with the original set of inputs. In an analogous way, one can retrieve a tuple from a relation by supplying values from a set of key domains and naming the relation. After retrieval, one knows the values of each item in the tuple.

Regarding a program as constituting another relation achieves uniformity between programs and data within the KS. Such uniformity is useful for a number of reasons. It simplifies the conceptual design of the DSS by reducing the number of different kinds of objects that must be handled. It permits the problem processor and user to be indifferent between information which is stored and information which is generated. Essentially, the uniformity allows a simpler logical design of the KS.

This uniformity does have a price. Some difficulties arise when a relational view of programs is taken. These arise largely because the tuples of a program do not exist and because a program has different uses from those of a relation (e.g., optimization and sensitivity analysis).

3.3. A Data Model for Decision Support

We will now go into a data model for decision support. The data model of DSS is a realization of a structure as defined above. We do this by extending the higher-level data model[7] to include programs. To make programs a part of the

---

†He uses the term "models" instead of "programs."

higher-level data model, we insert a new element which will be called a dynamic relation. The data model consists of domains, relations, relational domains, higher-level relations, links, virtual relations, dynamic relations, data dictionary, inference rules, and integrity rules. Figure 1 gives the correspondence between the formalism and the above elements of the data model. It is important to realize that the data model is an implementation oriented structure for the formalism. Looking at Fig. 1, we see that sort symbols are mapped to domains and higher-level domains; predicate symbols are mapped to relations, higher-level relations, virtual relations, and dynamic relations; and function symbols are mapped to links. The formalism provides a language for describing modeling (in the DSS sense of the word) knowledge. The wffs of the formalism contain knowledge about the state of the world and about modeling. The DSS provides a implementation of the structure for supporting the semantics of the formalism.

The role of dynamic relations in the data model is unusual due to their differences from real relations. Since their tuples do not explicitly exist, some of their behavior is reminiscent of virtual relations. For instance, a dynamic relation will not appear in an integrity rule. As in the case of virtual relations, the tuples of a dynamic relation are inferred. This is done, not by inference rule, but by execution of the code associated with the program.

Schema information about dynamic relations would be stored in three relations within the data dictionary. The old relation DICTRL would hold dynamic relation names, their levels, and the notation D (as opposed to V or R). There would also be a new binary relation DICTDI defined over dynamic relations and their input domains. Finally, there would be a second new binary relation DICTDO defined over dynamic relations and their output domains.

There are two uses for relations in the system. One use is to determine whether or not a particular tuple satisfies a predicate. For real relations, this is done by a table lookup. If the tuple is in the relation, then it satisfies the associated predicate. Dynamic relations determine truth by the method of procedural attach-

DSS FORMALISM	DSS FORMALISM	
SORTS	DOMAINS	
HIGHER LEVEL SORTS	RELATIONAL DOMAINS	
PREDICATES	RELATIONS VIRTUAL RELATIONS DYNAMIC RELATIONS	
HIGHER-LEVEL PREDICATES	HIGHER-LEVEL RELATIONS	
FUNCTIONS	LINKS	
ATOMIC FORMULAS	TUPLES	
WELL-FORMED FORMULAS	INFERENCE RULES INTEGRITY RULES	FIGURE 1. Correspondence between elements of higher-level DSS formalism and
META-LANGUAGE	DATA DICTIONARY	elements of higher-level DSS model.

ment. They use the input items of the tuple as inputs to their execution code. If the resulting output agrees with the remaining items in the tuple, then that tuple satisfies the associated predicate.

The second use of relations is retrieval of information. In the case of real relations, the retrieval is performed by reading stored data. Which stored data are read is determined by the values of the key domains. What would be a retrieval operator for a real relation will instead be an invocation of the code associated with a dynamic relation. The values of the input items determine the output produced by the code.

The overall DSS keeps track of what items may serve as keys or inputs by means of functional dependency information. Functional dependencies can be described by wffs and would be part of the knowledge about modeling stored in the DSS.

There is no notion to correspond to tuple-by-tuple modification of relations for dynamic relations. A dynamic relation is modified by means of changes in its execution code. Such a change modifies the entire relation.

A question that comes up is what set of programs make sense to execute together? In other words, what joins can be properly made upon a program set so that they combine to form a model (in the DSS sense of the word)? Roughly speaking, this can be done as long as there is an ordering among programs so that the inputs of a given program are not computationally dependent upon that program's outputs. Blanning[1] gives an algorithm for detecting when this condition is satisfied. He also gives a solution to the problem for the case when the condition is not satisfied. We feel, however, that his solution is not satisfactory.

We will explain this shortly in our discussion of some examples. The examples are intended to illustrate the use of the formalism and to show that our formalism suffices to express much of what various workers in the DSS are doing.

3.4. Knowledge Space Diagrams

We can formulate a diagrammatic representation of a knowledge space including both data and programs. This representation gives a DSS structure which can serve as a prompt to the user of the system. The prompt guides the user by showing the programs which are available and their relationships. The prompt gives a diagram of data and programs and their relationships within the knowledge space. The prompt is a tool for program synthesis; it guides the user in constructing a program from building blocks supplied by the DSS.

The approach to the diagrammatic representation is graph theoretic. The diagram that represents the KS is a directed hypergraph. A hypergraph is a generalization of usual graph, in which an edge may be an arbitrary set of nodes. In our case, the hypergraph is constructed by starting with a representation of the database portion of the KS according to the network data model. This is extended by adding a collection of new set relationships among record types. A new set is added for each program in the KS. The inputs to the program are considered to be owners of the set. (we will generally have multiple owner sets. This requires a slight generalization of the CODASYL network data model. We will also need multiple member sets.) The outputs from the program are considered to be members of the set. The sets and records that now make up the KS can be represented by arrows and boxes, in accord with the standard representation of a network database schema. Alternatively, the KS can be considered as a directed hypergraph. In this hypergraph, the boxes are nodes and the sets are directed arcs from one set of nodes to another. Whichever view is taken, this representation can serve as a guide to program data requirements, relationships among programs, and how programs may be sensibly used in the DSS.

The data requirements of any program are quite clear in such a representation. Any program must have the data corresponding to its owners. A program produces output corresponding to its members. If a system user demands an information item, he can query directly for it if it exists in the database portion of the KS. If it does not exist, he can attempt to generate it by executing a program which has the item as an output which has existing items for inputs. If no such program exists, he may attempt to construct one from the base programs using the KS representation as a guide.

A program may be built from base programs using four operators: concatenation, concurrency, branch, and iteration. The concatenation of two programs is a program which results from running the first program and then running the second. The concurrency of two programs is a program which results from running both programs so that their executions overlap in time. A branch of two programs is a program which results from running either the first program or the second but not both. An iteration of a single program is the execution of that program zero or more times, one execution after another. The KS representation provides a guide as to when each of these constructs may make sense.

Figure 2 illustrates these four ways to combine programs. (Any two programs may be combined arbitrarily. This discussion only gives the cases where something new is achieved by means of the combination.) Figure 2a shows the generation of C from A by running PROGRAM1 and then PROGRAM2 with B being an intermediate output of 1 and input of 2. Figure 2b shows two programs with no interaction. They have no inputs or outputs in common. Concurrency between two programs is generally permissible when the output of one does not become the input of the other. This can be tested in the diagrammatic hypergraph to see when programs may be executed concurrently. As shown in 2b, PROGRAM3 and PROGRAM4 may be executed concurrently. Figure 2c gives the case where two programs have identical inputs and outputs. An example where such a situation would naturally arise is when a system provides a number of alternative forecasting models. Each model would accept the same historical data as input. Each

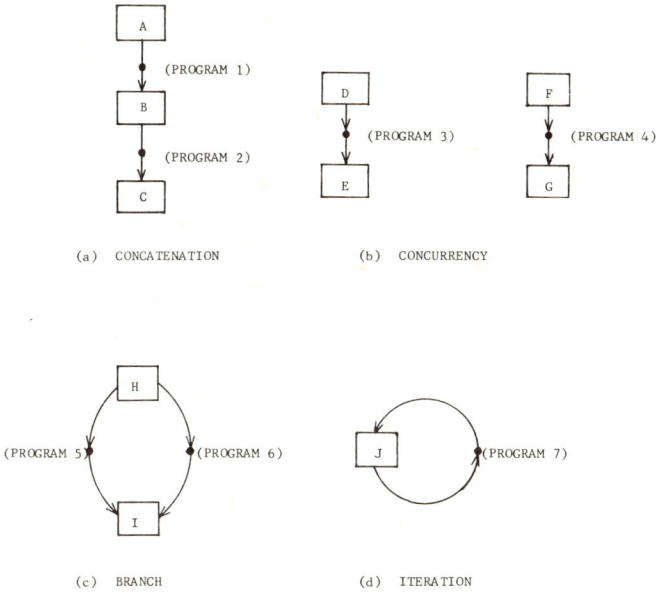

FIGURE 2. The four ways to build programs.

would provide forecasts for the same data item as output. It is left to the user to decide which forecast is the more useful. The system is only aware of the branch situation. The user's knowledge of the semantics of each program must be used to decide which branch is more useful. The system's knowledge and that information given in the diagram about the programs are restricted to input–output information. The user must choose which program to take in a branch situation. Figure 2d gives a case where iteration makes sense. Here a program has the same collection of data items as inputs and outputs. (If they are completely different, we can iterate, but the iteration produces the same result as a single execution since the program is necessarily idempotent.) Example 2, query 3 below gives a case where iteration is useful. As with branching, the control of the number of iterations is defined by semantic considerations outside of the diagram. The diagram only suggests the possibility of iteration.

3.5. Example 1

This is the first of three examples which will continue through the paper. We consider a DSS for inventory management found in Ref. 3. The data structure is shown in Fig. 3. The standard network conventions apply to this figure, with record types represented by rectangles and the items listed within the rectangle.

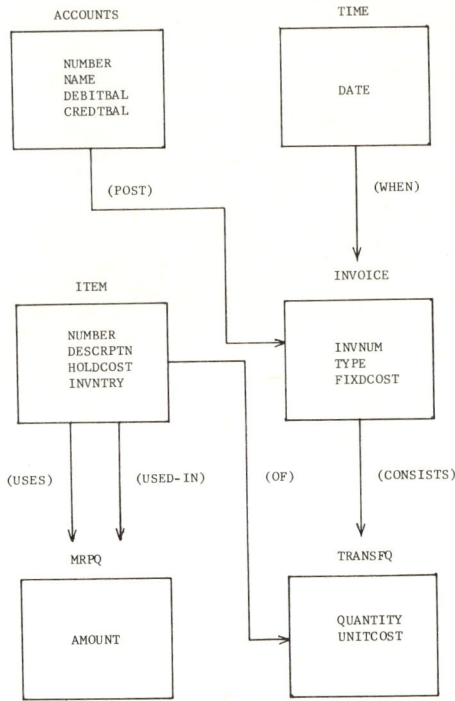

FIGURE 3. Data structure for Example 1.

The relationships are depicted as arrows pointing from the "owner" to the "member." A model that interfaces with the database is the EOQ model. EOQ model computes the optimal reorder quantity $Q*$ of item I in period P, given the holding cost C_h, ordering cost C_o, and a demand D. OC refers to the ordering cost C_o for item I at time P. DMD refers to the demand quantity D for item I at time P. And HC refers to the holding cost C_h for item I. ORDER refers to the historical record of ordering information for item I. REGRESS performs a linear regression on its input. SALES refers to the historical quantity sold and the time period array. IC retrieves the inventory holding cost and the time period for item I. And AHC is for the computation of the average holding cost C_h.

The following wffs describe the important properties of the example:

$$\phi_1 \equiv OC(C_o, I, P) \land DMD(D, I, P) \land HC(C_h, I) \land EOQ(C_o, D, C_h, Q*)$$
$$\rightarrow O(Q*, I, P)$$

$$\phi_2 \equiv ORDERS\ (I, C, T) \land REGRESS(T, C, P, C_o) \rightarrow OC(C_o, I, p)$$

$$\phi_3 \equiv SALES(I, Q, T) \land REGRESS(T, Q, P, D) \rightarrow DMD(D, I, P)$$

$$\phi_4 \equiv IC(I, H, T) \land AHC(H, T, C_h) \rightarrow HC(C_h, I)$$

A language L of the higher-level formalism useful for this example consists of the following parameters:

1. A set of sorts {INTEGER, REAL, STRING};

2. A set of predicate symbols:

ACCOUNTS: sort of (INTEGER, STRING, REAL, REAL);
TIME: sort of (INTEGER);
ITEM: sort of (INTEGER, STRING, REAL, REAL);
INVOICE: sort of (INTEGER, STRING, REAL);
MRPQ: sort of (INTEGER);
TRANSFQ: sort of (INTEGER, REAL);
EOQ: sort of (REAL, INTEGER, REAL, INTEGER);
ORDERS: sort of (INTEGER, REAL INTEGER);
REGRESS: sort of (INTEGER, REAL, INTEGER, REAL);
SALES: sort of (INTEGER, INTEGER, INTEGER);
IC: sort of (INTEGER, REAL, INTEGER);
AHC: sort of (REAL, INTEGER, REAL);
O: sort of (INTEGER, INTEGER, INTEGER);
OC: sort of (REAL, INTEGER, INTEGER);
DMD: sort of (INTEGER, INTEGER, INTEGER);
HC: sort of (REAL, INTEGER).

3. A set of function symbols:

WHEN: sort of (INTEGER, STRING, REAL; INTEGER);
CONSISTS: sort of (INTEGER, REAL; INTEGER, STRING, REAL);
POST: sort of (INTEGER, STRING, REAL; INTEGER, STRING, REAL, REAL);
USES: sort of (INTEGER; INTEGER, STRING, REAL, REAL);
USEDIN: sort of (INTEGER; INTEGER, STRING, REAL, REAL);
OF: sort of (INTEGER, REAL; INTEGER, STRING, REAL, REAL).

4. A set of constant symbols:

INTEGER-constant: $\{x \mid x$ is an integer$\}$;
REAL-constant: $\{x \mid x$ is a real number$\}$;
STRING-constant: $\{x \mid x$ is a character string$\}$.

The structure M of the data model maps to the following:
1. Domains:

$$I = \{0, 1, \ldots\}: \text{INTEGER};$$
$$R = \{x \mid x \text{ is a real number}\}: \text{REAL};$$
$$G = \{x \mid x \text{ is a character string}\}: \text{STRING}.$$

2a. Relations:

$\text{ACCOUNTS}^M \subseteq I \times G \times R \times R;$
$\text{TIME}^M \subseteq I;$
$\text{INVOICE}^M \subseteq I \times G \times R;$
$\text{MRPQ}^M \subseteq I;$
$\text{TRANSFQ}^M \subseteq I \times R.$

2b. Dynamic relations:

$\text{EOQ}^M \subseteq R \times I \times R \times I;$
$\text{ORDERS}^M \subseteq I \times R \times I;$
$\text{REGRESS}^M \subseteq I \times R \times I \times R;$
$\text{SALES}^M \subseteq I \times I \times I;$
$\text{IC}^M \subseteq I \times R \times I;$
$\text{AHC}^M \subseteq R \times I \times R.$

2c. Virtual relations:

$O^M \subseteq I \times I \times I;$
$\text{OC}^M \subseteq R \times I \times I;$
$\text{DMA}^M \subseteq I \times I \times I;$
$\text{HC}^M \subseteq R \times I.$

3. Links:

$\text{WHEN}^M\!: I \times G \times R \rightarrow I;$
$\text{CONSISTS}^M\!: I \times R \rightarrow I \times G \times R;$
$\text{POST}^M\!: I \times G \times R \rightarrow I \times G \times R \times R;$
$\text{USES}^M\!: I \rightarrow I \times G \times R \times R;$
$\text{USEDIN}^M\!: I \rightarrow I \times G \times R \times R;$
$\text{OF}^M\!: I \times R \rightarrow I \times G \times R \times R.$

4. Constants: We associate with every constant symbol of sort **REAL** or **INTEGER** the numerical value which would normally go with it. That is, numerals represent their associated number. We associate with every constant symbol of sort **STRING** the symbol itself. That is, character strings stand for themselves.

The following wffs, listed earlier, form the set of rules for the example:

1. $\text{OC}(C_o, I, P) \wedge \text{DMD}(D, I, P) \wedge \text{HC}(C_h, I) \wedge \text{EOQ}(C_o, D, C_h, Q^*) \rightarrow$
$O(Q^*, I, P)$

2. ORDERS(I, C, T) $\wedge$ REGRESS(T, C, P, C_o) $\rightarrow$ OC(C_o, I, P)
3. SALES (I, Q, T) $\wedge$ REGRESS(T, Q, P, D) $\rightarrow$ DMD(D, I, P)
4. IC(I, H, T) $\wedge$ AHC(H, T, C_h) $\rightarrow$ HC(C_h, I)

All of the above wffs are inference rules that define the extent of certain virtual relations and define the relationships among models and data. We do not have any integrity conditions listed since they are not of interest in the operation of the PPS. Also, there are no functional dependency wffs listed although they are necessary for operation of the system.

Figure 4 gives a diagrammatic representation of this knowledge space, excluding the rules. The diagram illustrates the path of information in the system from raw data to the generation of a recommended order quantity. The arcs in the diagram represent the set relationships among data or program executions. The nodes in the diagram represent intermediate data items which the system can generate.

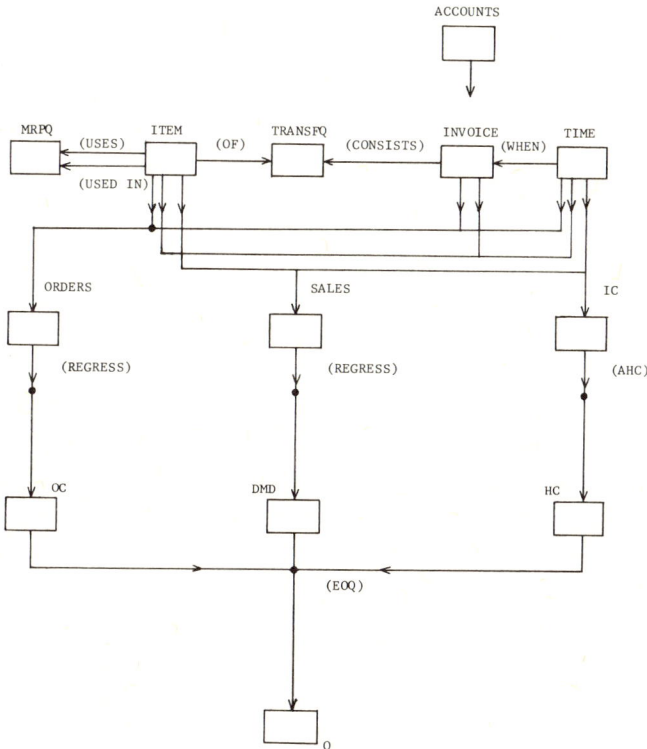

FIGURE 4. Diagram of knowledge space for Example 1.

Besides being useful for illustrative purposes, this example is intended to show that our formalism can serve to describe knowledge about modeling in accordance with the approach of a different set of investigators. This particular example was not very difficult since the source[3] was phrased in terms of mathematical logic. The next example is from a worker who does not use a mathematical logic as formalism. Our formalism is general enough to describe his system, which is reassuring.

3.6. Example 2

As a second example, we will consider an example proposed by Blanning.[1] The example includes four programs: (1) a manufacturing model that calculates manufacturing expense (e) as a function of sales volume (v) and raw material price (r); (2) a pricing model that calculates sale price (p) as a function of v and e; (3) a marketing model that calculates v as a function of p and advertising expense (a); and (4) a financial model that calculates net income (n) as a function of a, e, p, and v. The four models form the basis for four programs represented as follows:

MFG(v, r, e);
PRI(v, e, p);
MKT(p, a, v);
FIN(a, e, p, v, n).

To add interest to the example, we will assume that there are two relations that hold historical data about v and r. These two relations are represented as follows:

SALES(time, v);
MATERIALS(time, r).

We will also assume the existence of another program, RG, which does a time series regression of historical data and makes a prediction. The input to RG is a relation containing historical data and a time. Its output is a single prediction. With a relational domain h consisting of the relations SALES and MATERIALS and a new domain $v \cup r$ being the union of the domains v and r, the program RG is represented as follows.

RG(h, time, $v \cup r$)

We shall now express this example in terms of the extended higher-level formalism. In terms of the formalism, this comes to nine sorts: v, r, e, p, a, n, time, $v \cup r$, and h. The dynamic predicates are RG, MFG, PRI, MKT, FIN, SALES, and MATERIALS. Their types are as given above. There are no function symbols. The set of constant symbols that go with each of the sorts v, r, $v \cup r$, e, p, a, n, and time is the set of all integers. The set of constant symbols that does with the sort h is given by {SALES, MATERIALS}. The level of all elements of the above language is one with the exception of h and RG, which are second-level.

The above constitutes the set of parameters which define the particular higher-level formal language in use. These parameters can be combined with variable symbols and the logical connectors (,), $\sim$, $\wedge$, $\rightarrow$, $\forall$, and $\exists$ to form well-formed formulas to express various queries and facts. We will adopt the convention that a variable symbol for a sort will be an uppercase character identical to the name of the sort; e.g., V is a variable for the sort v.

A set of wffs to express the functional dependencies (and hence, the input and output variables) of the relations in this example is the following. The first wff says that, for the predicate MFG, the sorts v and r functionally determine the sort e. The meanings of the other wffs are similar.

$$MFG(V, R, E) \wedge MFG(V, R, E') \rightarrow E = E'$$
$$PRI(V, E, P) \wedge PRI(V, E, P') \rightarrow P = P'$$
$$MKT(P, A, V) \wedge MKT(P, A, V') \rightarrow V = V'$$
$$FIN(A, E, P, V, N) \wedge FIN(A, E, P, V, N') \rightarrow N = N'$$
$$SALES(TIME, V) \wedge SALES(TIME, V') \rightarrow V = V'$$
$$MATERIALS(TIME, R) \wedge MATERIALS(TIME, R') \rightarrow R = R'$$
$$RG(H, TIME, VUR) \wedge RG(H, TIME, VUR') \rightarrow VUR = VUR'$$

The conversion of the formalism to the data model is straightforward. Sorts become domains. Predicates become relations or dynamic relations. The difference between the formalism and the data model is that the formalism is a syntactic language while the data model is (presumably) implemented on a computer.

Figure 5 diagrams the knowledge space for this example. The knowledge space shows that there are several useful concatenations of programs. For example, sale price (P) may be calculated from sales volume (V) and raw material price (R) by executing MFG and then PRI. There is also an opportunity for parallelism. For instance, V and R may be calculated concurrently by regression (RG—two independent executions of the same code) from SALES and MATERIALS. Finally, iteration makes sense in this example since MFG, PRI, and MKT form a cycle.

3.7. Example 3

This example is intended to illustrate many of the unique capabilities of the higher-level formalism as an expressive tool. It also shows the desirability of the

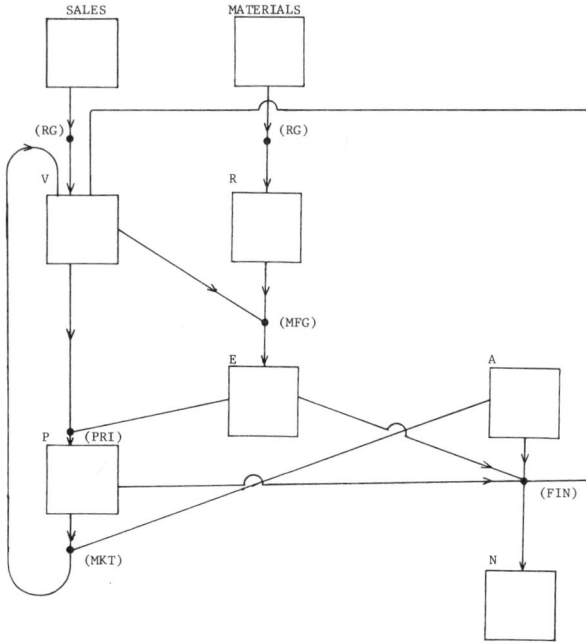

FIGURE 5. Diagram of knowledge space for Example 2.

higher level data model as a semantic model of data. We consider a matrix generator system, i.e., a DSS to support linear programming. In the interest of brevity, this DSS will only be outlined. Figure 6 will illustrate this example.

At the highest level (other than system dictionaries) of the system, there is a sort which we will call LP. This sort will consist of a collection of predefined linear programming models (in the DSS sense). Any constraints in the system which deal with all linear programming models will be quantified over the sort LP. All LP models will be represented in the system by third-level 4-ary predicates. For example, we might have LPTYPICAL over the sorts A, B, C, and X where A is a second-level sort over second-level predicates representing matrices of coefficients, B is a first-level sort over first-level predicates representing vectors of right-hand side elements, C is a first-level sort over first-level predicates representing vectors of cost coefficients, and X is a first-level sort over first-level predicates representing vectors of solutions to the problem MINIMIZE $C'X$ SUBJECT TO $AX \geq B$. It is obvious that one constraint upon the LP relations which implement these predicates is that the number of members in the relations must be compatible. Also, it is assumed that the predicates in the sort LP will be implemented by an LP processor which can handle relations as means of input and output.

The relations that serve as inputs and outputs for **LPTYPICAL** could be structured in the following way. A relation *a* in the domain *A* would be a unitary relation over a domain of **ROWNAMES** (which would be second level). A relation, call it *r*, in the domain **ROWNAMES** would be a first-level binary relation over **COLNAMES** and **VALUES** (each a first-level domain). *B*, *C*, and *X* would have structures similar to *r*. Each would be a binary relation over item names and item values. Each would be at the first level.

The levels in this example serve as a means of structuring information. At the first level, the system contains numerical data which can serve as inputs or store outputs for a linear programming solution routine. At the second level, the system stores matrices as sets of rows. At the third level, the system can associate various first-level data with various predefined models. The third level also permits the user to consider various classes of linear programming models. Further, the third level permits the system to group all linear program models as a class for unified handling. An example of this capability of the third level is given below. Although this example does not go further, it would be possible for a fourth level to contain general information about classes of models including linear programming as well as other optimization models. Beyond that, a fifth level could contain general information about both statistical models and optimization models.

To illustrate, suppose the sort LP has two members, **LPFIRM** and **LPE-CONOMY**. Presumably, these members stand for two classes of linear program models, one dealing with a firm and another dealing with an economy. Now, we may imagine that **LPECONOMY** is a 4-ary relation over the domains **TECH-**

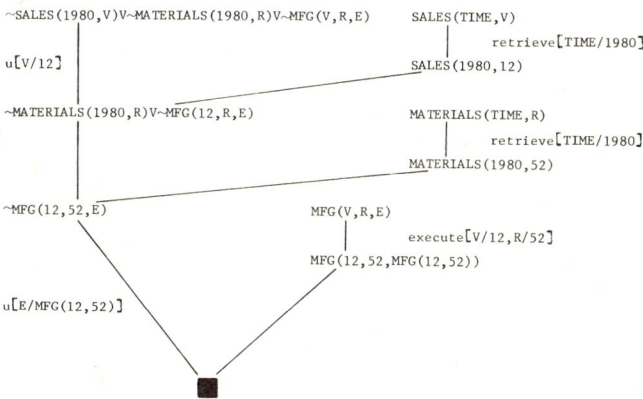

FIGURE 6. A relation from Example 3.

NOLOGY, CONSUMPTION, PRICES, and PRODUCTION. (This may be assumed to be a standard Leontief input–output model.) Each domain has three members: TECHNOLOGY = {TECH1980, TECH1981, TECH1982}, CONSUMPTION = {CONS1980, CONS1981, CONS1982}, PRICES = {PRI1980, PRI1981, PRI1982}, and PRODUCTION = {PROD1980, PROD1981, PROD1982}. This is illustrated in Fig. 6. Thus, we have a predefined class of economic models, one for each year. The user could also "mix and match" in order to see what one year's prices combined with another year's technology and consumption requirements would result in the way of industrial activity according to the model. A similar class of models can be predefined for LPFIRM. A decision to run a new model would require a redefinition of a second-level domain. This required effort might discourage the user from casually defining nonsense models. The use of sorts results in a discipline upon the user in terms of what inputs may be given to the solver.

So, this example has a formalism with three levels of sorts and predicates. The third-level predicates are all implemented as dynamic relations with the semantics provided by (probably) some version of the simplex algorithm. The first and second level predicates are implemented by relations in the database portion of the knowledge system.

4. The PPS

The PPS may be any theorem prover. We will consider resolution for now but will discuss other possibilities later in this section. Resolution is the driver of the PPS. Resolution is the sound and complete mechanical thorem prover explained by Chang and Lee.[4] It may be applied to the higher-level formalism after expressions in the higher-level formalism have been converted to fopc (which is trivial).

The use of resolution in the PPS goes as follows. The user presents the LS with a query. This query is translated by the LS into a wff in the higher-level formalism. The first step of the resolution procedure is to negate the wff and convert it to fopc clause form. The negated query in clause form is then processed by the resolution procedure in an attempt to find a contradiction between it and the set of acts in the KS. From such a contradiction, we infer that the query is a theorem of the KS and that we may respond either yes or with the instance which satisfied the theorem. The procedure of finding the contradiction is the procedure of finding a resolution proof.

The two components of resolution are unification and cancelation. Unification is of greatest interest since it involves retrieval of information from the KS. Unification involves matching of terms between two clauses being considered for cancellation. Unification substitutes terms for variables within a clause. Since at least one of the clauses must come from the KS (the only other possibility is that it comes from the query), unification involves trying to find a match with the KS. A unification with a predicate constitutes a retrieval operation or a program execution. The two appear identical to the unification algorithm.

Unification will retrieve data or invoke programs. The process of finding a match involves a search for a particular tuple in the KS. If the tuple come from a relation, this search involves a retrieval operation, typically of the SELECT variety. Should the tuple come from a dynamic relation, the search involves either executing the program to see if it can produce some given inputs and outputs (this would be a form of procedural attachment) or else executing a program with given inputs to see what the output turns out to be.

4.1. Example 1 (Continued)

Returning to the inventory management example, let us see how the system can process a query such as "Recommend the EOQ order quantity for item i' and period p'." (In this example, variables are upper case and actual quantities are lower case with a prime.) This query, when translated by the LS into the formalism, becomes $\exists Q^* O(Q^*, i', p')$. The rules for the system, translated into clause for resolution are

(1) $\sim OC(C_o, I, P)$ or $\sim DMD(D, I, P)$ or $\sim HC(C_h, I)$ or $\sim EOQ(C_o, D, C_h, Q^*)$ or $O(Q^*, I, P)$

(2) $\sim ORDERS(I, C, T)$ or $\sim REGRESS(T, C, P, C_o)$ or $OC(C_o, I, P)$

(3) $\sim SALES(I, Q, T)$ or $\sim REGRESS(T, Q, P, D)$ or $DMD(D, I, P)$

(4) $\sim IC(I, H, T)$ or $\sim AHC(H, T, C_h)$ or $HC(C_h, I)$

The resolution graph of this query against these four rules, the relations, and the dynamic relations is given in Fig. 7. In Fig. 7, the finding of specific values for variables in the KS is represented by execute when a program is run and by retrieve when a retrieval is performed. The theorem prover is indifferent whether an item is retrieved or calculated. Unification of a term t for a variable v in a clause is represented in the figure by $u[v/t]$. Cancellation is represented by two lines coming from the originating clauses which are cancelled with each other going to the resulting clause.

There are three blocks of processing in the graph of Fig. 7 which are marked by left brackets (]) on the right margin. It turns out that these three blocks may be interchanged with one another. They may be executed in any order with no change to the final result. Hence, these three blocks may be executed concurrently on separate processors.

4.2. Example 2 (Continued)

Let us now turn to several examples of user queries and consider how these would be handled by a PPS based upon resolution. All these sample queries will

```
HIGHER LEVEL DOMAINS:
   LP = [LPECONOMY, LPFIRM]
   TECHNOLOGY = [TECH1980, TECH1981, TECH1982]
   CONSUMPTION = [CONS1980, CONS1981, CONS1982]
   PRICES = [PR11980, PR11981, PR11982]
   PRODUCTION = [PROD1980, PROD1981, PROD1982]
   TECH1980
   TECH1981
   TECH1982

DYNAMIC RELATION:

LPECONOMY
```

TECHNOLOGY	CONSUMPTION	PRICES	PRODUCTION
TECH1980	CONS1980	PR11980	PROD1980
TECH1981	CONS1981	PR11981	PROD1981
TECH1982	CONS1982	PR11982	PROD1982

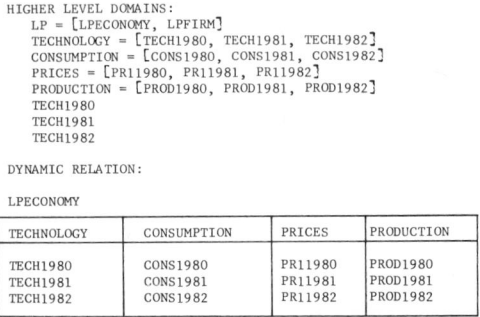

FIGURE 7. Resolution graph for query in Example 1.

refer to the example higher-level database whose schema was defined in the last section.

Query 1. Suppose the user asks, "What was the sales volume for year = 1980?" This would be represented by the wff $\exists v$ SALES (1980, v). Resolution would be in one step. The negation of the query put into clause form is $\sim$ SALES(1980, v). Cancellation wants to find a wff of the form SALES(1980, x) to cancel against the negated query. Unification would be able to find such a wff in the KS with some actual value substituted for x, by means of ordinary database retrieval. This value would be passed back to the user as an answer. Had no tuple been stored for SALES in 1980, the proof would have failed and no answer would have been available.

Query 2. The second sample query is not as simple as the first. Suppose the user asks, "What is the manufacturing expense for year = 1980?" Although similar in construction to the first, this query requires a lot more work on the PPS. This query is translated by the LS to $\exists E$ SALES(1980, V) $\wedge$ MATERIALS(1980, R) $\wedge$ MFG(V, R, E). In negated clause form, this query becomes

$\sim$SALES(1980, V) or $\sim$MATERIALS(1980, R) or $\sim$MFG(V, R, E)

The attempt to find a contradiction between this wff and the information in the KS is illustrated in Fig. 8. In Fig. 8, unification by substituting the term t for variable v is represented by $u[v/t]$. Cancellation is represented in Fig. 8 by two lines going from the initial clauses to the resulting clause.

Initially, the theorem prover cancels SALES. This is done by retrieving a tuple from the SALES relation for which time = 1980 (this is essentially a unification). Unifying v with 12 (the assumed 1980 sales volume) gives a match so that cancellation of SALES may take place. Cancellation of MATERIALS occurs in exactly the same way. Finally, the cancellation with MFG occurs. This time, the unification of MFG results in a program execution instead of database retrieval.

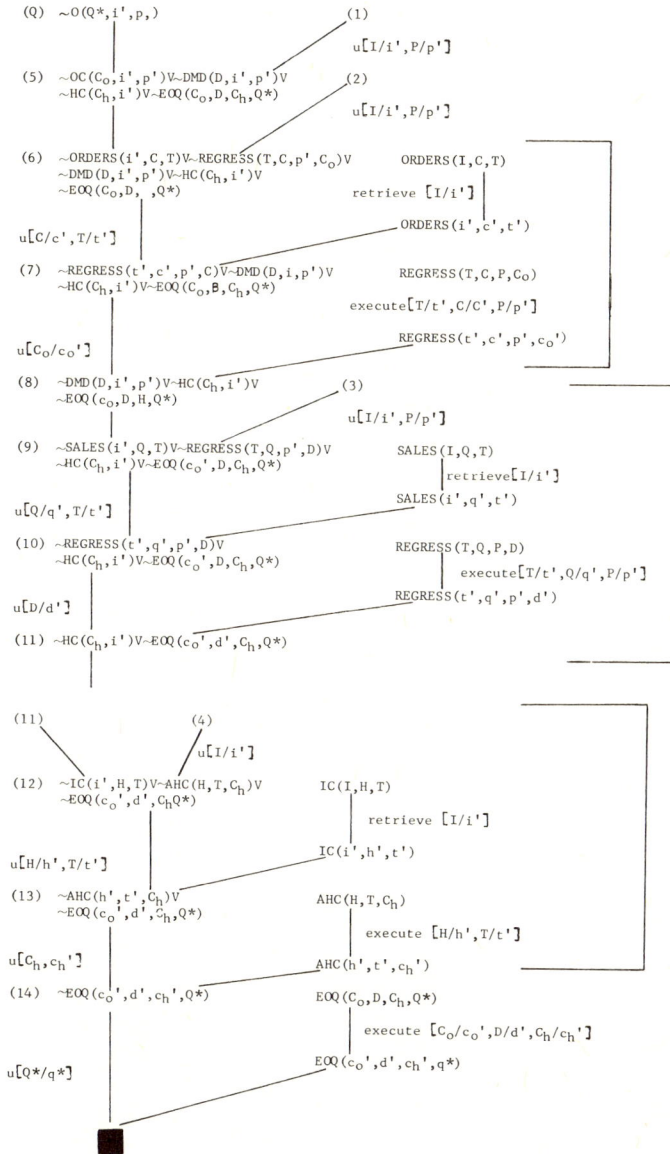

(Q) $\sim O(Q*,i',p,)$ (1)

$u[I/i',P/p']$

(5) $\sim OC(C_o,i',p')V\sim DMD(D,i',p')V$ (2)
$\sim HC(C_h,i')V\sim EOQ(C_o,D,C_h,Q*)$

$u[I/i',P/p']$

(6) $\sim ORDERS(i',C,T)V\sim REGRESS(T,C,p',C_o)V$ $ORDERS(I,C,T)$
$\sim DMD(D,i',p')V\sim HC(C_h,i')V$
$\sim EOQ(C_o,D,\ ,Q*)$ retrieve $[I/i']$

     $ORDERS(i',c',t')$

$u[C/c',T/t']$

(7) $\sim REGRESS(t',c',p',C)\overline{V}\sim DMD(D,i,p')V$ $REGRESS(T,C,P,C_o)$
$\sim HC(C_h,i')V\sim EOQ(C_o,B,C_h,Q*)$

   execute$[T/t',C/C',P/p']$

$u[C_o/c_o']$ $REGRESS(t',c',p',c_o')$

(8) $\sim DMD(D,i',p')V\sim HC(C_h,i')V$ (3)
$\sim EOQ(c_o,D,H,Q*)$

$u[I/i',P/p']$

(9) $\sim SALES(i',Q,T)V\sim REGRESS(T,Q,p',D)V$ $SALES(I,Q,T)$
$\sim HC(C_h,i')V\sim EOQ(c_o',D,C_h,Q*)$

   retrieve$[I/i']$

$u[Q/q',T/t']$ $SALES(i',q',t')$

(10) $\sim REGRESS(t',q',p',D)V$ $REGRESS(T,Q,P,D)$
$\sim HC(C_h,i')V\sim EOQ(c_o',D,C_h,Q*)$

   execute$[T/t',Q/q',P/p']$

$u[D/d']$ $REGRESS(t',q',p',d')$

(11) $\sim HC(C_h,i')V\sim EOQ(c_o',d',C_h,Q*)$

(11)   (4)

$u[I/i']$

(12) $\sim IC(i',H,T)V\sim AHC(H,T,C_h)V$ $IC(I,H,T)$
$\sim EOQ(c_o',d',C_hQ*)$

   retrieve $[I/i']$

$u[H/h',T/t']$ $IC(i',h',t')$

(13) $\sim AHC(h',t',C_h)V$ $AHC(H,T,C_h)$
$\sim EOQ(c_o',d',C_h,Q*)$

   execute $[H/h',T/t']$

$u[C_h,c_h']$ $AHC(h',t',c_h')$

(14) $\sim EOQ(c_o',d',c_h',Q*)$ $EOQ(C_o,D,C_h,Q*)$

   execute $[C_o/c_o',D/d',C_h/c_h']$

$u[Q*/q*]$ $EOQ(c_o',d',c_h',q*)$

■

ANSWER: $Q* = q*$

FIGURE 8. Resolution graph for Example 2, Query 2.

Note that if the user had asked for manufacturing expense in 1984, a use of the RG program would have been necessary in order to fill in a value of v and r in SALES and MATERIALS (since future values would not be stored in relations of historical material).

Query 3. This last query brings up some issues considered by Blanning. Suppose the user asks "What will be the net income if the raw material price is 67 and the advertising expense is 100?" Suppose this query is translated by the LS to $\exists N$ MFG(V, 67, E) $\wedge$ PRI(V, E, P) $\wedge$ MKT(P, 100, V) $\wedge$ FIN(100, E, P, V, N). This wff is a conjunction of atomic formulas. No predicates are involved, so the answering of the query will not involve any retrieval of data from relations. What would seem appropriate is to run the programs in turn in such a way that the output of one becomes the input of another. This is not possible. There is no ordering for which the variable V can be generated from existing information. Nor is it a matter of missing data or a misspecified query. The same symbol V would appear as both input and output of the program formed by composition of the three programs MFG, PRI, and MKT. This means that V is a fixed point. In fact, a fixed point is the only value for V which can satisfy the query as stated. Figure 4 leads one to suppose the possibility of this iteration due to the presence of a cycle. Conceptually, it is possible to compute fixed points for most programs (since many functions will have fixed points). It is, however, algorithmically difficult and is currently an active area of research by numerical analysts. Blanning suggests a very simple iterative procedure to find a fixed point. Such iteration is beyond the scope of the system we have proposed. However, it is captured by the diagrammatic representation pointing out the possibility of iteration by the presence of a cycle. It is beyond the capability of our resolution-based PPS to cause the unifier to successfully stumble upon the fixed point. Some initial investigation into the use of dynamic logic looks promising and we hope to soon have a formalism which will express the use of iteration in a DSS.

4.3. Example 3 (Continued)

The PPS for the linear programming DSS would be a very simple one. It would need to be able to process queries from the LS. It would need to be able to commence the execution of the simplex algorithm. There would not be a need for a true inference mechanism, since the system has no inference rules embedded in it. There would not be a need for building complex programs since there is only one base program and all its inputs and outputs are predefined.

4.4. Other Deductive Mechanisms

Thus far, the only PPS considered was based upon the resolution principle. Resolution has several advantages. It is sound; i.e., it only deduces that which is true. It is complete; i.e., it does not deduce that which is false. It is machine oriented. It is rigorous.

These advantages are disadvantages in many contexts. Soundness results in a theorem prover that is overly cautious. A sound theorem prover will fail to deduce a theorem unless the facts require it to be true. Yet a decision maker occasionally (perhaps often) finds it necessary to reach a conclusion based upon insufficient evidence. Consequently, an unsound theorem prover may be more useful than resolution if the PPS is trying to model or enhance actual decision making. An overly cautious theorem prover may not be useful.

Completeness results in an inefficient theorem prover. Resolution can deduce anything implied by a set of axioms. This requires the consideration of all possibilities. This results in comparing axioms which, for a given problem, are irrelevant. We may be willing to lose the capability of deducing all theorems in order to achieve a more efficient search. An incomplete theorem prover may reduce the combinatorial problems which have prevented the resolution principle from achieving any significant new proofs.

The precision and rigor of mathematical logic may also be a problem. Logic assumes a binary world of truth and falsehood. Reality is often difficult to describe in these terms. A decision maker may find gradations more useful. Some systems that have been proposed to accommodate various levels of truth include Shortliffe's model of inexact reasoning in medicine[10] and Zadeh's fuzzy reasoning.[11]

A class of logics of particular interest in the area of decision support are the nonmonotonic logics. A nonmonotonic logic has the property that the introduction of new axioms can invalidate old theorems. This is useful because it is often important, in a DSS, to infer information which is not, strictly speaking, deducible from what is known. The deduced information may turn out to be untrue in the light of knowledge obtained later. Default reasoning is an area where nonmonotonic logic is useful. An example of defaut reasoning is the following: By default, we assume that if something is a bird, then it can fly. If we are told that Tweety is a bird, then we deduce that Tweety can fly. When told that Tweety is an ostrich, we are forced to revise our conclusions. Although there are several proposed formal reasoning systems that have nonmonotonic properties, we are particularly impressed with Reiter's[9] approach. It is machine oriented and provides for reasoning by default. We intend to pursue the implications of a PPS based upon nonmonotonic theorem provers in a later paper.

5. Summary

This chapter has defined a higher-level formalism for decision support. Accompanying the formalism is a semantic structure and a theorem prover. These three components combined with a user interface form a decision support system.

As defined, a DSS is a very general abstraction. Information about the state of the world and about modeling is contained in the formalism. The approach to implementation is defined by the structure which goes with the formalism. The formalism turns out to have a sound and complete theorem prover in the form of the resolution principle. A proof may be found in another work.[7]

At this time, the formalism cannot describe iteration of programs. We hope to remedy this in future work by using dynamic logic as a formalism to model programs. We also have not considered any theorem provers other than resolution. We hope to consider nonmonotonic logic as well as fuzzy logic in future papers.

References

1. R. W. BLANNING, A relational framework for model management in decision support systems, *DSS-82 Transactions,* Gary W. Dickinson (ed.), 16–28 (1982).
2. R. H. BONCZEK, C. W. HOLSAPPLE, and A. B. WHINSTON *Foundations of Decision Support Systems,* Academic Press, New York, 1981.
3. R. H. BONCZEK, C. W. HOLSAPPLE, and A. B. WHINSTON, Specification of modeling knowledge in decision support systems, working paper, Krannert Graduate School of Management, Purdue University, West Lafayette, Indiana, January, 1982.
4. C. L. CHANG, and R. C. T. LEE, *Symbolic Logic and Mechanical Theorem Proving,* Academic Press, New York, 1972.
5. E. F. CODD, A relational model of data for large shared data banks, *Commun. ACM* **13**(6), 377–387 (June 1970).
6. H. B. ENDERTON, *A Mathematical Introduction to Logic,* Academic Press, New York, 1972.
7. S. S. PAN, R. A. PICK, and A. B. WHINSTON, A higher level data model, working paper, Krannert Graduate School of Management, Purdue University, West Lafayette, Indiana, June, 1982.
8. S. S. PAN, R. A. PICK, and A. B. WHINSTON, Behavioral semantics of the higher level data model, working paper, Krannert Graduate School of Management, Purdue University, West Lafayette, Indiana, July, 1982.
9. R. REITER, A logic for default reasoning, *Artificial Intelligence* **13**, 81–132 (1980).
10. E. H. SHORTLIFFE, *Computer-Based Medical Consultations: MYCIN,* American Elsevier, New York, 1976.
11. L. A. ZADEH, Fuzzy sets as a basis for a theory of possibility, *Fuzzy Sets Syst.* **1**, 3–28 (1978).

7

DECISION SUPPORT IN ENTERPRISE ANALYSIS

BENN R. KONSYNSKI AND JAY F. NUNAMAKER

1. DSS and Enterprise Analysis

This chapter discusses the application of decision support systems principles to an ill-structured problem—the planning of organizational information systems. It is difficult to separate the high-level information strategic planning process from the detailed determination of requirements specifications necessary for design and implementation of information systems. Both offer dilemmas in the determination of conduct and establishment of process objectives. As these are important steps in the information systems development process, it would be useful to offer computer-aided support wherever necessary in support of these activities.

Several problems face the enterprise analyst:

- It is difficult to elicit requirements from users who (1) do not perceive their requirements, (2) feel that they are not now able to determine those requirements, and (3) have no means of communicating requirements in a meaningful way.
- The volume and complexity of the requirements offers a significant roadblock to the analyst.
- The volatility, inconsistency, and incompleteness of the requirements offer special problems in identification and resolution.
- The cost of organization resources required to facilitate the analysis in terms of user, manager, and analyst time is prohibitive.
- Generally accepted enterprise analysis methodologies and techniques are lacking.

These problems, along with others, face the analyst in determining how to proceed and deciding what resources to apply to conducting the enterprise analysis. We

BENN R. KONSYNSKI and JAY. F. NUNAMAKER • Department of Management Information Systems, University of Arizona, Tucson, Arizona 85721.

shall now discuss the development of a decision support system (DSS) for enterprise analysis. The system draws together a collection of models and techniques under a central control facility that manages the dialogue, models, and data necessary in the analysis process.

Several requirements of a DSS in support of the enterprise analysis process have emerged:

- The system should offer a planning and requirements determination "environment" that allows participation by management, users, and analysts.
- Many models and techniques are available and applicable under differing circumstances.
- The "procedure" is not well defined and analysts must have the capability, with the systems assistance, to select appropriate models and techniques as applicable.
- The system serves as a memory of the process as well as the plans and requirements, thus assumptions, decisions, and procedures are documented as well as the results. These activities are then subject to review and evaluation, as are the resulting plans and requirements.
- The system must serve as a dynamic documentation of the processes and results, offering insight for future efforts.

The behavioral problems, data and model management problems, and analysis and design problems in enterprise analysis must be addressed in a support system. The ill-structured characteristics of the problem are not unlike those of the classical DSS problems—capital budgeting, portfolio analysis, and planning. The dilemmas created by having to balance problem and goal identification, solution procedure determination, and sensitivity determination also exist in enterprise analysis situations.

2. Alternatives in Enterprise Analysis

Several approaches may be taken to eliciting the information necessary in the formulation of system requirements from its ultimate source, the user, who often has difficulty providing it. Among the approaches are several classes:

1. Direct elicitation—Solicitation of requirements directly from the user community. Problems in completeness, consistency, requirements perception and communication, and analysis of impact frequently occur.
2. Recapture from existing systems—The extraction of requirements from documentation and source representations of existing systems. Problems

of the currency and integrity of the existing systems and propagation of control failures, as well as neglect of future demands arise.

3. Iterative development—Prototyping as a means of surfacing requirements ments offers convergence opportunity. Tool availability auditability, and integration of subsystems create significant problems in application of this approach.

4. Strategic planning in requirements determination—Most methodologies currently available attempt to derive requirements from analysis of current systems, assessment of future information needs through strategic planning, and synthesis of information requirements.

As mentioned above, most current methodologies are based on analysis of current and future information requirements consistent with a management view of future information needs.

Some of these techniques attempt to analyze information needs from a top-down analysis of the organizational environment, independent of the current applications. An example of this is the normative approach called business information analysis and integration technique (BIAIT). In this approach, seven questions are asked about the conduct of business, the handling of an order. Based on the answers to these questions, the organization is classified according to perceived generic requirements.

Another approach, critical success factors, is a method of determining important decision factors in the conduct of business. Through this process, a small number of factors usually surface, but little capacity for determining follow-up requirements.

The analysis of business processes has been a popular approach to the determination of requirements and has significantly influenced the development of the PLEXSYS methods. Examples include the approach advocated by the ISDOS project (with the authors' past participation) and its use of PSL/PSA and the business systems planning (BSP) methodology developed and promoted by IBM. These two approaches, more than the others, have influenced the development of the methods incorporated in the PLEXSYS system.

Below we briefly discuss the general characteristics of the first two phases of the PLEXSYS approach, the determination of strategic information requirements, and the determination of logical system requirements. It should be noted that while the ISDOS and BSP methodologies significantly influenced the determination of models and analysis techniques, no procedural biases are transfered to the system until the logical analysis reporting begins at the end of the second phase. The authors support the application of DSS principles in the early stages of enterprise analysis because no single structured approach appears to be complete or applicable in all situations and environments.

3. Overview of PLEXSYS

PLEXSYS methodology and system was designed and constructed to provide computer-aided assistance in the system development process, facilitating front end problem definition and strategic planning phases as well as actual production of executable code for a target system.

Some of the tasks included in this process are creation of a business system plan, structure of the problem definition, specification of a set of requirements, analysis of requirements, logical and physical design, specification of file structuring, construction of the target system in a common language form (e.g., PASCAL or COBOL), and review by the user for requirements modification.

PLEXSYS extends the work of the ISDOS (PSL/PSA) project, directed by Professor Daniel Teichroew at the University of Michigan. PLEXSYS includes all of the features of PSL/PSA with several added dimensions. In one direction, it addresses the front end problem structuring required prior to the use of PSL/PSA, in this phase, PLEXSYS deals with the development of the business systems plan. The second major distinction is the consideration given to problems dealing with detailed logical and physical design, leading to automatic code generation.

The following discussion focuses on the prototype that has been developed to demonstrate the feasibility of the approach. The number of langauges and processors involved may at first appear cumbersome. It should be understood that in the integrated PLEXSYS life-cycle support system under development, the various features of languages and processors meld into a single "dynamic" language and analyzer.

Efforts have been made to develop facilities which permit nonprogrammers to define problems for computer solution through direct interaction with a computer. Despite these developments, defining, analyzing, designing, and construction of information systems are primarily manual, ad hoc operations; there has been very limited application of analysis and design techniques as computer aids in the construction of software systems.

PLEXSYS consists of four interconnected parts or subsystems, structured to aid the participants in the system development process. An overview of PLEXSYS is presented graphically in Fig. 1. The four phases of PLEXSYS overlap, as no clear phase boundaries are identifiable. As mentioned earlier, the intent is to support the continuum that is the system development process.

The four "phases" and the supportable activities are as follows:

1. System problem structuring
   Strategic planning
   High-level feasibility studies
   Problem definition

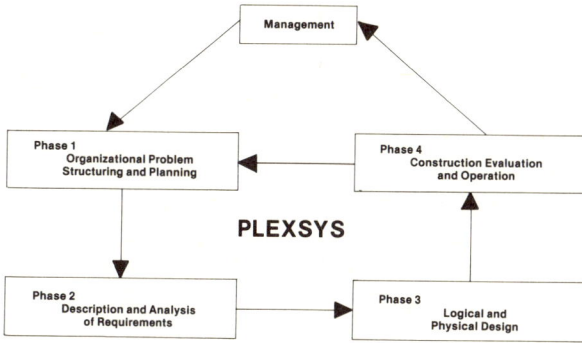

FIGURE 1. PLEXSYS system development system.

Determination of system boundaries
Coordination with organizational planning
2. Description and analysis of requirements
Specification of requirements
Capture of requirements
Documentation of requirements
Logical consistency and completeness analysis
3. Logical and physical design
Logical structure of data and databases
Logical structure of processes, modules, and programs
Physical structuring of processes
Configuration of hardware and software
Performance estimation
Optimization of system interconnection
4. Construction and evaluation
Code generation
Initialization of databases

4. Phase 1: Problem Structuring and Planning

Phase 1, problem structuring, is concerned with problem definition and business systems planning at a conceptual level. The essence of system structuring is to address the aspects of problem boundary identification and to deal with the strategic planning process. (See Fig. 2.)

In system structuring, one must continually ask: Is this really the problem we should be addressing? Am I unnecessarily constraining the problem definition

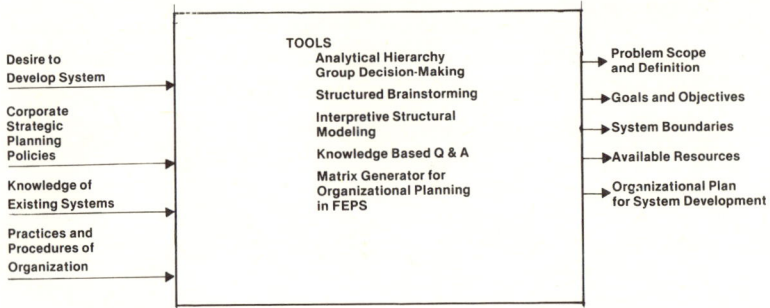

FIGURE 2. Phase 1: Organizational problem structuring and planning.

based on the group's experience? We should avoid constraining the problem at too early a point in the system development process. This front end phase involves the definition of objectives and goals of the organization or subunit. The resources of the organization that can be utilized in the system development process must be included in the organizational plan.

The primary function of Phase 1 is to produce the system plan for the organization. In order to generate the system plan for the organization, the analyst must get everyone concerned with the system involved in the process of defining the system's objectives, goals, and so on. Everyone talks about how to do this; however, very few organizations have been provided with tools to assist with the structuring of the problem. Phase 1 is a collection of cognitive aids to assist in this process. In addition, the analyst must determine characteristics of the user, so we can match system characteristics to the style of the user. The analyst must develop a user profile(s) and classify user types, taking into consideration the experience and education of the user in order to facilitate proper customization on the information system to "profile" the level of sophistication of the intended users.

The objective of Phase 1 is to determine the goals and objectives of the system. To accomplish this, considerable information on the resources available for system development must be obtained. The analyst must develop an accurate "picture" of the type of system desired or necessary. The analyst must document interfaces with all other systems in the organization. The interfacing process is extremely critical to planning an integrated corporate data base. Frequently, insufficient time and energy are devoted to understanding and recognizing the constraints and restrictions that may be involved.

Most corporate systems today have hundreds and hundreds of subsystems that must be interfaced. PLEXSYS is a tool for organizing the information needed to develop an overall strategic plan. The interfaces, goals, and objectives must be considered from the beginning—at Phase 2 or Phase 3 it will be too late. Designs will already be constrained and it will be difficult to accommodate the design desired by the users. This means the designer needs to know things like availability of data, whether it will be machine readable or whether it must be transcribed repeatedly. The scheduling requirements, inputs, outputs, and processes must be known, at the front end conceptual level, because the analyst needs to understand the constraints, not discover them in the detailed statement of requirements. Certain constraints imbedded in the system and cannot be changed. Therefore, it is important to establish system boundaries early on and determine whether the boundaries are fixed or flexible.

The analyst must test the boundaries and evaluate this definition against the statement of goals, objectives, and constraints. A checklist of items that must be considered is generated by PLEXSYS through a system for keeping track of information that may appear to be unrelated and/or extraneous at the start of a project. PLEXSYS Phase 1 provides the software for organizing information needed to develop the strategic plan. The PLEXSYS software triggers questions and provides reminder lists so the user or analyst or manager will not overlook important relationships. Even very experienced people forget when they go through the same procedures frequently; they often overlook considerations that are quite important. The surgeon sometimes leaves a sponge in a patient's stomach, although everyone knows that you should not leave sponges in stomachs. PLEXSYS Phase 1 "keeps track of sponges." As each routine is completed, completion is indicated on the terminal until the system can respond affirmatively to the question, "Have you removed all sponges?"

The checklist feature can trigger continuous evaluation of goals, objectives, and system boundaries. By going through a standard set of questions, we are often surprised by responses that we did not anticipate. Often we find we can relax one constraint or another. We find that the system constraints or boundaries are not as fixed as we assumed. This is very important, for with this new information, the system takes on different characteristics. We must spend considerable time on the front end problem, because situations and systems are often very different than they appear to be at first glance. Different perspectives must be presented and different views evaluated. PLEXSYS has the capability of presenting information from alternative perspectives and viewpoints. The PLEXSYS routines are designed to effectively assist the user in challenging system boundaries and constraints. This is, in effect, a way to restructure the problem. This may involve a reformulation of the problem in a different context so that issues may be reviewed. If users can obtain alternative views of a situation, they can better consider different perspectives.

PLEXSYS Phase 1 provides, in addition to the checklist systems, the question generation system and the tests for systems boundaries. In addition, it provides support for an activity called structured brainstorming system (SBS).

SBS is a methodology for capturing the information emerging from a brain-storming session in a very structured way. It can be accomplished at a terminal, with users in various locations around the country. SBS can be implemented on an electronic mail system or as a manual system. Manually, the procedure is very simple. A set of related questions concerning issues to be addressed in the planning processes is identified. The questions are placed, one per page, at the top of a sheet of paper. Each user responds to each question and passes the sheet to the next person, who then comments on the question and the previous comments. This process is continued for about one-half hour. After the exercise has been completed, the leader of the exercise has documentation or possibly a database recording the structured brainstorming process.

Examples of the type of questions that might be used in this exercise in the development of a strategic plan might be as follows:

Question 1: What are the major long-term business problems facing Company Z?

Question 2: What are the major disadvantages of the present information system with respect to Company Z's business?

Question 3: What are the major advantages of the present information system with respect to Company Z's business?

Given a particular situation, the questions would be specific to the organization and would be related to the application domains in question. We have found this to be an extremely enlightening exercise for both the analysts and the participants.

SBS provides a structured way to get started on the planning process. It also involves parallel processing, rather than sequential processing. The process is much more efficient than oral discussion. Further, intimidation is reduced, participants retain a degree of anonymity when writing comments on paper. It is clearly not as intimidating as challenging the boss in a discussion during a meeting. The prior documentation of comments is helpful in structuring one's own comments. In an oral discussion people are thinking of what they are going to say instead of listening to the speaker. They are concerned with the response they plan to give and do not listen. SBS, then, provides a mechanism for concentrating on the task. The set of responses can be grouped and categorized and then listed and reviewed so that they provide a starting point for further discussion.

The issues raised in SBS can then be structured and another technique called, ISSUE analysis, can be used to evaluate the set of alternatives available to address the issues. The computer-aided nature of these tools adds value to PLEXSYS as a tool in the planning process, including other features similar to the ones just described.

5. Phase 2: Description and Analysis of Requirements

A few of the statements of the PLEXSYS language are used in Phase 1 to assist in the structuring of the problem and in general design of the business systems plan. The majority of the problem description takes place in Phase 2. The PLEXSYS analyzer includes computer-aided techniques for structure documentation and analysis of information processing systems. It is a tool for describing system requirements, analyzing the descriptions, recording the descriptions in machine processable form, and storing them in a database. The PLEXSYS language and analyzer were designed to be "user friendly," unlike earlier requirements definition languages. The inputs and outputs of Phase 2 are described in Fig. 3.

The PLEXSYS language was developed as a single comprehensive language that can be used at very high level as well as the procedure definition level. The objective of PLEXSYS is to translate a very high level descriptive statement of a system into executable code for a target hardware–software configuration. Creation of a system using PLEXSYS includes the generation of a nonprocedural statement of requirements, selection of file and data structures based on data utilization, determination of the interfaces with a data management system, and generation of program code for the target system in COBOL or PASCAL.

It should be remembered that the PLEXSYS system is concerned with supporting the decision-making process at all levels of systems development. The capability of the PLEXSYS language ranges from high-level conceptual definitions down to the "nitty-gritty" decision level required to produce executable code.

The PLEXSYS language supports descriptions at five levels. A user operates at whichever level is of interest at a particular time and place in the life cycle. The PLEXSYS language is not made up of distinct sublanguages, however. The PLEXSYS language can be roughly divided into the following levels.

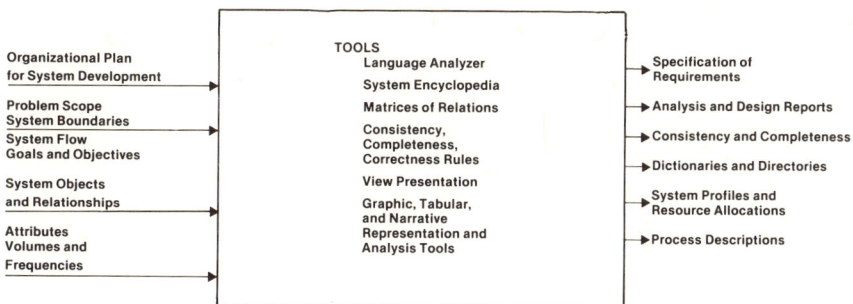

Inputs	TOOLS	Outputs
Organizational Plan for System Development	Language Analyzer	Specification of Requirements
Problem Scope System Boundaries	System Encyclopedia Matrices of Relations	Analysis and Design Reports
System Flow Goals and Objectives	Consistency, Completeness, Correctness Rules	Consistency and Completeness
System Objects and Relationships	View Presentation	Dictionaries and Directories
Attributes Volumes and Frequencies	Graphic, Tabular, and Narrative Representation and Analysis Tools	System Profiles and Resource Allocations / Process Descriptions

FIGURE 3. Phase 2: Description and analysis of requirements.

Level 1
  System flow
  System activities
Level 2
  Data definition
  Process definition and structures
  Procedure definitions
Level 3
  Logical structure
  Process organization
  Data
Level 4
  Physical environment
  Hardware description
  Software description
Level 5
  Code generation
  Procedural primitives

6. Form of Problem Description

The user of PLEXSYS has a choice of form of expression in specification of the problem description. The user can select from among the following types of representation:

1. Statement
2. Graphical
3. Tabular

The user selects the mode of representation with which he/she is most comfortable. The usefulness of PLEXSYS is enhanced considerably through the effective use

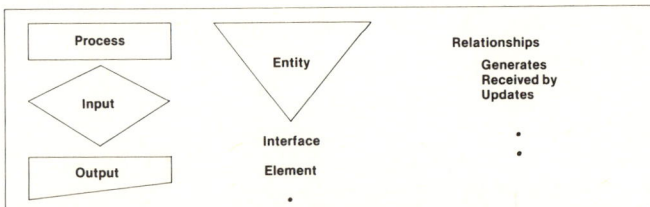

FIGURE 4. Objects and relations.

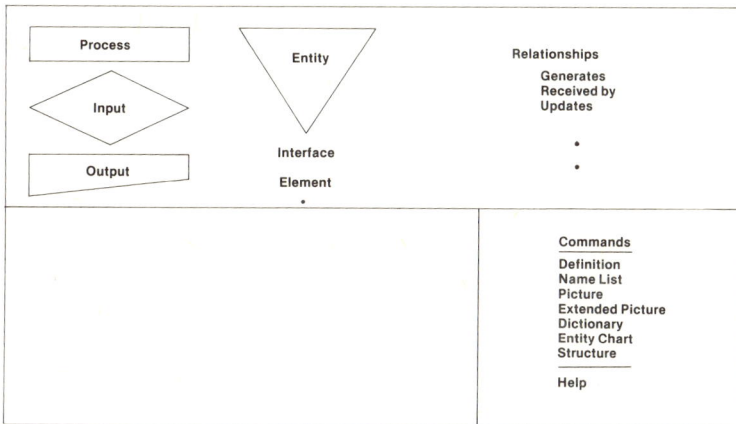

FIGURE 5. Analysis report commands.

of a graphical display. Using color graphics terminal offers the obvious advantage of being able to enhance and display output system flow descriptions and logical designs in a more useful and appealing form. However, the most important advantage appears to be related to the entry of information. The graphical approach, as illustrated in Fig. 4, describes how the user is prompted from one stage to the next in the problem definition process. Figure 5 illustrates the prompt commands used to describe the objects and relations in the PLEXSYS system and the prompt commands used to run various analysis reports.

Figure 6 illustrates the full screen of the graphics terminal with the objects and relationships of the PLEXSYS language shown on the top of the screen. The list of reports available to be run is shown to the right of the screen. A typical system graph of objects with associated relationships, built by a PLEXSYS user, is shown in the center of the display scope.

The activities involved in Phase 2 begin once the conceptualization of the system has been completed and the business systems plan has been prepared. The requirements to be derived in Phase 2 include the definition of the required inputs and outputs and the computations necessary to produce them. We need to be able to express these requirements. The PLEXSYS system was developed with the following characteristics in mind:

- The language must be capable of describing all requirements: conceptual; system flow; data structures; hardware environment; software environment; and detailed procedural levels.
- The language must be extremely user friendly so management will interact with the system.

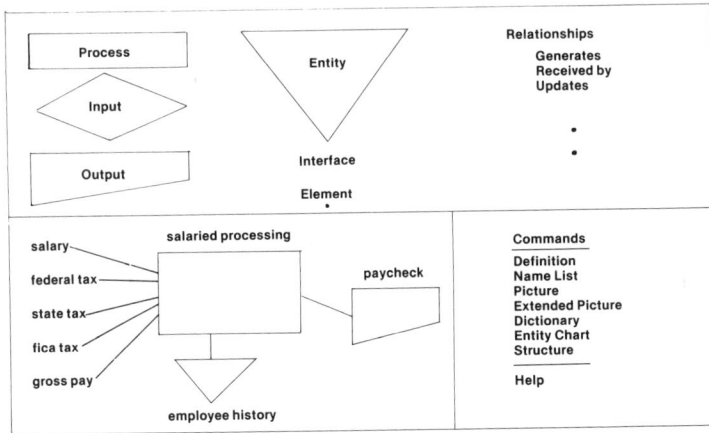

FIGURE 6. Screen layout for PLEXSYS.

- The structure of the language must allow for evaluation.
- The language must permit ease of modification of the requirements contained/stored in the various data bases.
- The requirements delineated using the language must be compatible with the use of the language in the design and code generation phases.
- The language must facilitate portability.
- The language must facilitate documentation

The PLEXSYS language was derived from the best features of other systems. However, it can best be described as a significant extension of PSL in terms of scope. Two important principles remain with respect to language structure:

- The language is as nonprocedural as possible and it is, at the same time, as procedural as necessary to produce code.
- The language supports hierarchical structuring in both process and data definition.

The first of these points is especially important. By stating "what is to be done" rather than "how it is to be done" we prevent the premature bindings that hinder the portability of the design and the consideration of alternative designs. Second, PLEXSYS releases the user from many bookkeeping aspects of programming. Therefore, there is less chance for error because the user need concentrate on only those aspects relevant to the problem at hand. The problem definition phase of system design and construction is necessarily an iterative procedure. The user cannot be involved until he or she has something to "grasp" such as feedback from the analyst regarding the form of the initial system requirements proposal. Thus, the problem definition process is handled in an interative manner facilitated by the many reports available through the PLEXSYS analyzer.

The interactive procedure of problem statement development is also enhanced by features which facilitate a top-down approach to the requirements definition. The basic language structure allows for hierarchical structuring.

A procedure definition facility (PDF) was included to make definition of logic easier at all levels of design. The PDF portion of PLEXSYS is based on the constructs determined necessary for structured programming top-down definitions.

Hierarchical structuring facilitates problem definition and assures a degree of correctness. Using a top-down structured approach, correctness can be established at the higher levels and maintained at each succeeding level.

To appreciate the benefit of a requirements statement tool, one must remember that the problem statement definition is an iterative procedure and each component is defined as the user builds the problem statement through the use of feedback from the analyzer.

6.1. PLEXSYS Analysis

The process of defining system requirements is handled in an iterative fashion by use of a PLEXSYS analyzer. The problem definers periodically process the problem statement or interactively update a problem statement through use of PLEXSYS. Thus, PLEXSYS serves as a tool in the problem statement process by continually providing feedback about many aspects of the system to the problem definer.

PLEXSYS-Phase 2 functions include the following:

- Accepts and analyzes PLEXSYS language input.
- Maintains a data base containing an up-to-date problem statement.
- Provides output of the present system requirements in PLEXSYS language.
- Allows several problem definers to state requirements of different parts of the system while maintaining a coherent system requirements definition.
- Produces reports on demand which allow alternative views of the status of the requirements statement.
- Analyzes the problem statement for completeness and consistency.

The reports produced by PLEXSYS can be used by project management as well as the problem definer. Reports are produced under defined conditions or on demand and each type of report can provide detailed or summary information. Further facilities are provided for the generation of special reports according to user specifications. In addition to aiding in the problem definer's work, the reports aid him or her in communication with the user and thus speed the problem statement process. After the system requirements are fully defined, the PLEXSYS outputs and data base serve as detailed documentation of the system.

The reports produced by PLEXSYS at various phases in the system's development life cycle are from among the following classes:

- Graphical presentation of static relationships;
- Graphical presentation of system flows;
- Tabular representation of relations;
- Tabular representation of similarities;
- Dictionaries and directories;
- Statistical presentation of completeness, frequency, etc.;
- Evaluation of consistency and completeness;
- User friendly help commands and presentation control commands;
- Data base manipulation such as update, delete, input, report; and
- Data base query processing.

Following the process of analyzing the reports and cleaning up the set of requirements, the data base of requirements is passed to the next phase, which consists of the logical and physical analysis and design. Experience has shown that numerous iterations are required to generate a complete, consistent, and correct problem statement.

7. Summary

DSS principles of flexible dialogue, model management, and data management have significantly influenced the development of the PLEXSYS approach. It is clear that no rigid set of formal procedures exists that completely address the needs in strategic planning and requirements determination in enterprise analysis. Until such a methodology appears, we require a flexible decision environment in which to conduct enterprise analysis. PLEXSYS offers such an environment.

The use of flexible dialogue forms (statement, tabular, and graphical) and application of color graphics in eliciting and presenting information have enhanced user–analyst communication. The variety of internal models supported for representation and analysis have accommodated a wide range of approaches that can be pursued by the analysts. Finally, flexible data management practice allows PLEXSYS to accommodate defined entity, relation, and attribute definitions.

In conclusion, PLEXSYS adopts several principles and structures of BSP, PSL/PSA, BIAIT, CSF, and other enterprise analysis approaches. The DSS approach of flexible dialogue, model, and data management have facilitated necessary support requirements in accommodating enterprise analysis.

8

PLANNING AND CONTROL SYSTEMS FOR R&D ORGANIZATIONS

Bala V. Balachandran and Richard W. Srch

1. Introduction

The attitude towards information systems in most research and development (R&D) organizations ranges from benign neglect to open rejection. Despite the expenditure of millions of dollars, few R&D organizations possess information systems whose quality and data integrity equal those found in major corporate profit centers. This chapter provides a constructive model framework for a decision support system combining the financial, operational, and functional needs of any R&D organization. However, the objectives are not profit oriented and, thereby, are different from those of a general corporate structure.

Several important reasons can be described which illustrate why information systems designed for corporate business applications are not effectively adaptable to an R&D application:

- Most of the systems for information management were planned, designed, and tested for profit-oriented corporations, which may not be relevant to R&D.
- Most of these are accounting, finance, and return-on-investment (ROI) oriented.
- The objectives and goals of an R&D organization are quite different from a sales and profit oriented division.
- R&D organizations invariably are viewed as the suppliers of services and

BALA V. BALACHANDRAN ● Department of Decision Sciences, Accounting and Information Systems, J. L. Kellogg Graduate School of Management, Northwestern University, Evanston, Illinois 60201.   RICHARD W. SRCH ● G & W Electric Co., 3500 West 127th Street, Blue Island, Illinois 60406.

not the consumers of services. Thus, to accept the discipline of the marketplace is inappropriate in an R&D organization.

● The kind of information needed by the R&D organization is both organizationally and functionally based. The planned projects and assignments that cut across organizations and functions are the resultant activities initiated by the inputs from both areas.

Provocative and purposeful articles have appeared in the literature which discuss the R&D problems and provide useful insight to the needed solutions.[1−3] For instance, in a recent article, Mechlin and Berg[1] state that, to measure the true value of a company's research, supplemental information beyond the ROI calculations are needed. One has to take a hard look at the overall strategic benefit of research activity, examine the cash flow in relation to the lifecycle of products resulting from the activity, and evaluate thoroughly all the revenue stemming from products and licenses connected with research. This means we need a management information system (MIS) that has breadth and depth to provide meaningful summary information, permitting management to assess the long-range value of R&D activities beyond the short-term (i.e., annual) return on investment, and the tax consequences.

There are often other needs for effective, timely information which have equal or greater importance than financially based information. One classification of such information is that which is required to direct the operations of the organization. Each organization as well as each constituent part has a purpose for its existence and a set of functions which accomplish that purpose. A constituent part may have a purpose which does not contribute directly to the profitability of the parent organization. To accomplish its purpose, which may enhance the future profit capability of the organization, the most important function may be the effective management and control of its operation. One example is a research laboratory whose primary objectives are the creation of new ideas for scientific application and investigating the feasibility of engineering applicability. No new products are developed at this point, but the foundation for future product development has been established.

In this chapter we develop a framework for an integrated MIS model that is uniquely directed towards satisfying R&D organizational objectives. In this framework, we identify three interrelated subsystems: a financial subsystem emphasizing cost minimization; an operational subsystem concentrating on time and scheduling; and an interactive interface with the database design focusing upon the functional hierarchy of R&D instead of organizational line hierarchy. The framework permits us to directly address all R&D planning and control needs instead of adapting an existing MIS model that is generally suited for ROI oriented firms. Later, using this structured framework, we identify the appropriate parameters to achieve the informational needs of all levels of R&D management. The final section provides a case illustration of an actual application of our R&D framework. The benefits are realizable by both the R&D organization and the parent organization because important operational information needs of R&D management can be effectively satisfied as well as the necessary financial information needs of corporate management.

2. R&D Environment and Information Needs

The R&D organization has a nature of its own which differs from a profit center. Its objectives are long term, often extending beyond a fiscal year, many inputs and outputs are intangibles, there is minimal interaction with the day-to-day operations, and the benefits from the investment are realized after the R&D work is completed. In this section, we examine the environment of the R&D organization and discuss its particular planning and control needs. Such an examination of the needs of an R&D organization permits us to develop an MIS study approach. This approach, in turn, aids us in identifying the informational parameters required to satisfy the organizational needs relative to planning and control.

2.1. Environment

Current literature on MIS systems are applications which focus upon a profit center type of organization. The dominant characteristic of the information and the management of the organization is financial. Aggregation of operational data is done to provide statistics on financial aspects of the profit center's performance. Operational data are provided principally for the purpose of directing more cost-effective operations or a more highly profitable performance. The R&D organization does not easily, if at all, fit into this perspective, and the received information is less than totally satisfactory.[6,8]

Any technical support or R&D organization will have a structure which is compatible with the parent organization hierarchy. The general functional hierarchy (shown in Fig. 1) contains those functions which any organization must perform or have performed for it. The organizational constraints that an R&D organization must contend with depends upon the corporate structure and the allowed degree of independence.

For example, the R&D organization may have the total responsibility for the fiscal function (including accounting) or may use the parent organization's function. Full responsibility implies greater independence and flexibility to meet R&D information needs with periodic reporting to the corporate function. If, however, the corporate function is used, all activities and transactions must follow corporate

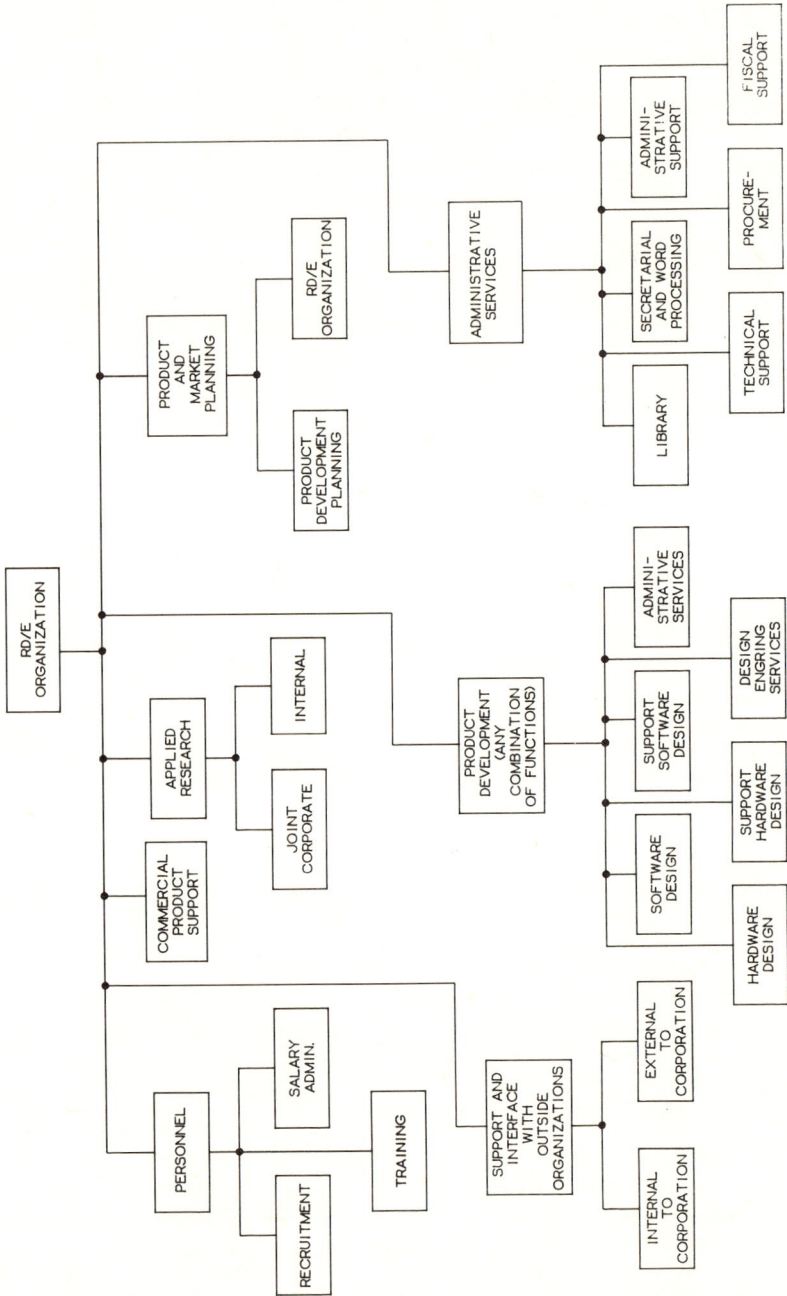

FIGURE 1. General RD/E functional hierarchy chart.

procedures, which usually reduces flexibility and independence. The effective trade-off is to have a means by which both corporate and R&D information needs are simultaneously satisfied.

2.2. Information Needs

A number of constraints, both external and internal, impose a requirement upon the organization to have an effective means to access timely and needed information. Pressure applied by external factors, such as a changing product market or a changing technology, cannot be relieved without good data. If future product planning is to be fruitful, the R&D organization must be able to easily interact with corporate functions, such as marketing.

The information needs can be described as having effective means of answering inquiries for periodic or ad hoc reporting. The principal needs are comprised of both operational and financial information which can be extracted from the available data and capability to answer "what if" type of queries. Often the data that satisfy an operational information need vary from financially based data through the relationships by which they are collected and aggregated. To identify the exact informational needs of an R&D organization, a questionnaire, similar to the one in the Appendix, could be developed, aimed at the end users of the information. Emerging from the response to a survey employing such a questionnaire will be a list of the primary informational needs which are described in the following categories:

- Project and resource planning for both current and future activities;
- Budgetary planning, preparation and control;
- Product planning in conjunction with marketing and corporate planning;
- Project scheduling and control of current activities;
- Appropriate information supplied to all levels of management;
- Coordinating at various levels of management the decision making capacity and information needed to execute it;
- Strategic planning of the organization's direction and goals in concert with the overall corporate goals.

The information requirements for a decision maker of an accountable subdivision depends upon dimensions that define the above categories. The type of decisions for different levels of management can be characterized as shown in Fig. 2.

2.3. MIS Study Approach

First a specified set of goals and objectives must be identified by management, who is responsible for the efficient operations of the organization. These R&D

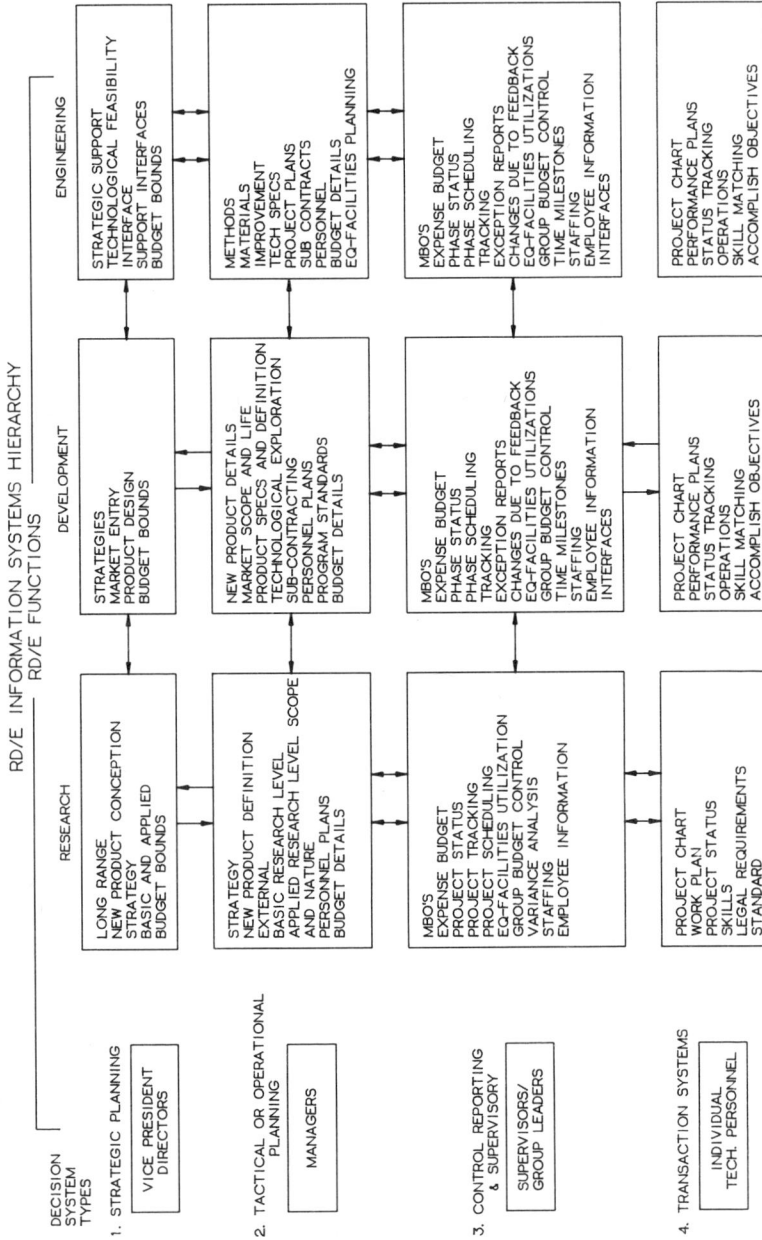

FIGURE 2. RD/E information systems hierarchy.

objectives are used as guidelines for the study and should indicate both long- and short-range goals. Once this is done, it is the duty of the study team to operationalize and characterize the project with major and minor milestones. This leads to a development program identifying major milestones with a complete time profile.

There are several study approaches which are currently followed in corporations and other organizations. For instance, the classifications described below by Rockart[4] may be a good enunciation:

- By-product technique: summarized information is only a by-product of the transactional/clerical processing system.
- Null approach: no "hard" information is provided due to the inadequacy in meeting the dynamic needs of executive activities.
- Key indicator system: providing on-line visual display of key financial indicators in the organization.
- Total business system: comprehensive system approach to meeting needs with "top-down" analysis and "bottom/up" implementation.
- Critical success factors: approach which extracts management's definition of factors critical to the successful operation of the organization.

The approach presented in this paper has drawn from the best of the approaches and formed a hybrid on the key indicators, the total business systems and the critical success factors. Our approach stresses and identifies the operational factors that the CEO defined as critical success factors for the organization, and encompasses the entire management hierarchy in order to acquire a comprehensive perspective and to attend to important budgetary indicators. Because of this cross section of needs to be addressed, this framework seemed best suited. It proposes an integrated systems method, utilizing central data base concepts, in addressing the information needs of management from senior level to first level supervision.[5] A system composition would primarily include the following:

- A financial information system (FIS);
- An operational information system (OIS);
- An interface between the two decision support systems.

Each of these subsystems will be discussed in greater detail in the following sections, which consider several dimensions and levels including time, management levels, functions, and responsibility.

2.4. Definition of Information Parameters

The success of implementing an overall management information system depends upon a unified systems approach. It should be oriented toward the general goals of the organization, the particular subgoals of its constituent subunits, and the activities associated with achieving those objectives. The development of a network of unified information systems requires a sequence of several phases which consists of identification of information needs, definition of requirements and their boundaries, general macro design, detailed micro design, development and testing, installation, and operation of the systems.

A set of questions can be identified which gathers information about the "critical success factors" for each interviewee to identify their information needs (see Appendix). Later, a set of projects are identified which are the subsystems of the total system and have a weight (for example, 1 to 5) assigned by each interviewee. Then based on an interactive process of data gathering, feedback, updating, and discussion, a final implementation plan with priorities emerges. During this process, a set of standards, procedures, and practices are identified which define input needs, input format, input frequency, and time intervals of input collection.

Irrespective of the mechanics and format of the informational output of the integrated MIS, it is obvious (e.g., the questionnaire) that the system should address parameters oriented toward the end users. Three specific parameters or dimensions must be considered in the MIS model, namely, level of end users, organizational functions, and time horizon.

2.4.1. Level of End Users. The hierarchy of end users who may be supported include, at least, four levels as given below:

- Transaction oriented (clerical and technical);
- Operational (first-level management);
- Tactical (middle-level management including planners);
- Strategic (top-level management).

In the R&D environment, the transaction oriented activities include entry and maintenance of data flowing through a department by clerical staff, entry or use of design data by technical staff, and documentation capture through word processing and inputting transactions. First-level and middle management have needs for access and availability of operational data for management of projects and development resources and to control and successfully meet schedule date. Finally, upper management has needs for current and historical data to forecast future products and effectively estimate future development projects. They also need external data which provide relative information about competition, economic conditions, and technological advances.

2.4.2. Organizational Functions. In these days of changing organizational structure, the integrated information system for R&D should be primarily oriented towards the functions that the R&D division performs, and only secondarily based on the organizational hierarchy. The delineation could be based upon the physical functions, which include finance, manufacturing, marketing, accounting, research, and development. Within each of the major functions, there can be further subdivisions. Thus, in the model design a functional parameter with an appropriate indexing system identifier is required.

The crucial function performed by a R&D organization is the definition and timely development of products for the marketplace. The single important factor in performing that function is the ability to effectively apply human resources, both experience and expertise, to the defined projects and identify gaps in that resource which must filled. By being able to easily access accurate information about human resources, as well as other resources, the R&D management can provide more dependable and useful development forecasts.

2.4.3. Time Horizon. A third major dimension in the model design is the time horizon factor. The decision making, planning, and control objectives need to also be concerned with the time orientation, e.g., short range, medium range and long range. Within each time span certain further refinements are conceivable. The aggregation or details of information can vary quite significantly depending upon this time focus. Thus, a parameter identifier for the time dimension is also needed.

Considerations of time horizons for an R&D organization include the constraints of tactical and strategic plans. Tactical constraints impose project schedule demands, responses to manufacturing problems which may affect development schedules, or reactions to market pressures. A strategic time horizon, for example, could be the time interval to develop a portion of the technical staff with the knowledge and skills to implement a new design technology in future products.

There can be other relevant dimensions depending upon the specific organization. Associated with each dimension, a parametric identifier with appropriate levels is to be designed. Other dimensions could include a country identifier for a multinational organization or a regional identifier for a multilocation unit. Depending upon the user organization and the span information support needed, one can design and model a customized MIS system toward the identified needs. We discuss a data model design along these lines in the next section.

3. Integrated MIS Model

3.1. Model Definition

An integrated system which meets all information needs can be defined in terms of its parts, namely, a financial information system, an operational information system, and an interface.

- The financial information system (FIS) provides all costs and/or benefits information on a timely basis in terms of monetary or utility units and aids management to control as well as plan for budget analysis and forecasting. Though there can be several types of related information, the main emphasis is summarization information expressed in dollar form or monetary units which in turn provides various rates and ratios for cross sectional and time series consideration. Such a system permits the R&D organization to more easily manage their budget and operate as a more effective cost center based upon target outputs from the parent organization.

- The operational information system (OIS) prepares, schedules, monitors, and reports all operations details by every resource including human resource, equipment utilizations expenditures for each project, and productivity indices for each system or job. Major aspects of consideration are scheduling, machine loading, logistics, distribution, tracking and monitoring, and other productivity measures. It should be noted that the monetary unit (dollar) has little significance, though it can be related. This is of major importance to an R&D organization in effectively managing and controlling development projects.

- The interface links one or more subsystems from each of the financial and operational systems. Responsibility accounting, incentive compensation plan, performance evaluation, productivity analysis, and project management can have access to both financial and operational information.

The general system model consists of two conceptual information models and interconnecting relationships or information bridges. The two sets of attributes fall into one of the three classes, namely, unique FIS attributes, unique OIS attributes and common attributes shared by both models.

3.1.1. Model Outputs/Objectives. The financial information system spans the entire informational needs oriented toward fiscal conditions at all levels of the organization. This system includes the following:

- Budget preparation for a time interval (annually) or budget maintenance within each period (quarterly).
- Budget tracking (monthly) current periods costs by organization (section/group level), year-to-date comparison with budget (actual vs. budget), budget variances, and control. Expected output is received in less than a week from input and is categorized by department/section/group.
- Project assignment tracking through the organizational hierarchy and tracks labor hours for projects for reporting costs on a periodic (monthly) basis.
- Financial reports at top management level. Product performance reports are produced which could use certain planning code categorization by project, etc., to facilitate cost and pricing decisions.

The operational information system has the primary objectives of timely completion of activities utilizing resources efficiently. This system can accommodate the following needs:

- Manloading and scheduling of jobs with capability to schedule, monitor, and update task data.
- Operational data having labor hour and other resource (e.g., automated robots) data based on related subtasks and dollars expenditures on an actual and budgeted basis.
- Scheduling projects for department/section/group by work station, work activities, and functions (product/project management).
- Scheduling within a section shows current activity and future work for forecasting workloads and manpower needs.
- Logistic and distributional information.

3.1.2. Financial Data Model. Based on the needs identified in the questionnaire and collected via the interviewing process, certain attributes of the financial data models (see Fig. 3) are identified in the following:

- Organizational attribute (index i): For responsibility and control purposes this identifier is needed so that information can be related to the smallest organizational group. This parameter may change from time to time.
- Functional attribute (index j): No matter what the organizational identifier is, the type of activities performed can be exhaustively enumerated. This is a permanent identifier which permits the analysis of functional needs and costs for planning and control purposes.

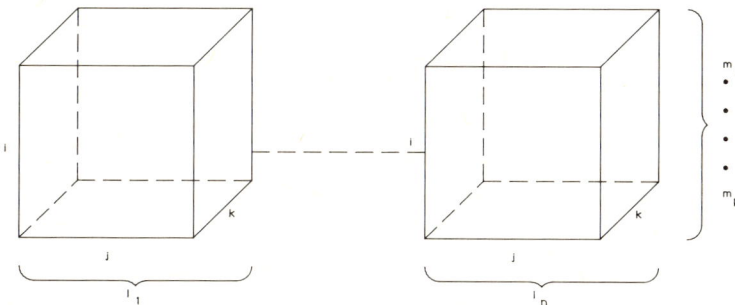

FIGURE 3. Financial data model. Parameters: i, organization structure; j, functional definition; k, effort logging; l, product; m, accounting.

- Effort logging attribute (index k): This attribute can track costs by an assignment or a project which cuts across several organizational units in the financial system as well as project time via the cost center concept of operational system. Thus, this attribute represents an ideal interface between the two information systems.
- Product attribute (index l): This attribute is the product identifier as currently defined in the organization and links to the financial reports of organizational units.
- Financial attribute (index m): This attribute is necessary to provide a viable interface with the financial accounting system of the units and to permit the generation of detailed financial reports by different accounting rules.

3.1.3. Operational Data Model. In the operational data model (see Fig. 4), five attributes or parameters are proposed which accommodate requirements identified in the questionnaire and interviews.

- Organizational attribute (index i): (This is identical to the organizational attribute of financial data model and serves as one interface linking FIS and OIS.)
- Project attribute (index j): This attribute defines the project to be monitored by the OIS. Projects will be user defined and can be any level of magnitude.
- Effort logging attribute (index k): (This is identical to the effort logging attribute of financial data model and serves as a second interface to link FIS and OIS.)

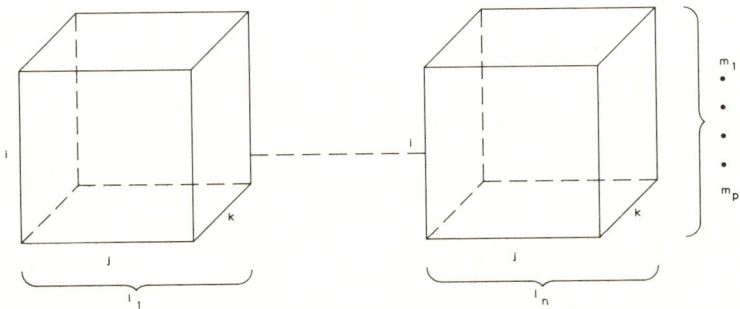

FIGURE 4. Operational data model. Parameters: i, organization structure; j, project; k, effort logging; l, task activity; m, organization resource.

- Activity attributes (index l): Data items encompassed by this attribute are: the task identifier, the type of task, required skill level, required resource level, required effort (budgeted vs. actual), and schedule interfaces (inputs, output, task successor).
- Organization resource attribute (index m): The model will facilitate all resources utilized by a project (i.e., technical personnel, administrative/clerical personnel, computer/DP service, automated robots, equipment for project aids).

3.1.4. Interface between Data Models. Technical personnel have payroll account numbers which uniquely identify the members of a group/section/department. They charge time against direct labor account (attribute of FIS) which is used by both the FIS and OIS. The primary data is *time* rather than *cost* which permits better tracking and monitoring of project schedules. Time information (a main ingredient of OIS) along with the corresponding, derived cost information provide the flexibility of tracking both the time and cost in reports per users needs. To be able to provide both the time and cost information requires a relationship that bridges the two information systems. The interface between FIS and OIS contains the relationships which provide the information bridge. Thus, the effort logging and organizational attributes comprise the interface and provide the integrating link between the objectives of FIS and OIS, creating a total MIS as shown in the general model in Fig. 5.

3.2. General System Attributes

3.2.1. Unique FIS Attributes. The unique attributes which provide the format to store financial and accounting based data are as follows:

- Accounting/fiscal—provides the viable and necessary interface with the parent company or encompassing organization's accounting system, to provide the required cost data, data aggregation by account, and generation of needed reports.
- Functional—identifies the major functions and subdivisions of those functions which are performed by the organization. It provides the access to data for analysis of the functional needs and costs to perform the planning and control task of management.
- Product—identifies the major products that are processed, handled, or developed by the organization. Pure research, for example, can be a product whose tangible embodiment is basic information collection about a technical subject.

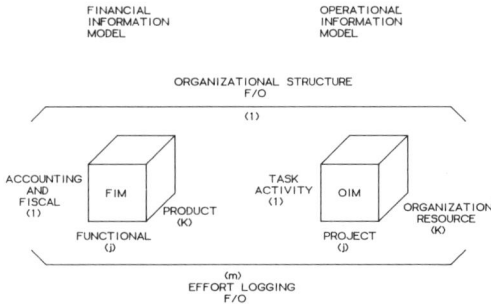

FIGURE 5. General model definition and structure. FIM attributes: (1) accounting/fiscal; (2) functional; (3) product; (4) effort logging; (5) organizational structure. OIM attributes: (1) task activity; (2) project; (3) organizational resource; (4) effort logging; (5) organizational structure.

3.2.2. Unique OIS Attributes. The unique attributes that provide the format to store operational information, related (nonfinancial accounting based) data are as follows:

- Task activity—provides means to define such information of data items as task identifier, type of work, required skill level, work level, work schedule, required effort, and schedule interfaces.
- Project—defines the activities which constitute outputs from an organizational subdivision, e.g., a computer program development or the fabrication of a printed circuit board.
- Organizational resource—defines all resources by the organization in completing a project activity with human resources, computer resources, computer equipment, and other such aids.

3.2.3. Common Attributes. The two attributes that are common to both FIS and OIS provide the information bridges permitting inquiries to access needed data in both models. The usefulness of the shared attributes can be seen when cost data for a product or project must be related to scheduled efforts and compiled with respect ot the level of support to a function by a subdivision of the organization.

- Effort logging—the mechanism for accounting for the expended efforts by human resources on projects in terms of cost and time.
- Organizational—identifies the various levels of subdivision in the organization that are formally recognized and which define the level of the individual.

With such a conceptual design we believe a framework for a unique MIS can be designed that is most appropriate and relevant to any R&D organization. We have applied this framework to a case study as given in the next section.

4. Development Laboratory Application

An investigative study was conducted at GTE Automatic Electric Labs (AEL) in 1979 to assess the information needs of this R&D organization.[9] The purpose of the study was to prepare a proposal for the development of a management information system for AEL. The proposed method described in this paper easily applies to AEL since it performs the functions of product development and technical engineering support.

The study team was assembled, which consisted of an outside consultant and knowledgeable personnel from within the organization. This approach created a team having broader knowledge of external MIS applications and intimate awareness of the organization's operations and needs. A survey of information needs was conducted of management personnel, ranging from the president of AEL to technical managers within several departments. Three departments were surveyed as a representative sample since all departmental operations and accounting functions are quite similar. The survey itself consisted of information gathered through a questionnaire (i.e., based upon the questionnaire in the Appendix) on an initial personal interview and a follow-up interview. The combined results of the survey were tabulated and prioritized, in a manner that was consistent with the viewpoints of the interviewed managers.

The information gathered through the survey focused upon information needs and related critical success factors for the representative organization. Both current and future needs were defined by the interviewees. They were asked to weigh each need, ranging from one (nice to have) to five (critically necessary). Current systems or needs include operational management factors, long-range planning factors, and financial management factors. Future needs had important factors identified in the following areas: operational management, long-range planning, financial management, quality measurement, work-efficiency, and personnel or staffing. A composite picture of the categories of factors or needs was then prepared which provided a prioritization by comparing average weightings for each category.

Analysis of the information needs of the R&D laboratory identified the most important factors as those which aided more effective project management and control, easier project planning, and more efficient budget control. Accounting and financial requirements, as required by the parent organization, were of lesser importance because they were expected to be easily satisfied from the primary information, i.e,. that which was needed to manage R&D organization.

The organizational relationships of AEL with GTE Automatic Electric Company can be described using the generic conceptual model developed in the paper and is shown in Fig. 6. AEL is a separate R&D organization and, yet, is an integral part of the company (GTE Automatic Electric Co.). It uses many functions of the parent company (e.g., accounting, payroll, plant facilities) and is part of the company's budget. It serves two major roles, namely, a product development laboratory and technical engineering support organization. As a product development laboratory it must work closely with different organizations within GTE besides Automatic Electric. As a technical engineering function, AEL provides specific and direct support to the company as products are released for manufacture and initial field sites are cutover.

The resultant output from the study was a development proposal for a management information system for a division of AEL. The system model consisted of a financial component and an operational component, with an interfacing mechanism between them. The focus of the system was the informational needs of the departments in the division and was intended to serve as a prototype for the entire R&D organization. These informational needs are nearly identical since each department must meet the requirements of both the laboratory and company. The conceptual model helped AEL to design the MIS architecture and identify all parameters, data models. and user applications which are currently used. Greater details are contained in the AEL internal report.[9]

A key element of the MIS definition was the integrated database structure under the administration of a database management system. Benefits which may be achieved by implementing the MIS in a database environment are: greater data independence where the data and the applications are independent such that either may be changed without adversely affecting the other; reduction or elimination of redundant data by permitting the MIS database to be the central data collection and management point; improved data integrity through administrative services and safeguards against hardware failures, software bugs, and erroneous data updates; increased privacy and security of commonly stored data to prevent unauthorized access to the information on both an individual and an application basis.

Once it had been determined that the conceptual data models do meet the information needs of the departments, their logical structure and physical implementation were considered. The major problem to overcome was the design of a network data structure which not only satisfies day-to-day processing requirements, but permits ad hoc management queries. The database management system selected for the application was IMS (IBM's database management system). One constraint imposed by IMS was that it basically is hierarchical in nature. A pseudonetwork structure under IMS was feasible provided that several considerations

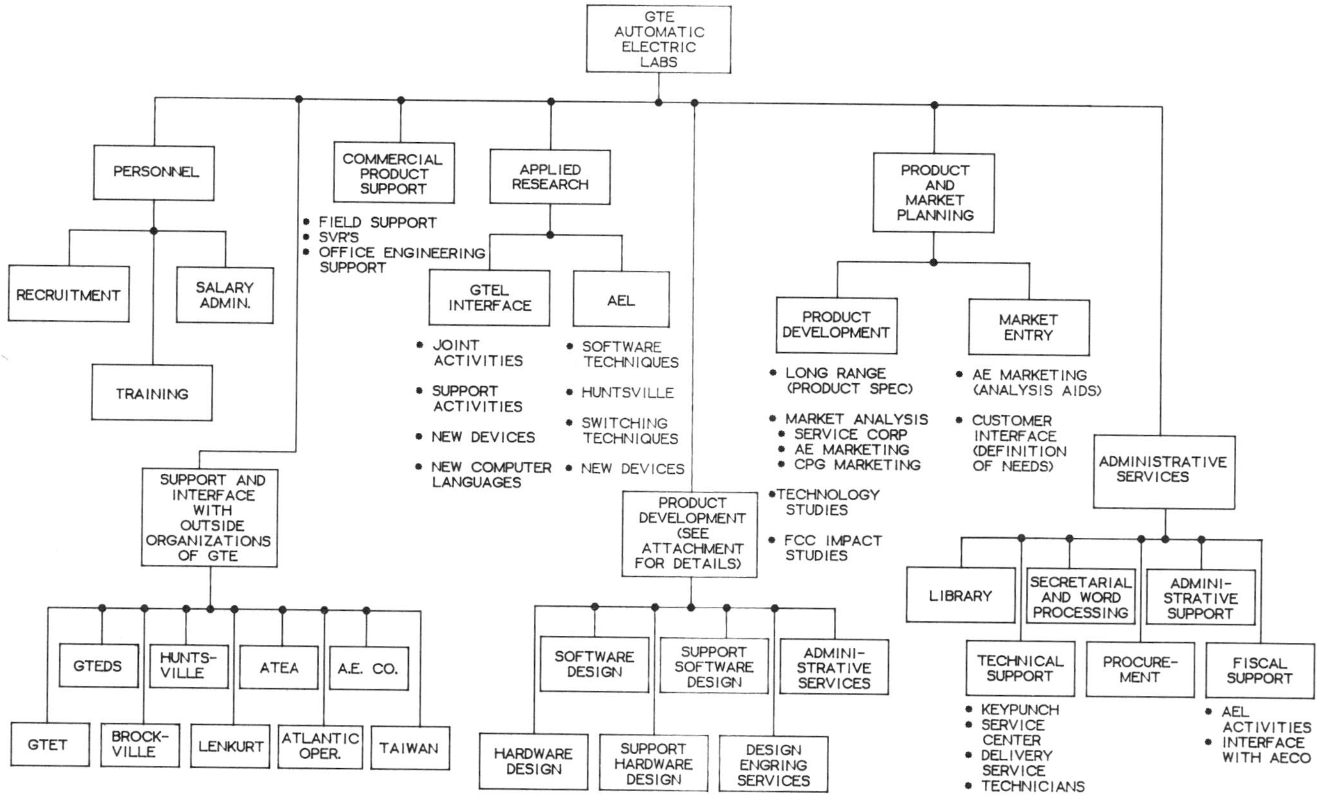

FIGURE 6. GTE AE labs functional hierarchy chart.

were made which defined the basic relationships that are a prerequisite to the design of physical databases:

- To provide financial monitoring on a functional basis, a relationship must be established between an assignment (i.e., project control instrument) and the functional areas within the scope of that assignment. This would presumably be accomplished using the task number as defined in the current lab planning system.

- The second consideration was a standardization of present policy concerning the association of an assignment to an organizational entity (i.e., department, section, or group). Briefly, no two entities at the same level in the organizational hierarchy can share a single assignment unless that assignment is "owned" by a higher-level common entity (e.g., one section may be common to two or more groups).

- One of the requirements of the operational information system (OIS) is accurate project management to perform scheduling and monitoring functions. If a project management system is integrated into the OIS, time reporting to the system would be a critical ingredient and would require collecting individual time charges against a monitored project.

Although the FIS and OIS can be considered distinct, the physical implementation will be common in keeping with the integrated MIS approach. At a

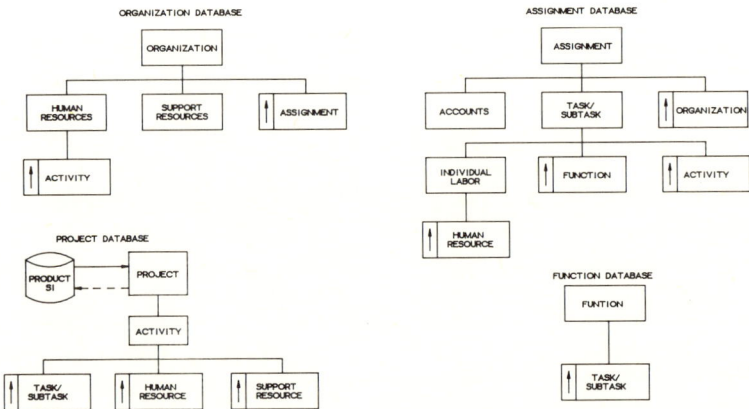

FIGURE 7. DBMS physical databases.

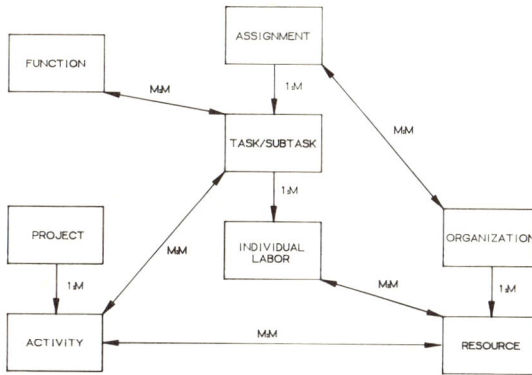

FIGURE 8. DBMS logical relationships.

high level, four physical databases encompassing both FIS and OIS have been defined. The design of each database constitutes a distinct entity and its associated relationships. Figure 7 illustrates the high-level physical design. These relationships (termed logical pointers in a database environment) determine the logical data structures (databases) which are related to the previously defined conceptual data models. The concept of the logical database is important when attempting to implement a network data structure under IMS. Although the logical databases are themselves hierarchical, the previously defined logical pointers are used by IMS to establish the pseudonetwork data structure as illustrated in Fig. 8. Associated with this concept is the flexibility to format the data per user requirements.

5. Conclusions

In conducting the MIS study at AEL, the methodology described in this paper was effectively employed to examine the feasibility of an MIS implementation in an R&D organization. A conceptual system model was defined consisting of an operational model, a financial model, and interfaces. The five-dimensional data model was applicable and did yield the broad system architectural definition. Further investigation confirmed the feasibility of physically implementing the data models under a database management system.

Our approach to defining critical success factors from management's input by using our technique provided good results. Important factors were not only identified by the CEO but by other levels of management, providing a comprehensive picture. Yet the approach did not attempt to exhaustively assess all possible needs, thereby incurring excessive time and costs. The project also provided several good break points where the interim results could be reviewed by management prior to any further work.

Appendix: Management Information System for an R&D Organization—MIS Questionnaire

Interview With:
  Date:
Job Title:
  Section:
Section Name:
Number of Employees:

1. Briefly, what are your technical areas of responsibility?

2. What is the relationship between your areas and the rest of the department/ labs?

3. How do you get your assignments?
  a. Do tasks come with restrictions (e.g., budget limits)?
  b. Is periodic accounting of expenditures required?
  c. What happens if you do not perform within these restrictions?
  d. Who sets priorities on tasks, besides the standard set of the labs?

4. How do you schedule your work?
  a. How are the end dates set?
  b. What is the estimation process?
  c. How are scarce resources allocated (e.g., man loading)?
  d. Who sets priorities on tasks, besides the standard set of the labs?

5. How do you track the work of your subordinates?
  a. What kind of reports are currently produced (which are optional and which are required)?
  b. What additional reports would you like?

6. How is your work tracked by your superiors?
  a. What kind of reports are currently produced (which are optional and which are required)?

7. What are your measurable objectives (goals) related to your technical areas of responsibility?

8. What are the critical success factors for your area?

9. What major technical problems have you encountered within the last year that made your job overly difficult or took an inordinate amount of your time?
   a. What prevented your solving it?
   b. What is needed to solve it?
   c. What types of signals or warnings could have helped?
   d. What would be the value to your area and the department if it were solved?

10. What major changes do you envision within the next two to five years that will have a major impact on your area of resonsibility (organizational or technological)?

11. What additional information of systems would improve the performance of your area?

References

1. G. F. MECHLIN and D. BERG, Evaluating research—ROI is not enough, *Harvard Business Rev.*, 93–99, Sept.-Oct. (1980).
2. R. H. HAYES and W. J. ABERNATHY, Managing our way to economic decline, *Harvard Business Rev.*, 67–77, July-Aug. (1980).
3. H. V. BALTHASER, R. A. BOSCHI, and M. M. MENKEL, Calling the shots in R&D, *Harvard Business Rev.*, 151–160, May-June (1978).
4. J. F. ROCKART, Chief executives define their own data needs, *Harvard Business Rev.*, 81–93, March-April (1979).
5. F. R. McFEDDEN and J. D. SWEVER, Cost and benefits of a data base system, *Harvard Business Rev.*, 131–139, Jan.-Feb. (1978).
6. R. HERZLINGER, Why data systems in non-profit organizations fail, *Harvard Business Rev.*, 81–86, Jan. (1977).
7. Data base systems: Fundamental to the future, *Infosystems*, October 1979.
8. R. W. SRCH, PIRAMED project: An integrated CAS/CAM system development, *Design Automation Conference Proceedings*, 437–444, June 1977.
9. R. W. SRCH, D. J. MAHER, and B. V. BALACHANDRAN, MIS study—Final report, AEL internal document.

DECISION SUPPORT SYSTEMS INFORMATION NEEDS ANALYSIS THROUGH A MANAGEMENT PROCESS FRAMEWORK

BAYARD E. WYNNE

1. Decision Support Systems

The move from batch information processing to transaction handling was the essential enabling difference between EDP and MIS.

Managers presumed that by replacing EDP with MIS they would drastically improve management processes. They felt that this would result from routinely supplying the current and historical performance data as information for corrective action.

Now decision support systems (DSS) are being installed based upon both a philosophical change in approach and further technological advances. The MIS approach has generally been "How can a given array of data be used more fully to inform a decision maker?" The contrasting DSS perspective is to ask "What data, assumptions, and structure may enable a decision maker to extend his judgments?"

1.1. The Underpinnings of DSS

The technological advances allowing the possibility of DSS are best illustrated by the typical "tool kit" of a DSS environment. Such a tool kit includes (1)

BAYARD E. WYNNE • Arthur Andersen & Company, 69 West Washington Street, Chicago, Illinois 60602.

external linkage capability, (2) "relational" data base manager, (3) analytical/statistical methods, (4) modeling capabilities, (5) graphics interaction, and (6) ease of report generation. All of these tools are combined in a user-friendly, interactive mode flexible enough to support in a single command structure the spectrum of individuals from end user through development programmer.

DSS are responsive, flexible computerized environments for interactive man–machine support of end users in improving the effectiveness of those individuals as they participate in critical management processes by extending their capacities for making judgments in pursuit of the organization's goals.

All these fine words aside, what enables us to expect that DSS may deliver where MIS failed?

DSS is based upon three distinct technologies. These are (1) information processing, (2) operations research, and (3) cognitive psychology as shown in Fig. 1. The latter two might be combined as management sciences in contrast to information sciences, but for the consequent loss of emphasis on the cognitive psychology. Figure 1 suggests the relevant primary elements of each of the three technologies which underlie DSS.

Information processing includes transaction handling, data base management (internal and external), graphic presentation capabilities, and inquiry and communications facilities. This information processing technology is ideal for structured repetitive operations. It makes use of existing data to describe *"what is."*

Operations research includes analytic/statistical capabilities, heuristics for problem solving, optimization to resolve complex trade-offs, and simulation to represent operations and their abstractions, accounting/finance outcomes. Collectively, these operations research modeling facilities operate on structurable issues using data and assumptions to describe and project *"what if."*

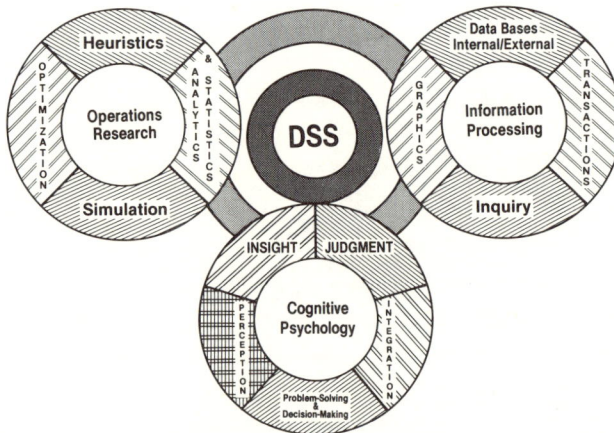

FIGURE 1. DSS technologies.

Cognitive psychology includes the human processes of perception, problem solving, and decision making in light of individual actions of insight, integration, and judgment. These human aspects operate in combination selectively upon whatever data and information are currently available to resolve the less formally structured issues before management by extending the individual intellects in a *"what could"* fashion.

With these historical and definitional notes out of the way, let us consider the lessons available from my own firm's DSS consulting experience.

1.2. A Pool of DSS Examples

An extensive set of our consulting engagements from around the world were examined. Each such engagement was identified by local professionals in response to "tell us about your recent client work to support management in the creation and exploitation of competitive advantages."

We were immediately struck by several facts. First, and obviously (now), the same application can be attempted as (1) an MIS system, (2) an OR project, or (3) a DSS installation. The key qualifier for DSS categorization appears to be whether they are user driven in extending a manager's judgment. Second, that a great many DSS applications had been done, but that few as yet were complete in several respects. That is, almost all the DSS applications appeared to be actively evolving. In addition, implementation to date in many of the DSS client engagements either lacked the full tool kit in the DSS environment, had only utilized a subset of the existing complement of DSS tools, or had only been extended to a portion of the obvious application areas.

These immediate findings required that we categorize the surveyed DSS engagements in order to utilize the survey results. Rather than publish here another DSS typology, I shall speak of our findings in terms of the DATAPRO typology.[2] Figure 2 is adapted from DATAPRO's typology. These seven types of DSS are ordered generally on the basis of increasing complexity.

We found examples of each category in our actual engagements. In addition, we identified examples of each of the seven categories in use or development within our own firm.

We also found it helpful to cross-categorize those DSS engagements on the basis of what I will call scale, or scope. The three scopes we found useful were the following:

- one time applications for specific individual projects,
- role support models for functional or strategic business unit managers,
- multiuser executive support systems for global pursuit of organization objectives.

Design and installation considerations, we found, varied among successful DSS both by the DATAPRO typology and the scope as given above.

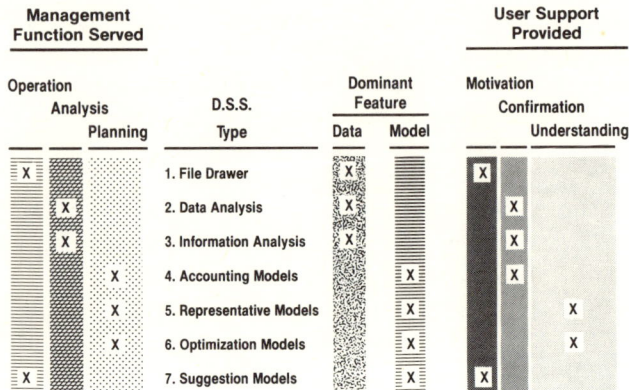

FIGURE 2. DSS typology.

1.3. Inferred DSS Guidelines

Arthur Andersen & Co. uses a product of ours, METHOD/1, as a standard methodology for the conduct of client systems engagements throughout the world. Thus, as we received the example DSS engagements, we had a standard against which to identify the experimental methodology changes which were adaptively made on each engagement. Integration of these departures enables us to create a variation of METHOD/1 for guidance in the conduct of DSS engagements. The key differences in this DSS methodology to date provide the substance of what I have to report here. Each of the key differences found is discussed in turn.

1. *Emphasis Upon Strategic Issues and Planning.* DSS are not inexpensive. Thus, their cost justification is much more liable to be judged adequate when they are applied to key management concerns or critical success factors.[3] Any DSS engagement must specifically address the question of how it contributes to accomplishment of organization goals.

2. *Strong Link to Financial Management Process.* This process serves essentially to provide a common management communications vehicle. Wealth of the individual organization ownership shares is a fundamental criterion for profit-making organizations. Strategic financial planning, as we view it, uses an extended decomposition of the "DuPont formula" to relate plans and performance to their impact upon increases in the intrinsic value of the organization. This decomposition enables all key ratios of (financial) performance to be interrelated in specific known ways. Most DSS we have seen successfully operating include a representation of how the management option being explored would probably impact these performance measures.

3. *Cross-Functional Impact is Significant.* We find that most DSS environments are first created within a single function or strategic business unit. How-

ever, dealing with critical success factors and key financial measures as they do, many DSS extend into sister functions and/or strategic business units. It is our experience that even a unit-level DSS must relate itself to a corporate perspective which enables the impact on related operations to be reliably indicated. Otherwise, the DSS generates more conflict than support.

4. *DSS Environment and Applications are Distinct.* Separate, compatible design and implementation methodologies are required for

- "architecting" a DSS environment,
- establishing management processes for a DSS environment, and
- developing specific DSS applications.

5. *Managers Need Processes, Not Products.* DSS are living entities in the sense that they evolve with the client users and are driven by or responsive to the human portion of the man–machine system. We find that a DSS must externalize a manager's model of his situation in order to utilize the computer's power to advantage. It must also assist him in identifying and utilizing his assumptions. And the DSS must make available for the user's browsing and selective consumption the relevant current internal and external data/information. Therefore, a successful DSS will be one which is created with the client and turned over to him as a process which he can manage as an extension of his current decision-making processes, rather than as a special purpose tool which rigidly responds in a fixed way when activated.

6. *Clients Need a Means to Manage the DSS Environment.* DSS are first and foremost a means of communication among an organization's executives. Either they provide for lower management a structured way of dealing with specified problems (case A), or they provide a standardized set of substructures which serve to ensure the validity of custom assembled results among executive users (case B). Focusing upon the case B class of DSS, the client needs to endorse and maintain certain models and analytic routines which are standard components to be relied upon by all parties. Similarly, the client needs to create, maintain, and continuously update the contents of valid external as well as internal data bases. In addition, the client needs to provide for segregated personal data bases. These issues (and related ones of tool additions and advances) all need to be managed, and to be supported by appropriate technical talent. In turn, this implies a need for continued client training and for internal user consultants or coaches as catalysts for continued user acceptance of the DSS process.

7. *Prototyping is Vital in DSS Applications.* Even when designing a fixed structure of analyses and cyclic reports for the typical MIS transactions systems as efficiently as possible, application project durations and backlogs can become lengthy. A typical DSS user is psychologically engaged in his application on a real-time basis—else it will fail because it is not "his" application. The DSS tools

should be viewed as user producitivty aids. As such they provide the vital ability, within a DSS environment, to bring up pilot or prototype DSS applications very rapidly. Used in conjunction with dummy, poor, and/or partial data, such prototypes are dynamic design laboratories for the fundamental man–machine process being evaluated. No longer is an application the end result of laborious system/coding specifications. Rather, the bulk of the specifications are defined by the polished version of the currently used prototype. This inside-out, or in conventional terms "cart-before-the-horse," application design philosophy is not a weakness, but is a major strength of the DSS technology—when well managed. The use of prototyping is integral to the DSS design methodology not simply to gain efficiency by use of the user productivity aids of the DSS environment. Prototyping is primarily a means of increasing managerial efficiency by enabling the user to encompass his perceived problem-space within the man–machine system which evolves.

1.4. DSS Architecture

Geoffrion and Powers[4] provide an excellent discussion of management support systems. Figure 3 is adapted from their article.

Appropriately, the user-manager is central to the illustration. In addition, an end-user coach[5] is shown providing assistance as desired by the end user. Flows to and from the "real system" are shown on left—decision in, while issues and data on operations flow out. Four classes of data are shown at the bottom: personal, transactions, environmental, and transformed accounting/MIS information.

On the right we have the decision support system. The DSS data base is made up of refreshed subsets of the operational data and its derivations. The DSS

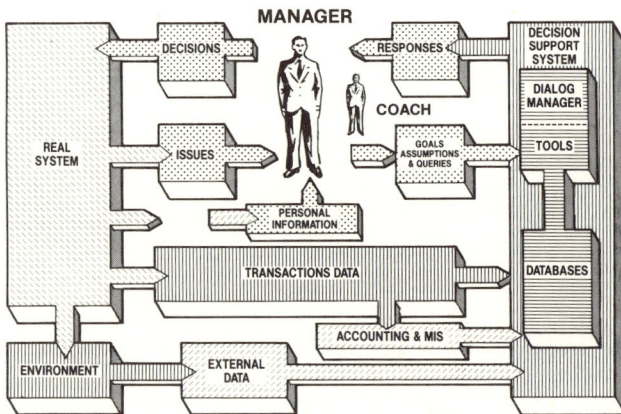

FIGURE 3. Generic DSS schematic.

also receives varied input from the user—responding to the human with ad hoc reports, model modifications, or solved results as appropriate.

Generally, the decision maker combines the DSS output with his other knowledge to generate decisions for the "real system" he is attempting to manage.

As we visualize DSS, there is an entire spectrum of support systems which fall within the overview just presented. On the one hand, a DSS model can be descriptive, in which case its utility is in gaining improved understanding about a relatively unstructured problem area. In contrast, a DSS model can be prescriptive, in which case its utility lies in suggesting a "best" response to the problem area under the assumed conditions. Some hybrid DSS applications will combine these two functions in linked or conglomerate systems.

1.5. Summary

We have reviewed a number of actual DSS installations. This pragmatic material, coupled with selective findings reported elsewhere, leads to these conclusions:

- DSS are based upon a different philosophy about the use of information.
- DSS are also developed differently than MIS.
- DSS must deal with the users' critical success factors in credible ways.
- DSS can be found throughout an organization, but the majority relate directly to strategic issues.

2. Organizations and CEOs

2.1. Organizational Background

Any active organization has a set of objectives. People who become organization members do so for mutual benefit. That implies greater collective goal attainment by means of interrelated work specialization. Management processes are put in place and evolve both to (1) enhance performance of individual roles and (2) coordinate activities of groups of individuals. The effectiveness of such management processes is measured by how they impact greater goal attainment toward objectives.

The description given above is idealized. It describes a "rational" model of organizational decision making. Following Huber[6] it should be noted that there are three additional models which occur in actual organizations. First, individuals and units within the organization behave in "political/competitive" ways to influence decisions to their own benefit. Second, organizational decisions can be made simply because the situation becomes "permissive" or even demanding of action on a given issue. Third, organizations "program" their activities, which can lead to habituated or enculturated decision making.

2.2. Executive Behavior

All four models of organizational decision making invoke selectively a variety of management processes within the organization. The management roles of individual decision makers are thus made up of management processes drawn from all four models of organizational decision-making environment. Mintzberg[7] found this behavior in his study of top executives who were each normally involved in a number of processes on a constant interrupt basis.

As Simon and others have suggested, Mintzberg found that chief (and other top) executive officers appear to evolve a set of programs for dealing with the issues they face repeatedly. They behave as though such programs are being invoked on an override basis as needed to handle stimuli.

The similarity between this CEO behavior and the man–machine process which we call a DSS is striking. So, too, is the similarity between each of these and what I referred to as management processes, evolving from all four descriptive models of organization decision making. If we can capitalize on these similarities, we can prescribe a way to derive meaningful strategic DSS information needs.

3. Management Processes Framework

3.1. Generic Top Management

Sprague[8] has adopted and extended Anthony's three levels of management: operational, tactical, and strategic/entrepreneurial for application to DSS issues.

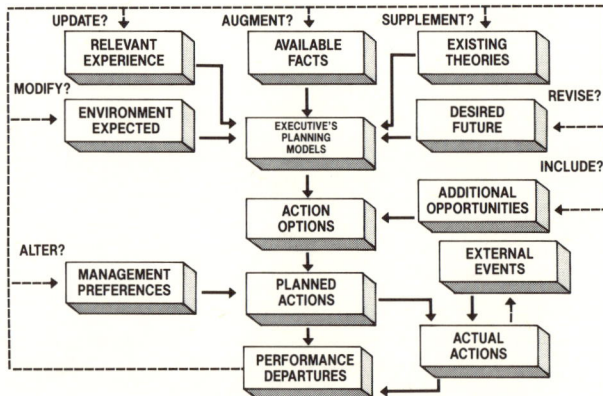

FIGURE 4. The nature of continuous planning.

OBJECTIVES

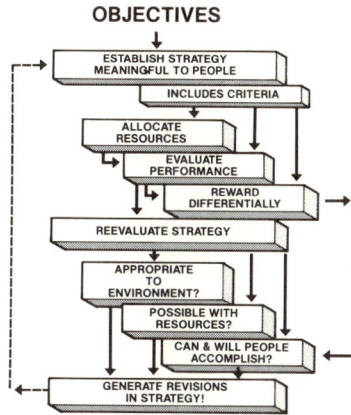

FIGURE 5. Continuing strategic task.

Both authors assert that a CEO spends most of his time planning or assembling planning information. On this premise I present Fig. 4, the nature of continuous planning, as a high-level conception of a CEO's business life. Those many specific things Mintzberg described the CEO doing can all be seen as a tributary to one or more of these basic planning issues.

Issues to be faced and information to be utilized by the CEO are identified. Regardless of what management processes he chooses to use, collectively they need to enable him and his organization to handle the myriad situations and actions that are implicit in Fig. 4.

We must assume that each CEO, as an individual surrounded by his team of individuals, will evolve a personalized set of management processes. For example, one CEO task is to "maintain an effective strategy." One man's translation of this task from the generic context of Fig. 4 is shown in Fig. 5. But our question of primary interest for information needs development is the total CEO activity set.

3.2. CEO Role Decomposition

Figure 6 is an attempt to capture the essence of the total CEO role. Again the weights put on each of the 36 elemental management processes of Fig. 6 are a function of the incumbent. The same might be said of the additional role aspects a given CEO might keep for his own ultimate actions.

In any case, Fig. 6 is taken as illustrative of the management process makeup of a typical chief executive role. Across the top the phases of "situation handling" are used to identify columns. If you view the CEO role as that of continued juggling of a variety of problem-solving activities, then these columns could be viewed as general stages in problem solving. Each of the rows represents a key role aspect of the CEO's total role in the organization.

CEO Role Aspects	Problems & Opportunities		Solutions & Responses		Policies & Operations	
	Scan Environment	Analyze Issues	Formulate Appropriately	Implement Selectively	Interpret	Evaluate
Evolve Organization's Objectives	Infer Limits Imposed by Society	Identify Desirable Objectives	Evaluate Alternative Sets of Objectives	Endorse Ambitiously Viable Set	Modify Organization Culture	Estimate Stakeholder Satisfaction
Maintain Effective Strategy	Study Suppliers Comps., Custs., & Industries	Appraise Threats & Potentials	Establish Performance Goals	Exchange Resources With Environment	Assign Resources for Results	Measure & Motivate Subordinates
Develop Human Resources	Identify Skills & Knowledge Available	Determine Talents Required	Perform Succession Planning	Conduct Training & Recruitment	Manage Compensation Systems	Monitor Employee Attitudes
Perform Financial Planning	Be Aware of Capital & Currency Markets	Perform Merger & Acquisition Activities	Integrate Capital Plans	Override Budgets as Appropriate	Direct Budgeting & Cash Planning	Compare Funds Slack & Lost Opportunities
Manage Value-Adding Activities	Predict Technology, Production & Sales	Understand Profitability by Unit	Maximize Present Value of Operations	Apply Contingency Scenarios	Specify Critical Success Factors	Highlight Extremes in Performance Results
Represent Firm to Stakeholders	Periodically Survey Each Group	Determine Leverages Available	Attempt to Modify Key Viewpoints	Cultivate Priority Influentials	Integrate Corporate Postures	Use External Consultants

FIGURE 6. CEO management processes.

At almost no time is the CEO concerned solely with one phase of one role aspect. Rather, he is typically and consciously simultaneously dealing with several key management processes at any one time. For example, in the midst of almost any substantive management process, he is probably also concerned with processes of motivating and measuring the person(s) with whom he happens to be dealing. In a deeper sense, this means that he is also almost always at least peripherally involved in the management process of succession planning as well.

Conceiving the CEO's role within the framework of Fig. 6 does not imply that the CEO has the luxury of dealing with the problem-solving stages of any one key role in the given conventional sequential order. Quite the contrary. It illustrates that a CEO is not only functioning in multiple roles, but also is simultaneously working many of the theoretically distinct problem-solving phases even within any one role aspect.

Even so, the decomposition of the CEO role suggested in Fig. 6 is useful. It enables the incumbent and his working associates to recognize the many elemental management processes in which the CEO has to participate to some degree. This, in turn, enables both (all) parties to focus more sharply on the required interactions/communications in working with the CEO.

Returning to the premise that the CEO is the central figure of this organization, one other point needs to be made. Each one of the representative 36 elemental CEO management processes of Fig. 6 is simply one link in one or more integrative management processes. Each of the other elements in each integrative management process will usually contribute to defining some management aspect of other roles at other levels in the organization. The combination of the CEO's role aspect (horizontal in Fig. 6) and integrative (backward into the organization layers behind Fig. 6) management processes serves to define how the CEO directs and controls the organization.

The very act of making that control structure explicit, and perhaps modifying it, can lead to both efficiency and effectiveness gains for the organization. Starting from the broad concept of Fig. 4 to create a specific, personalized version of Fig. 6 also enables the organization to identify better the many varied opportunities to employ DSS. Given such a survey, a CEO is in a position to selectively implement DSS to extend his and his team's judgments through improved analysis and communications on vital issues.

4. Information Needs Derivation

A firm basis for identifying fundamental information needs for an organization as a whole is one major result of this management processes approach.

The 36 elemental CEO processes of Fig. 6 can be taken as the top face of a cube. Then the successive layers of that cube can be regarded as the top, middle, and first-line management levels (after Anthony and Sprague).

Such a cube contains the supportive management processes to be carried out at each management level. Carried to extreme detail, it would be possible to describe all management roles in the organization within such a cube. Viewed this way, the detailed cube becomes a database containing each key job description in the organization. Such a data base chains job descriptions together as necessary to form each of the organization's important management processes.

4.1. One Example Process

Consider the CEO process "integrate capital plans." Viewing only those elemental management processes which chain with this CEO process we see Fig. 7

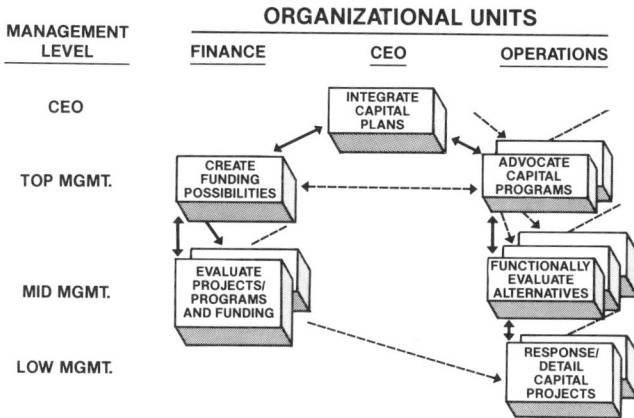

FIGURE 7. CEO management process support.

within the total cube. At the top is the CEO's process. Next are the essential supporting processes of the chief financial officer and of each operating group chief officer. The financial officer has one or more analyst-managers, here ranked as middle management. These individuals apply corporate criteria to projects and programs and to capital pool management, attempting to clarify alternative options for the decision makers.

Shown to the right, in each of the operating units, middle-level managers serve to relate specific capital projects, as detailed by lower-level project management, to major capital thrusts as advocated by their group chief executive.

In all cases, flows are shown to be both ways. This reflects the fact that the operating groups are competing with each other for vital resources. Yet at the same time, the organization as a whole is trying to determine how big a pool of resources to allocate now in the context of long-term financial strategies.

A process such as that of Fig. 7 must be recast as a cyclic project performed under a timetable before it can be proceduralized as routine corporate activity. Similarly, the process so stated can be extended to an information inventory and flow definition at the same time. Given the particulars of how each manager wants or is directed to perform his part of the overall process, the common data needs and the specific information addition/creation methods and timetables can be detailed.

We must note that the management process framework presented here (Fig. 6 and 7) is illustrative in nature. *It is not prescriptive.* That is, it is not set forth as being "the answer." Rather Fig. 6 and 7 show how a CEO in an organization might conceive and interpret his job for a period of time. The interpretation of Fig. 4 in a particular context results in a custom definition of the management process framework.

4.2. An Industry Case Study

This case study is drawn from a firm in the food distribution industry.[9] The management processes framework outlined here was not explicity used by that firm. However, the illustrative DSSs of the case study will show the utility of the framework. In each case a DSS was born of end-user needs. Each resulted in the identification of decision supporting information needs and the contingent structure for supporting man as decision maker in the man–machine environment.

As selected DSSs which were set up in that firm are described, the firm's successful evolution into a broader, higher-profit set of businesses will become obvious.

The firm in question provided foodstuffs and allied products to some 1800 supermarkets in about two dozen states. From a single distribution warehouse entity, the firm has grown, largely by acquisitions, to a complex of eleven warehouses. Facilities integral to or nearby four of the grocery warehouses were used in a sideline institutional foods business. Numerous services (accounting, site location, design, construction, finance, training, etc.) were provided on a fee basis to both sets of end customers. In addition, two of the warehouse locations had gradually created specialized food processing or packaging operations as satellite high-margin profit centers.

This organization operated with a basic functional structure. Line operations were directed through a combination of divisions and multiple-level subsidiaries. Most of the retail supermarkets served used one of six regional nameplates or logos such as IGA. Numerous private brands competed in the 1800-store system with the national manufacturers' brands.

Historically, acquisitions had been made on a highly personal "management chemistry" basis. Pressure for change of this management style came about when the firm listed itself on the NYSE. The first DSS to be noted here was an immediate result.

Financial performance objectives were formally established for the firm with the board of directors. Simultaneously, a few models were built and some selected databases were established for the purposes of (1) creating baseline financial planning projections of the firm's existing operations, (2) studying the firm's potential future with any given acquisition, and (3) portraying the impact of such a merger on each set of shareholders in a variety of measures to facilitate actual merger negotiation communications. The databases were for firms in closely related distribution industries.

To management, the most startling initial result from this DSS was that the firm simply could not meet its financial performance goals and remain in its basic industry. The low real industry growth caused the return-on-investment to decrease with time under the existing policies and practices. Several things happened as a result.

First, the firm's capital planning methods were thoroughly revised to rationalize them and make them a tool for all management rather than the domain solely of the financial vice-president. The need to become aggressive rather than merely do better became apparent to all for the first time.

Second, productivity improvement potentials for the firm's basic business were sought. The objective of course was to allow a greater share of earnings to be reinvested in the basic business, at acceptable standards. Several more DSS, to be discussed below, came out of this stimulation.

Third, an active search was begun to identify allied businesses into which some of the firm's newly defined unreinvestable earnings could be put.

Under the category of productivity improvements in the existing business, several logistic matters were attacked. The *physical distribution* system (company fleets) was modeled and changed. Warehouse territories were changed. Transcontinental supplier backhauls were integrated across the firm's several operating units. Food processing products and locations were restructured to lower the net cost at retail and to penetrate formerly diseconomic markets.

Outbound freight loads were put on a selective cycle basis which evened the day-to-day warehousing workload. Store resupplying was improved by keeping track of store inventories at the warehouses. Such data could then be used to generate compatible picking lists and truck route dispatching even including the individual stores' special orders.

One of the more notable DSS to come of this productivity push was the *interactive site selection* tool. Retail food stores typically have a five- to seven-year life before major renovation, enlargement, or replacement becomes an economic necessity. An individual store's ability to generate retail (and therefore wholesale) profits is a function of many attributes. Location, access, market socioeconomics, number and mix of departments, pricing policy and strategies, size, and personnel all have measurable impact.

Beyond these store level variables, there are the competitive issues of store image in the metropolitan area (Kroger's vs. A&P vs. Safeway, etc.). This introduces the market area advertising and aggregate-volume-dependent merchandising variables.

In this firm, every Thursday was given over to "storing meetings." Typically, most officers not out of town participated. A carefully created analysis of each retail-owner site location store size-styling was presented for go–no-go decision at these meetings. The primary focus was the specific financing arrangement which would or would not be made jointly by the retailer and the wholesaler. Also at issue implicitly in such decisions was the expected change in the wholesaler's share of the metropolitan market and the negative impact potential upon nearby retailers also served by the same wholesaler.

The DSS built and heavily used by management in this context was SLASH (site location and sizing heuristic). Databases of continuing market studies, consumer research studies, industry shipments data, warehouse operations, and retail operations were constructed for that model. The expected owner's financials for three different periods of store life cycle were generated. The specific impact upon sister stores was estimated, and the net impact for the wholesaler was also represented.

This system usually resulted in the evolution of a mutually satisfactory and better "storing" decision being made much more rapidly and with less uncertainty due to the greater number of alternatives which were explored. It is interesting to note that average store size rose dramatically using this tool. It is also worth mentioning that for the first time a true metropolitan campaign for engineering profitable gains into the metropolitan market storing plans could be constructed. In addition, it was accomplished in the context of integrated capital planning.

A wholly unexpected and highly profitable by-product was that SLASH was also used as a consulting service for noncompeting supermarkets. Later, this same DSS model was used for retail outlet decision making outside the food industry as well.

The existing minor business, *institutional foodservice*, was evaluated, centralized and expanded both by internal development and acquisition. This, too, was guided by models and databases in much the same way as was the primary supermarket business.

In addition to all these moves which were aimed at improving the existing businesses, *new business arenas* were explored. Obvious areas of familiarity (based primarily upon limited departments within foodstores) were soft goods, hard goods, restaurants, and primary food processing.

Today, that firm is a major factor in three additional, separately organized and operated distribution businesses. In each case the business is developed and managed analogously to the way in which the original business is now managed. These three added businesses are (1) a discount housewares–home goods chain, (2) a youth clothing chain, and (3) a chain of family-center supplies stores.

All three were entered by acquisition. All three have been remodeled and expanded in both market penetration and extent. Note that because of these sister distribution businesses, the firm is in a much more powerful position. Not only can it now bargain for much better space within major shopping centers under development, but also the firm can and does develop its own medium- and small-size shopping centers featuring itself as the primary tenant.

This once unsophisticated executive team, strongly motivated by the need for self-preservation, accomplished a lot. They

- greatly improved their basic business;
- created a viable business from a former stepchild;
- added three additional very similar businesses; and
- capitalized on the synergies among their new cluster of businesses.

Throughout this self-development period the firm was constantly modifying, replacing, and augmenting many of its management processes. Management was doing this, in part, through a variety of DSS. Some of their DSS applications were primarily of a project nature. Others, such as SLASH, were a wholly new set of integrative management processes. Still others developed whole new roles for a level of management—both marketing and finance gained new capabilities to perform their functions more productively.

5. Summary

When the generic continuous planning concept of Fig. 4 is used to generate a specific management process framework such as Fig. 6, then the power of this management processes approach to DSS and associated information needs becomes most apparent. The matrix of Fig. 6 becomes three dimensional. Each additional layer of the matrix shown in Fig. 6 displays more of the lower-level individual and collective management processes which bring life to the client organization. That was illustrated for one CEO issue in Fig. 7.

This method of inventorying an organization's elemental management processes ensures that key role and integrative management processes, together with their interrelationships, will be surfaced. This, in turn, provides a sound basis for ranking or grouping an organization's many potential DSS applications into a beneficial development sequence. Significantly, the information needs of managers throughout the organization are greatly clarified.

Perhaps most vital of all, this method greatly raises the probability that the resulting DSS will be perceived by management as an extension of themselves, rather than as a restraint. In other words, through careful attention to key management process identification, a sound basis is provided for a firm to move from EDP/MIS to MIS/DSS self-guidance.

References

1. 'What if' help for management, *Business Week* **January 21,** 73 (1980).
2. Classification of decision support systems, Systems Development E50-100, 1981, Datapro Research Corporation, Delran, New Jersey.
3. Chief executives define their own data needs, *Harvard Business Rev.* **March-April,** 81 (1979).
4. Management support systems, *Wharton Mag.,* (3), Spring (1981).
5. End user computing setup, John F. Rockart. Presented at Conference on Information Systems, The Society for Management Information Systems, Boston, 1981.
6. G. P. HUBER, Decision support systems . . . , in *Decision Making,* G. R. Ungson and D. N. Branstein, Eds., Kent Publishing Co., Boston, 1981.
7. H. MINTZBERG, Planning on the left side and managing on the right, *Harvard Business Rev.* **July-August,** 49 (1976).
8. R. H. SPRAGUE, Jr. A framework for the development of DSS, *MIS Q.* **4** (4), 1 (1980).
9. B. E. WYNNE, Keys to successful management science modeling, *INTERFACES* **9,** (4), 69 (1979).

10

THE ORGANIZATIONAL DIMENSIONS OF MANAGEMENT INFORMATION SYSTEMS IMPLEMENTATION
CASE STUDIES IN SINGAPORE AND INDONESIA

Juzar Motiwalla

1. Introduction

This paper has two objectives. Firstly, it illustrates organizational character-istics typical of major governmental institutions in Singapore and Indonesia. Sec-ondly, it reinforces the importance of understanding these organizational charac-teritsics before attempting to prescribe a management information system (MIS) for these institutions.

A priority program in Singapore is the provision of industrial infrastructure in order to support the right investment climate for multinational companies. To provide this infrastructure a profit-oriented quasi government institution has been set up. The organization develops land and multistoried factories in Singapore, which are leased to foreign and local industrialists. It conducts the planning, design, supervision of construction, and maintenance of its properties, although the actual construction is contracted out. Several departments, including Pur-chases, Marketing, Design, and Technical, have to coordinate on each property development project (see Fig. 1 for an organization chart). The environment is dynamic, with worldwide demand for industrial property.

JUZAR MOTIWALLA • Institute of Systems Science, National University of Singapore, Singapore.

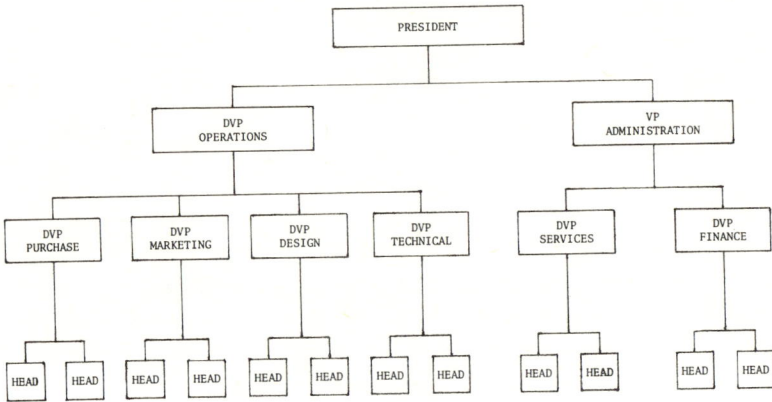

FIGURE 1. Organization chart of property development.

A priority program in Indonesia is the transmigration program, which desires to meet important national socioeconomic objectives through government-assisted large-scale movement of agricultural people from heavily overpopulated islands to organized settlements on underpopulated outer islands. The purpose of the program is to improve the standard of living of the transmigrants, lessen population pressures in the areas of egress, contribute to overall regional development, achieve a more balanced distribution of population, and create equitable development in Indonesia. Each project to transmigrate people to a specific area involves a considerable number of interrelated activities, including settler relocation, land clearing, site preparation, and village and community development. Although there is a Ministry of Manpower and Transmigration, in fact the project development is a complex interfacing of the joint efforts of at least ten Ministries, including Internal Affairs, Public Works, Agriculture, and Communications.

Unfortunately, most transmigration projects have not been successful. As a result, the Government of Indonesia, in conjunction with the World Bank and UNDP, had identified a specific transmigration project for which a project management and information system was to be designed and implemented. This project envisioned the move of 30,000 families from impoverished and ecologically threatened areas of Java and Bali to four sites in the province of Jambi in Sumatra. Figure 2 provides the organization chart for the project.

Table 1 provides a comparison of the organizational characteristics of the two institutions, which are elaborated on in this paper. These characteristics were investigated in the context of two management activities—strategic planning and project scheduling and control.

2. Strategic Planning

2.1. Property Development

The Singaporean organization faced a dynamic environment, and demand for the properties that it developed was mainly influenced by world economic trends, with the underlying assumption that the ASEAN region remained politically stable. Like any business organization it was important that sufficient inventory of developed property be available to meet fluctuations in demand. However, in the event of unforseen economic recession in tbe developed countries or political imbalances in the region, slackening property demand may result in high inventory levels, leading to high interest payments on loans without matching revenues. In contrast, at the time of this study, an unanticipated strengthening of demand had led to increased workload and early deadlines.

The organization had faced severe demand, inventory, and cost fluctuations in the past which had resulted in productivity and morale problems. The inability to anticipate these fluctuations could be attributed to the lack of a strategic planning system in the organization. Since development of property has a long lead time, the importance of systematic and careful planning was paramount. However, there was only a minimal attempt at planning, both long-term and short-

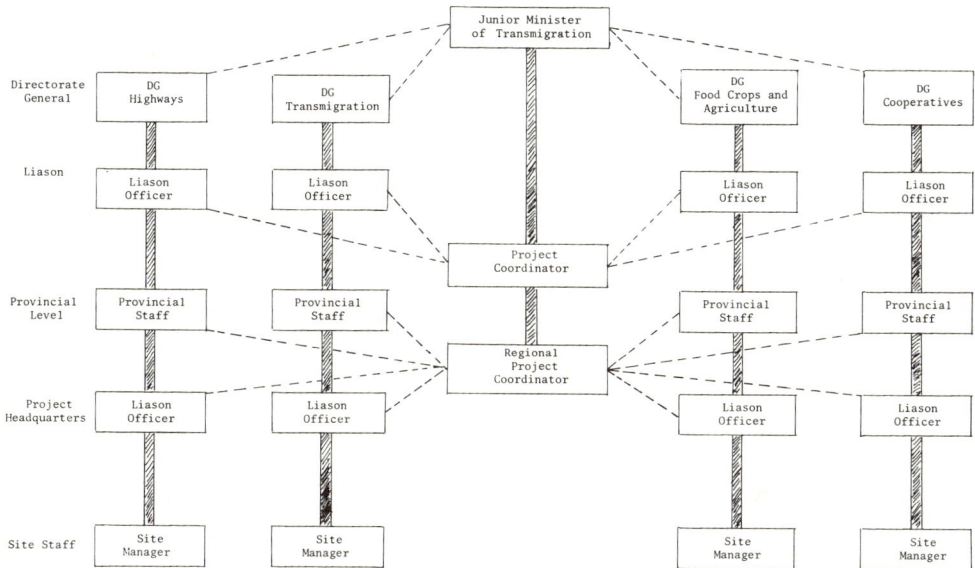

FIGURE 2. Indonesia transmigration project organization chart.

TABLE 1
Comparison of Organizational Characteristics

Organizational characteristics	Singaporean institution	Indonesian institution
Organization Structure	Single organization, departmentalized by function	Interorganizational, each organization decentralized geographically
Environment Type	Dynamic, influenced by economic trends in developed countries	Sociopolitical conditions in Indonesia
Decision making 1. Management style	Highly bureaucratic	"Musyawarah sampai mufakat" (consensus through consultation)
2. Reaction to environment	No formal scanning of environment, management by crisis	No formal scanning of environment
3. Management control	Structured	Lax
Coordination 1. Lateral linkages	Task force, one-way directives	Poor at project implementation level
2. Interunit communication	Formalized, little formal interaction	Little formal or informal flow
Information systems 1. Information system	Minimal computerization, considerable data collection but little structured analysis	No computerization, inadequate data collection
2. Implementation	Support for routine applications, but resistance to decision support systems	Low at all management levels
3. Constraint	Scarcity of technologically skilled manpower, though junior analysts may be trained rapidly	Lack of skilled manpower and teleprocessing difficulty for distributed systems

term, by top management. Planning meetings were only held on an ad hoc basis by the President with the Deputy Vice Presidents of Design and Technical.

The design of an effective strategic planning system required the design of an appropriate MIS. It was proposed that such an MIS for this organization would involve corporate and environmental modeling, with particular attention to economic research. However, there were two major organizational problems facing the implementation of this MIS:

(1) There was widespread scepticism on the part of several of the top managers to the idea of decision support. It was felt that an intuitive assessment of the environment and its effect on the organization would suffice.

(2) The institutionalization of the MIS function for strategic planning had serious implications for the power structure within the organization. The formalization of the planning process would have required the involvement of more top executives than the three who currently met on major decisions. Furthermore, the setting up of an important strategic planning section, reporting at a high level, would have meant the relocation and upgrading of the Research and Statistics Unit which reported to the Deputy Vice President of Services.

2.2. Transmigration Program

At the strategic level the main issues considered by the Ministers and their Directors-General were socioeconomic in nature. These issues included the following:

a. Overall project planning and scheduling;
b. Budget allocations;
c. Types of food crops to be cultivated on specific land opened up;
d. Appropriate target incomes of transmigrants, farm size, and village structure;
e. Government support to transmigrants; and
f. Interests of local population in settlement areas.

Typically strategic issues were decided at a meeting of all Directors-General of transmigration-related ministries. The Indonesian model for governmental decision making is one of discussion until a consensus is apparent, termed "musyawarah sampai mufakat." To persons from a different cultural background, this may appear to be an impossible way to run a government. Meetings are often protracted and decisions take a long time to reach. Values easily get intertwined with technical information at such meetings.

3. Project Scheduling and Control

3.1. Property Development

The architectural and engineering design for property development was carried out by the Design and Technical departments. The major work on each development project was handled by these two departments. The organizational climate within each department is represented in Table 2. The climate was assessed with

TABLE 2
Departmental Climate—Perceptual Measures

	Purchases	Marketing	Design	Technical	Services	Finance
Higher motivation	×	×				×
Lesser bureaucracy		×			×	×
Higher participation in decision making	×	×				×
Better leadership		×			×	×
Lower interdepartmental conflict	×	×				×
Higher departmental effectiveness	×	×				×

a 12-page questionnaire administered to 316 professionals in the organization. The questionnaire measured the perceptions of respondents on several structure, process, and performance variables.

It is interesting to note that both the Design and Technical department professionals (mostly architects and engineers) perceived lower motivation, as well as higher bureaucracy, lesser participation, and poorer leadership in their departments. In particular, analysis of the questionnaire responses indicated that Design professionals rated Technical as the department with which they had the greatest conflict, and similarly Technical professionals rated their conflict highest with Design.

With the increase in property demand, and consequent increase in workload for the professionals in Technical and Design, a good project planning and control system was needed. To ensure efficiency in project implementation, PERT networks utilizing a project data base were desirable. However, successful implementation of this MIS technique had several limitations posed by organizational characteristics:

(1) Successful project planning using PERT often utilizes a bottom-up approach with senior professionals being involved with management in identifying project tasks and task durations. Such an approach would have been quite a contrast to the management style present, which did not encourage participation in decision making.

(2) Effective project control using PERT not only requires structured feedback on task status, but also requires the communication of problem areas, and consequent revision of the PERT network based on problem resolution. For the two departments, resolution of problems was difficult at the professional level because of their high interdepartmental conflict. The high bureaucratic environment also led to rules being imposed on the channels of communication to be used

when coordination problems arose. The channel took the form of an inverted U, with problems going up through formal hierarchical channels to the managers, who would then liaise with their counterparts in the other department. This process lengthened the time for problem resolution and exacerbated conflict.

3.2. Transmigration Program

Each site development in the transmigration program consisted of several subprojects, including settler movement, site investigation and design, land clearing and site preparation, farm development and settler relocation, agricultural support services, and construction of community facilities, including schools, subhealth centers, places of worship, and other public buildings. A large number of agencies were involved, including the National Development Agency and the Directorates General of Highways, Transmigration, Food Crops Agriculture, Cooperatives, Agrarian Affairs, and Estates.

An MIS was then required for monitoring physical/financial progress, for coordination of work programs, and for budget coordination. An MIS was also needed for socio-economic monitoring because the final measure of success or failure of the transmigration program was whether the new settlements became permanent, self-sufficient, and viable communities providing better lives for their inhabitants.

The objective of the MIS was to develop a systematized timely information flow among all agencies concerned with the transmigration program. The major problems to operationalization of this objective were as follows:

(1) There were abundant reporting systems already in existence, put in place by each agency. However, the data collected at site by each agency were not uniform, and it was neither adequate nor comprehensive for effective monitoring of the transmigration program. Furthermore, information was generally not freely volunteered to another agency. It would have been politically difficult to establish a standard reporting system for all agencies. One possibility would have been to organize independent data collection, but this would have resulted in considerable duplication of effort to obtain the massive amounts of data required.

(2) Vertical information flows within each agency were characterized by untimeliness. There are several levels through which information had to flow. Figure 2 indicates the flow from site through project headquarters, provincial office, and Jakarta office before it reached the Directorate General. Lack of computerization resulted in both slow transmission of information as well as considerable filtering at each level to produce the summary reports requested at the next higher level.

(3) A pronounced feature of the Indonesian bureaucracy was the strength of its informal communication channels. These were partly a result of the necessity for bypassing excessive rules and regulations, partly a means of expediting work

which would otherwise go through formal hierarchical channels, and partly a reflection of the Indonesian culture.

4. Discussion

The effects of organizational characteristics on organizational communication have been explored by a number of researchers. Communication distortion and blockage is maximized in lateral relationships, where conflict is particularly present owing to greatest specialization and interdepartmental rivalry.[1] A bureaucratic environment tends to increase distortion of upward communication.[2] Although information that reaches decision makers is often modified or distorted,[3,4] such distortion usually involves omission, differential selection, and preferential placement rather than prevarication.[5]

Saunders[6] argues strongly that the success of the implementation of an MIS is dependent on consideration and appropriate adaptation of the systems to organizational workflows, information networks, and power structures. An MIS may be resisted because it may significantly shift the distribution of power in organizations.[7] The organizational impact of MIS on centralization and decentralization has been much discussed.[8] Furthermore, the decision maker may have problems adjusting to MIS because of new requirements for conceptual thinking,[9] diminished individual discretion,[10] or changed interpersonal work patterns.[11]

The problem that remains is one of identifying the strategies to ensure minimization of communication distortion and maximization of MIS implementation success.[12] The identification of such strategies, which involve the design of an organization structure and management control system in conjunction with a management information system, is bound to vary with different organizational contexts. It is useful then to understand how each specific context has been shaped.

The organizational characteristics of governmental institutions in Singapore and Indonesia illustrated in this paper have their roots in the political, cultural, and managerial systems which have evolved over time in each of these countries. The highly bureaucratic environment and the resistance to management systems change in the property developer are characteristics inherited from the Singapore civil service. The top managers in the organization are all former civil servants. Organizational conflict is also furthered by differences between an old guard, which has undergone tough economic trials during Singapore's growth, and a new guard, which has only tasted the affluent results of growth and demanded greater participation in decision making.

In Indonesia, the traditional method of major project implementation is to have different political agencies interface in the development effort. For instance, in the transmigration program, the Ministry of Transmigration is not directly responsible for "executing" the program, but is the coordinator of the executing agencies. This ensures that the careful alignment of power, particularly through budget allocations, remains. However, this is at the expense of a centralized, efficient project management and information system.

Part of the reason for the untimeliness and distortions of information transmission lies in the poor performance at the lower levels of the Indonesian administrative bureaucracy. Poor performance, which may take the shape of incompetence, unwillingness to take responsibility, and corruption, may be rooted in broader societal causation such as an inadequate educational system.[13] Finally, the cultural importance attached to consensus decision making is deeply entrenched, and is a practice adopted even at the village level.

References

1. H. R. WILENSKY, *Organizational Intelligence,* Basic Books, New York, 1967.
2. J. C. ATHANASSIADES, The distortion of upward communication in hierarchical organizations, *Acad. Manage. J.* **16** (2), 207–226 (1973).
3. G. T. ALLISON, *Essence of Decision: Explaining the Cuban Missile Crisis,* Little, Brown, Boston, 1971.
4. G. P. HUBER, Organizational decision making—The state of our knowledge, Presented at the *34th Annual Meeting of the Academy of Management,* Seattle, 1974.
5. C. A. O'REILLY III and K. H. ROBERTS, Information filtration in organization: Three experiments, *Organ. Behav. Hum. Performance* **11** (2), 253–265 (1974).
6. C. S. SAUNDERS, Management information systems, communications, and departmental power: An integrative model, *Acad. Manage. Rev.* **6** (3), 431–442 (1981).
7. P. EIN-DOR and E. SEGEV, Organizational context and the success of management information systems, *Manage. Sci.* **24,** 1064–1077 (1978).
8. F. W. McFARLAN, R. L. NOLAN, and D. P. NORTON, *Information Systems Administration,* Holt, Rinehart & Winston, New York, 1973.
9. C. ARGYRIS, Management information systems: The challenge to rationality and emotionality, *Manage. Sci.* **17** (6), B275–B292 (1971).
10. E. MUMFORD and H. SACKMAN, Eds, *Human Choice and Computers,* New York: American Elsevier, New York, 1975, pp. 325–342.
11. G. W. DICKSON and J. K. SIMMONS, The behavioral side of MIS, *Bus. Horizons,* 1–13 (1970).
12. M. J. GIBZBERG, Implementation as a process of change: A framework and empirical study, Report CISR-13, Center for Information Systems Research, MIT, 1975.
13. D. HADISUMARTO and P. SIEGEL, The optimum strategy Matrix and Indonesian administrative reforms, in A. F. LEEMANS, Ed. *The Management of Change in Government,* Martinus Nijhoff, The Hague, 1976.

DATABASE SYSTEMS

DATABASE DESIGN FOR DECISION SUPPORT SYSTEMS

Daniel T. Lee

1. Introduction

Adequate information is the prerequisite of decision making. Modern decision makers need internal operational data and external intelligence in their decision-making process. Current information-producing mechanisms, however, basically aim at providing static and operational information which are only fit for structured tasks. According to Refs. 34, 3 and 56, the typical tasks for decision makers are either semistructured or unstructured. Therefore, a new approach is required to face this new challenge.[11]

Prevalent literature and existing methodologies in DSS development are either conceptually conceived or rigidly structured. The former emphasizes personal decision making, cognitive structure of the decision makers, and often stops at the conceptual description of DSS. The latter is biased toward rigid structure and static development of DSS. The former conveys some vague ideas without indicating how to implement these ideas, while the latter, though more concrete, is only suitable for stable and structured tasks. As mentioned earlier, the tasks faced by a modern decision maker are largely either unstructured or semistructured. Therefore, we may conclude that the existing methodologies in DSS development are inadequate to meet the needs of a modern decision maker.

The purpose of this paper is to examine the existing technologies in DSS development and to develop a new approach in DSS design with special emphasis on database design because, as Donovan[27] said, database systems lie at the heart of decision support tools.

In the first part of this paper, the fundamentals of decision support systems (DSS) will be discussed to lay down a framework in the DSS development. In the

DANIEL T. LEE • School of Business Administration, University of Wisconsin-Milwaukee, P.O. Box 742, Milwaukee, Wisconsin 53201.

latter part, the database design methodologies will be fully covered with an eye on how to fit it into the overall DSS constructs. A practical example will be given to exemplify the basic concepts in merging the database design methodologies and DSS development into a unified whole. A prototype will be used to demonstrate the unified methodology which is not only theoretically feasible, but can be physically implemented.

2. The Basics of DSS

2.1. The Background

Decision support systems (DSS) were born from the natural evolutionary advancement of data processing.[63] They are basically used to enhance the knowledge workers in their decision-making activities. Over the past years, electronic data processing (EDP) has made contributions to the automation of paper work and labor saving, but has been fragmented and applied only at the operational level of the organization. Redundancy and inconsistency are considerable.

Management information systems (MIS) were named for their integration. They emphasize providing information for the decision makers. Unfortunately, they fail to fulfill their promises due to technological constraints. They usually only provide standardized periodic reports which are either irrelevant or indirectly relevant to the needs of the decision makers.

There are many incentives for improving decision making because (1) the payoff for improving the knowledge workers' productivity is high, and (2) the knowledge workers always try to take advantage of technological advancement for enhancing their performance. For example, owing to the technological progress in time-sharing systems, mini- and microcomputers, data communication systems, distributed systems, and database systems, the knowledge workers can personally interface with computers, models, and data in their decision-making process. This increases their productivity through such supportive tools and the result is thus called decision support systems. The main function of the DSS is to support the decision makers in their decision making activities, not just to take care of routine transactional processing.

Edelman[28] defines "knowledge workers" as all supervisory personnel plus all those who hold policy-making positions. The knowledge workers are supported by information workers. The present author believes that the knowledge workers should include analytical personnel who function as the intermediaries of the decision makers because the decision makers are busy and have no patience to sit down and interact with the computers.

2.2. The Characteristics of DDS

Morton[50] first defined DSS as interactive computer-based systems that help decision makers utilize data and models to solve unstructured problems. This definition was criticized as too restrictive, since few actual systems can completely satisfy it. Sprague and Carlson[56] adopt a "characteristics approach" for defining DSS. This approach indicates that DSSs tend to be aimed at the less well-structured problems, attempt to combine the use of models with database systems, focus on ease of use by noncomputer personnel, and emphasize flexibility–adaptability to accommodate changes in the environment. They further differentiate the DSS from MIS and EDP by delineating the EDP as data oriented, the MIS as information oriented, and DSS as decision oriented.

From these characteristics, it is true that DSS represents a natural evolutionary advancement, but it will not replace either one of them, nor merely aim exclusively at top decision makers. Therefore, we may fairly conclude that DSS seems to comprise a class of information system that interacts with the operational database, analytical models, and decision makers (including their intermediaries) to support the decision-making activities.

2.3. The Basic Components

In accordance with the basic characteristics discussed in the previous section, DSS constitutes a class of its own and requires a new combination of technology. Basically, it requires four components to satisfy three basic capabilities, the data, the model and the dialogue.

In the dialogue component, the dialog and query capability represent the whole system. Ease of use is their main concern. It consists of the end users, the terminals, and the software systems.[56,8] It is supposed to be able to support various input and output formats, a variety of dialog styles, and the knowledge base of the end users.

In the data component, it becomes the most important component of the four because adequate information is the prerequisite of decision making. Donovan said: "database systems lie at the heart of decision support tools." It is also the major concern of this paper. This data component comprises operational databases and DSS databases. The former is the transactional databases or the constitutional databases while the latter embraces model databases, derived databases, computational and statistical routines.

As to the model component, it consists of analytical model databases, computational and statistical routines. Actually, this component may be embedded within the operational databases or the derived databases as long as they can be incorporated with the main databases or the derived databases.[57]

The last component is the software systems which encompass the database management system, the model base management system, and other subroutine software systems. Figure 1 depicts the architecture of the DSS. It consists of the constitutional databases, the DSS databases, the derivation routines, and the software systems. It interacts with the outside world for obtaining its inputs. Its outputs in turn affect the firm itself and the outside world. The end users interact the DSS for obtaining information for decision making. Within the DSS, the constitutional databases obtain data from the data sources (internal or external) for inputs, and interact with the derivation routines through software systems for constructing the DSS databases. The DSS databases can also be constructed directly by obtaining data from the data sources through the software routines.[37,56]

Among the four components, the data component is the major component which acts as an integrating mechanism for the whole system. In order to execute this integrating role, the data component needs a new approach with a new combination of technologies.[56] Donovan[27] also indicated: "the characteristics of the problems associated with decision support are different from those to which database systems and other computation technologies have usually been applied in the past." Therefore, it is quite clear that a new approach with additional technologies is crucial for DSS development. Unfortunately, it is still not clear how to integrate

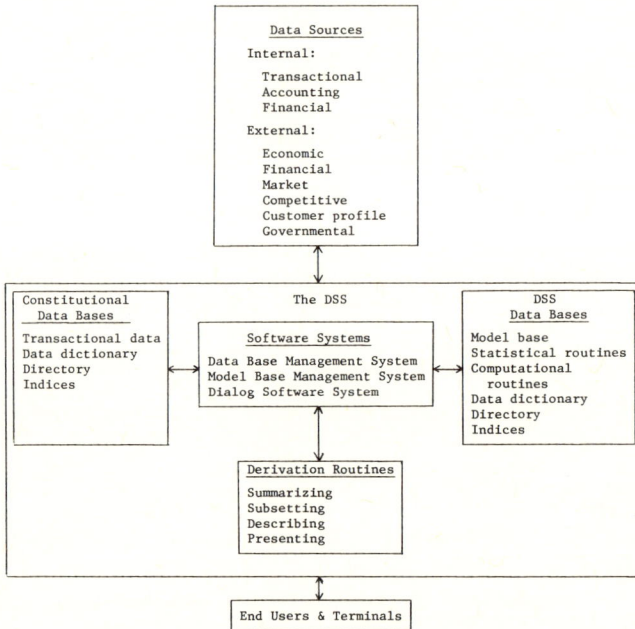

FIGURE 1. The architecture of decision support systems.

the various components into a unified whole. The purpose of this paper is to trace the existing technologies in DSS development with a special emphasis on database design, and to develop such a new approach with a new combination of technologies for DSS development. Before discussing the new approach, a brief review of the existing technologies in DSS development is essential for us to gain insight into the problem. It will be the topic of the following section.

3. DSS Design Methodologies

According to Lee,[39,40] currently there are generally two approaches in DSS design, the application-specific approach (ASA)[4,33,50] and the integrated MIS approach (IMA).[55,28,53,24,11,10] The existing DSS are basically based on the ASA approach, which has dominated the DSS development in the recent decade because of historical and technological reasons.

Historically, the MIS fails to live up to its promise; some knowledge workers want to improve their productivities by exploiting the existing new technologies and applying them to specific applications. Besides, the MIS personnel are busy in producing standard reports and have no interest or expertise in DSS development.

Technologically, the DSS represents a new invention. It requires a new combination of technologies which are basically nonexistent. Therefore, nobody knows how to integrate the various parts into a unified whole. Some inquisitive and ingenious knowledge workers always try to take advantage of technological advancement for enhancing their job performance and applying them to specific application areas.

The ASA approach, however, only tries to improve the efficiency and effectiveness in a specific application. It fails to take advantage of the existing information constructs such as the MIS which generally already exist in an organization. As Keen[23] indicated: "Improvisation, informality, and temporary project groups have substantial side-effects. They reinvent the wheel biweekly and are tangential to the ongoing activities of the organization. They lack economies of scale and do not draw on specialized capabilities and procedures." De and Sen[24] also criticized this approach: "the DSS designed under the ASA approach is not general. It will be more economical if the DSS supports multiple processes."

Since the ASA approach is neither efficient nor economical, development of an integrated MIS approach (IMA) was called for. It has the advantage of a total system concept which requires that everything is related to everything else. This would, of course, be desirable, but the question is how it could be achieved. With current technology, it represents the goal in DSS development, but is beyond our current capability.

In this transitional period, a step in compromise between the ideal and the doable is needed. Lee[39,40] suggested a unified approach instead for DSS development. It is based on a contingent view which moves down a level of abstraction to consider the midrange concept.[32] According to Lorsch and Lawrence,[45] the internal functioning of organizations must be consistent with the demands of the organization task, technology, or external environment, and the needs of its members if the organization is to be effective. Rather than searching for the panacea of one best way to organize under all conditions, investigators tend to examine the functioning of the organizations in relation to the needs of their particular members and the external pressures facing them. In other words, the functioning of the organization is contingent upon external requirements and member needs.

The underlying principles of the contingent view are to intensively investigate the organization to understand its environment, the nature of the business, and the decision process. Based on the major information flows, the patterns of their relationships, and the boundaries of each subsystem, a configuration of subsystems can be built up. The main focus of the contingent view is to pinpoint the major decision-making process and their information flows. It prevents the collapse of the system designed under the total system fallacy but without losing sight of the whole.

4. Fundamentals of Database Design

The current technology in database design exists basically for static and stable environment. There are very few, if not nonexistent, design methodologies which are available for designing databases for decision support. As we know, database systems are vital for effective decision support. The purpose of this paper is to examine the existing technologies in database design and to develop a new approach, which is more appropriate for decision support. Before discussing the new approach, a brief review of fundamentals in database development is useful in paving the way for a better insight into the problem of database design for decision support.

4.1. Conceptual System Design

Information increasingly becomes a scarce resource for an organization. Efficient management and utilization of this scarce resource determine the successful operation of an organization. For efficient use of information, the information requirements for various decisions should be first identified through a conceptual model which is used as a communication tool between the system designer and the user. This conceptual model may be divided into local conceptual models and a global conceptual model. The local conceptual model is developed by examining (or talking to the personnel or the decision maker concerned) the information requirements for the various decisions. Then all these local conceptual models are integrated into a global conceptual model. It is pursued without consideration of physical aspects of database at this stage. These local conceputal views are equivalent to the external schema in the ANSI-X3-SPARC/DBMS[5] Interim Report which consists of three distinct types of schemas: external, conceptual, and internal. The external schemas are the definitions of the user's views of a database and their mapping to the conceptual schema (or global conceptual view of the organization). The conceptual schema is the definition of the real world (or the organization's view, or DBA's view) of the database and its mapping to the internal schemas. The internal schema is concerned with the physical storage and access path.[46,58]

The major reasons for using conceptual schema as the interface[16] are the following: (1) to reduce the number of mappings between the external schemas and internal schemas; (2) since the conceptual schema is not concerned with the physical storage and access path, it is relatively stable while allowing changes in external schemas and internal schemas, and it plays an important role in maintaining logical data independence and physical data independence; (3) the conceptual schema is the same as the enterprise schema. The entity–relationship (E/R) diagram proposed in Ref. 16 can be used to describe the conceptual schema. Furthermore, the external schemas may be expressed in terms of three logical data models, relational, hierarchical, and network (DBTG). The E/R diagram will be a very useful tool for translating the conceptual model of data into various logical data models. This paper will follow the basic concepts and the translation rules of the entity–relationship model in defining its conceptual model and subsequent mapping between the conceptual model and logical data models because the E/R model is very natural in defining a conceptual schema of an organization and its mechanism is easy to follow.

4.2. Logical Data Models

The logical view of data has been an important issue in recent years in database design because existing commercial systems are based on one of the three major data models,[23] relational, hierarchical, and network, and especially on hierarchical, or network models.[61] This situation might change in the near future toward a relational approach or a unified approach. These subjects will be discussed in the next few sections. When designing a data base, both problems of computer efficiency and human efficiency should be considered.[62] In terms of human efficiency, data should be presented to a user in a form suited to both his skills and the application concerned. As to which data structure should be supported at the user level, it is a factor that critically affects many components of the system. It also dictates the design of the corresponding data manipulation language(s), because each DML operation must be defined in terms of its effect on those data structures.[23] Thus the question "What data structures and associated operators should the system support?" is a crucial one. Before answering this question, we may briefly examine the three best known approaches, relational, hierarchical, and network.[60]

4.2.1. The Relational Data Model. The relational model is based on relational theory. The mathematical concept underlying the relational model is the set-theoretic relation, which is a subset of the Cartesian product of a list of domains. A domain is a set of values. The relational model consists of a collection of relations, each of which can be thought of as a simple table. Rows of such tables are generally referred to as tuples which correspond to entities. Columns are usually referred to as attributes. The ordering of rows and columns is immaterial. The attribute name usually corresponds to domain name provided no ambiguities occur, otherwise a role name should be used to qualify the domain name as the attribute name. The domain and the attribute are different concepts. The former is a set of values, the latter is a list of items taken from the domain. A particular item may occur several times in the column of attribute values while it occurs only once in the set of values in a domain. Sometimes, two or more attributes take values from the same domain. The attribute in a relational model is used to distinguish domains with the same name in the same relation and to map attribute names to values in the domains of the attributes.

The list of attribute names for a relation is called the relation scheme which corresponds to a record format. A relation corresponds to a file and a tuple to a record. The collection of relations with their values is called the relational data base. We are free to create relations with any set of attributes from the relation schemes. Since the number of basic constructs in the relational data model is one, namely, the relation itself, all information in the data base is represented by this simple construct. We need only one operator for each of the four basic functions, retrieve, insert, delete, and update. In order to avoid the operation anomalies, the relational model is usually operated under normalized relations. It possesses a body of theory applicable to database problems such as normalization theory for designing a relational schema,[22,65] and the theory of relational completeness for comparing relational languages.[23]

In summary, the structure of a relational model is best since it describes each domain, with its possible data type, and each relation, identifying its attributes and primary key which uniquely identifies each type within a relation. Tuples correspond to entities, and relations correspond to entity set. Both the entities and relationships among entities are represented by one construct, relation. One–many and many–many relationships are treated the same.

It is very clear that relational structure is simple and easy to understand, and it is predicted that it will become the major contender in the logical data model selection.

4.2.2. The Network Data Model. The specification of the CODASYL Data Base

Task Group (DBTG) for defining and processing network-oriented data bases was recorded in the 1971 Report of CODASYL DBTG[18] and the discussion of the network data model is in detail in Ref. 52. This report, written by a group of voluntary representatives from computer manufacturers, users in U.S. industry and government, and university researchers, has become the basis for some sort of standardization of a generalized data base management system.

The basic constructs of a network data model are logical record types represented by rectangles which correspond to entity sets and DBTG-set types represented by arrows which correspond to relationship types in the E/R model (which will be discussed in detail in the following sections). The most important construct in the network model is the set which goes from the owner record type to one or more member record types. In case of many–many relationships it must create a link record type between the two record types, the owner record type and the member record type, and then these two record types can be in one-to-one correspondence. According to DBTG Data Definition Language (DDL), one–many relationships are usually required; of course, it can be one–zero, one–one, or one–many. Record occurrences correspond to entities, data items to attributes, and set occurrences to relationships.

The network model compared with the relational model shows that repeating groups are allowed in the network model while they are not allowed in the latter; the former does not have to have a tuple identifier while the latter must have; the former uses predefined access paths through set mechanisms while the latter does not and all possible routes are dynamically materialized; the former specifies certain integrity constraints to the data structure while the latter does not and only declares them as adjuncts to the data structure. According to Ref. 49, of the four major areas of data definition—structure, physical placement, access path, and integrity and privacy constraints—the relational model includes neither physical placement nor access paths, and there is clear separation between structure and constraints, while the network model includes all these four areas of description. From these structure comparisons, the network structure is more complex than the relational. From the DSS point of view, the relational model is more appealing than the network. Current implementation of database management systems, however, exists either in the network model or hierarchical model. We might still have to deal with the network structure either by translation between the relational and the network or by a unified design at the very beginning. These are subjects of the following sections.

4.2.3. The Hierarchical Data Model. Hierarchies are special cases of networks; any network can be translated into hierarchical structure. The data are represented by a tree structure. The record type at the top of the tree is known as the root or the parent, and the elements at the lowest levels which have no children are called leaves or children. The root may have any number of leaves; each of these may have any number of lower-level leaves. A tree is a hierarchy of records because the root and the leaf are both organized as records. This has led to the term hierarchic data base. No child record type may have more than one parent segment type while it is allowed more than one parent (owner) in the network structure as long as the child is in a different set. A set type represents the relationship between the owner record type and member record type in a network sense and it is formally declared; but it is implied in the hierarchical model. Many–many relationships also cannot be handled directly. It must be treated by creating a pointer segment for each of the two segments (IMS's terms of IBM), while in network structure, it is handled by creating link record types (or two-way connectors). No child segment occurrence can exist without its parent while it is allowed in the network model by a singular set for which the owner is the "SYSTEM" where the SYSTEM has only one occurrence.

From this comparison between a network model and a hierarchical model, we can visualize that the hierarchical structure is even more complex and rigid than the network structure. When more record types are brought into the structure, it will get worse. The user, as Date[23] pointed out, is forced to devote more time and effort to solving problems that are introduced by the hierarchical data structure and that are not intrinsic to the questions being asked. Of course, hierarchies are a natural way to model truly hierarchical structures from the real world. Besides, virtual logical record types are very useful mechanisms in connecting two physical data bases or in converting the network structure into hierarchical ones. From an updating operation point of view, however, the hierarchical model possesses even more undesirable properties than the previous two logical data models. As mentioned before, since many current implementations of data bases are in the hierarchical model, we probably still have to deal with them either by transformation among the three approaches, or by adopting a unified design approach of logical data models.

4.3. Data Model Assessment

So far three logical data models, relational, network, and hierarchical have been briefly reviewed for laying the foundation in the subsequent analysis. Hopefully, it will give us some guidelines for evaluation among them to see which is the best fit for the environment of a DSS. Since there is a diverse community of users facing a DSS, it should provide information to all levels of management in a batch or in an interactive mode. Besides, decision makers at all levels need standard reports and analytical data for solving their structured, semistructured, or unstructured problems. Based on these capability requirements, the three logical data models discussed will be further scrutinized to see which is more appropriate for decision support.

As mentioned earlier, since the hierarchical structure is a special case of the network, the comparison between the relational and the network approaches will suffice. Michael[49] outlines five factors for evaluation. Date[23] uses two factors and Ullman[61] also uses two factors; it does not matter how many factors they pick up for evaluation. The easy to use, easy to understand, easy to manipulate, and easy to implement factors are vital for a database designed for meeting the diverse requirements of a DSS; besides, operational data and analytical information are also critical for decision making.

From these six capability requirements, the relational structure meets all these factors except "easy to implement." Therefore, the relational model is very promising because of its nonprocedural languages, its separating structural elements from physical elements so as to maintain data independence, and its simplicity in data structure and data manipulation. It does not mean that there are no problems in implementing a relational database model. As Ullman[61] indicates, the multilist data structure and the pointer-based implementation of variable length records do not generalize readily to many–many mapping. Theoretically, it is always possible to implement relations by a hierarchical or network structure, but it is not always clear how to do so, especially in a cost-effective way.

The network model is more complex than the relational because of its procedural language, its rigid structure, and its bundling four areas of data definition so as to make it lack data independence.[42] Its relative merit, however, is that it is readily available for implementation. Many of the inedequacies are not inherent in the network approach. The initial DBTG specifications have undergone subsequent development and refinement as reported by two CODASYL groups.[20,21]

Generally, the relational model is more appealing in the environment of a DSS, but we are not suggesting that any one model should be dominant[23,36,49] because the user demands are so diversified that no one model can meet the needs of users completely under all circumstances.

4.4. The Unified Approach

Many researchers have made contributions in this area[2,9,16,38,23,25,31, 36,48,51,58,59,62,64] such as Date's[23] Unified Database Language (UDL), Chen's[16] entity–relationship model, Zaniolo's[64] multiple external schemas for designing and supporting relational and hierarchical views over CODASYL network schemas, Vetter's[62] structure-type coexistence, Deen's[25] a Global Schema for supporting interfaces to other systems, etc., just to name a few. There are generally two types of data structure coexistence: top-down and bottom-up. The bottom-up approach is done by creating normalized relations as the basic ingredients, and then the three data structures, relational, hierarchical, and network are derived from them.[23] The top-down approach[16] is exemplified in an entity–relationship model as a generation from which the three existing data models may be derived. Either way is all right. The latter approach utilizes the semantic information to organize the data in the form of entity–relationship relations which are similar to 3NF relations. As Chen puts it, his E/R model can reduce the transformation process to the minimum. This feature is excellent because the normalization process can only get rid of a certain degree of operation anomalies, and sometimes it is a messy and tedious operation in the transformation process.

The Unified Database Language (UDL) proposed by Date,[23] is very attractive and theoretically sound. It intends to support the three data structures, relational, hierarchic, and network in a uniformed way. The "onion-layer" structure is the basis for the construct of the UDL. It indicates that the language features, the operators and the operands of a relational database are the subset of those required to declare a hierarchical database, and these in turn are a subset of those required to declare a network database.

The relational structure is one of the most promising approaches in database development such as system R, which is one of the typical examples.[15,23] It is capable of supporting both repetitive transactions and ad hoc queries that are very attractive for the environment of a DSS. The network structure and the hierarchical structure, however, will continue in use for some time because of configuration compatibility requirements of data processing structure in an organization. Tremendous investment by the business world has been in these two approaches. All these lead to the development of data structure type coexistence. Though at the present time there is no DBMS that can support the three approaches at the same time, a strong foundation has been built up. As Date pointed out, theoretically, the structure type coexistence is feasible and desirable for the diversified community of users.

5. Illustration

Conceptualization of the organization for which the information system or database will be designed is one of the most important steps in information system or database development. Conceptual system design begins with information requirement analysis by identifying the major information flows, then grouping them into a configuration of subsystems. It becomes the conceptual model of the organization, and reflects the true structure of the organization and information needs of the end users. Physical storage is not considered at this stage.

Based on this conceptual model and the semantic meaning of the organization, the entities and relationships between entities are identified. The entity–relationship model (E/R model) is born.

5.1. The Basics of E/R Model

As we mentioned earlier, the entity–relationship mode (E/R model) proposed by Chen[16] is very close to the conceptual model (or the global view) of the organization. The entity and relationship relations in the E/R model are similar to 3NF relations. The steps in logical database design following the E/R approach are simple and close to human thinking. The E/R diagram is independent of the processing frequencies. Therefore, it is more stable. The translation processes from an E/R diagram into logical data structures—hierarchical, network, and relational—are easy. For these reasons, the E/R model is adopted for demonstrating the logical database design concept and the transformation process from the E/R diagram into the three major logical data structures. Since the user's environment of a DSS is diverse, a powerful approach such as the E/R model is required for such an environment. In addition to its simplicity of design, its capability in synthesizing the three major logical data models into a unified design which can meet the requirements of a DSS is also most appealing.

5.2. Procedures in Logical Database Design

Since, as we mentioned earlier, following the E/R model for logical database design is handy, let us now illustrate this by an example of technological transfer. Suppose that a company has many projects. Each project needs technologies which are available in the organization, or has to be purchased from outside domestically or internationally. Some technologies are not readily available in the market and have to be searched through a potential market so that a potential supplier list can be built up. If the necessary technologies are not available in its own capability file which can be drawn out for immediate use, or if the technologies to be developed by itself are cheaper than purchase from the outside, the company has to develop them by their own capability.

For simplicity, we only list six entity record types and six relationship record types in the E/R diagram in Fig. 2. The six entity record types, PROJ, TECH,

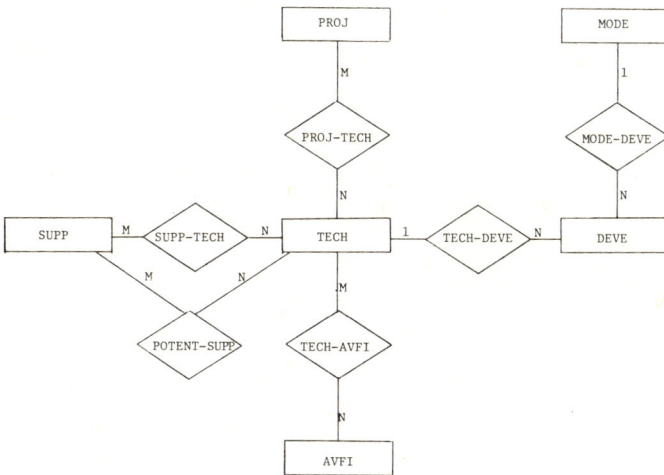

FIGURE 2. Entity–relationship diagram.

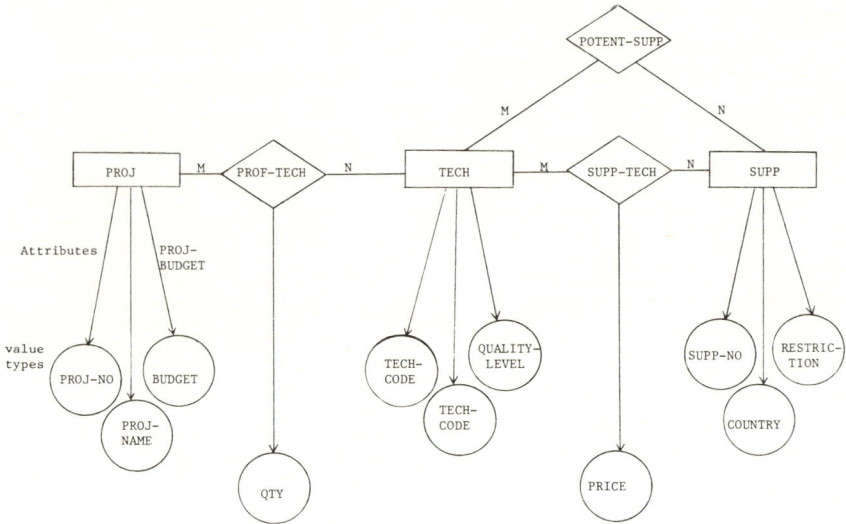

FIGURE 3. Attributes and values of PROJ, TECH, SUPP, PROJ-TECH, SUPP-TECH, POTENT-SUPP.

SUPP, AVFI, DEVE, and MODE, are represented by rectangular boxes. The six relationship record types, PROJ-TECH, SUPP-TECH, POTENT-SUPP, TECH-AVFI, and MODE-DEVE, are represented by diamond boxes. These relationships can be classified according to their association types between the entity types as one–one (1:1), one–many (1:N), and many–many (M:N).

After identifying entity types and relationship types and drawing the E/R diagram according to their semantic meaning. the attributes and value types within each entity record type and each relationship record type should be identified as shown in Figs. 3, 4, and 5.

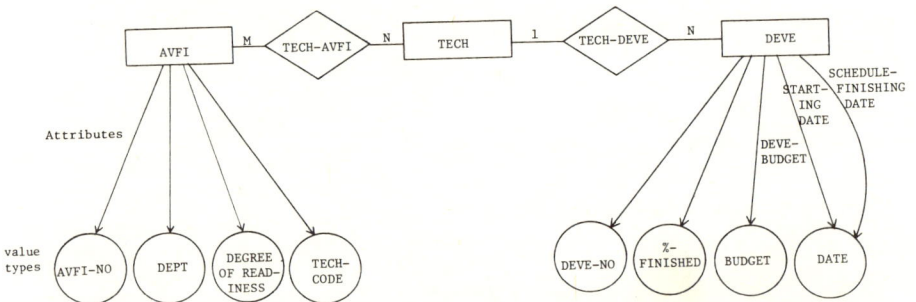

FIGURE 4. Attributes and value types of TECH, AVFI, DEVE, TECH-AVFI, and TECH-DEVE.

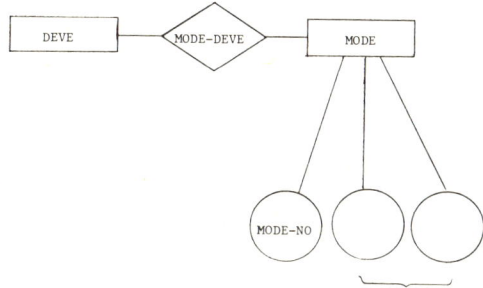

FIGURE 5. Attributes and value types of DEVE, MODE-DEVE, and MODE.

Here rooms are left for these empty value types. As soon as they are defined, they can be added on at any time.

The next step, a data-structure diagram in Fig. 6, can be derived from the E/R diagram in Fig. 2. All the entity types in E/R diagram become record types in Fig. 7 in the data-structure diagram. One–many relationships are translated into a data-structure set (i.e., an arrow), and many–many relationships are translated into a record type (a linking record type) in Fig. 8.

The last step is to group attributes into records and decide how to implement the data-structure sets by using pointer arrays, chains, or other methods. This paper emphasizes conceptual aspects of database design. As to physical aspects, please refer to Refs. 16, 17, 61.

5.3. Data Model Coexistence

In logical database design, we first talk to the decision makers or analyze the information requirements for various decisions. then combine these local concep-

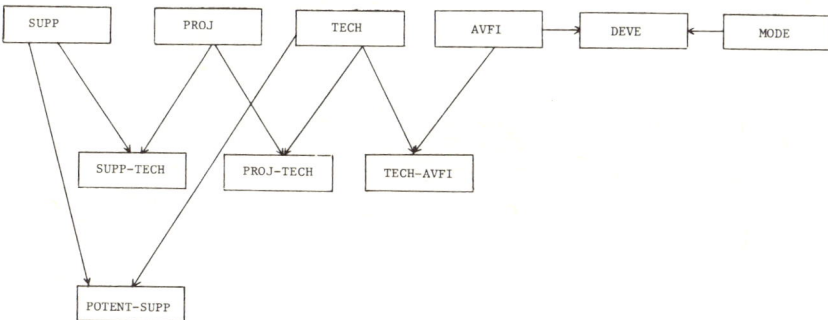

FIGURE 6. The data-structure diagram transferred from the E/R diagram in Fig. 1.

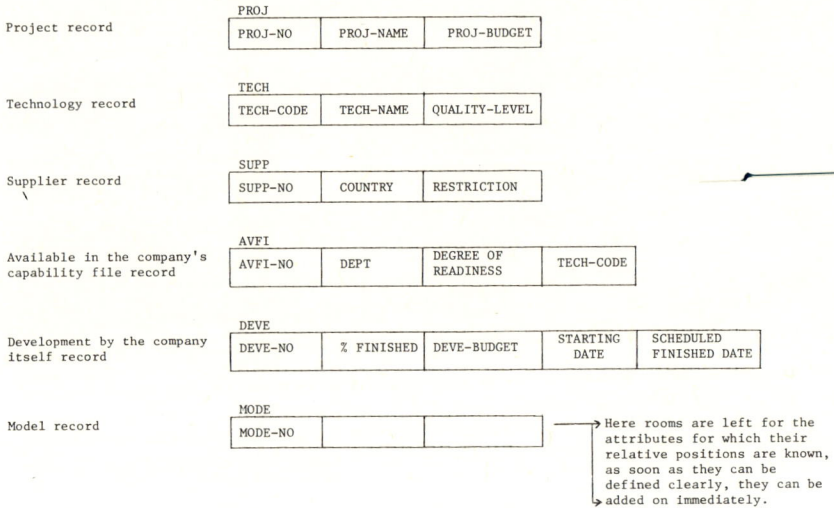

FIGURE 7. Record formats of entity record types.

tual models (or we may call them external models) into an integrated global conceptual model. After identifying all the entities and relationships, we draw an entity–relationship diagram. Next we identify the attributes and value types of all the entities and relationships, and translate the E/R diagram into a data-structure diagram. Finally record formats are designed in accordance with the attributes and value types identified.

Since the record formats are equivalent to the relation scheme in the relational data model, if all the record formats (or relation schemes) are loaded with actual values, it becomes a data base. Though all the record formats are very close to the normalized relations, we might go ahead to split or merge all the relations (traditionally, they are called files) through the normalization process[7,9,22,23,29,41,44,58,59,61,62,65] as the situation warrants. Detailed discussion of normalization is beyond the scope of this paper; please refer to the above references.

One thing is clear: the E/R approach is flexible and close to human thinking. If some particular relationship types change from, e.g., one–many to many–many, a relationship record type is simply added; the program or the database does not have to be changed. If the one–many relationships are already translated into relationship record types, even this process can be omitted.

The most important feature is that the E/R diagram may be translated into many different data structures to meet the needs of different data processing environments. For example, it can be translated into relational, hierarchical, or network data structures without any difficulties.[1,2,16,25,31,43,48,51] All the entity records

and relationship records are in the form of universal relations which can be immediately and conveniently used in a relational data model logically or
physically.[25,31,61,65]

Translation from the global E/R diagram into hierarchical data structures
is easy. The entity record types of the E/R approach are equivalent to the segment
types of the hierarchical data model. First the root segments should be identified
as the starting points and then based on the conceptual and semantic meaning, the
hierarchical trees can be structured. Through pointer segments, the many–many
relationships can be handled. The most important features in the hierarchical data
structure are that the logical parent pointer or the logical child pointer can be used
for integrating several hierarchical organizations into a unified one and by virtual
storage, physical redundancies can be avoided. The set concepts are implied
through the parent–child relationships.

Translation from the global E/R diagram into network data structures is
also very simple. The entity record types of the global E/R diagram are equivalent
to the DBTG record types. The relationship record types are equivalent to the
DBTG-set types. The set mechanisms are the most important concept and can be
formally declared and used as access paths and navigation routes. Many owner
records can be accessed through hashing mechanisms or other methods. Any member records can also be set up as the entry point if that is desired.

Translation from the global E/R diagram into relational data structures is

Project–Technology Relationship Record	PROJ–TECH		
	PROJ–NO	TECH–CODE	QTY

Supplier–Technology Relationship Record	SUPP–TECH		
	SUPP–NO	TECH–CODE	PRICE

Potential–Supplier Relationship Record	POTENT–SUPP	
	SUPP–NO	TECH–CODE

Technology-Available in the Company Relationship Record	TECH–AVFI	
	AVFI–NO	TECH–CODE

— —

Technology-Development by the Company Itself Relationship Record	TECH–DEVE	
	DEVE–NO	TECH–CODE

Model-Development Relationship Record	MODE–DEVE	
	DEVE–NO	MODE–NO

Remarks: (1) The Technology Development by the company itself Relationship Record is
a one-many relationship, it may or may not be translated into a relationship record type. It is up to the Data Base Administrator (DBA). If he
wants more data independence, all one-many relationships may be translated
into relationship record types.

(2) For simplicity, only the basic entities and relationships are translated
into record types. Actually, all the logic and coefficients of management
models can also be translated into record types.

FIGURE 8. Record formats of relationship record types (many–many relationships).

straightforward.[47] The entity record types are translated into relations (tables). The major attribute or the combination of attributes which can be used to uniquely identify an entity (or a record) are selected as the primary key of the record. Every record must have a unique primary key for identification of the record. Sometimes, a foreign key which is the primary key value of some tuple in some other relation can be used to help identify the record involved.[23] The relationship record types are also translated into relations. The primary keys of the entities involved in the relationship are used as the primary key. If the relation is not in a simple form (e.g., including repeating groups in the relation), or all the nonprimary attributes of a relation are not fully dependent on its primary key, or there exists transitive dependencies or multivalued dependencies, a normalization process should be used to produce the 3NF or higher-level normalized relations.

6. Implementation Issues

6.1. The Unified Approach

Theoretically, the data model coexistence and the unified design has been demonstrated to be feasible. How to implement it is the next subject for concern.

There are several methods in which the unified approach can be implemented. The set mechanism in the network model is one of the important constructs for maintaining the record sequence and navigating through the stored records in the database. There is no comparable construct in the relational model because the set mechanism is carried out dynamically through relational operators during executive time while it is implemented by pointers and indexes in the network model. This dynamic association between relations in the relational data system (RDS) exemplifies a great flexibility but it suffers performance penalty because it requires a great amount of computer resources. Recently, a prototype, system R[14,6,23] adopts a compromise by implementing pointers for the anticipated links or structured associations, and dynamically implementing additional pointers for unanticipated links or unstructured associations when demand arises.[6,12,14,23] This dynamic feature is vital for decision support because decision support environment is always volatile. The anticipated links can be used for solving structured tasks while the unanticipated links are used for unstructured or semistructured problems. The former is good for supporting repetitive transactions while the latter is good for ad hoc analytic queries. The combination of both features is excellent for implementing management decision support. Technological progress such as associative or parallel computer will ease the performance penalty in maintaining the pointers and dynamically construct additional pointers.

Another is by way of issuing relational statements which can be operated in a network system. It may have performance problems because it involves two data-bases. The best way is to convert them into a common database by a unified design as demonstrated earlier or by converting the existing CODASYL database through pushing down the keys and adding sequence fields for maintaining the coset mechanisms.[12,13]

System R allows to create and load part of the database and begin to operate, and later on the database can be expanded or destroyed without affecting the functioning of the system. This is also extremely valuable for decision support.

The unified approach for database design stresses to put the related part into a unified whole. It does not mean that we have to build a gigantic database which holds everything in one place. Sometimes, an all-inclusive database is not economical or feasible. What is being stressed here is to put the related things together into a unified whole. The database can be divided or distributed for economy of storage or use.

6.2. The Distributed Approach

In addition to the above unified features, the database designed under the E/R approach can be logically integrated but physically distributed.[13] Data distribution will be done by clusters. Each cluster is organized in accordance with the guidelines of the E/R model, and stored wholly at a single computer site. The system is a network which supports one logically integrated database under one data model and allows the user to enter repetitive transaction processing or ad hoc queries at any computer site. A user may access a part of the database, which may be stored at a remote site, and the system will connect the user to the portion of the database.[14,42] A set of standard functions has to be provided to the user and it can be activated in a uniform manner by all the users. All the DBMS connected on the network are actually a unified and standard DBMS. It is called, according to Gardarin,[30] a virtual DBMS.

6.3. Techniques

Clemons[18] outlines five guidelines in database design for decision support: (1) Exploit the knowledge of traditional and file-based inquiry systems, such as using auxiliary data structures, inverted organizations, indices, for quick access. (2) Design for the specific rquirement of DSS. (3) Keep auxiliary and derived data in summary form for use by DSS. (4) Separate operational database from derived database for saving cost in storage, and reducing response time, redundancy, and inconsistency. (5) Keep additional data for recalculating the derived data. These permit rapid recalculation without degrading the operational data-base. There are many more techniques in Refs. 18 and 56.

7. Conclusion

Decision support is one of the most complicated phenomena in human activities. It involves a wide range of disciplines, computer technology, quantitative models, and organizational management. The constructs of DSS are also complex. It consists of four components, the operational databases, the DSS databases, the derivation routines, and software systems. The DSS obtains its inputs from data sources and is used by the end users.

Though there are so many constructs mutually interacting each other, they should be designed in a unified fashion under a unified guideline. A practical example has been used to demonstrate this unified approach in database design for decision support.

A prototype, system R, has illustrated that the theoretical principles of the unified methodologies is not only feasible but implementable in the real system for decision support.[26,14,6,23]

References

1. M. ABIDA, C. DELOBEL, and M. LEONARD, A unified approach for modeling data in logical data base design, *Modeling in Data Base Management Systems,* G. M. NIJSSEN (Ed.), North-Holland Publishing Company, Amsterdam, 1976.
2. M. ABIDA and C. DELOBEL, The problem of the corporation between different D.B.M.S., *Architecture and Models in Data Base Management Systems,* G. M. NIJSSEN, Ed., North-Holland Publishing Company, Amsterdam, 1977.
3. S. ALTER, A taxonomy of decision support systems, *Sloan Management Rev.* **19,**(1), Fall 1977.
4. S. L. ALTER, *Decision Support Systems: Current Practice and Continuing Changes,* Addison-Wesley Series on Decision Support, Reading, Massachusetts, 1980.
5. *ANST-X3-SPARC/DBMS, Study Group Report* published by the American National Standard Institute, Washington, D.C., 1975.
6. M. M. ASTRAHAM *et al.,* System R: A relational data base management system, *Computer* **12,**(5), May (1979).
7. C. BEERI, On the membership problem for functional and multivalued dependencies in relational databases, *ACM Trans. Database Syst.* **5**(3), September (1980).
8. J. BENNETT, User-oriented graphics, systems for decision support in unstructured tasks, in *User-Oriented Design of Interactive Graphics Systems,* S. TREU, Ed., ACM, New York, 1977.
9. P. A. BERNSTEIN, Synthesizing third normal form relations from functional dependencies, *ACM Trans. Database Syst.* **1**(4), December (1976.)
10. R. H. BONCZEK *et al.,* Aiding decision makers with a generalized data base management system: An application to inventory management, *Decision Sci.* **9**(2), April (1978).
11. R. H. BONCZEK, C. W. HOLSAPPLE, and A. B. WHINSTON, Computer-based support of organizational decision making, *J. Am. Inst. Decision Sci.* **10**(2), April (1979).
12. R. H. BONCZEK, C. W. HOLSAPPLE, and A. B. WHINSTON, The evolving roles of models in decision support systems, *Decision Sci.* Vol. **11**(2), April (1980).
13. O. H. BRAY, and H. A. FREEMAN, *Data Base Computers,* D. C. Heath and Company, Boston, 1979.
14. O. H. BRAY, *Distributed Database Management Systems,* D. C. Heath and Company, Boston, 1982.
15. D. D. CHAMBERLIN *et al.,* Support for repetitive transactions and ad hoc queries in system R, *ACM Trans. Database Syst.* **6**(1), March (1981).

16. P. P.-S. CHEN, The entity–relationship model—Toward a unified view of data, *ACM Trans. Databse Syst.* **11**(1), March (1976).
17. P. P.-S. CHEN, The entity–relationship approach to logical data base design, *Q.E.D. Monograph Series,* No. 6, 1977, Q.E.Q. Information Sciences, Inc., 141 Linden Street, Wellesley, Massachusetts, 02181.
18. E. K. CLEMONS, Data base design for decision support, *Proceedings of the International Hawaii Conference on System Sciences,* January 1981.
19. CODASYL data base task group report, 1971, CODASYL Association for Computing Machinery, New York, April 1971.
20. CODASYL Data Description Language Committee, Proposed Revision of the 1971 DBTG Report, February 1973.
21. CODASYL Data Base Language Task Group, Proposed Revision of the 1971 DBTG Report, June 1973.
22. E. F. CODD, A relational model of data for large shared data banks, *Commun. Assoc. Comput. Mach.* **13**(6), June (1970).
23. C. J. DATE, *An Introduction to Database Systems,* 3rd ed., Addison-Wesley, Reading, Massachusetts, 1981.
24. P. DE and A. SEN, Logical data base design in decision support systems, *J. Sys. Manage.* May (1981).
25. S. M. DEEN, A canonical schema for a generalized data model with local interfaces, *Computer J.* **23**(3), August (1980).
26. E. M. DIECKMANN, Three relational DBMS, *Datamation,* September (1981).
27. J. J. DONOVAN, Database approach to management decision support, *ACM Trans. Database Syst.* **1**(4), December (1976).
28. F. EDELMAN, Managers, computer systems, and productivity, *MIS Q.* **5**(3), September (1981).
29. R. FAGIN, Multivalued dependencies and a new normal form for relational databases, *ACM Trans. Database Syst.* **2**(3), September (1977).
30. G. GARDARIN *et al.,* An approach towards a virtual data base protocol
31. L. A. KALINICHENKO, Relational-network data structure mapping, *Modeling in Data Base Management Systems,* G. M. NIJSSEN, Ed., North-Holland Publishing Company, Amsterdam, 1976.
32. F. E. KAST and J. ROSENZWEIG, General system theory: Applications for organization and management, *Acad. Manage. J.* December (1972).
33. P. G. W. KEEN and M. S. S. MORTTON, *Decision Support Systems: An Organizational Perspective,* Addison-Wesley Series on Decision Support, Reading, Massachusetts, 1978.
34. P. G. W. KEEN, Decision support systems: Translating analytic techniques into useful tools, *Sloan Manage. Rev.* **21**(3), Spring (1980).
35. P. G. W. KEEN *et al.,* Building a decision support system: The mythical man-month revisited, in *Building Decision Support Systems,* J. F. BENNET, Ed., Addison-Wesley Series on Decision Support, Reading, Massachusetts, 1980.
36. L. KERSCHBERG, A. KLUG, and D. TSICHRITZIS, A taxonomy of data models, *Systems for Large Data Bases,* P. C. LOCKEMANN and F. J. NEUHOLD Ed., North-Holland Publishing Company, Amsterdam, 1976.
37. L. J. LANING *et al.,* A DSS oversight: Historical databases, *DSS-82 Transactions,* Second International Conference on Decision Support Systems, 1982.
38. D. T. LEE *et al.,* Quintary tree: A file structure for multidimensional database systems, *ACM Trans. Database Sys.* **5**(3), September (1980).
39. D. T. LEE, The contingent model of decision support systems, *The Proceedings of Western AIDS,* 1982.
40. D. T. LEE, the unified approach for designing decision support systems, *DSS-82 Transactions,* Second International Conference on Decision Support Systems, 1982.
41. D. T. LEE, United database for decision support to appear in the *Int. J. Policy Anal. Inf. Syst.* 1982.
42. E. Y. LIEN *et al.,* Design of a distributed entity–relationship database system, *Proceedings of COMPSAC,* 1978.

43. Y. E. LIEN, Hierarchical schema for relational databases, *ACM Trans. Database Syst.* **6**(1), March (1981).
44. T.-W. LING et al., An improved third normal form for relational databases, *ACM Trans. Database Syst.* **6**(2), June (1981).
45. J. W. LORSCH and P. R. LAWRENCE, *Studies in Organizational Design,* Irwin-Dorsey, Homewood, Illinois 1970.
46. J. MARTIN, *Computer Data-Base Organization,* 2nd ed., Prentice-Hall, Englewood Cliffs, New Jersey, 1977.
47. W. E. MCCARTHY, An entity–relationship view of accounting models, *Accounting Rev.* **LIV**(4), October (1979).
48. I. I. MERCZ, Issues in building a relational interface on a CODASYL DBMS, *Data Base Architecture,* BRAECHI and NIJSSEN, Eds., North-Holland Publishing Company, Amsterdam, 1979.
49. A. S. MICHAELS, A comparison of the relational and CODASYL approaches to data-base management, *ACM Comput. Surv.* **8**(1), March (1976).
50. S. M. S. MORTON, Management decision systems: Computer-based support for decision making, Division of Research, Harvard University, Cambridge, Massachusetts, 1971.
51. E. NAHOURAII, L. O. BROOKS, and A. F. CARDENAS, An approach to data communication between different generalized data base management systems, *Systems for Large Data Bases,* P. C. LOCKEMANN and E. J. NEUHOLD Eds., North-Holland Publishing Company, Amsterdam, 1976.
52. T. W. OLLE, *The CODASYL Approach to Data Base Management,* John Wiley & Sons, New York, 1978.
53. T. R. PRINCE, *Information Systems for Planning and Control,* 3rd ed., Richard D. Irwin, Inc., Homewood, Illinois, 1975.
54. H. A. SIMON, *The New Science of Management Decision,* Harper and Row, New York, 1960.
55. R. H. SPRAGUE, A framework for the development of decision support systems, *MIS Q.* December (1980).
56. R. H. SPRAGUE, Jr. and E. D. CARLSON, *Building Effective Decision Support Systems,* Prentice-Hall, Englewood Cliffs, New Jersey, 1982.
57. E. A. STOHR et al., A database for operations research models, *Int. J. Policy Anal. Inf. Syst.* **4**(1), (1980).
58. S. Y. W. SU, A semantic association model for conceptual database design, *Entity–Relationship Approach to Systems Analysis and Design,* P. CHEN, Ed., North-Holland Publishing Company, Amsterdam, 1980.
59. S. Y. W. SU, H. LAM, and D. H. LO, Transformation of data traversals and operations in application programs to account for semantic changes of databases, *ACM Trans. Database Syst.* **6**(2), June (1981).
60. D. C. TSICHNTZIS and F. H. LOCHOVSKY, *Data Model,* Prentice-Hall, Englewood Cliffs, New Jersey, 1982.
61. J. D. ULLMAN, *Principles of Database Systems,* Computer Science Press, Potomac, Maryland, 1980.
62. M. VETTER and R. N. MADDISON, *Database Design Methodology,* Prentice-Hall, Englewood Cliffs, New Jersey, 1981.
63. G. R. WAGNER, Decision support systems: The real substance, *Interfaces* **11**(2), April (1981).
64. C. ZANIOLO, Multimodel external schemas for CODASYL data base management systems, *Data Base Architecture,* BRACCHI and NIJSSEN, Eds., North-Holland Publishing Company, Amsterdam, 1979.
65. C. ZANIOLO, On the design of relational database schemata, *ACM Trans. Database Sys.* **6**(1), March (1981).

12

TOWARD AN ENTERPRISE INFORMATION SYSTEM DESIGN METHODOLOGY

C. R. Carlson and Adarsh K. Arora

1. Introduction

During the past decade, the growth of enterprise information systems based on large, integrated databases has focused attention on the need to develop structured guidelines for the design of such databases. This need is underscored by the demand for increased productivity on the part of information system developers, the fact that database design responsibility often falls on inexperienced individuals and the increased expense for maintaining complex databases. Despite considerable research efforts focused on developing design guidelines, the concept of logical database design remains a distant, elusive, and poorly understood art for many in applications development. As a result, the quality of database design varies from one individual to another based on their experience, knowledge of the application, etc. Design methodologies are clearly needed which are effective, easily learned and based on sound engineering principles.

The methodology proposed in this chapter tries to apply some sound engineering principles to the problem of logical database design. The methodology builds upon the DARTS (design aide for relational database schemas)[1-3] prototype whose implementation was based on an earlier version of this methodology. The extensions to DARTS incorporate comprehensive facilities for semantic information modeling. The methodology consists of a four-phase process comprising requirements analysis, view modeling, view integration and model mapping. This process conforms to the three-schema framework defined in the ANSI/X3/SPARC documents.[4,5]

The first phase of the methodology—requirements analysis—concerns itself

C. R. CARLSON • Standard Oil (Indiana), 200 East Randolph Drive, Chicago, Illinois 60680. ADARSH K. ARORA • Department of Computer Science, Illinois Institute of Technology, Chicago, Illinois 60616.

with the analysis of an enterprise and the identification of its information processing requirements. It yields requirement specifications for every user expressed in an enterprise model which best suits the needs of that user. View modeling, the next phase, is a computerized process whereby these user requirements are translated into Update Protocol Model (UPM) expressions,[6,7] thus providing the remaining phases of the methodology with precise representations of the corresponding user views in a uniform language, UPM. View integration, the third phase, checks for a wide variety of possible semantic conflicts amongst separate user requirements. User assistance is required to resolve some of these conflicts. Once resolved, view integration proceeds by combining these views into a global, composite view which "supports"[2] the operational requirements associated with each user view. Finally, in the model mapping phase the composite view is mapped onto the available database management system software. Critical to the sound engineering claims for the proposed methodology are the Update Protocol Model and the view integration phase, both of which are the focus of this paper.

2. Requirements Analysis

Requirements analysis, as currently practiced, is clearly an unstructured process whereby through many iterations the analyst obtains more precise descriptions of user requirements from fuzzy, unstructured thoughts about an enterprise. The advantage to using an application defined enterprise model to structure these thoughts is that it facilitates dialogue, and hopefully agreement, between the requirements analysis and the enterprise community regarding user requirements. Requirements analysis results in enterprise model descriptions for the relevant business procedures (e.g., processing orders, paying vendors, moving inventory). To clarify these procedures the enterprise modeler must identify (1) the *operations* required to carry out these procedures, (2) the *things* to which these procedures are applicable, and (3) the *constraints* by which operations on these things are controlled.

Unfortunately, the field of enterprise modeling is still in its infancy. While considerable recent research has focused on the entity–relationship model,[8,9] no widely accepted general purpose enterprise model has yet emerged.

3. View Modeling

View modeling is a translation process which yields a precise, uniform description of each individual user view. The output of view modeling consists of a relational subschema for each user view together with the necessary UPM expressions to describe the semantic aspects not covered by the relational model.

UPM was chosen because of its theoretically comprehensive information modeling facilities. Also, it has proven[6,7] to be a tool with which a wide range of enterprise models are precisely and uniformly defined. This section focuses on UPM and leaves questions regarding the translation of enterprise requirements into UPM for future analysis.

The UPM extensions to the relational model define a powerful collection of update protocols over one or more relations. While only normalized relations are used to illustrate UPM in this paper, there is no reason that they could not also be applied to unnormalized relations. Further, UPM assumes that the following relational update statements are supported:

Update-Statement ::= Insert-Statement | Delete-Statement |
                    Replace-Statement
Insert-Statement   ::= INSERT tuple IN relation-name
Delete-Statement ::= DELETE tuple FROM relation-name
Replace-Statement ::= REPLACE tuple BY tuple IN relation-name
Tuple ::= /* Each component of a tuple can be either a constant, a variable or a
        function value. */

For both INSERT and DELETE type statements involving individual relations, the database designer can associate an "update protocol." The purpose of this protocol is to both enforce semantic constraints and trigger appropriate semantic repercussions of the particular update statement. The protocol is invoked when an update of that type is attempted on the specified relation.

An update protocol consists of two parts, an optional list of constraint expressions followed by an optional list of trigger expressions as described below. Following conventional notational practices, square brackets are used to denote that the enclosed syntactic unit is optional.

Update-Protocol ::= [Constraint-Expression-List] [Trigger-Expression-List]
Constraint-Expression-List ::= Constraint-Expression
                          [Constraint-Expression-List]
Constraint-Expression ::= PRECOND Predicate-Expression |
                    POSTCOND Predicate-Expression
Predicate-Expression ::= [Range-Expression] Tuple-Boolean-Expression
Tuple-Boolean-Expression ::= * The class of boolean expressions is dependent
                        on the choice of data types over which tuples
                        are defined. Various built-in functions, e.g.,
                        INPUT, MAX, MIN, etc., may also be
                        required. */
Range-Expression ::= [Quantifier] Tuple-Variable ∈ Relation-Name [Range-
                Expression]

Quantifier ::= $\exists$ | $\not\exists$ | $\forall$
Trigger-Expression-List ::= Trigger-Expression [Trigger-Expression-List]
Trigger-Expression ::= IMPLIES {Update-Statement | Predicate-Expression}

Each constraint expression must be satisfied in order for the update to be committed. Each constraint expression is either a precondition, i.e., must be satisfied before the update changes the state of the database, or a postcondition, i.e., would be satisfied on the assumption that the state of the database already has been changed by the update. Each trigger expression identifies a predicate expression definable set of relational update statements whose execution is automatically triggered subject to the successful committment of the aforementioned update statement.

4. UPM Illustration

To illustrate the enterprise modeling capability of UPM, let us consider an enterprise model in which entities, relationships and "semantic constraints" are thought of as the primary information components. Further, let us assume that all entities (and relationships) having the same "attributes" are represented by a distinct relation and all semantic constraints are represented by UPM specifiable expressions.

4.1. Semantic Constraints Involving Relationships

Entities can be involved in many relationships with other entities. These are termed *simple relationships* if only the referential integrity constraint[10] is needed to characterize the involvement of the entities in these relationships. Expressed in UPM, relation R0 defines a simple relationship involving the entities represented by relations R1, . . . , Rn, n $\geq$ 2, if for each relation Ri with key set Ki, Ki is contained in the key set K0 of relation R0 and the following protocol holds.

1. Simple Relationship Protocol

INSERT t0 IN R0	PRECOND $\exists$ ti $\in$ Ri t0[Ki] = ti[Ki]
DELETE t0 FROM R0	No Protocol
INSERT ti IN Ri	No Protocol
DELETE ti FROM Ri	IMPLIES {DELETE t0 FROM R0 |
	ti[Ki] = t0[Ki]}

If a relationship with another entity must be established when an entity enters a realm of the business, then that entity is involved in a *prerequisite relationship*. For example, it could be a company policy that one prerequisite for employment is that the individual be assigned to work for some cost center. Assuming that employees and cost centers are represented by relations R1 and R2, respectively, and that work assignments are represented by relation R0; then the protocol for inserting tuples in relation R1 described in protocol (1) must be changed to the following:

2. Prerequisite Relationship Protocol

INSERT t1 IN R1   IMPLIES {INSERT t0 IN R0 |
$$t0[K1] = t1[K1] \text{ AND}$$
$$t0[T1\text{-}K1] = \text{INPUT AND}$$
$$t0[K2] \neq \text{NULL}\}$$

Here, INPUT denotes a built-in function which makes a request to the user to furnish information regarding attributes denoted by T1-K1, i.e., all attributes of relation R1 other than K1. NULL denotes the "unknown" value.

Entities are involved in a *permanent relationship* provided the relationship can be dissolved only if one of the entities involved in the relationship no longer exists. For example, it could be a company policy that all history information relating vendors to cost centers for which they have completed some contract must be maintained until either the vendor or cost center no longer exists. Expressed in UPM, a relationship is permanent if the protocol for deleting tuples from relation R0 in protocol (1) is changed to the following:

3. Permanent Relationship Protocol

DELETE t0 FROM R0   PRECOND $\forall$ t1 $\in$ R1 ... $\forall$ tn $\in$ Rn
$$t1[K1] \neq t0[K1] \text{ OR } \ldots \text{ OR}$$
$$tn[Kn] \neq t0[Kn]$$

An entity, represented by relation R1, is involved in a *required relationship* provided the entity "exists" only as long as it is involved in at least one relationship, represented by relation R0. For example, in order to be classified as a payee entity a vendor may have to maintain a contract relationship with some cost center. Expressed in UPM, a relationship is required if the deletion protocol for relation R0 in protocol (2) is changed to the following:

4. Required Relationship Protocol

DELETE t0 FROM R0   IMPLIES {DELETE t1 FROM R1 |
$$\forall t3 \in R0$$
$$t3 = t0 \text{ OR}$$
$$t3[K1] \neq t1[K1]\}$$

Note that the deletion of the entity, denoted by tuple t1 in relation R1, only occurs if it is not involved in at least one relationship of the type denoted by relation R0.

4.2. Property Defining Semantic Constraints

Let us now consider two relations R1 and R2 such that the key set K2 of relation R2 is a subset of the nonkey attributes of relation R1. The entities represented by relation R2 can be viewed as properties of the entities represented by relation R1. These properties are either "optional" or "prerequisite" and either "independent" or "dependent." Relation R2 defines an *optional property* if the following protocol holds.

5. Optional Property Protocol

INSERT t1 IN R1   IMPLIES {INSERT t2 IN R2 | $\not\exists$ t3 $\in$ R2
                                  t1[K2] = t3[K2] AND
                                  t1[K2] = t2[K2] $\neq$ NULL AND
                                  t2[T2-K2] = INPUT}

Here, T2-K2 denotes the non-K2 attributes of relation R2. For example, the terminal defined by relation R2(Terminal#, . . .) could be an optional property of the employees defined by relation R1(Emp#, Terminal#, . . .). That is, not all employees are assigned a computer terminal.

The entities represented by relation R2 are considered *prerequisite properties* if the following protocol holds.

6. Prerequisite Property Protocol

INSERT t1 IN R1   PRECOND t1[K2] $\neq$ NULL
                    IMPLIES {INSERT t2 IN R2 | $\not\exists$ t3 $\in$ R2
                                  t1[K2] = t3[K2] AND
                                  t1[K2] = t2[K2] AND
                                  t2[T2-K2] = NULL}

For example, the departments defined by relation R2(Dept, Mgr, . . .) could be considered a prerequisite property of the employees defined by relation R1 (Emp#, Dept, . . .). That is, no employee is hired without a departmental assignment.

The properties defined by relation R2 are considered *independent* of the entities defined by relation R1 if the following protocol holds.

7. Independent Property Protocol

DELETE t1 FROM R1   No Protocol
INSERT t2 IN R2   No Protocol
DELETE t2 FROM R2   IMPLIES {REPLACE t1 BY s1 IN R1 |
                      t1 $\in$ R1 t1[K2] = t2[K2] AND
                                  s1[T1-K2] = t1[T1-K2] AND
                                  s1[K2] = NULL}

For example, the departments defined by relation R2(Dept, ...) could be considered an independent property of the employees defined by relation R1(Emp#, Dept, ...). That is, a department can exist independent of there being any employees in that department.

The properties defined by relation R2 are considered *dependent* on the entities defined by relation R1 if the following protocol holds.

8. Dependent Property Protocol

DELETE t1 FROM R1	IMPLIES {DELETE t2 FROM R2 | t2 ∈ R2 $\nexists$ t3 ∈ R1 t2[K2] = t1[K2] AND t3[K2] = t1[K2]}
INSERT t2 IN R2	PRECOND ∃ t1 ∈ R1 t1[K2] = t2[K2]
DELETE t2 FROM R2	PRECOND $\nexists$ t1 ∈ R1 t1[K2] = t2[K2]

For example, the projects defined by relation R2(Project-Name, ...) could be considered dependent properties of the employees defined by relation R1(Emp#, Project-Name, ...). That is, only those projects are described on which at least one employee is working, and as long as one employee is working on a project that project cannot be eliminated.

4.3. Constraints Involving Categorical Abstractions

Consider the relations R0, R1, ... , Rn, n ≥ 2, such that K denotes the key set for all these relations. The entities defined by relation R0 represent a *generalization* of the entities defined by relations R1, ... ,Rn if the following protocol holds between relation R0 and each relation Ri, 1 ≤ i ≤ n.

9. Generalization Protocol

INSERT t0 IN R0	PRECOND ∃ ti ∈ Ri t0[K] = ti[K]
DELETE t0 FROM R0	PRECOND $\nexists$ ti ∈ Ri t0[K] = ti[K]
INSERT ti IN Ri	IMPLIES {INSERT t0 IN R0 | t0[K] = ti[K] AND t0[T0-K] = NULL} where t0 denotes the attribute set of R0
DELETE ti FROM Ri	IMPLIES {DELETE t0 FROM R0 | t0 ∈ R0 t0[K] = ti[K]}

For example, the personnel defined by relation R0(School-Id, ...) could represent a generalization of the staff and faculty represented by relations R1(School-Id, Job-Title, ...) and R2(School-Id, Faculty-Rank, ...), respectively. That is, on becoming either a staff or faculty member of a university one automatically obtains the position of university personnel.

Additional examples detailing tbe richness of UPM's information modeling capability can be found in Refs. 6 and 7.

5. View Integration

The next phase of the design process is view integration. The following algorithm describes the analysis which must be performed in order to identify semantic conflicts between different user requirements and produce a composite database design which "supports" each user view.

Step (0). The algorithm is provided with a collection of relational views V = $\{Vi(Ti, Ei) \mid 1 \leq i \leq m\}$ together with a collection of UPM specified expressions defining update protocols amongst these views. Each view Vi is defined over a set of attributes Ti. Ei denotes the set of functional dependencies (FDs) which the value set associated with view Vi must satisfy. The notation $X \rightarrow Y$ is used to denote an FD relationship between attribute sets X and Y. Simply stated, an FD relationship holds between the X and Y values of view Vi if, at all times, these values define a functional mapping between X and Y.

Step (1). Naming and FD consistency are checked for across all views.

For each attribute name that appears in more than one view, the users of the algorithm are asked whether or not it has the same interpretation in all of these views. If not, then the users are asked to rename the appropriate attributes and the algorithm is reinitiated. If multiple occurrences of the same attribute name have the same interpretation across all views, then naming consistency is said to hold for these views.

View Vi is said to be FD consistent with all views $\{Vj \mid j \neq i \ \& \ 1 \leq j \leq m\}$ if the following condition holds:

$$X,Y \subseteq Ti \ \& \ X \rightarrow Y \in (\cup_{j \neq i} Ej)^+ \Rightarrow X \rightarrow Y \in Ei^+$$

where Ei^+ denotes the FDs in Ei and all those that can be deduced from this set (2). If the property $X \rightarrow Y \in Ei^+$ is not desired, then these attributes must be renamed in view Vi so that FD consistency across all views holds. If any renaming takes place, then the algorithm must be reinitiated. FD consistency is a UPM specifiable constraint which has been isolated from the other UPM constraints because of its special role in the last step of the algorithm.

Step (2). Multiple FD derivations across all views are examined to determine whether the conflict-free or semantic equivalence properties are to be maintained. Two derivations of the FD $X \rightarrow Y$ are said to be conflict-free if whenever these derivations yield tuples of the form (x,y1) and (x,y2) where $x \neq$ NULL, then either y1 = y2 or y1 = NULL or y2 = NULL. Note that this property is slightly weaker than saying that the two derivations are semantically equivalent.

For each occurrence of a multiple FD derivation where neither property is desired, the appropriate users are asked to rename the necessary attributes and reinitiate the algorithm.

If the conflict-free property is desired, then UPM specifiable expressions which check that updates do not violate this property are associated with these view relations. For example, if the following views were provided, it might be desirable to maintain the conflict-free property for both the

COURSE → PROF → DEPT   and   COURSE → TA → DEPT

derivations of the FD COURSE → DEPT:

V1(COURSE, PROF, TA)   COURSE → PROF | TA
V2(PROF, DEPT)   PROF → DEPT
V3(TA, DEPT)   TA → DEPT

On the other hand, if the semantic equivalence property is desired, then the necessary UPM specifiable expressions must be generated. Note that the semantic equivalence property is difficult to maintain and is also quite restrictive regarding the database updates which are allowable. For example, the semantic equivalence of the two COURSE → DEPT derivations can be maintained only if the appropriate values for both the PROF and TA attributes are known. On the other hand, the conflict-free property can be maintained whether or not these values are known. After this step of the algorithm, it can be assumed that at a minimum the conflict-free property is to be maintained for multiple derivations of the same FD.

Step (3). Maximize data sharing through view redefinition. Consider the following views:

V1(EMP, DEPT)   EMP → DEPT
V2(DEPT, MGR)   DEPT → MGR
V3(EMP, MGR)   EMP → MGR

It can be assumed that all the derivations of the FD EMP → MGR embodied by views V1, V2, and V3 are to be maintained in a conflict-free manner. If these derivations are represented by separate relations, then appropriate UPM expressions must be utilized to maintain this property. On the other hand, the users are presented with the option of redefining specific views so that some redundancy can be eliminated. For example, if view V3 is redefined as (EMP, DEPT, MGR), where DEPT → MGR, then multiple representations of the FD EMP → MGR are avoided by actions taken in Step (5). This redefinition, while it affects the user's view of the database, does not require that the algorithm be reinitiated.

Step (4). UPM expression conflicts are checked for across all views.

The following example illustrates one possible conflict which is identified in this step. It involves three distinct views of the database. The first view is held by the Payroll department, which has the responsibility of issuing checks to payees who work on projects. Payroll might assume that the following PAYS relation defines a required relationship involving PAYEES and PROJECTS:

PAYS (Payee#, Project#, . . .)

PAYEES(Payee#, . . .)

PROJECTS(Project#, . . .)

Employee Relations might need a different view to handle employee benefits for employees who work on projects. Employee Relations might assume that the PAY-EMPLOYEES relation defines a simple relationship between EMPLOY-EES and PROJECTS:

PAY-EMPLOYEES(Employee#, Project#, . . .)

EMPLOYEES(Employee#, . . .)

PROJECTS(Project#, . . .)

Finally, the Controller department might need the following view in order to monitor external contracts. The Controller department might assume that the PAY-VENDORS relation defines a simple relationship between VENDORS and PROJECTS:

PAY-VENDORS(Vendor#, Project#, . . .)

VENDORS(Vendor#, . . .)

PROJECTS(Project#, . . .)

If additional information is available which indicates that PAYEES is a generalization of EMPLOYEES and VENDORS and that the PAYS relationship is a generalization of the PAY-EMPLOYEES and PAY-VENDORS relationships then a semantic conflict exists regarding whether these relationships are simple or required as indicated above. Thus, the users who furnished these protocols must be asked to redefine the appropriate view descriptions. If only the protocols are revised, then only this step must be reinitiated. On the other hand, if the views are redefined, then the algorithm must be reinitiated. It must be noted that not all conflicts are easy to detect. A general algorithm for detecting such conflicts would have to employ theorem-proving techniques, which points out the "difficultness" of the general problem. Further analysis of the problem is currently underway to determine if this step can be simplified for specific enterprise models.

Step (5). Maximize data sharing through normalization. Using the synthesis approach to normalization as outlined in Ref. 2, an update preserving 3NF representation of the views is constructed subject to any redundancy imposed in Step (3). If the database management system chosen to support the resulting design includes a generalized view mechanism, i.e., one which supports both view retrieval and update operations, then the update protocols can be handled at the view (external schema) level. If not, then the update protocols must be translated into update protocols involving the normalized 3NF representation of the views since it is at this level that the updates will be given.

6. Conclusion

The methodology outlined in this article has several desirable properties. First, due to the rich facilities that UPM has for modeling both static and dynamic information, it is expected that the proposed methodology could facilitate the design of a broad range of enterprise information systems. Second, because it is based on the relational model, it takes advantage of the trend toward relational database management systems. Finally, due to the theoretical soundness of the view integration algorithm, it can be shown that the methodology produces database designs in which (1) the retrieval, insertion, and deletion operations for each user view are supported, (2) consistent interpretation of the composite view is held by all views, (3) only well-defined tuples (non-NULL values in key attributes) in all views are allowed, (4) a conflict-free representation of FDs is supported, and (5) the redundant representation of FDs is minimized.

References

1. A design aide for relational database schemas—User manual, Bell Laboratories, September 1981.
2. C. R. Carlson, A. K. Arora, and M. M. Carlson, The application of functional dependency theory to relational databases, *Comput. J.* **25**, 1 (1982).
3. A. K. Arora and C. R. Carlson, On the flexibility provided by conflict-free normalization, COMPSAC 82.
4. The ANSI/X3/SPARC DBMS framework, Interim report of the Study Group on Database Management Systems, *File and Data Translations* **7**, 2 (1975).
5. *The ANSI/X3/SPARC DBMS Framework, Report of the Study Group on Database Management Systems*, Tsichritzis and Klug, Eds., AFIPS Press, Arlington, Virginia, 1977.
6. C. R. Carlson and A. K. Arora, The update protocol model: A unified approach to semantic data modeling, The Informal DBMS Workshop, Naperville, Illinois, 1981.
7. C. R. Carlson and A. K. Arora, Toward a unified, formal approach to semantic data modeling, Technical Report, Bell Laboratories, 1981.
8. P. Chen, The entity–relationship model: Toward a unified view of data, *Association for Computing Machinery—Transactions on Data Systems* **1**, 1, 1976.
9. Entity–relationship approach to information modeling and analysis, Proceedings of the Second International Conference on Entity–Relationship Approach, P. Chen, Ed., ER Institute, 1981.
10. E. F. Codd, Extending the database relational model to capture more meaning, *Association for Computing Machinery—Transactions on Data Systems* **4**, 4, 1979.

13

LANGUAGE DESIGN FOR RELATIONAL MODEL MANAGEMENT

ROBERT W. BLANNING

1. Introduction

Within the past decade there has emerged a small but growing literature suggesting that (1) decision models, like data, are an important organizational resource that should be managed effectively, (2) a discipline of model management be developed to guide managers in the performance of this task, and (3) software systems, called model management systems, should be implemented to assist in the application of this emerging discipline.[1-9] That the thinking in this area has not coalesced into a unified view is not surprising, for no such coalescence has occurred in the far more established discipline of data base management. One of several propositions put forth is that the relational view of data, which has given rise during the past decade to an outpouring of theoretical research and several implemented systems, be extended to model management. It is suggested that just as a database may be viewed as a set of relations with key and content attributes and appropriate functional dependencies between them, so also may a model bank (as it is called) be viewed as a set of relations with input and output attributes and with appropriate functional dependencies.[10]

There are two reasons for examining decision models from a relational point of view. First, many operations in relational model management appear to have counterparts in relational data management, and an understanding of one may help in understanding the other. For example, selection of data from a file and the execution of a simulation are logically similar: in each case a tuple having specified values for certain of its attributes is selected (from the file) or generated (by the model), even though the procedures for selecting or generating tuples are quite different. Similarly, an operation analogous to a join in relational data man-

ROBERT W. BLANNING • Owen Graduate School of Management, Vanderbilt University, Nashville, Tennessee 37203.

agement occurs in model management whenever the output of one model is also the input to another. The second reason for examining model management from a relational perspective is that such an examination may lead to a unified view of information which is independent of the source of the information—data or models.[11]

We are interested here only in the logical view of models, not in the physical implementation of model management systems, which will differ substantially from the implementation of data management systems. An important facet of the logical view is the language with which a user communicates with the system to define models and to request information from them. Criteria for relational completeness of model query languages have been arrived at, and they have been codified into a relational algebra for model management.[12] In addition, a primitive nonrelational query language for both data and model management has been developed,[13] and its transformational properties have been studied.[14] The research presented here is a synthesis of these two approaches—we will present a relationally complete model query language and will study its linguistic properties.

In Section 2 below we examine briefly the similarities and differences, both linguistic and nonlinguistic, between the relational views of data and of models. In Section 3 we present the criteria for relational completeness of model query languages. Section 4 describes MQL—a model query language that satisfies these criteria—and examines several of its linguistic properties. In Section 5 we discuss the possibility of integrating data management, model management, and knowledge management (that is, the management of concepts and associations between them) in a unified relational framework.

2. Databases and Model Banks

We begin with the view that both databases and model banks are collections of relations with certain attributes and functional dependencies between the attributes and ask how this view may be articulated and in what way it should be modified. To answer this question we examine two issues that arise in relational database management and determine how they differ when the physical realization of the relations are models rather than files of data.

The first issue is the structuring of the set of relations—that is, the specification of the various relations (defined by their attributes) that make up the database or model bank. In relational database systems functional dependencies within relations are used to define a sequence of normal forms. For example, a relation is in first normal form if all of its attributes identify domains of attribute values and not the names of other relations; it is in second normal form if no nonkey attributes are functionally dependent on a proper subset of the primary key; and it is in third normal form if there are no transitive dependencies in the relation. The reason for these definitions (and of other definitions for still higher normal forms) is that projecting lower-form relations into a higher normal form eliminates certain types of update anomalies—problems that can arise in adding, changing, or deleting a tuple in a relation. For example, if a relation contains a transitive dependency (and therefore, is not in third normal form) and all tuples containing information about a component of the dependency are deleted, then information about other components is deleted as well.[15,16]

Arguments of this type are not valid in relational model management for a very simple reason—in relational model management tuples do not exist, and therefore, neither do update anomalies. However, other anomalies, called processing anomalies, do exist. They describe difficulties that can arise when users input data to models, execute the models, and receive the output, and they lead to normal forms that are similar, but not identical, to the normal forms found in relational data management.[17]

The second issue is determining the criteria for relational completeness of database languages and sublanguages. A set of criteria based on such maintenance operations as insertion and deletion of a tuple, such algebraic operations as union and intersection, and such topological transformations as projection and join (or composition) have been identified. This has led to the construction of a relational algebra and to a demonstration that the first-order predicate calculus is complete with respect to the algebra.[15,16]

Criteria for relational completeness of model management languages have also been articulated. They differ from the criteria for relational data base systems in that (1) the maintenance operations are not present, (2) the algebraic (i.e., set) operations are not present, (3) the operations of optimization and sensitivity analysis have been added, and (4) the join operations, although it exists, is transparent to the user. A relational algebra (explained in Section 3 below) has been constructed, and it has been demonstrated that the first-order predicate calculus is relationally complete for model management.[12]

The transparency of the join operator results from the fact that if more than one model is used to respond to a specific query, then no output attribute can appear in more than one of the models. For example, there may be several models available for calculating total cost as a function of certain decisions, but only one of them may be used to respond to a specific query—there can be only one total cost. If we define a *model bank* as the collection of all models managed by a model management system and a *model set* as the collection of models (which may consist of only one model) used to respond to a specific query, then any output attribute can appear in only one of the models of a model set. Thus, the lossy join problem, which arises when there is more than one way of joining data relations,[18] does not arise in relational model management, and any joins in a model set can be implemented by the system and need not be specified by the user. (See Refs. 12,17 for other problems that can occur when a model management system implements joins.) In summary, the principal difference between the criteria for relational completeness of query languages in data management and in model management is that in model management joins do not appear but optimization and sensitivity analysis do appear.

Although optimization operations are occasionally performed by database systems (e.g., to find the salesman with the highest sales or the product with the lowest inventory), nothing like sensitivity analysis is found in database management. An example of sensitivity analysis in such a context would take place if one wished to use a file whose key is inventory part number and whose content is inventory level to estimate the sensitivity of inventory level to inventory part number. This would presumably be accomplished by selecting an inventory part number that is close to the number at which the sensitivity is to be calculated (the base case), determining the inventory level of that part, and dividing the increment in inventory level by the increment in inventory part number. This, of course, is ludicrous. Yet models are often used to provide analogous information. For example, a simulation of a production facility whose input includes a targeted production quantity and whose output includes the resulting production cost can be used to calculate the marginal cost of production by incrementing the production target and observing the change in production cost. In this case the tuples are not stored in a file but are generated by the model as needed. Yet the calculation procedure and the interpretation of the output is the same.

This represents an important difference between the relational views of data and of models. In the first case certain content attributes of a relation are functionally dependent on certain key attributes, and in the second case certain output attributes of a relation are functionally dependent on certain input attributes. Yet when the physical realization of the relation is a model, determining the sensitivity of the dependent attributes with respect to the independent ones is frequently done, and when the physical realization of the relation is a file, it is not done.

The reason, examined in detail in Ref. 11, concerns the nature of the functional dependencies found in databases in model banks. They are not the same. The functional dependencies found in data bases are *assigned* dependencies (e.g., an inventory part number is assigned to a type of finished product, and changing the number will not change the product and therefore, will not change the inventory level). Thus, there is an entity in the real world corresponding to each tuple in the relation, and it does not change even if its identifier were to be changed. The functional dependencies in model management, on the other hand, are *causal* dependencies (e.g., there is a causal connection between production target and production cost, such that a change in the first will induce a change in the second). In this case there is only one entity in the real world corresponding to the entire relation, and the (virtual) tuples describe causal relationships between sets of possible attribute values for that single entity. When the functional dependencies in a relation are assigned, sensitivity analysis is of little or no use, but when they are causal, sensitivity analysis is meaningful and useful.

3. The Relational Completeness of Model Management Languages

We now enumerate and describe in algebraic form the criteria for relational completeness of a query language with which the users of a model management system may instruct the system to perform the operations described above. We assume the existence of a model set (which may consist of a single model) in relational form $\langle \alpha | \beta \rangle$ with inputs α and outputs β. Consider for example, a model set in which inputs are a sale price P (decision variable) and a raw material price R (environmental variable) and the outputs are raw material expenses E and net income N. Thus, $\alpha = (P, R)$ and $\beta = (E, N)$, and if CORP is the name of the model set, we have CORP $= \langle P, R | E, N \rangle$. The relational algebra for model management consists of three operations performed on (relational) model sets: (1) execution, which is a synthesis of selection and projection in relational data management, (2) optimization of an output over one or more inputs, and (3) sensitivity analysis.

In some cases the attribute values in the model set may be constrained. The constraints are described in a *specification set,* which is a set of triples consisting of an attribute name, one of the symbols "$\leq$," "$=$," or "$\geq$," and a number. (We assume that all attribute values are quantified and that more complex constraints, of the type found in mathematical programming models, are contained in the models themselves.) For example, if we want the sale price to be between $5 and $17 and the raw material price to be no greater than $25, then the specification set, here denoted σ_1, will be $\sigma_1 = \{(P, \geq, 5), (P, \leq, 17), (R, \leq, 25)\}$. We note that constraints of this type (e.g., $R \geq 0$) may also be found in the model set, and that the specification set may also contain constraints on the outputs (e.g., $E \leq$ $2 million). We also note that the specification set may be null—that is, it may contain no triples, and hence, may specify nothing.

The execution operator $\epsilon(\quad , \quad)$ determines the outputs of the model set for all values of the inputs, where both are constrained by the specification set. It has two arguments—the names of the model set and of the specification set. For example, to determine the values of P, R, E, and N for which $5 \leq P \leq 17$ and $R \leq 25$, we execute $\epsilon(\text{CORP}, \sigma_1)$. The form of the output will not be considered here but will presumably be controlled by means of a report writer in the model management system.

It is possible to concatenate specification sets so that the constraints contained in both are met. This may be accomplished in either of two ways—by creating a new specification set containing both of the existing ones or by imbedding one execution operator in another. For example, if we wish to execute CORP with its attribute values constrained by the two specification sets σ_2 and σ_3, we can create a new specification set $\sigma_4 = \{\sigma_2, \sigma_3\}$ and execute $\epsilon(\text{CORP}, \sigma_4)$. [We could also have written $\epsilon(\text{CORP}, \{\sigma_2, \sigma_3\})$.] The second approach is to exploit the fact that execution is a relational operation—that is, it operates on a relation to produce a relation. Thus, we may obtain the same result by executing $\epsilon(\epsilon(\text{CORP}, \sigma_2), \sigma_3)$ or $\epsilon(\epsilon(\text{CORP}, \sigma_3), \sigma_2)$. In deriving the model query language in Section 4 below, we will assume for simplicity that the first approach is used and that execution operators are not concatenated.

The optimization operator determines the values of one or more inputs that maximize or minimize a single output within the constraints contained in a (possibly null) specification set. The operator is $\mu(\quad , \quad , \quad , \quad , \quad)$, whose arguments are the names of the model set and the specification set, a nonvoid subset of the inputs, a single output attribute β, and the symbol "$+$" or "$-$", depending on whether the output attribute is to be maximized or minimized. For example, to determine for each value of $R \le 25$ the value of P in the interval $[5, 17]$ that maximizes N, we execute $\mu(\text{CORP}, \sigma_1, P, N, +)$. To determine the value of P that maximizes N when $R = 7$, we define $\sigma_5 = (R, = , 7)$ and execute $\mu(\text{CORP}, \sigma_5, P, N, +)$.

Since optimization, like execution, is a relational operation, we can imbed one optimization operation within another one. For example, the model set CORP may be used by the raw material supplier to determine the raw material price that will maximize raw material expense (the revenues of the supplier) assuming that his customer will then set the sale price to maximize net income. In other words, we wish to find the value of R that will maximize E assuming that P will then be selected to maximize N. If the specification set is σ_1, then we write $\mu(\mu (\text{CORP}, \sigma_1, P, N, +), \sigma_1, R, E, +)$.

This imbedding of optimization operations is of special interest for three reasons: First, for model sets with a large number of input attributes, a sequence of many optimization operations may be performed; the only requirement is that the sets of input attributes over which the optimization operations are to be performed (in this case R and P) must be pairwise disjoint. This has a significant impact on the properties of the model query language described in Section 4 below. The second reason is that the interaction between supplier and manufacturer has some of the characteristics of an agency relationship, in which the supplier is the principal and the manufacturer is its agent.[19,20] In this case the functional form of the fee schedule (i.e., the procedures for calculating E) is contained in the model set, and the principal needs only to determine a parameter in the schedule (i.e., the value of R). The third reason is that the imbedding of optimization operations may serve as a useful test query to determine the ease of use of a model query language. An unofficial but widely used test query in relational data management is "Select all employees whose salaries exceed those of their supervisors," applied to a relation each of whose tuples identifies an employee, his salary, and his supervisor. (It is assumed that supervisors are also employees and that tuples describing them are in the relation as well.) Imbedded optimization has the same self-referential property as this test query for relational data management, and it may serve the same purpose.

We now turn to the last of the operations—sensitivity analysis. There are five types of sensitivity analysis, each of which calculates the rate of change of one attribute in a model set with respect to another. The sensitivities thus calculated may be point estimates (e.g., first derivatives) or tables or graphs demonstrating how a change in one attribute will affect the other. As before, we assume that the output format (including the form in which the sensitivity is to be reported) will be controlled by the user through a report writer in the model management system. We note that although sensitivity analysis is included in the criteria for relational completeness, it is not a relational concept (i.e., a sensitivity is not a relation); thus, sensitivity analyses cannot be combined with each other.

The first type of sensitivity, called a *partial sensitivity,* is the rate of change of an output with respect to an input with all other inputs held constant. It is written $\Delta_1(\quad,\quad,\quad,\quad)$, where the arguments are the names of the model set and the specification set and of the input and output attributes. If more than one value of the attributes is allowed by the specification set, then the sensitivity is calculated for all allowable values. For example, to determine the sensitivity of net income to the sale price for all values of the sale price when the raw material price is \$7, we write $\Delta_1(CORP, \sigma_5, P, N)$. The partial sensitivity operator Δ_1 is a primitive operator; the remaining sensitivity operators $\Delta_2 \ldots \Delta_5$ described below can be derived from it.[12]

The second type of sensitivity, called a *substitution sensitivity,* is the rate of change of one input with respect to another where a single output is held constant. It is written $\Delta_2(\quad,\quad,\quad,\quad,\quad)$, where the arguments are the names of the model set and the specification set and of the two input and the output attributes. For example, to determine the sensitivity of sale price to raw material price where raw material price is \$7 and expense is \$2 million, we let $\sigma_6 = \{\sigma_5, (E, =, 2000000)\}$ and write $\Delta_2(CORP, \sigma_6, R, P, E)$. If the specification set were $\sigma_7 = \{NULL\}$, then the sensitivity $\Delta_2(CORP, \sigma_7, R, P, E)$ would be calculated for each value of R and P and the resulting value of E.

The third type of sensitivity, called a *tradeoff sensitivity,* is the rate of change of one output with respect to another output, where the changes in both are caused by a change in one of the inputs. It is written $\Delta_3(\quad,\quad,\quad,\quad,\quad)$, where the arguments are the names of the model set and the specification set and of the two output and the input attributes. For example, if to find the rate of change of net income with respect to expense as the sale price changes for a raw material price of \$7 and for all values of the sale price, we write $\Delta_3(CORP, \sigma_5, E, N, P)$.

The fourth and fifth sensitivities, called *total sensitivities,* are rates of change of an output with respect to an input where a second input will be adjusted in response to the change in the first one. In a *total sensitivity with optimization* the second input is adjusted to maintain the designated output at its maximum (or minimum) value as the first input changes. For example, to obtain the rate of change of net income with respect to raw material price when the raw material price is $7 and the sale price is adjusted to maximize net income as the raw material price changes, we write $\Delta_4(CORP, \sigma_5, R, N, P, +)$. We note that only one quantity (number, table, or graph) is reported here, even though the value of P is not determined by the specification set, because this sensitivity is defined for only one value of P, the value that maximizes N when $R = 7$. Finally, in a *total sensitivity with invariance*, the second input is adjusted to hold a second output constant. For example, to determine for each sale price the rate of change of net income with respect to raw material price at a raw material price of $7 and the sale price is adjusted to hold expense constant as the raw material price changes, we write $\Delta_5(CORP, \sigma_5, R, N, P, E)$. These two types of sensitivity are examined in detail and illustrated with numerical examples in Ref. 21.

4. The Properties of MQL

We now present MQL (model query language), an English-like query language that is relationally complete with respect to execution, optimization, and sensitivity analysis. After illustrating each of the features of MQL, we examine its linguistic properties. A BNF syntax of MQL appears in Appendix A.

We assume that a model set CORP with inputs P and R and outputs E and N has been defined, as have a specification set SIGMA and a report writer RPT. All other words are MQL reserved words and are underlined. The relational operations and their illustrations are as follows:

1. *Execution.* Execute the model set: $\epsilon(CORP, SIGMA)$.

> EXECUTE CORP
> WITH SIGMA
> PUT RPT

2. *Optimization.* Select the sale price that will maximize net income: μ $(CORP, SIGMA, P, N, +)$.

> MAXIMIZE N
> OVER P
> WITH SIGMA
> USING CORP
> PUT RPT

(For a minimization problem, the first word would be <u>MINIMIZE</u>.)

    3. Imbedded Optimization. Select the raw material price that will maximize expense assuming that the sale price will then be selected to maximize net income: $\mu(\mu(CORP, SIGMA, P, N, +), SIGMA, R, E, +)$.

<u>MAXIMIZE</u> E
<u>OVER</u> R
<u>WITH</u> SIGMA
<u>USING</u>
      <u>MAXIMIZE</u> N
      <u>OVER</u> P
      <u>WITH</u> SIGMA
      <u>USING</u> CORP
<u>PUT</u> RPT

We note that the first use of <u>WITH</u> SIGMA is redundant, since the specification set in the imbedded operation constrains the enveloping operation as well.

    4. Partial Sensitivity Analysis. Calculate the rate of change of net income with respect to sale price: $\Delta_1(CORP, SIGMA, P, N)$.

<u>EXECUTE</u> CORP
<u>WITH</u> SIGMA
<u>IMPACT</u> P
<u>ON</u> N
<u>PUT</u> RPT

    5. Substitution Sensitivity Analysis. Calculate the rate of change of sale price with respect to raw material price where expense is held constant: $\Delta_2(CORP, SIGMA, R, P, E)$.

<u>EXECUTE</u> CORP
<u>WITH</u> SIGMA
<u>IMPACT</u> R
<u>ON</u> R
<u>CONSTRAINING</u> E
<u>PUT</u> RPT

6. *Tradeoff Sensitivity Analysis*. Calculate the rate of change of net income with respect to expense as the sale price changes: Δ_3(CORP, SIGMA, E, N, P).

EXECUTE CORP
WITH SIGMA
IMPACT E
ON N
VARYING P
PUT RPT

7. *Total Sensitivity Analysis with Optimization*. Calculate the rate of change of net income with respect to raw material price assuming that the sale price will be adjusted to maximize net income: Δ_4(CORP, SIGMA, R, N, P, $+$).

MAXIMIZE N
OVER P
WITH SIGMA
USING CORP
IMPACT P
PUT RPT

8. *Total Sensitivity Analysis with Invariance*. Calculate the rate of change of net income with respect to raw material price assuming that the sale price is adjusted to hold expense constant: Δ_5(CORP, SIGMA, R, N, P, E).

EXECUTE CORP
WITH SIGMA
IMPACT R
ON N
VARYING P
CONSTRAINING E
PUT RPT

We conclude by this section examining two sets of properties of MQL that determine (1) the way in which sentences in the language may be parsed for translation and (2) the complexity of the language. The first set of properties identifies the type of grammar that generates MQL and hence, the type of automaton needed to recognize or translate sentences in the language. We note that the generative grammar defined in Appendix A contains input, output, modset, and specset as terminals. However, in its implementation for any particular model, these will be variables, and the grammar will contain transformational productions of the form $\langle \text{input} \rangle ::= P$ and $\langle \text{output} \rangle ::= N$, converting a deep structure sentence with terminals such as input and modset into a surface structure sentence with terminals such as P and CORP. Thus, the transformational constraint (that all input terminals in sentences generated from Productions 3–7 be different) is implemented at the transformational level. (See Ref. 14 for a more general discussion of the transformational properties of DSS languages.)

By considering MQL with and without the transformational constraint (and hence, without or with the set of transformational productions), we can derive three results. The first is that for a given model set (with a fixed number of inputs and outputs). MQL with its transformational constraint is generated by a linear grammar. Hence, it can be parsed by a finite automaton.[22,23] Second, even if (1) the transformational productions are not considered, (2) the transformational constraint were removed, and (3) the model set may have an arbitrarily large number of inputs (so that sentences of infinite length, some of them semantically meaningless, are possible), sentences in the language are still generated by a linear grammar and can be parsed by a finite automaton. Finally, if we allow model sets with an arbitrarily large number of inputs and insist that the transformational constraint be observed, then the language is context-free and, hence, can be parsed by a pushdown automaton whose stack is used to detect violations of the transformational constraint. These three results are proven in the following theorem.

THEOREM 1: *(1) MQL for a given model set is generated by a linear grammar; (2) MQL for an arbitrary model set with the transformational constraint removed is generated by a linear grammar; and (3) MQL (including the transformational constraint) for an arbitrary model set is not linear but is context-free. (See Appendix B.)*

The second set of properties concerns the complexity of the language. (This is not the same as the computational complexity of combinational algorithms.) Two such properties are the star height of the language and whether the language possesses the finite power property (see Chapter 3 of Ref. 24). Neither property directly affects the design of translators or the efficiency of processing; rather, they indicate the relative degree of simplicity and complexity of MQL.

To define the star height of a linear grammar we must first define a regular expression in the language. It is defined recursively as follows: (1) the null symbol and each terminal are regular expressions and (2) if α and β are regular expressions, so are $\alpha \cup \beta$ (the union of α and β), $\alpha\beta$ (the Cartesian product of all strings in α concatenated with those in β), and α^* (the union of the null string and all strings obtained by concatenating any strings in α any number of times). Thus each regular expression is a language over the terminals. The star height of a regular expression is defined recursively as follows: (1) the null symbol and the terminals each have a star height of zero; (2) if α and β are regular expressions, the star height of $\alpha \cup \beta$ and $\alpha\beta$ are the maximum of the star heights of α and β; and (3) the star height of α^* is one plus the star height of α. We now define the star height of a language $\mathcal{L}$ as the smallest integer I such that for some regular expression equal to $\mathcal{L}$ the star height of the expression equals I.

The purpose of defining star height is to measure the "loop complexity" of a language. Any language with finite number of sentences is of star height zero, and any language based on a single terminal (but with possibly an infinite number of strings containing repetitions of the terminal) has a star height of at most one (see Theorem 3.1 of Ref. 24). Languages with larger star heights will have "loops" or repetitions of star (i.e., α^*) operations. It is clear that for a given model, MQL with the transformational constraint is finite and thus has a star height of zero. It will be shown below that MQL in its generative form with the transformational constraint removed (i.e., with all input and output terminals labelled "input" and "output" and not distinguished from one another) is of star height one. Since this is the smallest star height that an infinite language can have, MQL has a low degree of loop (or star) complexity.

The finite power property measures a different kind of complexity. If $\mathcal{L}$ is a language generated by a linear grammar, then $\mathcal{L}^2$ is the language consisting of the catenation of all sentences in $\mathcal{L}$ with all sentences in $\mathcal{L}$, $\mathcal{L}^3$ is the catenation of $\mathcal{L}$ with $\mathcal{L}^2$, etc. $\mathcal{L}^0$ is the null language. We say that $\mathcal{L}$ possesses the finite power property if the infinite sequence $\mathcal{L}^0$, $\mathcal{L}$, $\mathcal{L}^2$, $\mathcal{L}^3$, ..., $\mathcal{L}^n$ contains a finite number of distinct elements. (This does not mean that the number of sentences thus formed is finite, but that the number of distinct languages in the sequence is finite.) The finite power property can also be defined in terms of the order of the language, which is the smallest integer n such that $\mathcal{L}^n = \mathcal{L}^{n+1}$. If no such integer exists, the language is said to be of infinite order. It can be shown that a language possesses the finite power property if and only if it is of finite order (see Lemma 3.6 of Ref. 24).

The order of a language, and hence the existence of the finite power property, indicates the results of generating indefinitely many sentences in the language and concatenating them with previously generated sentences. We note that a nonvoid language containing a finite number of sentences is of infinite order, because for any $n \geq 0$ the longest sentence in $\mathcal{L}^{n+1}$ will be longer than the longest sentence in $\mathcal{L}^n$ and therefore, $\mathcal{L}^{n+1} \neq \mathcal{L}^n$. But if the language contains an infinite number of sentences, then a point (value of n) may be reached at which no new sentences are added as a result of concatenation. Since MQL in its transformational form with the transformational constraint contains a finite number of sentences, it is of infinite order. We will see that even in its generative form without the transformational constraint (and thus, with an infinite number of sentences), it is still of infinite order.

The results concerning star height and the finite power property are demonstrated in the following theorem.

THEOREM 2. *MQL in its generative form (without the transformational constraint) is of star height one. In addition, it is not of finite order and thus, does not possess the finite power property. (See Appendix C.)*

That MQL is of infinite order does not mean that it is inordinately complex. On the contrary, MQL is of infinite order for the same reason that a finite language is of infinite order—there are sentences of bounded length in MQL (e.g., the EXECUTE sentences) that are not contained in any of the unbounded sentences (i.e., the nested optimizations). But if MQL were modified so that any concatenation of queries were a valid sentence in the language (as is done in natural languages by joining clauses with conjunctions or subordinating adverbs), then MQL would be of first order and would possess the finite power property.

To demonstrate this, we define an extended MQL, which we will call EMQL. The syntax of EMQL is specified as follows:

1. Replace the variable ⟨sentence⟩ in Productions 1 and 3 of Appendix A with the variable ⟨subsentence⟩.

2. Add Production 8: ⟨sentence⟩ ::= ⟨subsentence⟩
                                              | ⟨sub-sentence⟩ ⟨subsentence⟩.

We can now prove the following theorem.

THEOREM 3. *EMQL in its generative form is a first-order language and hence possesses the finite power property. (See Appendix D.)*

We note that from this point of view, EMQL is not a very complex language, for the only language of lower order is the null language—the language that contains no sentences.

We have examined here the linguistic properties of MQL and found it to be fairly simple language. The examination revealed the type of grammar that generates the language, the properties of the automaton that recognizes sentences in the language, and the ways in which sentences or fragments of sentences adjoin. Other approaches to studying the complexity of decision support systems, that focus on the tasks performed[25] and the cognitive characteristics of the people performing the tasks,[26,27] have been proposed. Analyses such as these must await implementation of the language, but we may expect on both intuitive and linguistic grounds that decision support systems based on MQL (or EMQL) will not be difficult to implement and use.

5. Data Management, Model Management, and Knowledge Management

Those familiar with relational database systems will note that MQL is similar to SEQUEL[28] in that it uses terse imperative English sentences to describe the manipulation of tuples, and multiple optimizations are executed as a sequence of relational mappings similar to those used to implement joins in SEQUEL. These and other similarities between the relational views of data and of models suggest that it may be possible to synthesize a unifying relational framework for data management and model management.[11] Such a synthesis would be consistent with some of the recent literature on decision support systems (DSS) that examines the relationships between data and models. For example, a functional view of DSS that encompasses both data and models has been proposed,[29] and this has led to the construction of a rather primitive nonrelational language for manipulating both data and models.[13,14] In addition, several studies have been conducted on the ways in which data and models interact[30–32]; it has even been suggested that models may be viewed as "data abstractions"—that is, the relationships in a model may be thought of as aggregations (often statistical) of stored data.[33]

Relational structures may also be useful in describing a third type of information managed by some DSS: knowledge. The term "knowledge base" is now being used in two contexts in DSS research. The first context parallels model management; the coefficients in a model are considered part of an organization's knowledge base.[34] The second context arises from the more general perspective of artificial intelligence; it is suggested that knowledge is a set of concepts and a set of associations between them and that a DSS should maintain information on important concepts and their associations in order to help decision makers diagnose problems as well as solve them.[4] The methodologies proposed are those of knowledge representation[8,35]: both the network-oriented approaches of declarative knowledge representation[36,37] and the production-oriented approaches of procedural knowledge representation.[38] No attempt has yet been made to construct a relational framework for knowledge management, but the algebraic character of graphs and production systems[39,40] suggests that these structures will soon succumb to a relational approach.

The possible success of a single analytical framework for data management, model management, and knowledge management should not be surprising. The topological principles that lie at the heart of relational algebra are the distillation of mathematical techniques developed over several centuries to investigate natural phenomena, and it is not unreasonable to expect that similar priniciples will be useful in describing the world of artifacts that managers wish to influence or control. A final determination of the efficacy of these principles must await the implementation of model management systems and knowledge management systems, followed by competent behavioral research. But it is well within the realm of possibility that a unifying algebraic, topological, and linguistic representation of the three types of information managed by decision support systems will eventually be realized.

Appendix A: Syntax of MQL

The following is a BNF description of MQL, in which the upper case terminals are reserved words and the lower case terminals denote the model set, its inputs and outputs, and its specification set. The first two productions generate sentences that begin with EXECUTE (i.e., simulation and all sensitivity analyses except the partial sensitivity analysis using the optimization criterion). The remaining productions generate sentences beginning with MAXIMIZE or MINIMIZE—that is, optimization (including indefinitely repeated optimization) and partial sensitivity analysis with an optimization criterion.

This grammar generates all meaningful sentences in the languages once the names of the model set, the specification set, and the appropriate inputs and outputs have been inserted. That is, we assume that in the final implementation of MQL input, output, modset, and specset will be variable names, and productions such as ⟨input⟩ ::= input(i), ⟨output⟩ ::= output(j), ⟨modset⟩ ::= modset(k), and ⟨specset⟩ ::= specset(l) for certain values of i, j, k, and l will appear in the final sentences. All sentences generated by the final form will be meaningful with one exception: the input terminals of any sentences generated by Productions 3–7 should be different. The grammar presented here will be called the generative form of MQL, the extended grammar with names for input, output, modset, and specset will be called the transformational form of MQL, and the requirement concerning input terminals will be called the transformational constraint.

The generative form of MQL is as follows:

1. ⟨sentence⟩ ::= EXECUTE modset WITH specset IMPACT ⟨remainder⟩ PUT rpt
2. ⟨remainder⟩ ::= input ON output | input ON input CONSTRAINING output
   | output ON output VARYING input
   | input ON output VARYING input CONSTRAINING output
3. ⟨sentence⟩ ::= ⟨optimize⟩ output OVER inputs WITH specset USING ⟨object⟩ PUT rpt
4. ⟨object⟩ ::= ⟨relation⟩ | modset IMPACT input
5. ⟨relation⟩ ::= modset | ⟨optimize⟩ output OVER ⟨inputs⟩ WITH specset USING ⟨relation⟩
6. ⟨inputs⟩ ::= input | ⟨inputs⟩ input
7. ⟨optimize⟩ ::= MAXIMIZE | MINIMIZE

Appendix B: Proof of Theorem 1

We prove Theorem 1. (1) MQL for a given model set is geneated by a linear grammar, (2) MQL for an arbitrary model set with the transformational constraint removed is generated by a linear grammar, and (3) MQL (including the transformational constraint) for an arbitrary model or model set is not linear but is context free.

Proof. For a given model set, the number of inputs and outputs are finite. Thus, all sentences in MQL are of finite length, because (a) the sentences generated by Productions 1 and 2 of Appendix A are always of finite length and (b) the nonsyntactic constraint requires that the length of the sentences generated by Productions 3–7 be finite. Since any finite language is generated by a linear grammar, MQL is generated by a linear grammar.

(2) If the transformational constraint is removed, then each sentence generated by Productions 3–7 is generated by a finite set of productions of the form ⟨sentence⟩ ::= α ⟨relation⟩ β and ⟨relation⟩ ::= γ ⟨relation⟩, where α, β, and γ are strings of terminals. However, we may create a new variable ⟨newvar⟩ and decompose the first type of production into the two productions ⟨sentence⟩ ::= α ⟨newvar⟩ and ⟨newvar⟩ ::= ⟨relation⟩ β. The three types of production can easily be expressed in linear form.

(3) MQL for a model set with an arbitrarily large number of inputs cannot be generated by a linear grammar, for it could then be recognized by an automaton with a finite number of states. This is impossible because the automaton must check for duplications of an arbitrarily large number of input terminals. On the other hand, the language is context-free, because the left side of each production contains a single variable and an (infinite) stack can be used to check for violations of the nonsyntactic constraint by checking each input to see if it has occurred before.

Appendix C: Proof of Theorem 2

We prove Theorem 2. MQL in its generative form (without the transformational constraint) is of star height one. In addition, it is not of finite order and thus, does not possess the finite power property.

Proof. With regard to the star height of MQL, we note that the sentences generated by Productions 1 and 2 of Appendix A are of finite length (and thus, finite in number) and hence, are of star height zero. Thus, the regular expression consisting of the union of these sentences is of star height zero. The sentences generated by Productions 3–7 consist of sentences of the form $\alpha(\beta\gamma^*\delta)^*\epsilon$, where α, β, γ, δ, and ϵ are finite regular expressions generated by implementation of

α: ⟨optimize⟩ output OVER inputs WITH specset USING
β: ⟨optimize⟩ output OVER
γ: input
δ: WITH specset using
ϵ: PUT rpt

However, it can be shown that an expression of the form $(\beta\gamma^*\delta)^*$ is of star height one (see p. 34 of Ref. 24), and hence, each expression $\alpha(\beta\gamma^*\delta)^*\epsilon$ is of star height one, and MQL is of star height one.

With regard to the finite power property, we note that for any integer $n \geq 0$, $(MQL)^n$ contains each sentence generated by Productions 1 and 2 concatenated with themselves n times but not $n+1$ times. Thus, MQL is not of finite order and does not possess the finite power property.

Appendix D: Proof of Theorem 3

We prove Theorem 3. EMQL in its generative form is a first-order language and hence, possesses the finite power property.

Proof. Let θ be a regular expression equal to the set of sentences in MQL. Then because of Production 8, the sentences in EMQL are the same as those in θ^*. But concatenation is idempotent when applied to θ^*—that is, $(\theta^*)^2 = \theta^*$. Therefore, $(EMQL)^2 = EMQL$, and EMQL is a first-order language and possesses the finite power property.

References

1. H. J. WILL, Model management systems, in *Information Systems and Organization Structure*, E. GROCHLA and N. SZYPERSKI, EDS., pp. 467–482, Walter de Gruyter, Berlin, 1975.
2. R. H. SPRAGUE, JR. and H. J. WATSON, Model management in MIS, in *Proceedings of the 7th National AIDS*, pp. 213–215, 1975.
3. J. J. ELAM, Model management systems: A framework for development, in *Proceedings 1980 SEAIDS*, pp. 35–38, 1980.
4. J. J. ELAM, J. C. HENDERSON, and L. W. MILLER, Model management systems: An approach to decision support in complex organizations, in *Proceedings of the First International Conference on Information Systems*, pp. 98–110, 1980.
5. R. H . BONCZEK, C. W. HOLSAPPLE, and A. B. WHINSTON, The evolving role of models in decision support systems, *Decision Sci.* **11**, 337–356 (1980).

6. R. SPRAGUE, A framework for the development of decision support systems, *MIS Q.* **4,** 1–26 (1980).
7. G. FICK and R. H. SPRAGUE, *Decision Support Systems: Issues and Challenges,* Pergamon Press, Oxford, 1980.
8. R. H. BONCZEK, C. W. HOLSAPPLE, and A. B. WHINSTON, *Foundations of Decision Support Systems,* Academic Press, New York, 1981.
9. R. H. SPRAGUE, JR. and E. D. CARLSON, *Building Effective Decision Support Systems,* Prentice-Hall, Englewood Cliffs, New Jersey, 1982.
10. R. W. BLANNING, Model structure and user interface in decision support systems, in *DSS-81 Transactions,* pp. 1–7, 1981.
11. R. W. BLANNING, Data management and model management: A relational synthesis, in *Proceedings of the 1982 Southeast ACM Regional Conference,* pp. 139–147, 1982.
12. R. W. BLANNING, A relational framework for model management in decision support systems, in *DSS-82 Transactions,* pp. 16–28, 1982.
13. R. W. BLANNING, A decision support language for corporate planning, *Policy Analysis and Information Systems* **6** (4), 313–323, 1982.
14. R. W. BLANNING, Ambiguity and paraphrase in a transformational grammar for decision support systems, in: *Proceedings of the Fifteenth Hawaii International Conference on System Sciences,* Vol. 1, pp. 765–774, 1982.
15. C. J. DATE, *An Introduction to Database Systems,* Addison-Wesley, Reading, Massachusetts, 1977.
16. J. D. ULLMAN, *Principles of Database Systems,* Computer Science Press, Potomac (1980).
17. R. W. BLANNING, Normal forms for relational model banks, Owen Graduate School of Management, Vanderbilt University (1982).
18. A. V. AHO, C. BEERI, and J. D. ULLMAN, The theory of joins in relational databases, *ACM Trans. Database Syst.* **4,** 297–314 (1979).
19. S. A. ROSS, The economic theory of agency: The principal's problem, *Am. Economic Rev.* **63,** 134–139 (1973).
20. S. A. ROSS, On the economic theory of agency and the principle of similarity, in *Essays on Economic Behavior under Uncertainty,* M. Balch, D. McFadden, and S. Wu, Eds., pp. 215–240, North-Holland, Amsterdam, 1974.
21. R. W. BLANNING and R. H. CRANDALL, Heuristic modeling and technological impact analysis, *Technol. Forecasting Social Change* **15,** 259–271 (1979).
22. M. A. HARRISON, *Introduction to Formal Language Theory,* Addison-Wesley, Reading, Massachusetts, 1978.
23. J. E. HOPCROFT and J. D. ULLMAN, *Formal Languages and their Relation to Automata,* Addison-Wesley, Reading, Massachusetts, 1969.
24. A. SALOMAA, *Jewels of Formal Language Theory,* Computer Science Press, Potomac (1981).
25. B. KONSYNSKI and J. KOTTERMAN, Complexity measures in system development, in *Proceedings of the Second International Conference on Information Systems,* pp. 173–199, 1981.
26. P. R. WATKINS, A measurement approach to cognitive complexity and perception of information: Implications for information systems design, in *Proceedings of the Second International Conference on Information Systems,* pp. 7–20, 1981.
27. P. G. W. KEEN and G. S. BRONSEMA, Cognitive style research: A perspective for integration, in *Proceedings of the Second International Conference on Information Systems,* pp. 21–52, 1981.
28. D. D. CHAMBERLIN, M. M. ASTRAHAN, K. P. ESWARAN, P. P. GRIFFITHS, R. A. LORIE, J. W. MEHI, P. REISNER, and B. W. WADE, SEQUEL 2: A unified approach to data definition, manipulation, and control, *IBM J. Res. Dev.* **20,** 560–575 (1976).
29. R. W. BLANNING, The functions of a decision support system, *Inf. Manage.* **2,** 87–93 (1979).
30. E. A. STOHR and M. TANNIRU, A database for operations research models, *Int. J. Policy Analysis Inf. Systm* **4,** 105–121 (1980).
31. R. W. BLANNING, Model-based and data-based planning systems, *Omega* **9,** 163–168 (1981).
32. M. S. Y. WANG and J. F. COURTNEY, Formulating a conceptual model for developing decision support system generators in *Proceedings of the Fifteenth Hawaii International Conference on System Sciences,* Vol. 1, pp. 812–819, 1982.

33. B. B. KONSYNSKI, On the structure of a generalized model management system, in *Proceedings of the Fourteenth Hawaii International Conference on System Sciences,* Vol. 1, pp. 630–638, 1981.

34. F. MORI, T. HAMAGUCHI, and K. YAMASHITA, AREQS: An integration of database, knowledge base, and simulator for business decision support systems, in *Proceedings of the Fourteenth Hawaii International Conference on System Sciences,* Vol. 1, pp. 654–663, 1981.

35. J. J. ELAM and J. C. HENDERSON, Knowledge engineering concepts for decision support system design and implementation, in *Proceedings of the Fourteenth Hawaii International Conference on System Sciences,* Vol. 1, pp. 639–643, 1981.

36. R. D. HACKATHORN, Task representation and management of task descriptions: an approach to decision support, in *Proceedings of the Fourteenth Hawaii International Conference on System Sciences,* Vol. 1, pp. 439–447, 1981.

37. R. D. HACKATHORN and R. A. FETTER, Toward a formal definition of task representations, in *Proceedings of the Second International Conference on Information Systems,* pp. 277–297, 1981.

38. R. H. BONCZEK, C. W. HOLSAPPLE, and A. B. WHINSTON, A generalized decision support system using predicate calculus and network data base management, *Operations Res.* **29,** 263–281 (1981).

39. H. GALLAIRE and J. MINKER, Eds., *Logic and Data Bases,* Plenum Press, New York, 1978.

40. N. ROUSSOPOULOS and J. MYLOPOULOS, Using semantic networks for data base management, in *Proceedings of the Conference on Very Large Data Bases,* pp. 211–223, 1975.

14

FUNCTIONAL AUGMENTATION OF RELATIONAL OPERATIONS IN ARES

Masahito Hirakawa, Tatsuo Shimizu, and Tadao Ichikawa

1. Introduction

We have proposed a novel scheme called ARES which associates stored information through *relevancy estimation*.[1] ARES was then applied successfully to information retrieval in a relational database environment allowing users to give a certain amount of ambiguity in describing queries.[2,3]

In this retrieval system, QBE (*query by example*)[4] has been adopted for query description with an additional comparison operator ($\risingdotseq$) which implies ". . . be similar to . . .". The measure for controlling the degree of similarity between a query and retrieved data is given by users through a graphic terminal, and modified interactively when necessary. The effectiveness of the system has already been demonstrated through experiments of retrieving automobiles available in a market.

In this paper, we report a trial to improve performances of the system. Here let ARES imply the *a*ssociative information *r*etrieval *s*ystem in an extended use of terminology. In the following, we briefly describe the outline of ARES.

The information retrieval system ARES based on an augmented relational model has two types of relations, namely, the conventional and semantic relations. The semantic relation represents the relatedness between elements in a domain. The relatedness is designed so as to reflect user's requirements.

When users describe a query with a certain amount of ambiguity in retrieval

MASAHITO HIRAKAWA, TATSUO SHIMIZU, and TADAO ICHIKAWA • Faculty of Engineering, Hiroshima University, Shitami, Saijo-cho, Higashi-Hiroshima 724, Japan.

conditions, the system first executes SELECTION operation for semantic relation which corresponds to a domain of an attribute containing ambiguous conditions, and then creates a new relation. Next, it executes JOIN operation between the conventional and new relations. Thus, the queries with ambiguous conditions are translated entirely into the sequence of conventional relational algebra operations.

When the similarity estimation is thus completed, the tuples which satisfy retrieval conditions are sorted in the order of their relatedness to the query. This contributes again to the improvement of the efficiency in selecting a reasonable number of output tuples.

In addition to the improvement of performances on similarity estimation, a tool for designing semantic relation is provided so as to put the system in practical use. The design tool employs the display of semantic graphs on a graphic terminal to help design and modification of semantic relations. Semantic graphs are also valid for the verification of logical consistency of semantic relations.

2. Semantic Schema and Design Tool

2.1. Representation of Semantics

The relational model proposed by E. F. Codd[5] defines events in a database environment as n-tuple relations which form a subset of Cartesian products of n domains. Each of the domains which construct n-tuple relations is classified into three types in connection with semantics as shown in Fig. 1.

Type 1: A domain whose elements are distinct to each other having no relatedness in their semantics (see Fig. 1a).

Type 2: A domain where elements are connected one-dimensionally to each other in their semantics (See Fig. 1b).

Type 3: A domain which allows multidimensional connections between elements (See Fig. 1c).

In the prototype ARES[3] which we first developed in a relational database environment, the degree of mutual relatedness of elements in a domain was rep-

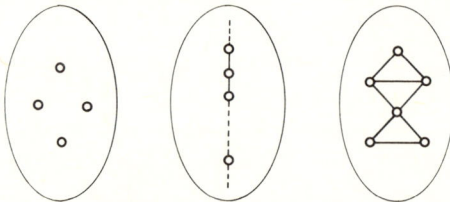

FIGURE 1. Classification of domains: (a) distinct; (b) one-dimensionally connected; (c) multi-dimensionally connected.

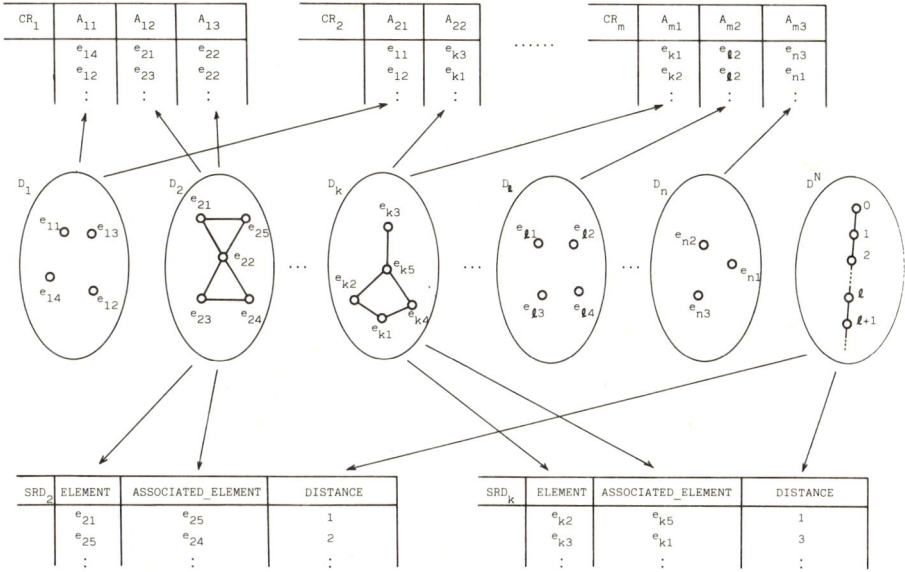

FIGURE 2. Relationships between conventional and semantic relations.

resented by Hamming distances between the codes assigned to them, and retrieval was carried out by calculating distances between a pair of elements every time for each retrieval. Though the system offered functional flexibility to users, the improvement on retrieval efficiency remained to be investigated.

Now we employ relations to represent mutual relatedness of elements instead of code distances.

2.2. Conventional and Semantic Relations

A conventional relation CR is the relation which represents the events in a database environment, and is defined as a subset of Cartesian products $D_1 \times D_2 \times \cdots \times D_n$ of n domains D_j $(1 \leq j \leq n)$.

A semantic relation presents similarity between an arbitrary pair of elements, and is defined for each Type-2 or Type-3 connection structure, separately. It consists of three attributes (ELEMENT, ASSOCIATED_ELEMENT, DISTANCE). Let a domain which has values for representing the degree of similarity in reverse order of their magnitudes as elements be denoted as D^N. Then the semantic relation SRD_j corresponding to D_j is represented as a subset of Cartesian products $D_j \times D_j \times D^N$.

Figure 2 illustrates relationships between conventional and semantic relations. In this figure, for example, a conventional relation CR_1 is defined on $D_1 \times D_2 \times D_2$, where D_1 and D_2 assume Type-1 and Type-3, respectively. Relatedness between elements in D_2 is represented in semantic relation SRD_2 in terms of attributes ELEMENT, ASSOCIATED ELEMENT, and DISTANCE. DISTANCE is represented by mapping $\bar{D}^N$ structure to the value obtained by the application of a shortest-pass algorithm to the corresponding graph of D_2 structure.

2.3. Tools for Designing Semantic Relations

There is a real need for a tool to assist in designing semantic relations so as to put the system into practical use. Direct-neighborhood specification and categorical clustering have been proposed as the methods for specifying relatedness of elements. Both methods generate a graph which specifies a semantic relation. The graph is thus simply called a semantic graph, hereafter. In a semantic graph, a vertex corresponds to an element and a direct connection between a pair of elements is represented by an edge. Degree of semantic nonsimilarity between an arbitrary pair of elements is then evaluated by the number of edges connecting them.

In the direct-neighborhood method, strongly related elements are specified by directly connecting vertices which correspond to these elements by an edge.

In the categorical-clustering method, some categories are selected in advance to the characterization of partial features of elements, and each element is encoded following these categories. Then the repetitive application of prototype ARES to the retrieval of related elements generates clusters of strongly related elements. And next the structure of this clustering is translated into a semantic graph. This method is valid for the case that the number of elements contained in a domain is large.

The application of these tools which generate semantic graphs makes the system reflect the user's personal view of its performance, and makes it easy to update semantic relations at the same time.

Figure 3 illustrates the process of specifying semantic relations.

3. Implementation of Retrieval Based on Semantic Schema

3.1. Translation of Ambiguous Queries

The additional comparison operator ($\leftrightharpoons$) which implies " . . . be nearly equal to . . ." requires the system to provide a similarity estimation facility, and this allows users to describe queries with a certain amount of ambiguity in conditions.

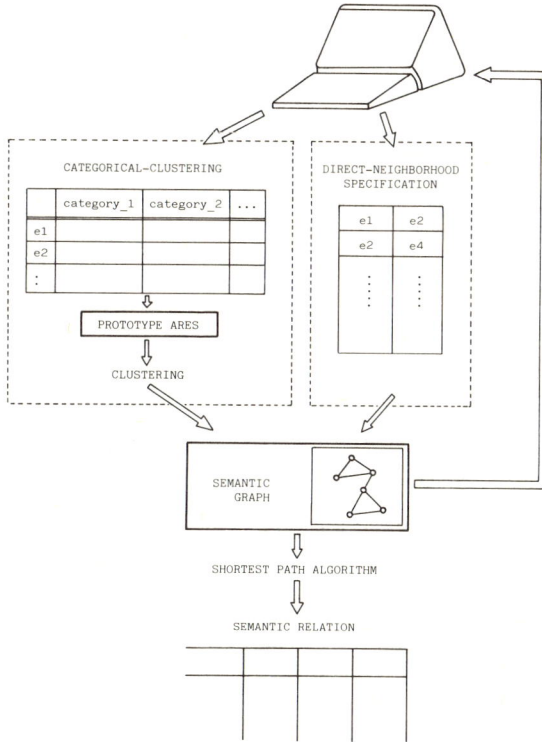

FIGURE 3. Design tool for semantic relations.

Generally, queries described by users are translated into the sequence of relational algebra operations before the execution of retrieval. Here we extend the relational algebra so that SELECTION, RESTRICTION, and JOIN can be activated in connection with the additional comparison operator ($\rightleftharpoons$). Then the queries with ambiguous conditions are translated into the sequence of extended relational algebra operations. Figure 4 illustrates this.

Here it is noted that the extension of relational algebra is limited to SELECTION, RESTRICTION, and JOIN. The connected use of "$\rightleftharpoons$" to other operations will make the result semantically meaningless. The extended use of SELECTION, RESTRICTION, and JOIN forms an ambiguous relational algebra.

Retrieval is executed after the extended relational algebra operations have been translated into the sequence of conventional relational algebra operations. In the next section, we describe how this could be done.

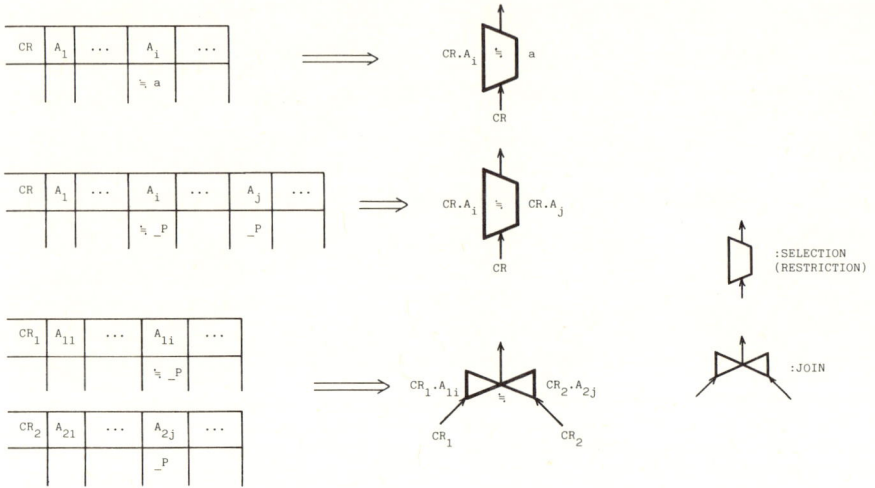

FIGURE 4. Translation of ambiguous conditions into extended relational algebra.[6]

3.2. Translation of Ambiguous Relational Algebra

In the previous section, we introduced three types of ambiguous relational algebra operations; ambiguous-SELECTION, ambiguous-RESTRICTION, and ambiguous-JOIN. These operations, however, require neither additional tools nor specific mechanisms specially provided for executing them. They are entirely translated into the sequence of conventional relational algebra operations, and then executed. In this translation, "natural-join" is adopted to connect the conventional relation CR and the semantic relation SRD_i which corresponds to the domain D_i of the conditioned attribute A_i.

The procedure of translating ambiguous algebra operations into the conventional algebra operations is shown in Fig. 5. The value t in the figure specifies the degree of ambiguity assigned to queries. Examples which explain the total flow of translations are given in Appendix A.

3.3. Regulation of the Number of Associated Outputs

It is hard to predict the number of output data which satisfy retrieval conditions, especially when ambiguity is assigned to conditions. Therefore, users are required to give a limit of the number of expected outputs along with the degree of ambiguity to the system before the actual retrieval operation starts. Output regulation is carried out as follows.

An additional attribute called TOTAL_DISTANCE is virtually accommodated in a conventional relation in the system, representing the degree of nonsimilarity between a query and each tuple which has been selected as candidate outputs by the query. TOTAL_DISTANCE is calculated by summing up the DISTANCEs defined in connection with semantic relation at each attribute. Next the tuples which satisfy retrieval conditions are sorted in terms of TOTAL _DISTANCE. Output regulation is then performed by selecting as many tuples as possible within the limit specified by users. The process is illustrated in Appendix B.

4. Conclusion

In this paper, we have presented a semantic schema to manipulate queries with ambiguous conditions in a relational database environment. The relation has

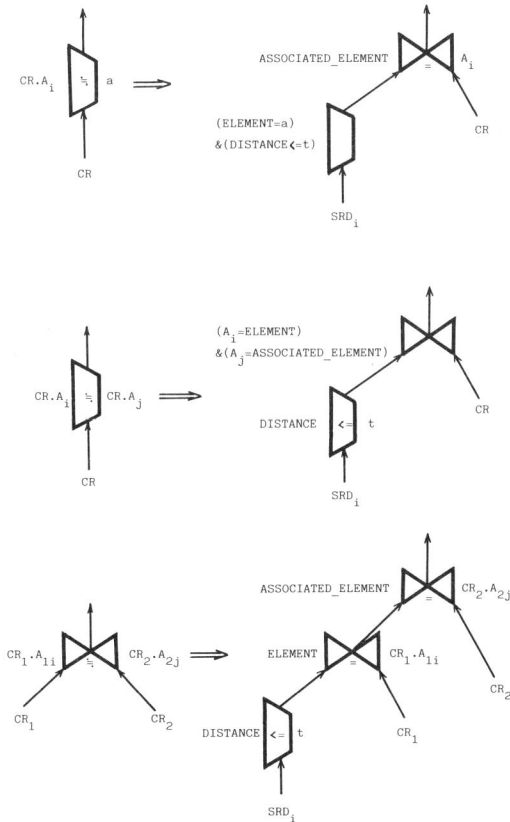

FIGURE 5. Translation of relational algebra operations.

been defined in terms of conventional and semantic relations. Semantic relation works for similarity estimation at the process of retrieving related tuples, and semantic data independency thus attained contributed to the improvement of system performances.

In addition to the improvement of performances on similarity estimation, we have provided a design tool for specifying semantic relations. Semantic relations are defined in terms of a linear graph displayed on a terminal, which assists both modification and verification of logical consistency of relations.

The system is now working on minicomputer HP-1000 in our research laboratory environment. Some displayed pictures are given in Appendix C.

Appendix A: Total Flow of Translations

Figures A.1–A.3 illustrate the total flow of translations for the following queries:

Query 1. Select automobiles of the price less than $8,000 and whose body color is similar to red.

Query 2. Select automobiles whose body color and seat color are similar to each other.

Query 3. Select automobiles whose seat color is similar to the body color of XXX.

Appendix B: Regulation of the Number of Outputs

Sample Database. A sample database is assumed to have three relations shown in Table A.1.

Query. Select automobiles of the body color similar to red and type similar to coupe, assuming that the degree of ambiguities are 3 for both the BODY-_COLOR and TYPE attributes, and the expected number of outputs is 4. (See Table A.2.)

A relational algebra tree representation of this query is shown in Fig. A.4.

Regulation Process. The steps the process takes are shown in Table A.3.

Q2:

CAR	CAR_NAME	BODY_COLOR	SEAT_COLOR
	P.	P._E	P._E

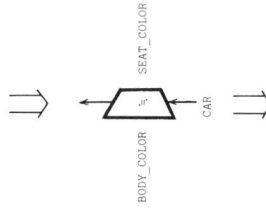

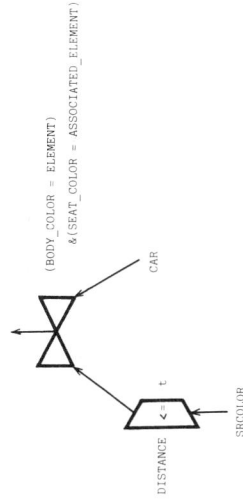

FIGURE A.2. Total flow of translation—Query 2.

Q1:

CAR	CAR_NAME	BODY_COLOR	PRICE
	P.	P. RED	P. <= 8000

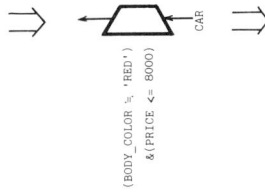

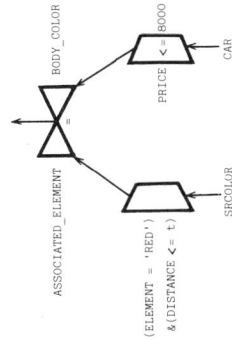

FIGURE A.1. Total flow of translation—Query 1.

Q3:

CAR	CAR_NAME	BODY_COLOR	SEAT_COLOR
	XXX	P. ≒ _E	
	P.		P._E

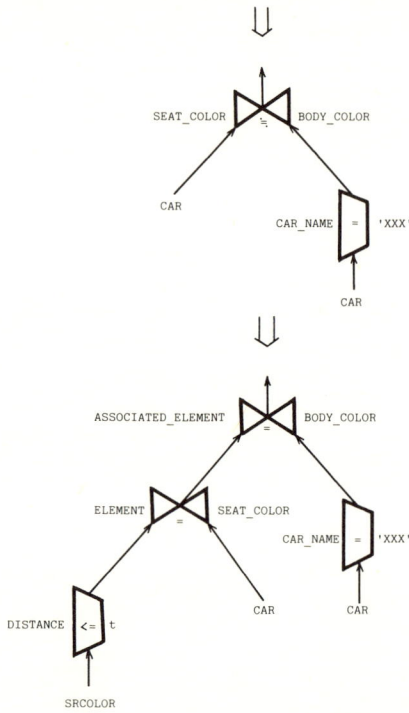

FIGURE A.3. Total flow of translation—Query 3.

TABLE A.1
Relations Defining Sample Database

CAR	CAR_NAME	BODY_COLOR	TYPE
	CAMARO Z28E	ORANGE	COUPE
	DATSUN 280ZX	RED	COUPE
	FORD LASER	YELLOW	HATCHBACK
	HONDA CIVIC	WHITE	HATCHBACK
	MGB	RED	SPORTS
	BMW 633csi	GREEN	COUPE
	VOLVO 760 GLE	BLUE	SEDAN
	LINCOLN CONTINENTAL	BLACK	SEDAN
	PEUGEOT 505TI	WINE_RED	SEDAN

SRCOLOR	ELEMENT	ASSOCIATED_ELEMENT	DISTANCE
	RED	RED	0
	RED	WINE_RED	1
	RED	ORANGE	1
	RED	YELLOW	2
	RED	GREEN	2
	RED	WHITE	3
	RED	BLUE	4
	RED	BLACK	5
	⋮	⋮	⋮

SRTYPE	ELEMENT	ASSOCIATED_ELEMENT	DISTANCE
	COUPE	COUPE	0
	COUPE	SPORTS	1
	COUPE	HATCHBACK	1
	COUPE	LIFTBACK	1
	COUPE	HARDTOP	2
	COUPE	SEDAN	3
	COUPE	WAGON	4
	⋮	⋮	⋮

TABLE A.2
Query for Sample Database

CAR	CAR_NAME	BODY_COLOR	TYPE
	P.	P. = RED	P. = COUPE

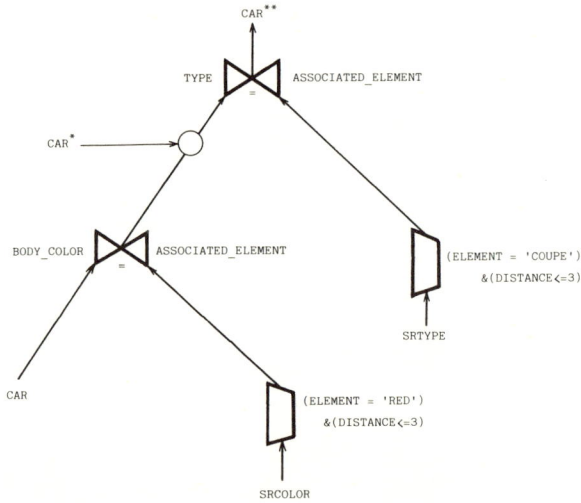

FIGURE A.4. Relational algebra tree representation of the query in Table A.2.

TABLE A.3
Process for Regulating Output Numbers

CAR_NAME	BODY_COLOR	TYPE	TOTAL_DISTANCE
Step 1 CAR*: results of JOIN between CAR and SRCOLOR			
CAMARO Z28E	ORANGE	COUPE	1
DATSUN 280ZX	RED	COUPE	0
FORD LASER	YELLOW	HATCHBACK	2
HONDA CIVIC	WHITE	HATCHBACK	3
MGB	RED	SPORTS	0
BMW 633csi	GREEN	COUPE	2
PEUGEOT 505TI	WINE_RED	SEDAN	1
Step 2 CAR**: results of JOIN between CAR* and SRTYPE			
CAMARO Z28E	ORANGE	COUPE	1
DATSUN 280ZX	RED	COUPE	0
FORD LASER	YELLOW	HATCHBACK	3
HONDA CIVIC	WHITE	HATCHBACK	4
MGB	RED	SPORTS	1
BMW 633csi	GREEN	COUPE	2
PEUGEOT 505TI	WINE_RED	SEDAN	4
Step 3 CAR***: sorted results in terms of TOTAL_DISTANCE			
DATSUN 280ZX	RED	COUPE	0
CAMARO Z28E	ORANGE	COUPE	1
MGB	RED	SPORTS	1
BMW 633csi	GREEN	COUPE	2
FORD LASER	YELLOW	HATCHBACK	3
HONDA CIVIC	WHITE	HATCHBACK	4
PEUGEOT 505TI	WINE_RED	SEDAN	4
Step 4 Outputs			
DATSUN 280ZX	RED	COUPE	
CAMARO Z28E	ORANGE	COUPE	
MGB	RED	SPORTS	
BMW 633csi	GREEN	COUPE	

Appendix C: Displayed Pictures Explaining the Process of
RESTRICTION

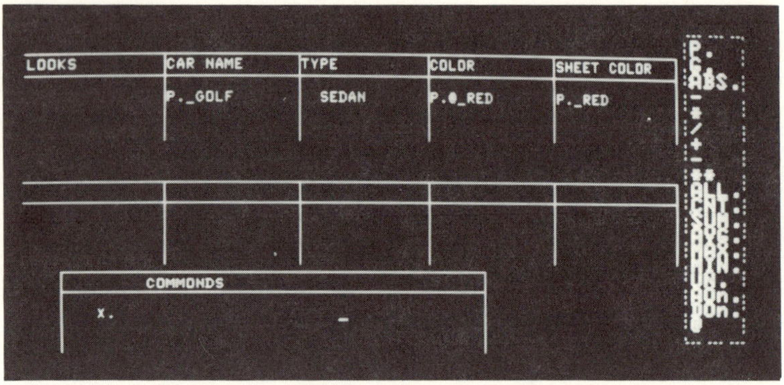

FIGURE A.5. Query.

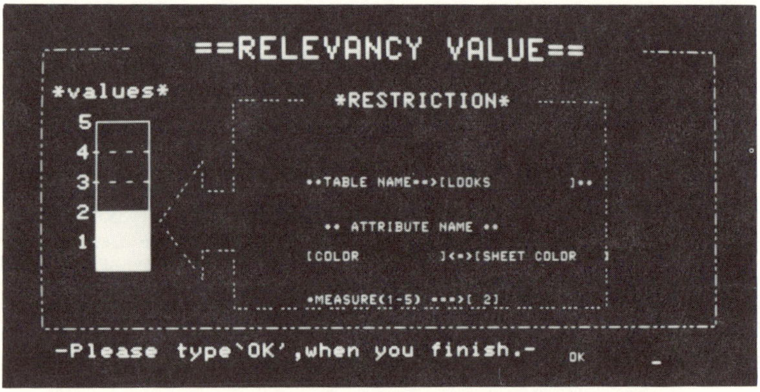

FIGURE A.6. Ambiguity assignment.

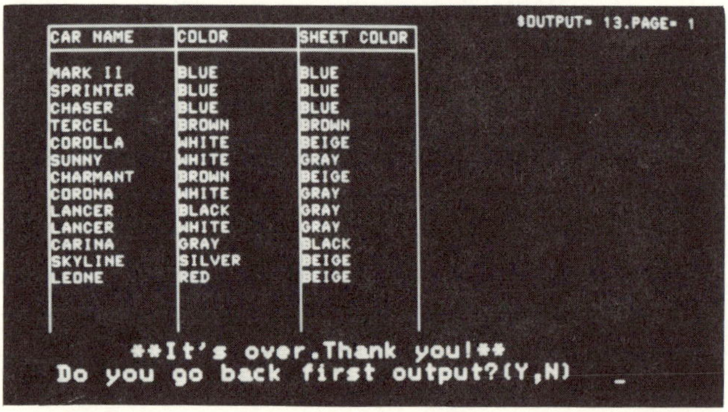

FIGURE A.7. Retrieved tuples.

References

1. T. ICHIKAWA, K. SAKAMURA, and H. AISO, ARES—A memory, capable of associating stored information through relevancy estimation, *Proc. AFIPS NCC* **46,** 947–954 (1977).
2. T. ICHIKAWA, T. KIKUNO, N. KAMIBAYASHI, and M. HIRAKAWA, ARES in relational database environments, Proc. COMPSAC'80, pp. 557–561, 1980.
3. M. HIRAKAWA, N. KAMIBAYASHI, and T. ICHIKAWA, An information retrieval system accepting ambiguous query descriptions, *Trans. IECE-Jpn* **J65-D**(1), 64–71 (1982) (in Japanese).
4. M. M. ZLOOF, Query by example: A data base language, *IBM Syst. J.* **16**(4) 845–853 (1977).
5. E. F. CODD, A relational model of data for large shared data banks, *Commun. ACM* **13**(6) 377–387 (1970).
6. J. M. SMITH and P. Y. CHANG, Optimizing the performance of a relational algebra database interface, *Commun. ACM* **18**(10), 568–579 (1975).

15

SIMILARITY RETRIEVAL FOR PICTORIAL DATABASES

Edward T. Lee

1. Introduction

Pictures and figures play basic and important roles in management and office information systems, picture database systems,[1] knowledge-based systems, decision theory, policy analysis, and artificial intelligence.

In examining the history of computer applications, we discover that the early electronic computers were developed primarily for scientific computation applications as in weather prediction, aerospace applications, and nuclear physics applications. At this stage, the computer served as a big calculator to perform in the main, scientific computation. Then we discover that computers could also be used for business applications, information storage and retrieval, word processing, and report generation.

New frontiers in computer applications are picture representation, picture processing, picture storage, and picture retrieval. A brief summary of the history of computer applications is shown in Fig. 1. Types of pictorial information amenable to computer processing include geometric figures, chromosome and leukocyte images, maps, fingerprints, and human faces. Work is also being done in the areas of computerized tomography and the interpretation of earth resource satellite photographs (e.g., to identify the rivers and highways in a particular area and to discriminate vegetation types).

2. Concept of Similarity Measures

A fundamental difference exists between alphanumeric information and the information conveyed in pictures. Alphanumeric information can be considered as

EDWARD T. LEE • Department of Computer Science, Louisiana State University, Baton Rouge, Louisiana 70803.

```
┌─────────────────────┐
│ Computers are used  │
│ to perform scientific│
│ computation (to     │
│ manipulate numbers) │
└─────────────────────┘
          │
          ▼
┌─────────────────────┐
│ Computers are used  │
│ to perform business │
│ applications (to    │
│ manipulate alpha-   │
│ numeric information).│
└─────────────────────┘
          │
          ▼
┌─────────────────────┐
│ Computers are used  │
│ to perform picture  │
│ processing (to      │
│ manipulate pictorial│
│ information)        │
└─────────────────────┘
```

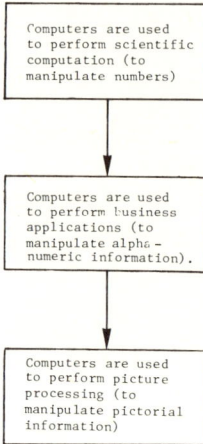

FIGURE 1. A brief summary of the history of computer applications.

exact or unambiguous because it is the symbolic representation of information which has already been structured. For example, computers are used to process payrolls and produce paychecks using categories which we provide (such as employee identification number, wage, and hours worked). Here, the computer is used only to manipulate data, not to make sense of it.

In order to use computers in the analysis of pictorial information, we must provide it with a method of classifying images. For instance, computer recognition of faces depends on a quantitative classification scheme of facial features.

Faces, like fingerprints and snowflakes, come in virtually infinite variety. Human identification of human faces is remarkably accurate, rapid, and inexpensive compared to the present state of the art of machine identification. A human face can be viewed from infinitely different angles. Thus, in human identification of human faces, it is reasonable to assume that we have not seen the same face from exactly the same angle before, yet we have little difficulty in recognizing a human face. Thus, similarity measures,[2] feature selection, and feature extraction play basic roles in the recognition of human faces. Automatic identification, classification, storage, and retrieval of human faces could have considerable utility in many personnel, commercial, security and law-enforcement applications.

Faces were classified in Ref. 3 by numerical judgment of selected features. Selected features are extracted from hair, forehead, eyebrows, eyes, ears, cheeks, nose, mouth, and chin. Hair features include coverage, length, texture, and shade. Eyebrow features include separation and weight. Eye features include opening, separation, and shade. Ear features include length and protrusion. Nose features include length, tip, and profile. Mouth features include upper lip thickness, lower lip thickness, lip overlap, and width. Chin features include profile.

In Ref. 4, attempts have been made to develop algorithms for defining unique individual description vectors from manually entered profile traces. A set of fiducial marks, lines, angles, areas, and other measures of the profile traces was developed and refined. Nine fiducial marks were used. These were: nose tip, chin, forehead, bridge, nose bottom, throat, upper lip, mouth, and lower lip. A way to obtain these nine fiducial marks may be found in Ref. 4. Examples of distance measures between fiducial pairs which can be used as vector components to identify individuals uniquely may also be found in Ref. 4. As a result, triangles, quadrangles, and polygons are formed. Furthermore, the nose tip, chin, and forehead form the basic triangle. Therefore, the concepts and results presented in the geometric figure[11,12] section may be applied to the automatic recognition of human faces.

Computerized recognition of fingerprints and handwriting samples would also be of use in security precautions common to business situations. However, just as these tasks are more difficult for humans to perform, so it is true with computers. Even for the same finger, fingerprints are different each time we make one because stretch and other related factors will vary. The same situation is true for handwriting and signatures. Thus, additional variables must be taken into account by the computer.

3. Pattern Description

Each of these cases (face recognition, fingerprint, and signature identification) requires a classification scheme based on features extracted from the image. Before this can be done, the image must be described in terms which can be handled by the computer. The first step in formulating a syntactic model for pattern description is the determination of a set of primitives in terms of which the patterns of interest may be described. The selection of pattern primitives will be largely influenced by the nature of the pattern, the specific application in question, and the technology available for implementing the system. There is no general solution for the primitive selection problem as stated in Refs. 6 and 7.

The precision of pattern description languages contrasts rather sharply with the imprecision of patterns encountered in typical pattern recognition problems. To reduce the gap between them, it is natural to introduce randomness into the structure of pattern description languages, thus leading to the concept of stochastic languages and their applications to pattern recognition as suggested by Fu.[8] Another possibility lies in the introduction of fuzziness. This leads to what might be called fuzzy pattern description languages or simply fuzzy languages as developed by Lee and Zadeh.[9] In this paper, shape-oriented similarity measures are used in the classification of pattern primitives. Three cases are described which use this method: the classification of simplified building types, chromosome images, and leukocytes.

4. Classification of Buildings

4.1. A House

Three building types will be considered: a house, a house with a high roof, and a church. We want to define a house in terms of its simplest building blocks and their relation to each other. For illustration purposes, let us define a simplified version of a "house" to be an isosceles triangle vertically concatenated to a rectangle. Thus, a house may be represented by a tree as

where I represents an isosceles triangle, and R represents a rectangle, and the syntactic relation between I and R is vertical concatenation.

By using the concept of a fuzzy language, an approximate house may be defined as an approximate isosceles triangle vertically concatenated to an approximate rectangle. Therefore, the tree representation of a "*fuzzy house*" is denoted by

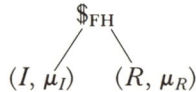

where μ_I and μ_R are grades of membership of "approximate isosceles triangle" and "approximate rectangle," respectively. $\mu_H(\$_{FH})$ denotes the grade of membership of "approximate houses" and is defined to be

$$\mu_H(\$_{FH}) = \mu_I \cdot \mu_R$$

For a triangle ΔABC with angles B and C as the base angles, a quantitative measure of the similarity of this triangle to isosceles triangles may be defined as

$$\mu_I(\Delta ABC) = 1 - \frac{|B - C|}{90°}$$

Example 1. For $A = 30°$, $B = 90°$, and $C = 60°$ as shown in Fig. 2b,

$$\mu_I(\Delta ABC) = \tfrac{2}{3}$$

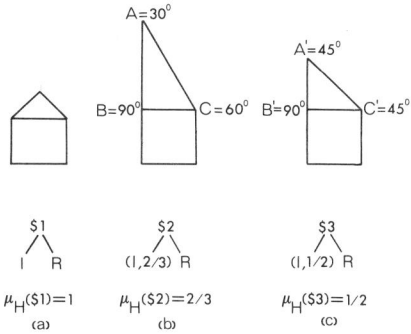

FIGURE 2. The grade of membership of "approximate houses."

For $A' = 45°$, $B' = 90°$, and $C' = 45°$ as shown in Fig. 2c,

$$\mu_I(\Delta A'B'C') = \tfrac{1}{2}$$

In the paper by Lee,[11] a quantitative measure of the similarity of a quadrangle with angles A, B, C, D to rectangles was defined as

$$\mu_R = 1 - \frac{|A\text{-}90°| + |B\text{-}90°| + |C\text{-}90°| + |D\text{-}90°|}{360°}$$

Example 2. The grades of membership of "approximate houses" for the three figures shown in Fig. 2 are

$$\mu_H(\$_1) = 1$$
$$\mu_H(\$_2) = \tfrac{2}{3}$$
$$\mu_H(\$_3) = \tfrac{1}{2}$$

4.2. House with a High Roof

For a triangle ΔABC with sides a, b, c and angles A, B, C, where B and C are the base angles, a quantitative measure of the similarity of this triangle to elongated isosceles triangles may be defined as

$$\mu_{EI}(\Delta ABC) = \frac{\mu_I(\Delta ABC) + \mu_E(\Delta ABC)}{2}$$

where

$$\mu_E(\Delta ABC) = \frac{\mu_{ab}(a,\ b) + \mu_{ac}(a,\ c)}{2}$$

and

$$
\begin{aligned}
\mu_{ab}(a,\ b) &= 1 && \text{if } b \geq 4a \\
&= b/4a && \text{if } b \leq 4a \\
\mu_{ac}(a,\ c) &= 1 && \text{if } c \geq 4a \\
&= c/4a && \text{if } c \leq 4a
\end{aligned}
$$

The rationale for this is that the definition of an elongated isosceles triangle may vary from person to person. Depending on its prospective applications, the constants $b/4a$ and $c/4a$ used in defining μ_{EI}, μ_E, μ_{ab}, and μ_{ac} may take on different values (e.g., $b/4a$ was chosen in Ref. 10 because it best modeled the acrocentric chromosome image.)

The tree representation of a house with a high roof is denoted as

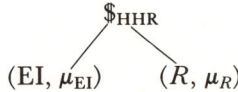

where $\mu_{HHR}(\$_{HHR})$ denotes the grade of membership of "*house* with a *high* roof" and is defined to be

$$\mu_{HHR}(\$_{HHR}) = \mu_{EI} \cdot \mu_R$$

4.3. A Church

A simplified version of a church may be defined as a cross vertically concatenated to a house with a high roof. The tree representation of a church is denoted as

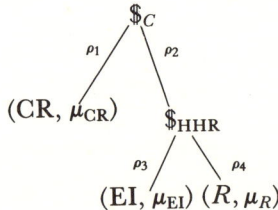

where CR represents a cross with intersection angles A and B and

$$\mu_{\text{CR}} = \frac{\min(A, B)}{90°}$$

Depending on its prospective application, μ_{CR} may take on different values. $\mu_C(\$_C)$ denotes the grade of membership of a simplified church and is defined to be

$$\mu_C(\$_C) = \mu_{\text{CR}} \cdot \mu_{\text{EI}} \cdot \mu_R$$

If the rectangle, cross, and elongated isosceles triangle are distorted, then the distortion can be entered into μ_R, μ_{CR}, and μ_{EI}, respectively. In addition, the vertical concatenation relation may be distorted and can be reflected in $\rho_1, \rho_2, \rho_3, \rho_4$, where $0 < \rho_i \leq 1$ for $i = 1, 2, 3, 4$. Thus, the general rule for membership value for all patterns is defined as

$$\mu_C(\$_C) = \mu_{\text{CR}} \cdot \mu_{\text{EI}} \cdot \mu_R \cdot \rho_1 \cdot \rho_2 \cdot \rho_3 \cdot \rho_4$$

In this paper, we assume that

$$\rho_1 = \rho_2 = \rho_3 = \rho_4 = 1$$

Example 3. For Fig. 3a

$$\mu_{\text{EI}} = 1$$

Hence, the tree representation of this figure is

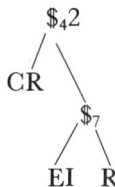

$$\$_4 2$$
$$\text{CR}$$
$$\$_7$$
$$\text{EI} \quad \text{R}$$

and $\mu_C(\$_4) = 1$. For Fig. 3b,

$$\mu_{\text{EI}} = 0.56$$

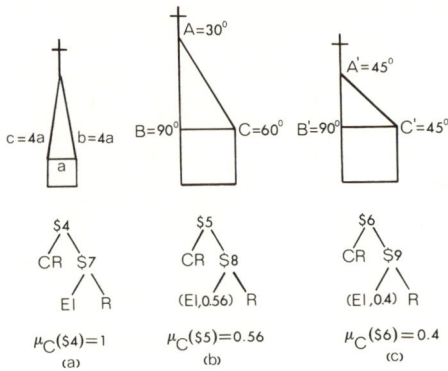

FIGURE 3. The grade of membership of "approximate churches."

Thus, the tree representation of Fig. 3b is

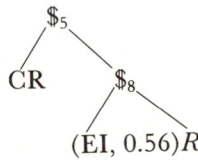

and $\mu_C(\$_5) = 0.56$. For Fig. 3c,

$$\mu_{EI} = 0.4$$

Therefore, the tree representation of Fig. 3c is

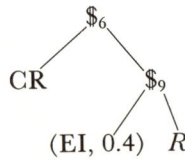

and $\mu_C(\$_6) = 0.4$.

5. Chromosome Types

A preliminary study of applying shape-oriented similarity measures defined over a pair of chromosome images to the classification problem was presented in Ref. 12. In this paper, the classification problem is studied through the use of shape-oriented similarity measures of a given chromosome image to symmetrical chromosomes, median chromosomes, submedian chromosomes, and acrocentric chromosomes.

The best fit skeletal "length and angle only" transformation with angles A_i and sides a_j is shown in Fig. 4. After connecting the tips of arms Nos. 1 and 2, and the tips of arms Nos. 3 and 4 as indicated by dotted lines, the best fit skeletal "length and angle only" transformation becomes a hexagon.

5.1. Symmetry of Chromosome Images

The preparation of chromosome images and the definition of metaphase chromosome images may be found in Ref. 13. At metaphase each chromosome has a twin, normally identical counterpart.

DEFINITION 1. A chromosome image with angles A_i and sides a_j is a *symmetrical* chromosome image if and only if $A_{2i-1} = A_{2i}$ for $1 \leq i \leq 4$, $a_1 = a_2$ and $a_3 = a_4$.

A shape-oriented quantitative measure of the similarity of a given chromosome image A to all symmetrical chromosome images may be defined as

$$\mu_s(A) = 1 - \rho_s \sum_{i=1}^{4} |A_{2i-1} - A_{2i}|$$

where ρ_s is a normalization constant to be determined.

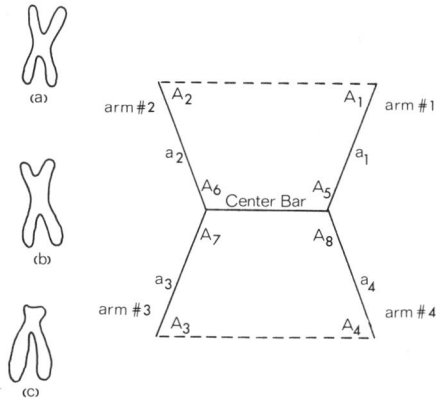

FIGURE 4. Chromosome images (a) median, (b) submedian, (c) acrocentric, (d) best fit skeletal "length and angle only" transformation.

LEMMA 1. *A chromosome image is a symmetrical chromosome image if and only if $\mu_s = 1$.*

In what follows, we assume that

$$A_i \leq 180° \qquad \text{for } 1 \leq i \leq 8$$

The angles of chromosome image A are represented in a vector form as

$$A = (A_1, A_2, A_3, A_4, A_5, A_6, A_7, A_8)$$

5.2. Determination of the Normalization Constant ρ_s

The purpose of ρ_s is to normalize the value of ρ_s between zero and one. In order to determine the value of ρ_s, we must first determine $\max \{\Sigma_{i=1}^{4} |A_{2i-1} - A_{2i}|\}$. After we find this value, we assume μ_s to be equal to zero at this extreme case, so that we can determine the value of ρ_s.

LEMMA 2. *For any chromosome image A with angles A_i*

$$\max_{A} \left\{ \sum_{i=1}^{4} |A_{2i-1} - A_{2i}| \right\} = 720°$$

DEFINITION 2. A chromosome image is a *most unsymmetrical* chromosome image if and only if $\mu_s = 0$.

THEOREM 1.

$$\rho_s = \frac{1}{720°}$$

PROOF. Assuming that the symmetry measure (μ_s) of a most unsymmetrical chromosome image is equal to zero, then

$$\mu_s = 0 = 1 - \rho_s \cdot 720° \quad \text{and} \quad \rho_s = \frac{1}{720°}$$

COROLLARY 1. *Given a chromosome image A with angles A_i*

$$\mu_s(A) = 1 - \frac{1}{720°} \sum_{i=1}^{4} |A_{2i-1} - A_{2i}|$$

5.3. Most Unsymmetrical Chromosome Images

Shape-oriented quantitative measures of the dissimilarities of a given triangle to isosceles triangles, right triangles, and equilateral triangles were defined in Ref. 12. According to the measures defined, it was also proved that the most dissimilar isosceles triangle is $(120°, 60°, 0°)$; the most dissimilar equilateral triangle is $(180°, 0°, 0°)$; and the most dissimilar right triangle is $(180°, 0°, 0°)$. It is of interest to ask whether the most unsymmetrical chromosome image is unique or not. If not then what are all the most unsymmetrical chromosome images? In order to answer this question in a concise form, we need to define an equivalence relation among chromosome images. We first define the following four permutations of the angles:

$$P_0(A) = A$$
$$P_T(A) = (A_2, A_1, A_4, A_3, A_6, A_5, A_8, A_7)$$
$$P_R(A) = (A_4, A_3, A_2, A_1, A_8, A_7, A_6, A_5)$$
$$P_{TR}(A) = (A_3, A_4, A_1, A_2, A_7, A_8, A_5, A_6)$$

P_0 is the identical permutation. P_T is the permutation which interchanges the right-hand side angles and the left-hand side angles. P_R is the permutation which interchanges the upper angles and the lower angles. P_{TR} is the composite permutation of P_T and $P_R \cdot P_{TR}$ may also be interpreted as the rotation of a chromosome image 180° about an axis perpendicular to its own plane.

Denote these four permutations as the set G:

$$G = \{P_0, P_T, P_R, P_{TR}\}$$

LEMMA 3. *Given a chromosome image A, μ_s is invariant over G:*

$$\mu_s(A) = \mu_s(g(A)) \qquad g \in G$$

LEMMA 4. *The set G over A forms an Abelian group.*

DEFINITION 3. Given two chromosome images A and B, A is *angularly equal* to B, denoted as $A = B$, if and only if $A_i = B_i$ for $1 \leq i \leq 8$.

DEFINITION 4. Given two chromosome images A and B, A is *angularly equivalent* to B, denoted as $A \equiv B$, if and only if $A = g(B)$ for some g in G.

Example 4. Given chromosome images A and B with

$$A = (180°, 0°, 180°, 0°, 180°, 0°, 180°, 0°)$$
$$B = (0°, 180°, 0°, 180°, 0°, 180°, 0°, 180°)$$

then $A \equiv B$.

THEOREM 2. *There are six most unsymmetrical chromosome images, namely,*

$$A^1 = (180°, 0°, 180°, 0°, 180°, 0°, 180°, 0°)$$
$$A^2 = (180°, 0°, 180°, 0°, 180°, 0°, 0°, 180°)$$
$$A^3 = (180°, 0°, 180°, 0°, 0°, 180°, 0°, 180°)$$
$$A^4 = (180°, 0°, 0°, 180°, 180°, 0°, 180°, 0°)$$
$$A^5 = (180°, 0°, 0°, 180°, 0°, 180°, 180°, 0°)$$
$$A^6 = (180°, 0°, 0°, 180°, 180°, 0°, 0°, 180°)$$

PROOF. The expression $\mu_s(A) = 0$ implies that

$$\sum_{i=1}^{4} |A_{2i-1} - A_{2i}| = 720°$$

This implies that

$$|A_{2i-1} - A_{2i}| = 180° \qquad \text{for } 1 \le i \le 4$$

Therefore, either

$$A_{2i-1} = 0° \quad \text{and} \quad A_{2i} = 180°$$

or

$$A_{2i-1} = 180° \quad \text{and} \quad A_{2i} = 0° \text{ for } 1 \le i \le 4$$

Thus, there are 16 most unsymmetrical chromosome images not angularly equal to each other. By using the equivalence relation defined in Definition 4, these 16 most unsymmetrical chromosome images are degenerated into six equivalent classes, and, A^1, A^2, A^3, A^4, A^5, and A^6 are the representatives of these six equivalent classes. ∎

5.4. Median

When classifying chromosome images, different types and sizes are encountered. Three of these different types, median, submedian, and acrocentric will be examined. They all have the same general appearance. The difference occurs in the location of their centromere. Both figures and string representations of median, submedian, and acrocentric chromosome images may be found in Ref. 14. String representations were done by using the terminal set $V_T = \{a, \searrow b, \nearrow c, \searrow d, \nearrow\}$. The same terminal set was used by Ledley *et al.*[15] String representation of a median chromosome image is as follows:

$$x_{(\text{median})} = cbbbabbbbdbbbbabbbcbbbabbbbdbbbbabbb$$

Given a chromosome image A with angles A_i and sides a_j, a quantitative measure of the similarity of this chromosome image to median chromosome images may be defined as

$$\mu_M(A) = \mu_s(A) \cdot \left[1 - \frac{|a_1 - a_4| + |a_2 - a_3|}{a_1 + a_2 + a_3 + a_4 + a_5} \right]$$

$$\mu_M'(A) = 1 - \mu_D(A) \cdot \frac{|a_1 - a_4| + |a_2 - a_3|}{a_1 + a_2 + a_3 + a_4 + a_5}$$

where

$$\mu_D(A) = 1 - \mu_s(A)$$

LEMMA 5. *Given a chromosome image A with angles A_i and sides a_j, the following three conditions are equivalent:*

(i) $\mu_M(A) = 1$

(ii) $\mu_M'(A) = 1$

(iii) *chromosome image A is a symmetrical chromosome image and $a_1 = a_2 = a_3 = a_4$*

LEMMA 6. *Given a chromosome image A:*

$$\mu_M(A) \leq \mu_M'(A)$$

LEMMA 7. *Given a chromosome image A, let ·*

$$\mu_{DM}(A) = 1 - \frac{|a_1 - a_4| + |a_2 - a_3|}{a_1 + a_2 + a_3 + a_4 + a_5}$$

Then,

$$0 \leq \mu_M(A) \leq \mu_M'(A) \leq \mu_s(A) \leq 1$$

and

$$0 \leq \mu_M(A) \leq \mu_M'(A) \leq \mu_{DM}(A) \leq 1$$

LEMMA 8. *Given a chromosome image A, let*

$$L_M = \{0, \mu_M(A), \mu_M'(A), \mu_s(A), \mu_{DM}(A), 1\}$$

The set L_M with max *and* min *as the two binary operations forms a distributive but not complemented lattice.*

5.5. Submedian

By using the terminal set V_T, string representation of a submedian chromosome image is as follows:

$$\chi_{\text{(submedian)}} = cbabbbdbbbbbabbbcbbbabbbbbdbbbab$$

Given a chromosome image A with angles A_i and sides a_j, let

$$a_{\text{SM}} = \min \{|a_1 - 2a_4| + |a_2 - 2a_3|, |2a_1 - a_4| + |2a_2 - a_3|\}$$

and

$$a_T = a_1 + a_2 + a_3 + a_4 + a_5$$

A quantitative measure of the similarity of this chromosome image A to submedian chromosome images may be defined as

$$\mu_{SM}(A) = \mu_s(A) \left(1 - \frac{a_{SM}}{2a_T} \right)$$

or

$$\mu'_{SM}(A) = 1 - \mu_D(A) \frac{a_{SM}}{2a_T}$$

LEMMA 9. *Given a chromosome image A, the following three conditions are equivalent:*

(i) $\mu_{SM}(A) = 1$
(ii) $\mu'_{SM}(A) = 1$
(iii) *chromosome image A is a symmetrical chromosome image and (either $a_1 = 2a_4$, $a_2 = 2a_3$ or $a_4 = 2a_1$, $a_3 = 2a_2$)*

LEMMA 10. *Given a chromosome image A:*

$$\mu_{SM}(A) \leq \mu'_{SM}(A)$$

LEMMA 11. *Given a chromosome image A, let*

$$\mu_{DSM}(A) = 1 - \frac{a_{SM}}{2a_T}$$

Then

$$0 \leq \mu_{SM}(A) \leq \mu'_{SM}(A) \leq \mu_s(A) \leq 1$$

and

$$0 \leq \mu_{SM}(A) \leq \mu'_{SM}(A) \leq \mu_{DSM}(A) \leq 1$$

LEMMA 12. *Given a chromosome image A, let*

$$L_{SM} = \{0, \mu_{SM}(A), \mu'_{SM}(A), \mu_s(A), \mu_{DSM}(A), 1\}$$

The set L_{SM} with max *and* min *as the two binary operations forms a distributive but not complemented lattice.*

Depending on its prospective application, the constant 2 used in defining a_{SM} may be changed to other constants.

5.6. Acrocentric

By using the terminal set V_T, string representation of an acrocentric chromosome image is as follows:

$$\chi_{(\text{acrocentric})} = cadbbbbbbabbbbbcbbbbbabbbbbbda$$

Given a chromosome image A with angles A_i and sides a_j, let

$$a_{AC} = \min \{|a_1 - 4a_4| + |a_2 - 4a_3|, |4a_1 - a_4| + |4a_2 - a_3|\}$$

A quantitative measure of the similarity of this chromosome image A to acrocentric chromosome images may be defined as

$$\mu_{AC}(A) = \mu_s(A) \cdot \left(1 - \frac{a_{AC}}{4a_T}\right)$$

or

$$\mu'_{AC}(A) = 1 - \mu_D(A) \cdot \frac{a_{AC}}{4a_T}$$

LEMMA 13. *Given a chromosome image A, the following three conditions are equivalent:*

(i) $\mu_{AC}(A) = 1$
(ii) $\mu'_{AC}(A) = 1$
(iii) *chromosome image A is a symmetrical chromosome image and* (*either* $a_1 = 4a_4$, $a_2 = 4a_3$ *or* $a_4 = 4a_1$, $a_3 = 4a_2$)

LEMMA 14. *Given a chromosome image A:*

$$\mu_{AC}(A) \le \mu'_{AC}(A)$$

LEMMA 15. *Given a chromosome image A, let*

$$\mu_{DAC}(A) = 1 - \frac{a_{AC}}{4a_T}$$

Then

$$0 \le \mu_{AC}(A) \le \mu'_{AC}(A) \le \mu_s(A) \le 1$$

and

$$0 \le \mu_{AC}(A) \le \mu'_{AC}(A) \le \mu_{DAC}(A) \le 1$$

LEMMA 16. *Given a chromosome image A, let*

$$L_{AC} = \{0, \mu_{AC}(A), \mu'_{AC}(A), \mu_s(A), \mu_{DAC}(A), 1\}$$

The set L_{AC} with max *and* min *as the two binary operations forms a distributive but not complemented lattice.*

Depending on its prospective application, the constant 4 used in defining a_{AC} may be changed to other constants.

5.7. An Algorithm

An algorithm for classifying a triangle as an "approximate isosceles triangle," "approximate equilateral triangle," "approximate right triangle," "approximate isosceles right triangle," or "ordinary triangle," and a algorithm used to classify a quadrangle as "approximate square," "approximate rectangle," "approximate rhombus," "approximate parallelogram," "approximate trapezoid," or "ordinary quadrangle" were presented in Ref. 11. This section presents an algorithm for classifying a chromosome image into one of the following three classes: "approximate median," "approximate submedian," or "approximate acrocentric." This can be done in the following manner. Compute μ_M, μ_{SM}, μ_{AC} and set a threshold δ, where δ is a parameter and $0 \leq \delta < 1$. If we compare the max $\{\mu_M, \mu_{SM}, \mu_{AC}\}$ with δ, there are two possibilities:

(i) If max $\{\mu_M, \mu_{SM}, \mu_{AC}\} > \delta$, then there are two possibilities:
    (a) If the maximum is unique, then we choose the class corresponding to the maximum value and classify the image accordingly.
    (b) If the maximum is not unique, then we define a priority among μ_M, μ_{SM}, and μ_{AC} and classify the chromosome image accordingly.
(ii) Otherwise, the chromosome image is rejected as not belonging to any of the classes.

Depending on its prospective application, μ_M, μ_{SM}, μ_{AC} may be substituted by μ'_M, μ'_{SM}, μ'_{AC}, respectively.

5.8. Expansion or Contraction Constant σ

The expansion or contraction of a chromosome image will not affect the values of the eight angles. Let σ be an expansion or contraction constant with $\sigma > 0$. By applying an expansion or contraction constant σ to a chromosome image A with angles A_i and sides a_j, we obtain a new chromosome image denoted as σA with angles A_i and sides σa_j.

LEMMA 17. μ_s is invariant with respect to an expansion or contraction constant σ:

$$\mu_s(\sigma A) = \mu_s(A)$$

DEFINITION 5. A quantitative measure of a chromosome image is a *shape-oriented* measure if and only if this measure is invariant with respect to an expansion or contraction constant σ.

Example 5. μ_s is a shape-oriented measure.

LEMMA 18. μ_M, μ'_M, μ_{DM}, μ_{SM}, μ'_{SM}, μ_{DSM}, μ_{AC}, μ'_{AC}, and μ_{DAC} are shape-oriented measures, and are independent of the size of chromosome images.

LEMMA 19. *The classification algorithm described in subsection 5.7 is independent of the size of chromosome images, and is a shape-oriented classification algorithm.*

5.9. Conclusion

A shape-oriented classification algorithm has been described. As stated in Ref. 12, there are three advantages of shape-oriented similarity measures. These are as follows:

1. Two chromosome images may have the same shape but differ in area and dimensions and still be similar.
2. Shape-oriented similarity measures can be normalized between zero and one.
3. Shape-oriented similarity measures are invariant with respect to rotation, translation, or expansion or contraction in size.

As demonstrated in Ref. 31, the perception of form embodies the automatic assignment of a top, a bottom, and sides. Thus, orientation plays an important role in chromosome classification done by human beings. Due to the invariance of angle and length measurements with respect to orientation, shape-oriented chromosome classification would not be confused by the orientation of the chromosome. In this sense, shape-oriented chromosome classification is better than chromosome classification done by human beings. The results obtained in this section may have useful applications in the storage, retrieval, and classification of chromosome images and geometric figures. In addition, the results may be applied to other areas, for instance, to the work done by Pavlidis[32-34] in the area of approximating an arbitrary shape by polygons, or the work done by Dacey[35] in the development of a two-dimensional language that produces line picture of polygons, or the work presented by Harmon[3] on face recognition. The results may also be of use in pattern recognition, information retrieval and artificial intelligence.

6. Shape-Oriented Similarity Measures and Their Application to the Classification of Leukocyte Images

Let the universe of discourse $U_L = \{L\}$ be the universe of leukocyte images. Let the set of terms T_L be leukocytes with circular nuclear shape, leukocytes with elongated nuclear shape, leukocytes with spiculed nuclear shape, leukocytes with indented nuclear shape, leukocytes with slightly indented nuclear shape, and leukocytes with deeply indented nuclear shape.

The peripheral blood leukocytes have been classified into eight categories in

Ref. 16. The categories were: small lymphocytes, medium lymphocytes, large lymphocytes, band neutrophils, segmented neutrophils, eosinophils, basophils, and monocytes. Pictures of typical peripheral blood leukocytes can be found in Ref. 16. The features used in Ref. 16 were nuclear size, nuclear shape, nuclear and cytoplasmic texture, cytoplasm color, and cytoplasm colored texture.

As stated in Ref. 16 it is particularly important not only to classify the five major cell types, but also to determine "intraclass" differences, between younger and older cells in some classes. For example, intraclass percentage shifts relate to the production rates and maturation of new cells, and thus to the physiological response to stress. In this section, our attention will be focused on the study of the shape properties of leukocytes in order to determine "intraclass" differences.

In Ref. 17, it is stated that the nuclear shapes of lymphocytes, monocytes, eosinophils, and basophils are round, indented, segmented, two-lobed, and elongated, respectively. Four shape features (circular, spiculed, oblong, and irregular) were listed in Ref. 18 as typical features for computerized microscopic image analysis. However, how to measure these four shape features were not presented in Ref. 18.

The nuclear shape measure used in Ref. 16 was $(\text{perimeter})^2/\text{areas}$. Let f denote this measure. Then

$$f = (\text{perimeter})^2/\text{area}$$

A way to obtain perimeter and area measures can be found in Ref. 16.

Over all possible nuclear shapes, circular shapes minimize f and the minimum of f is equal to 4π.

6.1. Equal-Perimeter Circular Shape Measure

The range of f is from 4π to infinity. In order to normalize this measure between zero and one, a normalization constant ρ_1 is multiplied times the reciprocal of f as

$$\mu_1 = \rho_1/f$$

where ρ_1 is a normalization constant, and is set to 4π. The term μ_1 may be viewed as a quantitative measure of the meaning of an "approximately circular shape" or the meaning of an "approximately round shape."

6.2. Equal-Area Circular Shape Measure

Let P and A denote, respectively, the perimeter and the area of a nucleus. Let P' denote the perimeter of a circle with area A. Let A' denote the area of a circle with perimeter P. Depending on its prospective application, the meaning of an "appoximately circular shape" may also be expressed as:

$$\mu_2 = \rho_2(P'/P)$$

where ρ_2 is a normalization constant, and is set to one in order to normalize the value of μ_2 between zero and one.

The term μ_1 may be called an equal-perimeter circular shape measure and μ_2 an equal-area circular shape measure. The relationship between μ_1 and μ_2 is summarized in the following three theorems.

THEOREM 3. *For all possible nuclear shapes, the equal-perimeter shape measure μ_1 is always less than or equal to the equal-area circular shape measure μ_2.*

THEOREM 4. *For all possible nuclear shapes, the equal-perimeter circular shape measure μ_1 is always equal to the square of the equal-area circular shape measure μ_2.*

THEOREM 5. *For any two nuclear shapes A and B, $\mu_1(A)$ is greater than or equal to $\mu_1(B)$ if and only if $\mu_2(A)$ is greater than or equal to $\mu_2(B)$.*

The proofs of these theorems an be obtained from the author. Theorem 5 shows the order preservation property of μ_1 and μ_2 with respect to all possible nuclear shapes.

6.3. Elongated

The nuclear shape of the basophil cell type is elongated. A quantitative measure of the elongated visual concept of a nucleus may be defined as follows:

1. Determine its area and center of mass. A way to determine its area and center of mass can be found in Ref. 16.
2. Find the best fit rectangle with the same area and with the center coinciding with the center of mass of the nucleus.
3. Let a and b denote the sides of the best fit rectangle. Let μ'_e denote a quantitative measure of the elongated visual concept of the nucleus. Then,

$$\mu'_e = \frac{\max(a, b)}{a + b}$$

4. If the best fit rectangle is not unique, the μ_e is defined to be the maximum of μ_e'

$$\mu_e = \max(\mu_e')$$

6.4. Spiculed

A quantitative measure of the spiculed visual concept of a nucleus may be expressed as

$$\mu_{sp} = \mu_e^2$$

Depending on its prospective application, the exponent used in defining μ_{sp} may take on different values.

6.5. Indented

The nuclear shape of the monocyte cell type is indented. A quantitative measure of the indented visual concept of a nucleus may be defined as follows:

1. As shown in Fig. 5, determine points A and B such that the indented nucleus is symmetric with respect to AB. If the symmetric axis AB does not exist, then determine the axis AB which will minimize the symmetrical difference.
2. Determine points C and D such that the tangents at C and D are perpendicular to the tangent at A. If C is not unique, then determine the middle point as C.
3. Determine points E and F such that AE is equal to EC, and AF is equal to FD along the perimeter.
4. Determine θ_1, which is the angle formed by the tangents at points E and F. θ_1 may be called the *exterior angle* of an indented nucleus.

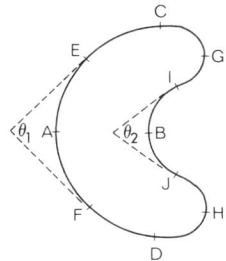

FIGURE 5. A quantitative measure of indented visual concept.

5. Determine points G and H such that the tangents at G and H are parallel to the tangent at A. If G is not unique, then determine the middle point as G.
6. Determine points I and J such that BI is equal to IG, and BJ is equal to JH along the perimeter.
7. Determine θ_2 which is the angle formed by the tangents at points I and J. θ_2 may be called the *interior angle* of an indented nucleus.
8. Let μ_i denote a quantitative measure of the indented visual concept of the nucleus. Then,

$$\mu_i = 1 - \rho_i \max(\theta_1, \theta_2)$$

or

$$\mu_i' = 1 - \rho_i' \min(\theta_1, \theta_2)$$

or

$$\mu_i'' = 1 - \rho_i'' \, \theta_1 \, \theta_2$$

where ρ_i, ρ_i', ρ_i'' are normalization constants, and are set to $1/180°$, $1/180°$, and $1/(180°)^2$, respectively, in order to normalize the values of μ_i, μ_i' and μ_i'' between zero and one.

Example 6.

(a) For Fig. 6a, $\theta_1 = \theta_2 = 0°$. Thus, $\mu_i = 1$.
(b) For Fig. 6b, $\theta_1 = 25°$ and $\theta_2 = 10°$. Thus, $\mu_i = 0.86$.
(c) For Fig. 6c, $\theta_1 = 84°$ and $\theta_2 = 70°$. Thus, $\mu_i = 0.53$.
(d) For Fig. 6d, $\theta_1 = 180°$ and $\theta_2 = 180°$. Thus, $\mu_i = 0$.
(e) For Fig. 6e, $\theta_1 = 90°$ and $\theta_2 = 180°$. Thus, $\mu_i = 0$.

It is of interest to note that μ_i is monotone decreasing with respect to the exterior angle θ_1 and the interior angle θ_2.

6.6. Slightly Indented

A quantitative measure of the slightly indented visual concept of a nucleus may be expressed as

$$\mu_{\text{si}} = \mu_i^{1/2}$$

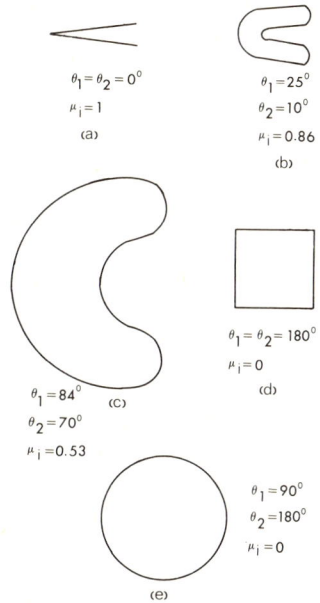

FIGURE 6. The grade of membership of indented nuclei.

Example 7.

(a) For Fig. 6b, $\mu_{si} = 0.93$.
(b) For Fig. 6c, $\mu_{si} = 0.73$.

Depending on its prospective application, the exponent used in defining μ_{si} may take on different values.

6.7. Deeply Indented

A quantitative measure of the deeply indented visual concept of a nucleus may be expressed as

$$\mu_{di} = \mu_i^2$$

Example 8.

(a) For Fig. 6b, $\mu_{di} = 0.74$.
(b) For Fig. 6c, $\mu_{di} = 0.28$.

Depending on its prospective application, the exponent used in defining μ_{di} may take on different values.

7. Dissimilarity Measures

A dissimilarity measure may be defined as the complement of a similarity measure.

7.1. Unary Dissimilarity Measures

We shall use triangles and chromosome images as illustrative examples. Some results are summarized in Theorems 6 and 7.

THEOREM 6. *According to the unary dissimilarity measures defined, the most dissimilar isosceles triangle is* $(120°, 60°, 0°)$; *the most dissimilar equilateral triangle is* $(180°, 0°, 0°)$; *and the most dissimilar right triangle is* $(180°, 0°, 0°)$.

7.2. Binary Dissimilarity Measures

Some results of the binary dissimilarity of triangles and chromosome images are presented.

THEOREM 7. *For any two triangles,* $A = 180°$, $B = C = 0°$, *and* $A' = B' = C' = 60°$ *are the unique pair of the most dissimilar triangles as shown in Fig. 7.*

For a given triangle $\triangle ABC$, algorithms for finding the most dissimilar triangles $\overline{\triangle ABC}$, and the dissimilarity measure between $\triangle ABC$ and $\overline{\triangle ABC}$ are presented in Ref. 12. It is found that the three possibilities for $\overline{\triangle ABC}$ are $(180°, 0°, 0°)$, $(60°, 60°, 60°)$, and $(90°, 90°, 0°)$. A flow chart of determining $\overline{\triangle ABC}$ and $\mu_D(\triangle ABC, \overline{\triangle ABC})$ is shown in Fig. 8.

A geometric interpretation of the dissimilarity of triangles is shown in Fig. 9. The horizontal axis denotes the value of A where $A \geq B \geq C$. The vertical axis denotes the value of B.

It is clear that there is an isomorphism between a point in $\triangle abc$, and an arbitrary triangle $\triangle ABC$. We obtain the following results:

   i. The most dissimilar triangle of all triangles falling in the area of the quadrangle *adec* is $b = (180°, 0°, 0°)$.

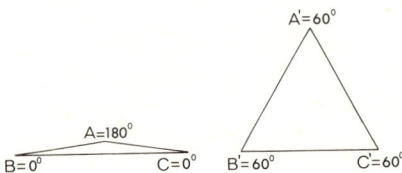

FIGURE 7. The unique pair of the most dissimilar triangles.

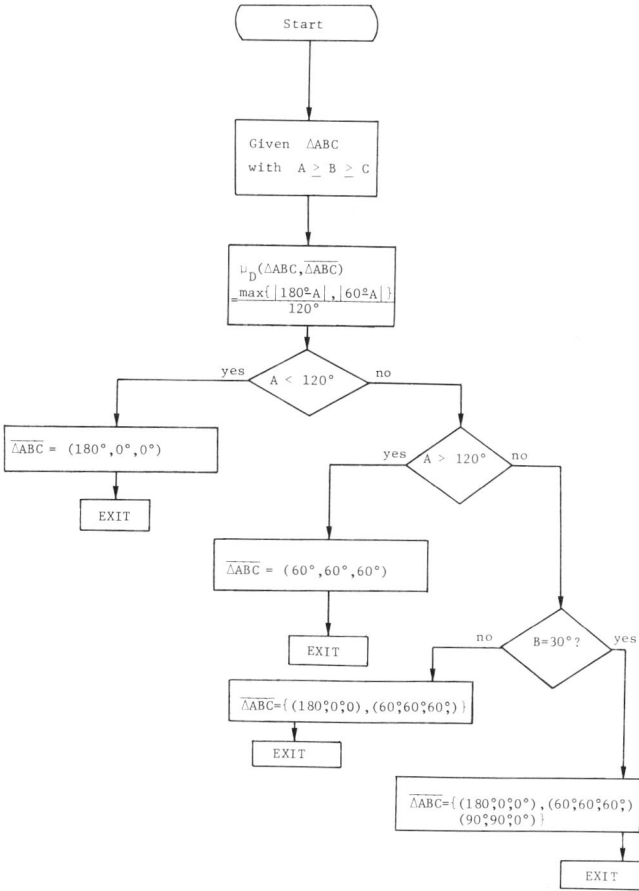

FIGURE 8. A flow chart of determining $\overline{\Delta ABC}$ and $\mu_D(\Delta ABC, \overline{\Delta ABC})$.

ii. The most dissimilar triangle of all triangles falling in the area of the triangle bde is $a = (60°, 60°, 60°)$.

iii. The most dissimilar triangles of all triangles falling in the line de are $a = (60°, 60°, 60°)$ and $b = (180°, 0°, 0°)$.

iv. The most dissimilar triangles of $d = (120°, 30°, 30°)$ are $a = (60°, 60°, 60°)$, $b = (180°, 0°, 0°)$, and $c = (90°, 90°, 0°)$.

THEOREM 8. *For any two chromosome images, $C = (0°, 0°, 0°, 0°, 180°, 180°, 180°, 180°)$ and $B = (180°, 180°, 180°, 180°, 0°, 0°, 0°, 0°)$ are the unique pair of the most dissimilar chromosome images.*

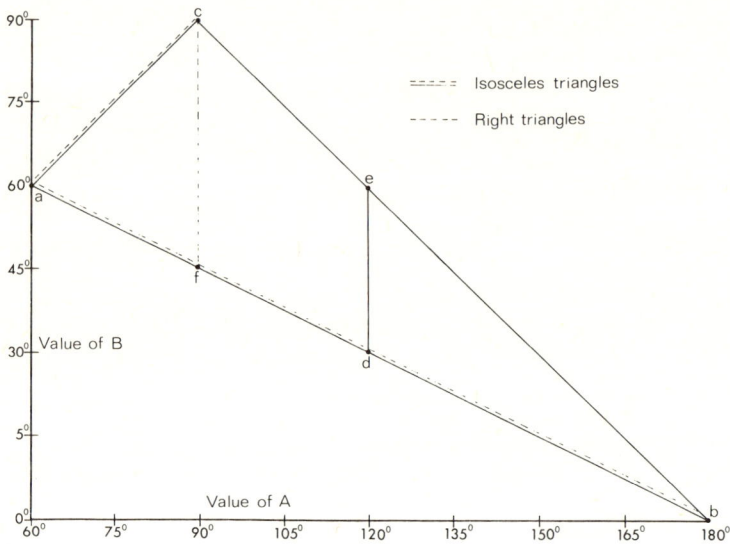

FIGURE 9. Geometric interpretation of the dissimilarity of triangles. $a = (60°, 60°, 60°)$; $b = (180°, 0°, 0°)$; $c = (90°, 90°, 0°)$; $d = (120°, 30°, 30°)$; $e = (120°, 60°, 0°)$; $f = (90°, 45°, 45°)$.

The unique pair of the two most dissimilar chromosome images is depicted in Fig. 10. The sides of chromosome images C and D are represented as c_i and d_i. E_1^C, E_2^C, E_1^D, and E_2^D are exterior biangles, and I_1^C, I_2^C, I_1^D, I_2^D are interior biangles as defined and investigated in Ref. 19.

By using chromosome images as a framework, algorithms for finding most dissimilar images and the corresponding dissimilarity measure are presented and illustrated by examples in Ref. 19. In terms of angles a chromosome image consists of two exterior biangles and two interior biangles. Biangles are defined and classified into 180° biangles, >180° biangles, and <180° biangles. The dissimilarity of biangles and its geometric interpretation together with various properties of biangles are also presented in Ref. 19. The uttermost dimensional similarity and the least dimensional dissimilarity of chromosome images are defined and investigated in Ref. 12.

A quantitative measure of the similarity of two chromosome images may be found in Ref. 12.

A quantitative measure of the similarity of two n-sided polygons may be found in Ref. 11. A quantitative measure of the similarity of an n-sided polygon and an m-sided polygon together with an illustrative example may be found in Ref. 12.

A way to represent a figure of arbitrary shape to its polygonal approximation can be found in Ref. 21. Thus, by using the polygonal approximation processing, similarity measures of polygons can be applied to figures of arbitrary shape.

8. Relationships between Pattern Space, Tree Space, and Fuzzy Languages

The correspondences between pattern space, tree space and fuzzy languages are shown in Table 1.

9. Pattern Classification and Recognition

We are using chromosome images to illustrate how the concept of fuzzy sets and fuzzy languages can be applied to pattern recognition and classification.

A stochastic context-free grammar was used to classify a string-encoded chromosome image into median, submedian, or acrocentric classes by H. Lee and Fu.[14] There is no sharp boundary between the class of median and submedian, nor between the class of submedian and acrocentric. Because the transition from membership to nonmembership in these three classes is gradual rather than abrupt, the concepts and techniques developed in fuzzy languages as developed by Lee and Zadeh,[9] may be applied to classify chromosome images. A median, a submedian, and an acrocentric chromosome image are shown in Figs. 4a, 4b, 4c.

In Ref. 11, a proximity relation is a fuzzy relation which is reflexive, symmetric, but not necessarily transitive. A quantitative measure of the proximity of two n-sided polygons is defined and various properties of angular and dimensional proximities of triangles are investigated.

In Fig. 11, triangles are classified into ordinary triangles and special types of triangles. Special types of triangles are further decomposed into right triangles and isosceles triangles. The intersection of right triangles and isosceles triangles is isosceles right triangles. Equilateral triangles are a special type of isosceles triangles.

In Fig. 12, quadrangles are classified into ordinary quadrangles and trapezoids. Parallelograms are a special type of trapezoids. Rectangles and rhombi are special types of parallelograms. The intersection of rectangles and rhombi is squares.

10. Pattern Storage and Retrieval

In pattern storage and retrieval area, we are using chromosome images and geometric figures as illustrative examples. Shape-oriented storage and retrieval of

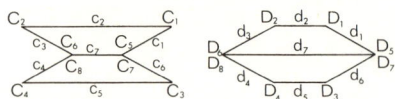

$$E_1^C = E_2^C = (0°, 0°) \qquad E_1^D = E_2^D = (180°, 180°)$$

$$I_1^C = I_2^C = (180°, 180°) \qquad I_1^D = I_2^D = (0°, 0°)$$

FIGURE 10. The unique pair of the most dissimilar chromosome images.

TABLE 1

Correspondences between Pattern Space, Tree Space, and Fuzzy Languages

Pattern space	Tree space	Fuzzy languages
Primitives	Nodes	Words with a membership function
Relative relation among primitives	Branches	The concatenation relations
Subpatterns	Subtrees	Phrases with a membership function
Patterns	Trees	Sentences with a membership function

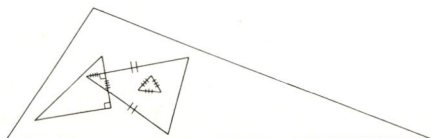

FIGURE 11. The classification of various types of triangles.

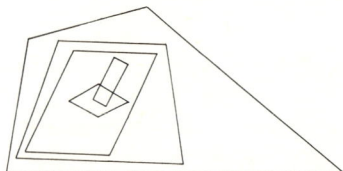

FIGURE 12. The classification of various types of quadrangles.

geometric figures and chromosome images may be found in Lee.[23] In this paper four advantages of storing and retrieving geometric figures and chromosome images through the use of shape-oriented similarity measures are presented.

Given a triangle $\triangle ABC$ with angles A, B, C, quantitative measures of the similarity of this triangle to isosceles triangles, equilateral triangles, and right triangles may be defined as

$$\mu_I(\triangle ABC) = 1 - \frac{1}{60°} \min\{|A - B|, |B - C|, |C - A|\}$$

$$\mu_E(\triangle ABC) = 1 - \frac{1}{180°} \max\{|A - B|, |B - C|, |C - A|\}$$

and

$$\mu_R(\triangle ABC) = 1 - \frac{1}{90°} \min\{|A - 90°|, |B - 90°|, |C - 90°|\}$$

respectively.

A quantitative measure of the similarity of $\triangle ABC$ to isosceles right triangles may be defined as

$$\mu_{IR} = \min\{\mu_I, \mu_R\}$$

or

$$\mu'_{IR} = \mu_I \cdot \mu_R$$

Since both μ_I, μ_R are in the range 0 to 1,[11] $\mu_{IR} \geq \mu'_{IR}$. Depending on its prospective application, μ_{IR} may be substituted by μ'_{IR} or vice versa.

A quantitative measure of the similarity of $\triangle ABC$ as ordinary triangles may be defined as

$$\mu_{OR} = 1 - \max\{\mu_I, \mu_R, \mu_E\}$$

For a triangle $\triangle ABC$ with $A \geq B \geq C$, we shall use the following vector representation for convenience:

$$\triangle ABC = (A, B, C)$$

LEMMA 20. *Given a triangle $\triangle ABC$ with angles A, B, C, if we assume that $A \geq B \geq C$, then*

$$\mu_I(\Delta ABC) = 1 - \frac{1}{60°} \min\{A - B, B - C\}$$

$$\mu_E(\Delta ABC) = 1 - \frac{A - C}{180°}$$

$$\mu_R(\Delta ABC) = 1 - \frac{|A - 90°|}{90°}$$

LEMMA 21. *Given a triangle* ΔABC, *the set* $\{0, \mu'_{IR}(\Delta ABC), \mu_{IR}(\Delta ABC),$ $\mu_I(\Delta ABC), \mu_R(\Delta ABC), 1\}$ *with* max *and* min *as the two binary operations forms a distributive but not complemented lattice.*

Example 9. μ_I, μ_E, μ_R, μ_{IR}, and μ_{OR} of the following 12 triangles are:

ID	ΔABC	μ_I	μ_E	μ_R	μ_{IR}	μ_{OR}
1.	(90°, 70°, 20°)	$\frac{2}{3}$	$\frac{11}{18}$	1	$\frac{2}{3}$	0
2.	(90°, 60°, 30°)	$\frac{1}{2}$	$\frac{2}{3}$	1	$\frac{1}{2}$	0
3.	(120°, 60°, 0°)	0	$\frac{1}{3}$	$\frac{2}{3}$	0	$\frac{1}{3}$
4.	(60°, 60°, 60°)	1	1	$\frac{2}{3}$	$\frac{2}{3}$	0
5.	(90°, 45°, 45°)	1	$\frac{3}{4}$	1	1	0
6.	(180°, 0°, 0°)	1	0	0	0	0
7.	(75°, 60°, 45°)	$\frac{3}{4}$	$\frac{5}{6}$	$\frac{5}{6}$	$\frac{3}{4}$	$\frac{1}{6}$
8.	(75°, 75°, 30°)	1	$\frac{3}{4}$	$\frac{5}{6}$	$\frac{5}{6}$	0
9.	(90°, 75°, 15°)	$\frac{3}{4}$	$\frac{7}{12}$	1	$\frac{3}{4}$	0
10.	(120°, 30°, 30°)	1	$\frac{1}{2}$	$\frac{2}{3}$	$\frac{2}{3}$	0
11.	(120°, 45°, 15°)	$\frac{1}{2}$	$\frac{5}{12}$	$\frac{2}{3}$	$\frac{1}{2}$	$\frac{1}{3}$
12	(150°, 15°, 15°)	1	$\frac{1}{4}$	$\frac{1}{3}$	$\frac{1}{3}$	0

In the paper by Zadeh,[24] "not," "and," and "or" are interpreted as "the operation of complementation (or, equivalently, negation)," "the operation of intersection," and "the operation of union," respectively. In the paper by Zadeh[25] a linguistic hedge such as "very," "more or less," etc., was viewed as an operator which acts on the fuzzy set representing the meaning of its operand. More specifically, "very" is interpreted as "the operation of concentration," which has the effect of squaring the membership function; and "more or less" is interpreted as "the operation of dilation," which has the effect of taking the square root of the membership function. Composite fuzzy queries can be answered by using linguistic hedges and quantitative fuzzy semantics.

Example 10. The grade of membership of triangle (90°, 75°, 15°) with respect to the class "very similar to isosceles triangles" is $\frac{9}{16}$, while the grade of membership of this triangle with respect to the class "more or less similar to isosceles triangles" is $\sqrt{\frac{3}{4}}$.

Example 11. Assuming the 12 triangles in Example 9 as the data base, the composite fuzzy query, "retrieve the triangles which are very similar to equilateral triangles and more or less similar to right triangles" may be answered by computing

a. μ_E^2, the membership function of very similar to equilateral triangles;
b. $\mu_R^{1/2}$, the membership function of more or less similar to right triangles;
c. $\text{Min}\{\mu_E^2, \mu_R^{1/2}\}$ denoted as $\mu_E^2 \wedge \mu_R^{1/2}$, the membership function of very similar to equilateral triangles and more or less similar to right triangles.

$\triangle ABC$	μ_E^2	$\mu_R^{1/2}$	$\mu_E^2 \wedge \mu_R^{1/2}$
(90°, 70°, 20°)	0.37	1	0.37
(90°, 60°, 30°)	0.44	1	0.44
(120°, 60°, 0°)	0.11	0.82	0.11
(60°, 60°, 60°)	1	0.82	0.82
(90°, 45°, 45°)	0.56	1	0.56
(180°, 0°, 0°)	0	0	0
(75°, 60°, 45°)	0.69	0.91	0.69
(75°, 75°, 30°)	0.56	0.91	0.56
(90°, 75°, 15°)	0.34	1	0.34
(120°, 30°, 30°)	0.25	0.82	0.25
(120°, 45°, 15°)	0.18	0.82	0.18
(150°, 15°, 15°)	0.06	0.58	0.06

If we set a threshold to be 0.6, then the answer of the above query is triangles (60°, 60°, 60°) and (75°, 60°, 45°). Absence of a threshold is interpreted as a threshold of zero. Thus, any element with a grade of membership greater than zero is part of the answer. Therefore, the answer of the above fuzzy query is the fuzzy set $\{(\triangle ABC, \mu_E^2(\triangle ABC) \wedge \mu_R^{1/2}(\triangle ABC))\}$ where $\mu_E^2 \wedge \mu_R^{1/2}$ is the membership function.

Discussion on the classification of linguistic hedges and the operations of contrast intensification, fuzzification, accentuation may be found in the paper by Zadeh.[25]

In Ref. 11, $\triangle x$ with angles $A \geq B \geq C$ and $\triangle y$ with angles $A' \geq B' \geq C'$, the similarity between $\triangle x$, $\triangle y$ is equal to

$$\mu_A(\triangle x, \triangle y) = 1 - \frac{1}{240°}\{|A - A'| + |B - B'| + |C - C'|\}$$

Example 12. Given a triangle $\triangle y$ with angles $A' \geq B' \geq C'$ and a tolerance ϵ with $0 \leq \epsilon \leq 1$, the fuzzy query "retrieve all the triangles which are similar to $\triangle y$ within a tolerance of ϵ" may be carried out as follows:
Let X be the set of triangles $\triangle x$ in the data base with angles $A \geq B \geq C$.

Since angles A, B, C are ordered from greatest to least, then the ranges for the angles must be

$$60° \leq A \leq 180°$$
$$0° \leq B \leq 90°$$
$$0° \leq C \leq 60°$$

Instead of testing each triangle Δx in X to see if $\mu_A(\Delta x, \Delta y) \geq 1 - \epsilon$, first form the subset X' of possible candidates by using one of the following three methods:

Method (a) Find the set of triangles $\Delta x'$ with A in the range of $\max\{60°, A' - 240°\epsilon\} \leq A \leq \min\{180°, A' + 240°\epsilon\}$

Method (b) Find the set of triangles $\Delta x'$ with B in the range of $\max\{0, B' - 240°\epsilon\} \leq B \leq \min\{90°, B' + 240°\epsilon\}$

Method (c) Find the set of triangles $\Delta x'$ with C in the range of $\max\{0°, C' - 240°\epsilon\} \leq C \leq \min\{60°, C' + 240°\epsilon\}$.

Those triangles $\Delta x'$ in X' where $\mu_A(\Delta x', \Delta y) \geq 1 - \epsilon$ satisfy the query.

Example 13. Let triangle Δy have angles $A' = 100°$, $B' = 60°$, $C' = 20°$, and $\epsilon = 0.20$. By using Method (a), the set of possible candidates for the fuzzy query "retrieve all the triangles which are similar to Δy within a tolerance of ϵ" consists of those triangles where

$$\max\{60°, 52°\} \leq A \leq \min\{180°, 148°\}$$

Thus, we obtain

$$60° \leq A \leq 148°$$

and

$$\mu_A(\Delta x', \Delta y) \geq 0.8$$

If $\epsilon = 0.10$ then the set of possible candidates becomes those triangles where $60° \leq A \leq 124°$.

A dissimilarity measure of Δx and Δy may be defined as the complement of the similarity of Δx and Δy as

$$\mu_{DIS}(\Delta x, \Delta y) = 1 - \mu_A(\Delta x, \Delta y)$$

Example 14. Given two triangles Δx and Δy, the fuzzy query "retrieve all the triangles which are more or less dissimilar to Δx or very very similar to Δy," may be answered by computing $\mu_{\text{DIS}}^{1/2}(\Delta t, \Delta x) \vee \mu_A^4(\Delta t, \Delta y)$ for all triangles Δt in the data base, where $\vee$ is an infix operator for max.

Therefore, other composite fuzzy queries involving chromosome or leukocytes can also be answered in the same manner. Examples of composite fuzzy queries involving chromosomes are "retrieve the chromosomes which are very similar to median chromosomes, but not similar to a given chromosome," and "retrieve the chromosomes which are more or less similar to median chromosomes and very very similar to a given chromosome." Examples of composite fuzzy queries involving leukocytes are "retrieve leukocytes with deeply indented nucleus or round nucleus," "retrieve leukocytes with elongated nucleus or slightly indented nucleus," etc.

In what follows, proposals are presented for an effective way of organizing a shape-oriented triangle, chromosome, or leukocyte database.

PROPOSITION 1. *For shape-oriented storage of triangles, it is advantageous to store the angles of a triangle in decreasing order of magnitude. This representation may be viewed as a normal form for shape-oriented triangle representation.*

PROPOSITION 2. *For shape-oriented storage of triangles, if we logically order all the triangles individually and independently according to the magnitude of the angles A, B, and C, then we can reduce retrieval time for answering queries.*

PROPOSITION 3. *For shape-oriented storage of triangles, we can use associative memory with match-on-between-limits and find-match-count operations[29] or other hardware searching facilities such as the Symbol 2R computer[30] in order to reduce retrieval time.*

As shown in Fig. 4d (A_1, A_2) and (A_3, A_4) are exterior biangles; while (A_5, A_6) and (A_7, A_8) are interior biangles.

PROPOSITION 4. *For shape-oriented storage of chromosome images, if we logically order all the chromosome images individually and independently according to the angular sums of exterior biangles and interior biangles, then we can reduce retrieval time for answering queries such as "retrieve the chromosomes which are very very similar to a given chromosome A."*

PROPOSITION 5. *For shape-oriented storage of leukocytes, it is suggested that leukocytes be logically ordered individually and independently according to the magnitudes of the grade of membership of approximately circular (round) nuclei, elongated nuclei, indented nuclei, slightly indented nuclei, and deeply indented nuclei, so that, for answering queries, the amount of leukocyte data neeed to be searched can be reduced and the response time improved.*

11. Conclusion

The foregoing analysis has shown that the concepts of the structural approach and similarity measures can be applied to the pattern description, classification, recognition, storage, and retrieval. Algorithms for finding most dissimilar images may be found in Ref. 19.

The application of tree structure and fuzzy languages to pattern recognition, storage, and retrieval offers what appears to be a fertile field for further study. The underlying ideas are interesting and easy for practical application. The results have useful applications in pattern recognition, artificial intelligence, shape-oriented pattern database study in Ref. 27, information retrieval, similarity retrieval techniques in Ref. 28, and pictorial information systems.

ACKNOWLEDGMENTS

I would like to thank my students Paul Cappannari and Karen Cappannari for helping me preparing this paper.

References

1. S. K. CHANG and K. S. FU, *Pictorial Information Systems,* Springer-Verlag, Berlin, 1980.
2. E. T. LEE, Similarity retrieval techniques, Chap. 6 in *Pictorial Information Systems,* S. K. Chang and K. S. FU, Eds., Springer-Verlag, Berlin, pp. 128–176, 1980.
3. L. D. HARMON, The recognition of faces, *Sci. Am.* **229,** 71–82 (November 1973).
4. L. HARMON and W. HUNT, Automatic recognition of human face profiles, *Proc. of 3rd Confer. on Pat. Recog.,* pp. 183–188, November 1976.
5. E. T. LEE, Similarity directed picture storage and management, *Proc. of 1977 IEEE Workshop on Picture Data Description and Management,* April 1977.
6. K. S. FU, *Syntactic Pattern Recognition and Applications.* Prentice Hall, Englewood Cliffs, New Jersey, 1982.
7. K. S. FU, *Syntactic Methods in Pattern Recognition,* Academic Press, New York, 1974.
8. K. S. FU, Stochastic automata, stochastic languages and pattern recognition, *J. Cybern.* **1**(3), 31–49 (1971).
9. E. T. LEE and L. A. ZADEH, Note on fuzzy languages, *Inf. Sci.* **1,** 421–434 (1969).
10. E. T. LEE, Shape-oriented chromosome classification, *IEEE Trans. Syst., Man, Cybern.* **SMC-5,** 629–632 (1975).
11. E. T. LEE, Proximity measures for the classification of geometric figures, *J. Cybern.* **2,** 43–59 (1972).
12. E. T. LEE, The shape-oriented dissimilarity of polygons and its application to the classification of chromosome images, *Pat. Recog.* **6,** 47–60 (1974).
13. B. WILDROW, The rubber-mask technique—I: Pattern measurement and analysis. *Pat. Recogn.* **5,** 175–197 (1973).

14. H. C. LEE and K. S. FU, A stochastic syntax analysis procedure and its application to pattern classification, *IEEE Trans. Comput.* **21,** 660–666 (July, 1972).
15. R. S. LEDLEY, L. S. ROTOLO, T. J. GOLAB, J. D. JACOBAEN, M. D. GINSBERG, and J. B. WILSON, FIDAC: Film input to digital automatic computer and associated syntax-directed pattern-recognition programming system, in *Optical and Electro-Optical Information Processing,* Chap. 33, pp. 591–613, M.I.T. Press, Cambridge, Massachusetts, 1965.
16. J. BACUS and E. GOSE, Leukocyte pattern recognition, *IEEE Trans. Syst. Man Cybern.* **SMC-2,** 513–526 (September, 1972).
17. I. YOUNG, Automated leukocyte recognition, *Automated Cell Identification and Cell Sorting,* Academic Press, New York, 1972.
18. J. BACUS, AGGARWAL *et al.* Computer recognition of microscopic images, *Proceedings of EASCON,* 1975.
19. E. T. LEE, Algorithms for finding most dissimilar images with possible applications to chromosome classification, *Bull. Math. Biol.* **38,** 505–516 (1976).
20. E. T. LEE, Algorithms for finding most unsymmetrical chromosome images, to appear in *Math. Biosci.*
21. T. PAVLIDIS and S. HOROWITZ, Segmentation of plane curves, *IEEE Trans. Comput.* **C-23,** 860–870 (August, 1974).
22. E. T. LEE, Shape-oriented classification storage and retrieval of leukocytes, *Proceedings of the Third International Joint Conference on Pattern Recognition,* November 8–11, 1976.
23. E. T. LEE, Shape-oriented storage and retrieval of geometric figures and chromosome images, *Inf. Process. Manage.* **12**(1), 35–41 (1976).
24. L. A. ZADEH, Similarity relations and fuzzy ordering, *Inf. Sci.* **3,** 159–176 (1971).
25. L. A. ZADEH, A fuzzy-set-theoretic interpretation of linguistic hedges, *J. Cybern.* **2,** 4–34 (1972).
26. E. T. LEE and N. LEE, Design of a fault tolerant microprocessor, *Proc. of the 1978 International Computer Symposium,* December 20–24, 1978.
27. E. T. LEE, A shape-oriented image data base, *Proc. of the Symposium on Current Problems in Image Science,* Sponsored by the Office of Naval Research, November, 1976.
28. E. T. LEE, A similarity directed picture database, *Policy Anal. Inf. Syst.* **1,** 113–125 (1978).
29. Y. CHU, *Computer Organization and Microprogramming,* Prentice-Hall, Englewood Cliffs, New Jersey, 1972.
30. H. RICHARDS and A. E. OLDEHOEFT, Hardware-software interactions in Symbol-2R's operating system, *Second Annual Symposium on Computer Architecture,* 1975.
31. I. ROCK, The perception of disoriented figures, *Sci. Am.* **230,** 78–85 (1974).
32. T. PAVLIDIS, Analysis of set patterns, *Pattern Recognition,* **1,** 165–178 (1968).
33. T. PAVLIDIS, Computer recognition of figures through decomposition, *Inf. Control* **12,** 626–537 (1968).
34. T. PAVLIDIS, Representation of figures by labeled graphs, *Pattern Recognition* **4,** 5–17 (1972).
35. M. F. DACEY, Poly: A two dimensional language for a class of polygons, *Pattern Recognition* **3,** 197–208 (1971).

OFFICE INFORMATION SYSTEMS

OFFICE INFORMATION SYSTEM DESIGN

SHI-KUO CHANG

1. Office Automation

> Are you genuine? Or merely an actor? A representative? Or that which is represented?
> In the end, perhaps you are merely a copy of an actor.
> —NIETZSCHE, *Twilight of the Idols*

Office automation can be defined as the replacement of manual office activities by equivalent or similar activities which automate means of doing office work. An *office activity* refers to any activity in an office, such as filling out a form, sending a message, entering information into a file, making a decision to route a form, etc. An *office procedure* refers to a structured set of office activities for the accomplishment of a specific office task, such as scheduling a meeting, processing a mortgage application form, reviewing a paper, etc. An office usually consists of a number of *work stations* or simply *stations*. The work stations are interconnected by a communication network to serve as a *message exchange system*.

The work stations in a manual system consist of the desks of clerks, secretaries, receptionists, managers, and other decision makers. A conventional message exchange system transmits paper messages (ordinary mail) via the mail system. The first step in office automation is usually the partial (or total) replacement (or enhancement) of the office desks by terminals, word processors, or small computer systems which are interconnected by an electronic message exchange system. In other words, initially office automation aims at the automation of devices and improvement of the communication network (message exchange system).

In the automated system, each work station can be a simple terminal, such as a printer terminal or a CRT terminal. It may also be a word processor, or a small desk-top computer, consisting of a microprocessor, floppy disks for local storage, a terminal, and other peripheral electronic equipments for office monitoring,

SHI-KUO CHANG • Department of Electrical Engineering, Illinois Institute of Technology, Chicago, Illinois 60616.

such as universal telephone interface for receiving incoming telephone calls and voice playback, analog-to-digial converters for monitoring fire alarms, burglar alarms, etc.

The electronic message exchange system is popularly called the *electronic mail system*. An electronic mail system can be defined as a message exchange system wherein information is transmitted between two or more terminals via a telecommunication network. Under this broad definition, there are many different types of electronic mail systems in existence today: telegraph; TWS/Telex; private line teletype; dial-up via DDD telephone network or specialized network such as Tymnet or Telenet; facsimile and OCR (optical character recognition) transmission; communicating word processors; message switching and computer-communications systems; hybrid systems such as Teletext systems (British Televax, French Antelop, etc.) with teletext pages broadcast from television stations to television units, and telephone dial-in for selection of teletext pages, which may serve in the future as basis of a home electronic mail system.

The electronic message exchange system can be one based upon an existing telephone network, with analog-to-digital data conversion at each work station. It can be one based upon an advanced business telephone system, such as a PBX (private branch exchange) system capable of providing an integrated means for communicating all types of information: voice, data, facsimile, and communicating word processing messages. It can also be a specially designed local network, such as Xerox–DEC–Intel's Ethernet using wideband coaxial cables, or a local network using fiber optics for communications. Depending upon the type of communication networks and communication bandwidth, communications may be voice-only, data-only, voice-and-data, voice-data-and-facsimile, etc. In the most sophisticated networks, we will have truly multimedia communications (voice, data, and picture) among the work stations.

Although electronic mail systems are rapidly proliferating, a number of shortcomings are yet to be overcome. Current electronic mail systems usually have limited coverage, which limits their usefulness. The lack of integration and compatibility among existing systems contributes to the limited coverage of each system. Electronic mail systems generally have very limited data storage and retrieval capabilities. The cost/benefits of electronic mail systems are yet to be proven. Because of these shortcomings, it is generally believed that electronic mail systems will gradually evolve as communications and equipment costs are reduced and data, facsimile, and word-processing devices consequently become more commonplace. This means that conventional mail and electronic mail will coexist in an evolutionary office environment.[19]

The second step in office automation is to take advantage of the electronic desks, and replace some manual office procedures by computerized procedures. At some work stations, manual intervention is still necessary for data entry and decision making. Some work stations may be partially automated, with some activities managed by the electronic desk. Some other work stations may be entirely automated using computerized office procedures.

It should be emphasized that the conversion of work stations from a "paper-oriented desk" to an "electronic desk" most likely will happen in an incremental and gradual fashion, with some stations computerized, and many other stations remaining as "paper-oriented desks." This incremental and partial conversion implies that an office will evolve gradually from a paper-oriented office to some intermediate stage. In other words, papers and manual activities will remain important components in an office information system. We must bear in mind this "mixed mode" of operation, when attempting to design and implement office information systems. For the foreseeable future at least, we cannot entirely eliminate either paper or paper-oriented desks.

In this evolution from a conventional office system to an electronic office information system, there are also opportunities to restructure office procedures, consolidate office activities, and streamline operations. This may arise partially as a by-product of computerization: when office procedures are automated, they sometimes must be restructured to suit computer operations. Files, messages, forms, activities, and procedures must be clearly defined. On the other hand, computerization also offers an opportunity to restructure office procedures so that they become more efficient in the new environment.

2. Key Concepts in Office Information System Design

Before we proceed, it is pertinent to summarize the key concepts in office information systems design. To manage information in an office information system environment, there are three aspects to be considered: How to manage data? How to manage communication? How to manage activities?

(1) Data Management. Files and databases are places where information is stored. Another name used is repository.[16] The techniques for file management and database management are well known. Various approaches for database design have been discussed by several authors in this volume. A distributed database system is needed to support a distributed office information system. Problems of concurrency control, consistency, and security need to be considered. To handle texts, pictures, and voice data, multimedia database management techniques remain to be developed. But above all, database systems must be enhanced for knowledge management. One approach will be described in this paper.

(2) Message Management. Messages and forms are the means of communication among work stations. A work station is a node in an office information system, where an agent (a process, an actor, a clerk) performs office activities (actions). A work station communicates with other stations via messages and/or forms. A work station stores information in files and/or databases. Since messages

and forms can also be stored in the database, it is possible to perform certain operations on messages, such as message creation, message modification, message filing, and forwarding of message to other work stations.[21] In this paper, we will describe how to integrate message management into office information system design.

(3) Activities Management. Since the first and ultimate goal of office automation is to automate office activities, it is important to understand the problem of office activities management, and how office procedures can be modeled in the office information system environment. As mentioned above, office procedures are the tasks performed at the work stations. Activity and action are synonyms. The agent which performs an activity or an action is variously called a process, an actor, an office worker, etc. Different models for office procedures emphasize different key concepts in office information system design.[9,16,22,23] A unified approach will be presented in the next section. It should be noted that activities management also includes knowledge management and model management, because in order to deal with activities, we must be able to deal with knowledge models. The office procedure model introduced later is such a knowledge model.

3. A Conceptual Framework for Office Information System Design

3.1. Event Monitoring Using Database Alerters

One of the major problems in office automation is the coordination and integration among various tasks. In the real world, actions are usually triggered due to a change of state of a certain event. Some of these actions are time-related routine operations, for example, routing a meeting notice among a group of people. Such routine operations are often periodically scheduled. Some of these actions are predetermined, for example, managing an editorial office which requires the coordination of a number of predetermined tasks. Such predetermined actions are usually both event-based and time-related. When we consider the design of an office information system, the monitoring of events, and the scheduling of predetermined and time-related routine activities are the main functions that an office information system can perform and thereby improve office efficiency and increase productivity.

An office information system requires the support of a database management system for the storage and manipulation of office information. Moreover, the database management system should also be capable of responding to external events. Database systems are usually passive, in the sense that they only respond to externally generated information retrieval/manipulation requests, but cannot take other actions spontaneously. The recent development of database alerting techniques have changed the character of the database system from a passive one to an active one. Database alerters were first introduced by Buneman.[2,3] To clarify the concept, consider the following examples:

Example 1. Report the name and temperature of any station at which the temperature falls below 10°C.

Example 2. Report the number and owner of any account from which more than $500 is drawn.

In each of the above examples, the user wishes to be informed when certain exception conditions occur. The exception condition and the prescribed message sending action form a ⟨condition, action⟩ pair. Such rules are called *alerter rules.*

Alerter rules can be used to monitor state transitions in a database. The current contents of a database determine its "state." If we aggregate the database states into two states, called the *IN state* (when an exception condition is met) and the *OUT state* (when an exception condition is not met), then an alerter is *triggered* and an *alert message* is generated or actions are invoked, whenever the database transits to an IN state. Such state changes are affected only by database updates. Therefore, to install *database alerters,* we need only monitor database updates. The alerting subsystem in Fig. 1 illustrates this concept.

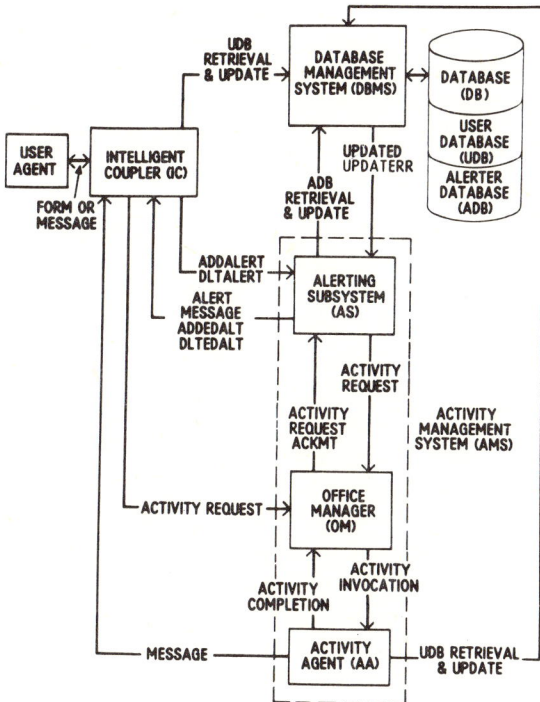

FIGURE 1. Component systems of an office information system.

Alerter rules therefore can be used to monitor database updates and trigger actions whenever certain conditions regarding database updates are satisfied.[15,18] With alerter rules, database updates will automatically cause prespecified actions to take place. Thus the database system can take on an active role in events monitoring.[20]

It should be noted that actions triggered by an alerter are viewed as side-effects of database updates. The failure of performing these actions does not necessarily cause the database updates to be rolled back. This constitutes the basic difference between alerters in an alerter system and triggers in an integrity system, such as the trigger mechanism proposed for system R.[17]

3.2. Activity Management in Office Information Systems

> Hobbes was right, as well as Rousseau: Man is a robustly active creature; activity alone keeps him from going crazy.
>
> —ERNEST BECKER, Escape From Evil

An office information system is a message-driven system. Work stations exchange messages, which cause certain office activities to be performed. In Fig. 1, we present the component subsystems of an office information system.

Figure 1 depicts the relationship among the database system (DBMS), the alerting subsystem (AS), the office manager (OM), the activity agents (AA), and the intelligent coupler (IC). The user agent communicates with the user interface, called the intelligent coupler, by messages or forms. The intelligent coupler performs the translation of user queries.[5,6] It can also interact with the user to complete an intelligent form[23] (or interactive letter[1]).

The intelligent coupler sends user database retrieval and update messages to the database system. The database consists of a user database and an alerter database, both managed by the database system. The *alerter database* is used to store the alerter rules. The database system sends messages to the alerting subsystem, containing descriptions of every completed update or failed update.

The alerting subsystem screens database updates to detect the occurrence of important events. Therefore, the alerting subsystem can be generally viewed as a screening program or a *filter* associated with the database system. When an event occurs, the alerting subsystem can either send an alert message to the intelligent coupler (which in turn informs the user agent), or send an activity request to the office manager to initiate office activities.

The office manager manages office activities. It receives activity request either indirectly from the alerting subsystem, or directly from the intelligent coupler. The office manager then schedules and performs office procedures by calling upon one or many activity agents. Therefore, the office manager is functionally analogous to the scheduler in an operating system.

An activity agent can be regarded as an office specialist, capable of performing some well-defined office activity.[23] For example, the activity agent can be a form generation program, a report generator, an editing program, etc. When an activity agent completes its task, it sends an activity completion message to the office manager, which may then schedule other activities.

The activity agent can send messages to the intelligent coupler, which then presents the information to the user agent. The activity agent can also perform database retrieval/update operations, which may lead to triggering of alerters and scheduling of additional activities.

The alerting subsystem, the office manager, and the activity agents, together form the *activity management system* (AMS), which monitors events and initiates, schedules, and performs office activities.[9] The activity management system is therefore the most important part of the office information system.

3.3. Office Procedure Model

To describe the relationships among office activities, databases, and alerters, we adopt the following formalism: a rectangular box is used to denote a file R_i, a diamond-shaped box an alerter rule A_j, and a circle any activity or process P_k. If an activity or process requires user interaction, it is denoted by a double circle. A message is denoted by u_i, and a form is denoted by F_j. The possible relationships are summarized as follows:

1. File Access.

$$R_i \dashrightarrow P_k$$

File R_i is accessed by process P_k.

2. File Update.

$$P_k \dashrightarrow R_i \quad \text{or} \quad A_j \dashrightarrow R_i$$

File R_i is updated by process P_k or alerter rule A_j. We say that P_k or A_j affects file R_i.

3. Alerter Triggering.

$$R_i \dashrightarrow A_j$$

Update of file R_i may trigger alerter A_j. The alert condition can be written beneath the directed arc. We say that A_j monitors file R_i for triggering.

4. Activity Invocation.

$$A_j \; -> \; P_k$$

Alerter A_j invokes process P_k.
5. Activity Precedence.

$$P_k \; -> \; P_m$$

Process P_k precedes (and invokes) process P_k.
6. Alerter Creation.

$$A_j \; => \; A_m \quad \text{or} \quad P_k \; => \; A_m$$

Alerter A_j or process P_k creates alerter A_m.
7. Alerter Deletion.

$$A_j \; =< \; A_m \quad \text{or} \quad P_k \; =< \; A_m$$

Alerter A_j or process P_k deletes alerter A_m.
8. Message Input.

$$u \; -\gg \; \text{MESSAGE}$$

Input message u is stored in a message file.
9. Form Output.

$$P_i \; -\gg \; F_j$$

Process P_i generates output form F_j.
10. Form Interaction Process.

$$P_i \quad \begin{array}{l} -\gg \; F_j \\ \ll - \; F'_j \end{array}$$

Process P_i sends form F_j to user agent to obtain additional information. When form F_j is completed by user, process P_i continues.
11. Alerter ON.

$$R_i \underset{\text{ON}}{\; -> \;} A_j$$

Update of file R_i may enable alerter A_j. The ON condition can be written beneath the directed arc. We say that A_j monitors file R_i for ON condition.

12. Alerter OFF.

$$R_i \; -> \; A_j$$
$$\text{OFF}$$

Update of file R_i may destroy alerter A_j. The OFF condition can be written beneath the directed arc. We say that A_j monitors file R_i for OFF condition.

13. Time Clock.

$$t \; -\gg \; \text{TIME}$$

TIME file is set to t. Since TIME file is often a conceptual device (see Section 5), the update of TIME file can be omitted in an OPM specification.

With these formal notations, we can graphically depict office procedures and analyze how they can be executed by an office information system. Such a formal model is called the *office procedure model (OPM)*. This knowledge model can also be stored in the database. It is accessed by the alerting subsystem to check for alerter database consistency. It is also accessed by the office manager to schedule and control concurrent activities invoked by the office manager, and to check for alerter system stability (see Ref. 9).

4. Simple Alerters and Implementation Issues

Simple alerters monitor database updates of *simple database objects,* usually records in a file (or tuples in a relational file, if we use the relational database terminology). To specify a simple alerter, we need to specify the following:

1. Name of Alerter. This is a unique symbolic name to identify an alerter.

2. Type of Update Operation to be Monitored. For updates of records in a file, there are three types of updates: insertion of a new record, deletion of an old record, and modification of an old record. The three update types are denoted by "i", "d", and "m", respectively.

3. Name of Database Object to be Monitored. For monitoring of record updates in a file, this will consist of two parts:

3.1. File name (or relation name), and

3.2. Field names (or attribute set).

4. Alert Condition. The alert condition is a logical expression involving atomic clauses. Each atomic clause consists of an attribute name and a literal, or two attribute names, related by a comparison operator such as " $=$ ", " $!=$ ", " $<$ ", " $>$ ", etc. In an alert condition for type "m" update (record modification), the attributes are prefixed by "old" or "new," indicating whether an attribute refers to the "old" or the "new" record. Similarly, in an alert condition for type "i" update (record insertion), the attributes are prefixed by the "new" keyword. In an alert condition for type "d" update (record deletion), the attributes are prefixed by the "old" keyword. In these two cases, however, the prefix can be omitted since there is no possibility for confusion.

5. Action. The *action* taken by a simple alerter when it is triggered is to send messages to various users or to invoke another process, or to perform database update operations.

6. Name of Creator of the Alerter Rule.

Alerter rules are stored in the alerter database (ADB), which is also managed by the database system. Referring again to the examples mentioned in Section 3.1, the messages to create the appropriate alerters are as follows:

(1) ADDALERT   a-name = "frostwarning", u-type = "m",
               rel-name = weather",
               attribute-name = "temp", condition = "new.temp<10",
               action = "ALERT user-a user-b",
               creator = "user-c"

(The alerter name is "frost-warning," update type is "m," relation name is "weather," attribute is "temp," condition is "new.temp<10," alert message should be sent to "user-a" and "user-b," and alerter is created by "user-c.")

(2) ADDALERT   a-name = "withdrawn-warning", u-type = "m",
               rel-name = "account",
               attribute = "balance",
               condition = "old.balance − new.balance > 500",
               action = "ALERT bank-manager",
               creator = "teller-a"

(The alerter name is "withdrawn-warning," update type is "m," relation name is "account," attribute is "balance," condition is "old.balance − new.balance > 500," alert message should be sent to "bank-manager," and alerter is created by "teller-a.")

An alerter can be removed by a deletion message:

DLTALERT "frostwarning"

Database retrieval/update requests from the user agent are sent to the database system. The ADDALERT and DLTALERT messages, on the other hand, are sent to the alerting subsystem, which then uses the database system to perform the actual updating of the alerter database.

When the alerting subsystem receives an ADDALERT message, it adds the appropriate alerter rule to the ADB, after checking that the rule is acceptable (e.g., the database object does exist, and the rule is consistent with other rules). A message

ADDEDALT alerter-name

is sent to the agent creating the alerter rule, where "alerter-name" is the symbolic name of the alerter rule. If the alerting subsystem finds the alerter rule unacceptable, an appropriate error message is returned.

Similarly, when the alerting subsystem receives an DLTALERT message, it deletes the specified alerter rule from the ADB and sends the following response to the agent deleting the alerter rule:

DLTEDALT alerter-name

When a database retrieval request is sent to the database system, it simply retrieves the appropriate information, and the response from the database system is forwarded to the user. No message is sent to the alerting subsystem. This is because we do not monitor retrieval operations. Retrieval could be monitored, if we intend to analyze *user profile* for security or protection reasons.

When a database update request is sent to the database system, it first performs the requested update operation. *Only after the update has been performed,* that the database system sends the following message:

UPDATED ⟨update-type⟩ ⟨obj-name⟩ ⟨old-record⟩ ⟨new-record⟩

to the alerting subsystem. The alerting subsystem then checks whether any alert condition is satisfied. The simplest approach is to scan through the alerter rules in the alerter database. The alerting subsystem can use the database system to retrieve alerter rules from the alerter database. To improve efficiency, the alerter rules could be indexed by (a) update type, (b) relation name, and (c) attribute name(s). With such an index structure, the lowest-level entries are pointers to the alerter rules. Only alerter rules pertinent to an update need be checked. Therefore, in practice, the required computation for checking ADB represents a small overhead on each update.

When an alerter is triggered, the alerting subsystem may send alert messages to the user agent, if the specified action is the ALERT command. The alert message contains the name of alerter, type of update, database object monitored, and value of database object before and after the update. The user agent is responsible for processing the ALERT message. On the other hand, the alerting subsystem may send activity request to the office manager for activity scheduling. The activity request consists of action names and other parameters, as specified in the alerter rules.

5. Existential Alerters and Time Alerters

Existential alerters are alerters with well-defined *duration*. To define duration of an alerter, we extend the concept of simple alerters as follows. Each alerter is associated with three conditions: an *alert condition,* an *ON condition,* and an *OFF condition.* When the On condition is met, the alerter is enabled. When the OFF condition is met, the alerter is disabled or destroyed. The alert condition, as defined previously, determines when the alerter rule is triggered. Each alerter thus monitors three database objects, one for each of the three conditions. These three monitored objects can be identical or different. The set of alerters that are currently ON is called the *ON-set.*

A *customized alerter* is an alerter of the form $A_k(c_1, c_2, \ldots, c_m)$ where the c_i's are parameters that may appear in the alert condition. A *customized existential alerter* is an existential alerter of the form $A_k(c_1, c_2, \ldots, c_m)$, where the c_i's are parameters that may appear in the alert condition or the duration (i.e., the ON condition and the OFF condition). All customized alerters of an alerter A_k have the same format as A_k, except the c_i's may have different values in each customized rule.

A *time alerter* is a special type of alerter for monitoring time-related events. In order to specify time alerters, we can assume there is a special relational file, called TIME, which has only one attribute—time. The system may update the TIME relational file periodically, the update frequency being dependent on applications. The TIME relational file may also be the system clock itself, and the update frequency is the same as the clock rate. With this conceptual time relational file, the system can treat time as an ordinary attribute, and the alerter rule can mention the time attribute in its ON condition, trigger condition, as well as OFF condition.

As an example, suppose we want to monitor incoming telephone calls. The alerter is in effect between 8 a.m. and 11 a.m., and the trigger condition is "caller = 'Smith'." The existential alerter is as follows:

(1) ON condition: time = 8 a.m.
(2) Alert condition: caller = 'Smith'
(3) OFF condition: time = 11 a.m.

For this application, the TIME file might be updated once every five minutes.

The above alerter rule can be modified to be a customized alerter rule as follows. The customized alerter $A(t_1, t_2, \text{caller-name})$ has the following conditions:

(1) ON condition: time = t_1
(2) Alert condition: caller = caller-name
(3) OFF condition: time = t_2

Other system parameters can be monitored similarly, by creating special-purpose system relational files containing such parameters. The system overhead is proportional to the frequency of updates for such system files, because every update of a system file will result in the evaluation of alerter rules monitoring this file. Therefore, we must exercise care in determining how often to update the system parameters, such as time, toggle switch, etc.

6. Journal Editing Example

As an example of office automation, we will describe the journal editing activities in an editorial office. Basically, there are three activities to be considered: (a) occurrence of real-world events, (b) database update activities, and (c) generation of forms.

The occurrence of real-world events causes input messages to be sent to the office information system. As illustrated in Fig. 2, each input message is considered a record insertion into a MESSAGE relational file in the user database UDB, which triggers alerters A_1 or A_6 to invoke user-defined processes. In actual implementation, the message file may be nonexistent, or it may serve as a log file to

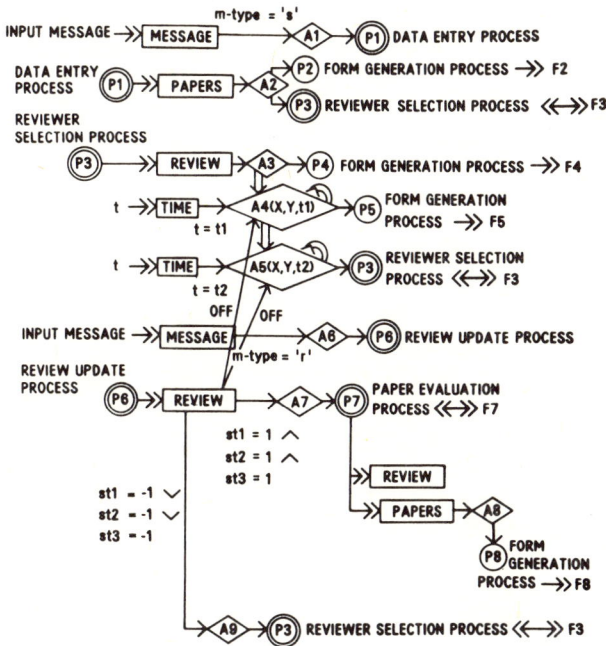

FIGURE 2. Office procedure model for the editorial office.

record all incoming messages. The message file may contain the following attributes: message-type, message-id, message-text.

One type of input message is the submission of a paper from an author. This message, with message-type 's,' represents an event which arises from outside the system. It triggers A_1 to invoke a (manual or automatic) data entry process P_1 to enter the relevant information into the user database. In this case, a new record is inserted into the PAPERS relational file. The PAPERS file has the following attributes: paper#, title, author, author-address, submission-date, paper-status.

The insertion of a new record in PAPERS relational file triggers alerter A_2 to invoke two concurrent processes: (1) a form generation process P_2 to send an acknowledgment letter (form F_2) to the author; and (2) a reviewer selection process P_3 to prompt the editor to select three reviewers. The form generation process P_2 is automatic. The process P_3 requires manual interaction. The interaction is accomplished using a form F_3.

After the editor has selected three reviewers using form F_3, process P_3 causes the insertion of a new record into the REVIEW relational file. The REVIEW file has the following attributes: paper#, reviewer$_1$, date$_1$, st$_1$, reviewer$_2$, date$_2$, st$_2$, reviewer$_3$, date$_3$, st$_3$. The status of a reviewer is initially 0. It is set to 1 when the reviewer sends back the review, and -1 when he declines to review the paper. The insertion of a new record in the REVIEW relational file triggers alerter A_3 to invoke a form generation process P_4, to send letters (form F_4) and copies of the submitted paper to the reviewers. The reviewer's name and address can be found in another relational file REVIEWER, which contains the following attributes: reviewer#, name, address, review-area.

The alerter A_3 also generates an existential time-alerter $A_4(X, Y, t_1)$, for reviewer X, paper Y, at time t_1. When a reviewer has not responded after a given time interval (say, three months), A_4 is triggered by the alerting subsystem. A_4 invokes a form generation process P_5, to send a letter (form F_5) to that reviewer asking for response. The alerter A_4 generates another existential time alerter $A_5(X, Y, t_2)$ and then self-destructs. It should be noted that A_4 is an existential alerter which is automatically destroyed when the reviewer sends back his review.

If the reviewer still does not respond after a given time interval, A_5 is triggered, which again invokes process P_3. The process P_3 prompts the editor to select another review, and again updates the REVIEW relational file. After firing, the alerter A_5 also self-destructs. A_5 is also an existential alerter which is automatically destroyed when the reviewer sends back his review.

Another type of input message occurs when a reviewer sends back his review. Again, this message, with message-type 'r,' is considered as an insertion into MESSAGE relational file, which triggers alerter A_6 to invoke a (manual or automatic) updating process P_6, to update the REVIEW relational file. The update of REVIEW may cause the destruction of existential alerters A_4 and A_5. If all three reviews of the same paper have come back (st1 = st2 = st3 = 1), this will trigger alerter A_7, which invokes an evaluation process P_7. P_7 will require manual interaction with the editor to determine the status of the paper. The interaction again is accomplished using a form F_7. A form F_8 is generated, to inform the author that his paper is (a) accepted, (b) required to be revised, or (c) rejected. If the paper is accepted or rejected, that record in PAPERS relational file may be moved to a backup file, and the corresponding record in REVIEW relational file may also be moved to a backup file. If the paper is to be revised, it stays in PAPERS relational file, and the corresponding record in REVIEW relational file is updated.

If a reviewer sends back a letter, saying he does not want to review the paper, then this reviewer's status is changed to "-1," and the update of the REVIEW relational file triggers alerter A_9, which again invokes process P_3 to prompt the editor to select another reviewer, and the whole procedure repeats.

From the above description, we can see that messages can be created by the user to represent outside events, or by the system because of updating of relational files, user time interrupts, etc. Each message may trigger one or more alerters, which usually invoke processes to perform some of the following: (a) request additional information from the user, (b) update the database, and (c) generate forms.

Figure 2 depicts a set of alerters to perform the journal editing task. There are two relational files: PAPERS and REVIEW. The MESSAGE file could be a nonexistent file, or a log file. Alerters A_2 and A_8 monitor the PAPERS relational file, and A_3, A_7, and A_9 monitor the REVIEW relational file. A_4 and A_5 are customized time alerters, and A_5 is generated only when A_4 has been triggered. A_4 and A_5 are both customized for a particular reviewer X of a particular paper Y, and they either self-destruct after firing, or are destroyed when OFF conditions are met, i.e., when the reviewer sends back his review. Figure 2 also depicts the relationship among various alerters. The notation introduced in the previous section is used, but duplicated relational files are drawn for the sake of clarity.

The above journal editing example illustrates the combination of manual and interactive activities (P_1, P_3, P_6, and P_7) with automated activities (P_2, P_4, P_5, and P_8). It also illustrates the usage of forms for office communications. Forms F_2, F_4, F_5, and F_8 are output forms. F_3 and F_7 are interactive forms, or so-called *intelligent forms,* which require manual interaction. P_1 and P_6 are also interactive processes, because if the input messages are paper messages (such is the case in a conventional editorial office), then these input messages must be encoded and entered into the system. However, if we have an electronic mail system, then the paper submission message is a form F_1, and the review update message is either the returned form F_4 or F_5, and in all these cases P_1 and P_6 are automatic processes. Notice also in Figure 2, A_1, A_4, A_5, A_6, A_7, and A_9 are conditional alerters. The other alerters do not have alert conditions.

Figure 3 illustrates the update of alerter database (Fig. 3a), the update of the PAPERS relational file (Fig. 3b), the generated form F_2 which is sent to the

```
ADDALERT          a-name = "A2",u-type = "i",rel-name = "PAPERS",condition = ""
       action=    "sendform F2 %author %author-address %title;
                   select-reviewer F3 %author %title".
       creator=   "Editor"


ADDALERT          a-name = "A3",u-type = "im",rel-name = "REVIEW",condition = ""
       action=    "sendform F4 %new.reviewer1 %new.paper#;
                   sendform F4 %new.reviewer2 %new.paper#;
                   sendform F4 %new.reviewer3 %new.paper#;
                   create-alerter A4 %new.reviewer1 %new.paper#;
                   create-alerter A4 %new.reviewer2 %new.paper#;
                   create-alerter A4 %new.reviewer3 %new.paper#".
       creator=   "Editor"
```

(a)

```
INSERT            (paper# = 12,title = "Hashing Technique",author = "John Doe",
                   author-address = "12 Main St.,Middletown,IL.",
                   submission-date = "7/17/1980",paper-status = "new") TO PAPERS
```

(b)

```
To: John Doe
    12 Main St., Middletown, IL.
From: Editor
Subject: Paper submission

This is to acknowledge the receipt of your paper entitled.
"Hashing Technique".
Thank you for your interest in our Journal.
```

(c)

```
To: Editor
From: Editorial Office System
Subject: Reviewer Selection

Please select three reviewers for paper entitled,
"Hashing Technique" by John Doe.

   reviewer1: _____

   reviewer2: _____

   reviewer3: _____
```

(d)

FIGURE 3. (a) Updates of alerter database ADB. (b) Update of PAPERS relational file. (c) Form F2. (d) Form F3.

author (Fig. 3c), and the interactive form F_3 which is sent to the editor to be completed and returned to the editorial office system (Fig. 3d).

7. Discussion

This paper presents a methodology for office information system design. We propose to use database alerting techniques for office activities management. The role of an activity management system in an office information system is clarified. This work is part of our project on methodology for intelligent system design. Our previous research results are summarized below.

(1) A model for information exchange has been developed to characterize the information exchange process among interacting agents.[7,8] (2) Techniques of high-level protocol analysis using automatatic-theoretic models have been developed.[10] (3) An office procedure model, called the OPM model, was defined to characterize activities in an information system.[9] (4) Translation and verification techniques for information system design based upon Petri-net theory were then developed.[13] (5) Techniques have been developed to compile the OPM model into a set of alerter rules, so that an alerting system can be automaticaly generated.[14] A computer program for the alerter rule compiler has also been implemented. (6) The concept of message filters has been developed.[11] Message filters can be used to (a) compress input messages, (b) check for validity of input messages, and (c) detect early-warning states. Techniques to abstract data description from database specification have been developed.[12]

A unified formalism to describe an office procedure model has been presented in Section 3.3. A diagram such as Fig. 2 then represents the office activities at one work station. Similar diagrams can be constructed for other work stations, and together they can be used to represent a *distributed office information system (DOIS)*. Such a model can be called a *distributed office procedures model (DOPM)*.

An example distributed office procedure model for a three-node (or three-station) distributed office information system is illustrated in Fig. 4. It can be seen that a distributed database management system (DDBMS) is needed to support a distributed office information system. Problems of infinite message loops, deadlocks, concurrency control, data consistency, and process conflicts must be analyzed carefully. Because of the complexity of distributed office information systems and the evolutionary nature of such systems, it is expected that more and more emphasis will be placed on the incorporation of knowledge (such as alerter rules, database skeletons,[4] and office procedure models) into such systems, so that it can function properly and provide adequate support for both routine activities management and decision making.

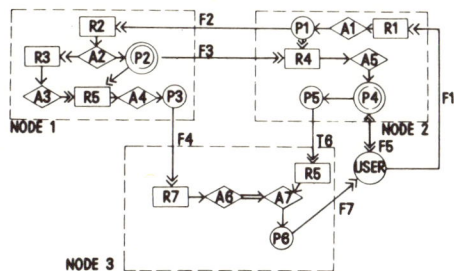

FIGURE 4. Distributed office procedure model.

References

1. R. A. ANDERSON and J. J. GILLOGLY, Rand intelligent terminal agent (RITA): Design philosophy, Rand Report R-1809-ARPA, Rand Corporation, Santa Monica, California, 1976.
2. O. P. BUNEMAN and H. L. MORGAN, Implementing alerting techniques in database systems, Proc. of IEEE COMPSAC Conference, November 8–11, 1977, pp. 463–469.
3. O. P. BUNEMAN and E. K. CLEMONS, Efficiently monitoring relational databases, *ACM Trans. Database Syst.* **4**(3), 368–382 (1979).
4. S. K. CHANG and W. H. CHENG, Database skeleton and its application to logical database synthesis, *IEEE Trans. Software Eng.* **SE-4**(1), 18–30 (1978).
5. S. K. CHANG and J. S. KE, Database skeleton and its application to fuzzy query translation, *IEEE Trans. Software Eng.* **SE-4**(1), 31–44 (1978).
6. S. K. CHANG and J. S. KE, Translation of fuzzy queries for relational database system, *IEEE Trans. Pattern Anal. Machine Intelligence* **PAMI-1**(3), 281–294 (1979).
7. S. K. CHANG, A model for information exchange, *Int. Policy Anal. Inf. Syst.* **5**(2), 67–93 (1981).
8. S. K. CHANG, On a theory of information exchange, *Progress in Cybernetics and Systems Research,* Vol. IX, Trappl, Pask, and Ricciardi, Eds., Hemisphere Publishing Corporation, Washington, D.C., 1981, pp. 313–323.
9. J. M. CHANG and S. K. CHANG, Database alerting techniques for office activities management, *IEEE Trans. Commun.* **COM-30**(1), 74–81 (1982).
10. S. K. CHANG, Protocol analysis for information exchange, *Int. J. Policy Anal. Inf. Syst.* **6**(1), 1–23 (1982).
11. S. K. CHANG and J. C. DORNG, Message filters for information exchange, Technical Report, Information Systems Laboratory, University of Illinois at Chicago, May, 1982.
12. S. K. CHANG and J. LIU, Indexing and abstraction techniques for a pictorial database, Proceedings of International Conference on Pattern Recognition and Image Processing, June 14–17, 1982, Las Vegas, pp. 422–431.
13. S. K. CHANG and W. L. CHAN, Modeling office communication and office procedures, Proceedings of National Electronics Conference, Chicago, October 4–6, 1982, pp. 250–257.
14. S. K. CHANG, Database alerters for knowledge management, Proceedings of NASA Workshop on Self-Describing Data Structures, October 27–28, 1982.
15. R. CONWAY, W. MAXWELL, and H. MORGAN, A technique for file surveillance, *Proceedings of IFIP Congress 74,* North-Holland Publishing Company, Amsterdam, 1974.
16. C. A. ELLIS, Information control nets: A mathematical model of office information flow, 1979 Conference on Simulation, Measurement and Modeling of Computer Systems, pp. 225–239.
17. K. P. ESWARAN, Specifications, implementations and interactions of a trigger subsystem in an integrated database system, Technical Report RJ1820, IBM Research Laboratory, San Jose, California, August 1976.
18. M. HAMMER, Error detection in data base systems, Technical Report, MIT Laboratory for Computer Science, 1976.
19. C. KLINCK, Electronic mail—Its place in the "office of the future", *Bus. Commun. Rev.* **July–August**, 3–11 (1980).
20. C. MCDONALD, B. BHARGAVA, and D. JERIS, A clinical information system for ambulatory care, Proc. of National Computer Conference, May 1975, Anaheim, California.
21. D. TSICHRITZIS *et al.,* A system for managing structured messages, *IEEE Trans. Commun.* **COM-30**(1), 66–73 (1982).
22. D. TSICHRITZIS, Form management, *Commun. ACM* **July,** 453–478 (1982).
23. M. D. ZISMAN, Representation, specification and automation of office procedures, Ph.D. Dissertation, University of Pennsylvania, 1977.

17

DATABASE TRIGGERS AND ALERTERS IN AN AUTOMATED LIBRARY CIRCULATION SYSTEM

A. C. Liu and D. A. Olson

1. Introduction

Much work has been done and many systems exist for automating library circulation systems.[2] Circulation systems lend themselves quite naturally to automation, as do payroll and inventory systems in data processing, primarily because many of the tasks performed by each are highly structured and repetitive.

Many existing circulation systems have merely mechanized the tasks that were once done by hand. The circulation functions become stand-alone, noninteracting tasks that are not integrated into a completely automated system.

This chapter discusses the interaction of both an integrity subsystem and an alerter subsystem with a library circulation database, and an attempt is made to show that this interaction will allow for a higher degree of automation of a library circulation system. By maintaining a database of alerters and triggers, a high degree of modularity can be obtained, allowing future additions or deletions of the alerter–trigger database to meet the ever-changing needs of an automated library circulation system.

In the following, Section 2 presents several definitions and clarifications of terms, and particularly the differentiation between, in this chapter's context, an alerter and a trigger. In Section 3 the concepts of alerter and integrity subsystems and their close association with the database management system (DBMS) are presented. A relational view of the data is assumed throughout this chapter. Section 4 presents an example of an automated library circulation system with alert-

A. C. LIU • Department of Electrical Engineering, Illinois Institute of Technology, Chicago, Illinois 60616.   D. A. OLSON • Ford Aerospace and Communications Corporation, Newport Beach, California 92660.

ers and triggers. Some implementation issues are also considered. Section 5 is the concluding remarks.

2. Triggers and Alerters

2.1. Triggers

A *trigger* is a predefined logical ⟨condition, action⟩ pair. The action specified is invoked when some condition is met. In Fig. 1a a trigger is shown being activated by some event, and the validity of that event (e.g., a modification of some field value) is ensured *before* the update is allowed. The action specified is to issue some warning message if the update is not valid.

The trigger is part of an integrity subsystem to prevent errors in the database and may not allow certain updates to occur at all. This integrity subsystem is discussed in Section 3.

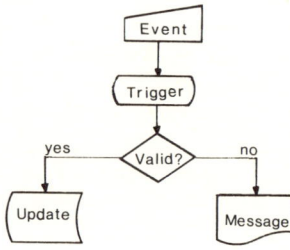

(a)

(b)   FIGURE 1. (a) Trigger vs. (b) alerter.

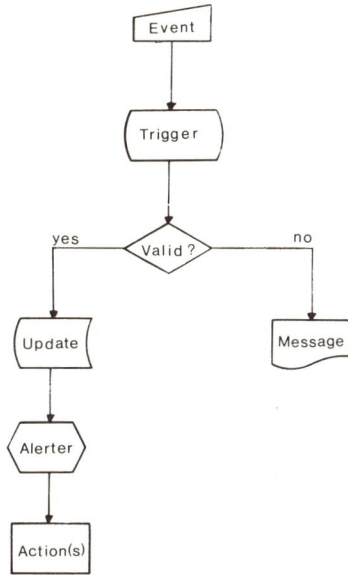

FIGURE 2. Trigger–alerter combination.

2.2. Alerters

An alerter also consists of a logical ⟨condition, action⟩ pair. Figure 1b shows that some event causes an update to the database. *After* the update, a condition the alerter is monitoring is met and the alerter invokes some resultant action. The fact that an alerter is activated *after* a modification is an important distinction between an alerter and a trigger.

2.3. Trigger–Alerter Combinations

Since alerters come into effect after the update of a database item they are monitoring, some alerting situations may require a combination of a trigger and alerter to ensure that actions invoked by an alerter are the result of a valid database update. Figure 2 shows this combination.

The invocation of an alerter is essentially a "side effect" of a database update, and the only way an alerter which monitors some update can change an invalid modification is to *undo* the update such that the system is restored to a previously valid state. For example, if a patron checks out even one more book than the library allows, the set of processes that were invoked by alerters to check out a book must be "backed-up" or undone, a potentially expensive task.

A prechecking trigger will determine ahead of time (by reading the number of books already checked out) if a patron can "legally" check out a book *before* any alerters are invoked.

2.4. Simple and Complex Triggers and Alerters

Most of a circulation system's alerters and triggers will be *simple* in nature, meaning that only one tuple need be monitored for any condition of interest. For example, a trigger that checks for too many books checked out need only monitor the number in the Books_Checked_Out field of the PATRON relation tuple (see Section 4). *Complex* alerters and triggers monitor the contents of several relations simultaneously, and are therefore difficult to implement. An added difficulty is the possibility of having to monitor *virtual* relations which are created from *base* (physically existent) relations via relational operators (e.g., join, project, etc.).[5]

2.5. Event- and Time-Dependent Alerters

We can define a Book_Out alerter which is activated by a patron checking out a book. Alerters of this type are *event dependent* in that some specific event occurs to activate them.

Much information needed in the management of a library circulation department can be generated by the use of *time-dependent* alerters. These alerters could be designed to monitor updates of a relation called "TIME"[6] which is updated on some regular basis by an application program. When a specific time occurs for which some alerter is monitoring, the action portion of the alerter can be invoked.

An "overdue" alerter might monitor TIME for "5:00 pm Friday," at which time it will search for all patrons who have overdue books and invoke a form generator to produce overdue notices.

Daily, weekly, monthly, and yearly statistical information, such as the number of books checked out in each of these time frames, could be automatically generated this way, obviating the need for manual queries. These alerters could be run at "off hours" when lengthy database searches would not slow down the on-line system.

2.6. Existential Alerters

In a college library setting, a faculty member may want to place on reserve a specific book which is currently checked out. Although the book is not available now, he may want to place the book on reserve when it is returned, but only if it is returned by some future date. This situation is well suited for using an existential alerter[6] which has a predefined duration and is destroyed when its actions are completed.

This type of alerter has three associated conditions: The "on" condition, which specifies at what time to begin monitoring returned books for the return of the specific book, the "off" condition, which states when to stop monitoring for the specific book, and the "alert" condition, which is the actual return of the specific book.

The "on," "off," and "alert" conditions for monitoring for the return of book number 1234 for a week are as follows:

1. "on" condition: 8:00 a.m.   mm/dd/yy   (e.g., Monday)
2. "alert" condition: Book # 1234   Returned
3. "off" condition: 5:00 p.m.   mm/dd/yy   (e.g., Friday)

The action(s) specified by the alerter would be to "flag" this book as reserved, and send a message notifying the faculty member that this book is now on reserve status for whatever duration was specified.

3. Integrity and Alerter Subsystems

The prechecking of database updates using triggers and the postchecking of updates which activate alerters have been discussed previously. These two different but very integral concepts must now be described in the context of an underlying DBMS. Figure 3 outlines the interactions between the integrity subsystem, the DBMS and the database itself, and the alerter subsystem.

The database is split into two *logical* components, information utilized by the alerters and triggers, called the alerter–trigger database, and information pertaining to patrons and the library collection itself, called the library database. The *physical* separation and storage of all items in this database is maintained by the DBMS, and as such is transparent to the user.

3.1. Integrity Subsystem

The integrity subsystem has two main functions. The first is assuring adherence to *semantic constraints* established by the designers of the circulation system. In defining alerters and triggers, it is obvious that data items referred to must actually exist in the database, and syntactically correct formats in the body of the triggers and alerters must be used. Of course the integrity subsystem must also be concerned with the syntax and validity of normal queries and the existence of data items they address (e.g., "List all patrons with overdue fines"), but these queries are merely *retrievals,* and as such are not of interest to alerters or triggers.

The second and perhaps more significant function of the integrity subsystem is maintaining data validity by testing against predefined *assertions* with triggers. The process of checking out a book, for example, has two assertions about the

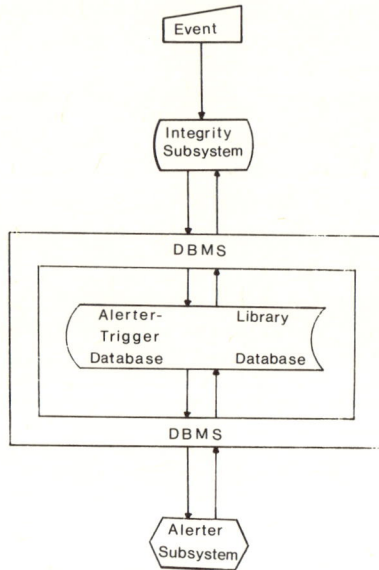

FIGURE 3. Integrity and alerter subsystems.

patron and one about the book that must be satisfied before he can check out a book:

1. A patron can have a maximum of eight books checked out at any one time.
2. Any unpaid overdue fines prohibit the patron from checking out a book.
3. A patron cannot check out a reserved book.

If, for example, a trigger fails to prevent a patron from checking out the ninth book, the assertion about eight books is not satisfied and the data item that stores the number of books checked out contains the invalid data value "9." This will not happen with a properly functioning integrity subsystem.

To make a decision whether to allow a modification or not, the integrity subsystem will need to query the DBMS about the contents of certain data items of interest, and the DBMS must send such information back to the integrity subsystem.

3.2. Alerter Subsystem

The alerter subsystem receives messages from the DBMS regarding information about all updates. The alerter subsystem acts as a type of screen or filter to determine which updates (which have already occurred) satisfy a condition monitored by some alerter. These alerters will then cause some specific, predefined process(es) to run. It is possible in the design of an alerter subsystem to have these processes in turn cause updates to the library database that might invoke other alerters or triggers. Extreme care must be used in this situation so that an infinite modification–alerter loop is not created.

Since many books will be checked out on any given day, a heavily utilized alerter will be the Book_Out alerter that detects an insertion (update) of a newly checked-out book into the PATRON–BOOK relation. The modification of this relation will result in several activities, such as incrementing the number of books the patron has checked out, flagging the book record itself as being "checked out," and collecting statistical information for library management purposes.

The following steps will result in the activation of an alerter:

1. An update notification is sent by the DBMS to the alerter subsystem.
2. The alerter subsystem must determine if this update is of interest to any predefined alerter that may be stored in the alerter–trigger database. This determination is made by a request to the DBMS to search for an alerter that monitors that update.
3. If an alerter is found, its condition must be tested to determine if the condition for activation has been met.
4. If the alerter's condition is met, the "action" (a process or processes) member of the alerter is run.

Note that if in step (3) no alerter is found or if in step (4) the condition for which an alerter is monitoring is not met, no action is taken.

As with the integrity subsystem, the communication between the alerter subsystem and the database is two-way, this being shown as double arrows at the bottom of Fig. 3.

4. Automated Library Circulation System

4.1. Library Database

Throughout the following discussion, the following three Library Database Relations will be assumed:

PATRON (Patron_ID,Name,Address,Phone_Number,Class,Sex,Major,
    Fines_Owed,Books_Checked_Out)
BOOK (Book_ID,Call_Number,Title,Author,Subject,Check_Out_Status,
    Reserve-Status)
PATRON–BOOK (Book_ID,Patron_ID,Date_Out,Date_Due)

The *PATRON* relation describes a set of library users, giving the Patron_ID, Name, Address, Phone_number, Class (e.g., undergraduate, graduate, or faculty), Sex, Major, Fines_Owed, and the number of Books-_Checked_Out a patron has.

The *BOOK* relation describes all books contained in the library database, and will be used not only for circulation (i.e., check-out) purposes, but also for an on-line catalog system for locating books in the library collection. The relation stores the Book_ID, Call_Number, Title, Author, Subject, Check_Out_Status, and Reserve_Status. Only those attributes of interest to alerters and triggers are shown, but of course much more data would be stored for each book by most circulation systems.

The *PATRON–BOOK* relation forms the link between a patron and a book. Its fields are Book_ID, Patron_ID, Date_Out, and Date_Due. This is a dynamically expanding and contracting relation since a tuple is added every time a book is checked out and a tuple is deleted whenever a book is returned.

4.2. Alerter and Trigger Database

The process of defining an example alerter and trigger is described below.

Trigger Example. When a patron arrives to check out a book the integrity subsystem must determine, through the use of a trigger, whether or not this patron has eight books checked out already. This precheck is necessary for maintaining the eight book assertion and a valid-state database.

A trigger which controls the books limit is shown in Fig. 4.

Each trigger is given a unique name, in this case "Books_Limit," which can be used for any subsequent referrals to it. The update_type specifies what operation this trigger concerns. The trigger then is activated when the patron attempts to check out the ninth book because the condition "Books_Checked_Out $>$ 8" is now met. As soon as a trigger is activated, the corresponding action(s) stated will be taken.

If an *alerter* were to monitor this same condition it would have to note the condition "Books_Checked_Out $>$ 8" *after* the attempted check-out and roll back

```
trigger_name = 'Books_Limit',

update_type  = 'modify',

condition    = 'PATRON.Books_Checked_Out >= 8',

action       = 'MESSAGE: Eight books checked out'
               'PROCESS:  Abort'
```

FIGURE 4. Defining Books Limit trigger.

```
alerter_name  =  ´Book_Out´,

update_type   =  ´insert´,

relation_name =  ´PATRON-BOOK´,

action  =  ´Update PATRON and BOOK relations´,

                ´Obtain statistical information´
```

FIGURE 5. Defining Book_Out alerter.

any processing that may have been initialized. The use of a trigger obviates any processing from occurring at all since the patron will be informed of having the limit of books checked out immediately.

Alerter Example. The Books_Limit trigger shown in Fig. 4 is a *conditional* trigger that was invoked on the condition that Books_Checked_Out $> =$ 8. What is described next is an alerter that monitors no specific condition, but rather is activated upon the insertion of a tuple into a relation.

The Book_Out alerter monitors the PATRON-BOOK relation for insertions of new tuples, which signals that a book has just been checked out. This alerter is defined in Fig. 5.

Book_Out alerter monitors insertions of whole tuples into the relation PATRON-BOOK.

The following three actions are initiated by the Book_Out alerter:

1. Update the PATRON relation such that the patron's Books-_Checked_Out field is incremented by one.
2. Update the BOOK relation such that the book's Check_Out_Status = 'Out'.
3. Obtain statistical information about the patron. It could be another insertion into a HISTORY relation, defined as

$$HISTORY \ (Book\_ID, Date\_Out, Patron\_ID).$$

Statistical data of this type are useful for managing a library collection. The number of times a book has circulated can determine whether to "weed out" the book from the collection or get more copies. Characteristics of patrons can be gleaned for possible studies of what type of people are using the library.

4.3. Adding and Deleting Alerters and Triggers

A high degree of modularity in the design of an automated library circulation system can be attained by the triggers and alerters database. In this context, alert-

```
trigger_name  =  'Fines',

update_type  =  'modify',

condition  =  'PATRON.Fines_Owed > 0',

action  =  'MESSAGE:  Patron owes overdue fines',

             'PROCESS:  Abort'
```

FIGURE 6. Defining Fines trigger.

ers and triggers then become mere database items that can be added or deleted. When various circulation processes must be changed or enhanced or future processes are to be installed, all that is needed to be done is to add or delete the associated alerters and/or triggers.

For example, a trigger "Fines" that monitors patrons attempting to check out a book to determine if they have any unpaid fines would be defined as in Fig. 6.

4.4. Implementation Consideration

Since triggers (or alerters) query the database very often, a flexible database design technique is needed to ensure efficient data access.

For example, the Book_Limit trigger and the Fine trigger are only interested in the fields Fine_Owed and Books_Checked_Out of the PATRON relation, respectively. If we decompose the PATRON relation horizontally into two sub-relations, PATRON1 and PATRON2, where

   PATRON1 (Patron_ID,Name,Address,Phone_Number,Class,Sex,Major)

   PATRON2 (Patron_ID,Fines_Owed,Books_Out).

then the above triggers just have to check PATRON 2. PATRON2 is supposedly much smaller than the undecomposed PATRON. So both the access time and response time are reduced.

In addition, if concurrent processing is allowed, PATRON2 can be further decomposed as PATRON21 and PATRON22, where

       PATRON21 (Patron_ID,Fines_Owed)

       PATRON22 (Patron_ID,Books_Checked_Out).

The idea of database decomposition has been developed in Ref. 7. The operation mentioned above is called horizontal concatenation.

As another example, the BOOK relation can be decomposed into BOOK1 and BOOK2:

> BOOK1 (Book_ID,CALL_Number,Title,Author,Subject)
> BOOK2 (Book_ID,Check_Out_Status,Reserve_Status).

In this case, a new trigger called Reserve_Book can be defined to check if a book is reserved. Since most books are not on reserve, BOOK2 is split verticaly as

> BOOK21 (Book_ID,Check_Out_Status,Reserve_Status)
> where Reserve_Status = 'yes'
> BOOK22 (Book_ID,Check_Out_Status,Reserve_Status)
> where Reserve_Status = 'no'.

As all the values of Reserve_Status in each subrelation are the same, the "Reserve_Status" field can be dropped as long as it is saved in the system with its characteristics, e.g., data dictionary. Thus the subrelations become

> BOOK21' (Book_ID,Check_Out_Status) where Reserve_Status = 'yes'
> BOOK22' (Book_ID,Check_Out_Status) where Reserve_Status = 'no'.

It is called qualified vertical concatenation. Similar operation can be applied to the Check_Out_Status field. For other operations, please refer to Ref. 7.

The problem with a decomposed database is when database update occurs. To insert a tuple, for example, the tuple must be checked against each subrelation to insert correct values into correct fields. Also tuples will move around when the characteristics of tuples are changed. For example, if a book is changed from "non-reserve" to "reserve", the book will move from BOOK21' to BOOK22'.

4.5. Library Circulation Flow Diagram

The triggers and alerters mentioned above are related to the check-out phase of the circulation process. To summarize, a flow diagram based upon a modified version of an information control net (ICN)[9] is shown in Fig. 7.

The concepts of alerters and triggers are not part of the original ICN model. They are incorporated in this diagram such that their role could be addressed.

We feel that ICN is a useful tool in modeling an automated library system. The notion of parallel processing can be shown so that the system, if possible, can take advantage of that. Each activity can be broken down into more detailed "subactivities." In other words, the levels of abstraction are controllable.

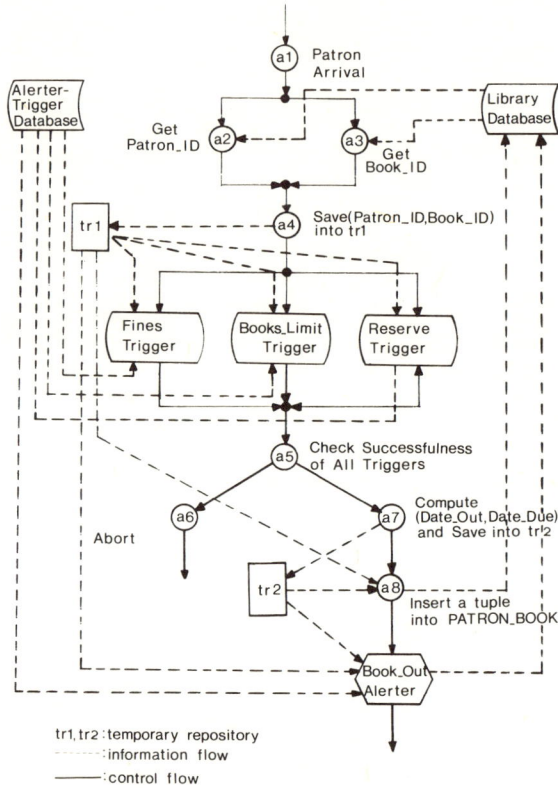

FIGURE 7. Check-out phase of a circulation system.

Other activities such as returning a book and overdue checking can be similarly implemented.

5. Conclusion

Triggers, alerters and their combinations applied to an automated library circulation system are discussed in this chapter. To enhance the efficacy of the system, an integrity subsystem which includes a database of triggers is added to an alerter subsystem.

The most significant advantage gained in using triggers and alerters, and in storing them as database items, is modularity. With an alerter–trigger database, future modifications that arise may only need the mere addition or deletion of a trigger or alerter. In any dynamic environment such as a library, new procedures and policies may be introduced frequently enough to take full advantage of this type of modularity.

To implement triggers and alerters efficiently, a database design technique using database decomposition is considered helpful.

References

1. R. W. Boss, Circulation systems: The options, *Library Technology Reports,* January–February 1979.
2. B. E. Markuson, Automated circulation control systems: An overview of commercially vended systems, *Library Technology Reports,* July 1975.
3. S. R. Salmon, Library automation: A state of the art review, Preconference Institute on Library Automation, American Library Association, 1969.
4. O. P. Bunemann and H. L. Morgan, Implementing alerting techniques in database systems, Proc. IEEE COMPSAC Conference, November 8–11, 1977, pp. 463–469.
5. O. P. Bunemann and E. K. Clemons, Efficiently monitoring relational databases, *ACM Trans. Database Syst.* **4**, 368–382, (September 1979).
6. J. M. Chang and S. K. Chang, Database alerting techniques for office activities management, *IEEE Trans. Commun.* **COM-30**(1), 74–81 (January 1982).
7. S. K. Chang and W. H. Cheng, A methodology for structured database decomposition, *IEEE Trans. Software Eng.* **SE-6**(2), 205–218 (March 1980).
8. C. L. Cook, Streamlining office procedures—An analysis using the information control net model, *AFIPS Nat. Comput. Conf. Expo. Conf. Proc.* **49**, 555–565, 1980.
9. C. A. Ellis, Information control nets: A mathematical model of office information flow, ACM Proc. Conf. Simulation, Modeling and Measurement of Computer Systems, August 1979, pp. 225–240.
10. C. A. Ellis and G. J. Nutt, Office information systems and computer science, *ACM Comput. Surv.* **12**(1), 27–60 (March 1980).
11. K. P. Eswaran, Specifications, implementations and interactions of a trigger subsystem in an integrated database system, IBM Research Lab., San Jose, California, Technical Report RJ1820, August 1976.
12. M. Hammer and M. D. Zisman, Design and implementation of office information systems, Proc. N.Y.U. Symp. Automated Office Systems, May 1979, pp. 13–23.
13. M. Stonebraker, Implementation of integrity constraints and views by query modification, Electronics Research Laboratory, University of California, Berkeley, Memorandum No. ERL-M514, March 17, 1975.
14. M. D. Zisman, Office automation: Revolution of evolution?, *Sloan Manage. Rev.* **Spring,** 1–16 (1978).

18

DESIGN AND IMPLEMENTATION OF A LIBRARY AUTOMATION SYSTEM

Jyh-Sheng Ke, Ching-Liang Lin, Chiou-Feng Wang, and Yuh-Ling Hwang

1. Introduction

In a modern library, the substantial part of typical information storage and retrieval activities concerns

1. Data entry and validation;
2. Documents cataloging and retrieval;
3. Query processing and telebrowsing;
4. Statistics generation;
5. Tabular output.

These functions not only include the traditional information retrieval facilities but also require very sophisticated computation and processing. Most of present-day library information retrieval systems are supported by conventional file-oriented software, which do not efficiently enable the more sophisticated data processing. Recently, the concept of database management systems (DBMS) has arisen, and provides a solution for integrating related data and facilitating sophisticated data manipulation. Among a variety of database models, the relational model has been recognized as the most promising for expanding the facilities of traditional information retrieval software towards the more advanced data processing.

JYH-SHENG KE • Institute for Information Industry, 6th Floor, No.116, Sec. 2, Hanking E. Road, Taipei, Taiwan, Republic of China.   CHING-LIANG LIN, CHIOU-FENG WANG, and YUH-LING HWANG • Institute of Information Science, Academia Sinica, Taipei, Taiwan, Republic of China. This work was partially supported by the National Science Council, Republic of China, under contract No. NSC70-0404-E001-01.

In a relational database, stored data are interpreted as two-dimensional tables. Manipulation of stored data by means of set-oriented relational operators may be interpreted in terms of operations acting on rows and columns of tables. The expressive power of these relational operators is at least equivalent to the first-order predicate calculus. Based on these relational operators, it is not difficult to implement a nonprocedural query language on top of DBMS to enable novice users to retrieve information in an easy straightforward way.

In this chapter we will present a library automation system which integrates the functions of both the information retrieval system and the management information system. The system presented is essentially the integration of a data entry and validation subsystem, an information retrieval subsystem, and a relational database management system with an intelligent user interface which provides an extensible nonprocedural query language for novice users to access data and retrieve information. Figure 1 shows the relationships among these subsystems.

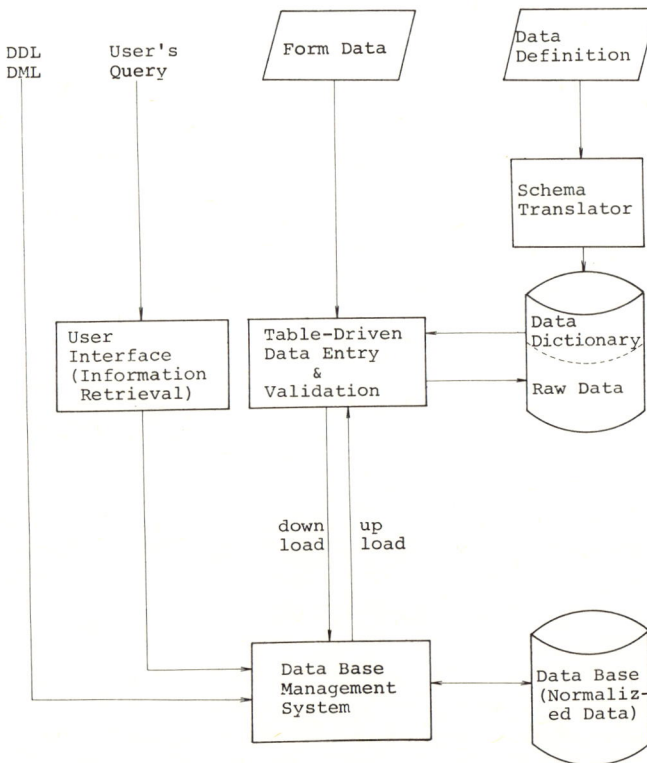

FIGURE 1. Library information management system.

There are four principal areas of library operations: acquisition, cataloging, circulation, and reference service. Automation of these activities may be complicated by their interactions and relationships. In order to reduce the implementation cost by detecting the improper system specification earlier, a Petri-net-based tool has been used to model the flow and transfer of information among work stations in the intended library system. The tool is essentially a very high-level specification language which can be used to define the library procedures and the associated work stations. Based on the concept of Petri-net hierarchy, the intended library system can be systematically top-down structured and specialized.

This chapter is organized as follows: Section 2 describes the data entry and validation subsystem. Section 3 describes the information retrieval subsystem and its underlying database management system. Section 4 illustrates the Petri-net-based tool for modeling the activities of library systems. Finally a conclusion remark has been made to investigate further research studies.

2. Data Entry and Validation (DEV) Subsystem

In a library, a substantial part of clerical work concerns data entry and validation of form data. For example, the acquisition of a book requires filling a request form and a purchase order form, and the arrival of a book requires catalog processing which is essentially to fill a specially designed form with relevant information. In the course of data entry, the DEV subsystem should guide the clerical staff in what sequence the entries are made, and with what codes to record it. For each different library function, there is a different form to be filled out. The complexity of the data entry sequence usually forces the system designer to design different DEV subsystems for different library functions. This results in spending a considerable amount of implementation cost. The problem will be worse if rules of library functions have been changed such that the DEV subsystem should be changed accordingly. For these reasons, we have implemented a universal data entry interface design tool to be used in designing a variety of data entry subsystems. The implemented data entry interface design tool includes a high-level data specification language (DSL) to be used to define each data item in the application domain, a high-level layout specification language (LSL) for defining the format of display layout, and a table-driven automaton with a report generator which can guide the clerical staff to enter/update data in a user-defined specific and relevant sequence.

To design data entry subsystems for each library function (e.g., cataloging, acquisition, etc.), the designer need only use the DSL and LSL to define data items and display layout, respectively. A schema translator will translate these definitions into internal table forms which will then be used to drive the automata and report generator. Figure 2 shows the specification of data items for cataloging

```
register_no()                /* registration number */
type is str;
pic is 4;;
class_no()                   /* classification number */
type is str;;
cutter_no()                  /* cutter number */
type is str;;
author()                     /* author name */
type is str;
sel is mul;;
authorship()                 /* author statement */
type is str;
sel is mul;;
title()                      /* book title */
type is str;
sel is mul;;
edition()                    /* edition */
type is str;
sel is mul;;
pub_place()                  /* publisher place */
type is str;
sel is mul;;
publisher()                  /* publisher name */
type is str;
sel is mul;;
pub_data()                   /* publish date */
type is str;
pic is 4;
sel is mul;;
preface()                    /* preface */
type is str;
sel is mul;;
page()                       /* number of pages */
type is int;;
illustration()               /* illustration */
type is str = {"ill."," "};;
height()                     /* height */
type is int;;
width()                      /* width */
type is int;

sel is mul;;
subject()                    /* subject heading */
type is str;
sel is mul;;
copies()                     /* copies */
type is str;
sel is mul;;
location()                   /* storage location */
type is str;;
check-out()                  /* check-out status */
type is char = 'y','n'
case is {series-name: (check-out == 'n')};;
borrower()                   /* borrower name */
type is str;;
data-due()                   /* due date */
type is str;
sel is mul;;
series_name()                /* series name */
type is str;
sel is mul;;
series_no()                  /* series number */
type is str;
sel is mul;;
reprint()                    /* reprint status */
type is str = {"Reprinted", " "};
case is {ISBN:(reprint != "reprinted")};;
reprinter()                  /* reprinter name */
type is str;;
ISBN()                       /* ISBN number */
type is str;
sel is mul;!
```

FIGURE 2. Book specification with DSL.

a book. Figure 3 shows the display layout specification of a catalog card. Figure 4 shows the computer display of a catalog card.

3. Information Retrieval Subsystem and Relational Database

The information retrieval subsystem (IRS) is the most important part of the library automation system. With IRS, the user can retrieve information on books by specifying titles, authors, subjects, keywords, or their logical connections. The underlying data storage system of IRS is a relational database management system (RDBMS). In RDBMS, a high-level data definition language (DDL) can be used to define the database schema (and subschema) which represents the information about data items and the association among data item. To retrieve information from a relational database is essentially to do manipulation on a set of related tables. Manipulation of relational tables can be accomplished by using set-oriented operations, namely, restriction, projection, join, division, union, intersection, and difference. In the relational database, there is a set of base relations which represents the structured raw data transferred from the data entry subsystem. The combination of above-mentioned relational operations possesses a powerful capability for deriving relations from the underlying base relations.[1] Figure 5 shows the architecture of the RDBMS. The designed RDBMS includes two subsystems, namely, relational interface system (RIS) and physical storage system (PSS). The RIS provides DDL, DML, authorization and integrity check, and supports for alternative views of stored data. The PSS maintains indexes on selected attributes, manages disk space allocation, file access, storage buffers, locking, and transaction consistence. In the following, Section 3.1 describes the RIS, Section 3.2 describes the PSS, Section 3.3 describes the interface between IRS and DEV, and Section 3.4 describes an extensible nonprocedural query language for use by novice users to retrieve data from the database.

3.1. Relational Interface System

The relational interface system provides high-level, data-independent facilities for data definition, manipulation, and retrieval. The data definition facilities

```
%class_no%-* %cutter_no%-* %author%-1
       {0&1}%title%-*  /  by  {0&1}%authorship%-*.     {1&0}    --
{0&1}%edition%-* ed. {1|0} -- {0&3}%pub_place%-* : {1&0}%publish-
er%-*, {1&0}%pub_date%-*.{1&0} %register_no%    {0|0}%preface%-*,
{1|0}%page%-*  p.{1&0}  : {0&1}%illustration%-* ; {0&0}%height%-*
{0&1}%width%-*cm.      {0|0}      --     ({0&2}%series_name%-*      ;
{1&1}%series_no%-*){2|0} %copies%!*
          %reprint%-* by {1&1}%reprinter%-*.{1&0} {1&1}
          %subject% *
          %ISBN%-* borrower :   {0&1}%borrower%-*   {1&1}%date-due%-*
location : {0&1}%location%-*
```

FIGURE 3. Layout specification with LSL.

```
130 K51      Kindred, Alton R
                     Introduction to computers / by Alton R.
        Kindred.  --  New   Jersey  :  Prentice-Hall,  1976.   0348
vi, 538 p. : ill. ; 21cm

                     Reprinted by Mei Ya.

                     1. computer fundamentals.

location : 1
```

FIGURE 4. Display of catalog card.

or the RIS allow the database administrator to define the data at conceptual level as well as internal level. They also allow a variety of external views to be defined upon common underlying data to provide different users with different views. The external views of the common data also facilitate some authorization checks and privacy control. The data manipulation facilities of the RIS allow data to be inserted, deleted, modified, manipulated, and retrieved by using a set of high-level relational operators which exempt the users from knowing the internal storage structure of the stored data.

3.2. Physical Storage System

The physical storage system manages disk storage allocation, indexed file access. B-tree structure has been used for indexing secondary keys of each relation. The disk space contains a set of files each of which is constructed by a set of fixed-size pages. For the purpose of saving space, we employ the concept of logical page number (what the relational operator sees) and physical page number (what the data is really stored on). A page table has been maintained to map logical page number into physical page number. Page identification is maintained by hashing and clustering. The PSS also supports concurrency control by using multilevel locking techniques. Details of RDBMS can be found in Ref. 2.

3.3. IRS and DEV Interface

As we mentioned before, the raw data of each book are entered into the transaction file through the data entry subsystem. After validation, the raw transaction file data are transferred into RDBMS. A down-load routine has been implemented to extract the data of each new transaction file record into several related relational tables for storage in the RDBMS. Similarly, an up-load routine has also been implemented to construct a transaction file data record from several related relational tables whenever an update or retrieval command has been issued by the user.

3.4. Extensible Nonprocedural Query Language

One of the practical problems of library information retrieval is that most of the users who want to borrow books or documents do not have programming or computer-related knowledge; an easy-to-use user interface badly needs to be provided for them to retrieve information. Focusing on this problem, an extensible query language (SQL) has been designed to allow casual users to retrieve information from the underlying database. The user's input query language has been made as easy as possible. With a few minute's learning, a user who knows the operational rules of the library should be able to enter his queries. Details of XQL can be found in Ref. 2. In the following we will present some examples to illustrate the expressive power of XQL in retrieving library information.

Example 1. Find all books written by James Martine.
XQL. Get book; author is James Martine.

Example 2. Get the titles of all books published by Plenum Press after 1980.
XQL. Get title; publisher is Plenum Press and year > 1980.

Example 3. Find the authors who write books in computer science or control theory.
XQL. Get author; subject is computer science or control theory.

4. Petri-Net Modeling of Library Procedures

The activities involved in a library system can be very complicated. At the initial phase of the system design, the designer may not be able to fully understand

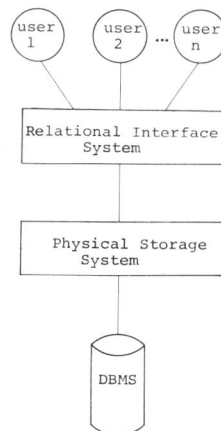

FIGURE 5. Architecture of RDBMS.

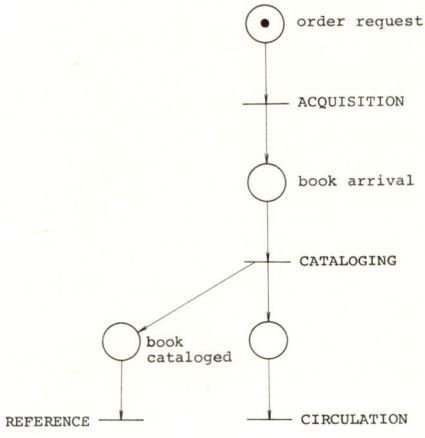

FIGURE 6. Petri-net modeling of library office system.

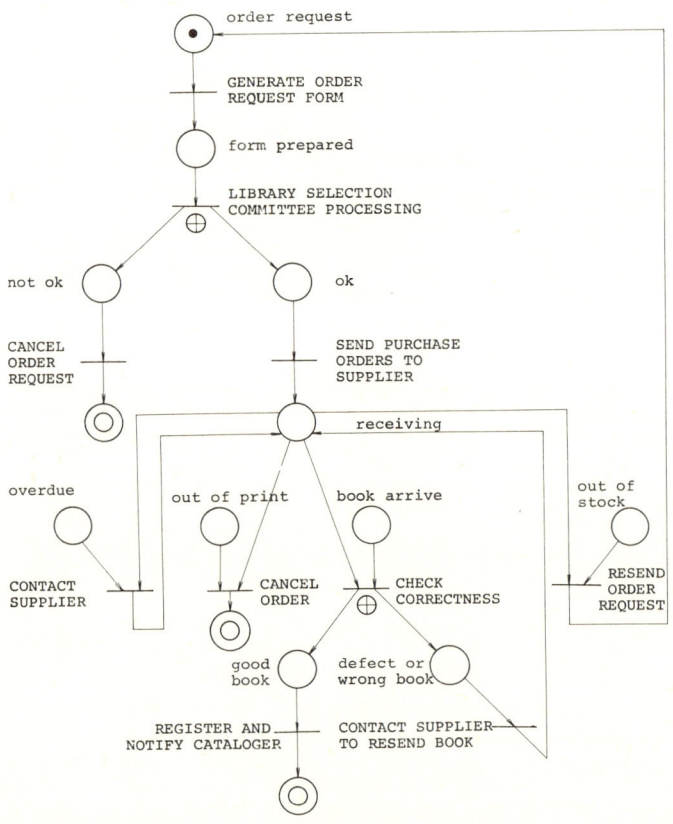

FIGURE 7. Petri-net modeling of acquisition process.

the procedures of the library system. In order to reduce the implementation cost by detecting the improper system specification earlier, we have developed a Petri-net based tool, PITSSL, to be used to model the flow and transfer of data among the work stations of the library system. This work is very similar to Zisman's.[3] PITSSL is essentially a very-high-level specification language which can be used to define the library procedures and the associated work stations. Based on the concept of Petri-net hierarchy, the intended library functions can be top-down structured and specialized. Details of PITSSL can be found in Ref. 4. In the following, Fig. 6 shows the relationships between the four major parts of the library system, Fig. 7 shows the Petri-net modeling of the acquisition process, Fig. 8 shows the form-filling process, and Fig. 9 shows the PITSSL description of Fig. 8.

5. Conclusion

In a library, most of the clerical work has been involved in form-filling. For each different library function, a different data entry subsystem is required to

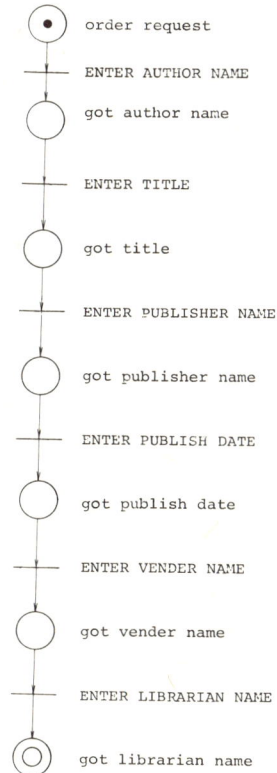

FIGURE 8. Petri-net modeling of generating order request form.

```
AUTHOR_NAME:
        receive  rl: order_request;
        transmit tl: got_author_name;
        actions
                Tell-user: sys-inf(id:"Author Name ?");
                Ask-user : sys-req(id:AUTHOR,m);
endt AUTHOR_NAME;
BOOK_TITLE:
        receive  rl: got_author_name;
        transmit tl: got_book-title;
        actions
                Tell-user: sys-inf(id:"Title ?");
                Ask-user : sys-req(id:TITLE,m);
endt BOOK_TITLE;
PUBLISHER:
        receive  rl: got_book_title;
        transmit tl: got-publ_name;
        actions
                Tell-user: sys-inf(id:"Publisher ?");
                Ask-user : sys-req(id:PUBLISHER,m);
endt PUBLISHER;
PUBLISH_DATE:
        receive  rl: got_publ_name;
        transmit tl: got_publ_date;
        actions
                Tell-user: sys-inf(id:"Publish Date(M/D/Y) ?");
                Ask-user : sys-req(id:PUBL_DATE);
endt PUBLISH_DATE;
VENDER_NAME:
        receive  rl: got_publ_date;
        Transmit tl: got_vender_name;
        actions
                Tell-user: sys-inf(id:"Vender Name ?");
                Ask-user : sys-req(id:VENDER);
endt VENDER_NAME;
LIBRARIAN:
        receive  rl: got_vender_name;
        transmit tl: got_librarian_name;
        actions
                Tell-user: sys-inf(id:"Your name ?");
                Ask-user : sys-req(id:LIBRARIAN,m);
endt LIBRARIAN;
```

FIGURE 9. PITSSL specification of form generation.

facilitate the clerical staff entering form data. The development of a universal DEV system design tool has greatly reduced the implementation cost of the data entry subsystem. The use of the relational model database in the application of information retrieval has several advantages; among them are data integrity, flexibility, and low cost of implementation. The nonprocedural query language makes the concept of access paths transparent to the user, which is particularly useful to the casual user. Specification of correct and consistent office procedures is usually a difficult job. In this paper we present a Petri-net-based modeling technique for hierarchically top-down structured-designing the library procedures. Although the modeling power of the regular Petri nets is limited to some extent, the use of the Petri-net model in specifying the library procedures has been proved to be successful and optimistic, and we are continuing to extend the modeling power of Petri nets by incorporating some program-proving techniques. Hopefully we are able to develop a more realistic and adequate modeling tool in the near future.

References

1. C. J. DATE, *An Introduction to Database Systems,* 3rd ed., Addison-Wesley, Reading, Massachusetts, 1981.
2. J. S. KE, S. K. CHANG, S. M. CHIOU, and Y. L. YAN, XQL: An extensible query language translation system, *Int. J. Policy Inf.* **5**(1), 147–161, 1981.
3. M. D. ZISMAN, Representation, specification, and automation of office procedures, Ph.D. dissertation, Department of Decision Science, The Wharton School, University of Pennsylvania, Philadelphia, September, 1977.
4. J. S. KE, W. M. GUH, and S. H. TAN, Design of information transfer systems, Proc. of National Computer Symposium, Taiwan, December 1981.
5. J. S. KE, C. L. LIN, C. F. WANG, and Y. L. HWANG, Design and implementation of a relational database management system, TR-81-009, Institute of Information Science, Academia Sinica, December 1981.

19

AN EXPERIMENTAL SYSTEM FOR OFFICE PROCEDURE AUTOMATION

Yang-Chang Hong, Yui-Wei Ho, Chen-Hshin Ho, and Te-Son Kuo

1. Introduction

Office automation has attracted and held great interest among computer science researchers and the office data processing community in recent years. There have been software- and hardware-intensive tools emerging as an aid in handling office tasks such as editing, filing, mailing, analyzing, and transforming data. Although these tasks can be automated individually, they are initiated and directed by people. Computer systems in this case do not play an active role, where the user is charged with the information flow control. In automated office systems, the design challenge is how the office tasks are coordinated and integrated in such a way that their initiation and control can be accomplished by the system.[2,6] People can then do more creative tasks.

Several software-intensive tools attempting to automate offices in the sense mentioned have been proposed and reported in the literature.[1,3,6−9] The system described in this paper tries to achieve the same purpose. It is mainly based on Petri nets[5] incorporated with data graphs which model office work as a set of predefined sequences of activities interacting with database and stations—i.e., processing units (see Appendix A and Ref. 4 for formal model definition and its details). It consists of five modules, which are processes of VAX-11/780: namely, supervisor, (Petri-net) execution monitor, mail manager, form manager, and data manager (see Fig. 1). Each has associated with it one or more VAX mail-boxes

YANG-CHANG HONG, YUI-WEI HO, CHEN-HSHIN HO, and TE-SON KUO • Institute of Information Science, Academia Sinica, Taipei, Taiwan, Republic of China. This work was supported by Telecommunication Labs, R. O. C.

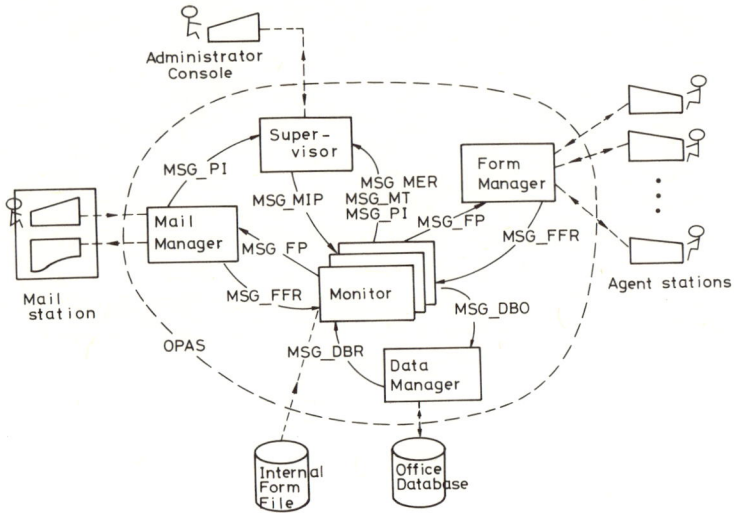

FIGURE 1. OPAS system architecture.

for interprocess communications. The mail manager provides facilities for communications between offices. In the current stage, a mail terminal is used to simulate communications with outside offices. The supervisor accepts requests for service from the administrator console, mail manager, or monitor (that is, from another office procedure). It creates a monitor process once a request for service is entered into the system and passes to the monitor the name of the procedure to be invoked and required parameters for initiation. A monitor process, once created, will be driven by the internal form of the invoked procedure. The execution of each procedure primarily follows the token machine concept (see Appendix B and Ref. 5 for details). Since the monitor is written in reentrant code, there is in fact only one single copy residing in the memory. The form manager deals with interactions between station and system. It receives commands from the monitor, displays forms or memos at stations, and passes worker-supplied messages back to the monitor. The data manager deals with queries which retrieve and manipulate data in the database. It provides a high-level interface between monitor and VAX file system. A high-level nonprocedural specifications language is also provided for describing office procedures, which could then be translated into an extended Petri net (in its internal form) and run.

The body of the chapter is divided into three parts. In the first part the overall system architecture is described. The second part is concerned with the internal forms (i.e., data structures) of the office procedures. The third part is concerned with detailed implementation of the system modules. This is followed by a summary and the status of the project.

2. Overall System Architecture

The architecture of the office procedure automation system (OPAS) is shown in Fig. 1. It consists of five modules: supervisor, (Petri-net) monitor, form manager, mail manager, and data manager. They are processes under VAX-11 VMS operating system. Each process uses VMS "event flag" and "mailbox" facilities as a means of interprocess communication. Interactions among processes are also shown in Fig. 1. These processes are functionally categorized into three classes:

1. System supervising—Supervisor
2. Petri-net driving (i.e., procedure execution)—Monitor
3. Activity serving—Form manager, mail manager, and data manager.

2.1. Supervisor

The supervisor controls the whole system, including

- Creating all other processes;
- Accepting procedure invocation demands from the administrator console, mail manager, or monitor;
- Interacting with the administrator console for system control; and
- Maintaining an office log file.

Its major function is the invocation of office procedures. A procedure will be invoked if a procedure invocation command is received from the administrator console or if an MSG-PI message is read from the mail manager or monitor processes (i.e., other office procedures). The invocation includes creating a monitor process and putting the procedure name (through which the monitor can obtain its internal form) and the initiation parameters in the supervisor's mailbox, which are then accessible by this created monitor. Once the internal form is initiated, it will drive the monitor. In this case, we say that a "procedure instance" has been created and is in progress.

The supervisor contains an office control table (OCT) for keeping track of information such as procedure instance ID, starting time, priority, status, etc., for instance management. The administrator console has the right to make inquiries about any instance status, adjust its priority, pause/stop its execution, etc. One entry is added to the OCT table whenever a procedure instance is created. Any termination messages (MSG-MT) or error message (MSG-MER) of procedure instances will be sent directly to the supervisor, which then reports to the administrators and records them in the OCT table and the office log file.

2.2. Monitor

A monitor process is created if a request for service is submitted to the supervisor. It then be driven by the internal form of the invoked procedure, which leads to the execution of the corresponding procedure instance. The execution follows the token machine concept (its realization is detailed in Section 4).

Office activities performed in the monitor are divided into five types:

- Working-data manipulation: Such as simple computation, assignment, etc.
- Form manipulation: Forms are interaction media between system and office station. Form manipulation is accomplished by the form manager.
- Database data manipulation: The monitor uses one simplified relational algebra to retrieve or update office data in the database.
- Security identification: The identification is accomplished by examining whether the password associated with the sensitive field of the form is matched against the worker-supplied password. This could be extended to sophisticated security process if necessary.
- Time scheduling: Time predicates such as WAITFOR, UNTIL, etc. are allowed to be specified in any above activities. The monitor has to be able to handle this type of scheduling.

In the current stage, we do not emphasize supervisor intervention to control the monitor process. Since the monitor is a subprocess of the supervisor, however, the supervisor can thus get full control over the monitor using the process control facilities provided by VMS.

2.3. Form Manager

The form manager deals with interactions between procedure instance (i.e., monitor process) and office station (or worker). The interaction media are forms. If a monitor process needs a "Form i/o," an MSG-FP request has to be sent to the mailbox of form manager. The request includes the internal representation of the form to be displayed and the destination terminal(s). Corresponding to each agent terminal is a request queue which holds all the MSG-FP requests using that terminal as destination. The requests in the queue are served on an FIFO basis. The form manager will then send worker key-in information back to the requesting monitor if input data to the monitor is needed. This completes the whole process of one form i/o activity. Note: Any sensitive field in the form could be associated with a password field to identify the worker/station (monitor's job).

2.4. Mail Manager

The mail manager deals with interactions between offices. Any executing procedure may need messages from the outside world. In this stage, this is accomplished by sending mail (MSG-FP messages) to the mail manager. Before a hard copy of the mail is made, it must be numbered and stored. This number would then be used as an ID of the mail for later references. When the mailed hard copy is filled in and returned, the operator uses that number to notify the mail manager. The manager is prompt to perform one form i/o for displaying the stored mail on the CRT terminal so that the values returned can be properly keyed in. The input data are finally sent back to the requesting procedure.

Invoking procedures from outside offices is another major function. This is done by sending the MSG-PI message (which includes the required information for procedure invocation) to the supervisor.

This mail process uses a CRT terminal plus a printer for communicating with outside offices. Note: In the second state (on going), it is designed to be supported by an electronic mail system with a set of communication protocols for office information exchange.

2.5. Data Manager

The data manager provides procedure instances with a high-level interface to the office data base. It can be seen as a rather simplified relational DBMS in the current stage. A high-level interface to a relational DBMS is under way.

All the executing procedure instances are users of this simplified DBMS. If data retrieving or updating is needed, they send to the mailbox of the data manager the relational algebra command (message MSG-DBO). The results are sent back to the requesting procedure via message MSG-DBR. Currently, the available algebra operations are SELECT, UNION, and MINUS.

3. Internal Forms

Internal forms basically are a set of data structures through which an office procedure described in a specification language is translated and run. This design must be able to provide information for the following tasks:

- Procedure execution control;
- Procedure execution (i.e., Petri-net driving); and
- Activity realization.

Corresponding to these tasks are the three types of data structures:

1. Procedure control data structure—It contains one block, procedure control block (PCB).
2. Petri-net driving data structure—The driving primarily follows the token machine concept. This type of data structure consists of two tables, namely, marking table (MT) and active transition list (ATL).
3. Activity realization data structure—It contains seven tables, namely, transition detail table (TDT), predicate expression list (PEL), predicate component list (PCL), activity list (AL), actual argument list (AAL), objects description table (ODT), and objects data area (ODA).

The following subsections are the layout and illustration of these data structures.

3.1. Procedure Control Block

The layout and explanation of procedure control block (PCB), one entry per procedure instance, are depicted below.

Procedure control block layout:

Type	Field	Comment
char*8	PRC-ID	Procedure-ID, i.e., the file name of the internal form of the procedure invoked
char*24	PRC-AT	Activation time, VMS ASCII time
int	PRC-PRI	Execution priority
char*1	PRC-STA	Execution status
int	PRC-CMK	Current Petri-net marking, pointer (ptr) pointing to one TMT entry
int array	PRC-CTR	Current executing transition, ptr to one TDT entry
int array	PRC-IPL(n)	Invocation parameter list, a list of ptrs to ODT entries which are invocation parameters

The PCB function is to provide information for controlling office procedure instances. The priority PRC-PRI of any executing procedure can be properly adjusted by the supervisor. Its status PRC-STA must reflect one of the states (e.g., ready-to-go, running, blocked, etc.) during execution. A procedure "instance" ID is formed by concatenating its activation time PRC-AT to the PRC-ID. We call it the procedure effective ID. It serves as the identification name of the corresponding instance in the system. The PRC-CMK and PRC-CTR record the current execution point of the corresponding instance. PRC-IPL is a variable list of pointers pointing to ODT entries. These entries will be established during the course of procedure instance creation.

3.2. Petri-Net Driving Data Structures

Two tables, namely, the marking table (MT) and the active transition list (ATL), are designed to realize the Petri-net driving.

Marking table layout—one entry per marking:

Type	Field	Comment
int	MK-NAT	Number of active transitions in the corresponding marking
int	MK-FAT	Ptr to the first active transition in ATL

One entry in MT stores one marking in a reachability tree derived from the token machine. All active transitions in a marking are stored in the consecutive entries of the ATL table. The MK-FAT, used to point to the first entry, and the MK-NAT are sufficient to fetch all the entries in the marking. The first entry in MT is the initial marking and the terminating marking is indicated by an entry with MK-NAT = MK-FAT = 0.

Active transition list layout—one entry per transition:

Type	Field	Comment
int	AT-TP	Ptr to the internal form of the corresponding transition (i.e., to one TDT entry)
int	AT-OMK	Ptr to next marking in MT (i.e., the output marking obtained from the firing of the corresponding transition)

Since each transition in a net could be active in more than one marking, the internal form associated with that transition is not stored in ATL. Instead, it is stored in TDT and a pointer, AT-TP, in ATL is used to point to it.

Figure 2 is an example illustrating the use of the tables MT and ATL.

3.3. Activity Realization Data Structures

This type of data structure includes the internal forms (TDT, PEL, and PCL) of transitions and their predicates, internal forms (AL and AAL) of activities in the transition, and ODT and ODA tables for storing the program objects used in the office procedure. They are explained below.

Transition detail table—one entry per transition:

Type	Field	Comment
char*20	TR-SN	Symbolic name of the corresponding transition
char*1	TR-FIRE	In-firing flag
int	TR-XCH	Exclusive chain link (ptr to next transition in the chain)
int	TR-PEP	Starting location of predicate expression of the corresponding transition in PEL
int	TR-NAC	Number of activities in the corresponding transition
int	TR-FAC	Ptr to the first activity in AL
int	TR-CAC	Activity counter

Each TDT entry (plus PEL, AL, etc.) describes an internal form of some transition in the procedure. It also contains some control items for transition selection and firing. The internal form must include predicates and activities associated with the transition. Since both predicates and activities are variable-length items, they are stored in PEL and AL, respectively. The TR-PEP and TR-FAC contains pointers pointing to the starting locations of these two items. The TR-CAC counts the number of activities of some transition that have been executed.

Predicate expression List:

Type	Field	Comment
int array	PE-PEL	Predicate expression list

Predicate component List:

Type	Field	Comment
char*1	PC-OPR	Atomic predicate operator
int	PC-OPN1	Atomic predicate operand 1, ptr to an ODT entry
int	PC-OPN2	Atomic predicate operand 2, ptr to an ODT entry

An atomic predicate (or called the predicate component) is of the form

$$[(\text{operand } 1)] \text{ op } (\text{operand } 2)$$

where op may be a comparison operator, or other operators, e.g., EXIST, UNTL, etc., and [ ] denotes an option. A predicate or predicate expression, in general,

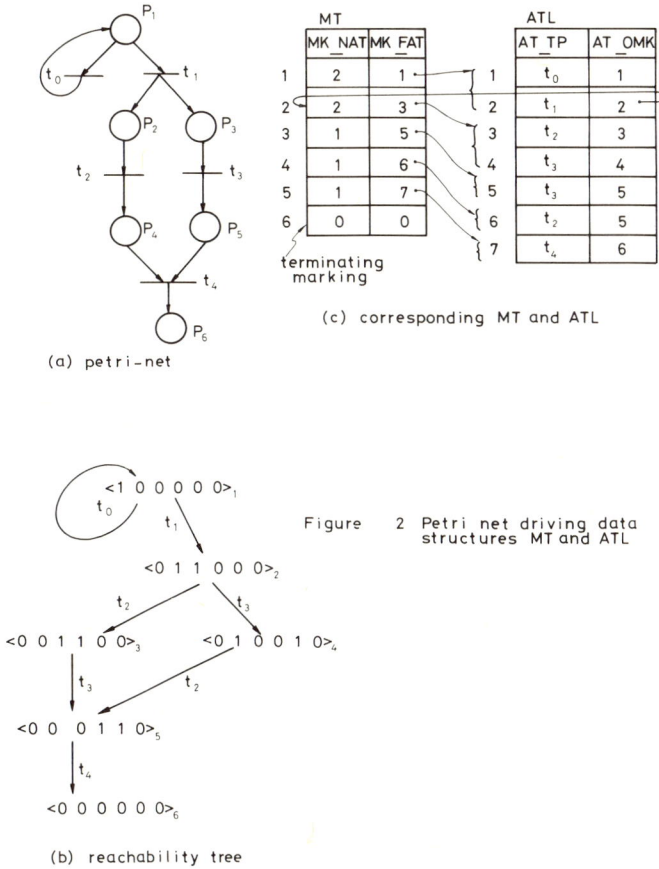

(a) petri-net

(c) corresponding MT and ATL

(b) reachability tree

FIGURE 2. Petri-net driving data structures MT and ATL. (a) Petri net; (b) reachability tree; (c) corresponding MT and ATL.

is a Boolean expression of atomic predicates. All the predicates of the transitions are stored in PEL and PCL. PCL stores the atomic predicates and PEL stores the predicate expressions in reverse polish notation. For example, consider the predicate expression

$$\text{``}(A = 0) \wedge (B = 1) \vee (C = 2)\text{''}$$

$A = 0$, $B = 1$, and $C = 2$ are atomic predicates and stored in PCL. The expression in PEL looks like

TR-PEP

| PEL array | $\cdots$ | 5 | p_2 | p_3 | $\vee$ | p_1 | $\wedge$ |

$\hookleftarrow$ length of expression

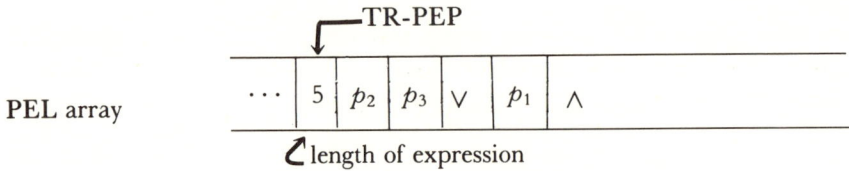

where p_1, p_2, and p_3 are the addresses of the three atomic predicates ($A = 0$, $B = 1$, and $C = 2$) in PCL, respectively, and "$\wedge$" and "$\vee$" are Boolean operators.

Activity list layout—one entry per activity:

Type	Field	Comment
char*1	AC-COD	Activity code
char*1	AC-NAG	Number of arguments in the corresponding activity (argument list length)
int	AC-FAG	Ptr to argument list in AAL

Actual argument list:

Type	Field	Comment
int array	AR-AAL	Array for arguments in some activity

AT and AAL describe activities in each transition. Each activity is assigned one code during translation. Like the case above, the variable item, the argument list is stored in a separate table AAL. The AC-NAG and AC-FAG are used to fetch this list.

Objects description table layout:

Type	Field	Comment
char*2	OD-TYP	Type information of objects
char*2	OD-LEN	Length information of objects
char*2	OD-XD	Additional description
int	OD-STA	Ptr to char array ODA

Objects data area:

Type	Field	Comment
char array	OD-ODA	Storage for all objects in a procedure

ODT and ODA allow the objects defined in an office procedure to be processed. The object values in ODA are stored as a string of characters whose starting location is in OD-STA.

4. Implementation of System Modules

4.1. Implementation Considerations

4.1.1. Form Handling. Forms are a major medium of communication between systems and office agent. Any form instance transmitted between monitor and form manager or between monitor and mail manager consists of a list of form fields, called the "form i/o packet." Each field is defined by two parts, namely, the descriptor part and the text part. The descriptor part describes the field in terms of its type, length, location, etc., and the text part gives the field value. A form driver routine residing in form manager and mail manager serves for displaying forms on DEC VT100 terminals as well as accepting field values input by the workers. Its design allows several simple editing functions to be performed. For example, the reverse-background display of input fields, automatic field advancing for a list of fields, and the ability to permit the worker to move the cursor freely are provided in the current stage. It will be extended to provide facilities for storing form i/o packets in a form database so that forms can be managed as they are done in manual office systems.

4.1.2. Initialization Parameters. Many procedures need some initialization data before they are invoked for execution. For example, in an order-processing procedure, the initialization data may include the customer ID, the amount of goods requested, etc. In OPAS, this kind of data is called the "invocation parameters." They are designed and defined by the office designer during procedure preparation. Whenever an office procedure is translated, the designer is asked to define an "invocation parameters entry form" using some facility provided by OPAS. This form will then be saved in the internal form file of the corresponding procedure. It will be displayed on the CRT terminal for accepting invocation parameters if any request for service is made.

4.1.3. System Generation. Before the OPAS system can get in operation, several tasks have to be done:

1. All the office procedures translated must be registered and stored in the system.
2. An Invocation Control Table (residing in the supervisor as well as in the mail manager for relating each registered procedure to its invocation parameter entry form) must be built.

3. All the global relations must be generated and stored in the office database.
4. All the OPAS terminals must be assigned.

These tasks can be accomplished by using the facilities provided by OPAS.

4.1.4. Bootstrapping OPAS.   OPAS is bootstrapped by running the supervisor process, which in turn creates other processes in OPAS in such a way that the system is ready to accept requests for service from the administrator console and the mail manager.

4.2. Use of VMS System Services

Three VMS System services make the implementation of the OPAS system successful. They are mail box, AST i/o, and event flag. As described previously, associated with each process is one or more VMS software mailbox for interprocess communication. The AST i/o (Asynchronous System Trap) plays a rather important role in the design of OPAS processes. It enables each process to deliver an asynchronous mailbox reading and continue. Once the message is ready to read, the process is interrupted (asynchronously trapped) to execute a special program section for accepting (and processing) the message. When finished, it goes back to its routine work. The AST i/o is also used by form manager for simultaneously handling all the agent terminal i/o's—i.e., i/o between system and station.

The event flag is another VMS-provided facility for interprocess communication. The monitor process uses it to handle reading mail from the mail terminal and forms in the system.

4.3. Implementation

4.3.1. Monitor.

Initializations.

1. Read in the MSG-MIP message.
2. Read in procedure internal form using procedure ID in MSG-MIP.
3. Get invocation parameter values.
4. Set PCB entries.
5. Create the monitor mailbox (mailbox name = procedure effective ID).
6. Start Petri-net driving.

Transition selection:

1. Start with the first active transition of the current marking, check its predicate expression; if the predicate expression is true, the transition is fired, else try rest of active transitions.

2. If all active transitions of the current marking have a false predicate, monitor hibernates.

Transition firing:

1. Fire the selected transition by performing activities associated with it one by one.
2. When one, go to marking advance.

Marking advance:

1. Set the current marking to the output marking of the current transition.
2. Go to transition selection.

4.3.2. Form Manager.
Initialization:

1. Read in "agent terminal assignment" file.
2. Assign agent terminals accordingly.
3. Create mailbox.
4. Issue an AST mailbox reading to get request.
5. Hibernate and wait for requests.

Main loop (once wakened from hibernating):

1. If "form completed chain" is not empty, process its entries (using input values gathered to build an MSG-FFN message) and send it back to the requesting monitor process; for any terminal whose request queue is not empty, start next form i/o in the queue.
2. If "Start i/o chain" is not empty, process its entries one after another. (A form i/o is started by prompting the form and issuing AST reads to accept input values).
3. If both chains are empty, then hibernate; else go to step 1.

Mailbox AST reading handler (activated once the reading is completed):

1. Insert form packet request into "request queue" of the corresponding terminal.
2. If this is the first request in the queue, put the corresponding terminal into "start i/o chain."
3. Wake-up form manager from hibernating.

Terminal AST reading handler (activated whenever any agent types a character on the terminal):

1. Store the character typed if it belongs to an input field.
2. Echo the character.
3. If the character is not a carriage return, issue the next one-character AST read; else (i.e., the form on that terminal is completed) put the terminal into "form completed chain."

4.3.3. Mail Manager.
Initialization:

1. Read in invocation control table.
2. Create mailbox.
3. Issue an AST mailbox reading to accept any requests.

Mailbox reading handler:

1. If the form is to be returned (having input fields), register and save it into "pending form table."

Main loop:

1. Prompt the ready message to the operator and wait for commands.
2. If the command is "enter form," use registration number given to retrieve the saved form packet and start form i/o; when done, use field values entered to build an MSG-FFR message and send it back to the requesting monitor process.
3. If the command is "invoke procedure," use the procedure ID given to retrieve the invocation parameter entry form and request for initialization parameters; after done, build and send MSG-PI message to the supervisor.
4. Go to step 1.

5. Summary

The office procedure automation system outlined in this paper has been implemented in a VAX-11/VMS environment. The data manager is now being extended toward a powerful, high-level interface to a database management system in such a way that the system can manage the messages (or forms). The mail manager is also being extended to provide interoffice communication facilities. We plan to extend this system to a distributed office system with Chinese data processing capabilities.

Appendix A: PNB Model Definition

A Petri-net-based model is a 6-tuple $\Omega = (T, P, D, \Phi, \Delta, \Sigma)$, where

   i. T is a finite set of transitions;
  ii. P is a finite set of places;
 iii. D is a finite set of depositories;
 iv. $\Phi = I \cup O: T \to P(p)$, the power set of p, where
     I is a mapping of a transition to its set of input places, and
     O is a mapping of a transition to its set of output places;
  v. $\Delta = i \cup o: T \to (P)D$, where
     i is a mapping of a transition to its set of input depositories, and
     o is a mapping of a transition to its set of output depositories;
 vi. Σ is a set of doublet (c_t, a_t) over T, where
     c_t Is a Boolean expression associated with transition $t \in T$, and
     a_t is a simple or compound action of $t \in T$.

Appendix B: PNB Execution Definition

The execution rule of a PNB diagram can be defined by a doublet $\Gamma = (m, \tau)$ over Ω, F, and B, where

   i. F is a set of incident markings. An incident marking f_t is a marking with only one token present in each place of $I(t)$, $t \in T$.
  ii. B is a set of outgoing markings. An outgoing marking b_t is a marking with only one token present in each place of $O(t)$, $t \in T$.
 iii. M is a set of "reachable markings" including the initial marking m_0. Of course, m_f, the terminating marking, belongs to the set, i.e., $m_f \in M$.
 iv. $\tau: M \times T \to M$ is a "firable function" of transition t in T. If a transition t fires under marking m, we say $\tau(m, t) = m'$, with $m' = m - f_t + b_t$, where $m, m' \in M$, $f_t \in F$, and $b_t \in B$. A transition t fires under marking m if
    a. $m \geq f_t$ and
    b. $c_t = $ True in (c_t, a_t)
    A transition is enabled if (a) holds.

References

1. J. M. CHANG and S. K. CHANG, Database alerting techniques for office activities management, *IEEE Trans. Commun.* **COM-30**(1), 74–81 (1982).
2. S. K. CHANG, *Knowledge-Based Database Systems,* Chap. 14 (a forthcoming textbook).
3. C. A. ELLIS and G. J. NUTT, Office information systems and computer science, *ACM Comput. Surv.* **12**(1), 27–60 (1980).
4. C. H. HO, Y. C. HONG, Y. W. HO, and T. S. KUO, An office workflow model, *Proc. NCS, Taiwan* 354–368 (1981).
5. J. L. PETERSON, Petri nets, *ACM Comput. Surv.* **9**(3), 223–252 (1977).
6. D. TSICHRITZIS, OFS: An integrated form management system, *Proc. VLDB,* 161–166 (1980).
7. D. TSICHRITZIS, Integrating database and message systems, *Proc. VLDB,* 356–362 (1981).
8. M. D. ZISMAN, Representation, specification, and automation of office procedures, Ph.D. dissertation, Wharton School, University of Pennsylvania, 1977.
9. M. M. ZLOOF, QBE / OBE: A language for office and business automation, *IEEE Comput.* **14** (5), 13–22 (1981).

20

PETRI NETS AND THEIR APPLICATION
AN INTRODUCTION

Tadao Murata

1. Introduction

A graph model now known as Petri nets originated in C. A. Petri's doctoral dissertation[1] in 1962 at the University of Bonn, West Germany. In the mid 1960s, Petri's work was introduced in the United States, and during the 1970s it spread over many parts of the world. At the time of this writing, the Europeans are most active in research and conferences on Petri nets: they have held a two-week advanced course on this subject in Hamburg, West Germany under the direction of Dr. Petri in 1979[2]; and held so far three workshops on applications and theory of Petri nets, one each in France (1980), West Germany (1981), and Italy (1982).[3] In this field two books, one in English[4] and the other in German,[5] are now available, and several tutorial articles[6-10] have been written. A comprehensive bibliography[11] is also available and is updated periodically.

Petri nets are a graph model particularly suited for representing and analyzing concurrent systems, systems in which several activities progress in parallel. A major strength of Petri nets is not only their descriptive capability as in block diagrams or flowcharts, but also their capability to perform analysis. Petri nets can be used by both practitioners and theoreticians. Thus, these nets provide a powerful medium of communication between them, i.e., practitioners can learn from theoreticians how to make their models more methodical, and theoreticians can learn from practitioners how to make their models more realistic.

This chapter stresses the analytic strength of Petri nets and provides several illustrative examples and applications. After explaining basic terminology and properties of Petri nets, we present in Section 4 the incidence matrix and state equations, which are a major analytic tool for Petri nets. Structural properties

TADAO MURATA • Department of Electrical Engineering and Computer Science, University of Illinois at Chicago, Box 4348, Chicago, Illinois 60680. This work was supported by the National Science Foundation under NSF Grant No. ECS 81-05649.

discussed in Section 5 show what kind of properties can be analyzed using matrix equations. Sections 6 and 7 are concerned with two subclasses of Petri nets: finite capacity nets and marked graphs. Section 8 contains four applications of Petri nets: performance evaluation, fault diagnosis, fair regulation in resource-sharing systems, and concurrency control in distributed database systems.

2. Transition Enabling and Firing

A Petri net is a particular kind of directed graph, together with an initial state called the *initial marking*. The graph has two kinds of nodes, called *places* and *transitions*. Places are drawn as circles, and transitions are drawn as bars or rectangular boxes. Directed arcs may exist only between different types of nodes (i.e., the structure of a Petri net is a bipartite directed graph).

A marking (a state) assigns to each place a nonnegative integer. If a marking assigns to place p a nonnegative integer k, we say that p has k *tokens*. Pictorially, we place k dots in place p. In modeling using the concept of conditions and events, places represent the former and transitions the latter. A transition (an event) has a certain number of *input and output places* representing the preconditions and postconditions of the event, respectively. The presence of a certain number of tokens in a place may be interpreted as either the holding of that number of data items or the truth of some conditions associated with the place. In order to simulate the dynamic behavior of a system, a token distribution or marking is changed according to the following transition (firing) rule:

1. A transition t is said to be *enabled* if each input place p of t is marked with at least as many tokens as the number of arcs from p to t. (A transition without any input places is always enabled by definition.)
2. A *firing* of an enabled transition removes one token (per arc) from each input place, and adds one token (per arc) to each output place.

Note that it is not necessary for a transition to fire even if it is enabled (i.e., the event may not take place even if it is allowed to do so).

Example 1. The above transition rule is illustrated in Fig. 1 using the well-known chemical reaction: $2H_2 + O_2 \rightarrow 2H_2O$. The transition t is enabled under the marking shown in Fig. 1a (i.e., the necessary ingredients for the chemical reaction are present). After firing the transition (after the reaction), the marking shown in Fig. 1b ($2H_2O$) will result. Note that the Petri net shown in Fig. 1a can be drawn as the one shown in Fig. 1c. That is, if there are k arcs between a place and a transition, they are alternatively drawn as a single arc having weight k (and if $k = 1$, normally unit weight is omitted).

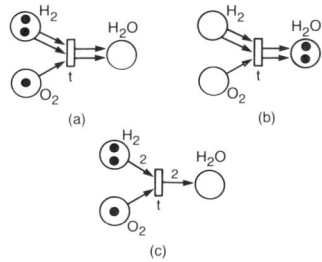

FIGURE 1. An illustration of a transition firing (Example 1): (a) before firing, (b) after firing, and (c) an equivalent drawing of (a).

3. Properties of Petri Nets

Among many other properties, three are characteristic of Petri nets and have been most frequently studied: reachability, liveness, and safeness (or boundedness). A marking M_n is said to be *reachable* from a marking M_0 if there exists a firing sequence which transforms M_0 to M_n. We denote by $R(M_0)$ the set of all markings reachable from M_0. A marking M_0 is said to be *live* for a Petri net if, no matter what marking has been reached from M_0, it is possible ultimately to fire any transition of the net by progressing through some further firing sequence. Thus, a Petri net with a live marking guarantees deadlock-free operation, regardless of the firing sequence chosen. A marking M_0 is said to be *m-bounded* if there exists an integer m such that each place of the net has at most m tokens for every marking reachable from M_0. Specifically, M_0 is said to be *safe* is $m = 1$. The concept of boundedness is related to the capacity bound of memory devices. For example, if registers with a single word capacity are used as places, then a safe marking will not cause overflow in these registers, regardless of the firing sequence chosen.

Other Petri net properties commonly discussed in the literature include persistence, coverability, reversability, and structural properties. A Petri net is said to be *persistent* if at any marking in $R(M_0)$ an enabled transition can be disabled only by its own firing. We denote a marking M as a vector and its pth component is denoted by $M(p)$. A marking M is said to be *coverable* if there exists a marking M_1 reachable from the initial marking M_0 such that $M_1(p) \geqq M(p)$ for each place p. A Petri net is said to *reversible* if for each marking M in $R(M_0)$, M_0 is in $R(M)$. Structural properties will be discussed later in Section 5.

4. Incidence Matrix and State Equations

Throughout this article, let m and n denote the number of places and transitions, respectively, in a Petri net. The incidence matrix of a Petri net, $A = [a_{ij}]$ is an $n \times m$ matrix of integers, and its typical entry is given by

$$a_{ij} = a_{ij}^+ - a_{ij}^- \tag{1}$$

where a_{ij}^+ is the number of arcs from transition i to the output place j, and a_{ij}^- is the number of arcs to transition i from the input place j. It is easy to see from the definition of firing that a_{ij}^-, a_{ij}^+, and a_{ij} represent the number of tokens removed, added, and changed in place j, when transition i fires once. Transition i is enabled at marking M if and only if (iff) $a_{ij}^- \leqq M(j)$ for $j = 1, 2, \ldots, m$, where $M(j)$ denotes the number of tokens in place j under marking M.

A *marking* or *state vector* M_k is an $m \times 1$ column vector of nonnegative integers. The jth entry of M_k denotes the number of tokens in place j immediately prior to the kth firing in some firing sequence. Specifically, M_0 denotes the initial marking or state. The kth *firing* or *control vector* U_k is an $n \times 1$ (0,1)-column vector containing exactly one nonzero entry, 1, in the ith position indicating transition i fires at the kth firing. Let M_k be the marking resulting from marking M_{k-1} by firing transition i. Since the ith row of the incidence matrix A denotes the change of the marking as the result of firing transition i, we can write the following state equation for a Petri net[12]:

$$M_k = M_{k-1} + A^T U_k, \qquad k = 1, 2, 3, \ldots \tag{2}$$

where superscript T denotes matrix transpose.

Reachability Condition. Suppose that there exists a firing sequence $\{U_1, U_2, \ldots, U_d\}$ that transforms M_0 to M_d, i.e., M_d is reachable from M_0. Applying (2) for $k = 1, 2, \ldots, d$ and summing, we obtain

$$M_d = M_0 + A^T \sum_{k=1}^{d} U_k$$

which may in turn be written as

$$A^T x = \Delta M \tag{3}$$

where $\Delta M := M_d - M_0$, and $x := \sum_{k=1}^{d} U_k$. Here x is an $n \times 1$ column vector of nonnegative integers and is called the *firing count vector*. It is well known that a set of linear algebraic equations (3) has a solution x iff ΔM is orthogonal to every solution of its transposed homogeneous system:

$$Ay = 0 \tag{4}$$

This condition can be expressed as

$$B_f \Delta M = 0 \tag{5}$$

where

$$B_f = [I \mid -A_{11}^T(A_{12}^T)^{-1}] \tag{6}$$

and

$$A = \begin{bmatrix} A_{11} & A_{12} \\ A_{21} & A_{22} \end{bmatrix} \tag{7}$$

Here A_{12} is an $r \times r$ nonsingular submatrix of A, r is the rank of A, and I is the identity matrix of order $m - r$. Note that $AB_f^T = 0$. That is, the vector space spanned by rows of A is orthogonal to the vector space spanned by the rows B_f. Therefore, we have the following theorem[12]:

THEOREM 1. *If M_d is reachable from M_0 in an unrestricted Petri net, then (5) must hold.*

An application of equations (3) and (5) will be discussed later in Section 8.2.

Example 2. For the Petri net shown in Fig. 2, the state equation (2) is illustrated below, where firing of t_3 transforms the initial marking $M_0 = (2\ 0\ 1\ 0)^T$ to another marking $M_1 = (3\ 0\ 0\ 2)^T$:

$$\begin{bmatrix} 3 \\ 0 \\ 0 \\ 2 \end{bmatrix} = \begin{bmatrix} 2 \\ 0 \\ 1 \\ 0 \end{bmatrix} + \begin{bmatrix} -2 & 1 & 1 \\ 1 & -1 & 0 \\ 1 & 0 & -1 \\ 0 & -2 & 2 \end{bmatrix} \begin{bmatrix} 0 \\ 0 \\ 1 \end{bmatrix}$$

The incidence matrix A of this Petri net is of rank 2 and can be partitioned in the form of (7), where

$$A_{11} = \begin{bmatrix} -2 & 1 \\ 1 & -1 \end{bmatrix} \quad \text{and} \quad A_{12} = \begin{bmatrix} 1 & 0 \\ 0 & -2 \end{bmatrix}$$

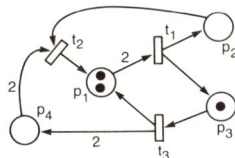

FIGURE 2. A Petri net used in Example 2.

Thus B_f can be found by (6):

$$B_f = \begin{bmatrix} 1 & 0 & 2 & \frac{1}{2} \\ 0 & 1 & -1 & -\frac{1}{2} \end{bmatrix}$$

It is easy to verify (5) for $\Delta M = M_1 - M_0 = (1\ 0\ -1\ 2)^T$.

5. Structural Properties

Structural properties are those which depend only on the topological structure of the Petri net and are independent of the initial marking M_0. Thus these properties can often be characterized in terms of the incidence matrix A and its associated algebraic linear equations. Here we discuss the following seven structural properties: controllability, structural boundedness, conservativeness, repetitiveness, consistency, S-invariant, and T-invariant.

A Petri net is said to be *completely controllable* if any marking is reachable from any initial marking. Applying the well-known controllability condition of dynamic systems to the state equation (2), we can state the following theorem[12]:

THEOREM 2. *If a Petri net with m places is completely controllable, then the rank of $A = m$.*

A Petri net is said to be *structurally bounded* if it is bounded for any initial marking M_0. A Petri net is said to be *conservative* or an *S-invariant net* if there exists a positive integer $y(p)$ associated with each place p such that the weighted sum of tokens,

$$\sum_{p=1}^{m} M(p)\, y(p) := M^T y = M_0^T y$$

is a constant for any marking M reachable from M_0. A Petri net is said to be *repetitive* if there exists M_0 and a firing sequence σ from M_0 such that every transition occurs infinitely often in σ. A Petri net is said to be *consistent* or a *T-invariant net* if there exists M_0 and a firing sequence σ from M_0 back to M_0 such that every transition occurs at least once in σ. The following results on structural properties can be derived using Farkas' lemma[13]:

THEOREM 3. *A Petri net is*
a. *Structurally bounded iff* $\exists\ y > 0,\ Ay \leqq 0$;
b. *Conservative iff* $\exists\ y > 0,\ Ay = 0$;
c. *Repetitive iff* $\exists\ x > 0,\ A^T x \geqq 0$;

TABLE 1
Corollaries of Theorem 3

Case	If		Then
1	Structurally bounded and $\exists$ a live M_0		Conservative and consistent
2	$\exists y \geqq 0$	$Ay \leqq 0$	$\exists$ no live M_0 and not consistent
3	$\exists y \geqq 0$	$Ay \gneqq 0$	Not bounded for a live M_0 and not consistent
4	$\exists x \geqq 0$	$A^T x \leqq 0$	$\exists$ no live M_0 for structurally bounded net; not conservative
5	$\exists x \geqq 0$	$A^T x \gneqq 0$	Not structurally bounded; not conservative

   d. *Consistent iff* $\exists\ x > 0$, $A^T x = 0$;
where $\exists$ *means "there exists."*

   As corollaries of Theorem 3, we can state the results such as those shown in Table 1, where $Ay \gneqq 0$ means that $Ay \geqq 0$ but $Ay \neq 0$.

   An m-vector y (or n-vector x) of (nonnegative) integers is called an *S-invarian (T-invariant)* iff $Ay = 0$ ($A^T x = 0$), i.e., iff $M^T y = M_0^T y$ for any markings M reachable from M_0 (there exists M_0 and a firing sequence from M_0 back to M_0 whose firing count vector is x). An upper bound for $M(p)$, the number of tokens in a place p, can be found from the relationship $M^T y = M_0^T y$ or $M(p)y(p) \leqq M_0^T y$. Thus, considering all independent nonnegative S-invariants y_i such that $y_i(p) \neq 0$, we have

$$M(p) \leqq \min_i \ [M_0^T y_i / y_i(p)] \tag{8}$$

   Example 3. Figure 3 shows a Petri-net representation of a readers–writers system, where k tokens in place p_1 represents k processes which may read and write in a shared memory represented by place p_3. Up to k processes may be reading concurrently, but when one process is writing, no other process can be reading or writing. It is easily verified that up to k tokens (processes) may be in place p_2 (reading) if no token is in place p_4 (no process is writing), and that only one token (process) can be in place p_4 (writing) since all k tokens in place p_3 will be removed when t_2 fires once.

   The incidence matrix of this net is given by

$$A = \begin{array}{c} t_1 \\ t_2 \\ t_3 \\ t_4 \end{array} \begin{matrix} p_1 & p_2 & p_3 & p_4 \end{matrix} \\ \left[\begin{array}{cc:cc} -1 & 1 & -1 & 0 \\ -1 & 0 & -k & 1 \\ \hdashline 1 & -1 & 1 & 0 \\ 1 & 0 & k & -1 \end{array} \right]$$

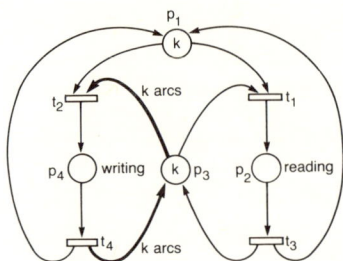

FIGURE 3. A Petri-net representation of a readers–writers system used in Example 3 and 4.

Since the rank of $A = 2 \neq m$, the net is not completely controllable. Using (6), we find

$$B_f = \begin{bmatrix} 1 & 0 & \vdots & -1 & 1-k \\ 0 & 1 & \vdots & 1 & k \end{bmatrix}$$

Linear combinations of the rows in B_f yield two independent S-invariants $y_1 = (1\ 1\ 0\ 1)^T$ and $y_2 = (0\ 1\ 1\ k)^T$. Using (8) and $M_0 = (k\ 0\ k\ 0)^T$, we have $M(p_4) \leq \min [M_0^T y_1/y_1(p_4), M_0^T y_2/y_2 (p_4)] = \min [k/1, k/k] = 1$. Thus at most one token can be in P_4, i.e., at most one process can be writing. This net is structurally bounded and conservative since there exists $y = y_1 + y_2 = (1\ 2\ 1\ k+1)^T > 0$ such that $Ay = 0$. It is repetitive and consistent since there exists $x = (1\ 1\ 1\ 1)^T > 0$ such that $A^T x = 0$. It is easily seen that the net is live for the initial marking M_0.

6. Finite Capacity Nets

The transition firing rule defined in Section 2 assumes that each place in a Petri net can accommodate an infinite number of tokens, and is often referred to as the *weak transition rule*. In a Petri net with finite token capacity, we need an additional condition for a transition to be enabled, i.e., a transition firing should not violate the constraint $M(p) \leq K(p)$ for each place p, where $K(p)$ is the capacity of place p. This rule with the capacity constraint is referred to as the *strict transition rule*.[2] A reason why we have not discussed Petri nets with the finite token capacity is that a Petri net with a strict transition rule can be transformed into its equivalent Petri net with the weak transition rule. This can be done by adding a complementary place p' to each place p so that each pair of places p and p' constitutes an S invariant as is illustrated in Figs. 4a and 4b. Note that $M_0(p_i') = K(p_i)$ and $M(p_i') + M(p_i) = K(p_i)$ for each M in $R(M_0)$ and $i = 1, 2$ in Fig. 4b, and that for each arc from p to a transition t (or from t to p), there is an added arc from t to p' (or from p' to t) shown by dotted lines in Fig. 4b.

Petri nets with finite token capacity can not have an infinite number of different markings (states). Thus they are a finite state machine and can be analyzed by an exhaustive method such as the reachability tree[4] or the marking graph.[40]

7. Marked Graphs

Marked graphs are a subclass of Petri nets for which many interesting analysis and synthesis results are known.[14,15] Since each place in a marked graph has exactly one incoming and one outgoing arc, a marked graph can be drawn as a directed graph, where nodes correspond to transitions, arcs to places, and tokens are placed on arcs. A directed circuit in a marked graph yields a vector corresponding to an S invariant, and plays an important role in the study of marked graph properties.

For example, it is known that (1) the token count in a directed circuit is invariant under any transition (node) firing; (2) a marked graph G is live iff G has no token-free directed circuits; and (3) a live marking is safe in a marked graph G iff every arc in G belongs to a directed circuit with token count one.

Condition (5) is necessary and sufficient for a live M_0 to reach M_d in a marked graph.[15] Equivalently, we can state that two live markings M_0 and M_d in a marked graph G are mutually reachable iff $\Delta M = M_d - M_0$ is a linear combination of a set of fundamental cutsets in G. This result has been applied to a synthesis problem in Ref. 15. Another synthesis approach described in Ref. 16 allows the user to prescribe properties of concurrent systems such as deadlock-freeness, overflow-freeness, the number of reachability classes, the maximum resource or cost, the maximum computation rate (performance), the number of states, and the number of system components (arcs and nodes).

To save space, we refer the reader to a tutorial article on marked graphs published elsewhere.[6,10]

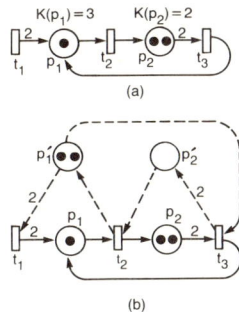

FIGURE 4. An illustration of: (a) Petri net with finite token capacity, and (b) its equivalent.

8. Some Applications

Petri nets and their related variants have shown the potential to model a wide variety of systems and concepts such as computer software,[17,18] hardware,[19,20] operating systems,[21] compiler optimizations,[22,23] legal systems,[24] office information systems,[25] formal language theory,[26,27,40] representation of mathematical knowledge,[28] communication protocols,[29,30] industrial process control[31]; in addition to those discussed in this section: performance evaluation, fault detection, fairness problems, and distributed database systems.

8.1. Performance Evaluation by Timed Petri Nets

How to introduce or not to introduce the concept of time in Petri nets has been a controversial issue. This is because it may not be practical to assume the availability of a universal time scale in distributed concurrent systems. Nevertheless, the introduction of delay times associated with transitions and/or places yields some results useful for performance evaluation and scheduling problems. Such a Petri net is called a timed Petri net.

We are interested in finding how fast one cycle of a computation can be performed in a timed Petri net, where a single cycle is defined as a firing sequence leading back to the initial marking after firing each transition at least once. Thus, it is assumed that the net under consideration is consistent, i.e.,

$$\exists\, x > 0, \qquad A^T x = 0 \tag{9}$$

where the ith entry of x denotes the frequency of firing transition t_i in one cycle (or in one unit of time). Suppose that a token spends at least d units of time in place j, and that the delay in each transition is zero (if not, split this transition into two, add a place between them, and assign the delay to this place). Comparing the mean number of tokens in each place with that of tokens arriving at that place, we obtain for each nonnegative S-invariant y_i[32]

$$y_i^T M_0 \geqq y_i^T D(A^+)^T x, \qquad i = 1, 2, \ldots \tag{10}$$

where D is the diagonal matrix of delays d_j's and $A^+ = [a_{ij}^+]$ is as defined in (1). Therefore, the maximum vector x satisfying (9) and (10) yields the maximum rate of computation. In particular, the vector x satisfying (9) and (10) with equality is the maximum possible rate of computation, if it exists. For a marked graph, we know that each directed circuit C_i corresponds to an S-invariant y_i. Let $x = [x_0]_{n \times 1}$ satisfy (9). Then, (10) reduces to

$$M_0(C_i) \geqq \tau(C_i) x_0, \qquad i = 1, 2, \ldots$$

where $M_0(C_i)$ and $\tau(C_i)$ denote the token count and the total delay for directed circuit C_i, respectively. Therefore, the maximum possible frequency x_0 or the minimum possible period T_{min} is given by

$$T_{min} = 1/x_0 = \max_i [\tau(C_i)/M_0(C_i)] \tag{11}$$

Example 4. Consider the Petri net shown in Fig. 3, where it is assumed that there are delays d_1, d_2, d_3, d_4 associated with the four places. In Example 3, we found that the net has two independent S invariants $y_1 = (1\ 1\ 0\ 1)^T$ and $y_2 = (0\ 1\ 1\ k)^T$. $[x_0]_{4 \times 1}$, $x_0 > 0$ satisfies (9). Thus, applying (10) to y_1 and y_2, we have

$$k \geqq (2d_1 + d_2 + d_4)x_0$$
$$k \geqq [d_2 + (1 + k)d_3 + kd_4]x_0$$

Therefore, the minimum possible period is given by

$$T_{min} = \max \{(2d_1 + d_2 + d_4)/k, [d_2 + (1 + k)d_3 + kd_4]/k\}$$

8.2. Fault Detection and Isolation

In Section 4, it has been shown that if a marking M_k is reachable from M_0, then we have

$$\Delta M = M_k - M_0 = A^T X \tag{12}$$

and

$$B_f \Delta M = 0 \tag{13}$$

Thus, by checking if (12) and/or (13) hold at some place(s) after executing some operations (firings), it may be able to detect and/or isolate fault(s) in the system modeled by a Petri net. There are two methods: one is based on (12) and the other on (13). Both methods have advantages and disadvantages.

Method 1. This method is based on (12):
1a. Store the initial marking M_0 and the incidence matrix A of a given Petri-net model of a system.
2a. At each or some stage k, record the kth firing count vector $X_k = [x_i]$ where x_i is the number of times that transition i has fired up to stage k, and compute $V_k = A^T X_k$.
3a. At each or some stage k, record the marking vector $M_k = [m_j]$, where m_j is the number of tokens in place j at stage k.

4a. Compute $\Delta T_k = M_k - M_0 - V_k$.

5a. If the jth entry of the m-vector ΔT_k is different from zero, then a fault is suspected in the subsystem involving place j.

Method 2. This method is based on (13).

1b. In addition to Step 1a, compute B_f by (6).

2b. Do Step 3a.

3b. Compute $\Delta S_k = B_f(M_k - M_0)$.

4b. If the ith entry of the vector ΔS_k is different from zero, then a fault is suspected in the subsystem involving the ith S invariant y_i.

It is required to record the firing count vector in Method 1 but not in Method 2. However, the former has a better resolution of isolating faults than the latter. Not all faults can be detected by these methods (nor many other methods), since (12) and (13) are only necessary conditions for reachability and certain combinations of multiple faults would yield $\Delta T_k = 0$ and $\Delta S_k = 0$. In a geographically distributed system, it may be difficult to find a global system state such as M_k. Nevertheless, we can apply the above methods to a local subsystem by computing V_k in Step 2a, M_k in Step 3a, and ΔT_k in Step 4a *only for a locally affected subset of places*, and by computing ΔS_k in Step 3b *only from the subset of places* corresponding to an S invariant (assuming that the local initial marking is updated whenever there is a flow of tokens in and out of the local places). The above methods are simple and suitable for real-time fault analysis since they require a very small amount of computation (essentially a few vector subtractions and multiplications at each test).

Example 5. Consider the Petri net shown in Fig. 5, for which the matrix B_f can be computed by (6). Suppose a marking $M_2 = (2\ 0\ 1\ 1)^T$ is detected at a certain stage when the initial marking was $M_0 = (1\ 1\ 0\ 0)^T$. By Method 2, we compute

$$\Delta S_k = B_f(M_2 - M_0)$$

$$= \begin{bmatrix} 1 & 0 & 0 & -1 \\ 0 & 0 & 1 & 1 \end{bmatrix} \begin{bmatrix} 1 \\ -1 \\ 1 \\ 1 \end{bmatrix} = \begin{bmatrix} 0 \\ 1 \end{bmatrix}$$

It shows that there is a fault in $\{p_2, p_3, p_4\}$, the set of the places associated with the second S invariant, while there is no fault in $\{p_1, p_4\}$, the first S invariant. Thus, it is likely that there is a fault in the subsystem involving $\{p_2, p_3\}$.

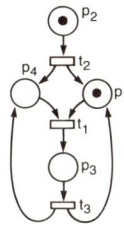

FIGURE 5. A Petri net used in Example 5.

As for other methods of fault diagnosis using Petri nets, Sifakis[33] has presented an elegant method of applying error-correcting coding techniques to the design of fault-tolerant systems based on Petri nets. Also, Merlin and Farber[29] have shown the use of "time Petri nets" (where each transition is allowed to fire only in a certain time interval) for the design of a message protocol that will automatically recover from an error caused by a loss of a token in a place.

8.3. Fair Regulation in Resource-Sharing Systems

Consider the Petri net shown in Fig. 6a which models a simple resource-sharing system where a single resource (p_3) is shared by two users (p_1 and p_2). User 1 (or user 2) starts using the resource by firing t_1 (or t_2) and releasing it by firing t_3 (or t_4). The Petri net in Fig. 6a is said to be "livelocked' in the sense that t_1 can fire any number of times without the need of firing t_2, i.e., user 1 may use the resource exclusively, and vice versa. It is not a fair way of sharing a resource. Suppose it is desired that one user may use the resource at most k times before the other user gets a chance. This fair regulation can be accomplished by adding a pair of places p_4 and p_5 between transition t_1 and t_2, as is shown in Fig. 6b. This is a simplest fairness problem and its solution. More complex fairness problems can be solved by using the concept of the weighted or unweighted synchronic distance defined for Petri nets.[34−36]

8.4. A Distributed Database Model

Various modifications of Petri nets have been proposed. Among them, predicate-transition nets[37] and colored Petri nets[38] are noteworthy because of their modeling power and amenability to matrix analysis methods. In this section we illustrate how a Petri net similar to these nets can be used to model the so-called, "small database system"[5,37,38] shown in Fig. 7. Here it should be noted that

    i. a token has a distinct name or color;
    ii. an arc has a label to specify which token(s) are removed or added when a transition fires; and

iii. a transition is enabled only when all the input places have at least as
many tokens of specified names as removed at its firing.

The net shown in Fig. 7 shows a method of concurrency control in a dupli-
cate distributed database system. Here a set of n database managers $\{d_1, \ldots, d_n\}$
communicate to each other through a set of four message buffers represented by
p_3, p_4, p_7, and p_8. The arc labels shown in Fig. 7 denote as follows: s, a sender;
r, a receiver; $\langle s, r \rangle := sr$, a message from s to r; $\Sigma_{r \neq s} \langle s, r \rangle := \Sigma$, the sum of
$(n - 1)$ messages; and $s, r \in \{d_1, \ldots, d_n\}$. We denote by $M(p)$ the sum of tokens
in place p under marking M. Let the initial marking M_0 be as follows:

$M_0(p_1) = 1$ (i.e., no update is in progress)

$M_0(p_3) =$ the sum of all possible $n(n - 1)$ ordered pairs taken from

$\{d_1, \ldots, d_n\}$

$:= MB$ (i.e., no messages are used)

$M_0(p_5) = d_1 + \cdots + d_n$

$:= DMB$ (i.e., all managers are inactive)

$M_0(p) = 0$ for all other places p

The states of the message buffers are represented by the following four places: p_3
(unused messages), p_4 (messages sent), p_7 (messages received), and p_8 (acknowledged messages). The states of database managers are represented by the following
three places: p_2 (waiting for acknowledgments), p_5 (inactive managers), and p_6
(performing update).

Since, at this initial state, no update is in progress, a manager s can start
updating his own data segment. This is done by firing transition t_1, resulting in
$M_1(p_4) = \Sigma_{r \neq s} \langle s, r \rangle$ (i.e., s sends the messages to all other managers), $M_1(p_2)$

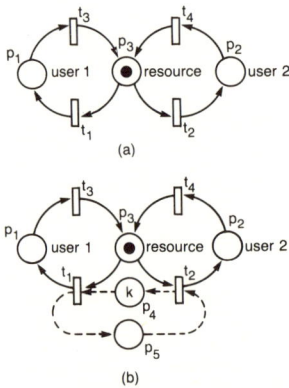

(a)

(b)

FIGURE 6. A Petri-net representation of a simple resource-sharing system: (a) without regulation, and (b) with regulation.

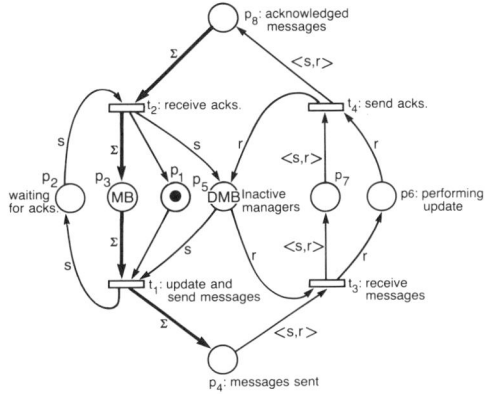

FIGURE 7. A distributed database system
model.

$= s$ (i.e., s waits for acknowledgments), and $M_1(p_1) = 0$ (i.e., an update is in progress). When a manager r receives the messages $\langle s, r \rangle$ (t_3 fires), he performs the update. After each of the $(n - 1)$ managers has performed the update [t_4 has fired ($n - 1$) times], all the acknowledgments, $\Sigma_{r \neq s} \langle s, r \rangle$ are present in the message buffer of place p_8. Then, the sending manager s can return to place p_5 (the system goes back to the initial marking M_0 by firing t_2). After that, another manager may start an update. Note that, at each firing, $(n - 1)$ tokens move through a heavy line arc labeled Σ, whereas one token moves through a light line arc in the model of Fig. 7.

Let us analyze this model by applying some of the analysis techniques discussed in Section 5. First, the transition-to-place incidence matrix A of the net shown in Fig. 7 is given by

$$
A = \begin{array}{c} \\ t_1 \\ t_2 \\ t_3 \\ t_4 \end{array}
\begin{array}{cccccccc}
p_1 & p_2 & p_3 & p_4 & p_5 & p_6 & p_7 & p_8 \\
\end{array}
\left[
\begin{array}{cccccccc}
-1 & s & -\Sigma & \Sigma & -s & 0 & 0 & 0 \\
1 & -s & \Sigma & 0 & s & 0 & 0 & -\Sigma \\
0 & 0 & 0 & -sr & -r & r & sr & 0 \\
0 & 0 & 0 & 0 & r & -r & -sr & sr
\end{array}
\right]
$$

For the above incidence matrix A, there are the following independent S invariants:

$$
\begin{aligned}
y_1 &= (\ 0 \quad 1 \quad 0 \quad 0 \quad 1 \quad 1 \quad 0 \quad 0\ )^T \\
y_2 &= (\ 0 \quad 0 \quad 1 \quad 1 \quad 0 \quad 0 \quad 1 \quad 1\ )^T \\
y_3 &= (\ s \quad 1 \quad 0 \quad 0 \quad 0 \quad 0 \quad 0 \quad 0\ )^T \\
y_4 &= (\ 0 \quad 0 \quad 0 \quad 0 \quad 0 \quad sr \quad -r \quad 0\ )^T \\
y_5 &= (\ 0 \quad \Sigma \quad s \quad 0 \quad 0 \quad 0 \quad 0 \quad 0\ )^T
\end{aligned}
$$

There is one independent T invariant: $x_1 = (1\ 1\ n-1\ n-1)^T$.

Thus, we can make the following observations:

1. The net is structurally bounded and conservative since there exists $y = y_1 + y_2 + y_3 = (s\ 2\ 1\ 1\ 1\ 1\ 1\ 1)^T > 0$ such that $Ay = 0$.
2. The net is repetitive (thus deadlock-free) and consistent since there exists $x_1 > 0$ such that $A^T x_1 = 0$.
3. Since $y_1^T M_0 = y_1^T M_0$ for every $M \in R(M_0)$, we get $M(p_2) + M(p_5) + M(p_6) = $ DMB, i.e., each database manager d is in exactly one of its three states: "inactive," "waiting," and "performing."
4. From $y_2^T M = y_2^T M_0$, we get $M(p_3) + M(p_4) + M(p_7) + M(p_8) = $ MB, i.e., each message buffer is in exactly one of its four states: "unused," "sent," "received," and "acknowledged."
5. From $y_3^T M = y_3^T M_0$, we get $sM(p_1) + M(p_2) = s$, i.e., while the update of one manager s is in progress, no manager can initiate another update.
6. The S invariants y_4 and y_5 can be combined with other S invariants to derive additional observations.[37,38]

In the above, we have used a simpler model of a database system for the purpose of illustrating the application of the analysis techniques discussed in earlier sections. The reader who is interested in more detailed models is referred to Refs. 37–39.

9. Conclusion

We have discussed Petri nets and their applications, with an emphasis on the use of the matrix and state equations. Petri nets may serve as intermediate hardware (or software) models between detailed circuit diagrams (programs) and block diagrams (flow charts), when the former are too complex to analyze or the latter too coarse to predict the behaviors of systems. A difficulty in the use of Petri nets, however, is that the net representation becomes too large even for a modest size system. To cope with this problem, some transformation techniques have been proposed.[41] Yet, there remains much research to be done in this and other areas of the Petri net theory.

References and Notes

1. C. A. Petri, Kommunikation mit Automaten, Univ. of Bonn, 1962; English translation by C. F. Greene, Jr. Communication with Automata, Supplement 1 to Tech. Report RADC-TR-65-377, Vol. 1 Rome Air Development Center, Griffiss Air Force Base, Rome, N.Y. 1965.
2. W. Brauer (Ed.), *Net Theory and Applications,* Lecture Notes in Computer Science, Vol. 84, Springer-Verlag, Berlin, 1980.

3. C. GIRAULT and W. REISIG (Eds.), *Applications and Theory of Petri Nets,* Informatik-Fachberichte, No. 52, Springer-Verlag, Berlin, 1982.
4. J. L. PETERSON, *Petri Net Theory and the Modeling of Systems,* Prentice-Hall, Englewood Cliffs, New Jersey, 1981.
5. W. REISIG, *Petrinetze: Eine Einführung,* Mit 111 Abbildungen, Springer-Verlag, Berlin, 1982.
6. T. MURATA, Petri nets, marked graphs, and circuit-system theory—A recent CAS application, *Circuits Syst.* **11**(3), 2–12 (1977).
7. J. L. PETERSON, Petri nets, *Computing Surv.* **9**, 223–252 (1977).
8. T. AGERWALA, Putting Petri nets to work, *Computer* **12**(12), 85–94 (1979).
9. T. MURATA, Modeling and analysis of concurrent systems, to appear as Chapter 3 in *Handbook of Software Engineering,* C. Vick and C. V. Ramamoorthy, Eds., Van Nostrand Reinhold Co. Inc., New York, in press.
10. R. JOHNSONBAUGH and T. MURATA, Petri nets and marked graphs—Mathematical models of concurrent computation, *Am. Math Mon.* **107,** October (1982); this is an updated version of Ref. 6, pp. 552–566.
11. E. PLESS and H. PLUNNECKE, A bibliography of net theory, ISF-Report 80.05, Second Ed., August 1980, GMD, St. Augustin 1, West Germany.
12. T. MURATA, State equation, controllability, and maximal matchings of Petri Nets, *IEEE Trans. Autom. Control* **AC-22**(3), 412–416 (1977).
13. G. MEMMI and G. ROUCAIROL, Linear algebra in net theory, pp. 213–224 in Brauer, Ref. 2, above.
14. F. COMMONER, A. W. HOLT, S. EVEN, and A. PNULI, Marked directed graphs, *J. Comput. Syst. Sci.* **5,** 511–523 (1971).
15. T. MURATA, Circuit theoretic analysis and synthesis of marked graphs, *IEEE Trans. Circuits Syst.* **CAS-24**(7), 400–405 (1977).
16. T. MURATA, Synthesis of decision-free concurrent systems for prescribed resources and performance, *IEEE Trans. Software Eng.* **SE-6**(6), 525–530 (1980).
17. C. V. RAMAMOORTHY and H. H. SO, Software requirements and specifications: Status and perspectives, in *Tutorial: Software Methodology,* IEEE Catalog No. EHO 142-0, pp. 43–164, 1978.
18. L. J. MEKLY and S. S. YAU, Software design representation using abstract process networks, *IEEE Trans. Software Eng.* **SE-6**(5), 420–435 (1980).
19. J. R. JUMP, Asynchronous control arrays, *IEEE Trans Comput.* **C-23**(10), 1020–1029 (1974).
20. S. S. PATIL, Micro-control for parallel asynchronous computers, Euromicro Workshop, Nice, June 1975. Also, Comp. Struct. Group Memo #120, Project MAC, MIT, March 1975.
21. J. D. NOE and G. J. NUTT, Macro E-nets for representations of parallel systesm, *IEEE Trans. Comput.* **C-22**(8), 718–727 (1973).
22. R. M. SHAPIRO and H. SAINT, A new approach to optimization of sequencing decisions, *Ann. Rev. Automatic Programming* **6**(5), 257–288 (1970).
23. J. L. BAER and C. S. ELLIS, Model, design, and evaluation of a compiler for a parallel processing environment, *IEEE Trans. Software Eng.* **SE-3**(6), 394–405 (1977).
24. J. A. MELDMAN and A. W. HOLT, Petri nets and legal systems, *Jurimetrics J.* **12**(2), 66–75 (1971).
25. C. A. ELLIS and G. J. NUTT Office information systems and computer science, *Comput. Surv.* **12**(1), 27–60, March, 1980.
26. M. HACK, Petri net languages, Report TR-159, MIT, Lab. for Computer Sci., March 1976.
27. J. L. PETERSON, Computation sequence sets, *J. Comput. Syst. Sci.* **13**(1), 1–24 (1976).
28. H. J. GENRICH, The Petri net representation of mathematical knowledge, Report ISF-76-05, GMD, Bonn, 1976.
29. P. M. MERLIN and D. J. FARBER, Recoverability of communication protocols: Implications of a theoretical study, *IEEE Trans. Commun.* **COM-24**(9), 1036–1043 (1976).
30. The 2nd European Workshop on Petri nets devoted itself to Petri net modeling of communication protocols and its proceedings, Ref. 3, contains many papers on this subject.
31. C. ANDRE, M. DIAZ, C. GIRAULT, and J. SITAKIS, Survey of French research and applications based on Petri nets, in *Net Theory and Applications,* Lecture Notes in Computer. Sci., Vol. 84, W. Brauer, Ed., pp. 321–346, Springer-Verlag, Berlin, 1980.
32. J. SIFAKIS, Use of Petri nets for performance evaluation, *Measuring, Modelling and Evaluation Computer Systems,* Beilner and Gelenebe, Eds., pp. 75–93, North-Holland, Amsterdam, 1977.

33. J. Sifakis, Realization of fault-tolerant systems by coding Petri nets, *J. Design Automation Fault-Tolerant Comput.* **IV**(1), 93–107 (1979).
34. A. C. Pagnoni, A fair competition between two or more partners, CP Project Report, Inst. of Cibernetica, Univ. of Milano, Feb. 1981; also in Ref. 3.
35. W. E. Kluge and K. Lautenbach, The orderly resolution of memory access conflicts, *IEEE Trans. Comput.* **C-31**(3), 194–207 (1982).
36. T. Murata, V. B. Le, and D. J. Leu, A method for realizing the synchronic distance matrix as a marked graph, *Procs. of the 1982 IEEE International Symposium on Circuits and Systems,* Rome, Italy, May 1982, pp. 609–612.
37. H. J. Genrich, K. Lautenbach, and P. S. Thiagarajan, Elements of general net theory, in W. Brauer, Ed., *Net Theory and Applications,* Lecture Notes in Comp. Sci., Vol. 84, pp. 21–164, Springer-Verlag, Berlin, 1980.
38. K. Jensen, Coloured Petri nets and the invariant method, *Theor. Comput. Sci.* **14,** 317–336 (1981).
39. K. Voss, Using predicate/transition nets to model and analyze distributed database systems, *IEEE Trans. Software Eng.* **SE-6**(6), 539–544 (1980).
40. M. Jantzen and R. Volk, Formal properties of place/transition nets, in W. Brauer, Ed., *Net Theory and Applications,* Ref. 2.
41. I. Suzuki and T. Murata, A method for stepwise refinement and abstraction of Petri nets, *J. Comput. Syst. Sci.* **27** (1), 51–76, August, 1983. An earlier version, A method for hierarchically representing large scale Petri nets, was published in the Proc. of the IEEE International Conf. on Circuits and Computers, pp. 620–623, October 1980.

21

MACROS
AN OFFICE APPLICATION GENERATOR

KIICHI KUMANO, YOSHIHIRO NAGAI, AND MITSUHIRO HATTORI

1. Introduction

Computer facilities, such as small business computers and computer terminals, are now almost ubiquitous in offices, thanks to the recent advances in computer and communication technologies, and more and more people have been accustomed to using these facilities to assist in their office activities. These situations create an opportunity and demand for the office system construction. However, just the presence of facilities and people who use them does not mean the realization of an office system. There must be office software, wide varieties of office application programs, which bridge computer facilities and people in offices. The key to the office system construction is to provide a wide range of office software which can become part of office activities and can be used easily by office workers. However, it is quite difficult to attain this, because there are few ready-made office application packages which can fit into office activities. Also, there are very few tools for designing, developing, and maintaining desirable office application programs.

The major reasons that office software development is difficult and troublesome are the characteristic natures of office application programs. They are quite large in number, versatile in function, and volatile in specifications. These aspects of office application programs stem from the nature of the office activities to which,

KIICHI KUMANO, YOSHIHIRO NAGAI, and MITSUHIRO HATTORI • Computer System Research Laboratory, C & C Systems Research Laboratories, NEC Corporation 1-1, Miyazaki Yonchome, Takatsu-ku, Kawasaki-city, Kanagawa 213, Japan.

or to part of which, they correspond. Namely, office activities have the following features:

1. Functional diversity—Quite a wide range of office activities are carried out in offices, such as budgetary planning, personnel allocation, purchasing, etc.
2. Office peculiarity—Office activities differ in detail from one office to another, depending on the mission, customs, people, and so forth, for the office.
3. Frequent changes—A particular activity in a particular office changes regularly or irregularly. For example, the information flow is changed due to organizational structure changes.

Therefore, it is virtually impossible to cover the whole office software development with classical approaches, which were to develop each office application program, using professional programmers. The reason is that these approaches consume a great deal of time and engender a large cost.

Accordingly, in order to provide abundant office software, it is of prime importance to realize a new approach to the office application program development, which can drastically reduce the cost and time required for the office application program development.

MACROS (*m*ulti-purpose *a*pplication *c*ustomizer for *r*etrieving *o*rganizational *s*tatistics), presented here, is a new kind of office application program generator. MACROS is based on the commonality found among a great variety of office activities in various offices. That is, the commonality is applied to the target application program framework design, which can be tailored to a particular office application. The commonality, which was abstracted, is that of a summary data processing and retrieving scheme. The summary data are used in various office activities to capture the status of various office indices, such as sales amount, office expenditures, etc., from many different viewpoints. The commonality-based approach makes it possible for MACROS to provide a comprehensive and compact target system description interface, which only requires a knowledge of office jargon, with which every office worker in the office is familiar. Therefore, even an ordinary office worker can design and develop application programs easily. In addition, the generated application programs provide systematized input and table/graph retrieving interfaces, through which office workers can easily and freely retrieve many different kinds of office summary data in table and graph forms, with just a few simple operations. The simplicity of the target application program user interface stems from the reflection of the retrieval structure in actual office activities. MACROS can be applied to a wide range of office activities in various offices, because it is based on the commonality widely found in many offices.

This paper presents the MACROS basic concept and an overview of the MAC-ROS prototype system, which is under development at present.

2. Objectives

The key factor in realizing a computer-based office system is software. Namely, it is very important to provide plentiful office application programs, each of which has a "user-friendly" interface, and can be used easily and freely by the ordinary office workers, a new breed of users who have no data processing training or background. At the same time when ordinary office workers are provided with an application program generator, and they can design and develop these office application programs by themselves effortlessly, it will be a great step toward the realization of "office automation." Herein lie the reasons MACROS was designed, to offer a comprehensive methodology and concrete measure for specifying, developing, and maintaining interactive office application programs, which can fit into and streamline office activities.

The MACROS objectives are to provide:

1. *Extremely "user-friendly" interfaces* for retrieving office summary data in a table/graph form. The term "user-friendly" means that casual users, including top executives, can retrieve easily and freely what data they want in a short time with just a couple of simple operations, without wrestling with voluminous users' manuals or taking boring lessons to use them. To meet these requirements, MACROS establishes an extremely simplified and standardized retrieval interface, through which users can specify the table/graph they want from a great amount of tables/graphs, just by pushing a few function-keys and figure-keys on the ten-key-pad.

2. *A practical and concrete measure* to generate interactive office application programs with the above-mentioned user interface, which supply the high-level program description interface. Namely, the description interface gives users the office application program design framework that helps them in designing and specifying the application programs they want. In addition, MACROS does not need dp-idiosyncrasies. In other words, users can specify the desirable application programs in entirely compact descriptions, composed in office jargon they are familiar with.

3. Basic Concept

The MACROS concept is worked out, based on the commonality in handling a class of data in offices. Those data are called *office summary data,* which have structure-driven nature. This section presents MACROS basic concept in terms of the office summary data nature and retrieval structure.

3.1. Office Summary Data

In offices, a great variety of data or information in various forms are created, handled, transmitted, filed, and so forth, in a way peculiar to each office. However, these exists a class of data which are quite systematically and regularly treated in offices. These are named office summary data, which include most of the office indices, such as office expenditures, investments, workload, and sales amount. These office summary data are obtained by collecting, grouping, and summing up the primitive data, normally written in specific business form configurations, such as invoices, etc. When these primitive data are sorted and grouped, the criteria are (1) office organization, (2) time period, and (3) object classification peculiar to a particular office application. In other words, office summary data are identified by these three criteria. For example, one office summary data can be specified, when section A (office organization), June in 1982 (time period), and product P sales amount (object classification) are indicated. Next, each of these criteria has its own structure, which is hierarchically organized, based on the inclusion. Each structure shows one aspect of the office summary data structure. Namely,

1. Office organizational structure (example: division–department–section)
2. Time period structure (example: year–half year–quarter)
3. Object classification structure (example: vehicle–automobile–van)

are structures which define the data structure for the office summary data. Therefore, they are named *basic structures*. These three basic structures are established in a mutually independent manner.

3.2. Office Summary Data Accumulation Procedure

Three basic structures, office organizational structure, time period structure, and object classification structure, indirectly define the data structure for the office summary data. At the same time, they designate (1) the summarization level and range for each office summary data, and (2) the summary data accumulation procedure. First, the three basic structures have, in nature, tree structures, because their structures are established based on the inclusion relations. Namely, each node in the structures has its own descendants, if it is not a terminal node. Assume a certain piece of office summary data corresponds to, for example, department A, a node in the office organizational structure. It means that the summarization level for the data is department level, and that the summarization range covers all the sections in department A. Secondly, according to the three basic structures, the summary data accumulation procedure is defined. Office summary data, which is identified by three nodes in the three corresponding basic structures, is named *entry data,* which is at the lowest summarization level. Office summary data for higher summarization levels are accumulated and summed up, based on the three basic structures, from the entry data. Namely, primitive data are grouped and summed up to present entry data. Then, they are collected and accumulated in a manner coordinated with each of the three basic structures to present higher-level summary data.

The office summary data accumulation procedures differ in detail among different application areas, because the basic structures are different from one application area to another. However, the structure-driven aspects are common. Therefore, the accumulation procedure framework, which can be applied to many different application areas, can be easily established. The framework is tailored, based on the three basic structures.

3.3. Retrieval Structure

Office summary data, which includes most office indices, are extensively used in a variety of office activities in various offices, because they represent the office status briefly and precisely. These office summary data are, in general, used in a table form (or graph form, as a variation of a table form). The reason is that office data, when arranged in a table form, enable office workers to make much more accurate and pertinent decisions than when the data are separately retrieved. These tables are mainly retrieved and used on a casual basis. Users are, in general, unwilling to specify troublesome commands or parameters. They wish to retrieve desirable tables effortlessly.

A table is a two-dimensional arrangement of captions and data. The caption arrangement specifications show the whole table specifications. Therefore, if there is a simple way to specify the captions and their arrangements, it can simplify the table retrieval interface. A table is used to arrange mutually relevant data. The typical relevancy for table arrangements for office summay data is that given by the three basic structures. When three nodes, each of them corresponding to the three basic structures, are specified, they identify a single piece of data. However, when one or two of the three nodes are interpreted to represent their direct descendants, these three nodes represent line/column arrangements and, consequently, a set of summary data, which can be arranged in a table form; namely, an office summary data table is specified, as shown in Fig. 1, when three nodes, each in a different basic structure, and one or two basic structures, whose nodes among the three nodes are to be interpreted to represent their direct descendants, are given. The last part of the specifications is called a *facet.* Clearly, this method drastically simplifies table specifications. On top of that, operations to change the summarization level for the table data, according to the basic structure, are easily specified

Organization: Department A
Time period : June in 1982
Object class : Product X
Facet : Organization, Object class

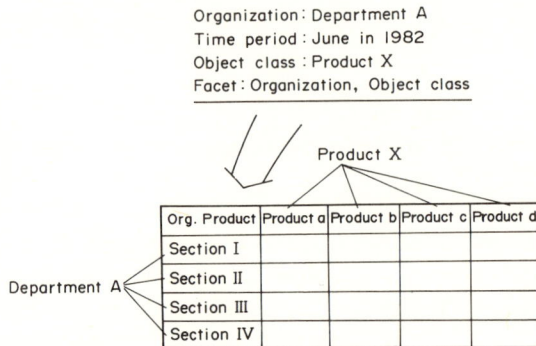

FIGURE 1. Table specification example.

by users. The table retrieval interface, presented here, is structure dependent, but not dependent on application areas, so that, together with the office data accumulation procedure framework, it can be used to construct retrieval-oriented application programs.

4. MACROS Prototype

The MACROS prototype was designed, based upon the concept described in the previous section, to demonstrate and verify the feasibility and usefulness of the MACROS concept. And the MACROS prototype development is underway at present. However, several MACROS target programs were developed, as trial programs, prior to the MACROS prototype development, and are currently used as managerial information retrieval systems. They have exhibited ease of use in the MACROS target programs. The MACROS prototype system excludes a certain portion of the function involved in the MACROS concept, for implementation convenience, as long as the restriction does not cause a significant reduction in MACROS adaptability. The major part is caused by the fact that the MACROS prototype is more of an interpreter for information peculiar to the application area, including the three basic structures, than a program generator.

This section presents an overview of the MACROS prototype, focusing on the target program description interface and the retrieval interface of the resulting programs.

4.1. MACROS Overview

The MACROS prototype comprises four major subsystems, as shown in Fig. 2. Among them, three modules, other than the MACROS translator, form the framework for a target program to be generated. Each subsystem has the following functions.

4.1.1. MACROS Translator. The MACROS translator furnishes a screen-editor-like target program description interface, which allows a user to specify a target program interactively, and translates the description into internal representations, which are to be used as messages and menus for the users, and summary data accumulation schemes and table/graph forming scheme. Target program descriptions are divided into general feature description division, organizational structure description division, and object structure description division. The information needed to specify the target program is merely the office jargon every office worker is familiar with. The description interface shows the design framework, i.e., what to specify. This allows users to concentrate heavily on the "what" in programming, rather than the "how." These features are especially useful to ordinary office workers who merely have a vague idea of what they want the program to do. When a target system has to be changed, due to, for example, changes in the office organizational structure, it can simply be accomplished by updating the relevant part of the specifications. This eases the maintenance procedures significantly.

Another MACROS translator factor is its capability of printing out various documents, which include users' manuals, maintenance documents, and file allocation documents.

4.1.2. User Register. A retrieval user of the MACROS target system is registered in terms of his personal ID, name and position in the organizational structure, as well as his personal default values for the retrieval parameters, which

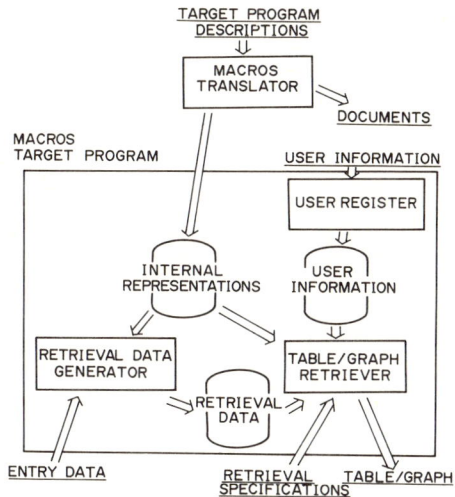

FIGURE 2. MACROS prototype organization.

show where his primary concern lies. This information is used to simplify the user's retrieval operations, and can be used to control security for systems operated under a multiuser environment.

4.1.3. Retrieval Data Generator.   The retrieval data generator presents two kinds of data entry interfaces. One is an interface for inputting the entry data, en bloc, which are data correspondent to the undermost nodes in all three structures, organizational structure, time period structure, and object classification structure. The other is for inputting of individual primitive data, which is to be summed up to the corresponding entry data. Hereafter, all the office summary data for retrieval are generated through the accumulation procedure, which is established based on the internal representations of three basic structures specified by the user. This module also provides functions for users inspecting and updating the data.

4.1.4. Table/Graph Retriever.   This module offers a comprehensive and standardized user interface, which even a casual user can use without taking a look at a voluminous user's manual. In order to retrieve a necessary table or graph, a user may just push a couple of figure-keys on the ten-key-pad and function-keys, because all the information needed to specify the table/graph for retrieval is given in the menus. This approach is especially effective in Japan, because it extremely simplifies the input of Kanji (Chinese ideographs) characters, which are used in names of organizations, object classification items, etc.

4.2. Program Description Interface

MACROS furnishes an entirely simplified program description interface. To exemplify the MACROS concept and features, a simple budgetary system for an imaginary research institute is described.

General Feature Description Division. This division is provided to specify the outline and terms used in the target system, as well as the description of the time period structure, which include

```
LEVEL NO., DEPARTMENT NAME, ACCUMULATION CODE

  O  Research  Group,
    1  Computer  Research  Laboratories, +
       2  Computer  Architecture  Research  Laboratory, +
          3 . . . . . . . . . . . . . . .
       2  Basic  Software  Research  Laboratory, +
          3 . . . . . . . . . . . . . . .
       2  Application  Software  Research  Laboratory, +
          3 . . . . . . . . . . . . . . .
       2  Peripheral  Equipment  Research  Laboratory, +
          3 . . . . . . . . . . . . . . .
    1  Communication  Research  Laboratories, +
       2 . . . . . . . . . . . . . . .
```

FIGURE 3. Organizational structure descriptions.

LEVEL NO., OBJECT CLASS NAME, ACCUMULATION CODE

```
0  Total expenses
   1  Personnel  expenditure, +
      2  Direct  personnel  expenditure, +
      2  Transportation, +
      2  ............
   1  Materials  cost, +
      2  ............
   1  Equipment  cost, +
      2  ............
   1  Miscellaneous  expenses, +
      2  ............
```

FIGURE 4. Object classification descriptions.

- System name;
- Terms used in the system, including retrieval parameter names;
- Data unit (yen, $, kg, etc.);
- Time period information (calendar year/fiscal year);
- Function-key arrangement.

Most probable choices for each term, except for a system name, are given in the corresponding menus so that users do not need to input lengthy terms, except when a user wants names or terms differing from those given in the menus. The time period structure is predefined as a couple of years, whose subnodes are half-years, and months, and specified in the system overview, in terms of calendar/fiscal year, and the number of years, partly because it simplifies the implementation, and partly because it does not seem to significantly restrict the MACROS prototype applicabilities.

Organization Structure/Object Classification Description Division. MACROS presents exactly the same interfaces for both organizational structure and object classification structure descriptions. Figures 3 and 4 show the organizational structure and object classification structure, respectively, for the example target budgetary system. The structure is defined in a fashion similar to the data structure definition in programming languages, such as COBOL and PL/I.

4.3. Retrieval Interface

The features of the MACROS retrieval interface lie in its simplified aspects, although it allows users to retrieve many different tables/graphs. When a user actuates the MACROS table/graph retriever, he is required to input his personal ID. The first panel displayed on the screen, when a user inputs his personal ID, is shown in Fig. 5. This panel shows the retrieval parameters and the user's most likely values for them, which indicate a set of office summary data which the user usually wants to retrieve. Consequently, the user can call up the table or graph (bar chart) onto the screen just by pushing a TABLE or GRAPH function-key,

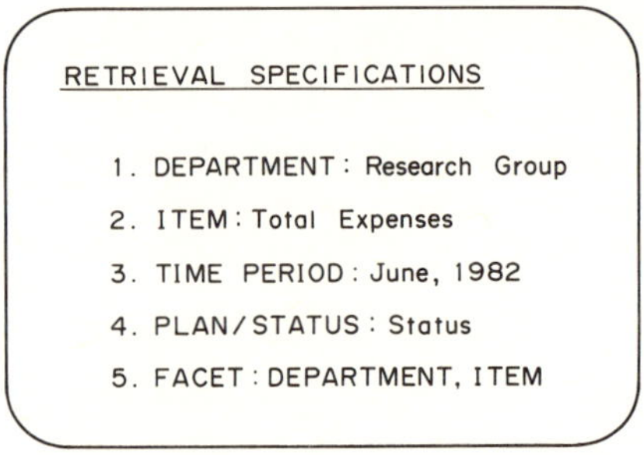

RETRIEVAL SPECIFICATIONS

  1. DEPARTMENT : Research Group

  2. ITEM : Total Expenses

  3. TIME PERIOD : June, 1982

  4. PLAN / STATUS : Status

  5. FACET : DEPARTMENT, ITEM

FIGURE 5. Panel for retrieval specifications.

respectively. The topmost three retrieval parameters are used to specify three nodes from the corresponding basic structures. The forth parameter is to indicate whether a user wants to know about the planned values and/or actual results for the retrieval objects. The fifth retrieval parameter shows which one or two nodes are to be interpreted to designate their subnodes in the corresponding structures. When the user wants another table or graph, he has to change some of the retrieval parameter values. When a user keys in a parameter number that he wants to change, the corresponding menu shows up, which shows alternatives for the parameter value. The menu example for the organizational structure is depicted in Fig. 6, which shows just part of the structure. The rest is displayed when a user pushes function-keys depicting arrow marks. Namely, menus for the organizational structure and object classification structure themselves are structurally organized by the MACROS translator and displayed, depending on the users' primary concerns and the target system status. In the sample menu, lines depicting the relation among entries are generated by the MACROS translator. The code for each entry is decided independently among menus to shorten the code length. When a particular code is selected, the target system converts it into the corresponding internal code.

Figure 7 shows an example of a table retrieved by MACROS, which corresponds to the retrieval specifications presented in Fig. 5. When all of the table cannot be shown on the display screen at the same time, the MACROS target system divides the table logically. It displays part of data and their related captions. A user can separate another part of the data and captions by using table shift function. Table shift is specified by pushing the arrow-marked function-keys. Valid arrow marks are always displayed on the screen. A table and a graph are mutually changeable in the MACROS target system. Namely, each of them is changed into the other form by pushing function-key TABLE/GRAPH. When a user wants to retrieve another table or graph, after calling up a table or graph, he has to push the ANOTHER RETRIEVAL function-key, which calls up the home panel, shown in Fig. 5, which displays the retrieval parameter values. A user can continue to retrieve tables and graphs of different or similar views, as explained above.

The simplicity of the MACROS retrieval interface is attained by (1) reducing the number of retrieval parameters by utilizing the structure-driven nature of the office summary data and (2) organizing two-dimensional retrieval interface, which uses the screen for the retrieval object specifications, and function-keys for the retrieval operation specifications. These features markedly reduce the number of key-pushings necessary for table/graph retrieval. At the same time, they make the interface natural to users. In short, MACROS simplifies the retrieval interface by adapting the retrieval view presentations to the user's actual viewpoint toward office data.

5. Conclusion

It is of prime importance to provide abundant office software in offices. However, attaining this goal is quite difficult, because office application programs are, in nature, large in number, versatile in functions, and volatile in specifications, reflecting the nature of the corresponding office activities. MACROS, presented in this paper, is contrived to offer a new approach to the office application generation. The MACROS objectives are to present a comprehensive methodology and concrete measure for the office software development. The resulting application programs provide an extremely simplified and standardized user interface, through which even casual users can retrieve tables/graphs from a large amount of tables/graphs easily and freely in a short time with a couple of simple operations. In addition, these application programs are specified by the compact and precise descriptions in the office jargon with which every office worker is familiar. Although the MACROS application program framework is rigid, and it can be applied only to a specific class of office software, retrieval-oriented application programs, it can be

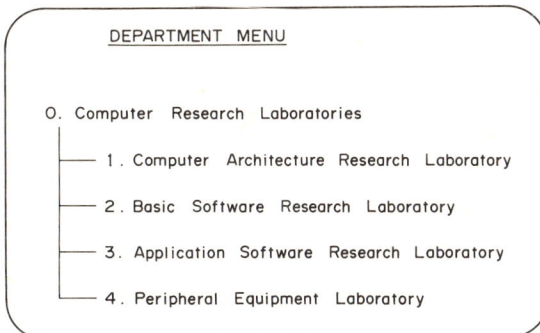

FIGURE 6. Example menu for organization structure.

June, 1982

Total expenses in Computer Research Laboratory

DEP\ITEM	Personnel expenditure	Materials cost	Equipment cost	Miscellaneous expenses	Total
Computer Architecture Reslab.					
Basic Software Reslab.					
Application Software Reslab.					
Peripheral Equipment Reslab.					
Total					

FIGURE 7. A retrieved table example.

adapted to a great variety of office activities in various offices. The MACROS concept is based on the nature of office summary data, which are extensively used in almost all offices. The processing and retrieving schemes for the office summary data are, in nature, common among most offices.

One of the merits in the commonality-based approaches is that they can furnish the design framework for designers. This is effective to lessen the design load, especially when designers are the eventual users who do not have a good idea of what they want the system to do. When program specifications are to be changed, due to, for instance, organizational changes, such changes are carried out merely by up-dating the related part of the program descriptions. This MACROS feature drastically reduces the maintenance burden. Therefore, MACROS can be used to support the software development life cycle in its entirety, although coverages are restricted to a specific class of office software.

Prior to the MACROS prototype system development, several target application programs were developed, by reprogramming the one application program which has the MACROS application program framework. These are at present practically used to retrieve managerial information, such as research expenditures, working hours, and the number of patents granted. Among the target program users is the general executive manager, who could freely operate the target program, after only a three-minute oral explanation of the user interface. To develop a MACROS application program by manually modifying the already-developed application program took only a seventh of the time required to develop programs entirely from scratch, because the application-dependent part is highly localized. These are considered to demonstrate and verify the MACROS concept feasibility and usefulness. The MACROS prototype can reduce the time needed for program modifications even more significantly.

The office activity commonality, namely, generality of the office summary data processing and retrieving, leads the MACROS system concept to a wider range of application, for example, as a component in decision support systems and as an end-user facility for database systems.

ACKNOWLEDGMENTS

M. Uenohara, Senior Vice President and Director of NEC Corporation suggested to the authors the need for a managerial information retrieval system with an extremely simplified user interface, and provided the requirements from a user viewpoint, which triggered and gave impetus to the MACROS concept development and refinement. The other members of Computer System Research Laboratory gave constructive remarks on the MACROS concept, which are reflected in the MACROS prototype development. The authors would like to thank all these people.

SYSTEMS AND
APPLICATIONS

AN INFORMATION SYSTEM APPROACH TO THE ANALYSIS OF JOB DESIGN

Peter S. Albin, Farrokh Z. Hormozi, Stergios L. Mourgos, and Arthur Weinberg

1. Introduction

In many structured job designs,* job content can be identified with the complexity of human–machine interfaces, with the computational or logical complexity of decision routines, and with interactive complexities associating with organizational or command structures. We have argued elsewhere[2] that such complexities may be measured or evaluated using established results in the theory of automata[3-5] and methods developed by us[6,7] to yield a practically small set of *complexity parameters* and *class indices* descriptive of an entire job and/or routines and tasks within the job. In turn, it is hypothesized that complexity parameters and indices so derived can be used to predict behavioral responses to the job. Appropriate job content can affect attitudes toward work generally, improve per-

---

*By "structured job design" we mean a formal assignment of tasks within an organization. The design may be embodied in a set of specifications, implied by an interface with technology, or implied by an assignment of decision responsibilities. See Ref. 1 for a broader discussion and bibliography.

PETER S. ALBIN, STERGIOS L. MOURGOS, and ARTHUR WEINBERG • City University of New York, John Jay College, 445 W. 59 St. New York, New York 10019. FARROKH Z. HORMOZI • Pace University, Bedford Road, Pleasantville, New York. This research was supported by the National Science Foundation and is a part of a continuing study of technological complexity carried out at the Center for Study of System Structure and Industrial Complexity of the City University of New York.

formance specifically, and may assist in developing responsibility. In an industrial setting, these effects would be partial determinants of general productivity and individual satisfaction. They may also associate with performance reliability for an operation or system and with the development of responsibility, efficiency, and sustainable interest for individuals and groups.†

This chapter addresses the problem of describing and measuring the content of a job design with analytical rigor. In Section 2, we propose a system for structural respresentation of a job design. Through a formal coding process, a job is described in terms of the circuit design of an automaton that takes actions and makes decisions implicit in the work specification. The parameters of this emulating automaton (or an equivalent data structure) are then used to identify behavioral properties of the job or proposed interactions affecting the individual within the job design. These broader considerations are discussed in Section 3 along with the general theory that underlies this approach.

2. The Coding of Job Designs

The problem considered in this section is that of translating technical, organizational, and decision-making features of a job design into a consistent format that permits complexity measurements for a specific job and enables comparisons among jobs or their content ordering and classification. There are, no doubt, a number of viable approaches to this problem. We have chosen a method of structural representation that associates critical elements in the job design with abstract automata that emulate the workers' task, decision, and communication responsibilities.

2.1. A Job Design Structural Language

In practice, we have identified two main stages in the structural representation of job design: first, the coding of separable basic elements or tasks, and second, the expression of these elements as symbol strings in what we label Job Design Structural Language (JDSL), where JDSL is a simple computer language with expressions denoting the entire job, routines, tasks, primitive operations, and control functions, as follows:

1. A job is viewed as a composition of routines, each of which can be isolated for purposes of analysis. A routine is set off by brackets: e.g., $\{N\}$ is the Nth routine.

---

†Controversy is rife over the effects of job content on individual and enterprise functioning. See Ref. 1.

2. Transitions from routine to routine are governed by an "autonomy function" which is set off by asterisks: e.g.,

$$\{N\} *A* \{N + 1\}$$

describes the transition from the Nth routine to the $(N + 1)$st routine governed by the Ath autonomy function. Autonomy functions range from *rigid sequencing* impelled by a clock, materials flow, or a current machine state; to *external control*, e.g., a direct order of a supervisor or a direction given by a sequencing plan; to *autonomous controls*, which include individual or group optimization decision or other choice functions, constrained or free. Corresponding to each autonomy function is a "pseudo-machine" to be described subsequently.

3. A routine is viewed as a sequenced composition of primitive tasks, e.g., $\{N\} = \{S_a \cdot S_b \cdot S_c \cdots S_n\}$, where the dots denote logical sequencing operators given by JDSL grammar.

4. Primitive tasks include:

   a. *Simple logical operations*, e.g., throwing a two-position switch;

   b. *Calculations* as described by the hardware and software required for their realization;

   c. *Standard manipulations*, such as turning a Vernier switch; and

   d. *Cognitive structures and physical skills:* These are designated by finite surrogates in the coding process, but are segregated for subsequent job-content analysis. A primitive is understood to mean a "distinguishable element which, for the purposes of analysis, is considered irreducible." It is also understood that at a later stage or in some other analysis a primitive might be further decomposed into more basic elements.

With a few additional finesses as described in Appendix A, these forms provide the basis for a hierarchical "compilable computer language"[8] in the sense that each of the language elements and logical operators associate with computer-logic building blocks, circuit-building devices, computerlike devices of greater or lesser integration, and pseudocomputers acting as surrogates for richer cognitive and physical primitives. Using standardized expressions (see Appendix B), notations, and grammar, the observer represents the routine, task, and decision structures of a specific job as symbol strings in the job-coding language. In turn, each grammatically acceptable string, when "compiled," associates with a parts-list and design blueprint for a "virtual computer" or "job surrogate."* Complexity analysis of the "surrogate" (to be described subsequently) serves as the source of information on complexities of the job itself. We also note the usefulness of a variant

---

*On Compiled Sequential Machines, see Refs. 3 and 9. JDSL is well adapted to LISP; we have used Timex-Sinclair Basic for an operational version of the language.

form of JDSL which treats the sequencing operators as "pointers" within a data structure or data management system.

The distinction between "autonomy functions" and "routines" in JDSL is admittedly artificial and requires further comment. We identify the former with points at which the worker can control the content, flow, or pace of work, or at which the worker interfaces with a control or authority structure that determines these matters. In general, the autonomy function designates a prominent point of intervention in work redesign, i.e., a feasible point for subdivision or reassignment of job responsibilities. An autonomy function in a rigidly structured design can be no more than an AND gate which directs the worker to replication of the assigned routine upon completion of the past replication and the arrival of fresh material at the work station. As such, the autonomy function has no more content than the trivial sequencing logic linking tasks within a routine. In more flexible designs, worker autonomy functions can, in effect, embody the management decisions[10] which are encountered by workers in more rigid designs only as control signals.* Note that our format permits separate identification of the job content within routines (logical, computational), that which associates with tasks (computational or athletic), and that which associates with control over the way in which work is to be done (decision and/or computational).

To illustrate the approach, we examine use of the coding procedure for a rigidly structured job design. We will consider more complex jobs in later sections.

2.2. Tightly Structured Jobs and Routines within a Process Technology

A process technology is used for production of a standard consumer good. Each job is identified and described by management to be a set of responsibilities and tasks at a specific machine position. (Rotation and reconfiguration of jobs within work groups are considered subsequently.) Tasks are further specified through instruction manuals and machine documentation. Direct observation verified that the work was actually performed as documented. At each machine position we (and the documentation) identified three separable types of routine:

   a. Start-up,
   b. Running maintenance,
   c. Trouble shooting.

---

*For example, if the relevant decision involves "scheduling," the emulating pseudomachine might be a linear-programming or critical-path algorithm (as appropriate). Computational complexity for the emulating pseudomachine could be considered as an index of the content embodied in the autonomy function. When workers' autonomy extends to adaptive reconfiguring of the work environment (e.g., active participation in investment decisions and technological choice), the emulating device is at the level of a "universal Turing machine" or cellular automaton.[5]

TABLE 1
JDSL Coding of Start-up Procedure

(a) Initiate start-up	(b) *A1* (start-up)	(c) *Aut1*
1. Turn the main power to *ON* position	S1 (turn to on)	L3
2. Open air valve to supply air	S2 (open valve)	L4
3. Turn the main switch to *ON* position	S3 (switch)	L3
4. Check supplies: P.V.A. seam seal adhesive	S41 (check)	L2
Garniture tape	S42 (check)	L2
Ink	S43 (check)	L2
Pare	S44 (check)	L2
5. Turn main selector switch to Heater	S51 (switch, heater)	L3
Fan	S52 (switch, fan)	L3
Hopper	S53 (switch, hopper)	L3
6. Turn to *ON* position Gummers	S61 (switch, gummer)	L3
Knives	S62 (switch, knives)	L3
Blower	S63 (switch, blower)	L3
7. Check indicator gauges; put to 80 lb	S71 (check) · S72 (Vernier) set	L2 · L4
8. Start the machine	+S8 (switch to on)	+L3
9. Check for quality	+S9 (quality check)	+L1
Proper operation of the machine and quality check transfers the operator to running maintenance	*A2*	*Aut3*

First compilation

Aut1 {L3 · L4 · L3 · L2 · L2 · L2 · L2 · L3 · L3 · L3 · L3 · L3 · L3 · L2 · L4 + L3 + L1}
Aut3→

Second compilation

$\overline{\text{MSTART}}_i{}^a$ = *Aut1* {(L1) (5L2) (9L3) (2L4) (15 ·) (2 +)} *Aut3* {running maintenance} *Aut4*

---

[a]Further reductions are possible if we represent the vernier check L2 as a tree structure of binary checks. The successor to $\overline{\text{MSTART}}_i$ is running maintenance. Hence the partial string ···} *Aut3* {running maintenance} *Aut4* {···.

In turn, each routine was further decomposed into a series of simple tasks performed in sequence or in isolation.

The instruction manuals specify the details of tasks and how to perform them. The procedure we followed involved a preliminary reading in which routines were distinguished, unusual types of tasks identified, and hypotheses formed as to authority and autonomy in the job control function. The first analytical stage was carried out in practice by recording the steps identified in the data on individual index cards. Rough verbal descriptions were included along with notes as to possible ambiguities, physical requirements, trouble spots, tentative codings, etc. The cards were organized, one-per-identified step in decks corresponding to identified routines. Table 1 gives an example of this stage of coding for the "start-up" routine. It is understood that the organization of cards at this stage will inevitably reflect the job-designers' image of the technology, their preconceptions as to the learning capabilities of workers, and their conception of power relationships in the workplace.

The second analytical stage involved translation of task cards into JDSL codes. Standard logical operations, e.g., binary choices, switch settings, finite calculations, sequencing instructions, etc., were located first. These are given by standard symbols in JDSL, as shown in Table 1, columns (a) and (b). The expressions in Table 1 column (c) give the final coding in our standardized logical format, employing a number of commonly encountered forms, described further in the Glossary (Appendix B).

Thus the coding procedure for the start-up routine identifies a collection of tasks and sequencing steps at the simplest logical level. The autonomy function "A2" (of type *Aut3*) controls the linkage from start-up to the running-maintenance routine and, in this job design, has no more content than the ($\cdot$) sequencer. Also note that the ($+$) sequencer at the last two positions permits a branch to the trouble-shooting routine. It is understood that the first ($+$) associates with a kind of mechanical failure, i.e., where the machine does not start; while the second ($+$) associates with product defect, i.e., the machine is in operation but the output does not meet the quality-control standards.

2.2.1. Running Maintenance. Running maintenance in a normal "trouble-free" condition consists of a series of quality checks every so often, supply replacement, and maintaining a clean working area. In addition, the worker is to watch for machine malfunctions and watch for warning lights and branch to trouble-shooting as appropriate. Analysis similar to that above shows that all of these tasks are primitives of the type L1, L2, and L5 (e.g., binary checks, Vernier checks, and simple physical primitives). However, the autonomy function Aut4 controlling running maintenance merits further comment. Whereas Aut1, Aut2, and Aut3 reflect shift of control according to an external signal (e.g., going on to the job or activating a routine on a command signal) and have the content of the simple task sequencer, Aut4 permits the worker's personal sequencing of tasks within the routine.

2.2.2. Trouble Shooting. Trouble shooting in this job setting is triggered by one of two error conditions: machine jam, or wearing out of parts. The worker is provided with a preset trouble-shooting protocol or check list. The protocol is designed to have the structure of a conventional decision tree, where the default condition at each test node is to call a mechanical or electrical technician with greater assigned responsibilities. The nodes themselves correspond to the steps in the start-up routine. The trouble-shooting routine thus has the content of the start-up routine, substituting ($+$) for ($\cdot$) sequencers and adding an element Lxx for the physical primitives of clearing tangles. The autonomy function for this routine has the basic form of an "idiot-free" checklist. However, experienced operators have the option of leap-frogging several levels into the decision tree to pick out a known or presumed condition.

2.2.3. Summary Calculations. It was revealed through the coding process that the logical structure of tasks and routines for each of the several types of machines at this facility was virtually identical. That is, the start-up routine for job–machine interface i coded (at the bottom of Table 1) as the composite automaton $\overline{\text{MSTART}}_i$ was virtually identical for interfaces j, k, ... , n—the differences being no more than 2 or 3 ($\cdot$) sequencers and simple L1 or L2 task operators. As argued in Section 3, these differences are of little cognitive significance and we are justified in defining a reference start-up routine $\overline{\text{MSTART}}$ as descriptive of all job positions. On similar reasoning the trouble-shooting routines were found to associate with a common emulating automaton $\overline{\text{MSTART}}^+$—identical to $\overline{\text{MSTART}}$ but substituting the ($+$) for the ($\cdot$) sequencers. Finally, running-maintenance operations on all machines were found to have identical structure to $\overline{\text{MRUN}}$, a control device with fewer logical components than $\overline{\text{MSTART}}$ but with some variety in (typically $k < 6$) physical primitives of the L4 type and the adjoined Aut4 autonomy function. The composite complexity (complication) of jobs in this category is therefore no greater than that of [$3\overline{\text{MSTART}}^+ \cdot$ kL4 *Aut4*].

There is nothing particularly remarkable in this calculation. Its significance derives from the implied predictions: first, that a job design which adjoins trouble-shooting responsibilities to the basic start-up and maintenance functions would not be perceived as adding qualitative complexity to work; and second, that offering job rotation to workers, e.g., the option of shuffling between machine types i, j, k, would not represent significant variety in job content. Both predictions went against the management view that the job design and rotation opportunities would be perceived as significant enrichments to work. The evidence on attitudes—post redesign—seems to bear out the predictions based on the formal structural model.

2.3. Coding of Machine-Shop Job Assignments

Having shown the feasibility of our methodology and some justification for its use, we are now prepared to approach a less rigid technology. The firm we examine next is a custom-order, specialty steel forge-and-finishing, job shop. As is common in many such shops, the automation level is low, product variety is high, production runs vary, and task cycles are relatively long. The main operations consist of (1) forging; (2) simple, one-worker machine operations on drill-presses and single-cut (e.g., outside-diameter) lathes; and (3) advanced machine operations such as multiple-cut, turret-lathe machining and finishing.* Our concern here is with a few aspects of the machining operations; elsewhere[11] we report in full on both machining and forging.

---

*Subsidiary operations, including cutting of steel, materials handling, packing, etc., are of standard type and are not considered here.

For the analysis of each machine job we assigned a specific operation to two or more observers, one of whom would make a direct JDSL transcription, the others would proceed from written notes and sketches to subsequent JDSL transcriptions, either individually or in committee. In one instance, an analyst set up and operated a machine and produced JDSL code based on his experience. He was observed independently and a third observer produced code for the same machine run by the regular machine operator. The purpose of multiple observation was to obtain some indication of the sensitivity of the coding procedures to the choice of observer. It turned out that codes produced by different observers corresponded nearly perfectly. (Hypothetically, two observers can differ in their identification of routines, but at the compilation stage their code could still produce identical complexity measures.) In addition, the coding was checked for completeness against job descriptions supplied by management and against job descriptions in the DOT* and in other sources.

2.3.1. Drill Press. Our coding identified two distinct routines: a "checklist, load, start-up, run, unload" procedure which on compilation was discovered to have logical content virtually identical to that of $\overline{\text{MSTART}}$ for process technology; and a "setup" involving translating blueprint parameters into machine settings (for centering, number of holes, etc.). This procedure was found to be reducible to a sequence of logical primitives virtually identical to that of $\overline{\text{MSTART}}^+$. As in the case of the process technology, all physical primitives were of the L5 type. Autonomy functions for the job† were of the Aut3 type, to initiate setups (triggered by a management signal delivered through a batch order) and to initiate a new run cycle (triggered by completion of the previous cycle and available pieces in process).

In short, the work day can be represented by the complication equivalent $b[\overline{\text{MSTART}}^+ + r\overline{\text{MSTART}}]$, where b gives the average number of batch setups per day and r the number of pieces per batch run. It is not surprising that the operating cycle can be learned reliably in minutes by an entry-level worker and the setup procedure in a matter of hours. (This also bears on our conclusion of management's overestimation of complexity for the process technology.)

2.3.2. Single Cut Lathe. The running routine for this machine can be described by a start-up and load subroutine corresponding to $\overline{\text{MSTART}}$, an internal autonomy function of type Aut4 (one that allows some operator flexibility) in choosing how to perform the operating routine, $\overline{\text{MOPR}}$. This subroutine contains

---

The Dictionary of Occupational Titles[16] (DOT) of the Department of Labor is a standard source of information on the complexity of actual jobs with respect to "data, people, things." For purposes of comparison, the DOT provides an *ordinal* scale of observer-classified complexities with no explicit foundation in cognitive theory or the information disciplines.
†In still more rigid designs, the setup and operating functions are assigned to different workers.

p primitive tasks of type L7 which permit some skill development in a logical format equivalent to $\overline{\text{MSTART}}^+$. Thus for the running routine as a whole we have the following "emulation equivalence" (described by $\simeq$):

$$\overline{\text{MSCLR}} \simeq \{\overline{\text{MSTART}}\} * \text{Aut4} * \{\overline{\text{MOPR}}\}$$
$$\simeq \{\overline{\text{MSTART}}\} * \text{Aut4} * \{\overline{\text{MSTART}}^+ \cdot p\text{L7}\}$$

Setup for this machine involves a preliminary choice of tools and feed speeds based on blueprint specifications, followed by iterative application of $\overline{\text{MOPR}}$ to bring the cut to tolerance. At this point, bench marks are placed to complete the setup and the machine is ready for production, during which the operator runs the machine ($\overline{\text{MSCLR}}$) to the benchmarks. The autonomy function for the setup is of the Aut4 type, governing tool choice and the iterative application of simple primitives required to complete a precision measurement. Let it suffice that the entire job of setup operation for the machine can be expressed as an application of subroutines of the $\overline{\text{MSTART}}^+$ type, Aut4 controls, and n physical primitives of the L7 type. We designate the entire job package as $\overline{\text{MSCL}}$.

2.3.3. Turret Lathe. The multiple-cut lathe or turret lathe can be thought of as a composite machine which enables $c = 1, 2, 3, \ldots , 10$ (or more) distinct single cuts to be made on a part once mounted. As such, the emulating automaton MT for the turret-lathe operator's job could be viewed as the equivalent of $c\overline{\text{MSCL}}$ (and, of course, the constituent primitives of $\overline{\text{MSCL}}$). This is only partially correct. For, as we shall see subsequently, the turret-lathe operator's job contains additional features of richness. For the moment, however, the composite machine description (which is formed by routine-by-routine coding of the job) is informative on how machinists' skills are acquired. Just as the single-cut lathe can be viewed as the drill-press content package plus additional discrete physical and cognitive primitives that can be learned individually, the routines for specific turret-lathe cuts and controls can be learned individually as increments to the basic single-cut lathe package of skills. Furthermore, once operator skill is mastered, the worker can progress to mastery of setup routines which combine precision measurement with operating control. In fact, such incremental accumulation of physical primitives and cognitive experience is a major stage in a machinist's education.

However, many of the individual physical primitives intrinsic to machine operation (e.g., intervening to compensate for tool wear or irregularities) are of the L7 type (those susceptible to improvement). Linked combinations of such tasks can be viewed as providing opportunities for athleticism (type L8) and are viewed so with pride by master machinists. Furthermore, although the incremental routines can be acquired through practice, their variety is such that good machinists eventually develop or seek our formal theoretical knowledge (generalized human capital) embracing the practice. Finally, the setup—although it can be produced by a check-list and rules of thumb—implicitly contains many opportunities for trade-off among machine functions, variant approaches and sequences, and opportunities to tailor the work to personal preferences, aesthetics, cost considerations, and standards of mechanical art. In short, the autonomy functions are potentially at the Aut5 level, embracing a computational level at or near the Turing machine*—an experienced machinist designs the setup to anticipate the logical structure of the eventual production run and most machinists can delineate distinct "cost-effective" versus "best-art" approaches to a setup. The rich physical content within routines and the significant cognitive content of the autonomy functions are recognized by machinists and are highly appreciated by them. It is also hypothesized that the skill package of the experienced machinist expedites productivity increases of the disembodied, "learning-by-doing" type.

2.4. Summary

The examples were selected so as to demonstrate several critical features of our coding methodology. These are, in brief:

1. Identification of separate components of control structure, task content, and logical sequencing of tasks and routines. Note that in some specific cases these components can be distinguished as associating with *technology* (as in the case of a sequence of primitive tasks within a routine), or associating with an organizational principle (as where a control function is assigned either to management or to a worker). Thus, the coding approach can prompt redesign and/or intervention.

2. Hierarchic compilation promoting job comparisons both within particular technologies and between technologies. Consider the manner in which the emulating machine for a major routine in the process technology appears as a recurrent "proper-submachine" at several levels of the metal-working technology. Job content comparisons are facilitated and the conclusions are obvious. Other empirical studies performed by our group suggest that the approach is quite general.

3. Hierarchic organization corresponding to the process of skill acquisition and education. This is an important conjecture. The coding reveals a hierarchic sequence of routines and skill levels in the metal-working technology. Whether or not actual processes of skill acquisition follow such steps is a matter for further empirical analysis.

---

*Note again that one purpose of the coding approach is to identify rich cognitive structures or the potential for such structures within a job design. Such structures are not subject to further quantitative analysis.[12]

4. Identification of the ingredients of rich and interesting work. Note especially the synthesis of elements in the work of the turret-lathe machinist. This is the only job among those described here in which content is self-reported as a positive value.

3. Complexity of Automata and the Complexity of Work

As shown in the preceding sections, a production system can be represented by a hierarchic code which is isomorphic to a structured composition of automata. Such representations allow one to compare ostensibly different systems in terms of primitive elements embodying a common general concept of machine complexity. It must be recognized, however, that "complexity" has been an elusive and impressionistic concept in the literatures of economics, behavioral science,[13] and management science. Thus, a major contribution of our paper is the development of an operational scheme which offers a link between "complexity" as it is loosely defined in the job-content literature, and "complexity" as a quantitative variable which is reasonably well defined within automata theory, system theory, and semigroup theory and which pertains to significant structural, cognitive, and organizational attributes.

In the industrial setting, we associate "automaton complexity" with attributes of job designs. Specifically, job designs may be said to embody four basic types of complexity:

1. There is a form of complexity associated with the range and scope of social interactions and interpersonal relations at the work site.* This complexity is discussed elsewhere.[7]
2. There is the complexity which relates to control over work, worker or group decisions, and relations with management. This complexity type—embodied in our autonomy-function specification—is the subject of a worldwide movement concerned with the quality of work life. Our scheme makes it possible to analyze the content of control decisions.
3. There is the complexity which associates with the logical organization of tasks within routines[14] the sequencing or assignment of routines. This complexity type—directly coded in JDSL—is the usual subject of management interventions of the enlargement type.
4. There is the intrinsic physical or cognitive content of individual tasks. This complexity type—associated with JDSL "rich primitives"—is perhaps most neglected in the literature.

---

*For an excellent treatment of this issue, see Ref. 1, particularly Chaps. 2 and 3.

Each of these complexity types can be found within a job design, and although different in connotation, each can be of essentially the same machine-theoretic genotype. As we have argued in the previous section, every routine and control of a particular job design can be resolved into JDSL elements. In general, these elements and their compositions generate a set of fundamental variables for analysis of "behavioral types" of complexity within the job design. Even though deriving "cardinal" or even "ordinal" measures of complexity for a particular man–machine interface may seem to be unrealistic (and antihumanistic), nevertheless the representation of job designs by emulating machines of standard type provides a foundation upon which a humanistic theory of job complexity can be built. We claim that the complexity of an emulating machine associates with the complexity of a specific behavioral attribute of a job design. Simple structures can be identified by their minimal attributes; rigid designs show their inflexibility and lack of adaptability to human performance. Finally, autonomy, decentralization, and opportunities for learning-by-doing will reveal themselves in the essential control structures.

As is apparent, machine emulation of a job design permits deeper analysis of structural attributes. Routines can be categorized according to intrinsic complexity; branch points, replications, and iterations can be compiled; and autonomy functions can be analyzed for cognitive content. This last point is significant. Autonomy functions, as we have defined them, are cognitive structures (note that we have incorporated explicit computable decision mechanisms into our specification of these functions). The complexity level of those mechanisms is doubly important since they are, operationally, the entry point for organizational interventions and job redesigns. Work redesign, as it has been practiced too often by management, may be little more than a reassignment of trivial routines. The complexity content of autonomy functions could be interpreted as an index of the political economy of the workplace.

Note, finally, that if positive job satisfactions can be related to higher-level autonomy functions and/or rich content, productivity can indirectly be related to these structural elements. This point would not seem to require argument, but is nonetheless the subject of some controversy. The claim is that *ceteris paribus* a more satisfied worker is a more productive one. Our own empirical studies support this notion.[11]* It is our view that a significant component of actual and potential productivity increase can be explained on a comparative basis by variables associated with job design and the man–machine interface.† As such, complexity

---

*R. B. Freeman[15] has found "job satisfaction to be a major determinant of labor market mobility. . . ."

†Furthermore, more autonomous designs appear intrinsically to be more open to adaptive change. It is not clear whether the satisfaction and adaptation effects on productivity can be disentangled.

parameters are the basic measures of a technology and provide an information basis for planning and directing technological change.

ACKNOWLEDGMENT

The authors gratefully acknowledge the contribution of Terrence Stoeckert at an earlier stage of this study.

Appendix A: Basic JDSL Symbols

A.1. Primary Symbols

Sxx   Name of an identified basic task in a job design.

Sxx ( )   Name of a basic task with descriptive data within parentheses.

Pxx   Name of an integral task which is isolated within the job design but not analyzed with respect to complexity. As, for example, where the task is physically or intellectually beyond evaluation by a finite automaton.

Pxx ( )   Name of a task like Pxx with descriptive data in parentheses.

Lxx   Name of a standard task defined in the glossary. Included are irreducible logical primitives or simple circuits of logical primitives.

Usage. The analysis begins with the labeling of basic tasks in the job design (the Sx's) and arraying them as they are sequenced within routines. One objective of the analysis is to substitute expressions of the form Px, or Px ( ), or Lx for the Sx's. The substituted forms are the standard elements in a job content analysis.

A.2. Job and Task Sequence Controls

A control to link discrete subtasks which must be performed as an integral unit, e.g.,

$$Sa \cdot Sb \cdot Sc \rightleftarrows Sxx$$

$+$ A control to link (a series of) basic tasks to a routine. It is understood that $(+)$ permits a branch to an emergency exit when an appropriate emergency signal is received.

$\{$ Beginning of a routine, a collection of tasks considered to be an integral functional unit.

}   End of a routine.
} ( )   End of a routine with an identifier or label. Thus,

$$\{Sa + Sb + Sc (\ \ )\}\,(14)$$

refers to routine 14 which contains the indicated tasks.

A   An "autonomy function" which governs the sequence from one routine to another. It is understood that *A*'s can be numbered as Axx, according to their sequencing position in the job.

n   An integer denoting replication. Thus, ·6Sx· indicates six replications of task Sx.

; . . . ;   Delineator for routines (such as trouble-shooting procedures) which are entered via a branch from the main sequenced design.

/y/   A marker which indicates that a particular task or routine is performed in association with or cooperatively with a named worker, individual *y*.

Usage. The logical controls govern the sequencing of tasks and routines. A grammatically acceptable string of primary symbols and logical controls is interpreted as an executable sequence of machine steps. Counts of logical controls can be used to indicate the degree of iteration, cooperative activities, etc., within the job design.

Appendix B: Glossary of Standard Tasks and Routines

The list below contains tasks which are often encountered in job analysis. These tasks may be identified in the initial steps of job coding or substituted appropriately at later stages.*

B.1. Primitives

L1 Binary checks, i.e., position of a two-way switch. Basic circuit building blocks, e.g., *AND, OR,* logical functions; functions that are emulated by simple neural nets, etc.

L2 Vernier check, i.e., level, ½ empty, 80 lb pressure, etc.

L3 Binary act, i.e., put switch to *ON.*

L4 Vernier act, i.e., restore level to xlb.

---

*Note that several of these primitives could be further reduced into basic hardware parts or, alternatively, indexed as the "computer memory" required to store their transition functions.

L5 Standard physical primitives: Standard movements or manipulations, e.g., lifting, turning, walking, pushing. These are not ordinarily identified in JDSL although they may have ergonomic content.

L6 Binary tree of depth (x) (note that a binary tree is reducible to a sequence of L1's and L3's), and other equivalent standard compositions of basic building blocks, e.g., finite algorithms, composite logical functions, etc.

L7 Physical primitives involving ordinary capabilities but susceptible to improvement in speed and/or accuracy; e.g., a docking procedure involving continuous feedback speed and position.

L8 Physical primitives involving recognized athletic capabilities. Athletic actions including motions and operations which can be performed with style, individuality, or finesse; require unusual abilities, or demand unusual training.

L9 Cognitive structures such as decisions or actions requiring judgments, interpersonal comparisons, optimizations, multiattribute calculations at or about the Turing machine level, creativity, etc. Note that a job design may specify decisions implying a rich cognitive structure for which finite machines or heuristics may be substituted in practice. Conversely, finite job requirements may be invested with nonessential content. Such antinomies would be identified in side commentaries.

B.2. Types of Autonomy Functions

Aut1 Clock-started.

Aut2 Command-started.

Aut3 Sequentially-started.

Aut4 Default constrained, personal control of task or routine sequencing, e.g., operator follows rule-of-thumb or arbitrary sequencing—subject only to not permitting a default condition. Inferentially there are no optimizations.

Aut5 Rich cognitive functions involving higher-order decision mechanisms. They require interpersonal optimizations and multiattribute computations.

B.3. Types of Composite Machines

$\overline{\text{MSTART}}(n)$ A composite machine representing n unbranched tasks of types L1–L5 in a simple check-list sequence.

$\overline{\text{MSTART}}^+$ A composite machine with two or more branched exits.

References

1. R. J. HACKMAN and G. R. OLDHAM, *Work Redesign,* Addison-Wesley, Reading, Massachusetts, 1980.
2. P. S. ALBIN and A. S. WEINBERG, Work complexity in structured job designs, *Human Syst. Manage.* (1983) (forthcoming).
3. A. GINSBURG, *Algebraic Theory of Automata,* Academic Press, New York, 1968.
4. K. KROHN and J. RHODES, Algebraic theory of machines, *Trans. Am. Math. Soc.* **116,** 450–464 (1965).
5. A. R. SMITH, Cellular automata complexity trade-offs, *Inf. Control,* **18,** 446–482 1971.
6. P. S. ALBIN, *The Analysis of Complex Socio-Economic Systems,* D. C. Heath & Co., Lexington, Massachusetts, 1975.
7. P. S. ALBIN, The complexity of social groups and social systems described by graph structures, *Math. Social Sci.* **1,** 101–129 (1980).
8. N. CHOMSKY, *Syntactic Structures,* Mouten, London, 1965.
9. M. MINSKY, *Computation: Finite and Infinite Machines,* Prentice-Hall, Englewood Cliffs, New Jersey, 1967.
10. C. FUTIA, *The Complexity of Economic Decision Rules,* Bell Laboratories, Murray Hill, New Jersey, January 1975.
11. P. S. ALBIN, C. BAHN *et al.* Worker perception of job complexity, Research Paper #RM.11. Center for the Study of System Structure and Industrial Complexity, CUNY, 1983.
12. P. S. ALBIN, The metalogic of economic predictions, calculations and propositions, *Math. Social Sci.* **3,** 329–358 (1982).
13. H. A. SIMON, Rationality as process and as product of thought, *Am. Econ. Rev.* **68**(2), 1–16 May (1978).
14. G. E. FLUECKIGER, A finite automaton model of behavior and learning, *Econ. Inquiry,* **XVI**(4), 508–530 (1978).
15. R. B. FREEMAN, Job satisfaction as an economic variable, Discussion paper #592, Harvard Institute of Economic Research, Harvard University, Cambridge, Massachusetts, 1977.
16. *Dictionary of Occupational Titles,* U.S. Department of Labor, 1977.

23

COMMAND DECOMPOSITION AS A DECISION-MAKING PROBLEM

PANOS A. LIGOMENIDES

1. Introduction

Large business, military, political, or economic systems are "open" to exchange of energy, materials, and information with their environments, and include regulatory processes which ensure the harmonization of their internal activities and nonlinear interactions. Such "cybernetic" systems with highly complex populations of units and groups can exhibit metastable evolutionary transitions.[14] Chance concatenations of inputs and of internal events may enforce or counteract local stability, so that it is only through dynamic programming and adaptive control that the behavior of the system may be maintained within desirable norms.

Metastable transitions are directed by two tendencies: a homeostatic drive expressing the "noiseless" dynamics of the system, countered by an "adaptive" component generated by "noise" that includes environmental fluctuations and external forces, which may force the system to move away from certain preferred states. These two components determine the time trajectory of the system's metastable behavior.

The engineering–cybernetic (EC) model was proposed in Ref. 14 to provide the framework for the development of means and methods for the prediction of the coherent component, and for the exercise of on-line control over the adaptive one. The EC model, shown in Fig. 1 is a distributed, multifeedback decision-making organization, which includes the descending, behavior generating, hierarchy of command decomposition, characterized by the $\mathcal{P}$ operator. Along it, strat-

PANOS A. LIGOMENIDES • Intelligent Machines Program and Electrical Engineering Department, University of Maryland, College Park, Maryland 20742.

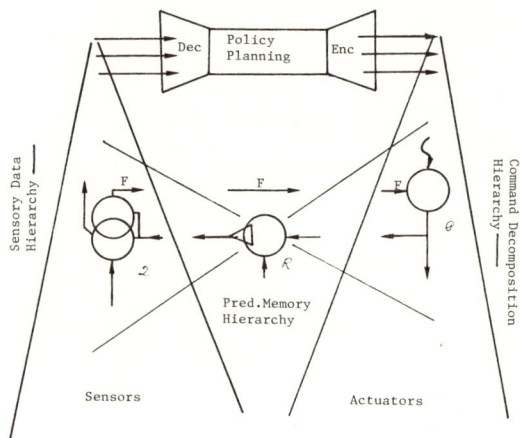

FIGURE 1. Conceptual configuration of the Engineering-Cybernetic model (from Ref. 14).

egies may be modified and implemented in a dynamically goal-seeking way. An ascending hierarchy of sensory data integration and information quality enhancement, characterized by the Q operator, generates feedback F for the on-line adaptive control of command decomposition. The predictive memory hierarchy, characterized by the $\mathcal{R}$ operator, links the $\mathcal{P}$ and Q hierarchies by accepting information about the current command traces and by providing context information for the filtering and evaluation of the sensory data. The function of the $\mathcal{P}$ operator, i.e., the command decomposition operation, is analyzed in this paper as a decision-making operation.

The adaptive implementation of strategies along the command decomposition hierarchy of a large cybernetic system involves the concurrent and dynamic decision-making functions of cascaded decomposition of slow-varying command trajectories into lower-level, fast-varying, subcommand trajectories, under conditions of incomplete information. The command decomposition is done in an environment in which the goals, the constraints, and the consequences of possible actions, are not, or cannot be, always known precisely. To deal quantitatively with such environments we use the measures and the calculus of probability, as well as those of fuzzy logic.

Command decomposition at each level of the behavior-generating hierarchy is also a local policy generating function aiming for the best monotonic attainment of the goals. The function is one of decision making within the constraints and goals defined by the input command statements and within the alternative options of action available, guided by some maximizing (payoff) or minimizing (loss) objective. Therefore, policy generation is also formulated as a decision-making endeavor which implements compositional rules of inference. In general, most such nontrivial problems are too ill defined and too complex, and thus virtually unsolvable or intractable with precise algorithmic ways and with classical, formal logic.

We must note here that, in a fuzzy environment and with fuzzy entities, there exists the possibility of a multiplicative action of "fuzzification" along the decomposition hierarchy, due to added fuzziness at each level. This effect may compile to a serious problem of "losing sight of goals and strategy objectives" along the hierarchy. This possibility necessitates the need for "restandardization," i.e., a "defuzzification" mechanism. Restoring sharpness of goals in the statements of the output decisions is mostly a human endeavor, but may also be assisted by machine-processed algorithms. Often, in business environments, excessive fuzzification of objectives reflects poor communications and problematic corporate organization. Restandardizing action becomes especially important when nonquantifiable information is used and the human link becomes prominent in the interpretation of statements.[1,21]

Informal verbal communication along the command and sensory hierarchies must be formalized to allow for mathematical analysis. The conceptually oriented schemas of human communication forms must be analyzed on the basis of formal rules. Algebraic representation of command statements are examined in Section 2.

Decisions at the various levels of a command decomposition hierarchy are related and occur in temporal sequences. This makes the command decomposition a dynamic behavior-generating activity. Decisions at one level directly affect the decision environment at other levels (both lower and higher ones) by determining the states and the alternatives available to other decision makers.

2. Command Trajectories—Algebraic Representation

A "command trajectory" is a dynamically evolving sequence of linguistic command statements issued as inputs to each level of the descending hierarchy. Each "command statement" is a directive on goals to be attained and constraints to be adhered to. Formally it may be expressed as an algebraic function of propositions, involving such operators as negation, union, and intersection. Command statements are normally coded in a natural or an artificial language with propositions, hedges, and linguistic labels, fuzzy relations, and max/min and other operators.[22] Such forms of linguistic representation and processing are of basic importance for the formalization of the decision-making procedures.

The logical propositions appearing in command statements are referred to as "command entities," each containing a command and a time determinant. Command entities may be stated in terms of either binary propositions or of linguistic labels of fuzzy sets in appropriate spaces, representing values of fuzzy or linguistic variables.[22] They refer to the assertion of either goals or constraints. An example of a fuzzy goal command entity may be "Production should be increased substantially during the following six months." This goal may be conditioned to the following fuzzy constraint command entity: "if market demand is sustained high during the same period, compared to last year's average." Here we should point out the symmetry in the treatment of goal and constraint entities (Ref. 3, p. B147).

The constrained command entities contained in a command statement are used in related groups, or individually, to define appropriate decision-making situations at each level. The constraint entities are manifested in the definition of the states of the decision-making "subworld." The goal entities are manifested in the definition of the alternative actions, related to the decisions of the decision-making situation.

As an example of an input command statement in a large manufacturing environment (along the hierarchy of a large business system), consider the following directive: "Increase production by about 10% over a period of six months, if the market demand is sustained high enough to justify raising the price of the product by 5% in the same period. The increase in production must not necessitate additional work force, and the added cost of production over the same period must not exceed 3%."

One may express the goal in this command statement ("increase in production") using conditional statements of implication of the form "IF A THEN B," or as an algebraic function of the component command entities, thus defining the decision-making situation. The decision to be reached will determine new command trajectories as inputs to this and other levels, thus leading to related action. Activities such as "market monitoring and reporting," "preparing for, and, if warranted, executing the increase in production," are possible consequences of the decision-making process. The fuzzy nature of some entities in the above statement, like "high" market demand, is apparent.

If we represent each command entity by an ordered pair of (event, time) determinants, then the statement of the goal entity may be represented as an algebraic function using only the union–intersection connectives. Thus for the above example we may have

$$G = V_1 \wedge V_2 \wedge \neg V_3 \wedge \neg V_4$$

where Δt is the six-month period, and

$$V_1 = (E_1, \Delta t) = (\text{"high market demand sustained" over } \Delta t)$$
$$V_2 = (E_2, \Delta t) = (\text{"price rise justified," over } \Delta t)$$
$$V_3 = (E_3, \Delta t) = (\text{"additional force required," over } \Delta t)$$
$$V_4 = (E_4, \Delta t) = (\text{"added cost exceeds 3%," over } \Delta t)$$

We may observe that an input statement to a certain level may generate or propagate more detailed command trajectories and related action at the same or other levels, by the more detailed goals and constraints contained in the decision reached. Therefore, input command statements are derived from the decision choices made before.

In some situations it is possible to define a "universal set," from which all command entities may be drawn, or even to define a specific "command language" as a set of (input or output) command statements formed from a vocabulary of command entities by the rules of the "language." Then, the decision-making situation may be presented as a language translation problem. Certain types of business, health care, or military environments, where the vocabulary and the semantic variability and syntax are more restricted and structured, are better suitable for the definition of such special decision-making languages.

3. DM Problem Formulation

The decision-making (DM) problem is specified essentially by a set $X = \{x_j\}_n$ of possible states of the system (i.e., the decision-making "subworld"), the set $Y = \{y_i\}_m$ of possible alternative actions (i.e., decisions) related to the goal entities of the input command statement, and by the "pay off" array of values $U = \{u_{ij}\}_{mn}$ which the decision maker can expect from each state-action contingency. Other determinants of the DM problem may be any action-related set of attributes $A = \{a_k\}_l$ with assigned weights $W = \{w_k\}_l$ and rating coefficients $R = \{r_{ik}\}_{ml}$.[2]

The payoff function U depends on the state $x \in X$, on the dynamically determined sensory feedback information F (Fig. 1), which updates the $\mathcal{P}$ operator's knowledge about the probable state x, and on the contemplated alternative action $y \in Y$.

If a continuous case may be assumed, $U = U(X, F, Y)$, with $p(X)$ being the probability density distribution over X, then the expectation of U

$$E_X[U] = \int_X U(X, F, Y)p(X)dX \qquad (1)$$

is maximized to determine the "optimum" action $y = y^0$. If, then, U is continuous with respect to Y, the necessary condition for finding the extremum of $E_X[U]$ is

$$\nabla_Y E_X[U] = E_X[\nabla_Y U(X, F, Y)] = 0 \qquad (2)$$

If $p(X)$ is known and $E_X[U]$ has a gradient at any point y^0 in the ordinary sense, then the gradient will be written in explicit form and the optimum value $y = y^0$ of the parameter vector Y will be found, at least in principle, by the well-developed methods of optimal control theory. However, if $E_X[U]$ is ill-defined, due to imprecise knowledge of X or U, and to "noisy" feedback information F, then y^0 must be sought heuristically in real time by continuously observing F and reassessing our knowledge about X and $p(X)$.

If the DM environment is discrete with X being an exhaustive and mutually exclusive set of hypotheses about the state of the system, $X = \{x_j\}_n$, Y being an exhaustive set of alternatives, $Y = \{y_i\}_m$, and U being a discrete two-dimensional array of values, $U = \{u_{ij}\}_{mn}$, then the expectation of U may be maximized

$$\max_{Y} E_X[U] = \max_{Y} \sum_{X} u_{ij}p(x_j) \tag{3}$$

to determine the optimum alternative $y = y^0$.

If the states of the system are better expressed by subsets $\beta_\nu \in B$ of X, then the expected payoff for β_ν and y_i may be *defined* by

$$u_{i\beta_\nu} = \sum_{x_j \in \beta_\nu} u_{ij}p(x_j) \tag{4}$$

or more pessimistically, by

$$u_{i\beta_\nu} = \min_{x_j \in \beta_\nu} \{u_{ij}\} \tag{5}$$

Again, the optimum alternative $y = y^0$ may be determined by maximizing the expectation over the set of alternatives, i.e.,

$$\max_{Y} E_X[U] = \max_{Y} \sum_{B} u_{i\beta_\nu}p(\beta_\nu) \tag{6}$$

where $u_{i\beta_\nu}$ is given by (4) or (5), B is the state-set of the system, and

$$p(\beta_\nu) = \sum_{x_j \in \beta_\nu} p(x_j) \bigg/ \sum_{\beta_\nu \in B} \sum_{x_j \in \beta_\nu} p(x_j)$$

We may note here that Y may also be partitioned in subsets and the expressions (4), (5), and (6) may be extended accordingly.

If, due to imprecise knowledge, the states of the system are better expressed by fuzzy subsets $\xi_\nu \in \Xi$ of X with a membership function $\mu_{\xi_\nu}(x_i)$, then the optimum alternative $y = y^0$ may be determined by maximizing the expectation, $E_\Xi[U]$, as in (6), where

$$p(\xi_\nu) = \sum_{X} \mu_{\xi_\nu}(x_j)p(x_j) \bigg/ \sum_{\xi_\nu \in \Xi} \sum_{x_j \in X} \mu_{\xi_\nu}(x_j)p(x_j) \tag{7}$$

and

$$u_{i\xi_\nu} = \sum_{x_j \in X} \mu_{\xi_\nu}(x_j) u_{ij} p(x_j) \tag{8}$$

Notice that $p(\beta_\nu)$ and $p(\xi_\nu)$ are properly normalized to satisfy the $\Sigma_N\ p_\nu = 1$ condition.

4. Uncertainty and Imprecision

4.1. X as a Random Variable

In the sense that we lack complete knowledge about it, the state of the DM system may be seen as a (discrete or continuous) random variable, whose trajectories are determined by the internal structure and couplings of the system, and by the external forces (e.g., the implemented management strategies) applied on it.[14] In a DM problem the state may also be described by a composite function of a number of, independent or not, random variables (e.g., "the Dow Jones average" and "the interest rates" in a business DM system). As an alternative to handling states which are composites of random variables, one may process a separate DM system for each random variable and formulate a composite of the outputs (decisions).

If the state of the system is represented by a composite function of random variables, e.g., $X = g(X_1, X_2)$, then joint statistics are used to determine the probability distribution of the composite random variable X from those of X_1 and X_2. Thus, the density function $p(X)$ is found in terms of $g(X_1, X_2)$ and the joint density function $p(X_1, X_2)$ (Ref. 17, p. 187).

4.2. Probability Distributions

Probability assignments based on prior knowledge about the state of the system are "subjective" only in the sense that they describe a "state of knowledge," possibly including subjective knowledge, rather than anything which could necessarily be measured by some repeatable "random" experiment. In this sense, the probability measure represents a quantification of the available "knowledge."

The emerging consensus among decision theorists is a view of probability that admits a subjective component. It is that component which takes into account that there is an element of human judgment, even in seemingly objective procedures, for determining quantitative probabilities. In frankness, this view does not require that there is only one correct value of probability assignment, unless the available evidence logically entails it.

The particular method which may be used for the quantification of prior knowledge in each instance may take into account the personal traits of the decision maker to the extent that this may be desirable. Weighing procedures and formulas, such as the maximum entropy formalism (MEF) and Bayes' rule,[10] may be employed for the assignment and updating of probabilities. If the circumstances of the inference or decision-making problem require that a "unique" prior probability distribution may result for a given state of knowledge, then the available "evidence" must be freed of any personal opinions and characteristics and must be reduced to "testable" information, as defined below.

It is apparent that, at present, we do not have formal methods to convert all kinds of prior information into unique probability distributions. We do not know of any parametric formulas and procedures by which the subjective component of the input in the assignment of probabilities may be consistently represented by parameter values that measure personality traits of individual decision makers. Therefore, any "objective" assignments of probability values, based only on the available state of knowledge, may have to exclude certain kinds of prior information.

There is a rather definite minimum requirement which prior information must satisfy before it can be used by any presently known methods for assigning a unique probability distribution, such as the MEF.[10] The requirement is that an "item of information" (such as a proposition or a statement of fact) must be "testable." An item of information I is "testable" if it concerns some identifiable parameter value η, or hypothesis h, of the problem's parametric or hypothesis space, and if, given any proposed prior probability assignment, $p(\eta)$ or $p(h)$, over the space η or h, *there exists* a procedure which will determine *unambiguously* whether $p(\eta)$ or $p(h)$ does or does not agree with the given information item I. This definition of testability also implies that $p(I/\eta)$ or $p(I/h)$ must exist and must be known or be calculable.

This maximum entropy formalism, as applied in the assignment of prior probabilities, says that the assignment should be the *one* which maximizes the entropy measure consistently with all, and nothing but, the available prior information. This formalism has an intuitive appeal in that it leads to the probability distribution which assumes the least about the unknown. If the available testable information is in the form of averages (more general constraints have also been treated[6]), then $p(x_j)$ is determined by maximizing

$$H = -\sum_{x_j \in X} p(x_j) \log p(x_j)$$

subject to

$$\sum_{x_j \in X} p(x_j) = 1 \quad \text{and to} \quad \sum_{x_j \in X} p(x_j) f_k(x_j) = F_k \tag{9}$$

$k = 1, \ldots, m$, where F_k represent testable information in the form of m pre-scribed mean values of functions $f_k(x_j)$, which represent prior observations on the variable x_j.

Assuming stationarity and using Lagrangian multipliers in the standard vari-ational technique, the solution takes the form

$$p(x_j) = \frac{1}{z(\lambda_1, \ldots, \lambda_m)} \exp\left[-\lambda_1 f_1(x_j) - \cdots - \lambda_m f_m(x_j)\right] \qquad (10)$$

where the partition function is

$$z(\lambda_1, \ldots, \lambda_m) = \sum_{x_j \in X} \exp\left[-\lambda_1 f_1(x_j) - \cdots - \lambda_m f_m(x_j)\right]$$

and the λ's are chosen so that[10]

$$F_k = -\frac{\partial}{\partial \lambda_k} \log z, \qquad k = 1, \ldots, m$$

If the distribution $p(x_j)$ cannot be determined uniquely but only as a collec-tion of possible probability distributions $p_\vartheta(x_j)$, $\vartheta \in \theta$, i.e., if the "best" distribution $\vartheta = \vartheta^0$ cannot be determined by the MEF or other technique (e.g., for lack of testable information), then we may be able to assign a probability distribution $p(\theta_k)$, $\vartheta_k \in \theta$, i.e., to assign "probabilities of $p_{\vartheta_k}(x_j)$," and to extend (7) and (8) by substituting $p_\vartheta(x_j)$ for $p(x_j)$ and by adding one more calculation of expectation (summation) over $\vartheta_k \in \theta$, before substituting in (6), so that the uncertainty about the choice of $p_\vartheta(x_j)$ is also accounted for.

4.3. Coping with Imprecision

Imprecision in the common linguistic forms of input information in DM problems may lead to the definition of states, payoffs, and alternatives in terms of fuzzy subsets represented with corresponding membership functions. This possi-bility was briefly discussed in Section 3 with the fuzzified equations (6), (7), and (8). Such techniques seem particularly suitable in DM problems related to com-mand decomposition along the behavior generating hierarchy of the EC model (Fig. 1). In practical situations, membership functions such as $\mu_{\xi_\nu}(x_j)$ are estimated from only partial information by statistical analysis or by subjective assignments.

The set of possible states, X, is defined by the linguistic variables[22] found in the input command statement. Represented either as a single random variable or as a composite of various random variables, X may be first defined as a collec-

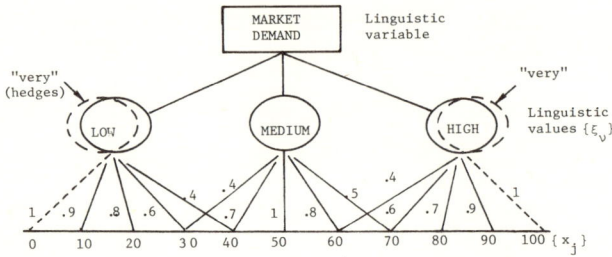

FIGURE 2. Primary fuzzy states of a DM system expressed by membership functions over a scale of "state indices," $\{x_j\}$.

tion of "primary" fuzzy states of the DM system, whose values are represented by membership functions specified over some (often arbitrary) scale, as illustrated in Fig. 2.

The MEF, or other technique, may be used to determine $p(x_j)$, and by the rules of fuzzy set theory to determine $p(\xi_\nu)$, where ξ_ν is a fuzzy subset over the scale $\{x_j\}$, or as modified with the help of linguistic "hedges," "connectives," and various *syntactic* and *semantic* rules of production.[13,22] A fuzzified version of Bayes' theorem[21] may then be used to compute the updated distributions $p(x_j/f)$ or $p(\xi_\nu/f)$ in view of any observed sample $f \in F$, if $p(f/\xi_\nu)$ may be determined (i.e., if f is testable).

In a similar fashion, the goals and constraints contained in the command statement may also be used to produce a description of the alternative actions as a collection of "primary" subsets, $\psi_\mu \in \Psi$, over a basic set $Y = \{y_i\}$. The solution of the DM problem may be either the determination of the optimum alternative, ψ^0, or of the ranking of the alternatives ψ_μ and the subsequent formulation of an optimum composite.

By applying the compositional rules of fuzzy set theory[22] we may also derive fuzzy payoff functions which correspond to pairing of fuzzy subsets from the spaces of states and alternatives, respectively. In this way, the payoff function is specified as a matrix representation of a fuzzy relation R on $X \times Y$ with a two-variable membership function, $\mu_R(x_j, y_i)$.

5. Formulation of DM in Command Decomposition

The goals and constraints contained in the input command statement, often in the form of linguistic entities (linguistic variables, values, and modifiers), are used to define and impose the framework of, often fuzzy, decision making under uncertainty.[3] In general, the command decomposition operator $\mathcal{P}$ may be represented as a DM problem on a ninetuple:

$$\{X,\ Y,\ U,\ A,\ W,\ R,\ F,\ p(X),\ p(X\,|\,F)\}$$

where X is a set of n states, Y is a set of m alternatives, U is a payoff relation on $X \times Y$ (an $m \times n$ matrix), A is a set of k attributes (or criteria) used in the ordering of the alternatives, W is a set of k weights, each denoting the importance of a corresponding attribute in the evaluation of each alternative, R is a relation on $Y \times A$, i.e., an array of rating coefficients $r_{ik} \in R$, each assessing the relative importance of an attribute $a_k \in A$ to an alternative $y_i \in Y$, F is the set of "observable" and possibly "testable" samples, $p(X)$ is the distribution function of prior probabilities (formulated by the MEF or other technique), $p(X/F)$ is the function that represents the weighing of observed samples $f \in F$ on each state $x \in X$(e.g., by Bayes' rule, or by the MEF).

The normalized weighted ranking for each $y_i \in Y$ (according to the simple additive weighing rule)

$$\rho_i = \frac{\displaystyle\sum_k w_k r_{ik}}{\displaystyle\sum_k w_k} \tag{11}$$

is used in the final composition and ranking of the fuzzy alternatives ψ_μ (i.e., decisions) on Y, after receiving an observed sample $f \in F$. Baas and Kwakernaak[2] have expressed the weights and rating coefficients as fuzzy sets, with membership functions μ_{w_k} and $\mu_{r_{ik}}$, respectively, defined in the interval $[0, 1]$. Cheng and McInnis[5] have used this approach to formulate a computational algorithm to rank the action alternatives. Also, Kahne[11] incorporated uncertainty in the problem of final ranking of the action alternatives (decisions) by letting the weights and rating coefficients be represented with random variables.

In order to evaluate how crucial a probability distribution is, like $p(X)$, or a membership function, like $\mu(X)$, which may have been specified somewhat imprecisely and on the basis of incomplete information, a *sensitivity analysis* can be carried out to determine how much the value of each p (or μ) would have to change before a recommended final decision is changed. If this kind of analysis reveals that some particular parameter p_k (or μ_k) is more crucial, and at the same time is measured by a least reliable number, possibly one whose value has largely been based on intuitive estimation or on rather diffuse intelligent information, then the recommended decision is highly risky, In fact, some "risk factor" reflecting the outcome of the sensitivity analysis may be associated with each possible decision. Also, our confidence (or lack of it) in the assignment of numerical values to such parameters as p or μ may be expressed by a "confidence coefficient" in the interval [0, 1].

The command decomposition problem, formulated as above, becomes a multiple weighted attribute, multiple alternative, decision problem, where the final ranking of the decision follows a sensitivity analysis, which reveals the extent of required changes in assigned probability and membership values in order to alter the ranking.

We may note here that in command decomposition problems the variety of possible alternatives, n, is characteristically limited. It can, therefore, be suggested that we may use a technique of "successive refinements" in reaching a desired level of detail and confidence in the final decision. We may begin with a very small number n (only a few possible alternatives), and, after applying a sensitivity analysis at each stage, move on to larger n (a more refined set of possible alternatives). This refinement procedure may continue until the risk factor reaches a maximum tolerable value. This characteristic of the set of possible alternatives, Y, in command decomposition is in contrast to other common DM systems, as for example in DM associated with medical diagnosis of diseases where the set of possible alternatives is large and totally specified from the start.[5]

6. Identification of the DM Feature Space

The problem of identifying the characteristic features of the DM situation is a goal-directed activity of basic importance in the design of formal DM systems. In a general case, the DM space may be characterized by feature space measurement vectors, $\Phi = \{\varphi_1, \ldots, \varphi_r\}$, where the components φ_i, $i = 1, \ldots, r$, are real-valued measurements or observations on characteristics of the various features, such as properties or attributes, of the DM environment. Normally, the raw data contained in Φ are voluminous, redundant, and diluted. Filtering and aggregation of information, in a way that the resulting data will reflect more densely the *relevant* properties and attributes of the DM situation in hand, is highly desirable.

If $X = \{x_1, \ldots, x_n\}$ represents a reduced vector of important features (note that X and its components are all functions of Φ), then a "feature space transformation," i.e., a mapping of Φ into $X(\Phi)$, is needed to (1) reduce the dimension of the problem from r (very large) to n (selected small), and (2) to weigh Φ so that the most important (semantically and pragmatically relevant) state variables are emphasized by such filtering of information.

Several techniques have been proposed to implement this transformation, $\Phi \to X(\Phi)$, under special circumstances. More often, however, the exceptional powers of human reasoning and association have been shown to be uniquely suited to this task.

The properties or attributes of the DM environment may be assigned real-number values using fuzzy-set or probability measuring notions and techniques. The real tough problem here is that we do not have as yet a reasonably general methodology for forming useful property measures, and we do not know whether such a universal method exists at all. Therefore, a general optimal selection (filtering) criterion for state variables, and a universal processing method for the enhancement of "info Q", may not be possible beforehand. Instead, the rather heuristic selection criteria and evaluation techniques for individual problems is probably more justifiable. Our hope is that, by the analysis provided in each case, some generalizations will be forthcoming for certain identifiable classes of problems. In any case, it is only the "survival of the fittest" under the scrutiny of test in real life DM problems that will determine the most suitable criteria and the most appropriate measures and methods for the treatment of semantic and pragmatic information. Performance in actual situations of decision making will serve as the final judgement, as the Court of Last Resort, that will tell us which method is preferable, in a way that will transcend all ideological doubletalk over the true meaning of probability, the subtle difference between "imprecision" and "uncertainty," and the philosophical arguments about the superiority of "fuzzy" versus "Bayesian" approach in handling imprecision on input information to DM analysis, etc., most of which often amounts to no more than an article of faith.

References

1. J. M. ADAMO, Towards introduction of fuzzy concepts in dynamic modeling, Conf. Dyn. Model. Control Nat'l. Econ., Vienna, North-Holland, Amsterdam, 1977.
2. S. M. BASS and H. KWAKERNAAK, Rating and ranking of multiple aspect alternatives using fuzzy sets, *Automatica,* **13,** 47–58 (1977).
3. R. E. BELLMAN and L. A. ZADEH, Decision making in a fuzzy environment, *Manage. Sci.* **17**(4) B141–B164 (1970).
4. S. K. CHANG, On the execution of fuzzy programs using finite-state machines, *IEEE Trans. Comput.* **C-21**(3), 241–253 (1972).
5. Y. M. CHENG and B. MCINNIS, An algorithm for multiple attribute, multiple alternative decision problems based on fuzzy sets with application to medical diagnosis, *IEEE Trans. Syst. Man Cybern.* **SMC-10**(10), 645–650 (1980).
6. R. B. EVANS, A new approach for deciding upon constraints in the maximum entropy formalism, in *The Maximum Entropy Formalism,* R. D. Levine and M. Tribus, Eds., The MIT Press, 1979.
7. A. N. S. FREELING, Fuzzy sets and decision analysis, *IEEE Trans. Syst. Man Cybern.* **SMC-10**(7), 341–354 (1980).
8. B. R. GAINES, Foundations of fuzzy reasoning, *Int. J. Man-Machine Stud.* **8,** 623–668 (1976).
9. R. JAIN, Decision-making in the presence of fuzziness and uncertainty, Proc. of the 1977 IEEE Conf. on Decision and Control, Vol. 2, pp. 1318–1323, 1977.
10. E. T. JAYNES, Where do we stand on maximum entropy?, in *The Maximum Entropy Formalism,* R. D. Levine and M. Tribus, Eds., The MIT Press, 1979.
11. S. KAHNE, A procedure for optimizing development decisions, *Automatica,* **11,** 261–269 (1975).
12. A. KAUFMANN, *Introduction to Fuzzy Set Theory,* Academic Press, New York, 1975.
13. W. J. M. KICKERT, *Fuzzy Theories on Decision Making,* Martinus Nijhoff, Leiden, 1978.
14. P. A. LIGOMENIDES, An engineering–cybernetic model for policy analysis and implementation, Int. J. *Policy Anal. Inf. Syst.* **6**(3), 273–284 (1982).

15. E. H. MANDINI, Advances in the linguistic synthesis of fuzzy controllers, *Int. J. Man–Machine Stud.* **8,** 669–678 (1976).
16. C. V. NEGOITA, Management applications of system theory, in *Interdisciplinary System Research,* Vol. 57, Birkhouser, Basel, 1979.
17. A. PAPOULIS, *Probability, Random Variables and Stochastic Processes,* McGraw Hill, New York, 1965.
18. M. SUGENO, Theory of fuzzy integrals and its application, Ph.D. thesis, Tokyo Institute of Technology, 1974.
19. M. SUGENO, Fuzzy measures and fuzzy integrals—A survey, in *Fuzzy Automata and Decision Processes,* G. Saridis and M. Gupta, Eds., North Holland, Amsterdam, pp. 90–102, 1978.
20. S. R. WATSON, J. J. WEISS, and M. L. DONNELL, Fuzzy decision analysis, *IEEE Trans. Syst. Man Cybern.* **SMC-9**(1), 1–9 (1979).
21. S. T. WIERZCHOŃ, Applications of fuzzy decision-making theory to coping with ill-defined problems, *Fuzzy Sets Syst.* **7,** 1–8 (1982).
22. L. A. ZADEH, Outline of a new approach to the analysis of complex systems and decision processes, *IEEE Trans. Syst. Man Cybern.* **SMC-3**(1), 28–44 (1973).

24

MATRIX OPERATIONS USING LINPACK
AN OVERVIEW

Houston H. Stokes

1. Introduction

This paper describes the use of 24 new SPEAKEASY LINKULES that have been developed to implement the LINPACK† subroutines as commands in SPEAKEASY. Figure 1 provides an overview of the capabilities of the_e LINKULES‡ that have been developed to utilize the modular design implicit in LINPACK and the BLAS. These LINKULES allow the SPEAKEASY user to factor various classes of matrices and to save substantial time, e.g., by avoiding the calculation of the inverse when it is not explicitly needed. The LINKULES are also useful in testing the accuracy of intermediate steps in matrix calculation in other programs.

LINPACK allows the user to check for matrix rank problems by testing the magnitude of the reciprocal of the condition of the matrix. In the SPEAKEASY implementation of LINPACK when the factorization of the matrix is computed, the reciprocal of the condition of the matrix is always tested, whether explicitly requested or not. Unless the user requests otherwise, error warnings are always given if there are rank problems.§ This paper will give an overview of the usage

---

†The basic reference on the SPEAKEASY system is *The SPEAKEASY III Reference Manual*.[1] The LINPACK routines are described in detail in *LINPACK User's Guide*.[2] Good references on the theory of matrix factorization include *Linear Algebra and Its Applications*[3] and the now classic *Handbook for Automatic Computation II, Linear Algebra*.[4] All LINKULES make extensive use of the BLAS routines (see Ref. 5).

‡Complete documentation for each LINPACK LINKULE is given in *SPEAKEASY Manual: Supplementary Help Documents, Level Pi*[6] and will not be duplicated here. More detail on the relationship between the LINKULES and chapters in the LINPACK manual is given in the Appendix.

§Reference 2, page 1.1; note that if the reciprocal of the matrix condition (RCOND) is approximately $10^{**}(-d)$, the implication is that the solution will have d fewer significant figures of accu-

---

HOUSTON H. STOKES • Department of Economics, University of Illinois at Chicago Circle, Chicago, Illinois 60680.

```
GMFAC      FACTOR GENERAL MATRIX.
GMINV      INVERT GENERAL MATRIX.
GMSOLV     SOLVE A SYSTEM OF EQUATIONS WITH FACTORS FROM GMFAC.
PDFAC      FACTOR A POSITIVE DEF. MATRIX.
PDINV      INVERSE OF A POSITIVE DEF. MATRIX.
PDSOLV     SOLVE A SYSTEM OF EQUATIONS WITH FACTORS FROM PDFAC.
PDFACUD    UPDATE A FACTORIZATION FROM PDFAC.
PDFACDD    DOWNDATE A FACTORIZATION FROM PDFAC.
SMFAC      FACTOR A SYMMETRIC MATRIX.
SMINV      INVERT A SYMMETRIC MATRIX.
SMSOLV     SOLVE A SYSTEM OF EQUATIONS WITH FACTORS FROM SMFAC.
HMFAC      FACTOR A HERMITIAN MATRIX.
HMINV      INVERT A HERMITIAN MATRIX.
HMSOLV     SOLVE A SYSTEM OF EQUATIONS WITH FACTORS FROM HMFAC.
TRFAC      ESTIMATE CONDITION OF A TRIANGULAR MATRIX.
TRINV      INVERT A TRIANGULAR MATRIX.
TRSOLV     SOLVE A SYSTEM OF EQUATIONS WITH TRIANGULAR MATRIX.
SVDCM      SINGULAR VALUE DECOMPOSITION.
QRFAC      QR DECOMPOSITION OF AN N BY P MATRIX.
QRSOLV     COMPUTE COORDINATE TRANSFORMS USING OUTPUT FROM QRFAC.
ZEROU      ZERO OUT UPPER TRIANGLE OF A SQUARE MATRIX.
ZEROL      ZERO OUT LOWER TRIANGLE OF A SQUARE MATRIX.
PL1FORT    ALTER STORAGE FROM BY ROWS TO BY COLUMNS.
FORTPL1    ALTER STORAGE FROM BY COLUMNS TO BY ROWS.
```

FIGURE 1. General overview of LIN-PACK LINKULES.

of the LINKULES. The examples given are by no means exhaustive and are only intended to be suggestive of possible use.

2. General Matrix Problems

The LINKULES GMFAC, GMINV, and GMSOLV will, respectively, factor a general matrix, calculate the inverse of a general matrix using these factors, or solve a system of equations using the LU factorization of the matrix without explicitly calculating the inverse. Figure 2 gives an example of the capabilities of these LINKULES. A general $k \times k$ matrix A can be factored into upper and lower triangular matrix U and L:

$$A = LU \tag{1}$$

Given b is a k element vector, the solution for the kx values of the system

$$Ax = b \tag{2}$$

can be shown to be equivalent to the solution of the two triangular systems

$$Ly = b \tag{3}$$

---

racy than elements of the basic matrix. Different LINPACK routines will give slightly different estimates of RCOND, because of differences in the factorization algorithm due to the characteristics of the matrix being factored.

and

$$Ux = y \tag{4}$$

Once A is factored, forward elimination yields a solution for y ($y = L^{-1}b$), which can be substituted into (4) to obtain, via backward substitution, the desired solution for x ($x = U^{-1}y$). The inverse of A can be calculated as

```
    X (A 3 BY 3 MATRIX)
    .038964       .0049338      .39384
    .067506       .83043        .10118
    .744          .12583        .74396

1/X (A 3 BY 3 MATRIX)
   -2.7976        -.21216       1.5098
   -.11583        1.2207        -.1047
    2.8173        .0056968      -.14806

GMINV(GMFAC(X,PIVOT),PIVOT,DD)  (A 3 BY 3 MATRIX)
   -2.7976        -.21216       1.5098
   -.11583        1.2207        -.1047
    2.8173        .0056968      -.14806
DD = -.21629
DET(X) = -.21629

    B (A VECTOR WITH 3 COMPONENTS)
    .14169        .098311       .018834

SOLUTION OF EQUATION SYSTEMS

(1/X)*B (A VECTOR WITH 3 COMPONENTS)
   -.3888         .10163        .39695
GMSOLV(GMFAC(X,PIVOT),PIVOT,B,0) (A VECTOR WITH 3 COMPONENTS)
   -.3888         .10163        .39695
(1/(TRANSPOSE(X)))*B (A VECTOR WITH 3 COMPONENTS)
   -.3547         .090061       .20084
GMSOLV(GMFAC(X,PIVOT),PIVOT,B,1) (A VECTOR WITH 3 COMPONENTS)
   -.3547         .090061       .20084

COMPLEX CASE

    X (A 3 BY 3 MATRIX)
    .51867+1.9739i      .13177+.70241i      .14012+6.2757i
    .13834+2.5982i      .08963+9.1128i      .23222+3.1808i
    .26312+8.6256i      .69012+3.5472i      .34524+8.6253i

1/X (A 3 BY 3 MATRIX)
    .019897+.22356i     .015493+.052725i    -.017955-.18208i
    .0037446+.016444i   -.0017238-.12416i   -3.6684E-4+.033823i
   -.020359-.23023i     -.0063955-.001586i  .018856+.052415i

GMINV(GMFAC(X,PIVOT),PIVOT,DD)  (A 3 BY 3 MATRIX)
    .019897+.22356i     .015493+.052725i    -.017955-.18208i
    .0037446+.016444i   -.0017238-.12416i   -3.6684E-4+.033823i
   -.020359-.23023i     -.0063955-.001586i  .018856+.052415i
DD = -22.647+299.68i
DET(X) = -22.647+299.68i

    B (A VECTOR WITH 3 COMPONENTS)
    1.4169+.037641i     .98311+.031355i     .18834+.013724i

SOLUTION OF EQUATION SYSTEMS

(1/X)*B (A VECTOR WITH 3 COMPONENTS)
    .032473+.35528i     .0063516-.092313i   -.023585-.31861i
GMSOLV(GMFAC(X,PIVOT),PIVOT,B,0) (A VECTOR WITH 3 COMPONENTS)
    .032473+.35528i     .0063516-.092313i   -.023585-.31861i
(1/(CONJ(TRANSPOSE(X))))*B (A VECTOR WITH 3 COMPONENTS)
    .03381-.28897i      .017122+.048099i    -.027322+.21443i
GMSOLV(GMFAC(X,PIVOT),PIVOT,B,1) (A VECTOR WITH 3 COMPONENTS)
    .03381-.28897i      .017122+.048099i    -.027322+.21443i
```

FIGURE 2. General matrix routines.

$$A^{-1} = U^{-1}L^{-1} \tag{5}$$

If B is a $k \times j$ matrix, the solution for the $k \times j$ elements X of the system

$$AX = B \tag{6}$$

would best be accomplished by saving the factors of A (calculated by GMFAC) and repeatedly calling GMSOLV with successive columns of the B matrix. GMFAC does not actually solve for L directly. U, when viewed with FORTPL1, is stored in the upper triangle and the multipliers necessary to recover L are stored below the diagonal. GMFAC, GMINV, and GMSOLV require the use of an INTEGER*4 work array to store pivot information. Figure 2 indicates how inverse, determinant, and equation solution problems can be done with the SPEAK-EASY matrix commands and the new LINPACK LINKULES.

3. Positive Definite Matrix Problems

The Cholesky decomposition LINKULES PDFAC, PDINV, and PDSOLV will, respectively, factor a positive definite matrix, use these factors to calculate the inverse, or use these factors to solve problems involving systems of equations. LINKULES PDFACUD and PDFACDD allow the factorization of a matrix to be updated or downdated when a new row of the basic matrix has been added or removed. A real matrix is positive definite if, and only if, it is symmetric and all eigenvalues are positive. If A is a $k \times k$ positive definite matrix, it can be factored such that

$$A = RR^t \tag{7}$$

where R is lower triangular. A complex matrix is positive definite if it is equal to its complex conjugate transpose $(A = A^h)$ and all eigenvalues are positive and real. The determinant of such a matrix can never be complex. In a manner similar to the general matrix problem, the solution of the system $Ax = b$, where x and b are k element vectors that can be reduced first to the solution of $Ry = b$ for y and second to the solution of $R^h x = y$ for x. The inverse of A, written in terms of the factorization, becomes $A^{-1} = (R^{-1})^h(R^{-1})$. The main advantage of the Cholesky factorization is that it is four times faster than the best general matrix routines. Once the factorization is calculated, often the inverse need not be directly calculated. In ordinary least-squares problems where there are N observations on k variables in X, A becomes $X^t X$. While PDFAC requires that $X^t X$ be formed directly before the factorization is calculated, the QR approach (see Section 8) allows calculation of R directly from the X matrix. Since the condition number of R is the square root of the condition number of A, in situations where the rank of the matrix is a possible problem, it may be wise to use QRFAC to obtain R directly from X without first forming matrix A.

Assume that a positive definite matrix A has been factored into RR^t and that $A = X^tX$. If an additional observation on the X matrix is added, it is possible either to recalculate a new A matrix (A^*) and factor this matrix, or, at some savings in cost, to update the original factorization of the A matrix. PDFACUD takes as input the old factorization of A and the new row of X that is added and returns a factorization of the new matrix (A^*):

$$A^* = A + xx^t \tag{8}$$

where x is the added row. In a like manner, PDFACDD will take as input the factorization of A^* and, given a row of X to be removed (x), calculate the factorization of A, where $A = A^* - xx^t$.

Figure 3a indicates how these LINKULES operate for real matrices. The matrix is first factored, the factors are checked to see if they are correct, and the inverse is calculated two ways. Next a system of equations are solved and the update/downdate LINKULES are shown. Figure 3b shows the same calculations for a complex matrix. While PDINV will correctly calculate the determinant as real, which can be verified by calculating the product of the eigenvalues, the SPEAKEASY LINKULE DET will show a small, close to machine zero, imaginary number. In this implementation of the complex matrix case, the equations system solved is $\text{CONJ}(A)^*x = b$ and for the update and downdate options the command CONJ must be used twice. At a later time this may be changed.

4. Symmetric Matrix Problems

The LINKULES SMFAC, SMINV, and SMSOLV will, respectively, factor a symmetric matrix, calculate the inverse of a symmetric matrix, using these factors, or solve a system of equations using these factors. If the real matrix is positive definite, the routines in Section 3 are approximately twice as fast. The symmetric matrix routines are themselves two times as fast as the general matrix routines (discussed in Section 1). Since the postive definite routines and the symmetric routines only use the lower triangular part of the matrix, it is important that they not be called in error if the matrix is not symmetric. If the matrix is complex and Hermitian (equal to its conjugate transpose) but not positive definite, the routines in Section 5 should be used.

If A is a symmetric real or complex matrix or a complex Hermitian matrix, it can be factored in the form

```
POSITIVE DEF. MATRIX
  PDX (A 3 BY 3 MATRIX)
  1.5723   1.2699   .9034
  1.2699   1.4351   .85719
   .9034    .85719  1.012

FACTOR POSITIVE DEFINITE MATRIX
PDFAC(PDX,RCOND) (A 3 BY 3 MATRIX)
  1.2539   0        0
  1.0128    .63981  0
   .72048   .1993    .67321
RCOND =  .067423

CHECK IF FACTORED CORRECTLY
PDFAC(PDX)*TRANSPOSE(PDFAC(PDX)) (A 3 BY 3 MATRIX)
  1.5723   1.2699   .9034
  1.2699   1.4351   .85719
   .9034    .85719  1.012

CALCULATE INVERSE TWO WAYS
1/PDX (A 3 BY 3 MATRIX)
   2.4599  -1.7511  -.71268
  -1.7511   2.657   -.6873
  -.71268  -.6873    2.2065
PDINV(PDFAC(PDX)) (A 3 BY 3 MATRIX)
   2.4599  -1.7511  -.71268
  -1.7511   2.657   -.6873
  -.71268  -.6873    2.2065

  BHOL (A VECTOR WITH 3 COMPONENTS)
  .019127   .71476   .41037

SOLUTION OF AN EQUATION SYSTEM TWO WAYS

(1/PDX)*BHOL (A VECTOR WITH 3 COMPONENTS)
 -1.497    1.5836   .40058
PDSOLV(PDFAC(PDX),BHOL) (A VECTOR WITH 3 COMPONENTS)
 -1.497    1.5836   .40058

ADD A ROW (BHOL) OF DATA AND UPDATE/DOWNDATE FACTORIZATION
  NEWPDX (A 3 BY 3 MATRIX)
  1.5726   1.2836   .91125
  1.2836   1.9459   1.1505
   .91125  1.1505   1.1804

PDFAC(NEWPDX) (A 3 BY 3 MATRIX)
  1.254    0        0
  1.0236    .94777  0
   .72665   .42915   .68427

PDFACUD(PDFAC(PDX),BHOL) (A 3 BY 3 MATRIX)
  1.254    0        0
  1.0236    .94777  0
   .72665   .42915   .68427

PDFACDD(PDFAC(NEWPDX),BHOL) (A 3 BY 3 MATRIX)
  1.2539   0        0
  1.0128    .63981  0
   .72048   .1993    .67321
```

FIGURE 3. Positive definite matrix: (a) Real case.

$$A = UDU^h \qquad (9)$$

where D is a block diagonal matrix with blocks of order 1 or 2 and U is a matrix that is the product of elementary unit upper triangular and permutation matrices. Given such a factorization,

$$A^{-1} = (U^{-1})^h D^{-1} U^{-1} \qquad (10)$$

```
COMPLEX POSITIVE DEFINITE MATRIX

PDXC (A 3 BY 3 MATRIX)
 63.965             46.983-.12153i    23.11+3.2927i
 46.983+.12153i     70.445            32.056+3.1288i
 23.11-3.2927i      32.056-3.1288i    18.65

FACTOR MATRIX
PDFAC(PDXC) (A 3 BY 3 MATRIX)
 7.9978             0                 0
 5.8745+.015195i    5.9946            0
 2.8896-.4117i      2.5168-.11116i    1.9455

CHECK IF MATRIX FACTORED CORRECTLY
PDFAC(PDXC)*CONJ(TRANSPOSE(PDFAC(PDXC))) (A 3 BY 3 MATRIX)
 63.965             46.983-.12153i    23.11+3.2927i
 46.983+.12153i     70.445            32.056+3.1288i
 23.11-3.2927i      32.056-3.1288i    18.65

CALCULATE INVERSE TWO WAYS
1/PDXC (A 3 BY 3 MATRIX)
 .031781            -.014384+.0040816i  -.013972-.010213i
-.014384-.0040816i   .07449            -.11093-.0048993i
-.013972+.010213i   -.11093+.0048993i   .26421
PDINV(PDFAC(PDXC),DD) (A 3 BY 3 MATRIX)
 .031781            -.014384+.0040816i  -.013972-.010213i
-.014384-.0040816i   .07449            -.11093-.0048993i
-.013972+.010213i   -.11093+.0048993i   .26421
DET(PDXC) =  8699.8+5.1039iE-13
DD =  8699.8
PROD(EIGENVAL(PDXC)) =  8699.8

ADD A ROW (CHOL) OF DATA AND UPDATE/DOWNDATE FACTORIZATION

CHOL (A VECTOR WITH 3 COMPONENTS)
 4.2378+.065098i   1.8585+.043111i   8.1188+.090104i


NEWPDX (A 3 BY 3 MATRIX)
 81.928            54.862-.059821i   57.522+3.146i
 54.862+.059821i   73.901            47.148+2.9462i
 57.522-3.146i     47.148-2.9462i    84.574
PDFAC(NEWPDX) (A 3 BY 3 MATRIX)
 9.0514            0                 0
 6.0611+.0066091i  6.0962            0
 6.355-.34757i     1.416-.13083i     6.4842
CONJ(PDFACUD(CONJ(PDFAC(PDXC)),CHOL)) (A 3 BY 3 MATRIX)
 9.0514            0                 0
 6.0611+.0066091i  6.0962            0
 6.355-.34757i     1.416-.13083i     6.4842
CONJ(PDFACDD(CONJ(PDFAC(NEWPDX)),CHOL)) (A 3 BY 3 MATRIX)
 7.9978            0                 0
 5.8745+.015195i   5.9946            0
 2.8896-.4117i     2.5168-.11116i    1.9455

SOLUTION OF AN EQUATION SYSTEM TWO WAYS

(1/CONJ(PDXC))*CHOL (A VECTOR WITH 3 COMPONENTS)
-.0062386+.075521i  -.82382+.049353i   1.8806-.03427i
PDSOLV(PDFAC(PDXC),CHOL) (A VECTOR WITH 3 COMPONENTS)
-.0062386+.075521i  -.82382+.049353i   1.8806-.03427i
```

FIGURE 3. (*continued*) (b) Complex case.

A system of linear equations $Ax = b$ can be solved by solving

$$U(D(U^h x)) = b \qquad (11)$$

remembering that if A is real, $A^t = A^h$. SMFAC does not explicitly form U or D but contains in its lower triangle (as seen without the FORTPL1 command) and diagonal the information necessary to construct matrix U and block diagonal

```
POSITIVE DEF. MATRIX
   PDX (A 3 BY 3 MATRIX)
   2.0642   1.5597   1.9879
   1.5597   2.2125   1.6744
   1.9879   1.6744   2.1061

CALCULATE INVERSE TWO WAYS
1/PDX (A 3 BY 3 MATRIX)
   5.3362    .1251   -5.1361
    .1251   1.1376  -1.0224
  -5.1361  -1.0224   6.1354
SMINV(SMFAC(PDX,PP),PP, DD,II) (A 3 BY 3 MATRIX)
   5.3362    .1251   -5.1361
    .1251   1.1376  -1.0224
  -5.1361  -1.0224   6.1354

DET(PDX) =   .34786
DD =   .34786
EIGENVAL(PDX) (A VECTOR WITH 3 COMPONENTS)
  .091252   .67924   5.6123
   II (A VECTOR WITH 3 COMPONENTS)
   3    0    0

SYMMETRIC, NOT POSITIVE DEF, MATRIX
   PDX (A 3 BY 3 MATRIX)
  -2.0642  -1.5597  -1.9879
  -1.5597  -2.2125  -1.6744
  -1.9879  -1.6744  -2.1061

CALCULATE INVERSE TWO WAYS
1/PDX (A 3 BY 3 MATRIX)
  -5.3362   -.1251    5.1361
   -.1251  -1.1376    1.0224
   5.1361   1.0224   -6.1354
SMINV(SMFAC(PDX,PP),PP,DD,II) (A 3 BY 3 MATRIX)
  -5.3362   -.1251    5.1361
   -.1251  -1.1376    1.0224
   5.1361   1.0224   -6.1354

DET(PDX) = -.34786
DD = -.34786
EIGENVAL(PDX) (A VECTOR WITH 3 COMPONENTS)
  -5.6123   -.67924  -.091252
   II (A VECTOR WITH 3 COMPONENTS)
   0    3    0


   BHOL (A VECTOR WITH 3 COMPONENTS)
   .72488   .78952   .65881

SOLUTION OF AN EQUATION SYSTEM TWO WAYS

(1/PDX)*BHOL (A VECTOR WITH 3 COMPONENTS)
  -.58318  -.31522   .48823
SMSOLV(SMFAC(PDX,PP),PP,BHOL) (A VECTOR WITH 3 COMPONENTS)
  -.58318  -.31522   .48823
```

FIGURE 4. Symmetric matrix: (a) Real case.

matrix D, given a work vector. SMFAC can be used to create and save the factorization of A for repeated use with SMINV or SMSOLV, or for checking the output of routines in user FORTRAN programs.†

SMINV allows the calculation of the inverse and, optionally, the determinant and the inertia (number of positive, negative, and zero eigenvalues). It must be

---

†An important use of the LINPACK LINKULES is to allow the user to check intermediate steps in user FORTRAN programs during the debug process. The LINPACK LINKULES are also very useful in SPEAKEASY programs and also when SPEAKEASY is being used in the manual mode as a super desk calculator.

```
COMPLEX SYMMETRIC MATRIX

PDXC (A 3 BY 3 MATRIX)
68.977+8.3602i    60.832+9.2764i    60.907+9.3792i
60.832+9.2764i    76.66+10.742i     56.018+10.321i
60.907+9.3792i    56.018+10.321i    75.879+12.023i

CALCULATE INVERSE TWO WAYS
1/PDXC (A 3 BY 3 MATRIX)
 .077033-.0023263i    -.034636+4.5402iE-4    -.036102+.0024421i
-.034636+4.5402iE-4    .043777-.001576i      -.0046953-1.3035iE-4
-.036102+.0024421i    -.0046953-1.3035iE-4    .045284-.0039383i
SMINV(SMFAC(PDXC,PP),PP,DD) (A 3 BY 3 MATRIX)
 .077033-.0023263i    -.034636+4.5402iE-4    -.036102+.0024421i
-.034636+4.5402iE-4    .043777-.001576i      -.0046953-1.3035iE-4
-.036102+.0024421i    -.0046953-1.3035iE-4    .045284-.0039383i

DET(PDXC) =   34223+8568.8i
DD =   34223+8568.8i
PROD(EIGENVAL(PDXC)) =   34223+8568.8i
EIGENVAL(PDXC) (A VECTOR WITH 3 COMPONENTS)
8.9328+.36001i    20.25+1.0491i    192.33+29.717i

SOLUTION OF AN EQUATION SYSTEM TWO WAYS

(1/PDXC)*CHOL (A VECTOR WITH 3 COMPONENTS)
 .047705+.0080485i  -.064625-.0060376i    .12206-.017219i
SMSOLV(SMFAC(PDXC,PP),PP,CHOL) (A VECTOR WITH 3 COMPONENTS)
 .047705+.0080485i  -.064625-.0060376i    .12206-.017219i
```

FIGURE 4. (*continued*) (b) Complex case.

noted that the inertia is only defined for real symmetric matrices and complex Hermitian matrices.

An example of the use of these linkules is given in Fig. 4a for real matrices and 4b for complex matrices.‡ In Fig. 4a SMFAC and SMINV are tested with both positive definite and positive indefinite matrices. The inertia is checked against the SPEAKEASY eigenvalue command. Finally SMSOLV is tested in the solution of a system of equations. An advantage of the SPEAKEASY language form of the problem [(1/PDX)*BHOL] is that it is easy to see what is being calculated. The advantage of the SMFAC, SMSOLV approach is greater speed for large-scale problems.

Figure 4b shows how the routines work with complex symmetric matrices. The matrix is first given, the inverse is calculated two ways, and the determinant is calculated three ways. Finally, a system of equations of the form $Ax = b$ is solved two ways.

5. Hermitian Case

Matrix A is Hermitian if it is equal to its conjugate transpose ($A = A^h$). The LINKULES HMFAC, HMINV, and HMSOLV will, respectively, factor A,

---

‡SMINV uses the LINPACK routines DSIDI and ZSIDI, which allows calculation of the determinant and the inertia without the inverse. This feature has not been implemented in SPEAKEASY, and SMINV will always attempt to calculate the inverse. Thus, SMINV must not be called if SMFAC indicates the matrix is not full rank.

```
POSITIVE DEF. HERMITIAN MATRIX

  CHX (A 3 BY 3 MATRIX)
  135               51.767-10.379i    51.846-10.458i
  51.767+10.379i    125.07            51.49-9.5985i
  51.846+10.458i    51.49+9.5985i     112.2

CALCULATE INVERSE TWO WAYS
1/CHX (A 3 BY 3 MATRIX)
  .0098251          -.002644449.7797iE-4   -.003410142.4079iE-4
 -.0026444-9.7797iE-4    .010748           -.0036191+.0011248i
 -.0034101-2.4079iE-4   -.0036191-.0011248i      .012268
HMINV(HMFAC(CHX,PP),PP,DD,II) (A 3 BY 3 MATRIX)
  .0098251          -.002644449.7797iE-4   -.003410142.4079iE-4
 -.0026444-9.7797iE-4    .010748           -.0036191+.0011248i
 -.0034101-2.4079iE-4   -.0036191-.0011248i      .012268

DET(CHX) =   1149038+1.1147iE-11
DD =  1149038
PROD(EIGENVAL(CHX)) =  1149038
EIGENVAL(CHX) (A VECTOR WITH 3 COMPONENTS)
  62.715   79.716   229.83
  II (A VECTOR WITH 3 COMPONENTS)
  3   0   0

SOLUTION OF AN EQUATION SYSTEM TWO WAYS

(1/CONJ(CHX))*CHOL (A VECTOR WITH 3 COMPONENTS)
  4.1644E-4+.0077055i   -6.8805E-4+6.2526iE-4  -6.484E-4-.0018652i
HMSOLV(HMFAC(CHX,PP),PP,CHOL) (A VECTOR WITH 3 COMPONENTS)
  4.1644E-4+.0077055i   -6.8805E-4+6.2526iE-4  -6.484E-4-.0018652i

HERMITIAN NOT POSITIVE DEF. CASE

  CHX (A 3 BY 3 MATRIX)
 -135               -51.767+10.379i  -51.846+10.458i
 -51.767-10.379i    -125.07           -51.49+9.5985i
 -51.846-10.458i    -51.49-9.5985i    -112.2

CALCULATE INVERSE TWO WAYS
1/CHX (A 3 BY 3 MATRIX)
 -.0098251           .0026444-9.7797iE-4    .0034101-2.4079iE-4
  .0026444+9.7797iE-4  -.010748            .0036191-.0011248i
  .0034101+2.4079iE-4   .0036191+.0011248i      -.012268
HMINV(HMFAC(CHX,PP),PP,DD,II) (A 3 BY 3 MATRIX)
 -.0098251           .0026444-9.7797iE-4    .0034101-2.4079iE-4
  .0026444+9.7797iE-4  -.010748            .0036191-.0011248i
  .0034101+2.4079iE-4   .0036191+.0011248i      -.012268

DET(CHX) =  -1149038-1.1147iE-11
DD =  -1149038
PROD(EIGENVAL(CHX)) =  -1149038
EIGENVAL(CHX) (A VECTOR WITH 3 COMPONENTS)
 -229.83  -79.716  -62.715
  II (A VECTOR WITH 3 COMPONENTS)
  0   3   0

SOLUTION OF AN EQUATION SYSTEM TWO WAYS

(1/CONJ(CHX))*CHOL (A VECTOR WITH 3 COMPONENTS)
 -4.1644E-4-.0077055i   6.8805E-4-6.2526iE-4   6.484E-4+.0018652i
HMSOLV(HMFAC(CHX,PP),PP,CHOL) (A VECTOR WITH 3 COMPONENTS)
 -4.1644E-4-.0077055i   6.8805E-4-6.2526iE-4   6.484E-4+.0018652i
```

FIGURE 5. Hermitian matrix.

invert A using the factors of A, and solve the system of equations $A^h x = b$. Since the Hermitian LINKULES factor and solve matrix problems using the same decompositions as the symmetric LINKULES [see equations (9), (10), and (11)], this method will not be repeated here.

Figure 5 shows how these LINKULES can be used with Hermitian matrices. The first example involves the factorization and inversion of a positive definite

Hermitian matrix. The determinant is also calculated three ways: with the DET command, with HMINV, and as the product of the eigenvalues. The DET command indicates a small imaginary component that represents a rounding error. Calculation of the determinant with the other two approaches does not result in this error.† The final example involves the solution of a system of equations two ways. In the present implementation, HMSOLV will solve the system $A^h x = b$. In the future this may be changed to $Ax = b$.

The second part of Fig. 5 repeats the above test for a Hermitian matrix that is not positive definite. In this particular example the positive definite matrix was made not positive definite by changing signs. The findings are similar to those obtained earlier.

6. Triangular Matrix Case

The LINKULE TRFAC will estimate the condition of an upper or lower triangular matrix T which can be inverted directly by TRINV since it is already in factored form. The system of equations $Tx = b$ can be solved by TRSOLV. By the appropriate choice of parameters $T^t x = b$ can be solved, where T can either be upper or lower triangular. TRINV and TRSOLV are substantially faster than their SPEAKEASY language counterparts and should be used whenever the structure of the matrix is known to be triangular. An example of the use of the triangular LINKULES is given in Fig. 6. If T is lower (upper) triangular, the inverse calculated by TRINV will always have zeros in the strict upper (lower) triangle. TRFAC and TRINV will not work as intended if the matrix passed is not triangular.

7. The Singular Value Decomposition

The LINKULE SVDCM will calculate the singular value decomposition of a real or complex matrix X. If X is $n \times p$, there exists a $n \times n$ orthogonal matrix U and a $p \times p$ orthogonal matrix V and diagonal matrix S of rank r, where r is the minimum of n and p that satisfies the following equations:

$$U^h XV = S \qquad \text{if } n = p \qquad (12)$$
$$U^h XV = [S \ 0] \qquad \text{if } n < p \qquad (13)$$
$$U^h XV = \begin{vmatrix} S \\ 0 \end{vmatrix} \qquad \text{if } n > p \qquad (14)$$

---

†This error is small and arises because the DET command does not know that the determinant of a Hermitian matrix *must* be real. The product of the eigenvalues approach, although costly in computer time, is accurate due to the accuracy of the EISPACK routines used in the SPEAKEASY EIGENVAL command.

```
LOWER TRIANGULAR
  TRL (A 3 BY 3 MATRIX)
  2.9381    0        0
  1.7532    2.2234   0
  3.3696    2.9654   4.7865
TRFAC(TRL) = .16488

CALCULATE INVERSE TWO WAYS
1/TRL (A 3 BY 3 MATRIX)
   .34036    0        0
  -.26838    .44977   0
  -.073336  -.27864   .20892
TRINV(TRL,0,DD) (A 3 BY 3 MATRIX)
   .34036    0        0
  -.26838    .44977   0
  -.073336  -.27864   .20892

DET(TRL) =  31.268
DD =  31.268
EIGENVAL(TRL) (A VECTOR WITH 3 COMPONENTS)
  2.2234   2.9381   4.7865

UPPER TRIANGULAR COMPLEX
  TRU (A 3 BY 3 MATRIX)
  5.8761+1.7141i   3.5064+1.3241i   6.7392+1.8356i
  0                4.4468+1.4911i   5.9308+1.722i
  0                0                9.573+2.1878i

CALCULATE INVERSE TWO WAYS
1/TRU (A 3 BY 3 MATRIX)
  .15684-.045749i  -.12662+.031832i  -.032147+.012535i
  0                 .20215-.067786i  -.129394+.035202i
  0                 0                 .099275-.022688i
TRINV(TRU,1,DD) (A 3 BY 3 MATRIX)
  .15684-.045749i  -.12662+.031832i  -.032147+.012535i
  0                 .20215-.067786i  -.129394+.035202i
  0                 0                 .099275-.022688i

DET(TRU) =  189.83+208.42i
DD =  189.83+208.42i
EIGENVAL(TRU) (A VECTOR WITH 3 COMPONENTS)
  4.4468+1.4911i   5.8761+1.7141i   9.573+2.1878i


  BHOL (A VECTOR WITH 3 COMPONENTS)
  .35072    .84132    .071579

SOLUTION OF TWO EQUATIONS SYSTEMS TWO WAYS

(1/TRL)*BHOL (A VECTOR WITH 3 COMPONENTS)
  .11937    .28427   -.24519
TRSOLV(TRL,BHOL,0) (A VECTOR WITH 3 COMPONENTS)
  .11937    .28427   -.24519

  CHOL (A VECTOR WITH 3 COMPONENTS)
  .35261+.61073i   .47202+.81756i   .2076+.35958i

(1/TRU)*CHOL (A VECTOR WITH 3 COMPONENTS)
  -.013729-.017795i   .11132+.094058i   .028768+.030987i
TRSOLV(TRU,CHOL,1) (A VECTOR WITH 3 COMPONENTS)
  -.013729-.017795i   .11132+.094058i   .028768+.030987i
```

FIGURE 6. Triangular matrix.

If X is real, $U^h = U^t$. Since U and V are orthogonal

$$U^h U = I \qquad (15)$$
$$V^h V = I \qquad (16)$$

If X is $n \times p$, where $n > p$, X can be written in terms of U, V, and S as either

$$X = U \begin{vmatrix} S \\ 0 \end{vmatrix} V^h \qquad (17)$$

or

$$X = U_1 S V^h \tag{18}$$

where U_1 is a $n \times p$ matrix that consists of the first p columns of U. Equation (18) is called the singular value factorization of X. The use of the LINKULE SVDCM is illustrated in Fig. 7, where both the real and complex case for X is given, equations (15) and)16) are verified for U and V, and equations (12) and (17) are illustrated. The singular value decomposition is one of the most useful factorizations in linear algebra. A full discussion of its use is beyond the scope of this paper. However, its relationship with the ordinary least-squares problem will be illustrated below.

The solution of

$$Y = Xb + e \tag{19}$$

for real X can be written as

$$Y = U_1(SV'b) + e \tag{20}$$

Given that

$$a = SV^t b \tag{21}$$

the principal components regression model can be written

$$Y = U_1(SV^t b) + e \tag{22}$$
$$= U_1 a + e \tag{23}$$

The coefficients of the principal components regression model, a, become

$$\hat{a} = (U_1^t U_1)^{-1} U_1^t y \tag{24}$$

which quickly reduces to

$$\hat{a} = U_1^t y \tag{25}$$

from (15).

The ordinary least squares (OLS) coefficients b are defined in terms of a as†

$$\hat{b} = VS^{-1}a \tag{26}$$

---

†Further discussion of these relationships can be found in Ref. 7.

```
REAL CASE

   X (A 3 BY 3 MATRIX)
   .78289   .91935   .49628
   .67707   .84562   .67822
   .60125   .16231   .81948
SVDCM(X,B,11,U,V) (A VECTOR WITH 3 COMPONENTS)
  2.0163   .56587   .10811
   U (A 3 BY 3 MATRIX)
  -.63387   .45531   .62522
  -.63091   .1632   -.7585
  -.44738  -.87525   .18382
   V (A 3 BY 3 MATRIX)
  -.59139  -.10478   .79955
  -.58964   .73255  -.34013
  -.55007  -.6726   -.49501

TRANSPOSE(U)*X *V (A 3 BY 3 MATRIX)
  2.0163        -1.6653E-16   4.4409E-16
  9.7145E-17     .56587      -4.1633E-17
  1.7347E-17    5.2909E-17    .10811
TRANSPOSE(U)*U (A 3 BY 3 MATRIX)
  1             1.249E-16     1.8041E-16
  1.249E-16     1             1.3878E-17
  1.8041E-16    1.3878E-17    1
TRANSPOSE(V)*V (A 3 BY 3 MATRIX)
  1             9.7145E-17   -1.6653E-16
  9.7145E-17    1             1.6653E-16
 -1.6653E-16    1.6653E-16    1
U*DMAT(SVDCM(X,B))*TRANSPOSE(V) (A 3 BY 3 MATRIX)
   .78289   .91935   .49628
   .67707   .84562   .67822
   .60125   .16231   .81948

COMPLEX CASE

   X (A 3 BY 3 MATRIX)
  -.78289+.88481i  -.91935+.95883i  -.49628+.70447i
  -.67707+.82284i  -.84562+.91957i  -.67822+.82354i
  -.60125+.7754i   -.16231+.40287i  -.81948+.90525i
SVDCM(X,B,11,U,V) (A VECTOR WITH 3 COMPONENTS)
  3.1419   .70055   .13117
CONJ(TRANSPOSE(U))*XX*V (A 3 BY 3 MATRIX)
  3.1419                 -4.4409E-16+2.3592iE-16   1.138E-15+3.9899iE-17
 -1.3878E-17+1.249iE-16   .70055                  -1.9429E-16+1.1102iE-16
 -2.2985E-16+1.8616iE-16  5.9848E-17-6.1583iE-17   .13117
CONJ(TRANSPOSE(U))*U (A 3 BY 3 MATRIX)
  1                        1.8041E-16-3.7297iE-17   1.5266E-16+2.4286iE-17
  1.8041E-16+3.7297iE-17   1                        9.7145E-17+1.2143iE-17
  1.5266E-16-2.4286iE-17   9.7145E-17-1.2143iE-17   1
CONJ(TRANSPOSE(V))*V (A 3 BY 3 MATRIX)
  1                       -1.3878E-17              -1.5266E-16+7.8063iE-18
 -1.3878E-17               1                       -8.3267E-17
 -1.5266E-16-7.8063iE-18  -8.3267E-17               1
U*DMAT(SVDCM(X,B))*CONJ(TRANSPOSE(V)) (A 3 BY 3 MATRIX)
  -.78289+.88481i  -.91935+.95883i  -.49628+.70447i
  -.67707+.82284i  -.84562+.91957i  -.67822+.82354i
  -.60125+.7754i   -.16231+.40287i  -.81948+.90525i
```

FIGURE 7. (a) Singular value decomposition.

or in terms of y as

$$\hat{b} = VS^{-1}U_1^t y \tag{27}$$

The estimated Y vector becomes

$$\hat{Y} = U_1 a \tag{28}$$

which is also equal to Xb. From (27) we see that the generalized inverse or pseudoinverse of $X(X^+)$ can be written

```
X (A 8 BY 5 MATRIX)
1          .40629     .84046     .32939     .55149
1          .35235     .29956     .95621     .79045
1          .49887     .68631     .73514     .12922
1          .96742     .46745     .2262      .41432
1          .26837     .69493     .81605     .86621
1          .098665    .16676     .73034     .88941
1          .67904     .30149     .46835     .82392
1          .33971     .28682     .20455     .79491
Y (A VECTOR WITH 8 COMPONENTS)
.73711     .032626    .52804     .66923     .82973     .27757     .70922     .017111


OLS RESULTS
(1/(TRANSPOSE(X)*X))*TRANSPOSE(X)*Y (A VECTOR WITH 5 COMPONENTS)
-.90168    .75702    1.1578    .16165    .61295

TEST FACTORIZATION   S=SVDCM(X,B,21,U1,V)    (SEE EQ 18)

U1*DMAT(S)*TRANSPOSE(V) (A 8 BY 5 MATRIX)
1          .40629     .84046     .32939     .55149
1          .35235     .29956     .95621     .79045
1          .49887     .68631     .73514     .12922
1          .96742     .46745     .2262      .41432
1          .26837     .69493     .81605     .86621
1          .098665    .16676     .73034     .88941
1          .67904     .30149     .46835     .82392
1          .33971     .28682     .20455     .79491

COMPUTE PRINCIPLE COMPONENT COEFFICIENTS A FROM EQ 25

TRANSPOSE(U1)*Y (A VECTOR WITH 5 COMPONENTS)
-1.3595     .46661   -.16407   -.20835     .40972

CALCULATE THE OLS COEFFICIENT VECTOR USING EQ 27

V*(1/DMAT(S))     *   TRANSPOSE(U1)*Y (A VECTOR WITH 5 COMPONENTS)
-.90168    .75702    1.1578    .16165    .61295

DEFINE A=TRANSPOSE(U1)*Y AND B =V*(1/DMAT(S))*A

   A (A VECTOR WITH 5 COMPONENTS)
-1.3595     .46661   -.16407   -.20835     .40972

   B (A VECTOR WITH 5 COMPONENTS)
-.90168    .75702    1.1578    .16165    .61295

   COMPARE THE PREDICTED VALUES   (SEE EQUATION 28)

U1*A (A VECTOR WITH 8 COMPONENTS)
.77026     .35097     .46864     .66243     .76895     .029322    .54217     .20788

X*B (A VECTOR WITH 8 COMPONENTS)
.77026     .35097     .46864     .66243     .76895     .029322    .54217     .20788
```

FIGURE 7. (*continued*) (b) Use of the SVDCM command in regression problems.

$$X^+ = VS^{-1}U_1^t \tag{29}$$

Figure 7b shows an example of the use of the SVDCM LINKULE to solve problems in regression analysis. First an X matrix is defined and a dependent variable y is listed. The SPEAKEASY language is used to calculate the OLS solution, vector b. The singular value factorization of X [see equation (18)] is calculated and tested. Using this factorization, the OLS coefficient vector b is calculated [see equation (27)], and the principal component solution a is calculated [see equation (25)]. Both coefficient vectors $\hat{a}$ and $\hat{b}$ are shown [using equation (28) and the relationship $Xb = y$] to generate the same predicted y vector.

8. The QR Factorization

If X is a $n \times p$ matrix, where n is greater than or equal to p and y is a $n \times 1$ vector, the OLS solution to the model given in equation (19) $\hat{b}$ is defined as

$$\hat{b} = (X'X)^{-1}X'y \tag{30}$$

Rather than explicitly calculating $X'X$, X can be factored directly into an orthogonal $n \times n$ matrix Q and an upper triangular matrix R such that

$$Q^t x = \begin{vmatrix} R \\ 0 \end{vmatrix} \tag{31}$$

Since $Q'X$ has zeros below the diagonal, we can partition $Q = (Q_1, Q_2)$, where Q_1 is $n \times p$. Then X and $\hat{b}$ can be written

$$X = Q_1 R \tag{32}$$
$$\hat{b} = (X'X)^{-1}X'y = (R'Q_1'Q_1 R)^{-1}R'Q_1'y \tag{33}$$
$$= (R'R)^{-1}R'Q_1'y \tag{34}$$
$$= R^{-1}Q_1'y \tag{35}$$

The LINKULE QRFAC will form the factorization in equation (32) and the LINKULE QRSOLV will form the coordinate transforms using the output from QRFAC. Various outputs are available that include the residuals of the model given in equation (19), the coefficients (b) of (19), the n-element vector Qy, the n-element vector $Q'y$, and the n-element vector of predicted y values Xb. Figure 8 gives an example of the use of QRFAC and QRSOLV for real and complex cases. QRSOLVE uses the LINPACK routines DQRSL and ZQRSL, which optionally have a pivoting option. The present implementation of LINPACK in SPEAKEASY does not allow pivoting. In the future, additional LINKULES may be written to allow the use of this option.

9. Other Useful Routines

ZEROU, ZEROL, PL1FORT, and FORTPL1 are LINKULES that were developed to utilize the BLAS to perform various utility functions connected with the other LINPACK LINKULES. For example, ZEROL will zero out the lower triangle or the strict lower triangle of a matrix, while ZEROU will zero out the upper triangle or the strict upper triangle of the matrix. FORTPL1 will change the storage convention of a matrix from by columns to by rows, while PL1FORT

```
OLS PROBLEMS DONE IN REAL AND COMPLEX DOMAIN
USING OLS COMMAND, FORMING XPX AND THE QR METHOD.

ORDINARY LEAST SQUARES REGRESSION

THE DEPENDENT VARIABLE IS  Y 1

INDEPENDENT VARIABLES...

NAME     COL   COEFFICIENT   STD ERROR   T-STATISTIC   SIGNIFICANCE
------   ---   -----------   ---------   -----------   ------------
X         1     .592384       .45904       1.2905        23.787
X         2     .153253       .44957        .34088       74.319
X         3    -.169466       .45657       -.37117       72.149

F-STATISTIC( 2, 7)= .21454       SIGNIFICANCE LEVEL OF F = 81.203

R-SQUARED = .05776                 CORRECTED R-SQUARED =-.2115
R-SQUARED FOR REGRESSION THROUGH ORIGIN =  .76824
NUMBER-OF-OBSERVATIONS=  10
SUM-OF-SQUARED-RESIDUALS=  1.0525
STANDARD-ERROR-OF-REGRESSION=  .38776
DURBIN-WATSON-STATISTIC=  2.5868


QRSOLV(QRFAC(X,PIVOT),PIVOT,Y,BAD,QTY,RES,YHAT) (A VECTOR WITH 3 COMPONENTS)
  .592383503959648   .153252700291641  -.169466273249361


          X          Y       FITTED    RESID      RES      YHAT
     ****************  ********  *******  ********  ********  *******
   1  .92779  .91758   .75421   .57907    .17514    .17514   .57907
   1  .30357  .85623   .092342  .4938    -.40146   -.40146   .4938
   1  .71704  .012197  .77233   .70021    .072123   .072123  .70021
   1  .65942  .26309   .81779   .64886    .16893    .16893   .64886
   1  .11637  .83133   .53958   .46934    .070246   .070246  .46934
   1  .99081  .59803   .91845   .64288    .27557    .27557   .64288
   1  .55077  .59682   .91669   .57565    .34104    .34104   .57565
   1  .48321  .792     .034141  .53222   -.49808   -.49808   .53222
   1  .19656  .6699    .83206   .50898    .32308    .32308   .50898
   1  .94118  .21075   .17432   .70091   -.52659   -.52659   .70091


(1/(TRANSPOSE(X)*X))*TRANSPOSE(X)*Y (A VECTOR WITH 3 COMPONENTS)
  .592383503959647   .153252700291642  -.169466273249359

COMPLEX CASE

QRSOLV(QRFAC(X,PIVOT),PIVOT,Y,BAD,QTY,RES,YHAT) (A VECTOR WITH 3 COMPONENTS)
  .16096178921037+15.7772149972784i     .328869581225175-6.74286220584952i
  .416363298895709-9.03705656708509i

(1/(CONJ(TRANSPOSE(X))*X))*CONJ(TRANSPOSE(X))*Y (A VECTOR WITH 3 COMPONENTS)
  .160961731651528+15.7772089934007i     .328869551224656-6.7428651884831i
  .41636326778454-9.03705962104546i
```

FIGURE 8. QR factorization.

will change the storage convention from by rows (the normal SPEAKEASY convention) to by columns. If the matrix is square, PL1FORT and FORTPL1 are equivalent to the TRANSPOSE LINKULE. If the matrix is not square, they are not equivalent since the number of rows and the number of columns are *not* changed in PL1FORT and FORTPL1. In the LINPACK LINKULES, FORTPL1 will allow a SPEAKEASY user to display a matrix that is stored by columns. An example would be the output from LINKULE QRFAC, which is usually only an intermediate step. SPEAKEASY allows direct calls to FORTRAN routines via the LINKULE FORTSUB and FORTFUN, provided the FORTRAN routines have been compiled and stored as load modules with all references resolved.

In this application, PL1FORT and FORTPL1 are not required, since TRANSPOSE can be used. However, use of PL1FORT and FORTPL1 facilitates transparency of programming, since the number of rows and columns of the matrix recorded in named storage remains unchanged, although the storage convention has been altered. Figure 9 gives an example of the use of these LINKULES.

10. Future Work

Possible changes in the SPEAKEASY LINPACK LINKULES include improvements in the complex versions of PDSOLV, HMSOLV, PDFACUD, and PDFACDD. Additional LINKULES are contemplated to solve systems of equations involving tridiagonal matrices and to factor, invert, and solve systems of equations involving band matrices. Finally, if there is interest, it might be useful to implement a routine to allow an update of a Cholesky factorization after a symmetric permutation of its rows and columns.

```
 X  (A 3 BY 4 MATRIX)
 1     2     3     4
 5     6     7     8
 9    10    11    12

 PL1FORT(X)  (A 3 BY 4 MATRIX)
 1     5     9     2
 6    10     3     7
11     4     8    12

 FORTPL1(X)  (A 3 BY 4 MATRIX)
 1     4     7    10
 2     5     8    11
 3     6     9    12


 X  (A 4 BY 4 MATRIX)
 .9557     .48732    .08084    .81328
 .11055    .025069   .17532    .82377
 .90908    .32307    .10907    .3084
 .58711    .60032    .16617    .017061

 ZEROL(X)  (A 4 BY 4 MATRIX)
 .9557     .48732    .08084    .81328
 0         .025069   .17532    .82377
 0         0         .10907    .3084
 0         0         0         .017061

 ZEROL(X,1)  (A 4 BY 4 MATRIX)
 0         .48732    .08084    .81328
 0         0         .17532    .82377
 0         0         0         .3084
 0         0         0         0

 ZEROU(X)  (A 4 BY 4 MATRIX)
 .9557     0         0         0
 .11055    .025069   0         0
 .90908    .32307    .10907    0
 .58711    .60032    .16617    .017061

 ZEROU(X,1)  (A 4 BY 4 MATRIX)
 0         0         0         0
 .11055    0         0         0
 .90908    .32307    0         0
 .58711    .60032    .16617    0
```

FIGURE 9. Utility routines.

SPEAKEASY began as a super desk calculator, was given the ablity to store and execute programs, and in recent years has undergone addition of applications LINKULES such as FEDEASY. As computer time decreases in price, many new procedures may be implemented in the SPEAKEASY language. The LINPACK LINKULES will be useful in this application and in testing and verification operations in SPEAKEASY in the manual mode. Any suggestions for improvements in these LINKULES are welcome.

ACKNOWLEDGMENTS

Computer time for this study was supplied by the Computer Center of the University of Illinois. Diana Stokes provided editorial assistance. Any remaining errors are my responsibility.

Appendix

The extract from the SPEAKEASY LINPACK Document given below shows the relationship between the LINPACK LINKULES and the LINPACK Manual. Further documentation for each LINKULE can be obtained via the SPEAKEASY HELP command.

A. GKeneral matrix (Chapter 1)

–GMFAC	– Compute condition and LU factorization.
–GMINV	– Computer inverse and optionally determinant using factors from GMFAC.
–GMSOLV	– Uses factors from GMFAC to solve system transpose(A) * X = B or A * X = B

B. Positive Definite Matrix (Chapter 3)

–PDFAC	– Factor and estimate condition of matrix (Cholesky Decomposition)
–PDINV	– Compute inverse and optionally determinant using factors computed by PDFAC.
–PDSOLV	– Use factors from PDFAC to solve system A * X = B
–PDFACUD	– Update Cholesky factorization from PDFAC
–PDFACDD	– Downdate Cholesky factorization from PDFAC

C. Symmetric Matrix (Chapter 5)

–SMFAC	– Factor and estimate condition of matrix
–SMINV	– Compute inverse and optionally inertia and determinant using factors from SMFAC.

–SMSOLV   – Uses factors from SMFAC to solve system of linear
                     equations.
D. Hermitian Matrix (Chapter 5)
–HMFAC   – Factor and estimate condition of matrix.
–HMINV   – Compute inverse and optionally determinate using factors
                     from HMFAC.
–HMSOLV   – Uses factors from HMFAC to solve system of linear
                     equations.
E. Triangular Matrix (Chapter 6)
–TRFAC   – Estimate condition of matrix.
–TRINV   – Compute inverse and optionally determinant.
–TRSOLV   – Solve triangular linear system of form $T * X = B$ or trans-
                     pose$(T) * X = B$
F. Singular Value Decomposition (Chapter 11)
–SVDCM   – Compute right singular values and optionally left and/or
                     right singular vectors.
G. QR Decomposition (Chapter 9)
–QRFAC   – Computer QR decomposition of an N by P matrix.
–QRSOLV   – Use the output of QRFAC to compute coordinate transform,
                     projections and least squares solutions.
H. Useful Routines
–ZEROL   – Zero out strict lower triangle of a matrix or array or option-
                     ally lower triangle.
–ZEROU   – Zero out strict upper triangle of a matrix or array or option-
                     ally upper triangle.
–PL1FORT   – Alter storage from by rows to by columns.
–FORTPL1   – Alter storage from by columns to by rows.

References

1. S. Cohen and S. Pieper, *The SPEAKEASY III Reference Manual,* Speakeasy Computer Corporation, Chicago, Illinois, 1980.
2. J. J. Dongarra, C. B. Moler, J. R. Bunch, and G. W. Stewart, *LINPACK User's Guide,*
   SIAM, Philadelphia, 1979.
3. G. Strang, *Linear Algebra and Its Applications,* Academic Press, New York, 1976.
4. J. M. Wilkinson and C. Reinsch, Eds., *Handbook for Automatic Computation II, Linear Algebra,* Springer, Berlin, 1971.
5. C. Lawson, R. Hanson, D. Kincaid, and F. Krogh, Basic linear algebra subprograms for
   fortran usage, *ACM Trans. Math. Software* **5**(3), 308–371 (1979).
6. *SPEAKEASY Manual: Supplementary Help Documents, Level Pi:* Speakeasy Computer Corporation, Chicago, Illinois, 1982. (1982).
7. J. Mandel, Use of the singular value decomposition in regression analysis, *Am. Statistician*
   36(1), 15–24 (1982).

25

THE CORPORATE PROVISIONING PLAN
A SYSTEMS APPROACH

Samir Chakraborty

1. Introduction

The prime task of a corporation's management is clearly the act of efficiently and effectively marshalling the *resources* of the corporation. This in turn results in the prime ongoing managerial effort being to *manage* corporate strategic constraints.

We define this effort as the corporate strategic management process, a key element of which is managing *cost* constraints. This in itself is a problem-solving activity defined as the corporate provisioning planning process. It is an integral part of and closely intertwined with the corporate strategic management process.

Three basic general systems concepts underlie our approach to the corporate provisioning planning process. The concept of the generalized managerial problem solving methodology is used to model and structure the generic elements of both the corporate strategic management process and the corporate provisioning planning process.

The concept of the process hierarchy framework is used to model and structure the information used in the two processes. These models are embedded in software and used for simulation during various stages of the corporate provisioning planning process.

Finally, the concept of the corporate strategic management process is used to model, structure, and define the specific elements and dynamics of the corporate provisioning planning process.

During both processes, once the relevant information has been structured using the *process hierarchy framework,* with simulation techniques, it is possible

SAMIR CHAKRABORTY • Consultant—Strategic Planning, Telecom Canada, 410 Laurier Ave. W., Suite 310A, Ottawa, Ontario K1P 6H5, Canada.

to pretest many alternative provisioning plans in searching for the most advantageous cost management opportunities.

Section 2 reviews the relevant general systems concepts. Section 3 reviews the main steps in the *process,* briefly outlines the *hierarchic information structures* used in the corporate provisioning planning process, and the information structure design considerations, Section 4 outlines the structure of the annual corporate provisioning plan, and Section 5 presents some conclusions.

2. Relevant General Systems Concepts

2.1. The Hierarchy of Epistemological Levels of Systems

Relevant information concerning the corporate strategic management process and the corporate provisioning planning process is modeled, structured, and simulated using the process hierarchy framework, which is based on the hierarchy of epistemological levels (e-levels) of systems.[17] This concept of the hierarchy of e-levels is based on the theory that any object of interest (automobile, planning process, the brain, a computer system, etc.) can be viewed by an examiner at different selected levels of knowledge (e-level) about it.

Thus, a given object of interest may be defined/described by a hierarchy of systems based on the levels of knowledge one wishes to view the object at (see Table 1). A higher e-level system entails all knowledge of the corresponding systems at any lower e-level and contains some additional knowledge which is not available at the lower e-levels.

2.2. The Generalized Managerial Hierarchy of Epistemological Levels of Systems

The hierarchy of e-levels of systems when applied to an organization/company/process in a general managerial context is redefined as in Table 2.[3-7]

TABLE 1
The Hierarchy of Epistemological Levels of Systems

Epistemological level (e-level)	System name
0	Source system
1	Data system
2	Generative system
3	Structure system
4	Metasystem
5	Meta-metasystem

TABLE 2
The Generalized Managerial Hierarchy of e-Levels of Systems

e-level	System name	Contents of system set
0	Source	Variables, space-time resolution level
1	Data	Source systems, activity matrix
2	Micro	Data systems, time-invariant relations/generating behavior
3	Functional	Microsystems, coupling variables/relations
4	Operation—I	Functional systems, managerial system-I
X	Operation—Y	Operation—(Y-1) systems, managerial system—(Y)

The managerial system defined on the process/company at an e-level is defined as the set consisting generally of the following two subsets of management information: The first subset (   ) generally represents the relatively time-invariant/"static" dimensions of the managerial system. The second subset (   ) generally represents the relatively time-variant/"dynamic" dimensions of the managerial system.

At any given e-level beyond 3, an operational system set can be defined as = ((lower e-level system), managerial system).

2.3. The Process Hierarchy Framework

The concept of the generalized managerial hierarchy of epistemological levels of systems when applied to any company results in the definition of the company using a framework based on the hierarchy of processes within the company.

The process hierarchy framework[3-7] can take on various forms depending on the problem-solving application[6-15] one is interested in. This section shows the process hierarchy framework in its role for the corporate information structure (Table 3).

2.4. The Corporate Information Structure

2.4.1. Logical Structure. The process hierarchy framework is used to model, structure, simulate, and communicate the information during the corporate strategic management process. It is described as in Table 3.

2.4.2. Information Set—Contents. The contents of the corporate information structure set at a given process hierarchy level/structure level is defined, generally, by two subsets:

a. Unit-names subset;
b. Unit-description subset.

TABLE 3
Process Hierarchy Framework: Corporate Information Structure

Process hierarchy level	Unit/set name	Contents of information set at given structure level
0	STEP	Function, STEP Description
1	METHOD	STEPS, METHOD Description
2	PROCEDURE	METHODS, PROCEDURE Description
3	SUBSYSTEM	PROCEDURES, SUBSYSTEM Description
4	SYSTEM	SUBSYSTEMS, SYSTEM Description
5	PROCESS	SYSTEMS, PROCESS Description
6	COMPANY	PROCESSES, COMPANY Description

The unit-names subset is a collection of descriptive names or phrases, one for each of the units, which are the building blocks at the given process hierarchy structure level, of the larger unit.

The unit-descriptions subsets at a given structure level are broadly catgorized to consist of two subsets each:

- Static information subset;
- Dynamic information subset.

2.4.2.1. Static Information Subset. The static information subset of the unit description set generally consists of the categories of information (or subsets), regarding the *unit* at a given structure level as described in Table 4.

2.4.2.2. Dynamic Information Subset. The dynamic information subset of the unit-descriptions set generally consists of the categories of information (or subsets) regarding the *unit* at a given structure level as described in Table 5.

2.5. The Generalized Managerial Problem-Solving Methodology

The next concept is that of the generalized managerial problem-solving methodology.[1,2] The problem-solving focus on the "object" of our interest requires the integrated application of two disciplines:

a. A systematic, manageable, complete, and efficient way of attacking the problem/"object" of our interest.
b. A createable, available, reliable, and maintainable framework for storing information regarding the problem/"object" of our interest.

Given the existence of item (b), which is described in Section 2.4, the main activity steps in the generalized managerial problem-solving methodology are briefly summarized in Table 6.

TABLE 4
Static Information Set: Corporate Information Structure

General introduction	Sequence schematic
Goals	Key decisions, measurements
Markets	Key planning areas
Products/services	Key results area
Objectives	Key activity cycles
Strategies	Approvals and controls
Budgets	Results
Subunits, building blocks for	Organization structure
Main functions	References to operating
Functions relationship	Information sources

TABLE 5
Dynamic Information Set: Corporate Information
Structure

Operating unit objectives	Unit results
Operating unit organization	Unit constraint
Structure	Resolution areas
Unit budget	Unit job description(s)
Unit work program	Unit notes
Unit manpower plans	Unit references

TABLE 6
Conceptual Model Relationship: Process Activity Steps

Generalized managerial problem-solving methodology	Corporate strategic management process
	Strategic planning:
(1) Preliminary analysis	(1) Develop future scenarios
(2) Synthesis	(2) Determine corporate issues
(3) Analysis	(3) Develop strategic direction for the corporation
(4) (a) Constraint identification and minimization (performance of) (b) Design modification and test	(4) Develop detailed strategies/plan recommendations and alternatives for implementing strategic direction
	Strategic decision making:
(5) Constraint identification and minimization (finalization of)	(5) Decision making on recommendtions
	Strategic implementation:
(6) Implementation	(6) Implementation of recommendations
(7) Monitoring and maintenance	(7) Maintenance and monitoring

2.6. The Corporate Strategic Management Process

The generalized managerial problem-solving methodology is used as the model for defining the corporate strategic management process.[10] The corporate strategic management process is viewed as a macro-problem-solving activity focusing on the corporation as a whole, and its activity steps are as shown in Table 6.[10]

3. The Corporate Provisioning Planning Process

3.1. General

The corporate provisioning planning process is a key component of the corporate strategic management process and focuses on the provisioning *costs* of the corporation. In a grossly simplified sense, managing the *costs* of the corporation is one of the ultimate measures of management performance.

3.2. The Provisioning Planning Process

The specific model, structure, and operational dynamics of the corporate provisioning planning process (see Table 7) are directly derived from that of the corporate strategic management process and its activity steps are as briefly summarized in Table 7.

TABLE 7
Structure and Logical Equivalency[a]

Corporate strategic management process	Corporate provisioning planning process
Strategic planning:	*Planning:*
(1) Develop future scenarios	(1) Develop provisioning environment scenarios
(2) Determine corporate issues	(2) Determine provisioning issues
(3) Develop strategic direction for the corporation	(3) Develop strategic provisioning direction for the corporation
(4) Develop detailed corporate strategies/ plan recommendations	(4) Develop detailed provisioning strategies/plan recommendations
Strategic decision making:	*Decision making:*
(5) Decision making on recommendations	(5) Setting specific provisioning targets, and plans to be executed
Strategic implementation:	*Implementation:*
(6) Implementation of recommendations	(6) Communication and initiation of implementation of the provisioning plan
(7) Maintenance and monitoring	(7) Monitoring, reporting, controlling the overall provisioning plan implementation

[a]Both processes are highly dynamic, interactive, iterative, formal/informal, nonsequential, and use simulation models for impact/contingency analysis.

TABLE 8

The Market Information Structure—Hierarchy: Revenue Model

Residential market:
   Metropolitan sector:
      Submetro segment:
         Customers by location:
           Specific customers:

   Nonmetropolitan sector:

Business market:
   Resource sector:

   Construction sector:

   Manufacturing sector:
     See Table 9 for more detail.
   ---------------------------- etc

3.3. Provisioning Planning Information Structures

The information structures used for key parts of the process during the modeling and computer simulation activities are derived from one or more elements of the process hierarchy framework—static information sets and dynamic information sets as shown by the following examples. They are finally integrated in the corporate financial plan as shown by the *hierarchy merge* in Table 14.

Thus, the *revenue forecast model* uses the hierarchies of *markets* (Tables 8, 9) and the hierarchies of the *products/services* (Tables 10 and 11) to structure its revenue information and perform simulation runs. Among the many simulation variables in this *highly complex* model are net/main station gain, inward/outward movement, intra/inter toll messages, general economic/demographic factors, revenues by market segmentation *and* product/services hierarchies, etc.

The *expense budget* model (Table 13) uses the ZBB (zero base budget) concept applied to the *costs* of the *organizational elements* of the process hierarchy framework defined on the company. The hierarchy of "decision units" and their "increments" for the ZBB applications match the process hierarchy based organization structure of the company. The cost simulation variables include: manpower, salaries, traveling, miscellaneous expenses, loadings, productivity improvement programs and their savings impact, inflation, etc.

The *construction (capital) budget* costs model (Table 12) use the ZBB concept in addition to portfolio management applied to the product/service elements of the static information set and the dynamic information set of the process hierarchy framework defined on the company. The resulting hierarchy of "decision units" and "increments" of the construction budget is actually the hierarchy

TABLE 9
Business Market—Manufacturing Sector—Hierarchy: Revenue Model

Business market:
  Manufacturing sector:
    Food and beverage segment:
      Meat and beverage subsegment:
        Customer's Ottawa/region X:
          Specific customer name and characteristics:

      Fish products subsegment:

      Fruit and vegetable products subsegment:

      Dairy products subsegment:

      Feed products subsegment:

      ------------------------- etc.

defined by projects, programs (and phases), estimates, jobs, work orders, etc. The simulation variables include the construction budget programs by category: basic growth, growth, discretionary, contract, contingency for the various classes of plant: station, loops, switching, facilities, data, special services, general equipment. This is also cross-indexed by key planning area and product/service segmentation hierarchy. Further, simulations for risk analysis use EPS, NPV, PWAC, Benefit Index, etc., variables.

In setting up the *corporate budget model* (Table 14), the hierarchy of the expense budget is matched with that of the construction budget requirements and "other" revenue and expense items. The simulation variables include the various budget variables and other income statement, balance sheet, use of funds, cash flow and financial planning variables (including debt/equity, payout ratio, etc.).

Thus, the models based on the process hierarchy framework provide a well-connected *hierarchy merge* and powerful mechanism (Table 14) for viewing via *simulations,* the inherent interrelationships between the many different causal elements that define the *costs* of the corporation.

3.4. Corporate Information Structure Software-Design Considerations

In this section we briefly highlight the key factors that influence the design of the simulation software for the corporate provisioning planning process. The traditional descriptions of the database structure, programming concepts and other important software principles that apply are not rehashed here.

TABLE 10
The Services/Products Information Structure—Hierarchy: Revenue Model

Business—information handling:
  Business group—telecommunications:
    Group services—toll:

    Group services—terminals:
      Service/product families—single access terminals:
        ----------------------------------- etc.

      Service/product families—multiple access terminals:
        Service/product lines—large terminal systems:
          Product—PABX System A1 (See Table 11)
          ------------------------ etc.
      -- etc.
-- etc.

TABLE 11
Large Terminal Systems—Product and Feature Hierarchy: Revenue Model

	PABX System A1	PABX System A2
System:		
Technology:		
System size features:		

Console features:		

Station instrument types:		
--------------------- etc.		
Special instruments:		
Key systems:		
Electronic instruments:		
------------------------ etc.		
Station operating features:		

Traffic analysis, control and routing features:		
------------------------ etc.		
Common equipment and control features:		

------------------------ etc.		
--- etc.		

TABLE 12
The Construction Budget: Costs Hierarchy (Capital Related)

Construction budget:
  Basic growth programs:
    Station equipment programs:
      Routine estimates:
        Routine jobs:
          Routine work orders:
            Green sheets:
      Specific estimates:
        Specific jobs:
          Specific work orders:
            Green sheets:
    Switching equipment programs:

    Loops equipment programs:

    Facilities equipment programs:

    General equipment programs:

    Building and land programs:

  Major growth programs:

  Discretionary programs:

  Contract programs:

  Contingency programs:

  Expense programs:

3.4.1. Users' and Designers' Needs. The operational software design of the process hierarchy framework based corporate information structure and its various elements has to meet the requirements of both the users and the designers.

Thus, in general, this process hierarchy framework, which is the basis of our corporate provisioning planning information structure, satisfies the following criteria:

1. Is universal, unrestricted, and compatible with "any" language;
2. Allows "all" information regarding the company/process to be included;
3. Allows various levels of knowledge to be expressed "fully" and "accurately";

4. Represents the hierarchical nature of the information generating mechanisms;
5. Allows synthesis and analysis to be performed on the information contained in it.

Specifically, the *users* require that the information structure be capable of

a. Describing different organizational and managerial dimensions;
b. Varying the formats of inputs and outputs;
c. Varying the number and type of variables in the structure; and
d. Allowing for the access, use and update (addition/deletion of discrete subsets of the information structure.

The needs of the *designers* (software) focus on the ability to

1. Design and operate components/subsets of the information structure independently;
2. Add/modify/delete components/subsets to the information structure without having to redesign the whole.

3.4.2. Constraints on Information Contents. The need the users and designers (software) have in common is the ability to change with ease the scope and depth of the corporate information structure. This ability to say "expand/contract" the

TABLE 13
The Expense Budget Hierarchy (People Related)

Company:
  Division:
    Departments:
     Sections:
      Groups:
       Decision units:
        Individuals:
         Salaries expenses:
         Traveling expenses:
         Miscellaneous expenses:

Division:

Subsidiaries:

TABLE 14
The Corporate Financial Plan: Revenue—Cost Hierarchy Merge[a]

Income statement and balance sheet:
   Corporate budget:
      Expense budget:
      Construction budget:
      Other expenses:
   Revenue forecasts:
   Financing plan:
      Source and use of funds:
      Debt:
      Equity:
      Etc.

[a]The financial hierarchy merge is a key part of the corporate business plan/ corporate strategic plan.

corporate information structure is a function of the following constraints on the information contents:

  a. Controlling the number of variables that have to be described;
  b. Controlling the number of coupling relationships between subsets;
  c. Ensuring that subsets describe complete functional relationships and do not share them between subsets; and
  d. Ensuring that the number of subsets that have to be activated to describe one subset is limited.

These constraints are of prime importance to the users, who in fact determine the scope and depth of the information required. Depending on the judgement applied, both the design and the use of the corporate information structure can be made simple or complex.

3.4.3. Software Design Guidelines. Given the users'/designers' needs and the constraints on information contents, the following are some of the prime thrusts and guidelines to be used during the design of the software for the corporate information structure:

(a) Proper definition of components/subsets that will define the boundaries of the Names and Descriptions subsets. This activity is not merely a question of asking users what subsets they can do without, because they may tend to over- or understate their requirements and not anticipate their own future needs. It is in fact a highly focused activity where one initially searches for a minimal number of subsets and then for the minimal number of incremental subsets that will describe the information structure.

(b) Identifying, separating, and codifying those portions of subsets or subsets themselves that are relatively time-variant and time-invariant. This allows for the isolation of the relatively time-variant portions or subsets and for the design of well-defined interfaces between these subsets and the rest. This results in some loss of structure generality but enables the structure to be a lot more efficient in its operation and modification for specific application.

(c) Using an access/use instruction set and variables in the Names and Descriptions subsets that in fact make the information structure appear "virtual" to its users.

(d) Defining components/subsets of the information structure such that

- They can be invoked and used independently of one another;
- They are hierarchically ordered where each level of the hierarchy provides testable and usable subsets; this is in fact assured by the use of the process hierarchy framework which uses the rules that
  1. Level 0 contains the subsets that use no other subsets (e.g., the STEP);
  2. Level i ($i \geq 1$) contains the subsets/components that use at least one subset at level i-1 and no subset at a level higher than i-1;
- Subsets (X) use other subsets (Y) under the conditions that
  1. Subset X is essentially simpler than subset Y, which it uses;
  2. Subset Y is not significantly more complex because it is not allowed to use subset X;
  3. There is a useful subset containing subset Y and not subset X;
  4. There is no subset containing subset X and not subset Y.

(e) Testing the subsets for completeness and logical consistency while aiming for their minimal number.

4. The Corporate Provisioning Plan

The main output document of the corporate provisioning planning process is the annual corporate provisioning plan. This plan[16] in general covers a 5-year planning period, of which years 1 and 2 are described in full detail and years 3, 4, 5 in some detail. Longer-term considerations or specific provisioning planning issues are described in provisioning planning memorandum which are issued as required.

The annual corporate provisioning plan is evaluated closely and then approved by the executive, and forms a key input to the financial and strategic plans of the corporation. It is the prime policy guideline document for management of corporate provisioning *costs,* and is updated quarterly.

4.1. Provisioning Plan Structure

The main structure of the corporate provisioning plan is as follows:

A. *GENERAL*
   1. *Plan Objective*
      Describes the corporate objectives that the plan is aimed at during the planning period. These objectives can and do change from time to time and result in a refocusing of corporate provisioning planning strategies.
   2. *Plan Content*
      Describes the structure and layout of the provisioning plan including key aspects of each section and subsection within it.

B. *PROVISIONING OVERVIEW*
   Describes in summary form each of the forecasts for revenues, operating expenses, and construction capital. In addition, the essential causal linkages are highlighted between the three forecasted elements.
   1. *Revenues*
      Describes the overview of the forecasts of revenues from the local, intra-toll, inter-toll, etc. businesses, derived from the corporate marketing plan and other documents.
   2. *Operating Expenses*
      Describes the overview of the forecasts of operating expenses covering items such as salaries, traveling, miscellaneous, benefits, maintenance expenses, depreciation, rents, etc.
   3. *Capital*
      Describes the overview of the forecasts of construction capital requirements covering major categories of expenditures in current and constant dollars, impact of accounting changes, etc.

C. *EXPENSE PLANNING*
   Describes the details of the expense planning assumptions, issues, strategies, forecasts and plans.
   1. *Summary*
   2. *Assumptions*
   3. *Issues Analysis*
   4. *Strategies and Substrategies*
   5. *Forecasts—General and Specific*
   6. *Specific Plans*

D. *CAPITAL PLANNING*
   Describes the details of the capital planning for the construction budget, and covers assumptions, issues, strategies, forecasts, and plans.
   1. *Summary*

      2. *Assumptions*
      3. *Issues Analysis*
      4. *Strategies and Substrategies*
      5. *Forecasts—General and Specific*
      6. *Specific Plans—Basic Growth Category*
      7. *Specific Plans—Growth Programs Category*
      8. *Specific Plans—Contract Programs Category*

E. *KEY PLANNING AREA ANALYSIS*

Describes the analysis of the operating expenses and the construction capital budget in terms of their *integrated* corporate bottom-line impact. This is achieved by creating "portfolios" of expenditures of both the expense and capital variety and analyzing their sensitivity to various underlying factors such as demand, inflation, staff levels, pre-set budget levels, etc. and evaluating the contribution of the various portfolios to earnings per share, return on investment, etc.

F. *RECOMMENDATIONS*

Describes the recomended portfolio of expenditures (costs) given corporate assumptions, forecast revenues, staff levels, etc.

G. *APPENDICES*

Describes the various inputs and supporting documents that underlie or guide the development of the provisioning plan.

5. *Conclusions*

The corporate provisioning planning process is a key part of the corporate strategic managment process of a corporation. Its focus is the costs of the corporation.

Three general systems concepts *among others* enable us to *better* model, simulate, analyze, and manage this process. These concepts impact the process design, its dynamics, information structures and software design, allocation of responsibilities, inputs/outputs, etc.

These concepts are

    a. The generalized managerial problem-solving methodology;
    b. The process hierarchy framework; and
    c. The corporate strategic management process.

These concepts have been selectively applied to modeling and *simulating* other corporate management activities including strategic planning, financial planning, organization redesign and change, market planning, budgeting, hardware systems design, etc., in a midsized, capital/technology-intensive Canadian telecommunications company since 1977.

References

1. S. CHAKRABORTY, A managerial problem solving methodology, in G. J. Klir, Ed., *Applied General Systems Research,* Plenum Press, New York, 1977.
2. S. CHAKRABORTY, Preliminary analysis in managerial problem solving, in F. Pichler, Ed., *Progress in Cybernetics and Systems Research,* Vol. VII, Hemisphere Publishing, Washington, D.C., 1978.
3. S. CHAKRABORTY, A hierarchy theoretic approach to structure management information, *Proceedings—International Computer Symposium—1978.* The Chinese Academy of Sciences, Taipei, Republic of China, 1978.
4. S. CHAKRABORTY, A process hierarchy framework for management information systems design, *Proceedings—12th Hawaii International Conference on Systems Science,* Honolulu, Hawaii, 1979.
5. S. CHAKRABORTY, Information structures for management process problem solving, *Proceedings—15th IEEE International Conference On Communications,* IEEE Press, New York, 1979.
6. S. CHAKRABORTY, Why managers avoid planning and what top management can do about it, *Planning Rev.* 7(3), 17–19, 34, 35 May (1979).
7. S. CHAKRABORTY, Hierarchic information structure design for management process problem solving, in R. F. Erricson, Ed., *Improving the Human Condition: Quality and Stability in Social Systems,* Springer-Verlag, New York 1979.
8. S. CHAKRABORTY, A general systems approach to redesigning corporate organization structures, in B. H. Banathy, Ed., *Systems Science and Science,* SGSR Press, Louisville, 1980.
9. S. CHAKRABORTY, The strategic planning process: A general systems approach, in Trappl, Hanika, and Tomlinson, Eds., *Progress in Cybernetics and Systems Research,* Vol. X, Hemisphere Publishing, Washington, D.C., 1980.
10. S. CHAKRABORTY, The acid tests of management performance—A systems view, in G. E. Lasker, Ed., *Applied Systems and Cybernetics,* Pergamon Press, Oxford, 1980.
11. S. CHAKRABORTY, The corporate business plan—A systems theoretic approach, *Proceedings—1980 IEEE International Conference on Cybernetics and Society,* IEEE Press, New York, 1980.
12. S. CHAKRABORTY, Hierarchical information structures for market planning software, *Proceedings—The International Computer Symposium—1980,* The Chinese Academy of Sciences, Taipei, Republic of China, 1980.
13. S. CHAKRABORTY, Developing marketing plans: A general systems approach, in W. J. Rechmeyer, Ed., *General Systems Research and Design: Precursors and Futures.* SGSR Press, Louisville, 1981.
14. S. CHAKRABORTY, Hierarchy theoretic structures for computerized market planning software, *Proceedings—The Third Hungarian Computer Science Conference,* The Hungarian Academy of Sciences, Budapest, Hungary, 1981.
15. S. CHAKRABORTY, The corporate financial management process: A problem solving activity, *Proceedings—The 1981 SGSR–SER Conference,* SGSR Press, Louisville, 1981.
16. S. CHAKRABORTY, *NBTel Corporate Provisioning Plan—Issue 4,* Planning Department, The New Brunswick Telephone Co. Ltd. Saint John, New Brunswick, 1981.
17. G. J. KLIR, Identification of generative structures in empirical data, *Int. J. Gen. Syst.* 3:d:89–104 (1976).

NOTE: This chapter does not necessarily reflect the views of the author's organization.

26

A GRANTS MANAGEMENT SYSTEM FOR COST ACCOUNTING
THE CASE OF NEW YORK CITY

Jae K. Shim

1. Introduction

The explosive increase in demand for services, relative to the increase in resources, has made essential the need for good financial management, including cost and managerial accounting. Municipalities have found grants from contracts with the Federal and State governments important sources of financing. According to a recent survey, nearly 40% of U.S. cities' general fund revenue is derived from Federal and State grants.[1] In the case of the City of New York, in 1978, for example, about 37.8% of the City's general fund revenue came from these sources. It follows that the generation of relevant information involving grant-related financial activities is necessary for the effective and systematic management of this source of the City's general fund revenue. To address this need, the City of New York has recently installed what is called the grants management system (GMS). Its objective is to provide in an accurate and timely manner specific accounting and reporting facilities needed to manage grants.

This paper describes the primary and key features of GMS. It also outlines how GMS functions and interfaces with other systems of the New York City's so-called "intergrated financial management system" (IFMS). Finally, a brief overview of output reports generated by GMS useful in grants management is presented.

JAE K. SHIM • Department of Accountancy, California State University, Long Beach, California 90840. Much of this paper was written while the author was a consultant to the City of New York for the period 1976–1979. The author is now a financial consultant to a Los Angeles County agency.

2. Types of Grants for Municipalities

There are two types of grants—expenditure-driven (or cost-reimbursable) and "fee-for-service." The former reimburses a certain portion of allowable expenditures, which include indirect costs such as fringe benefits and overhead as well as direct costs, according to the terms at the grant agreement. Many of the muncipality's grant revenues fall into this category. For example, the State may be obligated to reimburse 75% of the Department of Mental Health's yearly expenditure that were spent in pursuit of various mental health programs. For this type of grant, one can establish a *direct* relationship between expenditure and revenues because the grant revenues result directly from expenditures made. As a result of this relationship, revenue estimates can be made by the system on an *automated* basis.

"Fee-for-service" grants earn revenue on the basis of a fixed fee for every unit of service delivered, regardless of the cost of providing the service. For example, the school-lunch program is reimbursed by the Federal goverment based on the number of lunches served. Because of the difficulties involved in establishing expenditure/revenue relationships, the system may have to separately incorporate estimated earned revenue. Such revenues can be entered *manually* into the system. A grants management system should take into account the features of these two distinctly different types of grants.

3. The Grants Management System

The grants management system (GMS)* was designed to assist city agencies and the Office of Management and Budget (OMB) in achieving more effective and systematic management of grant programs.

The major purpose of GMS, which is a new capability of IFMS, is to provide grant-managing agencies and OMB with accurate, relevant, and timely expenditure and revenue information on reimbursable federal and state grants. Key attributes of GMS include

- Minimization of the delay in claims preparation;
- Maximization of reimbursements; and
- Monitoring ongoing grant-related activities.

The system's capabilities include:

- Cost acounting;
- Earned revenue estimation;

---

*Operating procedures are discussed in Ref. 2.

- Earned revenue plans;
- Determination of expenditures/revenue relationships; and
- Comparison of revenue estimates with actual revenue recognized.

These five areas are important because they meet the specific informational needs of the agencies as well as OMB. The key features of GMS are described below in relation to these five areas.

Cost Accounting

GMS provides an effective cost accounting feature, which uses cost pools called "claim categories" to identify and accumulate *all* reimbursable expenditures. These reimbursable expenditures essentially represent the basis for preparing grant claims.

The accumulation of reimbursable expenditures into claim categories also provides the basis for other functions of the grants management system, particularly the process of estimating earned revenue. Pooled expenditure data are important to this process because most of the city's grant revenues are expenditure-driven; that is, the grant revenue results dirctly from expenditures made in pursuit of a grant's goal.

The cost accounting capability also provides a mechanism for determining program costs for management purposes. For example, the Department of Health has several neighborhood clinics, each of which provides various services such as child health care, dental care, etc. GMS allows for the accumulation of expenditures by clinic (across all programs), by program (across all clinics), and by program within each clinic. GMS's capability to collect data in alternative formats is important because it provides management with the flexibility to organize expenditure data in whatever way is most useful for managing and estimating grant revenues.

Earned Revenue Estimation

The grants management system is designed to automatically generate earned revenue estimates for expenditure-driven grants. Its revenue estimating capability works as follows:

- All reimbursable expenditures are accumulated into designated claim categories.
- Each claim category defines a cost pool that has a unique reimbursement (rule-of-thumb) formula which approximates the reimbursement terms of the grant.

- The earned revenue estimates are calculated by the system by applying the associated rule-of-thumb formula to each claim category.

To illustrate, if the grant provides 50% reimbursement of expenditures, the rule-of-thumb formula is 50%. Each dollar accumulated into the claim category, therefore, represents 50 cents of estimated earned revenue. In addition, if the grant provides for the reimbursement of indirect costs, such as fringe benefits and overhead, GMS makes the necessary calculations and adds the adjustment(s) to the claim category total.

Estimated earned revenue is calculated for those IFMS revenue sources having budgeted grant revenues. Thus, estimated revenue is defined within the same budgetary structure as are invoices, accruals, and cash receipts. This allows agencies to determine whether

- a grant reimbursement has been unnecessarily delayed, necessitating an investigation to determine the cause, and if
- grant claims are being filed in a timely manner.

Earned Revenue Plans

IFMS[3] currently has two types of revenue plans: a revenue recognition plan and a cash collection plan. The grants management system adds a third type of plan, an earned revenue plan.

Grant revenues are earned by providing goods and services as specified by the terms of the grant. For expenditure-driven grants, revenue is earned when expenditures are incurred. For fee-for-service grants, revenue is earned when the service is provided.

An earned revenue plan is a series of estimates of how much grant revenue will be earned each month. For expenditure-driven grants, these estimates reflect the expenditures expected to be made each month. As might be expected, there should be a direct relationship between the monthly expenditures and the earned revenue estimates contained within the plan. The earned revenue plan serves as the basis for deriving the agency's revenue recognition plan, which in turn is used to calculate the cash collection plan.

Determination of Expenditure/Revenue Relationships

The grants management system provides a mechanism for determining effective grant reimbursement rates for each spending budget code and unit of appropriation. This allows grant-managing agencies and OMB to verify funding percentages and to determine the revenue implications of modifications in the expense budget.

Comparison of Revenue Estimates with Actual Revenue Recognized

As previously mentioned, estimated revenue for expenditure-driven grants is automatically calculated by GMS by applying the associated rule-of-thumb formula to each claim category. By interfacing with the IFMS revenue accounting module and its revenue recognition reports, the grants management system produces reports that permit the spending agencies and OMB to compare estimated revenue with actual revenue.[3] Figure 1 displays the IFMS accounting subsystem and how it relates to GMS.[4]

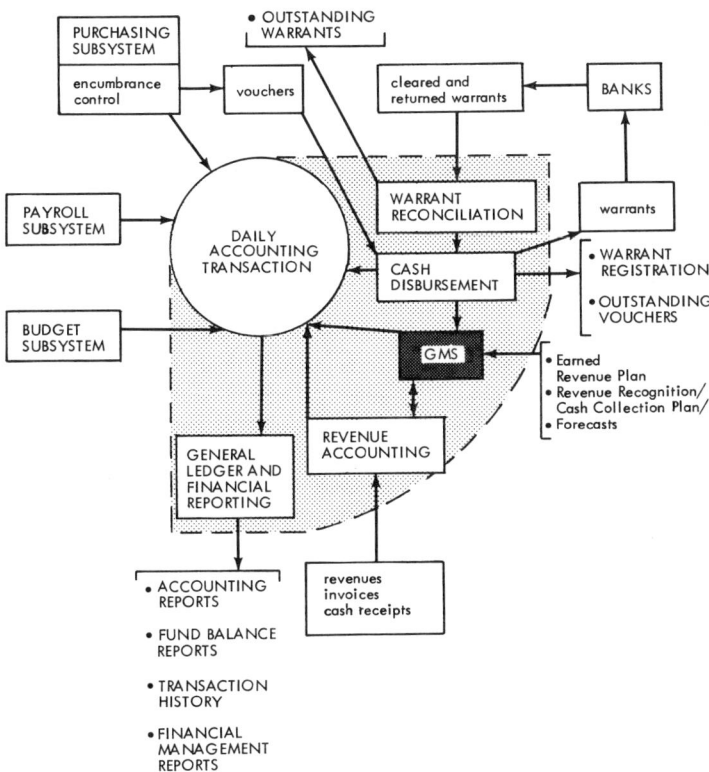

FIGURE 1. Accounting subsystem modules of IFMS and GMS. (Adapted from Ref. 4, p. 65.)

4. How the System Works

This section briefly describes how the GMS system works. In doing that, it introduces the following three important concepts: claim category, rule-of-thumb, and grant ceilings.

Claim Category

To provide the grants management system with necessary expenditure and revenue information, each revenue source should be examined and all the expenditures which would generate reimbursements identified.

The grants management system accumulates grant-related expenditures into costs pools called claim categories. All expenditures processed by IFMS are classified by a set of accounting attributes which include budget code, object or subobject, intra-city reference, or reporting category. GMS allows its users to define the accounting attributes for the group of expenditures to be accumulated into a particular claim category. In some instances, more than one claim category entry may be required for a particular grant.

Every month, GMS searches for, lists, and summarizes all transactions that satisfy the user's specifications, thus providing the user with expenditure data necessary for claiming. The specifications for each claim category are contained in the claim category master table.

Rule-of-Thumb

The amount of revenue that the expenditures are expected to generate for each claim category must also be determined. The key element here is that there are different types of reimbursable expenditures and that each claim category defines a cost pool that has a unique reimbursement formula associated with it. There are, in fact, many grant revenue sources which require more than one claim category since these grants reimburse different expenditures in different ways.

The terms under which a specific grant is reimbursed are stored in the rule-of-thumb master table. More specifically, the table contains the long and short forms of the grant title, the indirect cost adjustment percentages, the cost accounting report production specification, and up to a certain predetermined number of estimated earned revenue distributions.

Grant Ceiling

It should be determined if there is a ceiling imposed by the grantor. The terms of grant reimbursement may indicate that reimbursements will be made for all related expenditures up to a certain amount. Any limitation should be clearly defined in the table so that an agency can ensure that its grant-related expenditures fall within the grant parameters.

The claim category ceiling table provides agency personnel with a mechanism for monitoring their spending in relation to grant ceilings. However, the use of the ceiling table is *optional*.

5. Procedures for Implementation

As discussed in the previous section, there are three master tables in the data base. For proper computer implementation of the system, certain procedures are necessary, which include annual updates and routine maintenance of these tables, and manual entry and clearing of estimated earned revenues.

Annual Table Updates

Annual updating is a process whereby the GMS's master tables are provided with up-to-date grant information. These tables must be updated in a timely manner to ensure that accurate earned revenue estimates and proper reporting of grants data can be generated from GMS.

This annual table update is performed at the beginning of each fiscal year. Since each entry made in GMS's master tables is associated with only one fiscal year, a new set of entries must be prepared each year for each table. In addition, when new grants are awarded to grant-managing agencies during a fiscal year, new table entries in GMS's master tables are created, which in turn must also be updated at the beginning of the next fiscal year. Even if there were no changes in grant terms from one year to the next, master tables have to be changed since, as noted above, each entry is associated with only one fiscal year.

Routine Table Maintenance

To ensure proper processing of grant data and to maintain the usefulness of the reports generated by the system, table maintenance tasks must be performed routinely throughout the year. Essentially, these tasks cover all additions, changes, or deletions necessary to keep GMS's master tables up-to-date.

There are five situations which may trigger a need for table maintenance. These are the addition of a new grant; cancellation or closing-out of an existing grant; a change in grant terms; an expense budget modification; and/or fine tuning the rule-of-thumb tables.

Manual Entry of Estimated Earned Revenue

Most earned revenue estimates are generated automatically by the system. For expenditure-driven grants, GMS generates monthly earned revenue estimates from actual IFMS expenditure transactions using

- Claim categories specified in the claim category table;
- Indirect cost adjustment and reimbursement percentages stored in the rule-of-thumb table.

However, there are cases where earned revenues may have to be estimated and entered manually. For example, revenues for fee-for-service grants are generated on the basis of a fixed fee for every unit of service delivered. For fee-for-service grants, the amount of estimated earned revenue will be calculated separately and entered into GMS using an appropriate input form.

Clearing Process of Earned Revenue Estimates

The clearing process is performed to facilitate the effective use of the system. When the claim for a grant is prepared and the appropriate input form is entered into IFMS, the earned revenue estimate(s) which correspond to the revenue source(s) being recognized must be cleared. This clearing process is done by using the IFMS revenue accounting module.

The objective of this clearing procedure is twofold. First, managers can determine whether a grant claim has been filed in a timely manner and, second, managers can check to see if the amount of revenue claimed is what is expected, given the earned revenue estimates which have been previously made.

As a result of clearing earned revenue estimates, the IFMS revenue accounting module provides two reports which allow comparisons between *actual* revenue recognized or accrued and the earned revenue estimates which have been forecasted by GMS. Figure 2 shows the flow charts for the grants management system of the City of New York.

6. Reports

The output reports produced by the grants management system will provide agency managers and OMB personnel with the vital information needed to properly manage grants. Most reports produced by GMS are on a monthly basis. Six categories of reports are involved:

Table Maintenance Reports. Three reports are produced that list the active

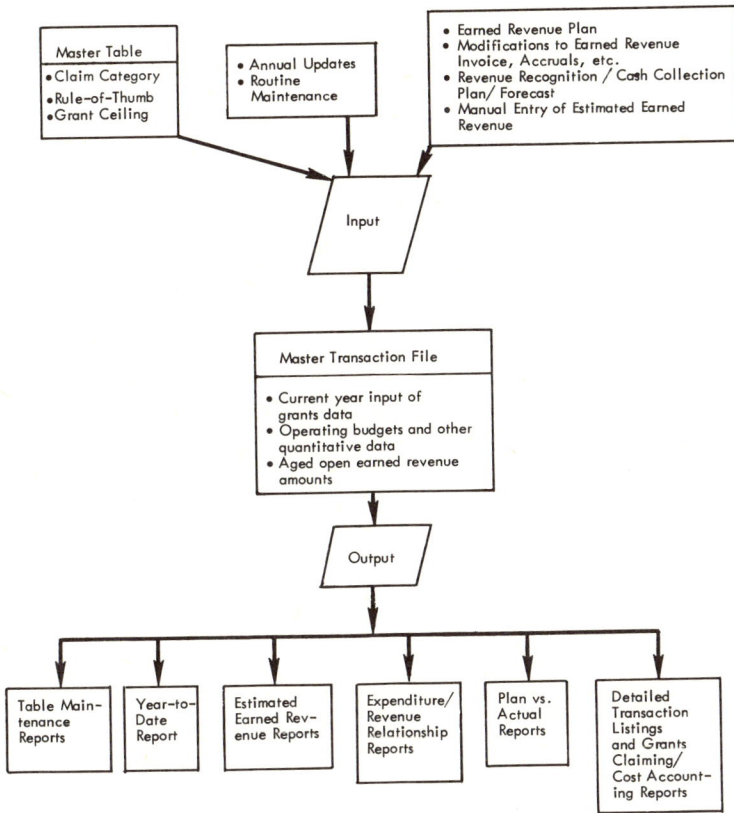

FIGURE 2. Overview of a grants management system.

entries in the claim category, rule-of-thumb, and claim category tables. Their data enable agencies to ensure that their tables are accurate and up-to-date.

Year-to-Date Reports. Three reports generated by the grants management system fall into this category. These reports provide year-to-date information on claim category spending.

Estimated Earned Revenue Reports. These reports display monthly earned revenue estimates and the calculations supporting each estimate.

Expenditure/Revenue Relationship Reports. These reports display the estimated earned revenue in relationship with the total spending made from each budget code and unit of appropriation. Each report is structured to provide direct evaluation and verification of funding percentages.

Plan vs. Actual Reports. Two plan vs. actual reports are produced. The first shows plans and actuals by revenue source; the second shows plans and actuals summarized to the revenue category level.

Detailed Transaction Listings and Grant Claiming/Cost Accounting Reports. Detailed transaction listings reports provide agency personnel with a list of transactions that have been accumulated into a particular claim category. The reports provide an audit trail that can be used to detail and analyze these expenditures. In addition to detailed transaction listings, summary reports of spending by claim category present the same spending data as the detailed transactions listings except that the transaction level details are omitted. The reports will be used by analysts who wish to see a more concise spending summary without the supporting detail.

The grants management system will allow agency personnel to select from among five transactions listing formats. Cost accounting reports, the detailed transaction listings by claim category, and the summary of spending by claim category will be available in five sort orders:

- Budget code and unit of appropriation subtotals;
- Reporting category* and object subtotals;
- Object and unit of appropriation subtotals;
- Object and reporting category subtotals;
- Subobject and object subtotals.

Both the detailed and summary reports will be forthcoming at the end of the month. The specific cost accounting reports received are determined by the agency.

In addition, the revenue accounting module of IFMS provides reports which allow agencies and OMB to monitor the clearing of estimated earned revenue documents by revenue invoices and accruals.

7. Conclusion

This chapter outlined the structure of the grants management system and its interface with other accounting subsystem modules of IFMS. Due to the fact that close to 40% of New York City's general fund revenue comes from grants, effective grants management is essential and largely depends upon an accurate cost accounting system. However, it should be noted that grants management is not

---

*Reporting categories are alphanumeric codes that each agency has the option to use to classify its own accounting data for internal cost accumulation and any other agency-specific purpose. The codes are defined independently for each agency. Their primary uses are in identifying cost reimbursement categories to assist agencies in obtaining reimbursement for federally funded and state-funded programs. This is a feature of the City's revenue accounting subsystem.

the same as cost accounting and thus GMS should not be regarded as a cost accounting system. Unfortunately, most cost accounting concepts and tools that are used in profit-making entities can*not* be applied to the governmental sector because of the difficulty of measuring outputs and productivity and the relationships between inputs and outputs.[5] Nevertheless, grants management can be construed as a significant part of an entire cost accounting system. In other words, the development of effective grants management is a stepping stone for what could turn out to be a cost accounting system for the municipal government.

References

1. L. E. HAY and R. M. MIKESELL, *Governmental Accounting,* Richard D. Irwin, Homewood, Illinois, 1974.
2. Urban Academy Management, Inc., *Grants Management System,* First Drafts, August 23, 1979, pp. 1–280.
3. Urban Academy Management, Inc., *Agency Revenue Accounting Procedures for New York City's IFMS,* April, 1977.
4. Urban Academy Management, Inc., *An Introduction to IFMS: New York City's Integrated Financial Management System,* 2nd edition, New York, December, 1977.
5. R. ANTHONY and R. E. HERZLINGER, *Management Control in Nonprofit Organizations,* Richard D. Irwin, Homewood, Illinois, 1980, pp. 54–60.

27

RELIABILITY AND MAINTAINABILITY MANAGEMENT

BALBIR S. DHILLON AND J. NATESAN

1. Introduction

The reliability discipline is one of the vital areas of assurance sciences. The beginning of the reliability engineering discipline goes back to World War II when the basic chain links concept was developed during the development of the V1 rocket. This concept was simply stated as that the chain's weakest link's strength is the maximum strength of the chain.

However, the reliability management had its beginning in the early Fifties. An ad hoc committee for guided missiles reliability came into being in the late Fifties.[3] Due to this committee, the reliability management aspect became more clear. During the same period, another ad hoc group was organized by the U.S. Department of Defense whose purpose was to study parts specification management for reliability (PSMR). The group's report was first published in 1960. Another report on reliability program management was published by USAF Ballistic Missile Division in 1969. Since then, several publications have appeared on reliability management. An extensive list of selective publications[1–105] on reliability management are listed at the end of the chapter. This literature search was mainly restricted to journal and conference publications. The various aspects of reliability management are discussed as follows:

2. General Management and Its Relationship to Reliability

The objective of this section is to briefly discuss the relations of the general management to reliability before we penetrate into the discipline of reliability

BALBIR S. DHILLON and J. NATESAN • Engineering Management Program, Department of Mechanical Engineering, University of Ottawa, Ottawa, Ontario K1N 6N5, Canada.

management. Basically the general management (manager) responsibilities may be divided as follows:[103]

   i. Manpower supervision;
   ii. Costs evaluation;
   iii. Operations analysis.

A major portion of a general manager's time is spent on organizing manpower, formulating policies, manpower development, and so on. The cost analysis or evaluation is another area of the manager's duties. In this case, the manager has to make decisions regarding new facilities, new departments or groups, purchasing or selling equipment and so on. He has to analyze advantages and disadvantages of each decision in the terms of dollars and cents in order to make rational decisions. The financial aspect of the organization is one of the main concerns of the manager. The third area of a manager's responsibility is operations analysis where he audits to see if his directives and policies are clearly understood and carried out properly. In this case, he carefully analyzes the feedback information regarding his policies, directives, decisions, and so on.

At the general management level, there are basically three objectives for reliability:

   i. Minimize errors which affect reliability by developing techniques of directing manpower;
   ii. Optimize system cost effectiveness by evaluating and backing the correct reliability effort;
   iii. Establish an operations feedback system; this system should provide enough information for management to discriminate activities which were instrumental in producing a product with expected reliability.

3. Reliability Budget and Tasks

The percentage of research and development budget for reliability in an organization gives a fair indication about the emphasis the company places on reliability. According to the U.S. Government missile contractors' survey reported in Ref. 67 about 0.3%–10% of the research and development funds are spent on reliability.

In order to have an effective and meaningful reliability program according to Ref. 67, there should be a central reliability group to control reliability tasks. In Ref. 67 there are 15 reliability tasks such as evaluation and modeling; reliability demonstration; maintainability; allocation of reliability; collection and dissemination of test data; analysis of failures; value engineering; developing statistical tests;

human reliability; developmental reliability testing; failure mode and effect analysis; standards, drawing checks, and specifications; approving engineering drawings from the reliability standpoint; characteristics classification, and trade-offs for reliability. The first nine tasks should be the direct responsibility of the central reliability group whereas in the remaining six, the group should act as an auditor. More clearly, these six tasks should be assigned to the usual groups.

4. Reliability Engineer and His Responsibilities

The reliability engineer is a well-qualified engineer like any other professional engineer. In many cases, the reliability engineers are the former design engineers who have gained knowledge of reliability through the special courses or other means. Because of these qualifications, the engineer in question is in a good position to determine the quality of the design. A reliability engineer provides information on parts failure rates, parts reliability requirements, predicting the effect of environment, maintenance and so on, which are useful in design decisions. In addition, he develops reliability evaluation models and techniques, reliability demonstration and evaluation test procedures, reliability growth monitoring procedures and so on. Other important aspects of the reliability engineer's duties are that he sits in the design reviews, monitors subcontractors from the reliabiliy aspect, reliability consulting, and so on.

Basically, the reliability engineer provides assistance to the management to define, evaluate and contain its risk, through the following three (or more) steps:

  i. Evaluating optimum reliability demonstration plan;
 ii. Analyzing requirements of the customer;
iii. Ascertaining the reliability prediction accuracy and evaluated reliability.

5. Reliability Management of a Short-Term System Development Project

The short-term projects do not differ that significantly as compared to the long-term project, especially from the reliability and functional point of view. However, there are significant differences in many other areas such as less time available to design the short-term system because a relatively larger portion of the time is spent on contract negotiation, specifications writing, defining the system, and so on. Furthermore, the project funding may be smaller and equipment development period is certainly shorter.

As far as the reliability personnel are concerned, the short-term projects are more demanding. This is due to the fact that because of a shorter development period, from the reliability point of view, any system defects have to be detected and corrected earlier. A short-term project[86] may be subdivided into the following five stages:

  i. Proposal stage;
  ii. Design and development stage;
  iii. Fabrication stage;
  iv. Test stage;
  v. Field operation stage.

In all of these five phases, a reliability engineer plays an important role. Therefore, the role of the reliability engineer in all of these five stages is discussed in detail in the following sections.

5.1. Proposal Stage

This phase is concerned with convincing the customer that the company can manufacture the required product satisfactorily at a minimum cost. The reliability engineer at the proposal stage performs the tasks such as preparing the reliability portion of the proposal, evaluating the new product fabrication processes, evaluating the reliability data to be supplied to the customer, evaluating and planning manpower requirements, determining cost estimates, and so on.

5.2. Design and Development Stage

This is one of the most important phases of the short-term project. Any design error generated at this stage may be a direct factor in the equipment's ultimate low reliability. Therefore, during this phase, the reliability engineer has to perform reliability analysis and other tasks so that the committed equipment quantitative reliability and other reliability related requirements are fulfilled without any difficulty. Furthermore, he sits in the design review meetings to ensure that the equipment reliability is not sacrificed, as well as making his own contributions in the meeting to improving equipment reliability. The team approach should be encouraged between reliability and design engineers so that the reliability problems are eradicated during the current phase because of the short-term nature of the project.

5.3. Fabrication and Test Stages

These phases are equally important and the reliability engineer has to play a vital role to ensure that the equipment fabrication and testing are correctly accomplished. The poor workmanship, wrong material used for fabrication, inadequate fabrication facilities, wrong blueprints, and so on, are the factors that may degrade the equipment reliability.

As far as the testing is concerned, the engineer designs the proper procedures to conduct required tests by the customer on the equipment. Furthermore, he analyzes the failure data obtained from these tests as well as carrying out other duties associated with equipment testing.

5.4. Field Operation Stage

In this phase the reliability engineer monitors the equipment reliability experienced in the field. The field failure data are useful to compare the designed or predicted reliability with the field reliability. These comparisons become quite useful for the subsequent similar equipment design.

6. Software Reliability Management

Computers are increasingly being used in military, industrial, and other fields. Therefore, the increase in the number of computers and their sophistication has led to the problem of computer software reliability. The last number of decades have witnessed significant advances in the field of hardware reliability. However, only from the last decade is attention being given to the software reliability. The overall system reliability evaluation has to take into consideration the reliability of the software; otherwise, the system reliability calculations will not be reflecting the actual reliability of the system because the system may fail due to software errors. Therefore, the management can play an important role to develop reliable software by taking advantage of the following recommendations[78]:

  i. To manage the software as a schedule unit, it should be treated as a configuration unit;
 ii. Make sure that the software configuration units are designed to fulfill the reliability requirements, by encouraging the development of procedures to fulfill this need;
iii. During the system conceptual and validation phases emphasize the need for software systematic requirement analysis;
 iv. Develop and expand further the current programs for software testing;
  v. For better management control, require the system development contractors to provide in advance their software procedures and controls (if applicable);
 vi. Specify the software requirements in the contract (if applicable);
vii. Programming languages proliferation to be controlled,
viii. Provide incentives to programmers for better software development.

These recommendations are the outcome of a workshop on Electronics System Reliability held at the Airlie House, Airlie, Virginia in 1975. The workshop was sponsored by the United States Armed Forces.

7. Reliability Training

Reliability engineering is one of the specialized areas of engineering. To the author's knowledge, this is not being taught as an undergraduate subject in very many universities or other institutions in North America. At the graduate level there are only a limited number of universities which have graduate courses on the topic. Therefore, in very many cases, the reliability personnel are trained through special courses or other means. The following are the basic purposes for the reliability training:

  i. To increase the awareness of the reliability field;
  ii. To enhance the knowledge of personnel involved in reliability so that they can perform their required tasks satisfactorily.

The following are the main channels which are used to train reliability personnel:

  i. Regular courses given at a local academic institution;
  ii. Special short courses organized by the company; these courses are generally taught by the company experts or the invited experts from the outside organizations;
  iii. Special courses organized by the professional societies such as IEEE Reliability Society, Society of Reliability Engineers, American Society for Quality Control (reliability division), and so on;
  iv. Special reliability workshops organized by the various government agencies;
  v. Reliability tutorial held at various reliability and maintainability conferences such as the Annual Reliability and Maintainability Symposium, Annual American Society for Quality Control Conference, and so on;
  vi. Short courses held at various academic institutions;
  vii. Sending personnel to various reliability and other conferences.

8. Manual for Reliability

Generally fair-size engineering manufacturing organizations have written manuals on organizational structure, quality control, and so on. These manuals are used to define responsibilities, outline work procedures, standardize activities or actions, define functional relationships between departments, outline authority, writing proposals, auditing, and so on. Therefore, a similar manual is necessary for reliability in order to carry out the reliability functions satisfactorily. The reliability documents[68] should include the following topics:

i. Organizational structure;
ii. Individual responsibilities;
iii. Reliability policy of the company;
iv. Procedures of reliability; these procedures are for use in engineering design; the procedures include design analysis and review, components selection, and so on;
v. Techniques and procedures to test equipment reliability;
vi. Procedures for failure data; basically, these procedures are concerned with failure data collection and analysis;
vii. Applicable reliability evaluation methods, models, and so on.

9. Reliability Survey Results

This section reports some of the results of a reliability survey[26] conducted in the United States. In this study, one hundred questionnaires were sent to randomly selected electronic companies. Only 56 of the 100 companies responded to this survey. The questionnaire was concerned with the following items:

i. Organizational structure;
ii. Department responsibilities;
iii. Size and age.

It is interesting to note that all the 56 companies reported that they have separate reliability and quality control departments. However, both the reliability and quality control functions were combined into departments in 16 companies. In addition, in 44 companies, the reliability manager was responsible to a top operating executive.

The reliability departments' responsibilities were in the areas shown in Fig. 1.

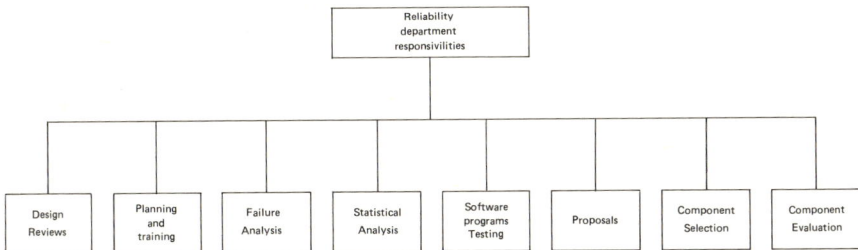

FIGURE 1. The reliability department's responsibilities.

Only 20% of the 56 companies responded to the size of the reliability department; therefore, no conclusions are drawn.

The last question in the questionnaire was concerned with asking the companies regarding recommendations to improve their reliability programs. Their recommendations were in the areas of specifications, budgeting, management, and data collection and reporting. The recommendations are given in detail in Ref. 26. Some of the important recommendations are presented below:

  i. Commercial data exchange system to be established on similar lines as one for the Armed Forces;
  ii. Quantify the reliability specifications needs;
  iii. All the company-wide reliability activities and costs should be the responsibility of the reliability manager;
  iv. In comparison to other similar company tasks, the reliability tasks should have the same status and weight;
  v. A reliability engineer should be a competent and experienced engineer;
  vi. The manufacturer and supplier should have meetings to overcome problem areas.

10. Summary

This chapter presents, briefly, the various selective aspects of reliability management. The following topics were discussed in the chapter:

  i. General management and its relationship to reliability;
  ii. Reliability budget and tasks;
  iii. Reliability engineer and his responsibilities;
  iv. Reliability management of a short-term system development project;
  v. Software reliability management;
  vi. Reliability training;
  vii. Reliability manual;
  viii. Reliability survey results.

The main intent of this chapter was to summarize the important areas of reliability management. Therefore, for further reading (if necessary), an exhaustive list of selective references is provided at the end of the chapter.

References

1. F. A. APPLEGATE, "Built-in" reliability for the Skybolt computer, Proc. Reliability and Quality Control Symposium, pp. 399–414, 1964. Available from the IEEE.

2. H. Ascher, Reliability analysis management, Annual Reliability and Maintainability Symposium, pp. 383–386, 1976. Available from the IEEE.

3. W. Austin-Davis, Reliability management—A challenge, *IEEE Trans. Reliab.* **R-12**(2), 6–9 (1963).

4. L. W. Ball, Impact of system engineering management requirements on the careers of reliability engineers, Proc. Tenth Annual West Coast Reliability Symposium, pp. 115–134, 1969. Available from the American Society for Quality Control.

5. L. W. Ball, Reliability in system design—Chairman's summary, Proc. Annals of Reliability and Maintainability, p. 354, 1966. Available from the IEEE.

6. D. C. Berman, Small sub-contractors in reliability programs, *IRE Trans. Reliab. Qual. Control* **11**, 38–41 (1962).

7. J. M. Biedenbach, Continuing education for the engineering manager, *IEEE Spectrum* **6**, 99–101, November (1968).

8. V. J. Bracha, The Air Force reliability program, MIL-R-27542 Reliability and Quality Control Symposium, pp. 17–23, 1962. Available from the IEEE.

9. E. J. Breiding, Purchasing reliability, *IRE Trans. Reliab. Qual. Control* **9**, 19–22 (1960).

10. W. C. Bullock, A managerial perspective of reliability engineering, *IEEE Trans. Eng. Manage.* **EM-14**(4), 163–165 (1967).

11. S. R. Calabro, *Reliability Principles and Practices,* McGraw-Hill, New York, 1962.

12. B. Camoin and J. P. Guerineau, Reliability oriented planning and management of telecommunications networks, NTC Conf. Rec. Natl. Telecommun. Conference, Vol. 2, pp. 28.6.1–28.6.5, 1980. Available from the IEEE.

13. J. L. Carpenter, Jr., Management of an integrated reliability, Proc. Aerospace Reliability and Maintainability Conference, pp. 175–177, 1963. Available from the IEEE.

14. M. T. Chambers, Reliability analysis computer programs for the management scientist, Proc. IEEE Eng. Management Conf. Rec., pp. 144–147, 1980. Available from the IEEE.

15. B. T. Colendene, Program costs vs. reliability, Proc. Reliability and Quality Control Symposium, pp. 386–394, 1964. Available from IEEE.

16. T. D. Cox and J. Keely, Reliability growth management of SATCOM terminals, Proc. Annual Reliability and Maintainability Symposium, pp. 218–223, 1976. Available from the IEEE.

17. J. C. Davis and J. R. Holmes, A field reliability data program, Proc. Reliability and Quality Control Symposium, pp. 415–430, 1960. Available from the IEEE.

18. M. Davis, Is a commercial reliability program feasible? Proc. Reliability and Quality Control Symposium, pp. 395–398, 1965. Available from the IEEE.

19. R. T. Dewey, The role of the buyer in reliability, Proc. Reliability and Quality Control Symposium, pp. 34–39, 1963. Available from the IEEE.

20. G. A. Dove et al., Program management at the subsystem subcontractor level for product reliability and maintainability, Proc. Annals of Reliability and Maintainability, pp. 345–353, 1966. Available from the IEEE.

21. W. A. Dwyer and J. P. Kornfeld, Effectiveness analysis and the new business area, Proc. Annals of Reliability and Maintainability, pp. 49–52, 1965. Available from the IEEE.

22. E. E. Fawkes, BIM.RAB and its influence on the BuWeps system effectiveness program, Proc. of Reliability and Maintainability, pp. 25–29, 1965. Available from the IEEE.

23. A. J. Finocchi, Reliability has failed to meet its goals, Proc. Annals of Reliability and Maintainability, pp. 111–117, 1965. Available from the IEEE.

24. J. W. Forrestor, Common foundations underlying engineering and management, *IEEE Spectrum* **2**, 66–67, Sept. (1964).

25. G. E. Fouch, Quality and reliability: Its role in logistics, Proc. Annals of Reliability and Maintainability, pp. 19–24, 1965. Available from the IEEE.

26. M. Freedberg, Reliability management—A survey, *Ind. Qual. Control* **10**, 224–226 (1966).

27. J. B. Garrick, Reliability analysis of bulk mail handling facilities, Proc. Annals of Reliability and Maintainability, pp. 394–399, 1971. Available from the IEEE.

28. H. L. Gimlore, Reliability's role in management, *IRE Trans. Reliab. Qual. Control* **11**, 36–37 (1962).

29. A. S. GOLDMAN, Planning and system selection under risk and uncertainty, Proc. Annals of Reliability and Maintainability, pp. 63–74, 1965. Available from the IEEE.

30. A. C. GARSKI, Reliability in practice, Proc. Annals of Reliability and Maintainability, pp. 97–101, 1965. Available from the IEEE.

31. M. B. GREENFELD, Responsive reliability proposals in a tight market, Proc. Annual Symposium on Reliability, pp. 133–138, 1971. Available from the IEEE.

32. J. W. GRISWOLD, Design reliability creation through management directives, IRE Trans. Reliab. Qual. Control 11, 49–55 (1962).

33. B. L. GROSE, Reliability can be predicted?—A negative position, Proc. Annals of Reliability and Maintainability, pp. 119–129, 1965. Available from the IEEE.

34. Handbook of Reliability Engineering, Published by the Bureau of Naval Weapons, 1964. Available from the Superintendent of Documents, U.S. Government Printing Office, Washington, D.C., 20402.

35. G. R. HERD, The case for reliability modeling and analysis, Proc. Annals of Reliability and Maintainability, pp. 103–104, 1965. Available from the IEEE.

36. D. HILL and J. WELLS, Cost–effectiveness guidelines for the design of a system with improved reliability, Proc. Annals of Reliability and Maintainability, pp. 53–62, 1965. Available from the IEEE.

37. T. D. HILL and T. A. MUSSON, Report on reliability design and acquisition management, Proc. Annual Reliability and Maintainability Symposium, pp. 374–477, 1976. Available from the IEEE.

38. C. J. HITCH, Cost considerations and systems effectiveness, Proc. Annals of Reliability and Maintainability, pp. 1–7, 1965. Available from the IEEE.

39. M. H. HOUCK and B. DATTA, Performance evaluation of a a stochastic optimization model for reservoir design and management with explicit reliability criteria, Water Resour. Res. 17(4), 827–832 (1981).

40. J. V. HUNT, Reliability management under automation, Proc. Annual Symposium on Reliability, pp. 15–20, 1968. Available from the IEEE.

41. W. L. HURD, Interpretation of reliability, maintainability, and safety requirements, Proc. Annals of Reliability and Maintainability, pp. 41–47, 1965. Available from the IEEE.

42. W. G. IRESON, Ed. Reliability Handbook, McGraw-Hill, New York, 1966.

43. R. F. ISAACS, Implementation of reliability and maintainability requirements for postal hardware systems, Proc. Annals of Reliability and Maintainability, pp. 392–393, 1971. Available from the IEEE.

44. J. R. ISKEN, The view from the bottom, Proc. National Symposium on Reliability, pp. 114–117, 1967. Available from the IEEE.

45. R. M. JACOBS, Quality and the courts, IEEE Trans. Reliab. R-22(4), 218–223 (1973).

46. L. N. JAMES, Obligations of a reliability organization, Proc. Annals of Reliability and Maintainability, pp. 131–134, 1965. Available from the IEEE.

47. I. K. KESSLER, The front office looks at reliability, Proc. Annual Symposium on Reliability, pp. 449–451, 1968. Available from the IEEE.

48. T. D. KIANG, IEC Guidelines, IEC Guidelines for Reliability Management, Trans. Annu. Tech. Conf. ASQC, pp. 402–408, 1977. Available from the ASQC.

49. J. KIMMEL, Management and organization of space-age reliability programs, Proc. Annual Symposium on Reliability, pp. 858–864, 1967. Available from the IEEE.

50. L. S. KLIVANS, An improved management approach to upgrade avionic system reliability, IEEE Trans. Reliab. 26, 23–28, Apr. (1977).

51. H. KNAPP and C. SEN-ALE, Organization for reliability, Proc. Reliability and Quality Control Symposium, pp. 219–224, 1958. Available from the IEEE.

52. C. H. KOHLER, JR. and W. Y. COOK, A manufacturer's corrective action system for reliability control, Proc. Aerospace Reliability and Maintainability Conference, pp. 190–197, 1963. Available from the IEEE.

53. R. E. KUEHN, Organizing for reliability, Proc. Reliability and Quality Control Symposium, pp. 123–125, 1957. Available from the IEEE.

54. W. B. LABERGE, Contractor management looks at reliability program activities, IRE Trans. Reliab. Qual. Control 9, 90–93 (1960).

55. F. P. Lees, Quantification of man–machine system reliability in process control, *IEEE Trans. Reliab.* **R-22**(3), 124–131 (1973).
56. S. N. Lehr, Reliability management of an incentive contract, Proc. Aerospace Reliability and Maintainability Conference, pp. 185–189, 1963. Available from the IEEE.
57. D. S. Liberman, A facelifting for NASA's reliability requirements, Proc. Annual Symposium on Reliability, pp. 121–128, 1971. Available from the IEEE.
58. D. K. Lloyd and M. Lipow, *Reliability: Management Methods and Mathematics,* Prentice-Hall, Englewood Cliffs, New Jersey, 1962.
59. A. A. MacDonald, What price reliability? Proc. Reliability and Quality Control Symposium, pp. 172–176, 1957. Available from the IEEE.
60. M. S. Majesty, Personnel subsystem reliability for aerospace systems, Proc. Reliability and Quality Control Symposium, pp. 199–204, 1962. Available from the IEEE.
61. P. N. Martin, Role of product evaluation facility in reliability, Proc. Annual Symposium on Reliability, pp. 36–42, 1970. Available from the IEEE.
62. V. Metcalfe, The assessment of reliability and maintainability from field data—The British army's methods and experience, Annual Reliability and Maintainability Symposium, pp. 387–393, 1976. Available from the IEEE.
63. V. O. Muglia, R&M management using risk analysis, Proc. Annual Reliability and Maintainability Symposium, pp. 230–233, 1976. Available from the IEEE.
64. J. D. Musa, Measurement and management of software reliability, *Proc. IEEE* **68**(9), 1131–1143 (1980).
65. J. D. Musa, Use of software reliability measures in project management, Proc. IEEE Comput. Soc. Int. Comput. Software and Appl. Conf., pp. 493–498, 1978. Available from the IEEE Comput. Soc.
66. H. M. Nachmias and T. J. Edwards, Management of equipment reliability activities at USASRDL., Proc. Reliability and Quality Control Symposium, pp. 32–36, 1962. Available from the IEEE.
67. R. S. Nelson, Integrating reliability progress into design and engineering: A study of management problem, Proc. Aerospace Reliability and Maintainability Conference, pp. 178–184, 1963. Available from the IEEE.
68. P. D. T. O'Connor, *Practical Reliability Engineering,* Heyden, London, 1981.
69. V. H. Pellicione, Tracking, growth and prediction (TGP) reliability growth: An integrated approach, Proc. Ann. Tech. Meet. Inst. Environ. Sci. 26th, pp. 76–81, 1980. Available from the Inst. of Environ. Science.
70. H. F. Perla, Outage planning and maintenance management impacts on reliability, Workshop Proc. Power Plant Availability Eng. and Product Improv., p. 20, 1979. Available from Pickard, Lowe & Garrick, Inc., Irvine, California.
71. E. G. D. Peterson, Some observations on quality assurance and reliability, Proc. Reliability and Quality Control Symposium, pp. 129–132. Available from the IEEE.
72. E. L. Peterson and H. L. Steverson, Operational readiness—A decision-making tool for reliability maintainability management, Proc. Annals of Reliability and Maintainability, pp. 75–86, 1965. Available from the IEEE.
73. W. J. Picker, Intra-corporation reliability coordination, Proc. Reliability and Quality Control Symposium, pp. 182–183, 1961. Available from the IEEE.
74. H. R. Powell, A customer looks at the reliability program activities, *IRE Trans. Reliab. Qual. Control* **9**, 108–111 (1960).
75. A. E. Puckett, The future of research, reliability and profits under fixed price contracting, Proc. Annals of Reliability and Maintainability, pp. 9–11, 1965. Available from the IEEE.
76. V. Rehg, Reliability management simulation exercise, Proc. Annual Symposium on Reliability, pp. 68–72, 1969. Available from the IEEE.
77. B. Reich, Management of electronic equipment reliability, Inst. of Environ. Sci. Annu. Tech. Meet., pp. 373–378, Institute of Environmental Sciences, Mount Prospect, Illinois (1976).
78. B. Reich and S. Grabman, Management of electronic equipment reliability, Proc. Annual Reliability and Maintainability Symposium, pp. 378–382, 1976. Available from the IEEE.
79. *Reliability Handbook,* AMCP 702-3, US Army Material Command, Washington, D.C., October 1968.

80. J. J. Riordan, The problem of cultism in logistics management, Proc. Annals of Reliability and Maintainability, pp. 31–33, 1965. Available from the IEEE.

81. J. W. Roach, Project definition—A tool of engineering management, Proc. Annals of Reliability and Maintainability, pp. 13–18, 1965. Available from the IEEE.

82. H. G. Romig, Quality engineering management implements reliability through production control, Proc. Aerospace Reliability and Maintainability Conference, pp. 268–277, 1963. Available from the IEEE.

83. S. A. Rosenthal, Implementing an effective product assurance program for high-reliability equipment, IEEE Trans. Eng. Manage. EM-13(3), 143–154 (1966).

84. C. M. Ryerson, Reliability from the program manager's standpoint, Proc. Reliability and Quality Control Symposium, pp. 169–181, 1961. Available from the IEEE.

85. M. H. Saltz, Supplier reliability assurance programs, Proc. Reliability and Quality Control Symposium, pp. 445–448, 1960. Available from the IEEE.

86. M. F. Schmidt and G. A. Raynoud, Reliability in the middle, Proc. National Symposium on Reliability, pp. 110–113, 1967. Available from the IEEE.

87. L. L. Schneider, Reliability contributions to Minuteman logistics, Proc. Annals of Reliability and Maintainability, pp. 105–110, 1965. Available from the IEEE.

88. F. M. Schriever, Ford Instrument Company's Reliability Program, Proc. Reliability and Quality Control Symposium, pp. 425–430, 1959. Available from the IEEE.

89. D. J. Sinkens, A reliability growth management approach, Proc. Annual Reliability and Maintainability Symposium, pp. 356–360, 1979. Available from the IEEE.

90. R. W. Smiley, Military management of missile quality control/reliability programs, Proc. Reliability and Quality Control Symposium, pp. 66–68, 1963. Available from the IEEE.

91. W. F. Stevens, .Management of the reliability effort, Proc. Reliability and Quality Control Symposium, pp. 379–385, 1964. Available from the IEEE.

92. F. A. Storall, Reliability management, IEEE Trans. Reliab. R-22(4), 232–237 (1973).

93. W. T. Sumerlin, Winning reliability management techniques—Vintage 1966, Proc. National Symposium on Reliability, pp. 104–109, 1967. Available from the IEEE.

94. M. M. Tall, Reliability management, Proc. Reliability and Quality Control Symposium, pp. 137–145, 1959. Available from the IEEE.

95. E. F. Thomas, Pitfalls in reliability program management, Proc. Annual Reliability and Maintainability Symposium, pp. 369–373, 1976. Available from the IEEE.

96. E. C. Towl, Fair price and fair play, Proc. Annals of Reliability and Maintainability, pp. 35–39, 1965. Available from the IEEE.

97. J. E. Vessley and J. W. Cowdery, Reliability, availability, maintainability: A management challenge, Proc. for the Annual Eng. Conf. on Reliability for the Electric Power Industries, pp. 70–72, 1980. Available from the American Society for Quality Control.

98. R. H. Weisler, Reliability and maintainability management for improved cost effectiveness by the first tier supplier, Proc. Annals for Reliability and Maintainability, pp. 338–344, 1966. Available from the IEEE.

99. R. Weller, Equipment reliability as a management problem, Proc. Aerospace Reliability and Maintainability Conference, pp. 125–127, 1963. Available from the IEEE.

100. R. Wellwe, Communication channels reliability operations, Proc. Reliability and Quality Control Symposium, pp. 126–128, 1957. Available from the IEEE.

101. A. P. White and J. D. Pavier, Reliability management of the avionic system of a military strike aircraft, Agard Conf. Proc. n 261 Avionics Reliab., Its Tech. and Related Discip., pp. 29.1–29.13, 1979. Available from the IEEE.

102. E. S. Winlund, Cost-effectiveness management, Proc. Annals of Reliability and Maintainability, pp. 87–96, 1965. Available from the IEEE.

103. L. A. Wood, Current management reliability objectives, IEEE Trans. Reliab. R-12(2), 1–5 (1963).

104. J. M. Wuerth, Policies for reliability organization in a multiproduct division company, Proc. Reliability and Quality Control Symposium, pp. 184–188, 1961.

105. P H. Zorger, Standards and education of reliability personnel, Proc. Annals of Reliability and Maintainability, pp. 464–471, 1967. Available from the IEEE.

INDEX

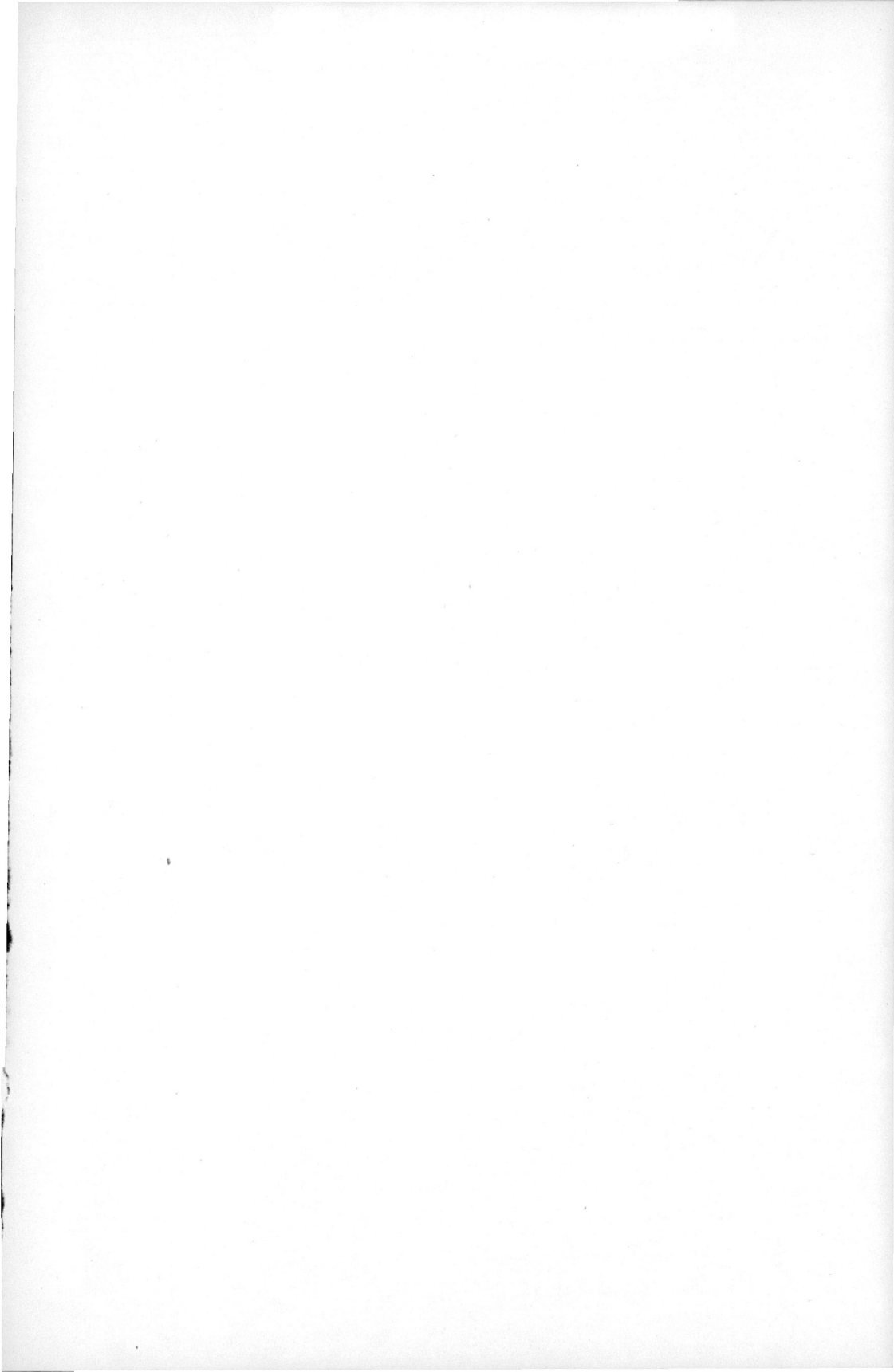